THE CALLAS IMPRINT

A Centennial Biography

THE CALLAS IMPRINT

A Centennial Biography

Sophia Lambton

THE CREPUSCULAR PRESS

THE CREPUSCULAR PRESS
London

First published in Great Britain by The Crepuscular Press 2023

Jacket design by Renée Clarke

Set in 10/12pt Constantia

Typeset by RefineCatch Limited, www.refinecatch.com

Printed and bound by Amazon Kindle Direct Publishing

A CIP catalogue record for this book is available from the British Library.

ISBN 978-1-7392863-2-3
ISBN 978-1-7392863-4-7 (pbk)
ISBN 978-1-7392863-9-2 (ebook)

https://thecrepuscularpress.com/

Contents

Acknowledgements

Liberty for many is deliverance from an unfinished self: a rediscovery of confidence too prone to fritter in our fragile adolescence.

Thanks in large part to the individuals here cited, mine remained for a long time unshakeable.

A stepping stool was granted me to board the rocky ship that is Maria Callas' historiography. In that vein I am first of all indebted to a swath of predecessors: the late Nicholas Petsalis-Diomidis—whose mountain of studies on Callas' formative years makes all others seem knoll-like; the insightful descriptions of Renzo Allegri, who introduced many to Callas the Veronese débutante; the belabored analyses of Stelios Galatopoulos—who made Maria look into herself—and all who have uncovered never-published correspondence since her death.

A nineteen-year-old nobody seems scarcely promising in the expended role of "new Callas biographer"—but many welcomed her into their home. Among that warm division pouring self-esteem into an antsy first-time documentarian were several who have since passed on. This book is gener-ously indebted to the late Janine Reiss—my first interviewee: a vocal coach and a delectable sophisticate *par excellence*. Luigi Alva bought me tea at Ristorante Savini (they still call it "Biffi Scala"). Sir John Tooley spent an afternoon regaling me with tales sat in his Cambridge kitchen and the speedy Natale Rusconi answered e-mails far beyond the needs of etiquette.

The tender Georganne Mennin graciously received me hours late after I'd shown up at an incorrect address in Brooklyn—making for a venture unfor-gettable. Athenian sunshine lit the backdrop of confabulations with the ever-lovely Marilena Patronicolas and the detail-oriented Korinna Spanidou; Taki Theodoracopulos provided entertainment on a drizzly London (evidently July) afternoon. Giovanna Lomazzi afforded hospitality both in Italian and French. Fabrizio Melano challenged my live Callas recording preferences: insatiable fun for a fanatic. Eugene Kohn dispensed

an irresistibly delightful opera-based exchange, John Copley and I traded
backstage anecdotes and the incalculably helpful Bettina Brentano became
a whole part of my life.

And then there were those lengthy phone chats—perhaps not dissimilar
to Callas' own spillages—stretched over timezones and ungodly hours. A
pleasure it was to delve deeply into Juilliard with Marko Lámpas—whose
own memoir is unmissable material for anyone who hankers to extract
more facts from the soprano's pedagogical immersion. Joan Lasker Sobel's
input became indispensable for this inspection also. Ninon Dimitriadou-
Kambouri and Mary Annexy elaborated on the Callas childhood, producing
Kalogeropoulou family portraits from tireless memory banks.

For tolerance of me I likewise thank Cordelia van Zuylen, Thérèse
Darras, Gregor Benko, Elaine Reynolds Duke, Sophie de Ségur, Pino Buso,
Aristides Embiricos, Carola Shepard, Piero Robba and his associate
Francesca Sgroi, Joseph Rescigno, Caterina d'Amico, Jake Tanner and the
late, warmhearted Barrie Smith: a gem gone far too soon.

I'm also grateful to my former editor Robert Matthew-Walker: a man
whose faith in me (as well as Callasian reminiscences) braced this unready
fledgling for her flight into the sphere of opera criticism.

Sharing portions of a life is one thing—digging into drawers to salvage
long-forgotten correspondence stored away another. For the long and hardy
undertaking of unearthing documents I owe a large bulk of this work to
Giovanni Mion—who threw in a free tour of Turin in the mix; Bruno
Antoniolli in Desenzano del Garda and his Elvira de Hidalgo remembrances; the late, eternally resourceful Fabio Gervasoni—a terrific correspondent and an even better archivist; Nicos Haralabopoulos, Gianni Tanzi,
Cristian Finoia and Federico Vazzola.

Even the most obsessive journalist cannot be torn across multiple
continents at once. For rifling, photocopying, scanning and identifying I'm
indebted to the following:

Constantina Stamatoyannaki at the Hellenic Literary and Historical
Archive in Athens (E.L.I.A.); George Iliopoulos at the Municipal School of
Music of Kalamata, Messinia; Giovanna Bosman and Eleonora Lattanzi at the
Fondazione Gramsci, Rome; Jeni Dahmus at the Juilliard School Library, New
York; Nathan Coy at the Stanford University Archive of Recorded Sound;
Natalia Guga at New York Public Library; Tara C. Craig at the Rare Book &
Manuscript Library of Columbia University, New York; Joy Austria at the
Newberry Library, Chicago; Arcadia Falcone at the Harry Ransom Center,
University of Texas, Austin; translator Fani Kanatzia of Athens and a heap of
people who remain anonymous at the British Library; the Bibliothèque
Nationale de France; the Bibliothèque de l'Opéra de Paris; the Koninklijke
Bibliothek in The Hague; the Victoria & Albert Museum Theatre and
Performance Archive, London; the Biblioteca Nazionale di Roma; the Library
of Congress, Washington D.C. and the State Library of Victoria, Australia.

Thank you for gifting me a dreamlike youth.

Permissions

Excerpts from MY LIFE IN AMERICA AND WHAT MARIA CALLAS TAUGHT ME by Marko Lámpas. © 2011.

Other permissions are cited in the endnotes.

The author has made her best efforts to locate the copyright owners of works herein cited. Any possible accidental omission is deeply regretted and can be reported to The Crepuscular Press through its website:

https://www.thecrepuscularpress.com

List of Illustrations

Prologue: "Break normality."

"Intangible" was her own epithet for it; that realm that Schopenhauer deemed the purest of the arts. Music inhabited a separate platform of existence. Singing was "no act of pride," in Callas' own words, but merely an "attempt to rise toward those heights where everything is harmony."[1] That fluster of tenacious instruments that fused and wrangled, clashed and melded was another stage whose lofty boards one deigned to tread.

"Stumbling by accident into the Sistine Chapel" was music critic William Weaver's description of a Callas performance.[2] Yves Saint Laurent became overexcited: "Empress, queen, goddess, sorceress, hard-working magician, in short, divine . . . You took away everything with you. Deprived of its enchantress, the red and gold pit functions no longer . . . Those overwhelming gold-fringed curtains, those shadowed ground-floor boxes, those loges, those galleries, those balconies, those rows of plush seats, those arc lights, those spotlights, those marble stairs, they are YOU!"[3]

Frenzy was awakened. Poring over books and journals from the fifties to the present day, we stumble upon lexemes taken from her name across a gallery of languages: "callasien," "Callasite," "callasiano."[4] The woman sparked a culture rather than a cult. Lines of fans who camped out in their sleeping bags could brave the frost for four successive nights. Like soldiers during a nocturnal vigil in the trenches they remained alert to spot suspicious prowlers.[5] Huddled together in the crowd were hippie teens and veterans from both world wars. At the peak of her career director Franco Zeffirelli wrote to her, "Marlene Dietrich . . . says that in American hospitals they play your records continuously because they have discovered that your voice helps those who are ill, giving them confidence, calming them, and helping them to recover from what ails them."[6]

Why were so many hypnotized? Their world was hardly an artistic wasteland. In the pop culture domain were Sinatra and Elvis; for classical connoisseurs there were Bernstein and Karajan. Marlon Brando warmed box office seats. Margot Fonteyn and Rudolf Nureyev electrified a scintillating onstage partnership that sent galvanic shockwaves through balletomanes and daydreamers alike.

But Callas lacked her colleagues' knack for ranking on a scale; no adjective selectable on a report card was ascribable to her. Albert Einstein's theory of relativity was still gathering steam; metaphorically she had already debunked it. "Relative" was she to no one.

Witnessing performances of hers was a surreal transgression; stolen chances to escape the rut of everyday existence and take steps into oblivion: a radiance accessible by different routes. Some inhale its heady aura strolling down the twisted path of Broadway; showered by caresses from a flurry of haphazard colored lights. Others stumble on it squeezing past the calligraphic swirls of tourists in the purple and mahogany mosaic of Venice, passing by its denizens of sprawled graffiti and the deluges of black canals encroaching on its banks. Eyefuls of it can be caught in hazy mists enshrouding the Niagara Falls: a bastion against ephemeral and seismic crises.

Some label it escape; others transcendence. What it really is is an encounter with the "other".

How do we map out the other? What are its co-ordinates? A plenitude of vivid sketches can account for it. The eyes were the first source of her narration: generous opulent gems of black opal. "If they were bullets, everyone in sight would be dead," photographer Diana Vreeland decreed.[7]

Onlookers cite her aquiline nose, the long tapers of fingers that helped her expression, a copious mane her admirers believed was jet black. Naturally brown, the locks were tinted with gold sun streaks. Sometimes she was even described as a redhead.

The fount of magic was the voice: an instrument that listeners attempt to liken to an oboe or a clarinet; at times even a flute. A natural sound was palpable somewhere beneath the portraiture of phrasings and inflections. Yet it's difficult to unearth the *raw* voice: a paradigm entirely stripped of character. An actor's instrument, it is a prop fluidly molded to create a role. Its pitch can oscillate; its volume slices human limits and an accent paints the personage.

The Callas voice could be a docile girl—Amina in Bellini's *La sonnambula*; an imitation of a pair of gently chinking glasses. Embodying the steely quality of Princess Turandot it threatens death to all her subjects in the aria "In questa reggia": an imperious execution of vindictive bloodlust. There was the eroticism of conniving Carmen; both beguiling and belittling in her prurient seduction.

At the polar end of this long line of roles was waif-like Violetta in *La traviata*. Callas would quote a letter from an English nurse who drew a parallel between the fragile voice that she had forged and victims of tuberculosis she had treated; in the singer's words a timbre "on a little *thread*. It can break from one minute to the other."[8]

So little of her is preserved on film yet photographs are incandescent. While other singers were content to raise their arms or lift their chins to indicate despair, Callas donned the flesh and mind of characters. Lord Harewood limned the vivid escapades of hedonistic Violetta in *La traviata*: a young woman who "kicked off her shoes, swept glasses and crockery off the front of a table and leant back on it to sing her *cabaletta* . . ."[9]

Others recalled a Cio-Cio-san in *Madam Butterfly* whose face lit up as she committed suicide. Stripped of her dignity because Lieutenant Pinkerton has left her for a bland compatriot, the ex-geisha commits seppuku to salvage her honor. A critic remembered how Pinkerton called out her name as she thrust the knife into her stomach: "Joy touched her, meeting death on the way."[10]

A phantasmagorical trance crystallized. When Callas sings the final phrases of the "Air des Lettres" piece from Massenet's *Werther*, "Tu frémiras" ("You will tremble"), a tremor chills the voice. The character Charlotte has just foretold her kindred spirit's suicide by reading one of his portentous letters. Callas' tremor is no vocal defect; neither is it excessive vibrato. Organic, it is woven in the voice of Charlotte. *Stylized*. Could Callas realize the aria if these disturbances were taunting her? Nobody could. They are the throes of agony and grief and murkiness we strive hard to avoid; the ugliness we seek to scrub off real life's scabrous surface.

It was the specter of the character through which she lived. Located just outside the entrails of the heroine, she gazed at her creation from afar—as though in retrospect. Charlotte is not the mirror of a woman visualizing her beloved dangling from a precipice. She is a ghost of it; an indefatigable echo. The threshold between simulated beauty and reality.

The purpose was to "break normality," in her words.[11] The gift she lavished onto opera had as many metamorphoses as a kaleidoscope. Walter Taussig, one of her vocal coaches, opined that while most singers were "reproductive artists," she was a "creative artist."[12] There is a difference between imbuing a role with emotion—even with a wealth of authentic intensity—and taking its contours to twist them. Picasso's sources were the same as Rembrandt's: physiognomies, eyes, noses, lips and limbs. Even fruit bowls. But the master took these forms and zigzagged over them, creating new contortions. Works of originality broke through.

Callas treated opera the same way. It was never about clasping roles to kindle them with vents of *fire*. Fire only has a use when subject to restraint. Callas yielded what she called a "strange interpretation which made [the public] work a little *harder* . . . instead of saying, '*Oh*, what a lovely voice, *oh* what a lovely note, *oh*, how *nice*, how *pleasant*—let's go home,' they were disturbed . . . anything that *disturbs* a person in the *beginning* creates a bit of a . . . *reaction*."[13] Previously pillaged of its sentimental truths and nuances to be a showcase for high notes, opera could now convert into a complex tapestry.

Callas rewrote a repertoire. An adorer of lesser-known, more difficult works of the bel canto period, she became their advocate for the sake of the triad: Rossini, Donizetti, Bellini. These were her gods. When Rudolf Bing—General Manager of the Metropolitan Opera from 1950 to 1972—responded to her suggestion of staging Donizetti's *Anna Bolena* with the bland comment, "it's an old bore of an opera,"[14] she took the idea to La Scala where director Luchino Visconti resurrected the work. Special effects like extra trills and scales and the interpolation of more high notes were anathema to her: "This sets my work back a hundred years."[15]

A good girl in real life who had contempt for anarchy, she broke into rebellion in art's sphere.

Her fantastical nature paved the way for a whole school of Callas mythology: an institution that expended gallons of black ink and dotted reams of paper. It's strewn with lies and stories cooked from scratch; half-truths, acrylic narratives, synthetic tales and fables stitched from semi-natural sources. It never stopped and doubtless never will.

Yet one can't be surprised by it. History has shown that geniuses are predisposed to feral conduct. Artistic greats who seem relatable make up a fraction of the sect. Run the gamut of them and the number of potential friends you'll find will hover close to zero. Nobody could argue they were ordinary—let alone *alike*.

There was Marlon Brando's rumored savagery and the occasion in which Rudolf Nureyev threw a chair and wrecked the furniture at his host's party.[16] Maria Malibran—the opera goddess of the nineteenth century—had a still-born child. During her next pregnancy she quipped, "I hope to get out of this fix like *last time*."[17] Dubbed the greatest actress of all time, Sarah Bernhardt yearned to sleep in a coffin. She had her mother buy one and was photographed in it.[18] Prokofiev referred to the wife he abused as an "infected tooth".[19]

They give us so much both aesthetically and soulfully.

Yet they fall short of meeting our criteria for friends or lovers.

Behind an overwhelming horde of stories that exploit her name it is precisely her normality that most incites suspicion. One of the recurring themes throughout her interviews is shyness. Callas was asked to name her complexes in 1970. "I'm very *timid*, oddly enough."—"Timid? Really?" journalist David Frost darted back. "Very timid." It was hard for Frost to get his head around this so she had to clarify it for him. "Not on *stage* . . . That's different . . . I'm shy of er . . . revealing my inner *self*. But I've understood that I suppose—*within* the limits of my possibilities, let's try and uncover myself." She laughed gently at her struggle to be open.[20]

American mezzo-soprano Sandra Warfield remembered spotting her at a restaurant near La Scala at the apex of her twinkling career. Warfield had never met her but approached her to alert her she and all her friends were hyped up for her imminent performance. Callas suddenly looked scared. "I hope they aren't expecting too much," she replied.[21] Constantly she claimed she didn't like to talk about herself because "I find *me* boring."[22]

Her aura emanated tenderness. Reared in an uncaring family, she seemed as much in need of love as an abandoned puppy; sometimes even rashly and naïvely. But it was something that she knew about herself.

A strong attraction to mother figures was a consistent motif in her life. The perennial one was Elvira de Hidalgo—a vocal coach who had granted sartorial advice and disparaged her nail-biting. Later Maria would financially support her.[23] Gestures from people she met only once could wrap this woman in a clutch of awe. Sat in the apartment of her friend, record producer Dorle Soria one day, she melted when the latter's mother gave her homemade jelly from wild grapes and noted: "This is the only thing I know wilder than you."[24]

Kindness was one of her foremost constituents. Eileen Farrell never forgot her first meeting with Callas. She had approached her in a London restaurant one day in summer 1959 and introduced herself. Having seen her on the Met stage, Callas recognized her. When Farrell mentioned she was due to travel to Milan in a few weeks Callas immediately asked, "How long will you be in Italy? Because I'm not using my house there, and I would love for you to use it for as long as you'd like."[25]

Photos present for the most part a giddy, warm and open creature. Her radiant, thick locks at times transcend her shoulders; in one candid still she holds her poodle in the air above her face and dotes on him. Enormous spectacles would shield her eyes. In silent footage of her at a party of two English friends, Louise and Ida Cook, she sits insouciantly, espies the camera and instinctively responds with a colossal wink. It isn't difficult to understand why biographer George Jellinek described her as a woman who "radiates an incredible aura of defenselessness men find irresistible, though they should know better."[26]

After a successful performance her excitement and buzz knew no bounds. She could spill out silly sentences and streams of garrulous affection. Her friend Stelios Galatopoulos recalled tailing her backstage on 22 June 1959 after a fearsome *Medea*. "I followed her through . . . the labyrinth until she heard my footsteps, stopped round a corner and caught me with both hands. We were chattering about the performance when suddenly she raised her voice, accusing me of making her late: 'Do you realize that the Queen is waiting for me?' 'It is not the Queen but the Queen Mother,' I informed her with a touch of smugness. [She had summoned the soprano for a dinner at Clarence House]. Waving her hand rather extravagantly, Callas declared, 'Same thing, isn't it!' "[27]

Touches of self-consciousness gloss many of her letters. In one to music critic Irving Kolodin she adds in a postscript: "I hope this letter makes sense to you because I was interrupted at least ten times whilst writing it."[28]

During a *Tosca* in May 1965 she unexpectedly neglected to remove her contact lenses. Because of her compulsive need to live inside a character Callas preferred to enter every stage in her myopic state. For those hours she lived in a fog—and when it had suddenly cleared, horror iced her. "A *terrifying* thing happened to me!" she gasped in intermission to her good friend Michel Glotz. "For the first time, I saw my partners, the props, the furniture, the set designs, the orchestra, the conductor, and *even* the first rows. And I felt *literally* overturned, because this is the first time this has happened to me!"[29]

All kinds of idiosyncrasies twitched in her personality. She had a habit of compulsively collecting recipes that she would never follow; something she referred to as "the only hobby that I have—isn't it *ridiculous? I know* it is, but there you are!"[30] Sudden urges to polish silver or rearrange furniture at three o'clock in the morning—and encourage her friends who had come round for dinner to join in the fun—were in no way uncommon.[31] Filming an interview in 1968, she fidgeted compulsively with a loose cushion thread, forcing technicians "to stop her . . . noises were coming over the microphones like pistol shots."[32]

The music that she worshipped was bel canto: swirls of mellifluousness. Yet her real-life speech pursued an altogether different rhythm. Callas' spoken warm contralto travelled at a speedy pace; phrases were often strangely syncopated. Unexpected words were stressed and pauses halted utterances unpredictably. Her art was opera but her speech was beats in music by Scott Joplin. It yielded long lines such as: "I talk with myself frequently, Mr. Downes . . . Every now and then, I just *withdraw* to myself and I calculate things and I say, 'Well, this happened and *that* happened, why should this happen, *why* did I do that, why *should* I do that, and why *don't* I do it better and why don't you have enough, er, *willpower* and, you know, you *reason* with yourself—doesn't it happen to *you?*"[33]

Every time she glowed with playfulness and giddiness there was an element of coyness in her; even a small dose of mischief. Ditziness conjoined in camaraderie with intellect. Neurotic and too nervous pre-performance, post-performance and *between* performances, she nonetheless kept her clear-headedness. Callas sparkled with the black and white gleam of the leading lady of a screwball comedy; Katharine Hepburn in *Bringing Up Baby.* You would have thought that she was an invention of the movies—but she wasn't.

In addition to this she was sometimes melancholy; even lushly senti-mental. Her favorite film was the 1939 Laurence Olivier *Wuthering Heights.*[34] Acutely aware of her dreaminess, she was self-deprecating about how much she allowed her mind to wander. "I still live in the atmosphere of those silly librettos, full of foolish innocence and naïve idealism!"[35] she wrote composer Renzo Rossellini.

Juxtaposed with the excited woman who would overemphasize her child-ish side that "loved westerns"[36] and adored tangos, Sinatra records, cha-chas; "nice soft music, sometimes even rumbas and things like that,"[37] was an artist eerily obsessed with her art.

"I'm perfectly normal—*possibly*," she once insisted to an interviewer.[38] Yet all the little and large actions that she implemented to create her work—to the detriment not just of her well-being but others'—reflect somebody light years beyond ordinary.

It was an addiction no external force could conquer and its name was "loyalty to the composer." She accentuated it in every interview, in every article she ever wrote; in every conversation that she ever had: "We *serve* art and we serve the composers that *were* geniuses; we are *not* geniuses."[39] At the end of a session with vocal coach Janine Reiss in the sixties she sat down with a much-needed coffee. "I hope he is happy," Maria despaired. "Who?" Reiss asked. "Donizetti."[40]

In this domain no shyness could blockade her wishes. She sought to have a hand in *everything*. Somehow she felt that she could contribute in a variety of ways to the fulfillment of composers' wishes. Her opinions fill the pages of a letter from director Alexis Minotis to conductor Nicola Rescigno regarding their forthcoming *Medea*: "She said that she would like her costumes not quite so Greek, but a little more barbaric ... About the scenery, she likes the first and second act very much. Not so the third. She finds it too closed in."[41]

Artists are called divas when they try to get their way. Callas went *out* of her way to make her life even *harder*. Twenty-hour rehearsals were part of her ritual. Luchino Visconti depicted her perfectionism as a drive devoid of care for her well-being. It was 3:30 am at one point during a rehearsal of *La sonnambula* in 1955 when Visconti insisted they stop. Callas made a rare concession: she sat down. Just when Visconti thought their work was over she got up and everything resumed.[42]

Every new success intensified her merciless self-loathing. "When I sing I wish that my voice would obey me always ..." she wrote. "At times I get to the point of invoking death to liberate myself from the torment and anguish that afflict me because I cannot succeed in attaining what I want."[43] Thousands of letters from her fans and endless lines of ticket-buyers petrified her; never did she view them as a metric of accomplishment. After spells of twenty- or forty-minute ovations she would retreat to her dressing room to sob furiously. Only *she* could know when she sang well: "For this is the paradox," she once wrote. "What an audience feels is a great performance does not necessarily mean the same thing to me ... Then at other times when *I* feel I have really given of my best the audience's reaction is not the same. So the mystery remains. It haunts me."[44]

Through such vignettes the portrait of a girl next door dissolves. Commentators have enjoyed dividing her into two individuals: genius and woman. Yet they co-exist. The Maria Callas who impaired her health to craft a memorable performance was the same frank woman who could openly express her complexes. She could barely give an interview without forewarning, "I'm not good at words."

Her parlance was a smorgasbord of motley, half-made-up expressions. Replete with purple sermons and pedestrian jargon, it incorporated phrases of her making such as, "But you have habituated me to a ball."[45]

"Prosaic reality" was how she termed an interrupting phone call.[46]

Yet during her time as a visiting teacher at the Juilliard School in the seventies, she so longed to appear hip to students, she used words such as "Gee whiz."[47]

At times it's difficult not to believe she was in parts conventional. In a letter to her husband dated 18 November 1948, she makes clear her reasons for being: "I live only for you and Mama—you share me between yourselves!"[48]

Sometimes her talk fazed intellectuals through its blunt deficiency of the cerebral. Making music was a thing that she described in culinary terms: "First of all you must have—well, as they say, to do *pastasciutta* you must have the 'farina'—the *flour* . . . But, er . . . after you have the flour and all the necessary ingredients you have to make the *pasta* . . ."

Her passion for cuisine was such that Leo Lerman would eventually "discover that when she asks me to order, in a Dallas restaurant, fifteen different varieties of ice cream, she will taste each and every one."[49]

Singing wasn't switching on a "genius" lightbulb. Callas' multi-facetedness covered a great scope. For someone who expressly never had a publicist or press agent, she contrived her image with more care than most imagined; arranging her comportment to suit others' expectations of her image.

It would trip people up. Watching her at a dinner party with the Queen Mother in 1959, philosopher Isaiah Berlin pondered: "They were like two prima donnas, one emitting white and [the] other black magic."[50] Through this Berlin unwittingly unveiled a secret. Integrity and honesty were her two highest principles. Callas was genuine. But she was also well-read in the art of self-adjustment: crafting a persona comely for the social context. This was the woman who in 1971 greeted a *New Yorker* interviewer not with "Hello," or "Good morning" but—fully attuned to the fads of the time— with the imperative, "Shoot."[51]

In situations of uneasiness she made a point of masking her malaise: an act that made her cherish solitude. "I *like* to be with myself every now and then . . ." she related. "I feel the *necessity* to be *alone—frequently*. It's our *work* . . . I have my own *interior* world . . . I can live with myself for *weeks*."[52]

The press envisaged her a raging shrew. Knowing they had termed her "tigress", she alluded to it almost casually. "That could be a lovely title. It looks good in the newspapers. It attracts attention. And the tigress as a beast is certainly wonderful to look at."[53]

Cracking the Callas code has been a daunting task for many. It has been easier to claim that she was binary, or even, in more slothful narratives, that she was "schizophrenic." Biographers have relished visualizing Callas twins perpetually engaged in a polemic duel with pistols blazing. They seem to favor the idea that genius cannot exist without the presence of some kind of mania.

But Callas was too mindful, too consistent in her ways, and far too conscientious—"conscientious" being her favorite word—to be removed from self-awareness.

Nobody could have inspired day-long periods of rehearsal or perform-ances she gave when she could barely stand; nobody forced her hand to cite her instrument throughout her correspondence. Many were written at a time when she was thought to be preoccupied by her liaison with a well-known billionaire. She spoke about her gift as though it were her ailing child—reporting on it as she might a separate person: "The voice is quite healthy . . . I want and desire it [for the performance to go well] more than anything you can imagine."[54]

At rare moments in her life one caught a glimpse of all of her: the contrasts that had fused to make an alloy and the human meshing with the superhuman. A friend once scrutinized her as she read the music of Verdi's *Lucrezia Borgia* for the first time while her husband dozed off at a type-writer. ". . . she was gone, completely immersed in the score. Occasionally, she looked at me and she smiled, but she didn't see me. This went on for a very long time, and I was enthralled . . . Maria took off her glasses, closed the book, put down the pencil, looked at me, and said, 'It's wonderful. It's really wonderful.' And I said, 'Do you know it all now?' And she said, 'Well, you know, you have to know it all, so that when you go out on the stage for the first rehearsal, you know who you are. Then I am free to breathe onstage.' "[55]

Her life is the story of a woman who subverts stereotypes. Back in 1859 composer Hector Berlioz assumed that he had found "the one." The man had fallen haplessly in love with mezzo Pauline Viardot. Under her bewitching spell he penned a declaration:

> *The whole of my life has been nothing but a long and passionate aspira-tion towards an ideal which I had created for myself. As soon as my heart . . . found in an individual one of the qualities, one of the charms of that ideal, it became fixed on that individual. Alas! disillusion soon came to tell me that I had made a mistake. My life passed like that, and, at the moment when I feel it to be near its end, the ideal, which I had had to give up as the fantastic creation of an insane imagination, suddenly appeared to my dying heart! . . . Let me spend the last days which remain to me in blessing you, in thanking you for coming to prove to me that I was not mad.*[56]

Eventually his love came to a standstill. Some time later he was swayed again and found another goddess to adorn with worship.

But she also disenchanted him.

And now we know the crux of Berlioz's quandary. The composer's problem was not fickleness: he simply lived a hundred years before the birth of his ideal.

1.

"Voluptuous intoxication"

Manhattan in the 1920s didn't have the aura of those cosmopolitan, resplendent cities known for cultivating artists. If anything it was an unsophisticated Paris or Berlin still on the cusp of evolution. Flooded with fresh immigrants left stupefied by the vernacular, the charged hub was an overflowing puddle of colliding crowds. Prohibition stirred a melting pot for vendors peddling taboo flasks. Walls flaked with peeling posters of parading ships and pinkish skylines vying to burn holes in tourists' pockets. An enviable residence for any gawping foreigner, the Big Apple was contemptible among the erudite elite.

Gleaming temptations that New Yorkers eyed in 1923 were miles away from the domains in which the greats of music had been reared. These were not the chandelier-lit, pearl-white halls that had once echoed the belabored steps of Mozart loath to play a rondo in the Prince-Archbishop's court; or the enchanting Milanese salons of Countess Clara Maffei that had served as Verdi's haunts. No Donizetti was on hand to offer tutelage to a Bellini; neither was the thirty-something Nadia Boulanger in search of sapling pianists to nurture.

The emergence of another kind of artist was apparent. Westerly a dawning Hollywood fed icons being bred. Neon signs of a jazz powerhouse blinked garishly across the South.

But no cane-carrying musicologist could have anticipated that the title of the greatest opera singer ever known would be ascribed to a shy girl from a Greek enclave in a run-down region of Manhattan.

Hometowns like to lay claim to their famed artists, striving to convert them into edifices as defining as the Eiffel Tower. It is perhaps befitting then that Callas—who would state, "I don't feel that my roots lie *anywhere*"[1]— was born into a bustling city swelling with diasporas of different roots.

At the time of her birth "Callas" did not exist; even "Maria" was far off from being her label. A person's date of birth is one of life's sole certainties;

in her case it was one of many factoids. Changed and variously recorded, the specific remained unconfirmed to Callas till the age of forty-four.[2]

The newborn struggled to incite festivities. Her mother's arms remained a foreign haven for the four days in which Evangelia Kalogeropoulou—a twenty-five-year-old Greek woman who had four months previously arrived in New York with her husband Yorgos—categorically refused to face the baby girl. The couple was Greek Orthodox; by no means terribly religious but a great deal superstitious. Both parents had been anxiously relying on the prophecy of an astrologer who had assured them their descendant would be male.[3] They had been certain God would grant them a male heir to compensate for their lost son, Vasily, who had died of meningitis at the age of three.[4] Already in possession of a girl—six-and-a-half-year-old Yakinthy—the baby daughter marred their expectations.

In New York Yakinthy became known as Jackie. Remembering her sister's birth, she told her readers it had been "disturbing news."[5] Their mother Evangelia Dimitriadou, known as "Litsa", was the daughter of an army officer.[6] Yorgos Kalogeropoulos—a student of pharmacy—hailed from Meligala in the Peloponnese. The name that Evangelia and her daughters took was "Kalogeropoulou".[i] Though they were not of a superior class her family looked down on Yorgos with cantankerous contempt.[7]

It was a loveless and disastrous marriage unimproved by the unwanted child.

Evangelia half-heartedly suggested that the girl be called Sophia, a classic Greek name borne by one of her sisters. Yorgos—whose name had now been anglicized to George—conflicted with his wife, insisting that she be Cecilia. Both names were written on the birth certificate—but incorrectly. "Sophie Cecelia [sic] Kalos" was how this little girl was registered. Her mother's maiden name Dimitriadou was recorded as "Demes."[8] Present in the delivery room together with the parents and Jackie was Dr. Leonidas Lantzounis, a friend of the Kalogeropouloses who still spoke no English and largely relied on their niche.

Since neither parent saw fit to remember such a date or keep the birth certificate, disputes surrounding it unfolded speedily. The girl had been born a month early.[9] While her birth certificate reads "2 December" Evangelia convinced her daughter it had been the fourth. "I couldn't tell you what originated these two versions . . ." a forty-one-year-old Maria wrote to her friend Herbert Weinstock. "I can only think that my mother mixed up the date of my birthday with my sister's [who had been born on June 4th]."[10]

She entered the world at Flower Hospital on Fifth Avenue near Manhattan's 105th Street: a facility now known as the Terence Cardinal Cooke Health Care Center. In the delivery room a plaque was later installed:

---

[i] In Greece the patronymic name women receive is the genitive declension of their father's name. Thus for the women the masculine "Kalogeropoulos" became the feminine last name "Kalogeropoulou."

"Maria Callas was born in this hospital on December 2, 1923. These halls heard for the first time the musical notes of her voice, a voice which has conquered the world. To this great interpreter of universal language of music, with gratitude."[11]

Can a toddler offer signs of genius? Likely only in the fantasies of (caring) parents. With curly raven hair and gaping chestnut eyes, the infant didn't seem extraordinary—but she made ungodly noise. Speaking in 1957 she remembered, "I can't remember when I first started to sing, but according to my parents I began very early—when I was barely out of the cradle." The neighbors heard her "hurling vocalizes and high notes so unusual for an infant that they found themselves stupefied."[12]

"They would be playing ball—whatever, and Maria would be singing,"[13] her second cousin twice removed, Mary Annexy, described her mother's memories in 2012.[14] The two- or three-year-old suffused the atmosphere with whirls of babbled melodies galore.

Sometime in the early months after her birth the family relocated to 87 Sixth Avenue in Astoria, where Yorgos Kalogeropoulos became George Kalous.[15] *Soft jobs are for soft people and that sort soon spoil!* preached a contemporary poster.[16] The rookie pharmacist expected to spruce up his English and acquire his drugstore in a handful of months.

Five years would pass. With shattered dreams George earned a living teaching Greek and working as a lab assistant.[17]

Maria was christened on 26 February 1926 in a Greek Orthodox cathedral, the Holy Trinity, at 319 East 74th Street. Her name was finally registered in the Hall of Records as Maria Anna Cecilia Sophia Kalogeropoulos: colloquially Mary Anna or Mary.[18] As the priest dipped the girl infant in the font she bonded with the water; an affiliation she would later resurrect in a capacity to swim great strokes. Her lungs protested as her parents finally began to dress her; fussing till they yielded to a piercing scream. An untrained voice.[19]

Legend (propagated by her mother and her sister) has it that Maria first became acquainted with an instrument aged four. Allegedly she was enchanted by the pianola Evangelia had bought. The latter recollected how Maria spent time pressing down its pedals: one of the first urban Callas myths.[20]

July 1928 laid bare a nervous disposition.[21] Jackie had just turned eleven. Evangelia's chronic hatred of the family's surroundings had provoked the clan to move more times than they could count: Washington Heights was now their neighborhood.[22] Maria was a lanky creature with thick tufts of bushy, coarse dark hair and dangling bangs; a timid girl already beaming with the love that she would radiate in later years.

"I was walking with my parents," she later recalled, "and suddenly I saw Jackie, who was playing ball on the other side of the street, with our house-keeper and a cousin. It often happens with me—it's a characteristic side of my personality—that I'm seized by sudden tender impulses and feel ashamed of them immediately afterward, I don't know why, perhaps because of excessive modesty about my feelings. At that time, too, catching sight of my sister, I ran to her to give her a kiss and then ran away, red and embarrassed, precipitously crossing the street just at the moment when a car was coming along at great speed."

The drama varies source to source. Incapable of summoning the recollections of her life at four, Maria tells us she was "dragged to the end of the street" and "unconscious for twelve days."[23] Her sister deflates the entire affair—insisting the length of Maria's hospitalization was less than a week.[24]

The aftermath was trance-like: "As far as I can remember, during the days I spent in the hospital after a road accident when I was five, the long hours of fever and hazy consciousness were full of strange kinds of music, melodious sounds that were confused but attractive and stimulating," she would recall.[25]

Tired of her husband and their constant monetary struggles, in summer 1929 a frazzled Evangelia took both her daughters on vacation to their cousins' house in Florida, where the three women stayed for no more than two months.[26] Newly bespectacled, the five-year-old Maria suffered from severe myopia.[27]

Their trip to Tarpon Springs was one of the rare times the girls were granted temporary respite: a luxury that spurred Maria on to offer an impromptu debut. Cousin Helen Arfaras (née Kritikou) was a little older than her at the time. In 2001 she remembered the visit. "She always sang wherever she went. My mother had on the piano a Spanish shawl, and Maria would take it and perform. She would go before the mirror and just sing. She warbled like a bird."[28]

By now George had learnt broken English and acquired a license to open "The Splendid Pharmacy," a Hell's Kitchen drugstore. In addition to this he had managed to squander their income. "A sweet, handsome man who was irresponsible and lied like all men," was Maria's description of him decades later.[29] Good friend Leonidas Lantzounis was on hand to loan ten thousand dollars.[30] Its use was limited when the destructive Wall Street Crash immersed the U.S. into chaos on October 24th.

They were living on 181st Street—having moved yet again. Evangelia was exasperating with her virulent invectives. The Crash provoked in her a most melodramatic stunt: when George was forced to close his pharmacy because of failing business, Evangelia hastened to the cupboard before closing time and grabbed some pills she swiftly swallowed. Immediately her husband took her to the hospital to have her stomach pumped. George's connections in the field of medicine assured him that the incident would stay a secret: suicide attempts were at the time illegal; punishable by imprisonment.[31] Twelve-year-old Jackie knew her mother never sought to kill herself. Evangelia's "one and only personal appearance in opera," was how she would term it.[32] The woman wanted more than anything to be a star.

Oblivious to her mother's inner workings, young Maria was still slow to understand that things were not quite right throughout the Callas home. Never did the family starve in New York—not even after the Crash. " 'Poverty' is not really the word because, I can't say I really suffered poverty," she later related.[33] On another occasion she stated, "We didn't have much money at the time, but there was nothing tragic about that, as a lot of nonsensical gossip has claimed."[34]

George began to prosper again when he became a traveling salesman for a drug company to market his treatment for gum disease; business took him away for long whiles. Later he told Jackie he cherished escapes from his onerous wife.[35]

*

Maria's first four grammar school grades took place at four different institutions.[36] A shadow of a musical formation started at the age of eight in 1932. The pianola was replaced with a piano Jackie heartily embraced. Maria scrutinized her sister as she played and soon the febrile fascination grew into her own tuition at the hands of one "Signorina Sandrina".[37]

Her first encounter with the instrument innate to her was zealously emblazoned in Maria's memory. "At the same time as the piano, my first bitter efforts to teach myself to sing . . . Up till then I had listened to music on the wireless, especially to light American songs which I picked up with great ease. But when the world of opera was opened out before me, I became infatuated, filled with a sort of voluptuous intoxication. I owe a great deal to Bizet. When I was still a child I was fascinated by *Carmen*; in fact it was probably *Carmen* that decided my life. I remember I went from room to room singing the enchanting 'Habanera' over and over again. And when my family could bear it no longer I switched over to Philine's song in *Mignon*—'Je suis Titania.' It was a good way of alternating the light soprano with the contralto and thus keeping all the doors open." An avid radio listener, the first opera that she heard was "*Aïda*, on the wireless."[38]

In September 1932 Jackie enrolled at George Washington High School on Aubudon Avenue; Maria was inducted into yet another school. Slowly the latter came to understand that Evangelia was a standout.

"My mother is very nervous, always moaning," Maria would describe in 1969. "When I was little I remember that she always complained about having to be our slave, of having sacrificed everything for us. So as not to hear her I would get away."[39] No tenderness—even a false one—could have emanated from the character of Mrs. Kalogeropoulou. Flaubert or Balzac would have balked at her gargantuan gradation of grotesque.

When the girls were little she would sprinkle pepper on their lips if she believed she heard a lie.[40] Sixteen-year-old Jackie wore a hat her mother didn't like. Evangelia responded with a brusque smack on the head with an umbrella. George attempted feebly to defend his daughter; insisting that she hit her on the rear if necessary.[41] Peeks into the family of high school friend Clare Poretz guided Jackie to discover something was dysfunctional about her own. Preferring not to dwell on these sore episodes, Maria was reluctant to divulge remembrances of early childhood. Sometime in her thirties nonetheless she showed her friend Giovanna Lomazzi a mark on her leg: Evangelia's blow with a chair.[42]

George lacked the impetus to hurry to their rescue. Mostly meek, he had a limited desire to gain affluence. Maria would speak fondly of the man— recalling how her shyness made itself apparent in their outings: "My father always used to say when we walked, and, especially if we passed by a[n] ice cream parlor [and] I'd all of a sudden *stop* walking—I'd pull my father's jacket—and I wouldn't say a word. I'd just look at him—wouldn't look at the ice cream parlor, I would look at *him*—and, well, he had caught on after a while, but he'd play the comedy and say, 'Well, what *are* you asking for, what *do* you want? Will you tell me?' And I wouldn't say a word; I was just *looking* at him like mad."[43]

Overall what George felt for the girls was not enough to qualify as love. In an interview in 1958 he listed his two daughters' birthdays incorrectly. Long absences from both their lives in later years suggest he never had a penchant for their company. At the peak of his daughter's career he insisted that he and Maria had always been close.

Although Maria's music lessons had been Evangelia's initiative, he lied and took the credit. In his broken English George announced in 1958 on television: "Especially *I* prefer to give Maria when she was eight years old [lessons], to start with her private teacher to give vocal voice, until the time she gone back [sic] Greece for a visit."[44] He also told George Jellinek about a year later that he was "very proud" of the way he had behaved during the girls' childhood, since he had never "let [his] wife go to work."[45]

In the early years of their relationship Maria didn't seek to question George's love. "[He was] a little weak, gentle," she would remember. "He was always travelling so I rarely got to see him."[46] Probed about her girlhood memories, she mostly complimented or defended George. "Perhaps he is too honest and too much a gentleman to succeed in elbowing his way into the business jungle," she scribed in 1957.[47]

Soon Evangelia's forceful hand began to have its way—and not just when it came to corporal punishment. As she discovered that Maria had a voice, her own hope of renown resurfaced. Convinced she would have been a singer or an actress if the world had treated her more fairly,[48] Evangelia ravenously plotted her two daughters' stardom. Jackie showed signs of becoming a promising pianist. Meanwhile the girls had barely realized their Hellenic roots.[49] Asked in the midst of her career about her mother tongue, Maria answered: "Of course we always favor our own home language which is, of course, English American."[50] The second language that she learned was French in grade school.[51]

There Maria knew no trouble. Attending at least six schools before puberty could not have been a relishable venture.[52] Yet whilst her childhood left a memory of bitter domesticity, her elementary education represented some form of relief. Recurrently she would compare the bliss of school days to the stressful atmosphere that plagued the peak of her career: "Well, very happy days, I must say—carefree days. I remember we had a principal that was very severe and he kept on saying, 'Now, children—self-control. Remember that all your lives.' I *am*."[53]

Her sole regret was having been too serious for merriment. From that perspective she was slightly envious of her sister's carefree attitude. "I was always much too mature for my age—and not very happy,"[54] Maria admitted. But she also made a point of saying, "I am supposed to have been consumed with jealousy of my sister. My goodness, she was seven [actually six] years older than I. What child does not look in longing at a sister so much older and in the ordinary course of nature, much lovelier than I could be then?"[55]

Ten-year-old Mary Anna couldn't help her introvertedness. Her deepest sentiments of isolation would be deftly blanketed and out of sight. Despite her amiability Maria struggled to appear outgoing. A hard-working student, she received A's, B+'s and B's from the ages of five to thirteen.[56] Miss Jessie Sugar at her last school, P.S. 189, spoke of the child as "a pleasant, well-behaved girl with no sign of temper."[57]

It wasn't just her mother steering her in the direction of the arts. Something was kindled in Maria every time her ears met music. A spark had been ignited in her infancy and she would later write regarding Evangelia's career choice, "I was quite happy to second her, but only on the condition that I be able one day to become a *great* singer. All or nothing."[58]

Criticizing others' voices as a child, Maria disliked Lily Pons. The radio aired a live performance of the Metropolitan's *Lucia di Lammermoor* with the soprano on March 3rd, 1934 as part of a tradition of Saturday matinee broadcasts. This may be the rendition referenced by biographer George Jellinek when he described how the young girl insisted, "I don't care if she *is* a star, she sings off-key! Just wait and see, one day I am going to be a star myself, a bigger star than she."[59]

Years later when Maria would be making her debut in a Saturday matinee broadcast, she nervously mused: "When I think that I stole so much of my homework just to listen to these Saturday broadcasts when I was a child it's just, er . . . well, it gives me, I suppose, the jitters to have to do it today, although I should be used to it."[60]

That same year the public caught her voice while dawdling on the sidewalk. As she sang "La Paloma" its current swept out of her window; passers-by stopped in their tracks.[61] Jackie reported that one of their neighbors, a Swedish man, later arrived at their doorstep to offer free lessons for her. Maria studied with him for two months.[62]

Soon she had her first steps in a theatre. It was the Hippodrome in New York on Sixth Avenue, a building later demolished in 1939. The opera was *Aïda* but it didn't feature cast members especially renowned.[63] Approaching her eleventh birthday, Maria was entered by Evangelia into a radio contest: the first of a few.

At one that took place a year later the master of ceremonies was comedian and actor Jack Benny. "I didn't win the first prize ..." Maria remembered. "Oddly enough ... Oh, I remember only Jack Benny [who] was *so* terribly disappointed, he just ... *couldn't*, couldn't believe it. There was a jury of ... er, *enfants prodiges*—you know, very famous children at that time. I don't remember who they were, but it was, I suppose, 1936, or '5 or '6, something like that ... I won a Bulova wristwatch. And the one that won first prize, I would be *most* curious to know what happened to this ... boy; he was an accordion player, imagine."[64]

Maria next met Benny at President Kennedy's Madison Square Garden birthday celebration, in which she was performing. It was May of 1962; he failed to recognize her: "We've met before, Mr. Benny. Don't you remember? I made my first radio appearance as a contestant on a *Major Bowes Amateur Hour* ... I came in second because you were the only judge who voted for me!"[65]

"The little singer of the school" was her identity according to her recollections.[66] Classmate Georgette Kokenakis attended P.S. 189 with Maria, later becoming a teacher there. She recalled the latter making her stage debut with the song "Play Gypsies, Dance Gypsies" from Emmerich Kálmán's *Gräfin Mariza* at the annual grade school graduation. This would probably have been in January 1935. By this time Maria—in her words—was "studying voice and piano with a kind of fury."[67]

This premiere was ingrained forever in her mind. "They always chose me to sing at some operettas or things like that [at school]," she would tell David Frost in 1970. "And I remember the first time—I *never* was terrified—I *thought*. But I went onstage and uh, I got such a dry throat that I couldn't open my mouth. Nothing came out. But anyway, I was quite good at it, I suppose ... And since then every year I was invited for the graduation play."[68]

Realizing later how much stress she had felt early on, Maria wrote in 1957: "My mother ... decided to make of me a child prodigy as quickly as possible. And child prodigies never have genuine childhoods. It's not a special toy that I remember—a doll or a favorite game—but, rather, the songs that I had to rehearse again and again, to the point of exhaustion, for the final test at the end of the school year; and above all the painful sensation of panic that overcame me when, in the middle of a difficult passage, it seemed to me that I was about to choke, and I thought, in terror, that no sound would emerge from my throat, which had become parched and dry. No one was aware of my sudden distress because, in appearance, I was extremely calm and continued to sing."[69]

Juvenile stardom was a feat deplorable. "I'm sorry for any children who grew up in that period of infant prodigies, when parents were getting such wonderful ideas about becoming rich and famous," Maria said in 1961. "As things turned out, of course, I can't complain. But to load a child so early with responsibility is something there should be a law against."[70]

Yet it's hard to know precisely how much Evangelia's exploitation tainted the girl's attitude toward a naturally delectable pursuit. The latter expressed her opinion on the subject with some ambiguity: "I couldn't continue school because my mother decided on my singing career," Maria told interviewer Norman Ross in 1957. "Your mother drove you very hard as a singer, didn't she?" he responded. "Yes, er . . ." She sighed. "I may be thankful for one thing, and I may not be thankful for another thing."

A coincidence befell the pair. The good-natured and hard-working student's wishes met her mother's merciless ambitions at the same point on a compass.

When Maria was around eleven George bought his daughters canaries. Altogether there were three of them, of which David belonged to Maria. Their chirping captivated her and she would watch the way their throats moved to examine them producing sound.[71]

In January 1936 Maria forayed into Gilbert and Sullivan, portraying a Japanese prince in *The Mikado*.[72] At twelve years of age, the pubescent Mary Anna was a comely girl: pale with puffy dark hair, svelte and lanky. "I hardly ever had breakfast," she would recall of the period. "My mother used to run after me down the front steps because I would go off in the mornings without even having had a cup of tea or a piece of toast."[73] At eleven she had weighed one hundred and nineteen pounds and was five foot three inches; eventually she would reach five foot eight and a half.[74]

In January 1937 Maria finished seventh grade at the age of thirteen. The school presentation that graduation day on January 28th was *H.M.S. Pinafore*, in which Maria sang the role of the sailor Ralph Rackstraw.[75] Around one hundred and forty students had gathered. In one of their autograph books Maria wrote the following message:

> *Being no poet, having no fame,*
> *Permit me just to sign my name.*

She signed it "Mary Anna Callas".[76] Most of the other students would advance to high school. This one was about to lose not just her scholarly advancement but her address and her name. The steadfast Evangelia had decided she was moving back to Greece together with her daughters— leaving George behind. Jackie had already left back in December 1936.

On 20 February 1937, the by now five-foot-seven Maria and her mother left 520 West 183rd Street, their final American residence, and boarded the *Saturnia* en route to Athens. Evangelia called the trip "a visit".[77] Maria would next clap her eyes on crystalline Manhattan in October 1945.

The Callas childhood is believed to be abysmal. Maria didn't help its bleak mien by admitting: "Children should have a wonderful childhood. I had not had it. I wish I could."[78]

Frequently fatigued by rumors and reports about her fabled ghastly infancy, she wanted to precise it hadn't been a torture chamber. "I am supposed to have endured a miserable childhood," Maria wrote in 1959. "Quite false. My parents are said to have quarreled all the time. Now when I was asked once 'Did you see your parents quarrel?' I very possibly answered 'Yes.' What child has not seen its parents quarrel at some time? . . . The truth is my childhood was normal. Distressingly so for would-be biographers."[79]

Since the day that statement was recorded over sixty years have passed. No biographer has ever felt distressed by the "normality" of these first years. The reader could conclude the statement hides denial.

Yet in the context of Maria's life they were proportionately easy. And in that vein she was right.

2.

"A sort of a straitjacket"

"The program was that of course er . . . I should become a singer, I should become an artist in any case; usually what parents say is, 'Well, I sacrificed myself for *you*, but *you* will do what *I* was supposed to do in life.' I suppose that's er . . . general."[1] Touching upon this discomfiting verity, Maria emitted a giggle. It was a 1968 BBC interview with her friend, opera critic George Lascelles, 7th Earl of Harewood. There was no understatement in her words except for the idea of "sacrifice". "Sacrifice" was not in Evangelia's behavioral register.

Halfway across the ocean back in February 1937 an enfevered Evangelia used another premise to parade her daughter. The *Saturnia*'s fifteen-day voyage allowed the perseverant stage mother to squeeze her novelty into the spotlight: thirteen-year-old Maria was recruited to perform at a party for the ship's first-class passengers.[2]

A veteran of amateur performances and radio contests, she was not a shaky ingénue. Precocious poise embellished the ebullient girl still scampering her way to adolescence as she sang an ode to promiscuity in Carmen's "Habanera". At the final line "Et si je t'aime, prends garde à toi!" ("And if I love you, then beware!")—where Carmen takes the rose set in her hair and tosses it to Don José—Maria reached for a carnation in a nearby vase and flung it to the captain.[3]

Patras, Greece—the destination of the family's arrival on March 6th—meant little to the westernized and anglocentric girl.[4] After living in Harlem and Washington Heights, attending seven U.S. schools and following the native ritual of yearbook-signing, she had little to associate with the "old country". "Broken Greek" was Evangelia's label for her daughter's dialect.[5] Supplementary lessons in the tongue were granted courtesy of Maria Trivella, her daughter's first voice teacher. By Evangelia's rules Maria was expected to address her mother with the formal "you": a Greek equivalent of the French "vous" or Spanish "usted".[6]

Overnight they traveled to Athens to stay with Evangelia's mother, Frosso Dimitriadou.[7] Bedridden and ailing at her home in Sepolia,[8] where Jackie had been living since December 1936, she was ill-prepared for the gorilla-like stampede of a harassing daughter advocating for the Callas brand. "Her campaign to advance Mary's cause got under way in earnest," Jackie described in later years. "There was Uncle Efthymios to be sent for, who had contacts at the Conservatory. There were unrestrained enquiries as to who might help finance all the plans she had been brooding over . . ."[9]

Strolling around the streets of Athens with her Uncle Doukas—one of Evangelia's eight siblings—on occasion young Maria would confide her dreams. Decades later Doukas' daughter Ninon Dimitriadou-Kambouri related his memories: "When she was thirteen, fourteen, she told him, 'Uncle, will you come and listen to me singing at the Scala in Milano?' And my father, because you know, 'Scala' in Greek are the stairs, joking, had told her: 'Maria, we have so many other "scalas". You want only the Milano Scala?' She said, 'Yes, uncle. It is *there* I'm going to sing.' "

Doukas may have been responsible for the recruitment of her earliest fan. At a nightclub where the local pianist Angelos Rakinas earned a living she was spotted. "Who is that girl?" the latter asked—and later on, "What can she sing?"

Dimitriadou-Kambouri recalled: "Maria said, 'Play the "Paloma" for me.' When she started, the pianist was so surprised, and also people started to enter the club; people stayed out [that night] to *hear* Maria. And to my father said the pianist, 'Douka, what is this? The first time I hear such a voice, and from such a young girl!' "[10]

References to George began to dwindle in the household. According to Jackie, for eight or nine weeks her father supplied a hundred dollars a month. Together with his aid and Evangelia's savings they could manage. Shortly afterward the pharmacist fell ill with pneumonia and was hospitalized. Obliged to pay medical costs, George cut off his funding.[11] Jackie took a job translating film titles—granting the family some relief.[12] Clouding her impression of the man with rosy tints, Maria nonetheless mistakenly assumed her father periodically supported them, later insisting to journalist Derek Prouse that the family "always had money sent over by [George]."[13]

Akin to Evangelia's radical need to move house in New York, the Kalogeropoulous intermittently inhabited seven Greek addresses from March 1937 to October 1945.[14] For the academic year of 1937–38 Jackie was already training with piano professor Tassia Filtsou.[15] Now Evangelia filled in Maria's application form for the Athens Conservatory, where sixteen was the minimum age for admission. "They laughed in my face," was all she remembered. "What were they to make—they said—out of a thirteen-year-old girl?!"[16]

Fortuitous was such an outcome for the makeshift businesswoman Evangelia: this institution wasn't able to serve up the kind of "get rich quick" McFame she craved. Students were forced to undertake compulsory subjects in theory and music history, pursuing the art academically as well as empirically.[17]

Suddenly her preference was the National Conservatory. Uncle Efthymios—another brother of hers—had connections with the Royal Theatre: at the time Greece's national opera house.[18] Close friends with Stavros Trivellas—voice teacher Maria Trivella's brother-in-law—he arranged an audition for Maria with her. A professor at the National Conservatory, Trivella was a woman of Greek origin Maria mistakenly remembered as being Italian.[19]

It was an intimate affair that took place at Trivella's house, 5 Hoffmann Street. "The plump girl was looking at me strangely, with a certain amount of nervous expectancy," Trivella later recalled. " 'What's your name?'— 'Marianna, Marianna Kaloyeropoulou.'—'What sort of voice do you have?'—'I've been told I'm a contralto.'—'Do you want to study singing?'— 'Yes! It's my one dream.' "[20]

Trivella recaptured the moment. "Her warm, vibrant voice, though somewhat primitive and completely untrained, attested to the great passion welling up in her heart. The tone of that voice was warm, lyrical, intense; it swirled and flared like a flame and filled the air with melodious reverberations like a carillon . . . a great talent that needed control, technical training, and strict discipline in order to shine." Following Evangelia's lament of the family's scarcity Trivella agreed to teach Maria privately and free of charge.[21] She also assumed the responsibility of carrying on the French language Maria had learnt back at school, together with teaching her diction in Greek.[22]

In later years Maria offered snippets of her thoughts regarding her first teacher's efforts. "Oddly enough she had a French method, which was placing the voice in the *nose*—rather nasal. It didn't do me that much harm, in fact. And erm . . . I had the problem of not having low chest tones—*essential* in the bel canto Italian music."[23]

Looking back on the unbridled instrument she would describe it as "dark, almost black . . . and I also had problems with the limits of my upper register. All my efforts . . . were directed toward lightening the tone and acquiring the tonal colors I would need for many—a great many—of the roles I dreamed of . . ."[24] "They say I was not even a true soprano, I was rather towards a mezzo, but I immediately took wing."[25]

Her speaking instrument was cymbal-like in depth and resonance— fluctuating in her interviews between a luscious silver mezzo and a somber dusky alto; ringing like a poker rolling on a fireplace's grid.

Most sopranos start with girlish and angelic voices that remain identical or, with the hand of solid training, grow the fortress of a sturdy technical support. Lined with palpable vibrato (the pulsation made by forceful emphasis of notes), Maria's instrument was bestial. "As soon as she started doing exercises I realized that she was not a contralto, as I had been told, but a dramatic soprano," Trivella would later report. "Previously, as far as I could see, some irresponsible, self-styled singing teachers had almost spoiled her voice assuming her an alto."[26]

Surrender to the military training of her art became an undertaking uncon-ditional: "Fanatical, uncompromising, dedicated to her studies heart and soul. She studied five or six hours a day and I was never in the unpleasant position of having to reprimand her . . ." Trivella would muse. "Within six months she was singing the most difficult arias in the international operatic repertoire with the utmost musicality . . . From time to time she would give me a hug and a kiss and say, 'I don't know how to thank you. I owe my progress to you.' And she was always saying, in her strong Greek-American accent, 'Darling, I love you so much. I shall take you to America, I shall make you a great music teacher!' I never believed any of her promises, I was only sure that she was extremely talented and that very soon she would be rising in the firmament and taking her place among the stars."[27]

Practice was chronic. "At home Maria would refuse to leave her piano for meals, and I would bring them to her in her room. She would put the plate in her lap and go on working,"[28] is one of Evangelia's scant reliable accounts. In retrospect Maria understood herself. "When one is very young one has a driving urge to assimilate everything, a sort of '*furie d'apprendre*' which is not so much ambition as a thirst to be able to satisfy the need for self-expression."[29]

Where else could she have channeled it but through her art?

After a few weeks of discreetly working with Trivella, Maria was officially accepted to the National Conservatory with a scholarship. Truth was tampered with again—giving Maria grounds for discombobulation: "They had to fake my age because of course I was then thirteen years old and no conservatory *would* accept you. And, I was . . . mm, very tall and well-built so I easily passed for seventeen years old . . ."[30] "It was the first lie I ever told in my life."[31]

Under the advice of Trivella the conservatory's director Manolis Kalomiris awarded Maria a scholarship.[32] Studies in vocal expression and the history of opera began with Head of the Opera School Yorgos Karakandas, later complemented by piano lessons with Professor Evie Bana.[33]

Most hours were devoted to self-loathing. Passing by her lessons, fellow student Yorgos Vokos recalled "vocal gymnastics—trills, runs, phrases, *legati*, *staccato*, scales—and every so often Trivella's voice exclaiming, 'Well done, Maria, well done!' 'But my passage-work was terrible, my trills were only half there, my legati were awful.' 'But, Maria . . .' 'No, no, I must do it from scratch! I need to meet my *own* standards, too. I'm sorry.' So once more *da capo*, until Kalogeropoulou gave it her O.K."[34]

Intuition and clairvoyance grew their presence. "I didn't give much time to the people who taught me because I was always so anxious to foresee what they wanted to tell me," Maria later remembered. "It was some sort of—not exactly a game—but at any rate I felt very upset if I didn't see what point they were going to make almost before they said it. When they started to tell me how I should sing a certain phrase I always prided myself on being able to say: 'I know what you mean. May I show you?' "[35]

Together with Yorgos Karakandas' tuition in acting, Trivella painted brushstrokes of the fast-evolving artist's expressivity.[36] Training in stage physicality began at this point. "I was taught then, when I was fourteen years old, the continuous flowing of a movement," Maria recounted. "It was always this movement of the arms and hands, which means freedom. Also how to fall down. It was really something to laugh [at]. To learn how to fall well—and you can't always fall the same way—you have to completely relax yourself and forget how you are going to fall. A slight tenseness and you hurt yourself. Then you also have to learn how this woman would fall and how that one should fall; it's catalogued in many—*many* ways."[37]

Excess weight plaguing the student pocked others' impressions. A philanderer and pedagogue, Manolis Kalomiris performed double duty when it came to protégés. On one occasion he ignored Maria's singing to extend some commentary on her size—inviting the introvert to sermonize on his professional duties. Her purpose was to stress that students should be judged only artistically and not by their appearance.

Short-tempered to a fault, irked Kalomiris suddenly expelled her. When she confided this to Evangelia the pair consulted Karakandas, Head of the Opera School. The trio then confronted Kalomiris and Maria offered an apology.[38]

Although it was believed that Kalomiris "could not stand Maria"[39] he warmed to her considerably later on. After watching her in *Parsifal* in Rome in 1950 he would scribe, "Please forgive me for not giving you any signs of life all this time, [and allow me] to express once more my admiration, and thank you for your kind welcome in Rome ... I hope that in September, we'll have you in Athens and arrange everything ... With fatherly kisses, Manolis Kalomiris."[40]

*

In early 1938 Jackie made the acquaintance of Miltiadis "Milton" Hariton Embiricos, a scion of a wealthy family.[41] He escorted Jackie and Maria to the latter's first exposure to the opera world on February 2nd 1938. A scrappy rendition of *La traviata* would stir on her senses: "It was ... the sort of thing that puts many people off opera for life," Jackie remembered. "I was deeply disappointed and worried, as I was sure Mary must feel the same. But no—as I turned to look at her after the final curtain I saw someone transformed with sheer pleasure. She was in another world, she had in fact entered her own world. Of course she knew that what she had seen was a poor thing but she had simultaneously experienced what it might be."[42]

It hadn't slipped Maria's mind where the "real world" of opera lay. Holding steadfast to the notion that its bastion still sat in the U.S., on 15

March 1938 she registered as an American citizen at the United States Consulate General, stating her intention to return within one year.[43] Jackie's beau Milton bankrolled all the family's expenses[44] and recruited tradesmen to equip their new house at 70 Harilaou Trikoupi.[45]

At this abode the sisters shared a room till the latter's liaison with Milton roiled moral Maria. "Prudishly shocked" was the term Jackie used; a description by no means surprising.[46] Aged fourteen, Maria had no interest whatsoever in the opposite sex.

11 April 1938 saw Maria Kalogeropoulou—as she was billed—give her first concert appearance at Parnassos Hall in Athens. An annual showcase recital where Trivella presented her students, in it Maria sang Agathe's recitative and aria "Leise, leise, fromme Weise" from Act II of Weber's *Der Freischütz* in Greek, the cavatina "Plus grand dans son obscurité" from Gounod's *La reine de Saba*, a song called "Two Nights" by a local composer and the duet from *Tosca* with tenor Yannis Kambanis.[47] Locally it was a non-event.

Behind closed doors the buzz began to scintillate. After just nine months of lessons at the National Conservatory Maria was entered in the annual proficiency exam held on 8 June: the intermediate step between the licentiate and the diploma.[48] Fellow candidate Marika Papadopoulou remembered the seductive sound as well as the sartorial spectacle: "She was wearing a white dress with lace trimmings and a colored belt round her waist . . . when I heard her I was stunned. I don't remember what she sang, but that was no voice, it was a whole orchestra!" Of the fourteen candidates Maria came fifth. A score of Kalomiris' own work, *To Daktylidi tis Manas* (*The Mother's Ring*) was given to her as a prize.[49]

Fifth wasn't good enough. The hunt was on for a new teacher.

Elvira de Hidalgo—a Spanish soprano renowned for performing alongside illustrious tenor Enrico Caruso and bass Feodor Chaliapin—had recently begun her tenure as professor at the Athens Conservatory. The day after Maria's proficiency exam de Hidalgo staged a student production of Bellini's *La sonnambula*, Puccini's one-act *Suor Angelica* and the first act of Humperdinck's *Hänsel und Gretel*. Talented soprano Zoe Vlachopoulou caught Evangelia's widely peeled eyes. According to the former's reminiscences, Evangelia approached her after the performance to announce her daughter would be working with her teacher.[50] It is unclear whether or to what extent Maria criticized Trivella's methods at the time.[51]

"I debuted er—imagine, I debuted, by the way, for the Americans—July 4th, in Greece," she later related to Edward R. Murrow.[52]

Everyone sang "The Star-Spangled Banner" in the concert at Rex Theatre, Panepistimiou Street that 4 July 1938. Launched by celebrated baritone Evangelos Magliveras, the concert served to introduce Maria to this well-known womanizer. According to his brother Christos, after singing a handful of both Greek and American songs she debuted "Casta diva": the aria from Bellini's *Norma* now known as her signature piece.[53]

It was already a staple in her day-to-day repertoire as Elvira de Hidalgo reported years later. "She was ready to sing anywhere, anytime, even if she was doing the dishes. No warm-up, no nothing; she'd go right into 'Casta Diva,' nothing less."[54] Maria requested supplementary lessons with Trivella through the summer. Other students went on vacation.[55]

In early September Maria auditioned for Elvira de Hidalgo.[56]

That afternoon impressed upon the pedagogue a visual mess. "She wore a school apron and worn out sandals on her feet . . . sat in a corner and being unsure what to do with her hands, she started biting her nails," de Hidalgo remembered. "This she continued to do until her turn came to sing. She stood up and came over to me walking heavily and swinging side to side . . . She was very tall and big and wore heavy glasses. If she removed them, she would look at you—but obviously she couldn't see you: big eyes steady and feverish . . .[57] Large and deep-set, [they] were the most express-ive things about her, but they were hidden behind very thick glasses . . . When she opened her mouth I was dumbstruck.

"Maria sang with exceptional power, she had a voice like a trombone. It was rough, but with a very individual timbre, quite extraordinary . . ."[58]

Despite acknowledging the raw material de Hidalgo discerned in Maria innately superlative technical qualities. "I had noticed right from the first audition, the first lesson, that she had a gift few others have; an extraordin-ary musical memory . . . The fact that she was extremely nearsighted was instrumental in developing this talent, as without her glasses, she could not even see the conductor or follow his beat."[59]

Apprised of her new student's training at the rival school, Elvira de Hidalgo waived payment for the upcoming lessons and decided to tutor her privately.

Gambling with a double deck of cards was Evangelia's forte. Maria would continue to have lessons with Trivella for the academic year of 1938–39, studying at the National Conservatory whilst dipping her feet in the tide of its foe. Lessons with de Hidalgo would be carried out in absolute discretion.

The latter had discovered in Maria an explodent charismatic creature she would have to curb: "Until then she had been 'on the wrong track,' " de Hidalgo elucidated. "An aspiring opera singer could hardly have done more things wrong . . . The colors she wore were 'over the top,' and it was the same with her voice too. Gifted as she was with phenomenal breath control (she could sing a whole melodic line in a single breath) and a natural flair for dramatic inflections, she thought the right thing to do was to open the floodgates and pour out everything she had inside her. So the first thing I had to do was to put a brake on her. 'You're young,' I explained to her, 'and for the time being you must get into the habit of singing lightly: think of it as delicate embroidery. Later on, we shall see.' "[60]

Alternating between two completely different teachers would have been no easy feat—and yet Maria never cited this peculiar quandary. Likely her determination and good vocal taste informed her vocal choices.

The fifteen-year-old fledgling made her operatic debut in the spring of 1939 in the National Conservatory's production of Mascagni's *Cavalleria rusticana* (in layman's terms, the opera featured in *The Godfather Part III*). Staged with a double cast, Maria was given the lead role of Santuzza in the second performance. It was one of the rare instances in history in which a female opera singer played somebody *older* than she is.[61]

The doomed heroine spends most of the opera in anguish: her beloved Turiddu has been fooling around with a peasant girl, Lola. Because it is *verismo*—late nineteenth- or early twentieth-century opera rich in simplified vocalization—the work is scarcely the steepest of challenges.

Swept up in psychological investigation, Maria sought to understand the core of the libretto. Puzzled about the line "Priva dell'onor mio rimango" ("I am left, dishonored") in the aria "Voi lo sapete," she posed a cogent question mid-rehearsal. "What does it mean by 'honor'?" the leading lady asked castmate Afroditi Kopanou. Heroine Santuzza sings it after being ostracized in a Sicilian village for an out-of-wedlock escapade with her beloved beau, Turiddu.

Kopanou couldn't put two and two together; neither could Maria. Upon the question being relayed to Karakandas he advised the pair to "ask their mothers".[62]

Three years would come to pass before Maria even *heard* of sex.

To avoid collisions with the props onstage the singer reserved time to practice on the roof of her apartment building. Using furniture and household items, she would imitate the distances of future props by marking their positions with a chalk. This way she memorized the whereabouts of every object.[63]

At a time when it's increasingly in vogue for denizens of Hollywood to suffer physically, have a psychotic break or starve in honor of the school of method acting this endeavor may seem trifling.

Yet the teenager had never heard of Stanislavsky let alone his creed.

"She would listen as if in a trance and sometimes she would walk nervously up and down the room repeating passionately to herself, 'I'll get there one day,'" Karakandas recalled the experience of watching Maria rehearse. "Even then her concern about the composer's markings and the importance of words were great. She may not have had full control of her voice, but I remember she made such a dramatic impact on 'Voi lo sapete' and the 'Easter Hymn' that one did not notice any vocal imperfections . . . this young debutante conveyed so memorably the conflict in the forsaken peasant girl who still loves but resents her betrayer."[64]

Throughout the year that led up to the country's entrance in the war what she recalled was liberty: the thrilling physical and psychic state unfettered in the luxury of youth. "When you are young to sing is in itself . . . an expression of your being, a being which is becoming. It is like the athlete who enjoys using and developing his muscles, the youth who runs and jumps, enjoying and growing at the same time, the girl who dances, enjoying the dance for its own sake, and learning to dance at the same time . . .[65] You simply love your work—this beautiful, intangible thing which is called music."[66] Her ravenous amorphous energy took relish in its spiritual house-hunting.

Something else posed a pestilent hindrance. "Everything went very well," Maria remembered *Cavalleria*. "But I was in despair because my face was swollen and contorted by a tremendous toothache."[67] It was an inaugural luck of the draw: persistently throughout her life an illness would afflict Maria on the cusp of a debut.

Literally blind to the audience, numbing herself to her muscles, the artist hurled herself into the role. Tenor Vyron Simriotis recalled Maria's immersion: "Nobody had ever really taught her how to do it, but when we were together on stage I could see that she threw herself into it with great feeling, and without suffering at all from nerves."[68] The performances were a success with critics and the minister of the capital, Konstantinos Kodzias.[69]

Her final exhibition concert for the National Conservatory took place on 25 June at the Olympia Theatre. She sang an excerpt from Verdi's *Un ballo in maschera*; most probably Amelia's lyrically complex entreaty, "Morrò, ma prima in grazia" ("I shall die, but first, in mercy"). Critic Dimitrios Hamoudopoulos wrote in newspaper *Proia* that Maria "had some really successful moments with her spontaneity of self-expression." She and fellow student Anna Remoundou received 1,000 drachmas to share.[70]

That summer she offered Trivella a parting memento: a photograph of her published in the paper *Eleftheron Vima* with an English dedication spelt out in italics: "To my darling teacher, to whom I owe all."[71] It is the earliest known example of Maria's signature; curvy and bombastic but less slanted than the fanciful calligraphy she would adopt in later years.

*

After switching serially between new dwellings, Evangelia selected her preferred abode in an apartment block at 61 Patission Street. There Jackie's lover would finance the family's rent and amenities.[72]

When "Maria Kalogeropoulou" became a blacklisted name to Filokitis Ikonomidis—Principal of the Athens Conservatory—de Hidalgo lobbied hungrily for her admission that September. Being a former student of the National Conservatory worked against the girl. It also didn't help that Evangelia wanted her to be exempt from mandatory music theory lessons.

Seditious in the face of in-school politics, de Hidalgo faced off fervently against her obstinate superiors: "I didn't manage to convince anyone but I had confidence in my judgment, so I brought the discussion to an abrupt end. 'All right,' I said, 'let's say no more about it . . . I'll take her on as my pupil at my own expense. You won't need to bother about paying me for any of the lessons I give her.'" But once Maria had auditioned with the aria, "Ocean, Thou Mighty Monster," from Weber's *Oberon*—the only piece in

English she would ever record—Ikonomidis and his colleagues were easier to appease. Finally she was granted official admission at the Athens Conservatory and awarded a scholarship for her four years of study.[73] The youngest of eight students in de Hidalgo's advanced voice class, Maria would be the sole first-year enlisted.[74]

Ecstasy for her was following her mistress's instructions. Speaking to Kenneth Harris in 1970, Maria recalled: "When I first studied under Elvira de Hidalgo we began work at 10 o'clock in the morning. We would have a short break for lunch, or maybe eat sandwiches in the school, and then we would begin again. We would work until eight o'clock at night. Now, this is what I am saying about work, you understand: some people would say, 'How does a girl work from 10 o'clock in the morning until 8 o'clock at night, and on a sandwich? Why doesn't she go home? Or maybe go out? Or have a good time?' But I did not want to go home. I wouldn't have known what to do if I had gone home, or gone out. My life was my work, and my work was my life."[75]

The artistic hatchling was aware of little. Never did she gulp down heavy tomes about composers; neither music theory nor the history of music was a strong suit. She couldn't have informed a fellow student how the voice worked; couldn't have designed a diagram consisting of the pharynx and the larynx and the vocal cords.

Yet still she qualified as the class nerd. "I loved to listen to all those different voices: *leggero soprano, lirico soprano,* and the men, too," Maria would recall. "It was all new to me, you see, a new exciting world."[76] This regular absorption gifted her with the impenetrable power to discern little by little what was vulgar and what tasteful; stylistic choices that aroused emotion as opposed to stale mimesis. It was a task of memorizing other people's faults as well as her own faults; of nailing to her mind a silent list of irrefutable instructions.

Prone to sentimental moments and sore spots, Maria lacked the poise of those more academically inclined. After de Hidalgo told her "That was wrong!" on one occasion she "dissolved into tears when we got out into the street."

Intimacy inched toward the precipice of volatility. "I often spoke quite sharply to her after our lessons when she was walking back home with me," de Hidalgo admitted. "I would tug at those awful clothes she wore, criticize everything she did, take her to task for the slightest fault. And nearly every evening she would burst into tears and grab my arm, sobbing, 'But what do I have to do to make you say I am getting on all right?' "

It was a form of worship, not hysteria. Maria would describe de Hidalgo as "this elect woman, who, besides giving me her precious teaching, gave me her whole heart as well, was a witness to my whole life in Athens, including both my art and my family. She could say more about me than any other person, because with her, more than with anyone else, I had contact and familiarity."[77]

Knowing that Maria lacked the money to buy scores, de Hidalgo lent her hers.[78] Ritually the former took de Hidalgo's terrier Gigi for her walks.[79]

"When Maria came in she generally looked awkward and uncomfortable," classmate Lola Ritsou recalled. "Usually she would go straight to the kitchen and do some odd jobs. This made her feel better, as she wasn't paying for her lessons and she knew that our teacher was rather mercenary-minded."[80]

Madame de Hidalgo was no typical maternal figure. If anything, she was a little pushy and the emulation of a diva: scarcely dissimilar to a theatrical agent. Buxom and stocky with a cigarette inextricably lodged between her fingers, the soprano unwound lectures about elegance yet exercised uncouthness. Student Ekaterini Politou remembered how "de Hidalgo got annoyed when we didn't do well. Sometimes she was so exasperated that she threw her books on the floor!"[81] Articles described her as "very self-centered and very possessive, she loved furs, jewelry, and above all money . . ."[82]

Decades later her ex-teacher would reproach the forty-three-year-old Maria for responding late to her most recent letter. "I felt jealously forgotten and I suffered in silence, being unable to understand your behavior toward me."[83] Yet for all of her soliloquies Maria never bore resentment. For a time she would financially support de Hidalgo and insist in one epistle: "You will find a check attached and yet my gratitude for your affection is immeasurable."[84]

Social Maria fell short of Student Maria. Her sartorial teenage tastes were something she recalled with humor. "Once, after . . . [de Hidalgo] entreated me insistently to put on my most chic outfit, because she was going to introduce me to an important person, she saw me turn up in a dark red skirt, a blouse another shade of red—gaudy and strident—and on my head, atop rolled-up braids, I had a ghastly [straw] hat of the 'Musetta' type. I thought myself quite elegant and was very crestfallen when Madame Elvira tore off that absurd headgear, yelling that she would not give me any more lessons if I didn't make up my mind to improve my appearance."[85]

de Hidalgo found the outfit unforgettable. "Her size made the whole thing rather comic."[86]

Maria piled on pounds for a twin cause: unbridled love of food and a hormonal problem. While biographers have relished an embraced conceit that has Maria compensating for a lack of love through excess calories, she liberally confessed indulgence was the core of her obesity. "Using the excuse that in order to sing well one needs to be hefty and blooming, I stuffed myself, morning and night, with pasta, chocolate, bread and butter, and zabaglione. I was rotund and rosy, with a quantity of pimples that drove me mad."[87] An underactive thyroid was the other reason for Maria being overweight.[88]

Despite the isolation that her fingers-to-the-bone resolve required, she was amicable. Welcoming tenor student Vangelis Lakadzis to her home, Maria helped him study *Aïda* and in his score wrote under the Italian text a

Greek transliteration of the words to "Celeste Aïda".[89] She was known as a shy girl who "withdrew into her shell and didn't mix with the others," according to student Spyros Salingaros. At the same time her misuse of certain words in Greek encouraged other classmates to regard her as "a blunt-spoken American, a very insolent girl who spoke familiarly to everyone from the first time she met them."[90]

It was not in her nature to open up. "I hate to show my feelings," Maria wrote in 1959. "That sort of thing can become boring. Of course such aloofness can be misunderstood. But that is the price I pay for being what I am."[91]

And yet she was uncomplicated. Her fondest memories consisted of rehearsing operas such as *Norma* and *La Gioconda* "in my mind, or on the top of a bus, or walking in the street . . . There is a great deal to be done in the mind: you do not always require a piano . . . the poet talks of the mind's eye: there is the mind's ear."[92]

June 1940 saw Maria assume the title role of Puccini's *Suor Angelica* in a Greek language version at the Athens Conservatory. de Hidalgo recollected how the podgy girl dissolved beneath the guise of a repentant nun in mourning for her secret son: "She disappeared under the white garb . . . It went down to her feet and covered her so much that even her figure seemed majestic. Even her face, wrapped up in the veil, appeared thinner, and her eyes, large, profound, expressive, rid of their glasses—were superb . . . I realized on that occasion that Maria genuinely had the potential to become a great actress, she had the sort of single-minded obsession that few artists in the world possess; and I determined that she had a wonderful future ahead of her."[93]

The pedagogue set Maria on the path of the bel canto schooling. A nineteenth-century, all-encompassing vocal technique, bel canto dictates that the voice be supple, limber and elastically malleable in any passage. Musicologists believe the twentieth century untied this doctrine's popularity by bolstering its operas with loud notes and simple melodies in place of arduous ascending scales and tapestries of trills.

At the dawn of the new epoch fashion and the arts were drastically divested of their frills. Just as Chanel crafted a new kind of chic through a little black dress or a white jersey jacket, the melodies of composers Puccini, Mascagni and Leoncavallo were luscious and easy.

Harrowing, at times interminable loops of operatic ornaments had wearied audiences. As waistlines lapsed vocal complexity grew loose. Lead singers who assumed the title roles were not obliged to spew unending series of fast notes: coloratura. Reluctant to enlist the most expensive talent of the highest quality, Italian opera houses' frugal managements appealed to poorer singers. Student vocalists discovered they could work less.

Everyone was happy.

A kind of cop out, this technique proved deleterious to any voice—especially for favored nineteenth-century works. Improperly trained singers found them mercilessly challenging; they *still* do. While contemporary couturiers stitched dresses that were simpler, they preserved a skill that could arrange the tessellates of tulle and taffeta. The same could not be said of singers struggling to string notes together.

de Hidalgo was one of a handful of coaches refusing to peddle the short-cut. In the confines of her home on Codringotos Street she resurrected the old-fashioned schooling. Adhering to the principles evolved by nineteenth-century pedagogue and tenor Manuel García, de Hidalgo taught her students to control the primary rudiment of vocalization, *legato*: smoothness across a vocal passage that ensures each note emerges with an equal strength and singers do not squeak or let slip excess air. Endowing them with the capacity to pace their breath along extensive phrases, she prohibited the sneaking in of stealthy breaths mid-word. Her protégés were trained to execute both grave low notes and sonorous high trills a couple octaves above middle C. Above all de Hidalgo buoyed all her students with the expectation of an almost limitless agility: the confidence and power to sing anything—and *well*.

"The method is usually *always* on the scales, trills . . . If you wrote a book, you must know how to read and *write. And* a little more than *that*," was how Maria clarified it. "Well—bel canto means how to learn to read and write and *become* a great writer. In other words, you have to *learn* to read and write, then learn how to compose *phrases* and *this* and *that*; it's a whole *science* . . . the exact schooling that *violinists, pianists,* all the *instrumentists* [sic]—go *through* . . . A *pure* attack, for instance—it's the *basis* of bel canto. The *legato*—the phrase *must* be *legato*; by *legato*, I don't mean *sliding* . . . It *is* a great schooling of *years* and *years* of dominating the voice . . ."[94] A sort of a straitjacket that you're supposed to put on, whether you like it or not."[95]

As well as solving her "problem of not having low chest tones"—notes in the bottom register that resonate in the chest area—de Hidalgo emphasized light roles; those founded mostly on swift, high notes. Her objective was the transformation of Maria's voice into a fluent resin: durable elastic.

Composing personalized exercises for each student, de Hidalgo crafted her tuition on the basis of the individual's flaws and virtues.[96]

Among the pieces that Maria studied were *Norma*, several Handel arias, Purcell's *Dido and Aeneas*, Rossini's *Stabat Mater* and *Semiramide*, Ponchielli's *La Gioconda*, Mozart's *Requiem*, the arias "La mamma morta" from *Andrea Chénier* and "Ah! perfido," from Beethoven's *Fidelio*: a piece Maria would accentuate when teaching at the Juilliard School years later.[97]

After her student production of *Suor Angelica* the sixteen-year-old signed her first contract as a professional singer with Greece's Royal Theatre. de Hidalgo urged General Manager Kostas Bastias not to give Maria great roles but instead equip her with enough small parts to earn an income. She would earn a fixed salary of 1,500 drachmas a month (around five dollars and the average low-tier wage in Athens). This would maintain her for a while, as she recalled in 1960: "He agreed with Madame de

Hidalgo that the National Opera would pay me a retainer while I continued to study. In this way they showed great faith in me and helped me in my first year, when I was most in need of help."[98]

That summer de Hidalgo took her students on their annual beach trip, where Maria practiced her abandoned gift of swimming, prompting onlookers to watch the singer "in her element in the water."[99] On this trip or another she bonded with classmate Zoe Vlachopoulou. Elsewhere Maria struggled to be bosom buddies: "I can't find anybody who takes her studies seriously enough to be a close friend."[100]

Vlachopoulou remembered her with fondness. "She was not at all gossipy and I never heard her say a bad word about any of the students at the conservatory . . . All Mary talked about was opera: the requirements of this or that role, the problems of staging and acting, the way a good leading man could draw out the best in his partner." On one of those beach trips Maria began singing "Una voce poco fa" from Rossini's *The Barber of Seville*. Vlachopoulou reacted to this by demanding to know: "Hey! You're so good at the vocalises and you've got such a lovely *pianissimo*! Why don't you ever sing at less than your full volume?" Diffident Maria shied away from the enquiry, unsure how to answer.[101]

*

That October Italy declared war on Greece. With no air raid shelter installed in the Royal Theatre, the entire troupe took refuge at the Pallas Cinema. All activities at the conservatory were suspended for three days as residents of Athens battled with encroaching chaos. Forced to huddle, the Athenian citizens began to share accommodation; Evangelia sublet one of the rooms at 61 Patission Street to a young woman, Mariana Papayeorgopoulou. Food became a luxury.

While others scavenged for nutrition the illustrious sapling stumbled on stage rivalry. Assigned to be the understudy for Nafsika Galanou—who was singing the small part of Beatrice in the Royal Theatre's production of Suppé's *Boccaccio*—Maria was alarmed by the soprano's green-eyed quest to soil her name.

The castmates slung some mud according to one chorus member, Galatea Amaxopoulou: "Even in rehearsal Mary's fantastic performing ability had been obvious and from then on the others started trying to find ways of preventing her from appearing. They went about it in the most awful way, insulting her whenever they had a chance. 'That American bitch that's come in, what right has she got to be here, the fat cow, taking our performances away from us?' and that sort of thing." Loudly in the corridors they laughed about Maria's "foreign accent".[102]

It's unclear how many performances of the seventy-one that took place between January and March 1941 Maria actually sang; likely only five or six. Nonetheless she was indelibly remembered by the kinder members of the cohort. "So we heard this rich voice, hysterical and terrifically alive, that swept you off your feet . . ." related bass Nikos Papachristos. "She made her entrance in a long green velvet dress, stormed around the stage, then went off and shut herself up in her dressing room, and we never saw her again."[103]

Two months after that the next stage of the war began: that of the reign of terror. Sixteen air raids sounded on 13 April. Occupation by both Germans and Mussolini's Italians commenced. While the latter held sway in the capital and other cities, Germans laid siege to Piraeus and the islands. The Athens Conservatory was closed till the middle of May. All contracts at the National Theatre were terminated.

This didn't stop Maria risking death by going to de Hidalgo's home for private lessons.[104]

Suddenly this adolescent's shoots were not the lilting leaves of stalks that swayed to wind's soft serenade. Excess bolts of sunlight served to expedite the spurts of her shy psyche's limbs through a blunt series of crude wake-up calls: the blackened skies of curfews and corrosive blares of sirens spear-headed her growth. Maria referred to this time as "the very, very sad war years, of which I don't like to speak even with the people closest to me, so as not to irritate wounds that have not yet healed."[105]

With the "every man for himself" frame of mind in full swing, the family elected the shy seventeen-year-old Breadwinner. Maria's function was to be the sole purveyor of the household. Evangelia even admitted in a letter to her daughter in September 1949: "[Jackie] carries on about having sacrificed herself for us [through the use of her fiancé Milton who supplied them with goods]. Shame on her! What are you to say then, you who were feeding your family at sixteen? I am not saying that she did not save us through that man. But it would have been better had she supported us by her work and in dignity, like you."[106]

de Hidalgo recalled how, "so as not to die of hunger and cold, Maria would have to walk for miles across the muddy countryside . . ."[107] The most excruciating period for the Kalogeropoulous took place in the early months of the Italian Occupation, sometime from April to December 1941.

Citizens were supine and emaciated on the streets. Maria endured lengthy treks into the countryside: "I had eaten only tomatoes and boiled cabbage leaves, which I managed to obtain by covering kilometer by kilometer on foot and begging the farmers in the neighboring countryside to spare me a few of their vegetables. For those poor people a basket of tomatoes or some leaves of cabbage could mean execution, because the Germans were implacable; nevertheless, I never returned empty-handed."[108] Her salary from the National Theatre was inconsequential: "no matter how much money they gave you, you could never *find* food in the market. Or rather *black* market where no amount of money was enough."[109]

In around December 1941 the family's other provider—Jackie's lover Milton—replenished their kitchen: "A friend of the family, then engaged to my sister, brought us a little cask of oil, corn flour, and potatoes; and I can't forget the incredulous stupefaction with which my mother, Jackie, and I looked at those precious goods, almost fearing that through witchcraft they could disappear at any moment," Maria recollected.[110]

Loath to contribute to the war effort, Evangelia enlisted Maria to raid cupboards in the home of her sister Sophia's equipped lover, Yorgos Goudelis. The teenage girl would use the pretext of a visit to her grand-mother and aunts who lived nearby to access his illegal storeroom. Goudelis would give her a hand on the five-mile expedition.[111] Maria also made a point of bartering her and her colleagues' complimentary opera tickets in exchange for food for the whole cohort.[112]

Throughout this horrific chimera the Kalogeropoulous began to live better. A sudden onset of relief unceremoniously entered: "His pity stirred by my progressive emaciation, a man who admired my voice, the owner of a butcher shop requisitioned by the invaders, introduced me to the Italian official in charge of distributing provisions to the troops," Maria related.

"Once a month, for a paltry sum, he sold me ten kilos of meat, and I strapped the package to my shoulders and walked for an hour under the sun, even in the hottest months, as lightly and happily as if I were carrying flowers. That meat, in fact, was our greatest resource. We didn't have a refri-gerator and so we couldn't keep it. But it was resold to our neighbors and with the proceeds we could get along by acquiring indispensable things."[113] By singing for Italians and Germans, Maria "finally had [her] first rice and spaghetti and meat."[114]

Meanwhile Evangelia developed a creative concept to elude starvation. Sometime in late 1941 she strived to set in motion an ambitious plan in which her daughters would earn food and money as Italian soldiers' prosti-tutes. Neither girl successfully fulfilled this project. Maria almost never spoke of it.

Decades later she confessed that she had been extremely reticent to go out with Italians but her mother had reduced the girl to tear-ridden consent.[115] Another time she told her friend mezzo-soprano Giulietta Simionato how, reluctant to defy despotic Evangelia, she experienced several outings with the soldiers and expectedly was incapacitated. Unable to proceed with the charade of flirtation—much less anything else—the tender creature wept and spilled the truth. Some soldiers felt sympathy for the girl, giving her unearned rewards. Maria remained virginal throughout the war and for a long time afterward—but managed to come home with cash for her mother.[116]

Later in life Maria allegedly claimed that one night at the conservatory a male teacher (who remained nameless) had attempted to rape her. She remembered running home and crying. Evangelia had scoffed. "A pity he didn't manage it—then we would have made him marry you and that would have been that!"[117]

In no way were circumstances going to vanquish her. As she sustained the household and kept studying, Maria prized the goal of learning a new language: "Madame de Hidalgo insisted that I learn Italian. 'It will be useful for you,' she would repeat, 'because sooner or later you will go to Italy. Only there will you be able to begin your real career . . .' I listened to her and tried not to allow myself to be charmed. Italy and La Scala represented an impossible dream for me, as though I might find myself on Mars or the moon, and I rejected them even at the back of my mind so as to avoid delusions.

"Nevertheless, I bet my teacher that in three months I would manage to converse in Italian with her. But I didn't know how to do it. I certainly couldn't go to the head office of the fascists, as some people suggested I do, because my compatriots naturally would have considered me a traitor. I couldn't manage the money for private lessons. At that time I had struck up a friendship with four young doctors who had studied in Italy, and I don't know how, perhaps because I immediately liked the language of Dante enormously, within three months I had won my bet."[118]

Life persevered. Maria sat some exams and skipped others deliberately. In June 1941 she purposely played truant at Principal Ikonomidis' assessments in solfège. That fall she chose to take the same class with a different teacher; a fact that hints that she and Ikonomidis had had some sort of conflict.[119]

A while later members of the Greek air force knocked abruptly on their door. Somehow they persuaded Evangelia to hide two British airmen—John Atkinson and Robert [last name unknown]. Two weeks later they were safely recollected. Nonetheless the following day Italian soldiers barged in and demanded to search the apartment. Since the room the men had occupied contained some relics of their stay, Maria dashed to the piano and began to play and sing. Such a beguilement worked as these Italians remained stoic in their stupor—neglecting to perform their check.[120]

Though her contract hadn't been renewed at the Royal Theatre for its lack of funds Maria was a guest performer in another iteration of *Boccaccio* in July 1941. This time the role of Beatrice was completely hers. For this engagement she received only 218 drachmas: the equivalent of two loaves of bread.[121]

In May 1942 Maria tackled the infuriating and bemusing plight of flunking her exam in music history. The test was no more than an oral exam. With the encircling events and her devotion exclusive to everything practical, Maria told her professor she "couldn't read Greek".[122]

August witnessed the debut of the eighteen-year-old in the Royal Theatre's *Tosca*. Much to her chagrin she also spent time singing in a nightclub on the infamous Omonia Square to supplement her fragile income. Later describing it as a "postribolo" (a "brothel"), Maria resented the songs that she had to perform there: ditties that included Arditi's "Il Bacio" and Leoncavallo's "Mattinata"; works Luciano Pavarotti later popularized.[123]

Tosca was shared between a double cast: one that performed in Greek, the other in the work's original Italian. So zealous was her study of Puccini's opus—her first leading role—that the naïve Maria accidentally sparked the jealousy of two unwitting wives. The soprano investigated the role with both *Tosca*'s conductor, Sotos Vassiliadis, and the baritone who sang lecherous Scarpia, Titos Xirellis. Whenever the two wives of the respective men were present she just happened to be lurking. Xirellis' wife caused a scene at the conservatory one day, absolutely certain that her forty-two-year-old husband was playing away with a teenager.

Haris Vassiliadis—Sotos' wife—remembered observing the girl she perceived as a threat: " 'You have no idea what a nitpicker she is!' he used to say. 'She drives you up the wall, always pestering you about the most trivial details. *"Shall we go through it once more, Maestro?"* Then she makes a circular movement with her hands and, whether you like it or not, she makes you do it all over again! . . .' [But he told me] 'Don't worry! The one person you needn't be afraid of is Mary . . . I felt reassured, not because Mary was overweight and had big fat legs, but because she was a very virtuous girl."[124]

"That voice of hers was strange, there was a natural sob in it that projected you straight into an atmosphere of drama," chorus member Andonis Kalaidzakis recalled. "A bit throaty, but attractively throaty, like the sound of a string instrument when not played absolutely true. It became crystal-clear only on the high notes."[125] Another recollected how, as Chief of Police Scarpia signed the safe-conduct for Tosca and lover Mario—a warrant he was issuing on the condition that she sleep with him—Maria walked diagonally toward the table, feeling for the dagger without looking as she stealthily concealed her actions from the foe: "[She] picked up the blood in your veins! It was as if there was a magnet drawing her hand toward the hilt!"[126]

Popular Greek opera critic Alexandra Lalaouni recorded in the national newspaper *I Vradyni*: "A true miracle . . . the deep natural musicianship, instinct and understanding of theatre are qualities that she could not have learnt at school, not at her age anyway; she was born with them."[127] A total of seven reviews were published about her performances; each of them laudatory.[128]

At the premiere of the Italian-language *Tosca* on 8 September 1942 Maria took seven curtain calls. Yet she was deeply imbued in self-loathing. In defiance of the public's roar her instinct was to rip herself to shreds. "After one performance I went up to congratulate her on her way back to the dressing room," Kalaidzakis remembered, "but she just shook her head without saying a word, as if she mistrusted the applause and had doubts about her performance."[129] The production earned her parcels of important foodstuffs from her fervent fans, Italian soldiers.[130]

Destiny had planted its first paving stones: Marianna Kalogeropoulou was rising. It did not adjust her vision with regard to people. Holes that had been pierced in sections of her common sense were left undarned. An iron wall of strength, Maria was ensconced in throngs of one-dimensional and noxious characters: whether the stereotypically evil and ambitious Evangelia, brutal Italian fascists or soprano Nafsika Galanou.

To the myriad of individuals between the polar opposites of "good" and "bad" she was oblivious. Perilously blinded, Maria was exempt from disillusionment in people: literally and soulfully myopic in destructive wartime Athens.

Slowly growing tusks of self-awareness were hard-pressed to rear their heads.

3.

"Strings of the heart and the *mind*"

Envy had punctured a hole in the vessel of one of Maria's scant sanctuaries. Now twenty-five and still encumbered with an older man hard-pressed to wed, Jackie found jealousy's beguilements alluring. Schisms had cast webs of crevices along the groundwork of their sisterhood: cracks stretching with the seismic triggers of Maria's onstage glory.

Later Jackie would assert she couldn't have become a star because she lacked Maria's "instincts of a killer".[1] Hariton Embiricos—brother of Milton, Jackie's eternal fiancé—recalled that she performed at one point in a bid to prove her vocal parity.[2] By 1992 a horde of Callas fans would find that Jackie hadn't much matured beyond these years. Although she had endured three quarters of a century by then, the non-musician gifted a recording of hers to the Callasites, hellbent on proving her misfortune as a victim of lost destiny.[3]

No shackles bonded members of this family. Evangelia's apathy toward her older daughter hurled a flask of acid in the boiling brew of Jackie's bitterness. According to the latter the horrific massacres that took place during the Greek Civil War of 1944–45 were "a just punishment for [Mother's] arrogance."[4]

It was now early 1943 and Casa d'Italia (the Italian Cultural Institute in Athens) was commissioning performances by singers without respite. At a concert there nineteen-year-old Maria was enlaced for the first time in the melodic swirls of Giacomo Puccini when her tenor colleague Andonis Delendas asked if she could sing the *Madam Butterfly* duet with him at the eleventh hour. With half a day remaining the experienced soprano dragged Delendas and his vocal partner Mitsa Kourahani to the tenor's home to channel the euphoria of "Vogliatemi bene": the newlyweds' ecstatic wedding night duet. Coating the recital's ceremony with a decadent *verismo*, Maria gave a sumptuous embodiment of the fey heroine that Kourahani labeled "just amazing".[5]

A handful of other concerts followed—some at the Italian Cultural Institute, others at the homes of private individuals to whom Madame de Hidalgo would present her eminent disciples. Far from desiring to transfer their audiences into a transcendental state, their object was procuring rudimentary gains: remuneration in the form of macaroni and potatoes.[6]

May 1943 ushered in Maria's last batch of exams at the Athens Conservatory. Following six years of zealous vocal study she left both her music schools without degrees, certificates or graduation ceremonies. In a mark scheme in which 1 was A, 2 B and so on, the last grades she earned were straight 1s for ability, progress and application in vocal performance and 1-2 for progress, 1 for ability and 2-1 for application in piano.[i] Since her disrespect for Ikonomidis had severed her attendance of the mandatory course in harmony, the student fell short of fulfilling the requirements to graduate.[7]

Though she continued to train privately with Elvira de Hidalgo her school days now trailed blissfully behind.

After a brief summer sojourn at the Meligalas home of her paternal aunt, Tassia Kalogeropoulou,[8] Maria plunged into the headiness of instant costume changes, slovenly orchestral warm-ups, stuffy crowds and the tenacious stench of stifling stage cosmetics. One of her first encounters with the hype and panic of the theatre was a night of multiple performances. Thirsty for the chance to tout her gifts, she accidentally double-booked herself.

Resolved to give her first solo recital, Maria booked a concert at the now defunct open-air Kosta Moussouri Theatre for 21 July 1943. Simultaneously she rehearsed for a revival of her 1942 blockbuster *Tosca* at Klafthmonos Square's open-air theatre . . . one of whose performances was scheduled for 21 July 1943.

"What am I going to do?" Maria yelped like a puppy to Zoe Vlachopoulou. "How am I ever going to appear on stage for the concert?" As fortune has it, Floria Tosca's entrance in the opera only takes place at the end of the first act. Zoe proposed Maria wear her costume for the concert's first half before dashing to the theatre to unleash the triple throb of: "Mario! *Mario!* MARIO!"[9]

Tosca's opening night stirred frissons in spectators. Maria found an advocate in Alexandra Lalaouni, who wrote, "Both her voice and, even more, her marvelous, natural, spontaneous talent rivet the attention and sweep the audience off its feet."[10]

---

[i] For the examination Maria played the relatively easy Prelude and Fugue in F minor by Bach and the third movement ("Scherzo") from Beethoven's Sonata No. 3 in C Major.

Reviewing another performance, Friedrich Herzog expounded on the soprano's rapt mystification: "Her voice possesses youthfulness, harmony, sweetness, gentleness, and roundness of tone, and with these qualities she imbued the title role with a high degree of expressiveness, which gives operatic singing great fluency and a radiant airiness." Nonetheless he noted that her Tosca "at times . . . appeared quite immature."[11]

One wonders whether it was Tosca's prima donna character or the teen actress who seemed green.

The pulse-accelerator of adrenalin was pumped into Maria four days after this performance when her scheduled *Tosca* was brought forward. With her concert set for half past six, the opera was now due to start an hour later. Between the two theatres lay a distance around twenty to twenty-five minutes by foot—plus it was wartime. Transport was no option for a denizen as strapped for cash as she but it was summer, there was natural light outside and why would she *not* do it?

Bursting onstage at the Kosta Moussouri Theatre, Maria sang Handel's "Care selve" which—for a singer adverse to Baroque—likely did little to boost her excitement. She proceeded to perform "Nacqui all'affanno": Rossini's greatest challenge from his *La Cenerentola*; an unknown aria from *Il trovatore*; the *verismo* piece "Io son l'umile ancella" from Cilea's *Adriana Lecouvreur* and a popular Greek song by Nikos Lavdas. After cramming into half an hour five eras of music, she raced frantically across debris and rubble spewed by the cracked city; rushing through its dust-strewn alleys to arrive in time for Tosca's jarring call intent on freezing lover Mario in his tracks.

With everyone oblivious, no review for her concert or *Tosca* could caption this frenzied trajectory. Herzog lauded her "pastoral style" in Handel's "Care selve," her "crystal-clear tone" in the *La Cenerentola* aria and the "inestimable nobility of her tone" as Leonora, the lady-in-waiting to the Princess of Aragon in *Il trovatore*.[12] Lalaouni waxed poetically about "the presence of a sacred flame burning in [her] soul." Tangible were these personas in a woman pressured by the fear of smothering charred ruins and a stranglehold of slipping time along her crosstown course.[13]

Steeped in confidence by the unfolding of this double drama, the prodigy prescribed herself a ritual she would make perennial: expressing gratitude to praising critics.

Sixteen years later Friedrich Herzog—once music critic for the newspaper *Deutsche Nachrichten in Griechenland* ("The German News in Greece"), where he had splashed propulsive praise about Maria—recalled the young soprano's visit to his office: "a strapping young girl wearing a sort of dirndl and holding a pair of glasses in her hand . . . I did not recognize her as the Tosca I had recently heard."

Her parents' separation still instilled in her a sense of sordidness—and so Maria claimed to Herzog that her family had "got stuck" in the city during a vacation. After her admission that she feared arrest for her possession of a U.S. passport, Herzog pacified her with the fact that General

Wilhelm Speidel, Greece's Military Commander, adored music. There was little cause to fret. Mostly she came off as an affable and anxious girl: encrusted in a town that didn't cater to her mother tongue; ensconced in an exhaustive war that cordoned off her chances.[14]

That September Italy surrendered to the Allies. Germans still presided over Athens while a different model of dominion held sway in the homestead. As she was dallying with former fellow student Katie Makriyanni, an invasive speck of dirt lodged in Maria's eye and made it swell, grow red and glisten amid tears. Grasping her friend's arm, Makriyanni led Maria back to her abode, where Evangelia was playing cards among a smoke-plumed group of men. Though she looked up and saw her daughter leaning on the girl, she made no comment. Confronted with a typical chagrin, Maria whispered into Makriyanni's ear, "You see what sort of mother I've got?" before bolting to the bathroom to wash out her eye.

Little could quell Maria's longing for companionship of a parental ilk. Next to de Hidalgo she now had another confidant in Dr. Ilias Papatestas, a tuberculosis specialist who lived in the apartment below theirs.[15] Maria would remember him with a tremendous fondness as the man whose gifts of food had saved her life on more than one occasion.[16]

In contrast, many of their gossip-gnawing peers dispersed the theory that the forty-something Papatestas had Maria in the torrid throes of an affair. Of their platonic kinship he averred, "I really loved that young girl. To me she was a very good friend and a very good companion in the rough times of the occupation." For the purpose of clarification, he added: "I am not trying to suggest that Mary was incapable of emotion . . . but it came out only in true love, not in sexual desire."[17]

The doctor's clinic comfortably became Maria's sanctuary whenever German soldiers flooded her apartment. It helped that he loved music.[18]

It wasn't just the home crowd that Maria had to shy away from. At the National Opera a collective contempt of the girl was fast brewing. Diatribes were darted at her with the speed of blazing arrows. At times it seemed that the entire company despised the singer on account of her accomplishments.

"She . . . never pried into other people's business . . . but would only comment favorably on their achievements," Galatea Amaxopoulou recounted. "Everybody really admired her, but many, deep down, hated her for her success, for her great talent . . . and by undermining her they strove to destroy her artistic career, hoping to banish her from the theatre world of her country."[19] Stefanos Chiotakis—then a tenor with the Greek National Opera—estimated that of around one hundred and seventy musicians in the ensemble thirty were neutral or liked her.[20] Maria "didn't join cliques,"[21] chorus member Kostas Dounias accentuated. In this querulous environment that attitude could only put her at a disadvantage.

The weeds of insults flourished till they stood in stacks of solidarity. One of the most salacious slurs originated in renowned mezzo-soprano Lysimachi Anastasiadou. Following an international career the singer had been unexpectedly demoted to the post of Grade-B soloist. When her petition to recover Grade-A status was rebuked by the board of the National Opera,[22] Anastasiadou hurled invectives at Maria. In the troupe's canteen at lunch she let her colleagues know Maria's voice was "vulgar", that she had "no talent"—and whatever instrument she did possess she would "soon lose it."

A tenor present opted to report this to Maria, who immediately took action. Approaching Anastasiadou the next day, she courteously requested that the mezzo keep her nose out of her business. Such a demand was met with a response of curse words, threats and calling Evangelia "the arch-bawd of all Greece."[23] Drafting a report, Maria wrote her version of events with the assistance of a tenor who had heard Anastasiadou's slander. Yet the board chose not to pursue disciplinary action.

Assailed by insolence in every corner of her life, Maria grew her sentimental needs with every cannon fired by the mob. She did not long to have her first romance. And yet she longed to have the love and mutual exclusivity attainable by means of one.

The first candidate to come in the vicinity of qualifying as a boyfriend was thirty-two-year-old businessman, Takis Sigaras. In 1942 the latter had encountered her at a surprise party in Athens; later in 1943 they started to spend time together. As a foreigner Maria ranked low in the hierarchy of Athenian society. The spoiled and scornful women constituting many of Sigaras' friends were scarcely amiable. "I'm glad your mind doesn't work the same way as theirs," he remembered Maria acknowledging, "All they think of is what they can lay their hands on, what they can get out of you."[24]

On one night in winter 1943 Sigaras was dropping Maria back home at Patission Street. After checking she had safely entered the apartment building, he drove off and crashed his vehicle violently into a German car. Following the accident Maria regularly visited and nurtured him in the three weeks it took him to recuperate.

She never sought or asked for money. Speaking of her in 1995, Sigaras emphasized that Jackie's beau Milton Embiricos had been the household's sole purveyor. Even when Sigaras tried to help Maria by equipping her with shoes, some nylon stockings and amenities unfindable in wartime, she expressed embarrassment: "I don't want to be under an obligation."

Perhaps Sigaras was the first example of another need that would sporadically spring up throughout Maria's life: a miniscule desire to experience escapism. One night in winter 1943 she pleaded with Sigaras to escort her to the beach despite the cold. The suitor took her to Kallithea Bay, where she exulted, "It's so lovely and romantic here. I'll sing for you!" before unbuttoning an aria. Sigaras was more interested in his entrapped car: it was stuck in sand. Maria disapproved of this transition to the trivial mundane—suspending her performance to denounce Sigaras as a philistine. While he conceded this may well have been the case, he made a blunt allusion to her lack of any high school education. His argument made sense, Maria openly admitted—taking care to point out, "But I'm not a jackass like you!"

It was not the sole occasion during which Sigaras' aculturality came into play. Maria couldn't help reminding her companion that he failed to understand her *raison d'être*: "it's impossible for you to enter my world," was the stately address. "I move in a different orbit, an artistic orbit, whereas you are a manufacturer."

She wasn't considering wedlock. "Art and marriage are incompatible," Maria stressed before the similarly uncommitted businessman—hastening to state that she was going to be a great and renowned prima donna: "You'll be proud of me one day!"[25]

For this reason Sigaras never viewed their idyll as a romantic affair—that and the fact that it was never consummated. "You could say that we were united by a sort of amorous friendship," he later confided. "When I took her home at the end of an evening we would kiss in the car, but Mary didn't give in. She simply didn't want it. She wouldn't let you . . ."[26] [there were] no surges of sexual passion on her part."[27] This was ironic since Zoe Vlachopoulou recalled that Sigaras was known as a "womanizer".[28]

Maria may have been too self-involved to notice.

Remarkably the nubile woman's dreamily romantic nature, empathy and thirst to love did not spark sexual interest. Though Evangelia scribed many lies about her daughter, the assertion, "Maria was not much interested in these frustrated Lotharios or even in the male animal" is likely a probable one.[29]

Her near-indifference toward sex was salient: throughout her life she didn't make a secret of it. In 1974 Maria recalled being as old as eighteen when she "learned how a baby is born." To her pianist friend enquiring how she managed to avoid it with her colleagues gossiping about their love lives, she responded simply that she had "not [been] particularly interested."[30]

*

The little-known 1902 opera *Tiefland* by Eugen d'Albert was Maria's next work. Evangelia would go into Maria's room and find her daughter sleeping on the carpet with the pages of the score dispersed around her. Arriving at the first rehearsal with no notes, she made the practice a perpetual axiom. Her colleagues instantly felt littler than she was. "We discovered afterward that she had shut herself up in her room [to study it], refusing to open the door to anyone," Zoe Vlachopoulou shared.[31]

Tiefland involves a dance inflicted by the opera's cruel protagonist on his tormented mistress Marta. Despite being heavyset and gawky, Maria trained herself to move more gracefully. Taking the production's pianist, Eleni Mangou, to the home of choreographer Louisa Kotsopoulou, she spent hours working out the dance's steps.[32] "We were rehearsing . . ." Maria later recounted. ". . . and because of the fear of bombing we had to perform in semidarkness that was diffused by acetylene lamps."[33]

By the advent of the first rehearsal she had phrased the paradox of a defenseless victim dancing: "She swooped and fluttered just like a bird!" colleague Mitsa Kourahani described. "Marta was forced to dance though inside she was grief-stricken and on the verge of tears, and Mary instinctively found a way of expressing that emotion in her graceful movements."[34] In the midst of a dramatic moment in the work where Marta breaks free from her keeper Sebastiano and defiantly declares her love for Pedro, she is hurled by her destructive lover to the ground. A photograph of Marta lying prostrate and despairing was the front of an installment of the music magazine *To Radiophonon*: Maria's inaugural cover.[35]

In hastening gradations Maria took further steps toward being an actress. These flights had been embarked upon during *Boccaccio* back in February 1941. "I didn't *really* know what to do with my hands—*but*, I remember then, we had a[n] . . . *operetta* director—he was Renato Mordo— he's dead now," Maria related, "and he *had* said then, two things that stuck to my mind: One—*never* move your hand, unless you follow it with your *mind* and with your *soul*. It's a . . . *strange* way of putting it, but it's so *true*. It *must*—be strings of heart and the *mind* . . . And, the *second* thing he said *was* that, when your colleague *sings* the role to *you*, sings his *lines*, try and forget what he's supposed to say and *your* reactions must be as though you had *never* heard what he's saying."[36]

These forays into acting were encouraged likewise by de Hidalgo—who expressly sought to strip her protégés of operatic clichés: "We were never allowed to have an arm outstretched with the palm upward, or to keep our arms pressed tightly to our sides," Zoe Vlachopoulou recounted.[37] de Hidalgo marveled at Maria's early physicality—the latter recalling years later: "*And* I asked her, 'Was I since a child—*always* . . . *easy* on acting?' She says, 'Yes, you were *amazingly* so, *I*, even then, I admired your—the way you moved your *hands*, your body—these were all new to *me*, and yet I *was* considered a good actress and I had seen the greatest—[even so] I saw that there was something *different*, and completely your own.' "[38]

An ailment popped the fervor of Maria's opening night of the revival of *Boccaccio* in late April 1944. Afflicted with a runny nose and temperature, "That day she went to the Olympia [Theater] before anyone else and locked herself into our dressing room," Vlachopoulou told. "When I arrived she refused to open the door, and I called Kalomiris [then Director of the National Opera], who asked her to let me in. 'I can't, I won't open it!' 'But, my dear girl . . .' 'Will you please leave me alone, Manoli?' . . . When she finally opened the door, I saw that her nose was running, her eyes were swollen from crying, and she was shivering all over with fever."[39]

Maria was distraught. Not only would her illness disempower her vocality, her self-esteem would have no chance to peak. Later that night a chorus member, Xenia Kouroussopoulou, spotted her looking "very upset with herself although she had acted her heart out and done fantastically well."[40]

Enamored critic Lalaouni now found rosy epithets reductive: "Kaloyeropoulou [sic] is one of those God-given talents that one can only marvel at. How does this twenty-year-old girl come to have . . . that truth, that honesty, that conviction? She sang and acted the part of Marta like an established artist, and there were moments—in the recitatives, for example—when she stirred you to the depths of your being."[41] Friedrich Herzog praised the "earthy naturalness" in her embodiment.[42]

But something else had happened—or *not* happened—during the rehearsals and performances of *Tiefland*. The role of Sebastiano had been played by popular and reputable baritone Evangelos Magliveras: a thirty-four-year-old small-time celebrity who was both married to an older woman and indebted to a mistress and some children on the side.[43] "Scathingly critical of any illicit relationship" in the words of her friend Papatestas,[44] Maria became a delectable must-have for the charged Magliveras. Another platonic idyll came to pass.

In their greedy need to graze on gossip's pasture the harmonic herd transformed this virgin territory into arable terrain. Intermittently they caught Maria waiting for the singer—"Vangelis" as she affectionately called him—"at the corner of Akadimias and Harilaou Trikoupi Streets, where there was a good basement restaurant," and expressed shock at her throwing her arms round the man in a "forward and intimate way."[45]

Was this relationship with someone of his reputation wise?

Not really. But it speaks to the criteria the juvenile Maria harbored when it came to men. Unconcerned with pinpointing a husband or a lover, she scarcely sought a fully-fledged liaison. What united her male interests of this era were the traits of being older, being patriarchal and behaving like chaste courtiers throughout thirteenth-century France. Under their aegis she enjoyed the privilege of pure companionship.

The consequences of this frowned-upon relationship produced another host of obstacles. Galatea Amaxopoulou recalled how Magliveras' notorious mistress, Kalliopi Vrettou, once extended her a warning. A solemn Maria declared in all earnestness: "I'm glad to meet you, but there is nothing between Vangelis and me. We just have a good working relationship and he encourages me—nothing more than that." Her entreaty must have had a favorable outcome since she subsequently sent her love to Kalliopi at the end of Christmas cards and letters that she mailed to Magliveras.[46]

Filling pages in his proverbial little black book, Evangelos felt undeterred. Though he and Maria rarely saw each other after *Tiefland*, impulse would propel him to propose to her before she left for the U.S. in 1945. Still married was he—and entangled with his mistress and their children.[47]

Apparently her snub was insufficient. "I did not stop considering you my best friend and loving you as such . . ." Maria consoled him months later in writing. "You knew well, Evangelos, that our lives were different. You had so many obligations and I could never live happily, even though I loved you, to the detriment and the misery of two women who have done me no wrong. So don't be angry with me!"[48]

On another occasion she scribed: "You are the finest of men but you are not free. Even if you were, my answer would have been the same. I can only be married to my art for the moment. You will always be a wonderful friend and that really is more important."[49]

Validity was lacking in these episodes of hers. Yet they built makeshift hearths of sentimental nourishment.

*

That summer the soprano elected to add a new role to her repertoire: Bringer of Justice. With Athens crumbling into destitution, singers were paid little more than what amounted to a daily meal at the soup kitchen per performance.[50] Bass Nicola Zaccaria would see Maria stood atop a cart amidst a wreath of bread each morning. From the spring of 1943 till the Italian surrender in September it was hoarded onto carts and pedaled to the theatre to feed staff. Maria had been chosen to distribute it because she spoke Italian.[51]

Tenor Stefanos Chiotakis told of how Maria found an anti-Nazi she persuaded to produce a warrant that would feed the company; an acquaintance of Takis Sigaras. According to Chiotakis, one morning Maria and a colleague "loaded a wheelbarrow with oil, sugar, cheese, lentils, beans, and I don't know what else, and pushed it up Pireos Street all the way from Piraeus to Ayiou Konstantinou Street [a journey of around a mile]. There they were met by other singers from the opera, including me."[52]

Questioned decades later about wartime in the occupation, her reply was undramatic: "Uh, that was hard. I confess that that was a bit hard, but er, it doesn't hurt anybody you know; hardship does one good."[53] Earlier in 1957 for an interview in German magazine *Der Spiegel* she had stressed: "[Herbert von] Karajan is always telling me, 'Come to Germany'. I've only been there twice . . . When I was in Athens during the war, I was in no way harassed by the Germans, even though I held an American passport."[54]

The summer of 1944 saw a quieter war on Maria. "I had my first scrapes with colleagues," she would recollect. "They were going to put on [Beethoven's sole opera] *Fidelio* and another prima donna had put herself out a great deal to get the part and had succeeded in getting it, but she was entirely too busy to learn it. Since the rehearsals had to begin immediately, I was asked whether I could replace her, and I naturally accepted, because I knew the score to perfection."[55] Maria maintains diligent discretion in this summary. The truth was uglier.

Singer Mireille Fléri—who had arduously strived to grasp the role of Leonore—wrote a petition to the board of the National Opera upon learning Maria had taken "her" role. Attached to it was a full list of her accomplishments over a decade. Following the Board's outright rejection of her protests, Fléri "insisted" to Hans Hörner—the upcoming production's conductor—that he "give" the role to Maria "because it was too heavy for [her] own voice"—despite her *already* possessing the part.[56]

This provoked an argument between the two sopranos. Soon it was suspended by Mireille Fléri's then husband, Nikos Glynos—who attacked Maria, labeled her a "whore" and publicly alleged that she had made her lyrical career the horizontal way and under Axis soldiers. Bystanders ushered them into the office of the company's director Kalomiris. There Glynos banged his fist on Kalomiris' desk and flung another insult at Maria: "dirty slut." Fléri later admitted that the dispute between Maria and Glynos had occurred because "he always had a belligerent streak."

The following day Maria sent Kalomiris a written account of the incident entreating the man to "take appropriate action."

Glynos was spared repercussions.[57]

Eleven performances of *Fidelio* were to take place at the open-air Herodes Atticus; all of them being in Greek.

Critics raved. The 1805 opera—which tells of a late eighteenth-century Spanish nobleman's unjust imprisonment and his beloved Leonore posing as a man to save him—granted worn-down Greeks drinkable hope: "[They] had glimpsed liberation," wrote Friedrich Herzog decades later, "had understood the tyrant was about to be expelled and that the end of their oppression by the enemy was near; that victory was finally approaching. When Maria performed [Leonore's duet with her saved husband Florestan] "O namenlose Freude", rendering the strength of her magnificent voice palpable ... the excitement in the auditorium began to swell until it reached the heights of an immense applause spurred on by true delirium amongst the people."[58]

Myopic Maria wasn't oblivious to the magic—later relating to Werner Schroeter: "*Fidelio* ... was given for the troops of the Occupying Forces ... When I was singing the part in 'Abscheulicher', 'Come hope, do not let fade your final star from weariness; illuminate my purpose; even if it is far, love will reach it,' The Shepherd's Star—which up to then had hidden in the clouds—appeared in the gray sky." This moved Maria to tears.[59]

Two months later on 14 October 1944 Athens was liberated by the Occupying Forces. A new government was then formed on the 23rd with Greece being split into two halves: radical right-wingers and left-wing extremists. The friction festering between the factions stifled every institution and domain including opera.

Given three months' vacation from the company, Maria was afforded new employment courtesy of Evangelia at the British Headquarters: "I was assigned to the office of distribution of secret mail. We started work at eight, but I had to get up at six thirty because in order to save money I made the whole trip on foot ... The British offered us an abundant noon meal, and rather than taking it at headquarters, I had it put in a pot and carried it home to share with my mother ... I had a break of an hour and a half in all, so I had a quarter hour, more or less, at home."[60]

This intermission from professional performance sparked another opportunity for an asexual love affair. The chosen one this time was twenty-something British officer, Lieutenant Ray Morgan, who had reached Athens with his troops on 14 October to liberate her. Later in life he would become a music teacher.[61]

For now he was a young man on the prowl. The night after his arrival he attended a "very respectable" party hosted by one Dr. Prapoleros. Some time had passed when the door opened and a guest regaled Maria with endearments. "Not only was she English," Morgan immediately thought, "she was good-looking. I became aware of an accent, a nasality on certain words. I realized that she was, in fact, not English but American ... She spoke perfect Greek but clearly missed using English."

Except for kinship fostered by a common language, little could bind Morgan to Maria. Accompanying him on breezy rambles, she buoyed his esprit with samples of banana liqueur, staying cagey in discussions of her private life. Moral embarrassment still plagued her: she recoiled from the admission that her parents weren't together. Morgan and Maria shunned embroilments in political dispute; the latter striving once to mitigate a contretemps between a pair of party guests.[62] Civil war was just a stroke of the clock's hand from its commencement.

He was taken with Maria as a woman. Takis Sigaras had been comparably enraptured by the twenty-something. With her nail-biting behind her, she would take care of her hands and sometimes switch her hair color from chestnut to peroxide blonde or auburn. Dusky shades of clothing minimized her hips. "She was full of life—she was terrific!" he'd recall.[63]

Although Maria shirked at the idea of sexual entanglements a lot of men were drawn to her precisely in this way—with Morgan being no exception: "Perched on a high stool, her eyes glistened. They had that unfocused dreaminess ... were slanted slightly upward, exotically almond-shaped. In her full relaxed face they suggested voluptuousness, but, made-up and with intensity of purpose, they could be very dramatic ... She had gawkish delicate movements like a large kitten ... I think I found her quite sexy in a way ... That's why it annoys me to hear people say she was fat and ugly. She wasn't at all so!"[64]

They courted only for six weeks. Two incidents struck blows to their relationship: the first was Morgan's swift enamorment with Maro Sariyanni: his future wife, the daughter of a general recently appointed Minister of War in Greece.[65] The second was the start of the atrocious civil war.

December 3rd saw Athens drowning in a mire of dissension. Known as "Dekemvriana", it consisted of ensanguined chronic clashes of the National Liberation Front—a Resistance group throughout the Occupation known by its Greek initials EAM-EDES—with the communist-controlled Greek People's Liberation Army ELAS. These had split Athens into the two zones of White and Red; the latter occupied by ELAS and the former believed safe. EAM-EDES was fortified by British forces.

Caught in the maelstrom, apolitical Maria hardly went unscathed: "I passed rather dramatic days then because . . . *when* the civil war broke out, I wanted to go back to the er . . . shall we call it 'Red Zone' because it so happened that it was divided into one zone where I *worked* [the White] and the General Headquarters—and the 'Red Zone' where it happened to be where I *lived* . . ."[66] "My superiors recommended that I not leave Headquarters [in the White Zone], because, having occupied such a delicate post as that of distributing secret mail, I would undoubtedly be a victim of communist reprisals and subjected to inevitable torture. But our house was located in the zone occupied by the Reds, and I did not want to leave my mother on her own. For that reason, I had myself taken, in a jeep, to Patissiou Street, and for several days I stayed locked in my room. I was racked with fear; moreover, I was sick thanks to a box of very old beans that, for the lack of anything else, I had decided to eat (and by the way, I have a real and genuine allergy to every kind of dry legume) . . ." Dr. Papatestas helped by bringing her more food.[67]

That same evening Maria attempted to call Ray Morgan, then stationed with his troops at his officers' mess. His general glared at him with menace as he picked up the receiver. Finding a pretext to avoid a conversation, Morgan next beheld Maria onstage in her London *Norma* eight years later. There she embraced him and his wife backstage.[68]

Several days into the war there came an unexpected knock. A terrified Maria saw "a pale and poorly dressed boy—he looked like a coal vender"— who claimed he had been sent by someone at the British Headquarters. Highly doubtful of his true intentions, Maria tried to shoo the pest away and was deliberately rude to him, but: "Since his insistence had become unbearable and nearly rabid, I resigned myself to listening to him. He was in reality a secret agent whom the British had sent to beg me to return to headquarters, because they feared for my life [in the Red Zone] and were amazed that the communists had not yet arrested me."

After calling Dr. Papatestas to request that he look after Evangelia, Maria travelled with the young man to the British Headquarters. The street on which they lived was "literally covered with broken glass and all sorts of wreckage that had fallen out of windows as a result of the constant machine gun fire . . . [There was] a tremendous, unnerving silence that would last sixty seconds, to be broken, once a minute, by the communists' terrible 'blind volley,' shots at regular intervals that could hit anyone and had the specific aim of wearing down the populace's nerves."[69]

A few days after that escape an unknown means let Evangelia also flee to the 'White Zone'. She and Maria spent the next few weeks cohabiting with Jackie and her lover Milton at their residence: a hotel on Ayiou Konstantinou Street.[70]

Hostilities had theatres closed till the end of the month.[71] It was perhaps their bloody horror that provoked Maria to renew her contact with her father. In November 1944 George had sent word to Evangelia that he was living now in San Francisco, where he ran a pharmacy. Enclosing a donation of one hundred dollars, he had asked in writing whether the three women would be coming to the States.[72] When at last mail service was resumed Maria sent an envelope to him containing two of her stage photographs: one from *Fidelio*, the other *Tosca*. "I send you a souvenir of what the newspapers here described as a historical event [*Fidelio*]," she wrote. "Your younger daughter, Maria."[73]

Dwelling in the midst of a dilapidated Athens lent her a lugubrious outlook. Maria's registration as a U.S. citizen had inauspiciously expired almost three years earlier. On 28 March 1945 she applied to renew her old citizenship and expressed the desire to return to her country and live with her father. It was granted her a little under three months later.[74]

Yet fate was unrelenting. Now that Maria had dodged bullets in a stream of civil conflicts, now that she was doggedly intent on heading homeward the next crisis was a ticking time bomb. On 6 April 1945 the Ministry of Finance commanded the board of the Greek National Opera to "streamline" their singers in a bid to recover the company's finances. It warned that if its issues remained unresolved, state funding for the GNO would cease and the entire troupe would be disbanded.

Maria found herself unjustifiably demoted eight days later. Without justification for the change she had been made a Grade-B soloist despite her critical acclaim and popularity. Records reveal that the director of the board of governors, Theodoros Synadinos, had requested that all members of the leadership accord new rankings to the then contracted soloists. These grades functioned in a fashion similar to marks Maria had been granted in her school exams: instead of A being the greatest, soloists were ranked either A-A, A-B, or B-A: A-A was the highest achievable grade. Evangelos Magliveras was awarded the exact same grades as she and yet retained Grade-A status.[75]

"It so happened though that I suppose I got on . . . my colleagues' nerves; they were older people, I don't blame them . . ." she reported. "And I was *so* young, and they couldn't understand *why* I was chosen for certain roles . . . the time had come to renew my contract with the Royal [National] Opera House, but I found out from a maternal uncle, a doctor at the Royal Opera House, [Professor Constantine Louros], that [Ioannis] Rallis, then the head of the Greek government, had received my colleagues en masse. They had gone to protest to him, and said that . . .[76] 'If she isn't brought down from first soprano to *second* soprano, well, we just won't sing with her, so she'll have to sing alone.' And of course the prime minister, which [*sic*] was a very dear friend of my uncle's, told him . . . 'Well, Maria can do just what she thinks, but I *can't* do otherwise because of course she can't sing by herself.' "[77]

The veracity in the story related by Constantine Louros to his great-niece Maria is dubious; the gist of it *less* so. Whilst the prime minister had then been Nikolaos Plastiras—rather than the former chief Ioannis Rallis cited by Maria—it's likely that her inexplicable demotion at the hands of

Synadinos had been prompted by nefarious intruders. Several singers threatened they would go on strike unless Maria would be stripped of leading roles. With the financial problems of the GNO already growing graver by the hour, Synadinos probably degraded the soprano to avoid sedition.

Maria's cravings to flee Greece intensified. "Here I just can't make myself not mind what people do to me," she lamented to fellow pupil of Elvira de Hidalgo, Maria Alkeou.[78] Her imminent departure for the States was made known by the local press on 26 April 1945.[79]

The alert was premature. Scouring for ways to fund her ship fare, Maria travelled to Thessaloniki to stay with her cousins the Moundouris and booked a recital. There she found an accompanist, Tonis Yeoryiou. Mawkish was the man the moment that he heard her sing: "I remember the first piece we tried was that aria of Donna Anna, where she asks Don Ottavio to take vengeance on Don Giovanni. So I play the chords of the recitative . . . and then Maria launches into 'Or sai chi l'onore.' As soon as she starts, I feel something welling up inside me, blocking my throat and clouding my eyes—they were completely misted over. I had to stop, my eyes were so wet that I couldn't see the notes, 'Go on! What's wrong?' she said in English, almost without stopping singing." Yeoryiou was so moved that he implored Maria to 'get out of here' and she enlightened him about her plans.[80]

Her aspirations to sail west somewhat deflated, Maria settled on performing as a Grade-B soloist and risked her self-worth for a salary.[81] It would involve one final Greek performance—this time in the role of Laura in the nineteenth-century Austrian operetta by Carl Millöcker, *Der Bettelstudent*.

At the same time she strived to book a concert hall for her "Farewell Recital", which took place on 3 August at Rex Theater. For the first and last time in her life Maria sang "Batti, batti, o bel Masetto", Zerlina's aria from *Don Giovanni*, as well as her customary signature pieces from *Semiramide*, *Aïda*, *Il trovatore* and *Oberon*. Critics mourned the loss of her strange instrument's "superabundant musicality."[82]

Her ticket for a voyage to New York was booked at last for 14 September 1945. The day after the final performance of *Der Bettelstudent* on 12 September, just twenty-four hours before her departure, she headed to Synadinos' office and barged through the door. An aura of theatricality was lent her revenge. "When the director told me, 'The whole theater is against you,' I said. 'Here is your contract,' and tore it across."[83] In later years Maria added: "I told them, 'I'm sorry, but I hope *they* won't be sorry for this kind of treatment.' But, you know of course—*then* I said it as a bluff, I was *most* unhappy, and I just couldn't *believe* that such a thing was happening. Only, er . . . you know, sometimes we just . . . keep up a front, as we say; I just said these words, never even *dreaming* that they would come true."[84]

The American Consulate had loaned her the cost of the voyage. As a ceremonial parting gesture, Dr. Papatestas managed to persuade the Mayor of Piraeus to present a goodbye luncheon. Embittered at Maria's departure, Evangelia and Jackie refused to attend.[85]

Acrimonious also was parting with Elvira de Hidalgo. Having assumed the role of second mother for a course of seven years, the teacher struggled to believe her former student was rejecting her sagacity. "We had an [sic] regrettable rift in our relationship . . ." de Hidalgo recounted. "At the end of the war Maria wanted to go to America, to see her father and have a more comfortable life while starting her career there. I was against this move. 'You must start in Italy . . . When you have become somebody in Italy the rest will follow.' Maria did not listen . . . On the evening of her departure she called me. 'My last words are for you,' she said. 'I will always think of you with gratitude. Tell me you forgive me.' 'You must not leave,' I repeated."[86]

Nevertheless she was gracious enough to supply her ex-student with a letter of recommendation addressed to conductor Romano Romani, who frequently worked with Maria's soon-to-be idol, soprano Rosa Ponselle.[87]

With nowhere to go and nowhere to stay Maria embarked on the MS *Gripsholm* on the morning of 15 September.[88] Since George was resident in San Francisco she had no idea whether her old acquaintances were living in Manhattan still.

The moment she set sail was hardly marked by auspices: "I hadn't written my father that I would be arriving; my mother had advised against it . . . A few minutes before embarkation I was fervently advised: 'Be careful and don't lose your money. Where have you put it?' 'There's no danger,' I replied. 'I don't have any.' They couldn't believe me. They took my pocketbook, turned it inside out, and didn't find anything."

The shackles had come loose, nevertheless—and that was emblematic of a victory. So much was she infused with joyous sentiment that she met danger not with bleak suspicion but beguiling hope: "I was going to meet the unknown; nevertheless, at that moment I felt with extraordinary clarity that I need not be afraid."[89] And her audacity was justifiable. Almost.

4.

"Thick as molasses"

"My secret, I think, is knowing how to say 'no'. Of course there will be anguish and pain and anxiety—but you have to know how to *wait*." Such was the ethos of the forty-five-year-old Maria—who revealed it was impossible to fetch an ice cream for the fear of paparazzi.[1]

Newly returned to New York's shores that 9 October 1945, the twenty-one-year-old denounced this as a dire dictum.

Tagalong tales of somber struggle tail most greats. Storming the Big Apple with the shirt on one's back and no more, the wannabe lurks haplessly by agents' hangouts; waiting on their tables during lunch.

But it's a narrative infrequently conveyed to stars of opera. Deemed miracles, a great deal get discovered in church choirs at the age of seven and the journey takes a rocket liftoff.

No rent was due for the newest Bohemian member of postwar Manhattan. Father George the pharmacist liked to peruse Greek-language newspapers. It was a time when every ship arrival was a ceremonious occasion; names of disembarking passengers were published daily in the press. Maria stepped ashore to find her father waiting for her in the port. Now resident at 544 West 157th Street,[2] he both housed and began to provide for his daughter—who would frequently spend her (completely) spare time at his drugstore.[3] These intervals afforded the young singer time to study the strained scope of her success in war-torn Athens.

Several new expatriates at George's drugstore—which was mostly servicing the Greek American community—would recognize and hail her as "the famous singer Maria Calogeropulos." Citing her "great Fidelio" of '44, they shared how they had "braved the raids of Germans" in a journey from Piraeus just to hear her sing.[4]

A whole year had passed since then. In showbiz minutes that was equal to a lifetime.

The fledgling was a foreign has-been in the eyes of U.S. industry insiders: one ashamed for the supposed crutch of a dark voice she termed "thick as molasses."[5] Bass Nicola Moscona—who had seven years before auditioned her in Athens and assured her of impending greatness[6]—was fed up with sapling singers snatching him as bait for their careers. She was old news and he refused to see her.[7]

Accompanist and composer Romano Romani—the recipient of de Hidalgo's letter of recommendation—made a somber impression. "He is nothing now," Maria wrote plaintively to her ex-teacher. "He gives few lessons and spends half the week in Baltimore seeing Rosa Ponselle . . . for the moment I'm going to see him for four lessons."[8] Whether or not these came to pass Romani quickly shunned the notion of tuition. "There's no point," he explained to her in January 1946. "Most of all, and really *all* you have to do, is *study*."[9]

Reflecting on the period later on, Maria recollected her nonplussedness: "At the end of the day I told myself that I had seven and a half years of a career already *behind* me. I was hoping, naïvely, to find engagements in New York. But who in America has heard of a country like poor little Greece? And who was going to listen to a twenty-one-year-old girl? I realized rather quickly—and with bitterness—that I would have to start all over."[10]

Unlike most artists in such circumstances she began to complicate them. When Maria learned her father was engaging in an untoward relationship with neighbor Alexandra Papajohn, she liberally expressed her moral outrage. Blindly she preserved the hope that Evangelia and George would reconcile. Years later Maria would speak of a "natural instinct to regard marriage as a permanent contract . . . the memory of my own parents' incompatibility has instilled in me an especial caution."[11]

At first Maria warmed to George's brazen efforts to assure her gratitude: "Thank God everything is going well with my father," she wrote to de Hidalgo. "He doesn't know how to prove his love—he gave me a present: a marvelous bedroom. I'm like a princess!"[12]

The sentiment was short-lived. Principled and righteous in her stance, she had to volley a bombastic blow to the vituperous liaison. Having no friend's couch on which to sleep, Maria made life harder by first moving to the Hotel Astor[13] then to the Hotel Times Square on Broadway[14] (now The Westin).

Desperately in need of contracts, she was hard-pressed to quit stalking the Metropolitan Opera's artistic director: laws were lenient then. After at least a dozen phone calls and successive letters supplicating Edward Johnson to accord her an audition, finally Maria won the longed-for day in every opera singer's life.[15]

3 December 1945. Paul Breisach—a guest conductor at the Met that season—was appointed to listen to her. On the roof stage she sang her customary arias: "Vissi d'arte" from *Tosca* and *Norma*'s "Casta diva."

"Exceptional voice—ought to be heard very soon on stage," Breisach wrote on the back of her note card. This commentary resulted in a second audition scheduled for 21 December—this time before Frank St. Leger, the

Met's Assistant Conductor. The same arias were performed together with "D'amor sull'ali rosee" from *Il trovatore*. On the back of that audition card was written "Good material—needs work on her voice." Mindful that her name was scarcely operatic, Maria had signed up as "Callas, Mary (Maria)".[16]

Johnson offered her a chance to sing *Fidelio*—which she had, as we know, performed already back in Greece—this time in English, as well as the lead role in *Madam Butterfly*.

It sounded good enough for a beginner, someone who had newly reached legal majority; a woman that New Yorkers would have deemed an "immigrant".

It wasn't good enough for *this* one.

Encrusted in her ways, Maria stuck to the pedantic mindset borne upon her by de Hidalgo: bel canto music was good; operas by Puccini were lowbrow. At the very least, Puccini was not very *tasteful*. Bel canto music was cinema; Puccini was television. *Haute cuisine* was bel canto; Puccini was Burger King.

"To sing *verismo*, one has to do certain things that are a little bit vulgar," Maria would later explain. "Obviously, it is not good for the voice either . . . And, well—a lot of Puccini is beautiful, yes. But, evidently—it can be sung well by a beautiful voice—whereas the operas of Bellini and Rossini, etc. *must* be well *sung*; if they're not, you simply are not able to sing them . . . Puccini brings a lot of good to the soul; not much good to the voice."[17]

A month later she filled fifteen pages for a letter to de Hidalgo: "You were perfectly right when you told me that the 'Metropolitan' is no longer what it used to be . . . They want to make everyone (young singers who don't have a name yet) study their way. Imagine! The German way. Which also happened in Greece. With the mouth open as big as an oven—so that when the top notes come they can't open any wider because the mouth is already so huge in the middle and low notes . . . And then, there aren't *maestri* such as Serafin, De Sabata, Toscanini—there's no one! . . . The theatre is consumed with Germanomania . . . Can you imagine—Johnson proposed that I sing Butterfly and *Otello*'s Desdemona. For the love of God! I turned it down and I said, 'Why would you make me sing Butterfly—I'd look ridiculous, considering my size . . .' It's better to just shut your mouth and never sing again than to sing all that stuff. It's true!!!"[18]

At the time Maria weighed one hundred and seventy-seven pounds: for a five-foot-eight-and-a-half woman, overweight—not obese. In her words she considered herself a "grassona": a "large lump of a girl."[19] In lieu of Butterfly and Leonore in *Fidelio* she offered to perform the title role in *Aïda* or *Tosca*—even for free. Mr. Johnson opposed this. Maria extended the following parting words: "One day the Met will be *inviting* me to sing. And I can say for certain that I'll sing the role I'm offered—but I won't do it for *free*."[20]

With *Fidelio* she had another issue: "Opera in English is silly. Nobody takes it seriously."[21] In Greece the Occupation had compelled her to perform the German work in Greek. Otherwise she held fast to the principle that opera be performed in its original vernacular. Speaking of the offer later, she responded somewhat shyly: "For a debut it wouldn't have been right . . . Other people pour funny ideas and I consider only . . . doing my job well . . ."[22] I refused the Metropolitan's offer to do *Butterfly*. I thought, why should I ruin my American debut in an opera which I can do better later on, or do without. Naturally everyone thought I was crazy."[23]

The "crazy" Callas image circulated long before she was a star. A couple days after her rejection of the Met, director Dino Yannopoulos signed his own contract with Edward Johnson. "By the way, do you happen to know a certain Callas?" enquired the latter. To the response of an assenting nod he followed up with, "Is she mad?"[24]

Johnson eventually admitted to the press that what he offered her was "frankly a beginner's contract. But she was without experience, without repertory . . ."[25]

Case closed. "Sometimes it seems that no opportunity will ever present itself," Maria mused. "But it's worth it to wait longer than to take a mediocre chance."[26]

After circumventing the trajectory successful singers heartily accept, Maria leapt onto a new one. Essentially it was a path identical to that of unpaid actors or aspiring rock stars.

At loss for what to do, she loitered at her father's drugstore once again. Sometime in early 1946 respected vocal coach and former opera singer Louise Taylor came in to collect her usual prescription. Invited to attend her lessons every Saturday to offer a critique of Taylor's students, Maria soon encountered Louise Caselotti: a fellow voice teacher and former opera singer whose successful sister Adriana had voiced Snow White in the 1937 film. Her husband Edward Richard "Eddie" Bagarozy was a lawyer trying— on the coattails of his wife—to make it as an opera impresario.[27] This faux entrepreneur elected to audition her and told Maria that she needed further training for the Big Time. After bumping into him a few weeks later, she agreed to begin complimentary lessons with his wife.

Caselotti was no master of her craft like Elvira de Hidalgo. Homogeneity strayed from the Callas voice—so her new teacher focused on its low notes and French horn-like darkness; molding it for heavy roles like Aïda and Tosca.[28] It remains unclear to what extent her lessons were a beneficial tutelage. "Caselotti never taught me a single note," Maria would claim thirteen years later. "She started teaching after she got back to the States [from Verona, after 1947]."[29]

Although her teaching methods appeared riskily regressive, she observed Maria's struggle in the top notes: a pernicious flaw to which the young soprano was already privy.[30] The instrument still sounded like an echo through a tunnel: notes were heavy, cavernous, deep-set; an alien phenomenon for the uncurious ear.

For this Maria envied her rolemodel Rosa Ponselle. The latter's voice was similarly viscous and imperious yet didn't fluctuate in shape across its registers, sustaining one smooth entity. Ponselle's career had dazzled at the Met throughout the twenties and the early thirties to create the only singer whom Maria emulated. Several years later she would probe the matter with a fan of hers: "To me Ponselle was probably the greatest singer of us all—but can you tell me how we differed on the stage?"[31] And she spent hours "wearing out the grooves" of Ponselle's records.[32]

Ironically the latter had abandoned her career for a luxurious Beverly Hills life. After attempting to negotiate some movie roles with Metro-Goldwyn-Mayer, Ponselle—to quote biographer James A. Drake—lived for "the expansive estate Rosa had envisioned, which originally included not only a seventeen-room house but also a swimming pool, three garages, a barn, a chicken house, a meat-dressing building, a dairy house and a climate-controlled underground-storage area for costumes and memorabilia."[33] The chance to brew a Ponselle-Callas rivalry was blown.

Yet listening to the notorious diva still unsettled juvenile Maria. "My idol and my despair," she called her, "because my own *timbre* was so dull and colorless (when I think of it the image of thick oil comes to my mind!) and I had great difficulty with the top register."[34]

The way her own strange instrument warmed up took her aback—preferring at the Met audition to dive deep into the low tones of "D'amor sull'ali rosee" from *Il trovatore* before stretching its extensile limbs into the higher "Casta diva." Maria called the process "astounding."[35] A year later she would write her old beau Evangelos, "My voice, thank God, is in splendid form and is getting steadily deeper. I am almost a mezzo-soprano now."[36]

Given the repertoire she practiced it was doubtful that she hoped to be one. This pipe dream was most likely an ephemeral escape from the perpetual plethora of grievances sparked by an instrument immutable. At her audition for world-famous tenor Giovanni Martinelli his response was an issue with the "breaks" between all of her registers.[37] "Who can *trust* you?" Director of the San Francisco Opera House Gaetano Merola asked. "You know, you're too *young* . . . I couldn't trust a twenty-one-year-old girl. You go to Italy and make yourself a *wonderful* career—then I'll engage you."[38]

"Well, thank you," Maria responded. "But by the time I shall have made my own career in Italy, I'm not sure that I'll need you."[39]

In those bleak days Maria felt "no one would have me."[40] Drifting in and out of cinemas, she spent her hours seeking comfortable distractions from the notion that her voice was short of being "natural".[41] For sure, it lacked consistency in timbre; lacked a sameness in its motley registers. This made a lot of people think that it was raw material: a voice untrained.

With the exception of some testy higher notes, not much was unprepared about the instrument. It was just shunned for being different—the exact *kind* of "different" that permitted this peculiar timbre to construct a cavalcade of characters; to shape their silhouettes like sticky fingers forging figurines with fondant.

No one as yet had realized that her voice was no constraint—but an *enabler*.

Destiny was her unfailing gospel. Corresponding to her Christian beliefs selectively, Maria's faith was vaguer and more fatalistic than submission to religion. Her use of the term "God" was more ambiguous than specifying Jesus Christ, his Holy Father or another deity. Often she would refer to herself as a "creature of destiny"[42]—relinquishing responsibility for her career yet simultaneously preparing for an oracle's fulfillment: "Destiny offers you contracts—but it doesn't tell you to stop working," Maria would later explain. "Always work for the day when destiny will come your way. When it comes, you must be ready to confront it."[43]

With zero means of making money she determined to facilitate her life-style. Shelving her principles, Maria moved back in with George, who was now living with his mistress. Following a guarantee from him that Alexandra Papajohn would not begin to run the home, Maria let him cover the hotel bills she had racked up.[44]

Ahead of her remained the scrappy task of finding a new way to earn. In Athens she had been a paid professional performer from her teenage days. Surely she wouldn't have to follow the same path as artists who had never earned a cent?

"Tighten the belt," Maria would advise young singers twenty-five years later. "Keep yourself alive as a waitress if you have to. No job is degrading."[45] Though she herself never admitted it, it was to Asti's Restaurant in Greenwich Village that Maria headed to seek work. Unlike most Italian restaurants, Asti's reeled its clientele in not with pizzas or calzoni but a service of bel canto waiters. So Maria waited tables singing *La Gioconda*'s "Suicidio" or "Casta diva."[46] "I'm not spending too much time entertaining myself as I want to save my strength as much as possible for the great moment [of my debut]," Maria had insisted to de Hidalgo back in January 1946.[47] It was an uphill climb.

Advised by Eddie Bagarozy of a family who sought a nanny, she was interviewed about her previous experience. Evidently she had none. The Failonis were newly arrived. Patriarch Sergio had recently moved to New York with his wife, Hungarian-born Nelly Klier, and their newborn little Nelly. Fortunately for Maria, he was an orchestral conductor.[48]

At first the deferring young woman said nothing. Clad in a black and white traditional maid's outfit, she was timid and reserved and held demonstrative respect for her employers. Without reservation Maria did everything from burping the baby to cooking the dinner. Nelly Failoni regarded her as a good cook and admired her "discretion and respectful tone of voice . . . even though we eventually began to talk about all kinds of subjects and became almost friends . . . She was well-cultured and had great moral elegance. I never suspected that she might have an artistic past."[49]

Maria's etiquette would rarely go unnoticed: her insistence on good manners could at times transgress all common sense. She once exited the opera house with several friends, awaited each of their emergences then went back to the door-holder to personally thank him.[50] Laments of the world's tawdriness such as, "I swear, I see so much vulgarity and banality nowadays that I am thankful for being the person I am" were ubiquitous.[51]

At the same time she could have never been a secretary. Maria's formal education had concluded at thirteen. Spelling choices would originate in a misfiring intuition; grammar was in critical condition. The woman would refer to "diffamation,"[52] cited "instrumentists" and without fail substituted "would've" in her letters for "would of".

So it was unlikely that sophisticate Nelly Failoni would catch on that her devoted maid and babysitter was an artist.

Till the Cunning Little Vixen made it so.

Nelly returned home one evening earlier than usual to espy Maria dusting to her voice's tune. "Why didn't you *tell* me you could sing?" preceded a shower of compliments. Persuaded to listen, husband Sergio poured praise on the instrument. To this the embarrassed girl whispered in shyness, "Thank you."[53]

While Failoni's find did not result in imminent engagements it was clear another useable connection had been forged.

Meanwhile Maria was beginning to rely more heavily on her rapport with wannabe svengali Eddie Bagarozy. As Christmas 1946 approached Eddie announced that he was on the verge of founding a new troupe—"The United States Opera Company"—and asked Maria once again to audition for him. After listening to her perform, he promised she would have the lead roles in both *Turandot* and *Aïda* . . . whenever these performances should fructuate.[54]

Bagarozy's pledges to Maria were accompanied by sentimental nourishment: the sore spot of her Achilles' heel. As he was married to her teacher she would never have embarked on an illicit fling. The virginal Maria was enraged enough to see her father settled with his mistress.

Yet it felt romantic just to feel a little close to Eddie; perhaps even to contemplate what might have been. Later correspondence suggests a certain level of intimacy: "Dearest Eddie—sweetheart—what are you up to nowadays? . . . Don't imagine that I have forgotten or will forget you . . . Next time I see you, I'll tell you everything! Know one thing: Maria doesn't change the way others do." And: "This morning, after waiting for two months, we finally received your letter. Naturally I use the term 'we', for Louisa [sic] and I are basically the same person . . . I want you to write to me immediately, with both clarity and spirit—not as my manager, but as Eddie, my friend."[55]

Although it would be easy to imply Maria was a hypocrite—judging her father's innocent relationship whilst being tacitly romanced by Caselotti's husband—she enjoyed the balm of never-to-be-consummated love. As a giving woman eager to experience the prized affection she had lacked in life, Maria was susceptible to strangers' kindness—and overtly so.

Approaches deviating from her mother's model of behavior constituted proof of goodness. In the hands of anyone who offered warmth or hoped to bolster her career she melted into putty.

"Well, you know that the mind does create many illusions," she would later admit.[56]

This nubile silliness extended far beyond her half-imaginary dalliances. She endured a sense of humor odd throughout her life: childish, simplistic or just abstinent. When asked in 1970 by David Frost, "What do you think is the great difference between a man and a woman?" she unleashed a great rhythmic laugh before timidly murmuring: "Well, I need *help*, here; I need help. What *are* the fundamental differences . . ."[57] Monikers such as cousin Mary Annexy's term "Lettucehead" for their uncle made her roar with insatiable mirth.[58]

Sensibility did not yield tact. Bumping into Peter Diamand of EMI Records on one occasion, she offered the greeting, "But you haven't changed in the ten years I've known you. You were always old."[59] In awe that she and music critic Lord George Harewood had been friends for some two decades, in 1968 she joked before his wife: "You know, George, if we had fallen in love when we first met, our son would now be twenty!"[60]

When Eddie Bagarozy—middle-aged and a notorious womanizer—lured her to the ambush of the dubious "United States Opera Company," the gullible singer believed her career was at last on the upswing. "My news, dearest, is that I am getting ready for my premiere at the Chicago Opera House in Turandot and Aida," she wrote to Evangelos on 12 January 1947. "May God give me the health and strength to succeed—as I want to."[61]

Given many theatres' wartime closure, Bagarozy saw exploitable material in the European opera artists recently arrived on U.S. shores.[62] Among them was Maria's now former employer, conductor Sergio Failoni, as well as bass Nicola Rossi-Lemeni, who would grow his own illustrious career. *The New York Times* announced the cast on 10 January 1947—reporting that the troupe would perform in Chicago and consisted of "Marie Calas [*sic*], Mafalda Favero and Galliano Masini."

Initially the opening had been set for January 6th, later postponed to January 20th. This touring company would give a three-week season of performances comprising *Turandot* and *Aïda*. Now opening night was being postponed till Monday, January 27th owing to a slowpoke ship that hosted many cast members.[63]

In truth Bagarozy had invested with another impresario, Ottavio Scotto—and mistakenly believed the funds sufficient to propel the enterprise. Scarcely enough to hire a rehearsal hall, the scant sum forced the singers to rehearse in Bagarozy's living room.[64] Guarantees had to be offered to the chorus members via a deposit to their union, the American Guild of Musical Artists, to ensure remuneration if the project fell to pieces.[65]

After traveling by train to Chicago the troupe anxiously awaited Maria's arrival. Many had heard Rossi-Lemeni refer to the "fire-in-ice princess, but possessor of one of the most fantastic voices that he or anybody had ever heard."[66] Back in New York she had elected to spend more time training with Louise.[67]

A few days before opening night the singers learned the project had been nixed: instead the company would opt to declare bankruptcy. In a bid to salvage its good name, Chicago Opera House engaged a publicist in Danny Newman, who promoted a "hello" and "farewell" concert that would fund the singers' journey home. Five thousand, eight hundred seventy-three dollars were raised. Studying at home for an already pre-empted debut, Maria was spared the debacle.[68]

The ambitious venture had been doomed from the beginning. According to Rossi-Lemeni, "Scotto was a scoundrel. He disposed of the entire amount that he had received for the season before it had even started."[69]

Dispatched back at Square Zero, the soprano weighed the value of her freshly made connections. The scrapped debut had led her to another contact in Rossi-Lemeni. Upon his return to New York he auditioned for Giovanni Zenatello, director of the Festival at the Arena di Verona: Italy's famed amphitheater opera house. He had voyaged to the States to scout for a soprano who could sing the title role in Ponchielli's La Gioconda. It was to be the first Arena di Verona summer festival since the conclusion of the war.

Rossi-Lemeni[i] right away suggested Zenatello hear Maria.[70] Reticent was he to listen to this singer unknown and so young. Hungering to lure Zinka Milanov, he had high hopes when it came to snapping up the legend.[71] Maria was sure nonetheless that, "Unfortunately, there didn't exist the kind of dramatic soprano who could sing La Gioconda ..." as she claimed two decades later. "It doesn't exist nowadays."[72]

Zenatello received Maria and the Bagarozys one day in the spring of 1947 at his Central Park West home. Louise was likewise auditioning. Maria first accompanied Louise on the piano; mesmerizing Zenatello with her sumptuous piano playing's musicality. He understood immediately that she was a professional and a musician—not just any vocalist-for-hire. After Maria sang "Casta diva" Zenatello ran up to the soprano and hugged her. Louise's chances were shot.[73]

Without gazing at the clauses stipulated in the contract, Maria signed the document that offered six performances of La Gioconda to take place at the Arena di Verona from the start of August.[74] These would pay 40,000 lire apiece (sixty dollars).

In the two months preceding her Italian departure she arrived at Zenatello's house each day for lessons. He believed her middle register had faults and worked hard to correct them, writing to his cousin

[i] The testimony of Sergio Failoni's daughter Donatella in Roberto Tumbarello's interview "La Mia Baby-Sitter si chiamava Maria Callas" (Oggi magazine, 4 August 1994) claims it was her father who wrote to Zenatello to suggest Maria as the soprano for La Gioconda. Failoni had a stroke and died a few months later.

Gaetano Pomari that he had discovered a "black pearl ... a truly exceptional voice."[75]

Still fearing that her luck would be ephemeral, Maria headed to the U.S. Embassy in early June to once again renew her passport. "My professional name is Maria Callas," she recorded officially for the first time.[76] As a precaution she additionally signed a contract with the shady Bagarozy just four days before she left.[77]

Though it is obvious to most that he was little more than an exploiter, the soprano still regarded him a friend and loyal confidant. The contract that she ratified appointed him as her "sole agent". It demanded Bagarozy channel his "best efforts" into finding work for her and be awarded "10% of all gross fees earned by her in Opera, Concerts, Radio, Recordings, and Television. Said fee becoming due and payable upon receipt of monies earned by Artist."[78]

This would have been quite valuable to Bagarozy at the time—for he was bankrupt.

He also promised to exchange a check she signed for tickets on a ship to Italy—insisting that he knew a guy who knew a guy who could obtain a discount.

Neither Bagarozy nor the tickets surfaced. Maria had to borrow money from her faithful godfather Leonidas Lantzounis, a friend of the family who had witnessed her birth.[79]

Despite all this she managed to forgive her questionable advocate's duplicity. Penning an epistle from Verona eight weeks later, she insisted, "Even though you treated me terribly in the last months before my departure, I said nothing and continue to be loyal to you."[80]

In retrospect Maria readily admitted: "I know I was a fool to trust and believe Bagarozy but I was young and I suppose I felt sorry for him going bankrupt. I quite a lot of times bought groceries for them—his wife promising to return the money—I never like saying things like that but it's the truth."

On 21 June the SS *Rossia* set sail for a two-week trip bearing Maria, Rossi-Lemeni and Louise Bagarozy; herself eager to establish a new, European career. With four women living in one cabin, Maria recollected that she "practically starved on it. We ate only potatoes and butter or some other rat."[81] Passengers were scolded by the filthy ship's harassing crew if they arrived late for a meal.[82] There were fifty dollars in her pocket and "a suitcase full of hopes."[83]

The prospect of creating a new home assuaged her anxieties. Though she had never voyaged to the Boot she was relying on de Hidalgo's reprimands en route to Naples: "Her 'screaming' at me in Greece that for my career I should go to Italy and not America was the greatest incentive and strength that enabled me to pull myself together and get on with my life."[84]

If young Maria had obeyed her mother figure in the first place, she could have avoided the mundanity that came with waiting tables, making dinner for the rich and being sensitive around superiors.

Yet sudden fortune would have been a cliché. Like Penelope anticipating the return of loyal Odysseus, she had to weave a web to keep herself distracted through the tribulations bent on testing her tenacity.

It had already taken her two years. But she was finally—albeit slowly—inching homeward to the stage.

5.

"Like going to church"

Enrobed in silvery bel canto drapes—with zigzag stitching of adorning trills, asymmetric hemlines of ascending phrases crowned with clambering cadenzas, pleats of perilous coloratura scales—daydreaming Maria was alarmed to see an Italy so threadbare.

Coated in a wreath of war-spawn wreckage, the beloved land of ancient ruins squatted under squalid chaos. Splintered walls and stripped-off paint comprised an empire of refuse.

Dropped off in these decrepit environs on 28 June, Maria disembarked in Naples. Together with her friend Rossi-Lemeni and the trailing Louise Bagarozy the team boarded a night train headed north to prosperous Verona. With no allocated seating the three alternated for a span of well over four hundred miles, following a roster to take turns to sit in the sole chair.[1]

Lodged at the Hotel Accademia by the Arena di Verona Opera Festival's administration, Maria was invited to have dinner with them on her first night in the city. In addition to the festival's director, his second-in-command, the principal conductor, the director of *Gioconda* and the chorus master there was a perfunctory addition present: the unwitting target of a matchmaking campaign.

Giovanni Battista Meneghini was a fifty-one-year-old respected business-man[2] who ran a large brickmaking company that had twelve factories in Italy. Heavyset and bald and of slight height, he had a head shaped like an upturned egg and a persistently surprised expression in his owl-like eyes. Smugly he believed himself to be a ladies' man. And yet in 1947's strictly Catholic Italy he was unmarried still.

At loss for what to do in his spare hours, Meneghini lingered close to the artistic management of the Arena. No patron was he of the festival—the man didn't *like* opera; expressing frequently his hope that the production "wouldn't last that long."[3] But after years of sacrificing his repulsion at the theatre to the cause of finding the right woman, his desire had become a feral hunt.

The eldest of eleven children, Meneghini—in his own words—had envisioned travelling the world and being a journalist before his service in the First World War had scrapped his dreams. Upon his father's premature retirement the latter had appointed young Battista as the new chief of his family's large enterprise. A self-elected father-surrogate for all his siblings, Meneghini proudly boasted of one doctor brother and another who was a professor of gynecology; a third who was a general and a fourth, a doctor in chemistry. All sisters were financially supported prior to their marriages. These feats he thought to be exclusively his own.[4]

Deeming himself "well-known and highly revered," proclaiming "all of the Veneto region's major industrial companies" would solicit his counsel, he was hardly a quotable figure or illustrious entrepreneur.

Meneghini wasn't multilingual, speaking mostly the Veneto dialect. Notorious was he for stinginess. Decades later a biographer would cite his meetings with the wealthy eighty-three-year-old who had survived two heart attacks:

"I'd go to his house in Sirmione two or three times a week . . . we'd have lunch at a local restaurant. On the first of these occasions, when Meneghini reached the bottom of the house's steps, he suddenly exclaimed: 'Good God, I left my wallet—I'll have to go and get it, or else I'll have nothing to pay with.' So he started up the stairs when I said, 'Signor—don't worry, it's on me.'—'Are you paying, or is it the publisher who pays?'—'The publisher pays.'—'In that case, it doesn't matter. Let's go.' "

The scene would then repeat itself some twentyfold—with Meneghini offering the pretext of his unexpectedly "forgotten" wallet every time.[5]

By summer 1947 his agenda had begun to stagnate. Bored of opera talk, the bachelor lamented to his friends in the administration: "What am I supposed to do? . . . Ballerinas aren't my type—skinny; all skin and bones. I like Titian women—fleshy women."[6]

At the time Meneghini—who had no permanent address and alternated between various hotels—was living with Gaetano Pomari: Zenatello's cousin and the administration's second artistic director. Too fatigued to go to dinner that night at the Pedavena restaurant downstairs, he was en route to the apartment when a hotel porter stopped him: "Sir, if you don't come to dinner Signor Pomari will be very upset."

The man had no choice but to dine with his old escort and the émigré soprano.

Sat across the table from the weary businessman, Maria at first thought: "I like this man—he comes across as someone honest and sincere." But in the fuzz of her myopia without her spectacles she struggled to discern him and forgot the guest. At the end of dinner Meneghini suggested that he take the new troupe—Louise, Rossi-Lemeni and Maria—out to Venice the next day. Her baggage still in transit on another train from Naples to

Verona, Maria was reluctant to present herself in public in the same clothes she had worn that evening. At the consent of her companions she was silent.[7]

Less than a day later Meneghini stood outside the Hotel Accademia with his purring car. Louise, Rossi-Lemeni and another friend of his, Giuseppe Gambato, came to tell him they had called on Maria, who was abstaining "for personal reasons". Meneghini persuaded Gambato to knock on Maria's hotel door and goad her.[8]

The way there was uneventful: she said nothing.[9] When late at night the passengers dismounted from the car and took a vaporetto (a Venetian public waterbus) to St. Mark's Square, the nubile woman was entranced by its nocturnal incandescence. Meshing her impressions of its marble glitter and the chessboard plaque of black and white with her new friend, she spilled out thanks to Meneghini in exalted gratitude.[10]

During their return Maria gradually unfurled herself. Too eagerly this tacit woman opened up and spoke of her rough childhood, her split family, her wartime famine and the struggles that New York had dashed in her direction. The performance of *Gioconda* was her final hope of making a career.

The vehicle halted in Vicenza for a break. It was 2 am: Maria was still talking. Having decided that he wanted this young woman in his life, Meneghini gave her a faint, tender kiss.

And she was bought.

Years later she reflected on these days with glee—insisting it had taken her five minutes to decide he was "the one": "I just—*loved* the way he smiled; it was just so open and er . . . well, you can't explain these . . . love at first sight, I suppose, and it *was* love at first sight—you can't explain these things."[11] She remembered Meneghini as "a man full of enthusiasm and energy:" hardly the somnolent signor we see in photographs.[12]

Inspecting images of Meneghini in this period, it is a near-impossibility to visualize a woman of Maria's age thrilled at the prospect of this most peculiar pairing. Such was her character nevertheless that almost any gesture of affection could immerse her into vulnerable enchantment. Bass George London would remember stopping by her dressing room before their 1956 *Tosca* to wish her "in bocca al lupo" (an Italian version of "break a leg"; literally "in the wolf's mouth"): "Miss Callas took my hand in both of hers and seemed deeply moved. She later told me that this insignificant courtesy had meant a good deal to her."[13]

Eternally surprised by the chicanery of certain individuals, she once expressed astonishment at what she overheard in a next-door hotel room as she took her morning bath: "A woman crying into the telephone . . . She wept for over half an hour," Maria wrote to Meneghini. "Then she finished that conversation and immediately telephoned someone else; a friend. She was laughing. It almost knocked me senseless—to think that she was faking tears to stop her boyfriend leaving her . . . Through my whole life, I have never been that startled by so many lies."[14] To her "the majority of people [were] really fine . . . *Basically*."[15]

Given her apparent absence of experience and age, the bachelor's pursuit was maybe too quick for the times.

And yet the concept of "ulterior motive" stayed beyond Maria's understanding.

With Meneghini in the picture she regarded him as no less than a guardian angel. "I considered him something of a screen for me—to protect me from the outside world . . . having had a very unhappy childhood and family life, I thought that . . . I would at least have affection."[16]

The next day he penned a love letter:

> *My dearest Signorina,*
> *I do hope yesterday evening's jaunt to Venice met with the approval of both you and your delightful friend; I hope you found in it a journey of relief and joy and flatter myself to imagine that we will return there soon and with less haste.*[17]

At the bottom he wrote down his telephone number. She dialed.

Three days later he escorted her to dinner on Lake Garda in Sirmione, a popular vacation resort and home of the great Roman poet Catullus.

Herein began the business conversations. Meneghini offered her his services not as a lover but as a manager/patron. The pair agreed they made a profitable team and formed a mutual understanding: Maria's hotel bills, restaurant checks, clothing and upkeep would be financed by him for a year. She would in turn devote herself to vocal training that included studying with coaches Meneghini personally selected with his "expert" status (he made sure to omit the part about him never liking opera). If at the end of this term both were satisfied with the results of the arrangement, they would draw up a new "deal" regarding future work.[18]

While it appears Maria was content with such an offer—as she had already been with Eddie Bagarozy's proposed contract—by no means did it demand the efforts of a courtesan. Bent on appearing gallant, Meneghini didn't expect sex from a shy, sanctimonious virgin in exchange for her material maintenance. His new companion saw this as the gesture of a suitor or a guardian and would have been incensed if he had crossed a line.

In this vein while Meneghini wrote her reams and reams of love letters, she never drafted a reply. Despite falling swiftly for her savior, she was reluctant to suggest that she was easy.[19]

The latter went out of his way to manifest his ardor in a manner cavalier. His correspondence was bestrewn with messages not just of tenderness but worship of a woman he already knew desired to become a star: "These first letters you receive in Italy come not from America but from Verona, where you have come to bring the smile of your blossoming youth and the promise of delight and the joy of your art . . .[20] Live the way I so want you to live: happy—always."[21]

Ashamed of her privation, Meneghini's consort let him know she had no jewelry. To her it was of scant significance. In her titular role as Gioconda however she would have to convince. An inexpensive bracelet in a shop window had arrested her eye; she would pay him back later. He accompanied its purchase with a note: "Light of my life, I have fulfilled the mission to which you assigned me . . . I pray that you accept my gesture as I wish you will—with a sentiment of amicable understanding."[22]

The beau bought her gardenias. On one occasion he requested that she specify what kind of gift she wanted. Timidly Maria replied he could buy her "whatever he wished". Having caught her open-mouthed before a little fifteenth-century rendition of the Virgin Mary, Meneghini offered her the miniature.[23] In later years Maria would be horror-stricken if her good luck mascot didn't make its way to every dressing room she graced.[24]

Together with this novel kinship the soprano found herself supported by the bosom of (some of) her suitor's close-knit family. Meneghini's sister Pia took the role of her new confidante; she funneled streams of worries through her ear.[25] Every Sunday she paid visits to his brother Nicola and his wife Liliana and had lunch with them at restaurants.[26]

It wasn't long before Venetian newspaper Il Gazzettino sought to interview Maria and Verona's local daily broadsheet L'Arena enclosed a profile of the lyrical newcomer "in love with Italy, its cities and its countryside, its courteous people—and . . . in her own words, already taken with a horrid Scala fever."[27]

As La Gioconda's rehearsals commenced Meneghini recruited a coach for Maria in chorus director Ferruccio Cusinati.[28] In the hierarchy of Maria's mentors he stayed wedged among the dregs. She was already studying with La Gioconda's maestro, Tullio Serafin. Himself a living legend, Serafin had been fourteen when he had seen Verdi conducting.[29]

Whilst many at the helm of the baton infuse each musical interpretation with an unmistakable élan—sometimes foregoing opera to avoid the hassle of its vocalists—Serafin was a self-termed "singer's conductor".[30] He made Maria see, in her own words, the maestro as "the master, the pilot, the train driver . . .[31] Conductors for us, once upon a time especially, were gods. We just, you know, sort of, went into the theatre—I still go into the theatre on tiptoes; it's like going to church, really. That's the way we were brought up."[32]

With Serafin she always felt secure: "We would look down and feel we had a friend there, in the pit. He was helping you all the way. He would mouth all the words. If you were not well he would speed up the tempo, and if you were in top form he would slow it down to let you breathe, to give you room. He was breathing with you, loving it with you. It was elastic, growing, living."[33]

In what Maria called their "great liaison of spirit"[34] she didn't need to adapt to the style of the maestro. Instead their creeds combined. They were remarkably artistically compatible in a unique creative bond she didn't share with the illustrious Herbert von Karajan. When first they studied Cherubini's famed *Medea* "not a single idea clashed", as Serafin recalled.[35]

His first exposure to the still unfinished instrument was not an awe-filled moment. Lending it the epithet "una grande vociaccia"[36]—"a great monster of a voice"—Serafin related that he "felt from the beginning that there was in her a future great singer, [but] she was not perfect. She had some difficulties with her diction and intonation, but looking back on it now, I believe that she began to progress and improve from the very first moment she sang in Italy. Can you imagine another singer who would come to orchestral rehearsals? At first she did this secretly but afterwards whenever I commented about it she always used to say, 'Maestro, am I not expected to be the first instrument of the orchestra?' "[37]

Whilst a great proportion of Maria's artistry was an intrinsic property, what Serafin proposed—although she may have come to an identical conclusion—was to interpret the minutiae of any score as cues for physical expression: "If you really *want* to *find* your movements, to *find* the *staging*, the composer has seen to that already. Listen *hard* to the music. Listen *well* to what we play—the orchestra plays—and you'll find all your gestures *there* . . ."[38] "There was a reason for everything . . . even fioriture and trills . . . have a reason in the composer's mind, that they are the expression of the *stato d'animo* [state of mind] of the character—that is, the way he feels at that moment, the passing emotions that take hold of him. He would coach us for every little detail, every movement, every word, every breath."[39]

To comprehend not just her character but others', Maria would request that if her colleagues were already present they attended her own sessions on piano with the "maestro sostituto": the assistant conductor.[40] *La Gioconda* marked the onset of a schooling that Maria leveled not just at herself but her entire entourage.

She was not unpopular. American tenor Richard Tucker—who was singing the male lead of Enzo—was notorious for being discourteous to colleagues. The woman he called "Mary" he made so at ease during their love scenes that she asked, "Why do I feel so comfortable with you and not with the others?", to which he replied, "Because, tonight, Maria, you are in the major leagues."[41]

As always her debut was marred by a marauding malady. In the midst of a July rehearsal her myopia caused her to overlook an onstage trap-door leading to a storage vault below ground. With her ankle sprained, Maria was determined to recover her performative control. By the third act it was so swollen that she couldn't stand her leg. Despite a doctor being called to bandage the sore limb she couldn't sleep that night for pain.[42]

Insisting on Meneghini—to whom she now referred as "Titta", short for "Battista"—being at her side throughout the whole performance, she appointed him to take his station in the wings that opening night on

August 2nd.[43] Performances at the Arena di Verona customarily begin at nine o'clock even today. A stadium of 20,000 seats, its premieres register as social highlights rather than artistic milestones.

Largely on account of that Maria was *more* terrified.

A British music critic would remember being introduced to her at intermission. Foregoing courtesies, she openly expressed that she was worried for two things: "[one was that] she had a rather badly sprained ankle and could only just limp about the stage, the other that we might not intend to stick out the opera's extreme length, and so would miss her big aria in the last act."[44] The soprano had "something individual—an almost steely power at full throttle, considerable flexibility, exemplary attack, and a silky-smooth *legato*; something hard to forget."[45]

But no "a star is born" explosion sizzled; no overnight success fed dynamite into the morning papers. Though other critics marveled, one described her as "dramatically gripping but spoiled by an obviously unfinished technique."[46]

"I was, immediately after my debut in Italy—not loved that much," Maria sourly remembered. "There were many people that used to say, 'Well, her high notes are beautiful, but her middle notes are *not*;' and the other ones say, 'Oh, the middle notes are *beautiful*, but the top one[s] no good;' and—er—well the other one would come out saying 'The low notes are beautiful, but *then* . . .' in other words, they wouldn't agree."[47]

The public's gut reaction to the voice and artistry of Callas was a little closer to the puzzlement provoked by the Parisian premiere of Stravinsky's *Rite of Spring* than Elvis Presley's breakout hype. It wasn't easy for the vast majority to get accustomed to a voice Chicago music critic Claudia Cassidy would term "part-oboe, part-clarinet".[48] Director Luchino Visconti was befuddled by the natural timbre of Maria's instrument, once telling her: "I'd like to cut you in a thousand pieces just to know what's in your voice."[49]

Its strangeness veered from visibility. "There are certain doctors also in London that wanted to look at my throat and see *how* my throat is made . . ." Maria would later recount. "They were surprised to see that my throat is—any normal throat."[50] EMI Records producer Walter Legge, one of her copious collaborators, called its center "basically dark-hued, her most expressive range, where she could pour out her smoothest legato . . . a peculiar and highly personal sound, often as if she were singing into a bottle."

He attributed this to "the extraordinary formation of her upper palate, shaped like a Gothic arch, not the Romanesque arch of the normal mouth. Her rib cage was also unusually long for a woman of her height. This, together with what must have been her well-trained intercostals muscles, gave her unusual ability to sing and shape long phrases in one breath without visible effort. Her chest voice she used mainly for dramatic effects, slipping into it much higher than most singers with similar range when she felt text or situation would gain by it."[51]

A laryngologist would later summarize Maria's larynx as "an extraordinary anatomical configuration [with] unique musculature around two vocal cords."[52]

Despite a near-faultless technique and approach, some critics still could not adapt to what one called "a fairly frequent lapse into a masked tone in the middle register, which at times makes her sound as if singing with a mouthful of hot marbles."[53]

Precisely that phantasmagorical echo enrobed her deep voice in portentousness.

It wasn't just the instrument *per se*. "They came to hear us push out notes and make beautiful sounds," Maria understood well. "*Yes*, they were music-lovers. But when they saw in me something that they were not *used* to, it wasn't their fault; they were accustomed to listening to another school of singing; they had been ruined by us singers *ourselves* . . ."[54] "The public *likes* good taste but cannot always understand what is . . . *liked*."[55]

Many people were and still are at a loss to understand why this chameleon's device changes so much not just from character to character, but stanza to stanza; phrase to phrase. "No one likes my voice the first time because they don't understand what I am trying to do with it," she would lament.[56]

Loath to hear the singer mold her voice to become someone *new*, a number of aficionados favored the predictable reliability of recognizable phenomena. In the words of American music critic Rual Askew, "Her joining of the soprano voice to the contralto—and its deliberate lack of homogeneity of timbre—is at once her peculiar stylistic triumph and the curse on which all who misinterpret rest their case."[57]

Following her pattern of perfidious fortune, on the day *Gioconda*'s mixed reviews came out Maria broke her glasses.[58] After another performance she met a fifteen-year-old Greek boy—later her friend, a music critic and a Callas biographer—who told her that her voice had made him feel "confused and rather frightened."[59] It made Maria laugh.

Being somewhat educated in the history of music, she was not dispirited by the absenting hype as much as Meneghini—who immediately fretted his investment in the germinating star would not pay off. Immediately his correspondence was suspended. Anxious, he consulted Serafin. The latter prescribed further study for Maria and immediately penned a letter of recommendation to his friend, vocal coach Emma Molaioli.[60]

The next six weeks saw not a single note from Meneghini to his new beloved.[61]

Maria didn't notice. On 20 August she wrote home to Eddie Bagarozy: "Thank God. He sent me this angelic person [Meneghini] and for the first time in my life I have no need of anyone else . . . As for an eventual marriage to him, I've thought about it a lot, I promise you. Because the truth is that one rarely finds such a gem of a soul . . . He is I and I am he. He understands me perfectly, I him. That's what counts the most—far more than some stupid career that doesn't even leave you a name . . ."[62]

No proposals of engagements came throughout the next two months except a trivial offer to sing *La Gioconda* in the tiny town of Vigevano near Milan. Serafin advised Maria to reject it so she did.[63]

By 17 September she finally landed an audition with Mario Labroca, La Scala's artistic director (a post lower in rank than Antonio Ghiringhelli, who was the "superintendent"—the manager). The response was that her voice had "too many defects; try to correct them. But you can go home now—I assure you that you'll definitely have the part of Amelia in *Un ballo in maschera*."[64]

He never called. "La Scala said I didn't know how to sing," was how Maria expressed it.[65]

Three days later she was ready to leave Italy and head back to the West; even writing Meneghini a letter of parting. But that night he convinced her—seemingly with endless declarations of *amore*—to remain. The farewell note was never handed to him. In lieu of it came her first love letter: "To leave you would be too great a punishment . . . Yesterday I was determined to leave because I thought you were fed up with me . . . Today depends on what you want. If you are tired of me, tell me and I'll leave right away . . . My Battista, you have all of me, all, to the ends of my deepest sentiments; to the reach of my littlest thoughts. I live for you. Your wishes are my wishes; I will do everything you want, but do not take this love and shut it in a closet. Try to love it . . ."

Thus began a stream of letters written in Maria's hand in partly literate Italian: notes with minimal respect for proper punctuation.[66] Her epistolary parlance was theatrical much like her speaking voice. In the words of composer Hans Werner Henze, "Her spoken voice was not so dissimilar to the sung one . . . 'uuuhh, uuuhhh . . .' "[67]

At the time her English was a fluctuating fusion of linguistic fragrances: *Mademoiselle* editor Leo Lerman described his first impression of it as "rich in varied associations: Manhattan sweet twang, Italian musicality, girlishness, a touch of diva resonance, a kind of Greek harshness."[68] Decades before it was a trend to incorrectly use the adverb "literally" Maria was suffusing speech with it. "I was literally lynched," she once said.[69] On another occasion: "Someone literally invented a story and published it."[70]

It was a habit of Maria's to loop languages together in her jargon. A friend limned her vocabulary as "a funny mesh of Veneto, Greek and English."[71] Despite the lattermost being her mother tongue—as she herself avowed[72]—comments such as "It's in the *spartito*" (the musical score) were aplenty.[73]

*

Returned to the title of manager, Meneghini escorted Maria to the office of Milanese operatic impresario Liduino Bonardi.[74] Despite her new credentials, he had naught to offer her.

On the way out she bumped into Nino Cattozzo—Artistic Director of the Teatro La Fenice in Venice. Surprised to see Maria, he expressed astoundment at her apathy toward singing Isolde (of Wagner's *Tristan und Isolde*) in Venice. The soprano was dumbfounded. "I didn't receive your telegram," he explained. "What telegram?" was her rejoinder.

He had telephoned Angelina Pomari—a singer and the sister of Gaetano Pomari, Second Artistic Director of the Arena di Verona—to request she ask Maria if she wanted to perform the role. With no response he had concluded that she wasn't after it. Standing in the threshold of the useless agent's office, suddenly she learnt the part was hers.

Partly because of her acrid experience with agents she never officially had one. Although Bonardi would arrange Maria's Mexican performances[75] and accompany her to an audition for Arturo Toscanini,[76] she never appointed a "sole representative". Wary of commercial matters crinkling operatic evolution, Maria disliked artists being sold in packages like flights and bed and board: "You see, if they have the name 'Callas' and a certain theatre wants me, they say, 'Sure, we'll give you Callas but on top of that you'll have to take this one, that one, the other one, and the other one'—and you know, by and by they manage to command the musical world," she ruminated. "Not being able to have me in their hands, of course they *lose* a lot of business and they lose the market, you know. And I'm . . . independent."[77]

Before Maria could be sent the contract the production's maestro, Serafin, had to audition her. In order to secure the role she had already lied to Cattozzo—alleging she knew the whole role off by heart.

When the test loomed she turned glacial. "I thanked my lucky stars that I had studied in the conservatoire because er . . . I had just looked at the first act by . . . *curiosity* . . . you know, they say that to learn Wagner is so difficult, and I know I'm a very quick learner . . . So I just *bluffed*, I said: 'Yes, of *course* I know Isolde and I *sight*-read the second act—I don't know *how, God* must have helped me—if I think of it even *now* after all these years! And he [Serafin] turned around and said 'Excellent!'—thank heavens he didn't ask for the third act 'cause I would have *died*. And he *told* me, he says, 'Well—*excellent* work; I must say, you know the role very well.' And then I confessed, 'Look, Maestro,' I said, 'I must say—I bluffed. I didn't know it; I sight-read the second act.' Well—he was *surprised* and he appreciated me even *more* then—but, *then* I had to study!" was Maria's memory of it two decades thence.[78]

The contract stilled the fears of Meneghini—who rained down on his inamorata a torrential stream of compliments: "I want you to be an incomparable Isolde. An Isolde of great class . . . An Isolde that's a real . . . Isolde!"[79]

Sent to Rome to study the exigent part with Serafin, Maria mourned her subsequent confinement. "Above all I want to make you happy," the soprano scribed to Meneghini. "Then, it's not just you, but I have to make Serafin happy also. What about me—who makes me happy? I make everyone happy and I'm left with this glory and my sentiments are worth nothing. Oh, well—I'll leave philosophy alone for now otherwise I'll become unhappy and sad."[80] It was one of many mood swings in Maria's sentimental carousel. The following day she was jubilant: Serafin's wife soprano Elena Rakowska had bestowed on Maria the wig she had worn as Isolde.[81]

Cloyingly clingy in her new rapport, she suffered textual tantrums if responses to her letters arrived tardily—beginning one with: "I awaited your letter with so much excitement today—but it didn't come; I don't know why. I don't want to believe that you didn't write to me. I'm sure that you did write to me, but that the mail is up to its old tricks again. But that ruined my day."[82]

Insecurities are manifest throughout her correspondence. Meneghini realized this and did his best to butter up her close ones—going so far as to send a telegram to Evangelia in Athens to announce her daughter's imminent engagement.[83] Later he would also be in touch with father George, who called the couple "My beloved children Maria and Battista" and thanked Meneghini for the newspaper clippings he'd sent.[84]

With her debut as Isolde five days away that December, Meneghini proposed. "Imagine: being in Venice, Christmas Day, with the person you love ..." Maria exulted years later. "Can you imagine *anything* more beautiful?"[85]

It was astonishing how many details of her life would lapse from Meneghini's knowledge. He would refer to sister Jackie as "Cecilia";[86] would cite Maria knowing "seven languages" when she spoke only four.[87]

Felicity enriched her foreseeable future; swelling the day that iconic soprano Renata Tebaldi attended her *Tristan*. The two had first met at a party in Verona during *La Gioconda*'s run and she and Meneghini had attended her Arena di Verona *Faust*.[88] Now the legend knocked on Maria's dressing room door. "Mamma mia!" she exclaimed, shaking Maria's hand. "If I had to sing so tiring a role, they would have to pick me up with a spoon."[89]

Tristan und Isolde is an ode to love: a love so fervid it can be at peace in death alone. "Tristan's last act is done like a dream world," Maria averred. "It must vibrate the heart."[90] During his work on the opus Wagner wrote to his friend and eventual father-in-law, composer Franz Liszt:

> *Since I have never enjoyed in life the actual happiness of love, I want to erect another monument to this most beautiful of all dreams, in which, from beginning to end, this love is going to satisfy its hunger properly for once. I have worked out a* Tristan und Isolde *in my head—the simplest and at the same time most full-blooded musical conception. Then I'll cover myself over with the "black flag" [a motif in the opera] flying at the end so I can—die.*[91]

What Isolde experiences prosaically is the death of her lover. Spiritually it is a lofty ascent to another realm via her subsequent death: a sphere superior.

Because of Italy's intolerance of all things German after World War II the opera was performed in the Italian language. Frequently interpreted by stocky, staggering sopranos, this Isolde stunned the crowd with: "[how she] sang it . . . lyrically and in utterly different fashion from the German style," in the words of her co-star Fedora Barbieri.[92]

Though there is no available complete recording of Maria in the role,[i] published recitals of the final aria, "Liebestod" or "Mild und Leise"—in Italian known as "Dolce e calmo"—stray far from stereotypical impressions of the heroine.

The 1949 Cetra rendition is no hammering declamation but an amorous outpour. In the words of *Washington Post* critic, Paul Hume: "in the Latin tongue . . . The results are an immediate upward leap in the sensuous appeal of the text, with Callas providing a legato and sustained sound not heard in this music since Kirsten Flagstad last sang it."[93]

Isolde limning her dead lover's "occhi belli" (beautiful eyes) is laced with an ebullient crescendo: ecstasy's upswing. Whirling round and round in a compulsive rhythmic pattern as it clambers into culmination, her accelerating speed and scaling sonancy convey the heroine into a long-craved other ether. When she finishes the aria with "Sommo ben" ("Supreme bliss"), we perceive at last her peace: security in a terrain intangible. The tentative diminuendo on the final syllable assures us that Isolde has come home. In death.

The Venetian incarnation scored well with the critics. They noted her "uncommon musical sensibility . . . she lived through the amorous passion through her part more with sweet femininity than with druidic virility."[94]

Speaking of the role two decades afterward, Maria noted that she "found [it] very easy. *Because* [Isolde's] supported by a *tremendous* orchestra, the notes are *not* extremely difficult, even the high notes are not all *that* many; not *nearly* as *Norma*—or even in *Verdi*."[95]

*

From the mellifluous *Tristan* she transported herself to the hazardous *Turandot* at the same theatre: the anti-heroine of the vindictive Chinese princess. In vocal terms she is a high-pitched, harsh and often strident ice queen. Later on Maria would admit the choice had mostly been careerism: "People wanted me to sing this role because of my big dramatic soprano voice . . . there were not many sopranos who could do it. It was a challenge and as I was young and totally unknown, a great opportunity to establish myself . . .[96] As soon as I could *stop* singing that, I *did*. Because—well, I was *happy* to because it's . . . not considered a very good role for the voice and

---

[i] In November 1968 Maria wrote to tenor Max Lorenz to ask if it was true he had a recording of their May 1948 Genoa performance of *Tristan*. The letter was published in *Maria Callas: Exposition, Hôtel de Ville de Paris, Salle Saint-Jean*, a catalogue for an exhibition held 27 March–28 June 1998. It is uncertain whether or not it existed but according to Frank Hamilton—who compiled annals of all her performances and exchanged letters with Lorenz's students—there may have been an "unlistenable" recording. (Frank Hamilton, *Maria Callas: Performance Annals and Discography*, 2010).

frankly also, *stage*-wise it's a . . . *very* static role and . . . When you hear everybody say, 'It's bad for you,' it's best that you listen to the *majority*."[97]

From a personal perspective, she "did not dislike Turandot. Shall we say I did not love her passionately."[98] Professionally she vacillated in her stance on which parts any given vocalist should have the capability to sing.

It was Maria's creed to stress *any* soprano be equipped to sing *any* soprano role; even some mezzo ones. At one point she espoused that there was no such thing as a distinction between "mezzos", "altos" and "sopranos": mere urban myths were these made up by none the wiser critics. Great singers should be able to do anything.[99]

And yet in criticizing the demands of *Turandot* Maria later noted, "It probably does *not* ruin your voice [but] you get the *idea* and you try and keep away from it anyway so . . . take no chances, there *are* lovely operas too."[100] Exactly where she stood on her insistence that a vocalist should be omnipotent was dubious.

Following a few performances of *Turandot* in the small town of Udine and a Trieste-based inaugural *La forza del destino*, the local press was congregating at Maria's feet. Forever in the wings, Meneghini was on hand to play both Assistant and Mentor—whispering backstage before every entrance: "Go on, Maria! There's no one like you. You're the greatest in the world!"[101]

At a further stage in their relationship he would buy diamonds. Each one would be named for a new triumph, with one being christened "Puritani" and another "La Scala".[102]

At the same time reporters failed to overlook how bored lethargic Meneghini looked in her recording sessions—sitting in a corner, head bowed and asleep.[103] His sister Pia recollected that at glamorous occasions when Maria met with colleagues, Meneghini would grow wearisome and bristly and eventually insult them.[104] Loath to hear live broadcasts by Maria when she was away, he would be urged by her to "try to listen to one if you can."[105]

In September 1948 Maria had another Verdi debut as Aïda in Turin.

"I'm gonna tell a story which is *true*—it happened to *me*," February 1972 saw her telling Juilliard student Barrie Smith and an audience of hundreds. "I was singing *Aïda* for the first time with Maestro Serafin in Torino—*and* the 'Cieli azzurri' is very difficult, I must confess—there are other pieces that are more difficult but I was *young* too and . . . so I ordered myself a *cognac*. 'Cause somebody told me that it would give me courage. Well, Maestro Serafin saw it pass by his dressing room. He says, 'Who's that *cognac* for?' So they told him, 'It's for Miss Callas.' He says, 'Take that *back!*' And he comes— very angry—into my dressing room and told me: '*This* is how you get into bad habits—*first* of all, of not using your *muscles*, reflexes . . . Once, you start drinking *one* cognac, and the next time it won't be enough, you'll be drinking *two* and by that time you'll have the *bottle*.' And . . . it's very true of very many of my colleagues." The audience burst out laughing. "When I practice I have *nothing*."[106]

Self-described as "practically a non-drinker, maybe a little wine but my friends provide all the spirit I need"[107]—Maria enjoyed brandy,[108] never drank liquors[109] and was tempted by concoctions like vermouth cassis.[110]

A predilection for incessant sugar had provoked proliferation of her cellulite. Her voraciousness discriminated nonetheless. Tasting was integral to her notorious dinner habits: unfailingly she used her fork to snatch a sample of companions' platters.[111] In those vernal days of Veronese inhabitation her routine was to go out at nine o'clock each morning to procure a mortadella-stuffed panini.[112] Years thence a publicist would see her shun the eatery of a luxurious hotel to patronize O'Connell's hamburger joint.[113]

Nothing could defeat her appetite for meat—except for maybe pasta, which the singer could appraise without restraint.[114] Bloody slabs of roast beef, steak tartare, and steak "alla fiorentina" were regular orders.[115] For a portion of a Tokyo television interview she couldn't resist waxing lyrical: "Your meat, I mean . . . it's out of this *world*."[116]

Dessert-wise, ice cream was the ruler of the culinary kingdom. At a formal dinner she could serve guests bowls of six scoops: each a different shade.[117] If she asked to have a small bite of a cupcake it was code for "I'm not going to give it back."[118]

All of this had lumbered her with weight she sought to shed. Asked to go shopping by the wife of Lord George Harewood—Queen Elizabeth II's cousin and the music critic who had met her during *La Gioconda*'s run— she replied by looking at her fatty arms and asking, "Who would want to drag all this around?"[119]

But she was polishing her physical demeanor. Meneghini's sister would allude to "fingers that spoke so delicately throughout her movements . . . her nails were always well looked after."[120] American music critic William Weaver expressed: "True, she was a big woman, Junoesque, heavy; but she knew— even then—how to move. Or rather how not to move. A single imperious gesture, her arm extended laterally, the forefinger firmly pointed, did more to establish Norma's drama than broad pacings or semaphore arm-waving."[121]

*

Maria's rapturous reception in the Turinese *Aïda* finally allowed her to acknowledge she was on a roll. In unabashed excitement she scribed to Elvira de Hidalgo:

> <u>Now</u> they say that I am the true Verdian voice—etc! etc! . . . Even so, the art is going down the drain. There are no longer fair judges! If it weren't for Serafin, I would never <u>sing</u> again. In their eyes I always have to refrain from singing, for, it seems to them that a powerful voice could never sing Verdi. They forget the voices of the past. Oh, well—the main thing is that I won and that's what counts!

I hope that Serafin finds a tenor for the Norma—*that will be my ulti-mate and definitive battle—and that way I shall have created that name that you and I so desire.*[122]

Her fears allayed by the elation sparked by her *Aïda*, she was on the warpath for a new success. In haste Maria informed Serafin that if she didn't find engagements she would hurriedly depart for the United States. Taken aback, he called his friend Francisco Siciliani, the artistic director of the Teatro Comunale in Florence.[123]

Siciliani had heard the radio broadcast of *Tristan und Isolde* in January. With Maria studying with Serafin in Rome, he turned up at the maestro's door and asked the young soprano to perform for him. She sang parts of *Aïda, Turandot* and *La Gioconda*.[124] "Let's forget we've scheduled *Butterfly* for opening night," Siciliani insisted to the general manager of the Teatro Comunale, Pariso Votto. "I've found an extraordinary soprano and we must do *Norma*."[125]

"This letter of mine will bring you great joy . . ." Maria began in her subsequent missive to de Hidalgo on 9 November.

My dear, pray that all goes well for me, pray I'm in good health, because after this performance, if all goes as we hope and dream, I am the queen of song in Italy, maybe even of everywhere, for the simple reason that I add to it the perfectionization of song, and that there is no other Norma in the whole world![126]

Demand for Maria was sluggishly growing. In the same letter she referred to her refusal of a Lisbon-based engagement: "After such a winter of such intense work I have to rest a little bit—I'd like to preserve my voice well! And then the reper-toire didn't suit me: they were offering me *Turandot*, two performances, then another *Ballo in maschera*, then one of *Don Giovanni*, and then a concert."[127]

Two weeks before *Norma*'s opening night Maria succumbed to a cold that included a blocked nose, a swollen sore throat and a fever. According to theatrical tradition in those days, it was her duty to provide at least a part of the role's costume. The director was insisting on a wig both "reddish blonde" and "90 cm long".[128]

Maria had already met with a great number of sartorial mishaps. During a Trieste run in 1948 of Verdi's *La forza del destino*, she had scribed of how the ill-kept theatre's costumes "stink of sweat so much, they almost make me faint. When my colleagues come into my dressing room they complain of the smell!"[129]

Taking care of costumes thus became a new component of the Callas Schooling. Her ritual would involve a visit to a shop owned by a dressmaker in Brescia—Meneghini's mother's hometown—to extract potential props and costumes.[130] As late as 1958 she was advising London's Royal Opera she would "bring her own costumes for LA TRAVIATA".[131]

Her acne-ridden skin had an adverse reaction to the commonly used greasepaint. Because of this Maria crafted her stage make-up and designed the upturned flicks of eyeliner that graced her generous eyes.[132] "For an hour and ten minutes, the public has *nothing* to do but *look* at you," she explained. "If you don't *really* fascinate them, *with* your voice—and no matter *how* much you *fascinate* them *with* your voice in your *role* they *still* have *all* the time—which means an hour and ten minutes—to *cut* you to pieces—take your costume and cut it to pieces; so if you *don't* really give it *the* best—you're *in* for disaster."[133]

Mired in self-preparation for the Florentine production, the soprano was subjected to new suffering. Eleven days remained till opening night when she wrote Meneghini:

> *I was studying* Norma *when I came back to the hotel after our first rehearsal with the mezzo-soprano, and suddenly I was overcome with the kind of melancholy that you couldn't imagine . . .*
>
> *You see—I want so much to give so much more of myself in everything I do. In art as well as in my love for you. When it comes to singing, I want to make my voice obey me <u>always as I</u> wish—but that seems to be too heavy a demand. The vocal organ is ungrateful and doesn't give you everything you want. I'd say that it's rebellious and resists being ordered or dominated. It always wants to escape and I'm the one who suffers for it. So much that if it continues in this vein, you'll soon have a neurasthenic on your hands.*
>
> *And in my love for you I suffer because I don't know how to give you more! I want—I don't know—to be able always to offer you more and more and I know that I don't have more to offer you because I'm just a human being.*

The corner into which she had painted herself was her life. Maria was solitary. To Meneghini she insisted: "I don't have friendships—neither do I want them. You know that I'm a misanthrope and I have solid grounds to be one. I live only for you and for Mama—you share me! People think art gives me everything. I think it doesn't give me even a *minimal* part of what I want."[134]

The self-loathing was invanquishable. And yet during *Norma*'s arduous rehearsals the artistic dictums that Maria chronically imposed evolved to be distinguishable for her listeners: a vocal part had to be treated like an actor's dialogue.

"Then you come back to the words. What do they say?" Maria rhetorically asked. "If I were to speak this recitative how would I say it? And you keep on saying it to yourself, noting the accents, the pauses, the little stresses that create meaning. You try to achieve the right balance between the different accents of speech and music. After that the trouble starts; or rather, the really rewarding part of the work. After you've learnt the music rhythmically then you say: 'Right, now *this* is the tempo of Bellini.'

Donizetti would have felt it this way, Wagner would have felt it another way. They might all write *allegro* or *adagio*, but each composer has his particular rhythm, and that is too elusive to put on a metronome.

"Coming back to the words and the music: you start to free yourself, and you apportion what you feel is the correct emphasis to each phrase; you come to an agreement about this with the conductor and the other singers. Together you decide the musical shape of each passage and how it will relate to the whole. It's like analyzing a balanced piece of architecture . . . Then the theatre person in you starts to judge, and you say to yourself: 'Now, wait a minute! If you do it this way, as the composer originally wished it, a modern audience will just die of yawning.' So you have to take little liberties, animating it a little more, adding a touch here and there."[135]

Some other technical necessities began to be encrusted in her thinking: a note had to be attacked directly—"never from underneath or from above." Two consecutive "fermata"s (long-held notes) were excessive; one would be scrapped. Was the composer always right? Yes. And no.[136]

Bellini's opera—delicately tender, militantly valiant—revolves around its titular heroine, the High Priestess of the Druids, in Gaul a few decades BC. To the dismay of her people, Norma has broken her vows and succumbed to Pollione, a Roman proconsul and one of her troubled land's occupiers. Though he is the father of her children, she has not become his wartime booty. Still at the helm of her seditious denizens, she pledges loyalty to them and promises to devastate the Romans. As she struggles to allay her people's bloodlust, Norma offers a serene prayer to the Moon Goddess: the incandescent "Casta diva."

When she learns that Pollione has betrayed her with her best friend, priestess Adalgisa, the lapsed Druidess is split asunder. Vindictive Norma hopes to vanquish Pollione and yet yearns for a revival of his love. Like Medea, she considers murdering their children to fulfill her vengeful quest. Instead she opts to have her people go to war against the Romans. Pollione must be killed so he can be the ritualistic sacrificial victim. Stoic in his presence, Norma is unable to perform her lover's execution and demands the slaughter of a priestess in his stead. Though everyone imagines she's referring to the traitor Adalgisa, she intends to kill *herself*.

This was Maria's most relatable protagonist. "She is a woman who cannot be nasty or unjust in a situation for which she herself is fundamentally to blame . . .[137] She just . . . *roars* like a *lion*, but *actually* she's *not* . . .[138] In the last act Norma thought that she was in control of the whole situation but lost her head completely when her emotions got the better of her. Nevertheless she remains a noble person to the end and sufficiently—so as to liberate herself without becoming a traumatic sentimental fool. That is her purification."[139]

Norma and Maria shared a purpose not dissimilar: the former was the ruler of her people and the latter of her art. Both feats would often seem impracticable. "It's an opera that lifts me beyond the heavens," Maria confided.[140]

By opening night on 30 November 1948 Maria had conquered her cold. Norma's address to her followers, "Sediziose voci, voci di guerra" ("Seditious voices, voices of war") earned ambivalence amid spectators. "The recitative diffused strange sensations over the public," tenor Mirto Picchi (Pollione) later wrote.[141] Serafin elaborated: "[they] were so puzzled by the uneven but dramatic delivery of the opening recitative that they did not really appreciate the ensuing 'Casta diva' as much as they should. You see at that time, in the late forties, most people unfortunately only had ears for pure lyricism and what they considered to be beauty of sound irrespective of the dramatic situation. However, I believe that by the end of her first Norma Callas' impact was so great that henceforth the audience, at least in their subconscious, were changing their approach to opera."[142]

Critics were kinder. Gualtiero Frangieri wrote of her "secure and perfectly commanded technique. With a single shade of color in the voice, with a schooling that is different to what we are accustomed to hearing, the instrument has undeniable merits. Callas created a character gifted with subtle and affecting accents of femininity, presenting in Norma—as well as the implacable priestess—a woman both in love and disillusioned in love; a mother and a friend."[143]

Five days later a sequential *Norma* felled Maria with the early symptoms of appendicitis. The cramping in her right leg was so painful Norma struggled to kneel. "I was sick and no one knew it," she recalled in 1954. "I was swollen, jaundiced. If I sat in a car for a short drive, my legs puffed up. I could not wash with soap and water. I could not sleep at night. I was tired and hoarse—it was as if a veil had dropped in front of me."[144]

Refusing to surrender to minutiae like these, it wasn't until 7 December that she went to hospital. Her fever was 41°C (106°F).[145] The ordeal resulted in Maria having to forego the scheduled Florentine *Aïda*s and spend ten days bedridden at Borgo Trento Hospital, not far from Verona.[146]

Maria was generally not in good health. Constantly complaining of her swollen legs,[147] she was subjected to sequential headaches and awakened by cruel migraines. "I thought I had a tumor or something. I swear," she wrote to Meneghini on one occasion. "That was how much it hurt."[148]

Racked with eczema, the soprano was observed after a performance by one fan to be "pitted with deep acne scars."[149]

At various points in her life she was anemic[150] but Maria's most dire affliction was plummeting blood pressure. "It was around 90 over something," recalled one of her friends.[151] Pia Meneghini noted that each time she and Maria stayed out late "the next day she would be in bed until two in the afternoon on account of [it]."[152] On the other hand it gave her a formidable excuse for downing copious amounts of coffee: ten cups a day if she was anywhere near an espresso machine.[153]

It didn't help that she suffered from allergies. Aware of her adverse reactions to dry legumes, a sly tenor once deliberately ate garlic prior to their onstage kiss. Excess saliva built up in her mouth and challenged her enunciation.[154] Though able to take aspirin, Maria was also allergic to antibiotics.[155]

*

Dispatched in Venice in the early days of January 1949 to realize Wagner's *Die Walküre* with Serafin, she stayed at the Hotel Regina near the Teatro La Fenice with her cast and composer-conductor Franco Mannino. At the time the latter was courting Uberta, a sister of director Luchino Visconti. After a journey to Cernobbio to meet his girlfriend, Mannino came back to the hotel at night to find Maria "at the entrance, stoic and frozen."

It was six am. He asked what she was doing up so late.

"I was waiting for you, sweetheart."

"Why?"

"Because at five o'clock in the morning *yesterday* you left the faucets on in your hotel bath so you could go meet up with your girlfriend. By seven o'clock all the furniture on the first floor were turning into gondolas. I mean—they were floating up and down like *gondolas*, honey." Following a long pause of suspense, she finished: "If the manager held you accountable for all damages, you wouldn't make enough money in a *lifetime* to meet all the costs. So last night all of us spent two hours trying to placate him. The bravest of us were Giulietta [Simionato] and Tito [Gobbi].[ii] I was in charge of standing here to warn you. Be careful, because the old man is already in his office." The latter's love of music spared Mannino the fallout.[156]

Departing the domain of the mundane for the Norse myths of Wagner, Maria debuted as the bellicose Brünnhilde in *Die Walküre*: "The Valkyries," from which the famous "Ride of the Valkyries" theme originates.

Assigned by the god Wotan to at first protect then sacrifice the mortal Siegmund in his duel with Hunding, Brünnhilde is an Amazonian woman cursed with alternating loyalties. After vowing to let Siegmund win the battle, she capriciously reverses her decision. Then she allows Siegmund's triumph; insisting to her father Wotan that he wished it all along. Her compassion for the human race—of which she's not at member—is invariably at strife with her intolerance.

The press was quick to warm to Callas as a German heroine performing in Italian. "She was a splendid Brünnhilde—through her musical attacks, her pride, her sweetness and her portamenti [melodic slides from one note to another]," a Venetian critic scribed. "After Isolde and Walküre, in Maria Callas Wagnerian theatre has found a new heroine."[157]

[ii] The references to Giulietta Simionato and Tito Gobbi are likely instances of misremembrance on Franco Mannino's part. Neither singer was participating in either *Die Walküre* or *I puritani* and Maria had yet to make their acquaintance. Fellow cast members were probably the ones who helped her.

Destiny determined one such feat was not enough. Simultaneously with *Die Walküre*, the Teatro La Fenice was presenting a production of Bellini's *I puritani* with soprano Margherita Carosio. Wagner's total opposite, *I puritani* is bel canto: fewer definitive vocal outbursts; more swirls of key-changing coloratura.

Suddenly Carosio was plagued with the flu. Serafin's wife Elena Rakowska was passing the hall in the Hotel Regina when her ears caught Maria's fortuitous warm-up. Unaware of the last-minute manhunt for a substitute Elvira, the soprano happened to be practicing *I puritani*. Rushing up to Maria, Rakowska advised: "You stay here and wait for Tullio—he'll be here any minute and you can sing this for him."[158]

Thinking it a joke, Maria performed some of the music.

The next day at 10 am she received a telephone call: " 'Please put your robe and come down.' . . . [it was] Maestro Serafin. I said, 'Maestro, I'm not washed-up, it'll take me about half an hour.' He said, 'No, no—come down the way you are . . .' And, er—I went down, and he said, 'Sing.' I said, 'What?'—'Sing what you sang to me yesterday.' There was the director of the theatre, [Nino] Cattozzo, and I said, 'Ah . . .'

"Anyway, I was *forced* to sing the aria, *and*, er . . . Sight-read, of course—which was the second time, the *third* time I sight-read it. I heard them talking and he says to me, 'Well look, Maria, you're going to do this role in a week.' I said, 'I'm going to do *what* in a week?' He says, 'You're going to sing *Puritani* in a week. I undertake that you study it.'—'But I can't—I have three more *Valkyrias*. Can't *do* it. It's ridiculous that I sing *Puritani*.' He says, 'I *guarantee* you that you *can*.' So I thought to myself, 'Well, if a man like Serafin—who is no child, knows his job—can guarantee *me* a thing like that—I will be a fool to say 'no'. And I said, 'Well, maestro—my *best*, I can *do*—more than my best, I cannot promise.' I was still young and you know, being young you *have* to gamble. I started working and I managed in five days to sing my three *Valkyrias*, to do the *prova generale* [general rehearsal] of *Puritani*."[159]

Brünnhilde was a piece of cake compared to this Elvira: a woman Maria regarded as having no variation of character "whatsoever. She does not have all these *abbellimenti* [ornaments] . . . She *is* one solid rock. More or less."[160] Often she would reference the renowned soprano Lilli Lehmann, who remarked that she would rather sing three *Götterdämmerung* Brünnhildes than one Norma.[161]

Having learned the music in five days, Maria sang the role of *Puritani* almost perfectly in her technique—with the exception of explicitly pronouncing "I'm a vicious virgin" (in Italian, "Son vergine viziosa") instead of "I'm a charming virgin" ("Son vergine *vezzosa*").[162]

The press now had a story on their hands. Callas had accomplished an endeavor quasi-unrealizable: "From the heavy roles of Turandot and Brünnhilde burst forth an agile creature, sensitive, vital in every note, who breathes melody filtered through a superior intelligence," one Venetian critic observed.[163] Whilst some admitted that they thought her voice was still too heavy for the light soprano sections of the role, they had no choice but to accept that she had outperformed their expectations. "To me she was the kind of artist whom, until then, one had only read about in operatic history books," mused Serafin in retrospect.[164]

From such a dazzling summit came a guillotine-like drop. During another *Walküre*—this time in Palermo—Maria arrived at the general rehearsal to see that the props were not ready. "The orchestra was blowing raspberries, the maestro [Francesco Molinari-Pradelli] talked a lot but didn't actually *do* anything," she wrote to Meneghini. "The bass—[Giulio] Neri—didn't even know his role! . . . The theatre actually called me up to remind me what time the performance was starting! It seems that over here some singers forget their engagements and must be reminded of them. Well, well, well!"[165]

During the last act of the opening night, Giulio Neri—who was singing the god Wotan—got vocally lost as he was putting his daughter to sleep for eternity. The conductor had to tell him to stop singing. He and Maria pantomimed most of the final scene.[166]

It was because of that—and a review that cited Neri's performance as "always so musical"—that Maria declared she would "never again set foot in Sicily."[167]

This followed the soprano's predictable pattern with cities and places: her relationship with sites depended on their treatment of her. Rome being the customary setting of her work with Serafin, she admired the "beautiful city—at least, the little I've seen of it."[168] New York was the despised location of her upbringing: "It's always so noisy and too crowded."[169] These preferences were liable to change according to the audience that greeted her in every town. And did.

Once again five days sufficed for the edacious singer to devour the new part of Kundry: the shrewd, witch-like seer of Wagner's *Parsifal*.[170] In Maria's words the costume for this role involved "a kind of bra so that the stomach shows. The rest of the dress is almost transparent. It has to be connected to my legs with some sort of clasp," she informed Meneghini.[171]

It was around that time in February 1949 that Luchino Visconti— already a controversial film director for his graphic depictions of sex and violence in *Ossessione* (1943) and *La Terra Trema* (1948)—was traveling to Rome for research. Having spotted a poster the previous year splayed with "Maria Kallas", he had recorded the name as a salient detail. A count descended from the great Visconti lineage of Milan, he wasn't at a loss to snare some complimentary tickets to Maria's *Parsifal*.

About to stage a play comprising costumes by Salvador Dalí, Visconti was surprised to see Maria onstage wearing, in his words: "pieces of veil . . . she was covered with yards and yards of transparent chiffon; a marvelous temptress, like an odalisque. On her head was a little tambourine that plopped down on her forehead every time she hit a high note. She would just bat it back in place."[172] Instantly he was hit by a realization: "I told myself that someone had to *dress* that woman—and someone needs to get her hats that don't fall on her nose when she is singing."[173]

Thereafter Visconti, a closeted gay man, became a frenetic admirer. "Every night she sang I secured a specific box and shouted like a mad fanatic when she took her bows," he proclaimed.[174] Visconti was not searching for the perfect actress. Though he tended to use some of the same actors in his cinema, there was no fervid hunt for legendary scenic gods and goddesses. The opera singer that he saw before him was his first prophetic muse.

A platonic courtship was the outcome. "Luchino is a gentleman ... I was *thoroughly* spoiled by him before we even started working together because he was the—the *grand seigneur* who was treating the prima donnas so *lavishly* and, er . . ." Maria bashfully remembered, "I *felt* that, he made a point of pointing it out and I enjoyed it *thoroughly*. I don't know whether I am really *always* on that pedestal for him or for others."[175] For every performance he attended she received not a bouquet but a *basket* of flowers and a freshly scribed compliment. A stage-hand once reached over to Maria to decry, "But this guy is impossible—he's a madman, this Signor Visconti!"[176]

Owing to Visconti's shooting schedules and Maria's operatic calendar a few months would delay their meeting. Maestro Serafin's Rome house hosted the introduction during which Maria sang *La traviata*'s "Sempre libera" and the chandelier began to chime frenetically in response.[177]

Prior to that night six months would pass.

*

On 1 April 1949 an unexpected Jackie Callas paid a visit to her sister.[178] Despite exchanging correspondence the estranged pair hadn't seen each other since September 1945. Arriving one morning at the Hotel Accademia, which was still Maria's residence, Jackie surprised a sleeping Meneghini with Maria at his side. The bespectacled latter was sitting up reading a score. Aghast to find the unmarried couple in bed, she heard Maria laugh off shock.[179] It's difficult to tell at what point Meneghini and Maria consummated their relationship, but they were now co-habiting.

Meanwhile Meneghini was stalling on the prospect of marriage. To meet his potential wife's heavy demands he would likely be forced to eschew his brick business and follow the globetrotting trail of her growing career. Maria was anxious to wed.[180]

The soprano threatened to leave Italy again if her fiancé failed to set a date. Implicating Meneghini's sister Pia in the conflict, she convinced the latter to persuade her brother or release Maria from his clasp.[181]

Determined was she for the wedding to take place before her imminent departure: she was traveling to Buenos Aires to perform three operas. A special dispensation was required from the Vatican as Meneghini was a Catholic and his bride Greek Orthodox.[182] Maria wanted to get married in a Catholic church but keep her Orthodox traditions.

Religion posed a tenuous relationship to her. Routinely she made the sign of the cross before every performance for luck.[183] She loved the ambience of the Greek Orthodox Church, preferring its calm to the pomp of Catholicism: "You see, I feel our church more than I do yours," she explained to Meneghini. "It's strange, but that's the way it is. Perhaps I'm used to it, perhaps it's warmer and more festive."[184]

Her faith eventually dissolved into an attachment to an unnamed higher power. "I am religious, but I do not stick that to my forehead," she would later precise.[185] "I have my own philosophy about that—I *feel* that—*we* call it 'God', other people call it—I don't know *what*, a 'superior *force*'—is with you all the *time*. You don't have to go to *church*. And then when there's a lot of people *around* me, I don't *concentrate* on . . . what I want to—express *inside* myself. So I really don't *feel* the necessity to go to *church*. Or if I *do*, I go when nobody's around and I light a candle."[186]

Prior to the wedding she would have to find a copy of her birth certificate and Evangelia was reluctant to begin the search. Writing to New York friend Harry Dardick, Maria urged the man to locate it[187] and finally he did.[iii]

Bureaucratic issues weren't the only obstacles. Most of Meneghini's brothers bore a grudge against Maria—fearing that his marriage to her would distract him from the factory and force him to desert his "real" family. When Meneghini telephoned the Roman Curia to ask if documents were ready to assure the marriage, he was notified that someone in his family had warned the union "wouldn't be in his best interests."[188] Because of the persistent loopholes the now fifty-four-year-old had to untangle, Meneghini could excuse his serial postponement of the wedding.

Maria was fed up with vacuous promises. "If Battista had wanted it, I would've abandoned my career," she insisted. "In the life of a woman— I mean to say, a real woman—love is more important—there's no comparison—than any artistic triumph."[189] It was something she espoused repeatedly.

So she extended Meneghini one last ultimatum: he would accompany her worldwide to each performance; if not, she would sever her career. They would get married prior to her Argentinean trip that *instant*—or her retirement would take immediate effect.[190] Was she being serious? It's too hard to figure out; too tricky to know how much of the warning was emotional blackmail, how much of it *real*. Perhaps *she* didn't even know.

And yet Maria got her way. On 16 April 1949 she felicitously announced to Elvira de Hidalgo that she was to marry.[191] The ceremony—which transpired five days later at a chapel of the Chiesa dei Padri Filippini in Verona—was rushed and rudimentary: no decorations, gifts or bridal gown. Maria stood attired in a blue suit and black hairpiece.[192]

[iii] As previously mentioned, Maria claimed not to possess a copy of her birth certificate in December 1967 when she asked her friend Fabrizio Melano to find the original in New York. It is likely that Dardick acquired a copy for her that she later lost.

After a three-week journey on the *Argentina* ship Maria disembarked in Buenos Aires on 14 May.[193] The impresario of the Buenos Aires opera company had hung a neon sign one story high on the Teatro Colón. It read:

ÓPERA NACIONAL CON
MARIA MENEGHINI CALLAS
LA SOPRANO ABSOLUTA DEL SIGLO[194]

The outsider was delighted to discover she had been selected—as opposed to local favorite Delia Rigal—to open that season as Turandot.[195] But the flu that she had suffered on her seaborne voyage stubbornly persisted. A bedridden Maria imbibed "three large glasses of cognac and honey and two coffees with aspirin. I was trying to feel drunk to fall asleep and start to sweat." She was terrified of being unable to sing.[196]

Her South American debut as Turandot on 20 May was ill received. "It was tied, in my memory, to the exhausting fatigue that I felt even just getting up out of bed—not to mention my fever," was Maria's souvenir of the evening.[197] "Evident nervousness and a slight vocal indisposition prevented a display of her full powers . . ." wrote the critic for national paper *La Prensa*, "though the facility of both her middle and low registers was noteworthy."[198] To Meneghini Maria lamented: "In *Turandot*, the public couldn't appreciate my art . . .[199] One paper said I have a small voice that has no real potential . . . Another says that I was indisposed and it was therefore impossible to critique me . . ."[200]

To her chagrin, on 27 May Delia Rigal sang the opening *Aïda*. Serafin—the maestro behind all Maria's Argentine engagements—had not yet managed to persuade Cirillo Grassi-Diaz, the director of the opera house, to let Maria sing a duo of *Aïda*s.[201] "La Rigal is *terrible!*" Maria wrote to Meneghini. "Really a horrible thing. But she is adored here! This is Argentina!"[202]

On 17 June there came another *Norma*. The general rehearsal had rendered Maria ecstatic: "Everybody cried at the 'Casta diva.' "[203] This time the press followed suit with the hype—calling her "decisively better here than in *Turandot* . . . she remained attentive and respectful in the face of the potential for excess of which some other *Norma*s have been guilty. She strived to tame, as much as possible, all claims to virtuosity to penetrate the personage's depths."[204]

Recorded partially that night, its tape gives us the earliest example of the Callas *Norma*. In contrast to the pyrotechnical exaggeration she could still exploit, Maria's singing is a plaintive contemplation in which slow crescendi suggest frailty. Whilst Norma is a fearsome character, in certain parts the voice intends for her to incarnate a damaged, confused girl. Through sumptuously slow diminuendi and demure staccati she succeeds.

"You see, my dear, God is great," Maria concluded in a letter to Meneghini. "It is enough to wait and do no wrong."[205]

Her eventual *Aïda*s were also a triumph. "I cleaned up here. The public loves me."[206]

After her return to Italy on 14 July the wedded pair embarked on a belated honeymoon. With her new apartment ready at 21 Stradone San Fermo, Verona,[207] Maria had switched mantles and was ready to immerse herself into the role of housewife.

6.

"In a room with little light"

"Maria had been studying her house as though it were a score she had to know from memory," Meneghini recollected.[1] After employing her first maid the budding housewife consecrated 1949's idyllic summer to the decoration of her marital abode: an apartment that would house a range of gilded objects, faux rococo curtains, variations on a theme of flowered wallpaper, a rosy marble bathroom and pink curtains.[2]

The bathroom was Maria's hearth. Writing letters[3] and consuming biographies of composers in the bath was a habit.[4] Soprano Shirley Verrett would recall Maria showing off her sanctuary—one that included a couch and a table with flowers.[5]

"It's where I like to work the most," she told Janine Reiss. The space was "full of scores," according to the latter.[6]

The design of the rest of the house had to vie for her hard-earned approval. With her maid Matilde Stagnoli, as well as two interior decorators, Maria would spend hours hanging and rehanging paintings, constantly enquiring from everyone: "Don't you think the wall would gain more if we swapped this painting with that other one?"[7]

Advice from experts went unnoticed.[8]

Like many local bourgeois housewives at the time Maria flaunted her ornate home to its visitors as though it were Versailles: its Brustolon picture frames and seventeenth-century landscapes and miniatures gave it like vibes.[9] Music critic William Weaver underscored how she deliberately "called downstairs" to show off her new gadget: a telephone with an extension.[10]

Engrossed in the laborious undertaking of this image, Maria was traditionally deferential to her husband when it came to everything domestic. A woman eager to claim independence on the stage, she ran a home of thoroughly old-fashioned values. "I have to dress for my husband, Signor Meneghini's sake," she told a journalist years later. "He likes me to look well-dressed *always*. He takes a vivid interest in my clothes, his favourite colour being red."[11]

It may appear pathetic by the standards of today—but for Maria it was yet another opportunity to shamelessly romanticize her marriage. In a house where screams and yells and sometimes smacking had been frequent, Evangelia had never asked George what to wear. Maria's conjugal demureness was not only a desire to succumb to the contemporary mores. As well as being the complete fulfillment of an operatic love—selfless and altruistic—it was also a rebellion against her early home environment.

Over years she would purport to realize domestic bliss. Her staff—from maids to butlers, cooks to secretaries—would behold her as a mother figure. One of these was Edda Zoraide Casali, who came to work for Maria at the age of seventeen in circa 1953. After hearing her confess that she had no experience and couldn't cook, Maria had insisted at her interview: "You don't need to do any of that. We'll just cook ourselves." Taking the teenager under her wing, she took to calling her "Frangetta" for her lengthy bangs.

Assuming some maternal traits, Maria didn't let young Edda stay out after hours: a curfew would curtail her nightly visits to the movies in the company of friends. When later she became engaged, Maria called her father to request permission. Her mistrust of Edda's groom led her to tell the maid that she believed the man was marrying her parents' wealth—not *her*. Edda's duties weren't restricted to the home: quite often she would linger in Maria's dressing room and help with putting on her costume.[12]

With each of her domestic staff Maria strived to break the barriers of hierarchy. Correspondence with her maids when she was out of town was frequent; in the sixties she would visit the family home of her butler, Ferruccio Mezzadri. The latter would describe the way Maria deemed him kin—sometimes by doling out spoonfuls of lessons: "You must never be impulsive," came one instruction. "Always *think* before you speak aloud."[13] These constituted her attempts to forge the family she never had.

The fall of 1949 saw the relationship between Maria and her mother come unhinged until it hung by its last nail. While George treasured his daughter's majestic career—insisting he took pride "in being one of the happiest fathers in the world"[14]—Evangelia exploited every new feat of Maria's to decry how little of her wealth she shared.

"Believe me, Maria, I do not recognize you. How you have changed . . ." she wrote that September. "Who should I blame? Your fame or your surroundings? I knew you to be selfish over your career, but not over your personal life . . . You decided to marry so soon, too soon . . . You should at least have opened your heart before deciding, asked my opinion even through our correspondence, out of courtesy and as a duty to the mother who bore you, if only as a point of form. But you went and married without further thought and without showing the superiority of your character even to your husband himself . . ."

Later in that letter Evangelia claimed Maria "didn't care" if her mother had to "mop floors and live in a cemetery," lamenting that Jackie had "offered herself solely in order to save you and me" when the relationship between her and Milton was clearly consensual.[15]

Maria didn't know how to respond to this—and very possibly she didn't. Two weeks later she drafted a note to Elvira de Hidalgo. "I know you haven't heard from me in a while . . ." Maria apologized. "I'm just writing to say hello and tell you that I have you on my mind . . . I hope to reach the height of a master like you. If you have any suggestions, write to me."[16] It seemed that Evangelia's trenchant words had sliced into Maria's conscience.

On 18 September Maria sang her first oratorio: Stradella's *San Giovanni Battista* at the Church of San Pietro, Perugia. Despite despising the art form—"a big bore" was her epithet for the genre[17]—what most distracted her this evening was the outcome of an unsolicited recording. Following her rendering of the first part she was abruptly played a tape. No one expected her reaction: "I cried—you don't know *how*," Maria disclosed. "I was so—I mean, I didn't want to go on with it—they were desperate [at the church]; they were desperate because I didn't want to continue with the second part. I said, 'No, no—that isn't *possible*.' "[18]

The first commercial Callas recording was released six weeks later. For the label Cetra in Turin Maria sang several arias including "Casta diva" and "Oh, rendetemi la speme . . . Qui la voce" from *I puritani*. Performing the first aria in the traditional key of F in which nineteenth-century icon Giuditta Pasta had sung it,[i] she exposed a solemn execution of still raw material: a ceremonious, cautious potency.

That December Maria debuted in a role she not only disliked but would finally shun: Abigaille in Verdi's *Nabucco*. In one of those crazy, nonsensical opera plots, Abigaille is the daughter of the king of Babylon, Nabucco.

Except she isn't. Ultimately she discovers she is illegitimate—which means her half-sister Fenena, who's in love with the foe—Ismaele, the king of Jerusalem—may inherit the crown. With the liberation of her father's trapped Israeli hostages, Fenena chooses to betray him out of love for Ismaele. This exhilarates Abigaille, who assumes the throne as Queen of Babylon. In typically operatic fashion, she repents, takes poison and implores punition from the God of Israel.

This warped psychology meant that the character could easily be traded in for caricature: something that Maria scorned. During rehearsals for the opera at the Teatro San Carlo in Naples, she complained to Meneghini: "[Vittorio] Gui is happy with me. I'm not with him. He's always talking about himself. The conductor doesn't know what *Nabucco* is! So I hope that onstage I'll be in my inspirations!"[19]

---

[i]Though the standard key for "Casta diva" is F, Bellini's autograph score puts it as G. It was altered after Pasta requested Bellini transpose it a tone lower. Maria performed "Casta diva" in the key of G in Rome and London in April and June 1953 respectively. However, there is no recording of her singing it in this key. (Scott, 122–23).

On 20 December, the day of the premiere, Maria wrote another morose missive to her husband:

> *Here I never know what to do. I don't want to go to the cinema alone because I'm scared of sleazy men and nuisances. That said, right now it looks like spring outside. And it is truly enchanting.*
>
> *Just to let you know: no baby! As usual, I was __furious__ on the 18th* [apparently the day Maria got her period]. *Together with a headache I would only wish on our enemies. I suppose I must be patient!*
>
> *Have you mailed the Christmas cards?*[20]

At the time Maria was already eager to conceive. Six months thereafter she would once again write: "There is a confession I must make. I have such a great desire to have a baby with you, I think it would also do good for my voice and my terrible skin. What do you think? Do you want one yet?"[21]

For the moment she was nevertheless busy tracing her terrain of timid stardom. A few hours after asking Meneghini if he'd sent the Christmas cards Maria had the audience in the clasp of merciless beguilement. When Abigaille seized the throne in her uphill ascent of an aria "Anch'io dischiuso un giorno"—a piece aswarm with sabotaging ornaments—she morphed into a lioness whose prowess rivaled Catherine de' Medici's.

A recording demonstrates Maria charging currents of abrupt crescendi with crazed tempi to convey the character's erratic nature. Shedding a smooth surface, the soprano narrowly skirts struggle in her execution of high notes. The timbre is pernicious and unpretty; almost corrugated with sharp ridges. A critic would recount:

> *The set was a challenge: a huge, steep flight of steps, with the throne on a confined platform at the top. Callas began the aria below the steps, then as she continued singing, she moved up the high flight, occasionally descending a step or two, as if physically to express her lingering hesitation about her plan; but then, as the aria ended, she climbed straight to the little platform and, on the final, ringing high note, she sat down squarely on the throne. Sitting down is not the usual way a soprano concludes a great scene. More likely, she will stride towards the footlights, or raise a triumphant arm, or—in more pathetic cases—faint. But Callas' taking her seat was such an unusual and dramatic assertion of power that the audience gave her an ovation.*[22]

The next day Maria cast a paler light on the premiere: "Everything went well until the second act [the one featuring "Anch'io dischiuso un giorno"]," she wrote to Meneghini. "At that point, instead of using the smoke machine, they burned paper and my throat became completely dry. So I don't know how I did after that. Acts III and IV went very well. My duet went splendidly and I gave a wonderful B flat. But nobody notices—neither the public nor the critics—so what's the use . . . And then *Nabucco* is beautiful but such a big Bore!"[23]

After several more performances and some Venetian *Norma*s, Brescian *Aïda*s and her final execution of a Wagner opera with Rome's *Tristan und Isolde* that February, Maria was rehearsing in Catania, Sicily for yet another *Norma* when she got an unexpected call: would she be willing to sing *Aïda* at La Scala in April? Renata Tebaldi was indisposed.[24]

Despite her vacillating fame reporters could extract a scoop from the eleventh-hour substitution. Milan's principal newspaper, *Corriere della Sera*, featured an article on it.[25] Paparazzi—who were not yet known as such, for the term "buzzing insects" would be popularized only in the sixties—lay in wait as the half-known soprano came to stay at her hotel with Meneghini on 12 April. Thirsting to collect salacious soundbites from Maria, they were kept at bay when she devalued the occasion:

"The public? What about the public? If I sing well they applaud, if they don't like me, they whistle. It's the same everywhere . . . They say my voice is uneven. Well, let them say what they want. I sing the way I sing . . . La Scala? Magnificent theater . . . Yes I am thrilled, of course I am thrilled. Great theater. But I am near-sighted, you see. For me all theaters are alike. If I am excited? La Scala is La Scala, but I am near-sighted; *ecco tutto*."[26]

Coincidentally, Aïda was another unpreferred role. "I did like the character, but felt for her up to a point. She is not very imaginative, perhaps too passive, and consequently not stimulating enough," Maria bemoaned. "Aida herself will become insignificant in a drama in which she should be the central character, despite her lack of imagination, and from whom the drama must emanate. This is why so often the emphasis is wrongly shifted to [antagonist] Amneris."[27]

In this take on the piece Maria would be veiled by a burqa-like headscarf baring only the eyes. Since Aïda is an enslaved princess, the gesture intended to showcase her shame.[28] After every aria, every recitative, every duet, she would immediately grab the nearest person in the wings—usually a fireman on duty—and demand to know: "How did I do?"[29]

Critics' response was tepid. "Though Maria Callas has been primed for a career at La Scala for a long time now, I was not enthused by her," Teodoro Celli of *Corriere Lombardo* stressed. "She has evident temperament and very good musicality, but her range is not equal across all the registers."[30]

Yet again Maria was alighting at an apex right before it detonated. The superintendent of La Scala, Antonio Ghiringhelli, was demonstrably reluctant to employ her as a "regular" performer assured x performances each season. During lunch with Serafin six months before she had been snubbed by him.[31]

This was in large part because Ghiringhelli bore a grudge against the maestro: they had crossed swords at the theatre in years past. Any singer looking for admission on his coattails would be ousted. Serafin thus struggled to convince La Scala's manager to stage a *Norma* and had recourse to a culinary simile: "I am from Rottanove. We have a famous dish in our area. Risotto alla pilota. Do you know what you need to make risotto alla pilota? The rice!" he signaled at Maria.[32]

"The trouble is opera house directors often use their position as a step to their own social advancement," Maria once commented.[33] Indeed, the position of superintendent at La Scala was an enviable one: this was no opera house attended only by musicians and their cliques; it was the second home of aristocracy like Count Visconti. Ghiringhelli wasn't even a great fan of opera. Originally a leather manufacturer, his youth had been suspended by a riding accident in which a horse had kicked him in the groin and left him permanently impotent.[34] According to soprano Birgit Nilsson, this didn't stop him "regaling" his singers with "stories of amorous escapades."[35]

It was the kind of headstrong stubbornness you couldn't beat. For that reason Maria's debut at La Scala resulted in . . . nothing.

*

Following a few token performances of *Aïda* in Naples Maria embarked on another South American tour. En route to Mexico, she met mezzo-soprano Giulietta Simionato, a soon-to-be regular colleague and friend of hers.[36] Simionato was to sing the Adalgisa to her Norma at the Palacio de Bellas Artes.

Evangelia had moved back to New York, where she was staying with George to save money. Stopping over in the city on their way to Mexico, that 6 May Maria and Giulietta paused at the apartment to escape the stifling heat. Evangelia was out. Unbeknownst to Maria, she was in hospital with iritis in her right eye. In the refrigerator stood a bottle of 7Up that Maria extended to the mezzo-soprano. "Scarcely had she consumed half the bottle when she suddenly vomited it," Maria later related. "It had, she told me, a strange taste: she thought it must be something like petrol. Terrified and dismayed, I picked up the telephone and called my father at the pharmacy. He advised me to give Giulietta milk and rush to hospital . . . So I went there. I will never forget the disconcerting candor with which Mother calmly told me: 'It's not petrol, it's insecticide.' "[37]

"Only a crazy woman like my mother could put insecticide in the fridge," Maria bitterly confessed to Giulietta one week later.[38]

Immediately Evangelia launched a bombardment of grievances: why hadn't Maria come to see her at the hospital? She hadn't known. Why hadn't she written? Why hadn't her *sister* written? She wasn't getting on with estranged husband George; George was a pain: he was ill. He always had problems on account of his diabetes; now his heart was in trouble.[39]

Maria was surprised that Evangelia could so casually neglect her sick and aging father. Although she felt compassion for her bout of iritis, she told her husband that her mother's only other maladies were diarrhea and the usual headaches. Her behavior on the other hand had bystanders convinced that she was dying.[40]

Using her "deathbed" as an opportunity to fiddle with Maria's heartstrings, Evangelia sought to know if she could come to live with her and Meneghini in Verona. Maria deflected the subject: in any case her mother was accompanying her to Mexico. Secretly she wrote to Meneghini: "May God forgive me but for the moment I would rather stay alone with you in our house, do you understand? . . . But how do you explain this to someone you love? How do you tell them that you love them the way they love *you* but it isn't the same as your love for your husband. I'm going to leave her money so that, if she wants, she can vacation somewhere in the countryside or in the mountains but I don't think she should be leaving her husband [sic] alone now. What do you think? Please don't speak of this to anyone. It's just between us, ok?"[41]

Upon reaching Mexico Maria awaited the news of her mother's arrival amidst her performances. "Mama hasn't written so I don't know when she's coming," anxiously she scribed to Meneghini—updating him with the same phrase days later.[42] Three weeks after coming to the city she received a cutting note from Evangelia again accusing her of being egotistical.[43]

When Evangelia eventually arrived, her daughter oversaw the sum of her expenses: accommodation, food, and souvenirs. She bought her mother a mink coat. A few months previously Maria had bestowed on her a thousand dollars (the equivalent of 12.6 today) on the condition that she make the money last a year.

Now in Mexico and healed from iritis, her mother once again proclaimed that she was broke—[44] demanding this time that Maria give her sister one of the two diamond rings that Meneghini had presented to his wife.[45] At their hotel the mordant Evangelia beset its manager with her prevailing grievances—alerting him his celebrated guest was "rude and selfish": owing to this most ungrateful daughter she had "terrible financial worries."[46]

Scarcely was Maria independently well-off. With her finances at Meneghini's managerial helm, it's possible she didn't even know exactly how much she was earning per performance. Money would be poured into their joint account. Maria never asked to look because it was the husband's duty to engage in matters of this caliber.

New York had compelled her to return the thousand dollars she had borrowed from the state to fund her trip from Athens to America, as well as seven hundred fifty that her godfather had lent her mother. Anxious not to demand more from Meneghini—"In the first year of marriage, one feels ashamed to constantly ask for money"—Maria was reluctant to give in to Evangelia's demands; afraid that she would put it to unworthy causes.[47]

One morning in Mexico Maria was making the bed in her mother's hotel room when she stumbled upon a bank statement. It turned out that Evangelia had around one thousand five hundred dollars at her disposal. Together with Maria's shock at Evangelia's nonchalance before her ailing father,[48] this resulted in another vicious argument. Upon her departure from Mexico City Maria was allegedly "tapped out" from all the expenses incurred by her mother.[49]

At the same time the soprano was still scaling the steep steps to stardom. It swiftly became evident that tenor Kurt Baum didn't know the score throughout the early preparations for *Aïda*. Because of this rehearsals with both orchestra and chorus were perennially delayed.[50]

"In the Greek soprano there exists the quality of pure gold," one critic had exulted of her *Norma* incarnation.[51] Yet the public hadn't been won over. When music historian Carlos Díaz Du-Pond dwelled on this, she dismissively noted: "People do not like my voice at first, they have to get used to it."[52]

It was therefore time—or so Maria thought—to make some compromises. "In the beginning of your career you can't get away with what you *want* so you have to give the public a little bit *of* its desire; in other words, a very *long* held note, and er . . . some of those things. But *later*, with the years, you tend to *under*act and under*play* these things."[53] Absorbing a recording of that Mexican *Norma*, one hears a Callas who is brazen, tacky: holding on to high notes before cutting them distastefully and brusquely short. Like many opera singers, she gulps notes for dramatic effect during moments of tragedy.

She's not her usual *self*.

Following *Aïda*'s dress rehearsal, the artistic director of the Palacio de Bellas Artes Antonio Caraza Campos invited Maria and Simionato to visit his home. He told the story of how nineteenth-century illustrious Mexican soprano Ángela Peralta had concluded the uproarious second act with a high E flat 6. Insisting the inclusion of the note would be a facile crowd-pleaser and shortcut to success, he nudged Maria to perform it. In turn she played her own card: that of wholesome art. "It is not written by Verdi and it is not nice. Besides, I should ask permission from the conductor and my colleagues."[54]

Conductor Guido Picco likewise sought to goad Maria into singing the notorious note. She decisively declined. Rumors began to circulate. Kurt Baum—the tenor who had barely known the score—began to counter them by promising he had his own E flat; that he was "going to eat Callas up." Faced with the promise of a contest, the soprano tackled the rogue note: "But mine was in my natural voice and his was in falsetto, so it was me everybody heard."[55]

As a recording proves, in this *Aïda* she relies on stereotypical soprano bombasticity. Her dense dynamics are broad strokes and sudden switches from swift outbursts to serene solemnity are many. Even the beseeching prayer of "Numi pietà del mio soffrir" in the key aria, "Ritorna vincitor" is designated militant resolve rather than somber desperation. So far does this *Aïda* overreach that when she learns her lover Radamès is still alive, Maria's exultation of relief in "Vive!" sounds like an explosion of exclamatory rage.

Critical reception was mixed. Whilst one wrote excitedly, "this woman's vocal organ rose to the most glorious heights, leaving us literally 'knocked out,' "[56] another insisted: "The note the singer executed was exceptional . . . for all the extraordinary nature of this, we still affirm Callas' voice is defective."[57]

In the recorded *Il trovatore* of 20 June we likewise hear Maria vacillating between pyrotechnics and refinements—and she strives to integrate another needless high note—D flat 6—into the climactic aria "D'amor sull'ali rosee."

It's worth remembering that most of what Maria offered through her Mexican travails was not symbolic of the Callas artistry. Sliding up to notes for dramatic effect, or gulping one to mirror tears, were vices for which she would chide her vocal students decades later. After a tenor at her Juilliard School masterclass ended the aria "Vesti la giubba" from *Pagliacci* by splitting the last note in two, she exclaimed: "You should *not* do that—that's *bad*. Don't *ever* do this again, ok? Because Caruso *had* that kind of thing but . . . that was *his* . . . You have *never* fallen so far into vulgarity and this is *vulgar*—what you did at the end. Right now I'm treating you a little harshly because you *never* do anything that way. It's very difficult to get away with a [Beniamino] Gigli; Gigli I *disliked*—he *cried* too much.[58]

Referring to the pirate tapes of these performances years later, Maria would lament to EMI producer Walter Legge: "Don't listen to them—they're awful! I was singing like a wildcat."[59]

For this brief episode her cravings for success surpassed her art. "I am furious with that tenor Baum," she wrote to Meneghini. "He is worse than a jealous woman. He continues to insult me and was furious because I finished the concertato in *Aïda* with an E flat. So basically, he's dying of envy because the public is raving over me and not him."[60] After trampling on Aïda's veils for two performances, Baum put his tail between his legs and finally apologized.[61]

Six days later Maria was endeavoring to restore her authentic self: "After the second act [of *Tosca*]," she wrote, "They gave me an ovation . . . They went crazy for 'Vissi d'arte.' Can you imagine—over five minutes of applause! They wanted an encore, but of course I didn't do it."[62]

She says "of course". But was she going to stay on such a route?

That fall the Meneghinis were in Parma for a day when they crossed paths with Luigi Stefanotti, a businessman and self-pronounced "great admirer" of Callas. It turned out he just happened to be pals with the indelible Arturo Toscanini. On September 20th Maria got a telegram from his resourceful daughter Wally that expressed his wish to hear her at his Milanese abode.

The much-cherished maestro had already heard about the singer and her seemingly elastic repertoire.[63] Dealt the information that Antonio Ghiringhelli had a mission to exclude her from La Scala, he referred to the administration of the opera house as "cretins".[64] In hot pursuit, Toscanini sought the consummate Lady Macbeth for an upcoming production of Verdi's Shakespearean opera.

After accompanying Maria's performance of several arias on the piano, Toscanini assured her that this was *her* role: she would embody it both at

La Scala and in the small town of Busseto, where Verdi had spent most of his youth.[65] "As you probably have heard he could not find the soprano for that part till he heard me," scribed Maria jocundly to Leonidas Lantzounis. "Are you satisfied, dear Godfather?"[66]

October brought a sycophantic plea from Antonio Ghiringhelli cordially requesting dates of her availability. Funds for the production were secured, as well as a recording contract that would air the premiere on the radio.

Toscanini never gave the go-ahead. Officially the reason was the clout of Maestro Victor de Sabata: a celebrated Verdian conductor and La Scala's artistic director. It was alleged he feared "eclipse" by the more famous rival at his theatre and preempted the production.[67] Rumors nonetheless abounded that the offer had been empty-handed in the first place.

Beppe Menegatti—who was working at La Scala at the time and frequently assisted Luchino Visconti—claimed Toscanini had described Maria to Visconti as a woman with "a needle in the voice."[68] "Vinegar" made up the simile Francesco Siciliani heard.[69] When Toscanini heard Maria's studio recording of *I puritani*, he wrote to his son that this "Calla" [sic] "[does not have] the right kind of voice for that music."[70]

So the entire near-performed *Macbeth* had been a series of false promises. Toscanini was notorious for treating singers with a shot of turbulence: Rosa Ponselle recalled they made him so mad in rehearsal he would take his watch off, hurl it to the floor and stomp on it. "They finally had to buy him a whole box of watches so he would stop ruining the expensive ones!" she reported. "That's why I never would sing under him."[71]

The legend's vilest criticism of Maria was his dubious avowal about her diction being "unintelligible".[72] About the matter there's a twofold truth. Her studio recordings speak to a crystal-clear diction; its clarity wavered onstage in her formative years. "I wasn't happy about my pronunciation . . . which is most important in singing," Maria admitted.[73] On the other hand she wrote to Meneghini back in 1948 regarding *Turandot* rehearsals in Udine: "They [the public] were above all impressed with my <u>marvelous pronunciation</u>."[74]

*

Maria forayed into comic opera that October with Rossini's *Il turco in Italia* in Rome. Set in eighteenth-century Naples, the work follows young housewife Fiorilla in her quest to eliminate boredom by enlisting a lover (the titular Turk).

Arguments about Maria's qualities as a comedic artist flit like fireflies parading in a jar. While certain critics persevere with the insistence that she was exclusively a tragedienne, others could embrace her humorous designs with greater ease. "In her voice there was just the subtlest hint of a suppressed giggle," critic William Weaver recalled of this *Turco*. "Suddenly the quiet matron I had met earlier sounded—and even looked—like a mischievous school-girl."[75]

The performance's conductor Gianandrea Gavazzeni described her appearance as "a little gawky, a little heavy; but what irony that lent to the character! ... The scenic rhythm was a balance between her physical stature and highly calculated art ... all under an unforgettable vocal color: wit, lyricism, lightness—all of these came together in miraculous fusions."[76]

The 1955 recording of the opera goes a long way to attest not only to Maria fashioning her voice in favor of comedic flair but to the methods that she used to mold a character's duplicity. Shrunk to a portion of its size, the instrument embodies what some critics call the Callas "little girl" voice: "Callas en fille". She sings the major aria, "Non si dà follia maggiore," with fervid fluency across the looping laces of coloratura, scales and swift arpeggios: a coquette who racily resents that she can't switch between her beaux like a "bee, breeze or brook that never loves only one flower."

Striving to seduce the Turk with slovenly, soft tones, some notes can scarcely scrape the surface of full-bodied sound. Sloth-drenched diminuendi across dimming drones embody a bored housewife's sleepy sighs. Where the score reads "with feigned tenderness" the voice diminishes with a pretend timidity.

Some listeners may find the incarnation saccharine; the voice a little cutesy. But as Maria's Fiorilla insists that the Turk is her lover—not thieving Zaida's—the "in-a-bottle" timbre of the lowest register as she sings "love gave me his bow and his torch" ("arco e face amor mi diè") evokes a woman battling with her bloodlust.

With the failed production of Macbeth La Scala's doors had once again been closed by Ghiringhelli. Composer Gian Carlo Menotti was ready to premiere his new opera Il consule at the theatre. Ghiringhelli gave him carte blanche regarding sopranos.[77]

"Maria Callas?! Oh my God—no, no—never, never, never!" was the superintendent's reaction to Menotti's suggestion. "Well, listen—you promised me I could have Maria Callas, de Sabata was present at our meeting—you cannot go back on your word," claimed Menotti. Ghiringhelli said, "I promised you that anything you chose would be acceptable to me. But I will not have Maria Callas in this theatre unless she only comes as a guest artist."

This proposition didn't shine so brightly in Maria's eyes. Not only did she highlight to Menotti her reluctance to be classed as a guest artist, on her way out of the meeting she turned round, stopped the composer in his tracks and pompously declared: "I want you to remember one thing. I will sing at La Scala, and Ghiringhelli will pay for this for the rest of his life."[78]

Four months later in February 1951 there came the same offer from one year before: La Scala, Aïda; Tebaldi was ill. No. Not again.[79] Her career-making became an art form in itself. Loath to accept the table scraps that came her way, she would be seated at the head or not appear at all. Sequence and chronology were most important and she wasn't going to be a has-been or a wannabe. She wanted to be it. "I think that the debut is most important; you *must* debut in *the* best opera or possibly *your* best opera."[80] So went the rule.

One year after settling into their apartment on Stradone San Fermo the couple was goaded to move. Through their recalcitrant resentment of his consort Meneghini's brothers were still making his life hell. In summer 1950 they had taken him to court in an attempt to annex his brick factory. Meneghini had refused to surrender the company for fear that without him the family wouldn't be able to run it.[81]

Maria was fed up with traveling long-distance on her own. While the couple had conjoined careers for one and a half years, Meneghini's troubles now provided an excuse to take on a new business. Parting ways with the beloved factory, he understood his venture as Maria's full-time manager would yield the greater profit.

After one brother refused to help Maria when she slipped down stone steps leading to their home, Meneghini chose to find another neighborhood.[82] Husband and wife moved to 9 Via Leoncino: another apartment Maria filled with *objets d'art* and chrome gadgets. This one had a terrace where she hoped to grow a garden and plant rambler roses.[83]

On her side of the family Evangelia was still playing Wicked Witch of the West. That same month as *Turco* in October 1950 she composed a letter to her son-in-law in Greek that Meneghini took to a translator. Though its contents are unknown it was, according to Maria, "full of recriminations, unjust accusations and crazy deductions" about her husband. When he countered this slander by informing her he had abandoned his business to be with her daughter, Evangelia's missives became more incendiary.

Elvira de Hidalgo subsequently received a letter from Maria describing the "crises of nerves" she had suffered because of her. "She says I'm swimming in money and that they [she and Jackie] are wretched and that isn't right!"[84]

A letter from the period offered an admission to her godfather Leonidas. "My mother wrote a letter cursing etc. as is her usual way (she thinks) of obtaining things, saying also that she didn't bring me into this world for nothing. She said gave birth [*sic*] to me so I should maintain her. That phrase I'm sorry but it's hard to digest."[85]

In later years Maria would recall her mother had "regretted my birth and cursed me . . . all because I refused to give her more money. She even declared me insane, as a result of a minor accident when I was a child. [The tale would make its way into Evangelia's 1960 ghostwritten book, *My Daughter Maria Callas*]. And yet I would have kept her if only she had stopped talking to the press, stopped blackmailing me, and I am talking about a period when I had to devote body and soul to my work and to the battlefield of the theatre."[86]

Evangelia wasn't finished with her smear campaign. Months after receiving Meneghini's defense, she advised George in writing: "If he happens to write to you too (for as you see he is a real swine), you must send us his letter and we will send you a letter in Italian to put him in his place. I have told them that to me Maria is dead, and as for him, I consider him a stranger and shall simply ignore him."

Although Maria stopped replying to her letters Evangelia taunted her with towers of pernicious hatemail—all of which Maria kept. As late as August 1951 she was still threatening her daughter: "I may never see you again before I die, but I shall tell you about a great secret of your father's, which I have been keeping to myself all these years." At the same time she began convincing George Maria was duplicitous—alleging that the wallet she had bought him back in Mexico had spurred the quip: "A wallet is more than he's worth."[87]

"As for my sister, I have tried to do my best, but that has only brought [me] insults—so to Hell with all that," Maria wrote to Leonidas in November 1950.[88]

No longer could she weather the barrage of hate. Resorting to the use of Meneghini as her advocate and shield, Maria bid him send a final message. It read: "I took your last letter to a Greek who translated it for me. To my great displeasure I saw that the letter was malicious, vindictive, and offensive, and those things cannot be written by a good mother . . . I will not allow you to indulge in the insulting and degrading language you have heaped on her, otherwise we shall reach the point of breaking off our friendly relations. Be very careful not to behave in a vulgar way, and do not utter any threats."[89]

Evangelia did not consent. Doing her best to turn the family against Maria, she would frequently consult the press in future years to speak of her unruly "ingrate"; once appearing on *The Johnny Carson Show* with her perfunctory excoriation.[90]

A salacious claim related that Maria had advised her to find work—and if she couldn't—to "jump out of a window or drown yourself."[91] The latter categorically denied that she had written something so sadistic: "Certain people, *dishonest* people, took advantage of *her* battle *against* me, to be put in the newspapers or to have *her* print stories and they would gain *money*."[92] Even in private she was horrified by the egregious nature of the tale.[93]

"My way of fighting is not fighting," Maria maintained in an interview once. "Once somebody declares war on me, that's when I freeze completely. I do not show anything. It costs me a great deal, of course."[94]

Thus communication ceased. The two never again had direct contact.

"For me it was the end . . . In some ways it was a relief," was Jackie's instinctive reaction. "Maria had gone."[95]

At the same time Maria didn't try to contact Jackie either—falling prey somewhat to the malicious misquotations of her sister's speech that Evangelia had spawned. It was easier for her to cling to the conviction that conspiratorial Jackie urged their mother to be cruel than vice versa: "It's probably my sister who's making her so angry," she had written to Elvira de Hidalgo. "What do you think?"[96]

Perhaps because of this Maria invited George to accompany her through her next South American season.[97]

In the meantime she performed her final Kundry: the potion-lender, seer-like figure of Wagner's Arthurian legend *Parsifal*. Kundry is a supernatural sorceress; able to recount to mythical knight Parsifal the secrets of his childhood as he zealously pursues the Holy Grail. After she is punished for laughing before Christ on the cross, Parsifal spurns her. The seething witch becomes a bloodthirsty beacon of vengeance.

In the opera Parsifal and Kundry have to make a kiss last the crescendi of three lengthy notes. Maria would recall that the rehearsals for her debut *Parsifal* in February 1949 had not been easy. "I was, er, sort of *shy* and so was the *tenor*, poor man, so we'd *leave* it [the kiss] for the first performance and he [Serafin] wanted to know exactly where we were *going*. So he—*angrily* stopped the orchestra and he walked up the steps . . . and said: 'Now if *I* can kiss a man on the lips like that—*you'd* better do it!' And he *did* it, my God! And I *had* to."[98]

Kundry also expels tuneless screams Maria hated doing—albeit admitting that the whole experience of the opera "was much fun."[99]

The recording of the 1949 interpretation excavates a Callas voice our ears shall never meet again: trenchant and grating, it is earthly; peasant-like. Kundry is not entirely human—neither is the voice. The sadistic laughs emitted by Maria are barbaric; cavernous concoctions of her chest voice no short of demonic. In this realm Kundry is a feelingless outsider. Her screams aren't high-pitched yells as much as they are long glissandi down the full length of a keyboard. Some stretched-out portamenti (melodic gliding between different notes) have pitches so bent they are devil horn-shaped.

Kundry's final words are languishing laments of a stray creature still transfixed in vengefulness.

*

After spending forty days in bed with jaundice[100] the soprano gave her first *La traviata* at the Teatro Comunale in Florence on 14 January 1951. Costume designer Piero Tosi recollected how he saw Maria's Violetta seated at her mirror with her back before the audience. "The phantom of [Eleonora] Duse or [Sarah] Bernhardt was onstage before my eyes," he marveled.[101] To perform without facing the public at that time—to imagine the "fourth wall"—was innovation in opera.

By this time so many wanted to hear Callas it was rumored "they had to call out the fire department and the police to control the mobs trying to get into the Comunale."[102] Serafin advised Maria to behave more like a prima donna. He disapproved of her for dressing blandly at rehearsals and denouncing divas' airs. "I prefer to be loved for my simplicity,"[103] was her dictum.

After more regional performances of *Il trovatore*, *Norma*, *Aïda* and *La traviata*, there came the opening night of Verdi's *I vespri siciliani* in

Florence with Erich Kleiber conducting. Hearing "in pearl-like clarity" the notes of an opera so rarely performed, Ghiringhelli at last lowered his sword.[104]

The offer was that of a regular at La Scala—with a contract set to include the theatre's first ever production of Mozart's *Die Entführung aus dem Serail*, *Norma*, Verdi's *Don Carlos* and *I vespri siciliani*. The last one was intended for the opening of the season.

Maria decided it wasn't enough: she wanted *La traviata*. Fresh off her reception in its Florentine debut, she understood her artistry would emanate more vividly; that she would linger with a greater palpability in people's minds as Violetta Valéry.[105]

An astute businessman, Ghiringhelli tried to coax her into signing a new contract that pledged "twenty performances" of operas without citing which ones.

She didn't.

In an unusual turn of repertoire Maria performed Haydn's *Orfeo ed Euridice* in Italian in Florence weeks later. She argued with Kleiber: "He told me I was wrong about something—and he was a wonderful conductor to work with—but I said, 'Maestro, I am not wrong.' We then turned to the original score and I was right. We laughed a lot about it."[106] Many critics however would likely mistrust her rendition of such a dispute. Maria Callas is not known as a performer of Classical works. Reviewers relish undermining her approach.

This instance was no different. Newell Jenkins of *Musical America*—himself a conductor of Classical operas—claimed that her interpretation of the opera "had more to do with the Sicilian Vespers [*I vespri siciliani*] . . . than with the classic style of Haydn."[107]

As select recordings can attest Maria didn't treat this music any differently than her approach to nineteenth-century bel canto. There is a school of thought—sometimes openly professed and sometimes lurking in subconscious shadows—that decrees a reverent approach to all works Classical and equates reverence with distance. It's a creed that mirrors the idea that Shakespeare should be showcased grandiosely with a stress on every word to honor the immortal master.

Maria called this pedigree of performance "on the tip of the toes". "Everyone tends, because it's Mozart, [to think] that you have to *overdo* the piano, that you have to overdo the *style* which becomes too *fragile*," she told a Juilliard student in 1971. "I think—I might be wrong—but I think we are doing Mozart an injustice by treating him too delicately."[108]

The Callas approach to Haydn was psychological. A 1961 recording in French of "Che farò senza Euridice" ("J'ai perdu mon Eurydice") extends a venerating attitude toward the aria in its technique. There are no added ornaments; no gulping or overdramatics. Yet to music one might class as less adventurous the voice lends lachrymose diminuendi and contrasts them with the anguishing vibrato of "Réponds-moi, réponds-moi!" ("Answer me, answer me!").

After a series of *Traviata*s and more *Aïda*s in Mexico, Maria moved on to São Paulo, Brazil in August 1951.[109] Swollen legs compelled her to withdraw from the production's opening night—which meant that she would have to alternate with a soprano recently arrived to sing at the same theatre: Renata Tebaldi.[110]

Becoming chummy, the two women, in Maria's words, "were very happy to see each other again (at least, I was, sincerely)."[111] Evenings were spent dining in each other's company with Maestro Serafin and wife Elena Rakowska. After Maria made her Latin American *La traviata* debut, Rakowska waxed lyrical about her prowess at the dinner table. Following this litany of compliments Tebaldi's attitude toward Maria started changing.[112]

A few days later the Teatro São Paulo announced an imminent benefit concert. Maria and Tebaldi made a pact: both would forfeit encores notwithstanding the reaction of the public. But when a generous applause vibrated in Tebaldi's ears, she launched into a thoroughly impromptu "Vissi d'arte." Having neglected to prepare an encore, Maria couldn't counter this with her own supplementary performance. She wasn't hurt, nevertheless—attributing Tebaldi's spontaneity to no more than "a childish caprice."[113]

Frostiness began to crust the singers' comity. Although Maria still made efforts to be friendly with Tebaldi, it was not so for the latter, who could pass by without greeting her hello. A few days following the concert she spent dinner with Maria and her husband "warning" her about the dangers of performing *Traviata* at La Scala; doggedly attempting to discourage her.[114] Coincidentally a month would pass until Tebaldi would fall ill again—and be replaced by a surprised Maria in that very opera.[115]

Chaos erupted on September 24th. Still suffering from swollen legs and feeling vocally impaired, Maria let her Tosca jerkily begin to flounder. As one critic of the live recording scribed, she was "dangerously close to being vulgar."[116] Soon enough the Rio de Janeiro public was intolerant. Many began heckling and stomping their feet.[117] A critic for *Jornal do Commercio* stressed: "An artist of the stature of Maria Callas ought not to have risked the kind of evident debacle that emerged when she performed the role of Floria Tosca last night . . . Her low and middle registers disappeared and her high notes, attacked with assuredness, were unpleasant and empty of beauty."[118]

The next day Maria was abruptly summoned to the office of Barreto Pinto, the artistic director of the Theatro Municipal opera house. Here was the verdict: she had been "protested". In operatic terms "protested" meant that there was no place left to go but home. The public didn't want her. In fact, Pinto averred, "For what you gave last night, I shouldn't even pay you."

Despite the fact that all of her performances—including those of *Traviata*—were sold out, Pinto insisted fiercely on Maria's banishment. She fought. Eventually he stubbornly relented: "Fine—sing in *Traviata*; but I'm telling you right now; no one will come to see you."

That meant Maria needed to be substituted in all future *Toscas*. Tebaldi was selected to replace her.[119]

Circumstances weren't much calmer when Maria returned home. Meneghini was still bent on wringing the best deal out of Antonio Ghiringhelli for the upcoming La Scala season; it was due to open in two months. *Traviata* was still on the table; Ghiringhelli still wanted to drop it. "Perhaps we can resume our conversation next year," he responded.[120]

Meneghini forced his hand—insisting that if *Traviata* couldn't feature on the roster, he should at least *pay* Maria for the missed performances. Ghiringhelli replied by asserting that this was illegal. Meneghini didn't care.[121]

It was not the only business matter he was tending to. Following her first commercial record's well-received release,[122] Maria sought to sign with Cetra Records, a company headed by husband and wife team Dorle and Dario Soria. In 1953 it would be sold to record label Capitol.[123]

To matters such as these the managerial husband's wife preferred to be oblivious—or had to, given her intrepid workaholism.

Maria's rehearsal routine could transcend what was widely regarded as "normal". Unlike most singers, seldom did she warm her voice up to arpeggios or scales. "When I come to the theatre and I hear a tenor vocalizing up to a high C, I tell myself he has it naturally—why is he wearing himself out for no reason? . . . Perhaps at the bottom of it all, I'm not a real singer, but rather a musician. What I love is sitting down at the piano and studying my score."[124]

In each rehearsal she would never "mark"—that is, sing in half-voice. Performers resort oftentimes to marking to preserve their instruments. Instead Maria would sing always in *full* voice regardless of the circumstance.[125]

Relying on her "maestro sostituto"—the conductor's assistant—to guide her through a score's vicissitudes, Maria would place calls at one or two at night to seek advice about a role. Invariably equipped with a piano, every dressing room that she inhabited would let her practice during intermission.[126]

"You slide into bad habits onstage," she explained. "So every now and then you must have *somebody* downstairs or you must have the *maestro* that calls you into rehearsal and says, 'Well, *now*—let us recapitulate. You do this, you do *that*, you do *that*. Take it off—it's not good. We have developed these bad habits—now you clean it up.' "[127]

It was fundamental to her mission to "participate in *every* detail of the production . . . Because you give life to the *whole* production."[128] As well as attending the conductor's orchestral rehearsals, Maria would come early in the morning to observe the chorus—even when instructed *not* to. "That way I will get in the right mood and know what I must do."[129]

If she turned up at La Scala and her colleagues were a couple minutes late, she would be furious. On one occasion she arrived to find that everyone was there. But the male members of the company were talking about last night's football game. That also kindled fury.[130]

Because of her myopia Maria had a policy of heading to the stage before the start of each performance to ensure the elements of the décor and set were all in place.[131] Once she had touched the objects their location would be printed on the raised-relief map in her mind.[132]

Despite no scheduled *Traviata* Maria opened the 1951–52 La Scala season with *I vespri siciliani* on 7 December. The role of Elena—a young woman suffering under French occupation in 1282 Italy—lopes around an elevated register; luxuriating in long coloratura swoops.

Simultaneously however she possesses dark Verdian moments: oil-like vignettes. While Maria's La Scala performance was never on tape, the recording of the May 1951 Florentine *Vespri* introduces the Callas Elena: a tender creature who can fluently descend from the most crystalline of high-pitched notes along a swift chromatic scale toward a growly pit.

This night Maria treated as her genuine La Scala debut: "I felt like I had never yet had such a difficult exam before me," the soprano wrote. "But the welcome of the Milanese audience, under the baton of Maestro De Sabata, was enough to free me from myself, proud of having conquered the most exigent public in the whole world."[133]

Hype was overflowing like the splashing glasses of colliding champagne coupes on New Year's Eve. *Corriere della Sera* alluded to her "phosphorescent beauty";[134] strict reviewer Emilio Radius rewarded Maria a triad of labels: "a light soprano, a lyric soprano, a dramatic soprano . . ."[135]

Three weeks later a *Traviata* in Parma led soprano Elisabeth Schwarzkopf—then an audience member—to humbly aver, "There is no point in my singing this role again."[136] Schwarzkopf was married to Walter Legge, a record producer for the British branch of EMI. Unaware of Maria's involvement with American company Cetra, he was eager to sign with her.

Meneghini kept Legge slyly on tenterhooks. Although negotiations had begun as early as March 1950, he would stay the signing of the contract endlessly—resorting to a weak excuse about Italians "never signing a contract until two weeks have passed;" it was a custom known as *"parola d'onore"*.

Following the passage of two weeks Legge got a telegram that read:

PAROLA D'ONORE UNKNOWN IN VERONA STOP
ONLY POSSIBLE SOLUTION YOU INCREASE TERMS

Despite Legge knowing of Maria's scheduled Cetra records, a contractual commitment was eventually made as late as July 1952.[137]

But Walter Legge was not the only puppet being dangled in the clasp of Meneghini. Artistic Director of the Metropolitan Opera Rudolf Bing had been striving to come to contractual terms with Maria for months now. Meneghini wouldn't yield.

When eventually she signed a contract with the Met to sing *La traviata* in the spring of 1953, the American consul in Italy refused to accord Meneghini a visa. Disempowered by the loss of her support, Maria couldn't bring herself to debut at the Met without him: "To the Metropolitan . . . I was supposed to come—I think it was about six years ago," later she recalled. "Only you see I have one . . . *mania* shall we say and I think it's quite understandable. You see, I was divided from my family years ago of course 'cause I started out coming to Italy alone and, from Greece to America alone so . . . I had put though—the only clause that I *did* put, *that* one—and I had my good reasons also—was having my husband with me."[138]

It's possible to be dumbfounded by her strange servility. Maria earnestly believed that Meneghini would confer to her the best career in history—and she was not the only one. Visconti was more willing to negotiate with Meneghini than he was with the soprano, writing: "Dear Maria and Dear Battista (Actually, Dear Battista because Maria will never read any of my letters and if anyone gets back to me, it's Battista . . .)."[139] In correspondence everyone from Elvira de Hidalgo to Leonard Bernstein would send "dear Battista" their love. He was reputable.

"By my very nature, I *never* like to ask for anything; perhaps it's shyness or else the fear that I will be refused and that I'll—*suffer*," Maria elucidated in 1966. "It's a complex of mine that nobody . . . *knows* about. I don't *like* to ask, I like it when things are offered to me."[140]

Meneghini was the perfect intermediary.

Maria's ignorance prevented her from understanding she was more of an investment to her partner than a wife. Later Meneghini shared his method with his wife's biographer: he'd treat the singer as he would a marketable load of bricks. Keeping all her payment records, Meneghini knew alone how much Maria was receiving. If she got 50,000 lire, he would demand 60,000 for the next performance. With every debut he would ask for more and more until—by the end of 1950—her performance fee had risen to 10 million lire (around $16,000 at the time).

These weren't specifics to which she was privy. Meneghini told his wife what *he* felt was appropriate. This meant her vision of their circumstances, in the words of one acquaintance, "was partial and distorted and did not reflect reality."[141]

A moment of impassioned haggling over a Swiss concert fee scrapped Meneghini's hustling when Maria saw her poodle cuddling up beside its organizer: "Look at the dog! He wouldn't be going to him if he weren't a good man. My mind's made up: I'll sing in Zurich."

Such was the star's attention span in the domain of enterprise.[142]

And she was hardly one for keeping numbers in her head. Admitting multiple times to a "poor memory," in one interview Maria failed to recollect if there were thirty days or thirty-one in June.[143] When she scribed her memoir in the early days of 1957 she alluded to the Wall Street Crash of "1928".[144] In later years whenever anyone would doubt that Meneghini had "made" Callas, he would anxiously insist: "This is history . . . When I met Maria, she was no one—even if she had already sung for seven years. At my side, very quickly, she became a world-class star. The secret of her success was having a manager like me."[145]

In the meantime a *La traviata* at La Scala went persistently unscheduled. After threatening the theatre's manager in telegrams and letters, Meneghini urged his wife to boycott her first rehearsal of *Norma* that January. On the 9th arrived the message: "I inform you that my wife will not be performing in *Norma*."[146]

The tactic was a flop. Ghiringhelli claimed he couldn't realize *Traviata*. Maria performed her first Scala *Norma* on 16 January with eight curtain calls.[147] Emilio Radius hailed her as a "new Maria Malibran," referring to the nineteenth-century operatic superstar whose life had been cut short when she had fallen off a horse aged twenty-eight.[148]

After several *Norma*s and *Traviata*s in Catania Maria brought Mozart's *Die Entführung aus dem Serail* to La Scala in its inaugural Milanese incarnation. Known as *Il ratto dal seraglio* ("The Abduction of the Serail") in Italian, the opera let the singer stun her critics with her handling of the Classical: a role known for its "acrobatics of the running passages, which she attacked and conquered with a vocal virtuosity that earned her unanimous admiration and clamorous ovations," as Mario Quaglia wrote.[149]

A 1954 recording of the aria "Martern aller Arten" (performed in Italian as "Tutte le torture")—in which heroine Costanza rejects the Turkish Pasha who threatens to rape her—rides on unheeding resolve.

It has been said that Callas hated Mozart. "[*Don Giovanni's*] Donna Anna is a bore," was her remark.[150] As for his other roles, she made her sentiments explicit: "I never considered singing the Queen of Night [*The Magic Flute*] either, nor the Countess [*The Marriage of Figaro*]. This does not mean that they are not good roles ... Mozart was undoubtedly an extraordinary genius and I cannot imagine the world without him. But generally speaking his operatic music does not really take me out of this world. It is the Mozart of the piano concertos that I love passionately."[151]

She did undertake nevertheless to study the notorious Queen of the Night from the great master's *Magic Flute* on one occasion. The result? As friend Christos Lambrakis later recollected, the musician shared, "There is a moment in the score where I must take a breath against the composer's wishes."—"So?"—"So?! I couldn't do that! That would be musical heresy!" And the portrait remained unembarked upon.[152]

Her penchant for bel canto buoyed the soprano to embellish her ambitious repertoire with the resplendent challenge of *Armida*: the tale of a medieval sorceress conspiring to rule over the Crusaders in Jerusalem. Blindsided by love in the form of their soldier Rinaldo, Armida vacillates between devotion to him and her great vindictive plan—and ultimately opts for vengeance.

Maria was "over the moon" when the opera was chosen: "I believe that the primary reason for the virtual disappearance of Rossini's *opere serie* was the unavailability of singers, both female and male, who could put the numerous florid passages at the service of dramatic expression. So it was a step forward and *Armida* opened the way to rediscover an all but lost repertoire."[153]

It was the start of what some call the Callas "bel canto revolution".

A pivotal shift in Maria's professionalism came about during rehearsals. To her despair she realized the director, Enrico Frigerio, planned to have the work's ballet take place at the same time as her seductive showpiece of an aria, "D'amor il dolce impero". Espying the dance as she sang, Maria stopped the mime with her demand: "What is this that's happening behind me?" The director specified: "It's part of the production."—"No, it *isn't*. Either I sing, or they dance. One or the other."[154]

They may have thought that she was bluffing—but she wasn't. Fed up with subpar standards—including a *Norma* whose maestro had forgotten to bring in the chorus and written to thank her for doing it[155]—Maria would no longer stoop to slovenly arrangements. In the eyes of others her rehearsal methods grew autonomous and difficult; in *her* perspective her approach to music grew austere. Rehearsing *Il trovatore* in London, she threatened to walk out when tenor James Johnston—a man more dedicated to his butcher's business than his vocal art—began to scuffle with her. And she lambasted conductor Alberto Erede for not employing her instructed tempi in the final aria.[156]

Many refer to such behavior as "ego"; Maria's demands were the opposite. By sacrificing easiness she was attempting to make music better. "If music is treated in a shabby or second-best way, I do not want to be associated with it. I do not want to be associated with inferior staging, taste, conducting or singing. I especially do not want to give an inferior performance myself. When I was young and trying to establish my career, I had to take whatever was given to me. Now, fortunately, I can afford to say no to inferiority . . .[157] I will never make a pact with mediocrity."[158]

Having seen her blasé colleagues turn a blind eye to bad discipline, it was her principle not to devolve into another lackey who could look the other way. "The minute you *make* concessions or *compromise*, you sell your *soul* to the devil. It's the beginning of the end because then you start making *one* little concession, and then the other and then you're *finished*," she explained.[159] "I don't like it. I don't like fights and I don't like quarrels. I hate the nervous mental confusion they engender. But if I have to fight—I'll fight . . . When I fight, it's almost always my fundamental beliefs—my artistic credo—which are at stake."[160]

Up to now a great deal of Maria's willpower had been devoted to conceiving a *career*; a name and her self-worth. Now it became a mission abstract: art's creation. An aim impossible and indescribable because of its elusive objectivity; because one goal-fulfillment merely ushers in another goal. "We must serve these poor people who created *music*, which is sometimes sublime—even *often* sublime," Maria would say.[161] "As interpreters, it is our duty in all humbleness to read between the lines, to search out his soul, his message, to mind-read his style, to bring out what he is trying to tell us . . ."[162]

It became a quest to contact—in her own words—"the inalienable property of genius".[163]

Self-preparation far surpassed the stage and was conceived in inner work. This artistic process would create a mental character so that Maria could envision her "in terms of basic gesture. I think of her age—her class—very important for the hands—her period and her fate. There are two or three gestures that are essential for the character and indissoluble from her, and until I have found them, I do not study her musically."[164]

The ritual would commence with indispensable darkness: "I close myself in a room, with little light, no noise and the score at hand. I try to discover. You must hear the whole thing put together in your own head."[165]

On 26 April 1952 *Armida* was an uncontested triumph. Conquering those running scales—some of which span two octaves—Maria added decoration as sopranos had in the Rossinian period; adorning the music with three extra top Ds [D6]. On one hand the unpredictable Armida was a juvenile in love: some of her chromatic scales in "D'amor il dolce impero" were executed timidly; even obedient and schoolgirl-like. On the other, she caught fire in an instant—letting rip a feral and omnipotent crescendo at the aria's conclusion. The indefatigable heroine crisscrossed between fragility and awe-inspiring furor.

It had been a fractious fight. But after hesitating between two at times concordant and at times conflicting loyalties—the service of her name versus the virtue of the art—Maria bowed to the superior force.

7.

"Everything seems in a dense fog"

No longer a starry-eyed novice, Maria was greeted in Mexico for her 1952 Latin American tour with luxurious hype. To Channel XHTV she gave her first televised interview broadcast on 27 May.[1] With microphones being hoisted in her face, radio stations registered her soundbites not just after and before performances but during intermission. In the middle of a *Traviata* a reporter flung at her the question: "How do you think you did in *I puritani*?"

Following a brief pause she replied insouciantly: "Well."

A longer pause ensued. *"Why?"*[2]

Certain *primo donnos* were not happy with her burgeoning success. While her incipient *Lucia di Lammermoor* distressed Maria despite sixteen curtain calls[3] ("beautiful top notes and all that—but it was not yet the *role*,")[4] a bombastic tenor was incensed at witnessing the frenzy for her final *Tosca*. When the orchestra traditionally feted the departing singer with the farewell song "La golondrina" after the performance, eager spectators began to sing. Since colleague Giuseppe Di Stefano's send-off had been more pedestrian, he stormed offstage before the curtain calls' conclusion claiming he would "never again" work with Callas.[5]

It wouldn't be the last of his exhausting outbursts. Di Stefano was known throughout his whole career for being crude and ill-behaved, throwing his weight around and using his renown as an excuse to disregard all etiquette. "I've always done exactly as I wanted," was his axiom.[6] Endowed with a colossal, ostentatious voice, Di Stefano desired to outshine his colleagues without respite. Almost always he upstaged his partners with a vulgar volume. Despite the tenor's irrepressible respect for Callas, his approach to other singers was persnickety and patronizing. Maria was the sole exception: "She gave the same a passion a man could."[7]

Their first *Rigoletto* in Mexico—another debut for Maria—came close to catastrophe when it opened that June. With an underrehearsed orchestra, no run-through and the need to learn the part of Gilda in the space of a few days, she begged off the production and advised the theatre to select an opera the entire party could perform to unimpeachable perfection.

They didn't.[8]

The outcome was a scruffy spectacle—and yet the first recording of Maria in a "little girl" role glimmers in its novelty. This is not the dark, sepulchral voice that has beset our ears.

Thin as a whip, the timbre shrinks to slenderness and revels in a limber incandescence. Serene staccati pop with a pitch equal to champagne corks: trepidation in a hybrid with temptation.

In the sixteenth century, Gilda is the nubile daughter of court jester Rigoletto, a subject of the dictatorial Duke of Mantua. Oblivious to his status, she is sheltered with no confidant except her maid, Giovanna. For this reason Gilda is impossibly naïve and desperate for affection. Unaware that the despotic Duke is actually her father's boss, she falls in love with him—opting to sacrifice herself to save his life despite his multiple betrayals with other women.

A recording exposes this germinal Gilda. Slim like the gossamer texture of butterfly wings, her voice slips into airiness. Maria shakes the "pa" of "Padre!" as the girl espies her father coming home with a vibrato palpable enough to shape the girl's sweet disposition. Before drifting to the dreamy aria, "Caro nome"—in which Gilda ponders her beloved's pretend name, Gualtier Maldé—she holds the long notes captive in drawn-out diminuendi: a tenacious trance.

And yet the Callas artistry has not alighted at an apex. In the aria's end the girlishness gets jammed as her enchanting instrument regresses to its lioness state. Bulky, broad and bestial, it grows into a fuller body that is alien to the piece.

Not only is Maria's Gilda lost in terms of personality, her words begin to wander through obscuring wilderness. Gilda and Rigoletto's duet, "Tutte le feste" becomes "Fra le tenebre;" other words are misplaced or *re*placed. Ever the law-abiding vocalist, Maria was contrastingly no fan of lyrics. "I can see what you're thinking . . . that I have a reputation for placing great values on the words?" she questioned a journalist many years later. "But let me tell you, sometimes I can't even remember them, they annoy me so much."[9]

As recordings testify, in those days every opera house had its own prompter: someone sitting in a box close to the stage who whispered the libretto to the singers. Frequently their susurrations surface over live recordings and subdue the atmosphere's sublime. One of these was eventual conductor Sir Edward Downes, who recalled Maria approaching him at the Royal Opera House with the whisper: *"più forte"*—"louder".[10] Missing words made up a specter that would haunt Maria at infrequent intervals—bedeviling her 1957 Athens concert when she sang "Ahimè" instead of lyrics in an ill-fated rendition of *La forza del destino*'s "Pace, pace, mio Dio."

Yet the role of Gilda excavated for Maria's public her most vulnerable and unassuming self. Describing how she taught a young soprano to approach the "Caro nome" aria in 1972, a music critic wrote: "Alert to the dangers of too much sweetness, Callas will now and then provide a shot of insulin. 'Don't get so cutesy there,' she warns a high-calorie Gilda. 'She may be a virgin, but don't forget she dies for love.' "[11]

Some find the "little girl" veneer with which Maria varnishes specific roles—notably Lucia di Lammermoor, Madama Butterfly and Amina of *La sonnambula*—specious and sugary. Yet through this vocal prism she invites us to identify an individual younger and more gullible than her emboldened early voice suggests.

By September 1955 the instrument has undergone a transformation for the studio recording. In moments of young Gilda's suffering the timbre is so thin it skates along the edge of breath support. Through tentative diminuendi Maria has made Gilda a woman unsure of herself: less excited, more lonely. Pondering that seclusion has kept her away from the city of Mantua ("né la cittade ho ancor veduta"), her already frail voice is chipped further by a sullen bashfulness.

This time, when Gilda confesses to Giovanna that she is in love with "Gualtier" her voice hangs by a thread in her guilt. In her duet with the perfidious Duke the jumpy lines of "Ah, de' miei vergini sogni son queste le voci tenere si care a me" ("Ah, those are the tender words that I have pined for in my dreams") are so alike, so statically identical we know this is no longer love but the magnetic trance of ironclad hypnosis.

Her quickfire but tiny voice commands "Uscitene!" ("Leave!"): terror and excitement charge the instrument. Music critic Teodoro Celli asked her why she used this "strange accentuation."

"Because Gilda says 'Leave!' but what she really means is 'Stay!' "[12]

Yet by the time the shame-struck girl confesses her illicit love to her stunned father she has morphed her voice into another. Their duet "Tutte le feste" opens up a timbre morbid and morose.

Gilda has grown world-weary. In a matter of days.

This studio Gilda makes us understand to what extent the 1952 Maria is a slow-to-grow artistic tadpole.

After another summer spent singing *La Gioconda* and *La traviata* at the Arena di Verona—and enduring an abrasive pimple on her spinal column[13]—Maria recorded her first complete opera: that same *La Gioconda* for Cetra. Reviews were ravenous but audiences were not. Upon its U.S. 1953 release, the disc accomplished only modest sales despite one critic advocating, "For years we have wondered where to find a true dramatic soprano with a solid, unwobbling tone, capable of ascending to a thrilling high C easily, and fully in command of all the nuances of great singing. Now we know. Her name is Maria Callas."[14]

Acclimatization to the Callas voice was still a *process*.

A fearsome debut followed next: *Norma* at the Royal Opera House beside young Joan Sutherland as her nemesis/ex-best friend, Adalgisa. Attempting to ingratiate herself with the ensemble, Maria fastened mistletoe around the theatre's Christmas tree but couldn't see what she was doing. Joan Sutherland was forced to "take La Divina by the shoulders and point her in the right direction."[15]

Although *Norma* was sold out[16] Maria suffered glacial burns of horror. "I remember that the moment I was due to go onstage my heart abruptly ceased to beat. I had been awaited in London with stupendous press—and I was terrified of the idea of being lower than the standards they expected from me."[17]

Having mustered all her energy to channel it into this night, she had been scaring members of the chorus with her prowess in rehearsal. Assistant conductor John Pritchard would remember how "she pulled her ocelot coat around her, walked up on to the stage and heaved the mallet as she went to strike the gong. As she approached the chorus shrank back and I had the distinct feeling that so did the gong . . . She approached it with a kind of manic fury."[18]

Conquering the public for Maria was like Norma reining in her rowdy rabble. "Until then Norma had not been heard in London since Rosa Ponselle had sung it there in 1930," she later pointed out. "She was the greatest singer of her time; and the British [are] not easy to please, after all, immortal names are written on Covent Garden's walls. I was given a great reception. I was hailed as 'the' new Norma. It was a tremendous compliment. Forgive me if I am prejudiced in favour of the British."[19]

Some had mixed reactions. *Norma* fired a passion in the heart of Noël Coward[20] but soured Isaiah Berlin. The philosopher wrote to a friend: "Madame C.'s gestures were somewhat Levantine when . . . she reproached the virtuous Roman Consul for leaving her, her gestures were rather like those of an Athenian landlady casting out a drunken lodger."[21] Berlin's reaction makes it clear the Callas of this period could sometimes stumble into ungroomed acting; a performance that skipped out on stylization.

Fans relish citing Callas as the most "emotional" performer; the most "soulful" soprano. Ignition is only a part of the story. Without the mind's cooperation, without slick, premeditated gestures and capped sentiments Maria would have been a vocalist unhinged: flames kindled by a drug-induced euphoria. What would that have symbolized? How *would* it have affected us?

Doubtless these features were dependent on a natural volatility: an inner ethanol. Before Maria was a finished actress, even in this period—she "had an extra: those eyes!" as one critic pronounced. "They, too, were Junoesque, ox-like in their breadth and their liquid softness. Even when she was standing stock-still, her eyes would do her acting for her: warm for one instant, icy with scorn the next. In moments of indignation, they would blaze like coals. In *Norma*, where the libretto portrayed her in many contrasting situations, the eyes often told the story: she was priestess, lover, mother, daughter, judge, and victim."[22]

A large part of her immersion happened on account of—not in *spite* of—her myopia. "My poor sight gives me another advantage. I can't see the people in the audience who are scratching their heads while I am lost in my role and giving everything I have to the drama!"[23] Maria accentuated. "Everything seems in a dense fog . . ."[24] One often forgets what is going on with the others, it's a little like—having *wings*, you know . . . You feel a lot of things, you become more *sensitive* to . . . many sensibilities . . . of the public."[25]

Her onstage mist provoked repulsion to disruptions of applause. "I call it 'atmosphere'—this *mysticism*, or whatever it is. Then all of a sudden just someone yells 'Brava!' or, you know, intending to do you so much good, and it *irritates* the one that just wants peace and quiet to *enjoy*, or to stay in that *atmosphere* . . ."[26] Maria conceded. "So you have to *rework* to recreate it. I *would* like at a certain point that applause *only* come at the end. But it's a bit difficult."

When David Frost asked whether the ovation at the end of the performance was "a thrill like no other," she wasn't enthused. "Not really—you feel a satisfaction; sometimes you feel that er . . . you don't deserve it, er . . . it's *gratifying*. It's not all that important; it *is* of course, but . . . you know, your *work* is more important."[27]

Slow to shake off any given role, she once came into the Biffi restaurant during *Medea*'s intermission armed still with her dagger.[28]

A switch of characters was due. That December 1952 Maria plunged herself into the part of Verdi's Lady Macbeth.

The composer had expressed his desire for the instrument to be "harsh, choked, dark. There are places that must not even be sung, but acted and declaimed with a veiled, black voice."[29]

In order to create this vocal caliber Maria darkened her soprano till it sounded almost trapped inside a vault. Sometimes it seemed the muffled groans of a gagged torture victim spawned these sounds; sometimes it was a sinkhole slurping all things in its path.

Frantically rubbing her two hands throughout Lady Macbeth's Sleepwalking Scene—[30] in which the villainess is certain that her fingers have been blotted with the blood of Duncan—Maria was determined to portray as many facets of the battleax as possible.

"She must *not* have been a terribly ugly woman," was her take on the character. "You see, I think she must have at least six mental thoughts that come to her here [in the sleepwalking scene], one completely different from the other . . ." Maria reflected. "One minute she's talking about the blood stains on her *hand*, that *terrify* her and she can never get them *clean*, and on the other hand right away she says, "Well, come now, we must get ready to *receive* these people, everything is *fine*," and all of a sudden she'd come back to *another* mental attitude. In other words she *is* out of her mind."[31]

The quotes above come from a 1968 analysis. As a live recording can attest, the 1952 performance fails to conjure these attributes. Lady Macbeth is barbarous: not yet ensnaringly attractive like her presence in a 1958 recording of three arias from the opera. By that time Maria will have sculpted the unwieldy instrument into a subtler source of might: no longer will it holler like a cave-bound sea monster.

Here there are rapid outbursts of abrupt crescendi. When the Lady scorches her comparatively weak-willed husband, bubbles foam atop her rage. "Immoto sarei tu nel tuo disegno?" ("Is your plan to be *stoic?*") her ego demands to know. This Lady Macbeth sees fit to test which of the pair is more *virile.*

Uttering "requiem" in "La luce langue" with a caustic, concave timbre, she is stimulated by the imminent extinctions of impending victims.

Yet when we hear the Lady toast her husband's victories—"Si colmi il calice di vino eletto" ("Fill the cup with the best wine")—the garishness presents a mistress wallowing in luxury. Lady Macbeth's eventual repentance is completely unforeseeable.

For some critics nonetheless it was the easiest domain through which they could habituate themselves to that chameleonic monster of an instrument—with one declaring: "Perhaps no other opera can be considered such a 'natural' for Callas as *Macbeth.*"[32]

"One cannot sing Lady Macbeth not having read Shakespeare," Maria had claimed.[33]

Funnily enough this axiom did not apply to all her roles. Whilst the singer eagerly did research in her quest to find out "about artists *in* the eighteenth century, nineteenth century, where they *improvised* cadenzas [an ornamental passage written to show off the singer] and *changed* many, many things *in* their operas"[34]—opera's source material was no crystal ball: it didn't help decode the art.

"I don't intend so much to frame my characters in their historical reality as I do to interpret them as figures of 'invention,'" was her dictum. "For example, I have to forget the true story of Anne Boleyn when I sing *Anna Bolena.* I have to portray her as a figure of someone's imagination, even if she was a part of history. So the basis of my interpretations is really my instinct."[35]

When asked if she had read Victorien Sardou's *La Tosca,* Maria clumsily insisted: "You try to . . . be exactly what the composer would have wanted and I'm sure that Puccini . . . was inspired by the libretto of Sardou."[36]

Her object was to excavate a character in music—not the text. At the same time she was fascinated with Alexandre Dumas *fils' La Dame aux Camélias*—the basis for *La traviata,* remembering with vividness how in the novel Armand (*Traviata's* Alfredo) "unburies" his lover Marguerite (Violetta).[37]

Literarily Maria wasn't one to dive into the canon during her spare time. A discourse on Greek philosophy with baritone Aldo Protti evoked the reply, "I don't really know."[38] Tea with Beverly Sills prompted the answer: "I don't read; I don't have the patience. I'm too fidgety."[39]

Although most of her pleasure-reading came from magazines—the periodicals *Annabella*, *Elle*,[40] *Vogue* and *Harper's Bazaar* lay across her coffee table[41]—she was sufficiently attuned to culture to refer to Graham Greene's *Life is a Battlefield*: a novel she would surely not have read.[42] Self-admittedly she wasn't one for poetry, "even if it's shameful on my part."[43]

Biographies of nineteenth-century singers like Maria Malibran and Pauline Viardot kept her attention.[44] She also adored books about composers—proudly once asserting that Puccini had desired to eliminate Tosca's famed aria "Vissi d'arte;" something she had read in an assortment of his letters.[45]

Next to these and magazines the only thing Maria ravenously read were recipes—collecting cuttings she could then paste into photo albums.[46]

*

Now a fixture at La Scala, the soprano settled in Milan while still residing in Verona. Staying at the Grand Hotel for every trip, she had befriended twenty-year-old Giovanna Lomazzi in 1951.[47] As a result of this Maria cherished a new family, treating Lomazzi as her younger sister.

The latter had been born into a family of music lovers known to Meneghini.[48] Little by little she began to learn that her new friend's dependence on her husband or the words of critics didn't always meet her needs. Instead Maria pined for that "best friend" proximity. It wasn't long before she started making trips together with Lomazzi's family to Salice Terme in Pavia—where she entertained guests with recitals of Chopin, played cards and swapped gossip.[49]

The urge to possess pals appeared a little limitless. Quickly Maria likewise cherished fans Louise and Ida Cook. The latter was a romance novelist who penned her works under the name Mary Burchell. "What is entirely endearing about her is that she never forgets a friend," she wrote of the soprano. "The most retiring, undemanding person who has been good to her will always be remembered and greeted in any part of the world."[50]

Easy and honest relationships with her colleagues were paramount to her work. Growing close to Giulietta Simionato, she confided, "To me, you're like chamomile."—"I don't understand ... is that a threat or a compliment?"

Laughing, Maria insisted: "No, it's a compliment—it's better for me this way."[51]

The compulsion to unveil the truth extended into a protective, matter-of-fact attitude. When eventually Lomazzi married, she was gifted by Maria with a bracelet and a card that read, "I'm not happy for you." Maria feared her dear friend had become involved with the wrong guy.[52] Years later Lomazzi divorced.[53]

Reined in by an unrelenting focus on her art and marriage, Maria was unable to fulfill this role in its entirety. "Maybe because I always approached my work with utter devotion, there was no time or inclination in me to make close friendships . . ." she would later confess.[54] "I'm a very good friend but—*unfortunately*, I'm not the kind who shows her affection the way others do. I'm not always *there*, I don't always call people, I don't see my friends frequently . . . And yet, in spite of that, my friends love me the way I am. They see me when I want to see them, they don't see me when I don't want to see them and . . . Perhaps they get annoyed sometimes, but they don't show it."[55]

Her letters frequently contain apologies regarding late replies and even, in one instance, an autograph with "Callas" crossed out and the message: "P.S. Excuse the habit of signing this way."[56]

For her deficiencies in friendship she would compensate with gifts. Making sure to wish both Simionato and her other colleagues good luck on their opening nights was a consistent must—and a frenetic schedule of performances did not derail her.[57] Free tickets to them were distributed with ease. Savoy Hotel concierge Tony Facciolo was always assured a seat "not for the back row, right in the front."[58] Maria sent a U.S. furrier sister-in-law Pia's measurements to buy a white mink coat for her.[59]

Despite displays of gestures such as these Maria was considered stingy by some members of her entourage. A more befitting word for her pecuniary disposition would be "flakiness". Apt to misuse money in her early years, she could tip a waiter the cost of a luncheon and a seamstress who had worked overtime fifty cents. Forgetting her cash was a frequent occurrence.[60]

Maria did at times demand—most probably at Meneghini's urgency— "high fees" for which she had, in her words, "earned the right".[61] Eager to avoid producing unpaid tax, in her peak years she profited from a Swiss bank account where she kept funds and often had to be reminded of unsettled taxes.[62]

Wartime destitution had most likely had a bearing on her attitude and yet it lacked rigidity. On impetus she could spend hundreds on completely inane gifts for friends: a gold swizzle champagne stick, for instance.[63] To one of her hairdressers, Alexandre of Paris, she donated a silver cross given to her by the President of Nigeria.[64] Whilst moving house Maria left for La Scala's *maestro sostituto* Antonio Tonini her piano, porcelain statuettes of a pianist and a violinist, most of her books and a painting.[65]

Whatever stinginess existed in her, it could easily be swayed.

By January 1953 Maria had already signed with impresario Sander Gorlinsky—manager to legends of ballet Rudolf Nureyev and Anna Pavlova. The title didn't swipe from Meneghini his own duties: while Gorlinsky would protect Maria's interests in the U.K. and U.S., France, Germany and several other European countries, Meneghini would arrange all her Italian affairs. Most opera contracts would be lengthily discussed by both before the application of her signature.

The first engagement that Gorlinsky offered was a couple of performances of Verdi's *Requiem* to take place on 1 and 2 April that year. Broadcast live over the BBC, it would help cement Maria's celebrity status.[66] When she and Meneghini hoped to leave Milan for London, however, a flu epidemic was brewing. The British Immigration Office wouldn't grant them entry.[67]

That was Part I of Maria's *Requiem* curse.

Back in January she was in the throes of yet another *Traviata*—this time in Venice—on the 100th anniversary of the opera's creation. With the Teatro La Fenice layered top to bottom in enrobing walls of pink and red carnations, the occasion stretched into a landmark moment:

> . . . *downstage left, quite apart, in solitude to be found in dreams, sits a monumental, Titian-haired, marmoreal figure, encased in her flounced but simple white gown, as she sits there casually, almost indolently, tossing white camellias toward the dancing guests. Am I imagining her? From her . . . the most haunting voice I have ever heard. It is filled with lost joys, permeated with present despairs. Here is desperate frivolity, and here is unavoidable tragedy . . .*
>
> *In Act III, this Violetta's great size completely vanished and even the voice was already in the other world and all dreamt.* [We witnessed] *The destruction of this monumental woman by her monumental passion for a weak, conventional man . . .*[68]

Wrote Leo Lerman, Contributing Editor to *Mademoiselle* magazine and a soon-to-be friend of Maria's. *La traviata* was followed by a Florentine *Lucia di Lammermoor*; the kind that prompted *Vogue* to feature an opera star in their regular column "People Are Talking About . . ."

> *The ecstatic performance of the New York-born soprano, Maria Meneghini Callas, at La Scala; in the mad scene of Lucia di Lammermoor, the singer's voice so perfectly matched the high notes of the flute that the audience came cheering down the aisles.*[69]

Having previously congregated at select sites—stage doors and singers' hangouts—fans began to splash like New York rain asplatter on the sidewalk. Pia had come across a band of students in the small town of Pavullo who were short of means to make the journey to Milan. So the soprano travelled there and roused them with her singing, thanking the adorers for their awe.[70]

Maria's first complete EMI recording was Donizetti's *Lucia di Lammermoor*. During the sessions Tullio Serafin began to pester her about her weight's enormity; flinging remarks about it as they scoffed down food at lunch. Amused, bass Tito Gobbi—a legendary singer and a fine friend of Maria's—proposed she weigh herself outside the cafeteria. Dissatisfied with the result, Maria dismounted the scales, handed Gobbi her handbag and kicked off her shoes. Dissatisfied with the second result . . . she couldn't disrobe out in public.

So she went quiet.[71]

Later Maria would describe the postwar fluctuations of her weight: "In 1945 up to the beginning of 1946 I ate a lot, too much, which in a certain way, is understandable, with the wonderful things I found here in America, especially coming from Greece in that period I reached 210 pounds. After I went on a diet and went down to 170. In Italy, trying to make a career, I went down to 150. After my operation of appendix, in December 1948, something went wrong and I gained weight."[72] At this point Maria weighed 92kg (203 pounds or 14 ½ stone).

Though the "weight machine" affair had brought embarrassment, the "wake-up call" Maria pinpointed occurred a little after that. "I was doing *Medea* then, and at the Maggio Fiorentino for the first time, and I remember that my *instinct*—which is *normally* good—my first instinct was saying that the face is too fat and I can't stand it because I needed the *chin* for expression, in certain very hard phrases and er, cruel phrases . . . I *felt* as a woman of theatre as I *was* and *am*, that I *needed* these—the *necklines* and the *chin* lines to be *very* thin and *very* pronounced," she determined.

"So I was *annoyed*, I er . . . *darkened* the color and all that but it's *nonsense*—you can't *do* that. Then . . . [in May 1953] I went to Rome to sing *Lucia*. Singing *Lucia* was such a *hard* ordeal for me in the first act—I was getting so heavy that even my *vocalizing* was heavy. So I was *tiring* myself, I was perspiring too much and I *really*—was working too hard. So then I said—'Well, now I've had enough of it'—and I wasn't really *well*, as health. I felt, 'Now, if I'm *going* to do things right, I studied all my life to put things right *musically*, why don't I just *diet* and put myself into a certain condition—that I am *presentable?*' "[73]

Myths have been forged over something that wasn't that interesting. In order to lose weight Maria did not give up food, and neither did she stealthily procure some quick-fix medication from a shady doctor. Her visit to a nutritionist resulted in a cumbersome reply: "I can't touch you, otherwise you'll lose your voice." Frustrated, Maria arrived home and recapitulated: "I said, 'Well, Maria, now that *was* a lot of *talk*. Supposing we come down to *earth* and say: you *always* had a voice, you had it when you were *thinner* because as a *child* I was not *fat* so—*what* are you going to do *about* it?' "[74]

Henceforth Maria's diet was reduced to little meat filets and small side salads. According to Lomazzi she had nothing but strong coffee for her breakfast and a tea a little later. Lunch would consist of meat and vegetables.[75] Occasionally she had chicken broth for dinner.[76] With no alcohol, no dessert and little fruit, Maria soon began to slim.

Quick was the singer to deny she had tested out "rubdowns", "cream oils" or "electric massages."[77] Over the course of 1953 her weight dropped from 92kg during *La Gioconda* at La Scala in February to 87 during *Aïda* in June. By January 1954 it had reached 75.[78]

Another source of weight gain had been the intrusion of hormonal problems. Having suffered from an underactive thyroid that had spiked her appetite in Athens, she at last found treatment for the overlooked disorder.[79]

One source of her increasing hunger[80] was a tapeworm she had accidentally ingested back in Greece. Because she would have never taken one deliberately—as many unimaginative tabloids have surmised—Maria didn't hide this medical condition. "I found I had a tapeworm. I treated myself," she admitted in 1954 to music critic Claudia Cassidy. "Fortunately, it departed."[81]

*

February of that year witnessed Maria's first *Il trovatore* at La Scala on the 23rd. Her relationship with the heroine Leonora—a fifteenth-century lady-in-waiting to a Spanish princess—was ambivalent. Leonora is lusted after by Count di Luna, the commander of the Royalist Aragon troops—yet in love with Manrico the Troubadour: leader of the enemy rebel forces.

In a recording of this Scala performance she oscillates between self-restraint and explosions of joy in "Tacea la notte placida," Leonora's admission of love. Some notes succumb to the poor practice of being held for too long once again; others glide gently in staccato, languorously lingering until they near *fortissimo*. There is a euphoric daze here—but it's comparable to Gilda, not the more august, maturer Leonora.

That did not deter Milanese critics. "In now listening to Callas, we have understood what Musset and Stendhal heard in their own times . . ." one began, "when, at the edge of a box watching a Malibran or a Pasta, they spoke of an 'extraordinary person'; even, of 'genius'."[82]

"Genius" might better be reserved for the eventual studio recording made in August 1956. Even so, the document of Callasian artistry misfires half the time. With Herbert von Karajan at the helm, the outburst of ecstasy in "Tacea la notte"'s cabaletta [an aria's enlivened last section] is surprisingly staid and reserved. "Remember, she *is* Spanish royalty," Maria would remind a Juilliard student.[83] She may be taking her conceit too far: regality devolves into near-impassivity.

Only when Leonora sees the Troubadour again—unwinding in a whirlwind of elation—does the instrument emit its sparkle; shimmering like bouncing sunrays off a river as she asks her would-be lover: "Are you descended from heaven, or am I in heaven with you?" ("Sei tu dal ciel disceso, o in ciel son io con te?").

Evolving a more elegant protagonist, the somber "D'amor sull'ali rosee" emerges a resigned, half-withered sigh: demure introspection. Technically it is exquisite.

Emotionally one wonders if an operatic noblewoman ought to suffer such repression.

As Leonora and Manrico vow to perish in each other's arms Maria finally allows a vehement vibrato to encroach on her insistent words: "With you forever, I will fall into my grave" ("Con te per sempre unita nella tomba scenderò"). In death her Leonora can let rip.

Comfortably ensconced in La Scala tradition, by early 1953 the Meneghini-Callases had moved to permanently live at Grand Hotel, Milan.[84] Whilst their perennial proximity ensured no need for amorous epistles, Maria relished avidly the role of Housewife. Messages of love were left around the house; notes scribbled with "I LOVE YOU, MY SOUL!!!"

Being especially cute with her husband, she would use his pet name for her, "paiassa"—the Veneto version of "pagliaccia" ("female clown")—but misspell it "payassa", and sign letters "Tua mugiera" in an effort to use the Veneto word "moier" ("wife").[85]

March 1953 saw the soprano lend her voice to a recording of Bellini's *I puritani*. Despite her telling opera director John Copley this was one of her favorite recordings,[86] her take on young, naïve Elvira—again a heroine embroiled in civil war, this time in the 1640s between Puritans and Royalists—is a heavy instrument unripe for the protagonist.

Wound around the notion that she thinks her groom has been unfaithful, Elvira's mad scene is perplexingly a paragon of peace. Her implorations of "vieni," ("Come") in "Oh, vieni al tempio" ("Oh come to the temple") are closer to chants than to cries of despair.

Recording wasn't palatable in Maria's eyes. "I dislike being—'hemmed in', as you say; I probably suffer of claustrophobia. So the minute I'm 'hemmed in' . . . we have no *atmosphere* there. You look at things so *plainly*, you see the musicians, you *hear* things too well . . . So, er—you get nervous . . .[87] The trouble is that you just project into the microphone . . . And the voice completely—you know, goes outside the doors and just goes around, it isn't closed into the—there isn't the acoustic box, shall we call it that way."[88] The circumstances meant she had to "tone it down" because the microphone would pick up every detail. Thus she felt restricted as an artist.

That didn't curb her craving to collect illegal pirate tapes of her performances she sneakily obtained through fans to scrutinize her instrument's behavior. Customarily she called up one of them, Charles Johnson, to enquire: "Have you found anything new?"[89]

Maria's next artistic feat marked a slight shift in style. "Dramatically the opera is more than Gluck, less than Beethoven, and far behind Verdi," one critic wrote of Cherubini's *Medea*.[90] Maria opted to explain: "This opera is not *bel canto* but recitative and theatre—straight acting, speaking with music. The strength of Cherubini's opera is not the aria but the recitative (which, incidentally, are not by Cherubini). And if we had done it in the classical style we could never have brought it to life."[91]

The credit for inducting certain operas back into the repertoire is not all hers. This particular revival came about after an almost-dare: "It started in 1953, when Maestro [Francisco] Siciliani pointed out that if I wanted to be taken more seriously, I must explore the possibility of classical works such as Gluck. I told him that I had sung Haydn's *Orfeo* earlier. He brought to my house Cherubini's *Medea*. I had very little time to prepare it, so I took the score to bed, and told my husband to go away."[92]

Stunned, the audience had expected it to be "a period piece". But *Medea* is a showcase for the anti-heroine herself: a shrew who sweeps the opera with soliloquies. Eliciting a comment from the Cook sisters—who had heard Rosa Ponselle in the role—Maria heard only: "You made a very good stab at it, didn't you?"[93]

Some regard her quest to reinvent the repertoire as a near-megalomaniacal compulsion to "sing everything". But bel canto and its historical neighbors charmed her for personal reasons. "It is the manner in which I can best express myself," she confided.[94]

Other singers with like sentiments were loath to mount this kind of music. French music critic Jacques Bourgeois averred, "She came about at a time when her repertoire was being sung *very* badly."[95]

In November 1952 Eric Blom of *The Observer* remarked, "The live performances of 'Norma' at Covent Garden seem to be doing extremely well. It is not altogether easy to see why. Is the public really interested in Bellini nowadays? ... Whatever the reason for this flash-in-the-pan success, we may be glad of a revival that gets opera away temporarily from the basic and doubtless necessary stock repertory."[96]

Regardless of how much she merited the label of a revolutionary, the seismic shift in opera houses' annual repertoires was undeniable.

It wasn't easy. As well as being challenged by administrators ruling opera houses all around the world—"*Anna Bolena* is an old bore of an opera"—disputed the Met's Rudolf Bing[97]—these selections raised a probing question. Whilst monologues or dialogues are rarely cut from plays, historically productions of long operas have removed cadenzas from their arias, excised the excess notes and severed those superfluous arpeggios. To cut or not to cut was not the pivotal debate: bel canto operas could last five-plus hours without cuts. *What* to cut and what was a "cruel" cut became the crux of conflict.

This didn't solely touch Bellini, Donizetti and Rossini. In Verdi's *Il trovatore*, Maria's first performances in Latin America tended to use Verdi's written top C and D flat [C and D flat 6] in "D'amor sull'ali rosee." Years later they were gone as she had changed her mind: it was excessive and not credible.

A December 1951 recording of *I vespri siciliani* finds Maria quarreling with Verdi once again. Where he has written two "fermata"s (long-held top notes), she spares one.

This was no precocious caprice on her part. Opera had not been written merely for artistic purposes. In the eighteenth and nineteenth centuries, singers had assumed the mien of gods; expecting their composers to add extra high notes, cabalettas and cadenzas as a showcase of their virtuosic splendor. Humility had scarcely been in vogue. Adornments had been written in the interest of a theatre's politics. It was a silent pact between performers and composers. One that led Rossini, in one instance, to exclaim: "How wonderful opera would be if there were no singers."[98]

Vocalists would get to pick and choose their ornaments like children in a candy store. With the share of musical biographies she had perused, Maria understood that this unspoken contract hadn't been the masters' preference: "I don't think that the composers *enjoyed* a lot of embellishments if not for means of expression. 'Cause I *read* frequently of their exclamations, of their dislikes, about artists *in* the eighteenth century, nineteenth century, where they *improvised* cadenzas and *changed* many, many things *in* their operas. It was the style; it was *florid*; it was like the way they used to *dress* then, they powdered, they used to wear wigs, and frills, and laces . . . [but] the musicians didn't like all that."

Abandoning such a Rococo custom led Maria into conflict with select conductors—not to mention singers. Tradition mandates that conductors make the cuts. Yet during her audition for Arturo Toscanini back in 1952, he had insisted she repeat Lady Macbeth's "Or tutti sorgete" cabaletta from "Vieni t'affretta" not once but *twice*. Maria had disputed this decision vehemently.[99]

At one point she and Maestro Gianandrea Gavazzeni contemplated a *Lucia di Lammermoor* without any additional ornamentation; even the mad scene's beloved cadenza. Fear of controversy nixed the concept.[100]

On the other hand Maria and her colleagues weren't the first to chop. Cuts had already been prolific in the last years of the nineteenth century. Some scholars claimed that several had been detrimental to the cause— and that abridged works such as Verdi's long *Don Carlos* should be sung unedited. Maria was at odds with such a principle: "Not *all* music is *really* delicious of every composer."[101]

Other musicians had various reasons for *opening* cuts. Karajan liked to do so in *Lucia di Lammermoor* to give the heroine more to sing than her colleagues.[102] The merciless Maria was against the process: "Great minds have *taught* me, *ages* ago, that—*nothing* should be repeated that much. *Repetition* . . . is *monotonous*."[103]

Most operas had been written in an era when the art had struggled to be taken seriously—like motion pictures in their nascent years. Whilst people still chew popcorn, slurp through straws and get a little frisky at the movie theater, in the nineteenth century the opera houses' patrons had chomped fruit and nuts and carried on in boxes. Maria recognized that changes in theatrical comportment would demand more patience from the audience than previously. "I, *myself*, being a *musician* . . . I *cannot* sit through a performance for five hours in the *same* seat, taking in *even* the most *gorgeous* music."[104]

Once again this was no rigid rule. In her performances of *Il trovatore*, she would make sure to open a major cut in the last act; a gesture she felt was "essential".[105]

Listeners can agree or disagree with Callasian tailorship. EMI producer Walter Legge approved of her artistic choices: "There were innumerable exquisite felicities—minuscule portamentos from one note to its nearest neighbour, over widespread intervals—and changes of color that were pure magic."[106]

Returning to London in June of that year, Maria opened an under-prepared, milquetoast *Aïda* under the baton of Sir John Barbirolli. Critics greeted her with mixed reviews that cited how she "disconcertingly changed vocal colour."[107]

Following a series of *Norma*s at the Royal Opera House Maria and Meneghini were invited to dine with British Labour MP Woodrow Wyatt. Uninterested in opera, Wyatt had left in the first interval for a cigar break and returned in time to catch the curtain calls. An oblivious Maria asked if Mr. Wyatt had enjoyed the opera. " 'What opera?'—'The one in which I performed tonight.'—'Excellent. I'm sorry I missed the entrance of the hero.'—'You mean Pollione, the Roman general?'—'No, I mean Norman.' "[108] At the time Norman Lamont had been Chancellor of the Exchequer.

Befuddled, Maria was at loss before all matters political—no matter *how* tiny. "An artist must *not* be a member of a political group," she would emphasize. "We belong to the whole *world*. We belong—to communists, to fascists—we don't *like* all that, because we are born *free*; art is free. Art is the freest ambassador in the whole world. When we speak of a 'passport', it's *our* passport. Music passes through the whole world, and above and beyond politics."[109]

At around this time Maria's sculpting of the voice began to change; alternating between episodes lugubrious, light, scintillating, seething or hypnotically entranced. "As the musician grows, you use 'flashes' *less . . .*" the performer would elaborate. "Essentially, the *music* that we do, the dramatic soprano—she is not exactly very *flashy*; she's usually an unhappy soul, oddly enough, ah . . . *suffering*, so you'd rather use a Chopin-ish kind of *color* in the voice—unhappy. Tragic, yes—finally tragic; but the *coloring* is rather a *melancholic* coloring."[110]

Throughout the *Tosca* recording that took place that August conditions were harsh. Different opinions persist over the number of takes of the end of Act I: some say sixteen, others forty-eight. A coal merchant delivering the heating system's fuel disrupted the first perfect take. Sessions were suspended when a spent Maria swiped her glasses off to warn Victor de Sabata: "Maestro, I cannot see you any more."[111]

The fruit it bore is an iconic *Tosca* that makes pale the live ones. Maria's heavy voice is at times stringent and seditious. Everything that Floria Tosca does in the first act is charged with coquetry or briskness. Slicing her vocal timbre in half to sing to Cavaradossi, "Non davanti la Madonna" ("Don't kiss me before the Madonna"), she is cutesy *par excellence*.

Here Tosca is one inelegant woman: a figure Maria did not deem intelligent. This is superlatively stressed in her audacious statement before Chief of Police Scarpia, her blackmailer, as he attempts to wring out information:

"Non so *nulla*" ("I know *nothing*"). When Tosca wants to know what she can offer in exchange for lover Mario's salvation, her "how much?" ("Quanto?") is both insecure and childlike. In Maria's eyes Tosca is a middle-aged woman behaving like an enamored, spoiled schoolgirl. The former appears in "Vissi d'arte" in the guise of an aria performed solemnly, slowly; engrossed in solicitous musings. The latter is the actress who makes even suicide a showy gesture.

This recording's mastery lies in the fact that it is Tosca who is gaudy and grotesquely garish—not Maria Callas.

Summer 1953 additionally marked Maria's studio recording of her first performed role, Santuzza in *Cavalleria rusticana*. Returned to her dark "bottle voice," she paints penetrant pathos. There is deference in the excommunicated woman's voice as she pleads frantically with her ex-lover's mother, "Dite, Mamma Lucia" ("Tell me, Mother Lucia"). Suddenly the urge to find out splits the glass restraints of her reluctant reverence as she cries: "Dite a me per *pietà*, dov'è Turiddu?!" ("Tell me, I *beg* you, where is Turiddu?!") and her vibrating voice charges the line with a zigzag of thunder.

Darkness serves her well. Having performed the pious Easter Hymn, Santuzza's duo with the treacherous Turiddu speaks to her possessiveness of the unworthy man. Through the overriding, harsh vibrato on "Tu l'ami dunque?" ("So you love Lola, then?") escapes the girl's irascible, wild nature: a corrupted psyche blind to reason.

After frightful nightmares led her to spend several days vacationing at the Lido with Meneghini and Pia,[112] Maria recorded *La traviata* and took the month of October to rest.

That Scala season Ghiringhelli had selected a strange opera for Maria in Scarlatti's *Mitridate Eupatore*—a work she didn't especially care for. Her reaction was to campaign for *Medea* instead. "I was anxious to do it at La Scala because it would have provided me with great possibilities ... although I had already been successful at La Scala, I was not yet firmly established there in the way I aspired."[113]

Ears peeled before a radio broadcast of a concert, Maria had discovered an unknown American whose single operatic feat had been conducting *Peter Grimes* at Massachusetts' Tanglewood Festival. She found a way to contact him—this Leonard Bernstein—and insisted that he take the podium for her *Medea*.[114]

Bernstein was reticent. With only five complete days of rehearsal available, friends had told him not to bother with "that Callas" who was known as "hysterical". Only at the tail end of a telephone exchange did she persuade him to commit to it.[115] Their relationship would turn into such scintillating warmth that he would write to her one day: "I go around saying 'Callas? Well of course. My private soprano.' Like a proud papa."[116]

A train carriage en route to Milan was the site where he studied *Medea*.

French director Margarete Wallman's vision of the opera was inspired by painter Salvatore Fiume's depictions of Ancient Greece. Installing a tiered ramp onstage, she visualized Maria opening the final act stretched out along the steps; her head at the bottom with the wig's scarlet curls splayed out "like a halo of fire, her cape spread out around her—the premonitions of the fire she will light in the temple to murder her children."

"Margherita! This is *impossible!* I cannot do it!" came the plaintive cry before it turned into a literal cry: Maria wept. To sing lying down—especially with the head sloping downward—is a challenge almost insurmountable. But Secretary of La Scala Luigi Oldani insisted, "It's so beautiful—you can't change it!" Wallman's reaction was to line the edges of the steps to make them clearer for the scared and short-sighted soprano.[117]

Over the years Maria's vision of Medea changed. Though in this performance she is more of a barbarian than a scorned woman, already critics had observed during the Florentine *Medea* her "grim vocality, fiercely intense in the low register; terribly shrill in the high. But she had heartbreaking accents for Medea the Lover, and likewise for Medea the Mother. In other words, she went beyond the demands of the vocal part."[118]

"This woman generates pure electricity on the stage," was Bernstein's description. "In *Medea* she is a power-station."[119]

The stirrings in a nuclear plant are palpable throughout this febrile incarnation. "Io, Medea" ("I, Medea"): the sorceress presents herself cholerically. Pronouncing the name of her husband Giasone—who has betrayed her with a juvenile princess—the voice constricts to emulate the throbbing of a taut elastic band. Throughout she blasts him with derision of his manhood: "Your old and new loves are at war in you," ("Il nuovo e il vecchio amor in te fa guerra"). It's a sardonic phrasing mimicking a child who fawns before a puppy.

Medea could annihilate that puppy.

Almost every sound emerging in the music thrives on a barbaric indignation. A foreigner in these parts, Medea has a nationality complex. She has killed her brother to allow Giasone to abscond with the desired Golden Fleece. Now she wants her clout restored. In *her* territory, Colchis, she was vicious and formidable.

In Crete she is a derelict, soon-to-be exiled wife.

In the midst of her near-shrill vibrato as she supplicates King Creon to allow her one last visit to her children ("Date almen per pietà"), fierceness genuflects to fear. Eventually her voice is worn away; its varnish scraped-off like old flakes of paint. So tired is she of suffering for children she will ultimately kill.

It's a monument to petrifying witches.

Yet it's not the stream of consciousness it will become.

Meanwhile the press was fervently deliberating fabricated instances of witchery. It had taken them a while but they were starting to refer to an alleged animosity between Maria and Renata Tebaldi. By this time the former had some friends in members of the press. Emilio Radius, a music critic for magazine *L'Europeo*, suggested that Maria and Tebaldi meet in public and shake hands as evidence of no hard feelings.

Whilst Maria wasn't going to take part in this trivial charade she did opt—just three days before *Medea*—to observe Tebaldi in *La Wally* at La Scala. Eight years later Lomazzi explained how Maria believed this would goad her faux rival to come see *Medea*; cementing a mutual amnesty. It was Lomazzi who accompanied Maria to *La Wally* on 7 December.

In an effort to appear approachable Maria applauded Tebaldi with endless aplomb; smiling directly at her during curtain calls. Guests of performers would be vetted by the manager at the stage door. Maria had anticipated her reception would suffice to gain admission to Tebaldi's dressing room. After all, Tebaldi had visited Maria during a Venetian production of *Tristan und Isolde*.

No signal came.

Tebaldi chose not to attend the opening of *Medea*; surfacing at its third offering instead. Meneghini reported to Maria that he was "very kind" to Tebaldi, removed her coat from her shoulders and enquired after her mother. He also noted he was "sure" that Tebaldi had struggled to recognize him and that—a few minutes into the first act—she had taken her coat and departed without a goodbye.

Maria took her husband's words as gospel.[120] Eight years thence Lomazzi would report how the notorious 1956 *Time* magazine quote that alleged Tebaldi had "no spine" had stemmed not from Maria but from *him*. Unbeknownst to her, he was a proxy in continuous communication with the media to flaunt his wife's career.

Privately the meanest things Lomazzi ever heard her best friend say of the soprano were, "She has the most beautiful voice, but she sings the wrong repertoire. If she had wanted to sing the dramatic soprano repertoire instead of continuing with only lyric soprano roles, it would have been much better for her career."[121]

To Dorle Soria nonetheless she labeled the soprano "as nasty and sly as they come,"[122] believing calumnious accusations likely conveyed by her husband. On account of Meneghini's stipulations she was wary of the woman. From the time of her performance as Lady Macbeth in December the previous year, Maria had weathered the booing and heckling of claques. Claques were groups hired by the singers' agencies to sabotage their clients' rivals mid-performance.

"Since 1952 . . . I have always had to contend with paid whistling. This is an unimaginable burden . . ." Maria would later recall. "Moreover, I will never be rid of them. The claque functions not only in Italy, it seems to me, but also in New York at the Metropolitan Opera, where there is a whistler at every performance."[123] The purpose of this—in Maria's words—was to have the newspapers believe "Callas is going downhill—they hissed her last night. *X* is rising like the sun—there was great applause for her."[124]

While Maria never blatantly accused Tebaldi of enlisting such a claque, she publicly confessed in 1957 that she feared this was the case: "Every time I reflect on this I repeat to myself that Renata could not have wanted to so disturb our friendship—and perhaps there is a misunderstanding, something difficult and incomprehensible, at the bottom of all of this."[125]

It was not long after her *Medea* that Maria met again with designer Elvira Leonardi Bouyeure: step-granddaughter of Puccini himself, commonly known as "Biki".[126] The dressmaker had once attired poet Gabriele d'Annunzio, as well as other luminaries in the Milanese elite.

Various sources attribute their very first meeting to different occasions— including a party thrown after this very *Medea*.[127] Most likely they had met at Wally Toscanini's party following Maria's debut at La Scala on 7 December 1951.

With a shrewd eye Biki scrutinized the heavyset Maria: "She was so fat! And with an evening hat on in the house! Black velvet with a wide brim. The hem of her jacket was at least five centimeters too long to cover her chest. As for her blouse—best to say nothing at all. A long, long skirt that didn't even manage to cover her huge legs and black leather shoes with a thin strap . . . Her handbag—also black—was as huge as a shopping bag. But what really shocked me were the earrings. Two long pendants . . . Plastic."[128]

Despite having lost tremendous weight, Maria hadn't been particularly scrupulous in matters of appearance. "I don't find myself beautiful. I think I'm rather ugly," she would state matter-of-factly.[129]

Endlessly she openly begrudged her stalks of peasant legs: "If you think I have beautiful legs you'd better have another look," she told a friend.[130] Sartorial advice was always welcome since Maria understood her clothing choices fell short of fortuitous.

Her fortune was about to shift.

8.

"Extreme poetry"

"Lithe, tall, and cool, tailored with a prim Jamesian elegance, Mme. Callas concentrates tremulous beauty in her great, anxious eyes. Reinforced by a generous mouth, she has the magnetism of the ancient world, at once enigmatic and blatant, as caught by Botticelli in *Primavera*. Her interviewer is soon in the grip of an Orpheus complex, racked by the contradictory urges to work and to look."[1] Such was the 1959 impression of a writer for *The Times*.

No more a bulky Christmas tree, Maria turned heads like another centerpiece: perhaps a twinkling ice sculpture reflecting moonlight. Bereft of the bad habit of enmeshing bold and vibrant colors, she compiled a look that lent to her a Snow White pallor: "At first glance she seems quite fair for she wears a powder paler than her skin, probably to intensify the contrast between her complexion and her hair which, surprisingly, is chestnut rather than black," described actress Arlene Dahl.[2]

By the late 1950s the soprano was transforming slowly into someone whose attire was the stuff of tabloid fodder: a style icon. Callas biographer George Jellinek avowed in 1957 that "the Callas wardrobe and the Callas jewelry have inspired many news comments. She never seems to wear the same dress twice, owns about three hundred hats—including a few 'wild' specimens for shock effect—at least six fur coats, and 150 pairs of shoes."[3] Her entrances at social functions could be captured in the papers with illuminating imagery: "Diva Callas—wearing a magnificent chinchilla coat over a green satin sheath with an overlay of black chiffon."[4]

Ignited once again was a debate: was Callas her own woman when it came to picking clothes? Was there a theme from which she stitched her image? Or was it yet another product of a team behind the work, or long-considered counsel, or the spell cast by the likes of *Vogue* and *Elle*?

Again it was a compromise. Callas cannot be accredited with the creation of a new or different kind of fashion style. Yet she worked shrewdly to ensure that it appeared that way.

Heeding the advice of Biki, she would carefully select the colors of her clothes—but under the designer's supervision. She preferred the blunt or flashy chromas: turquoise, emerald, black, red or white.[5] Furs were a craze of hers. A lot of evening dresses would be custom-made. When they were, the project would require the commitment of three people: Maria, Biki, and the latter's son-in-law and colleague, designer Alain Reynaud.

Reynaud would send Maria his designs awaiting the addition of her annotations: "Can't this be done for *pelliche* [sic] *interne* [fur on the inside]?" she wrote beside the sketch for one coat. "And light material quality?"[6] "This I like but in another quality of material."—or, "Excellent but I prefer another color." Next to such comments, Reynaud wrote in: "*Bon*". For each commission of Maria's she would be supplied with fabric samples she could choose. Extensive conversations would ensue over the phone: "Alain, I've chosen the orange but maybe I should pick the turquoise—what do you think?"[7]

Like a news reporter with an earpiece giving her instructions, the soprano guaranteed that Biki's counsel echoed in her conscious even when abroad. All her outfits and accessories were tagged with numbers. Beside them she would have a spreadsheet that instructed her which items to combine: dress number 23 with number 10 shoes; blouse number 4 with bag 7.[8]

There were rules to which she would adhere. Cashmere was the route to elegance; dark colors lined her soirées' runways. In Biki's words Maria's stagecraft lent to her "a very special allure . . . a style of wearing a gown that made it appear she was headed to a ball when she was just wearing a blouse."[9] In 1958 Italian weekly *Grazia* reviewed how Callas "sought to compliment her clothes with large cloche hats . . . and long elbow-length gloves."[10]

With a huge amount of weight now lost, even Maria's hands were altered. "They seemed to have grown long and beautiful," Reynaud later recalled. "It was a kind of miracle."[11]

It was on account of this new look—one that comprised small net hats, silky shawls and chic chignons—that Maria won the veneration of the haute couture elite. Manolo Blahnik ascribed one of the designs for his famed slingbacks to her custom-made footwear.[12] Nicola Bulgari, the creator of Bulgari jewels, evoked a meeting with Maria that had left the man "infatuated".[13] A 1958 Italian television program put her on a list of the world's ten most elegant women together with Anita Ekberg and Wallis Simpson.[14]

Enlisted at society balls and penciled in for photoshoots, Maria caused a stir partaking in the latter. Posing for a *Harper's Bazaar* feature for Louise Dahl-Wolfe, she felt so ill at ease surrounded by the guards appointed to protect the rented jewelry that she purchased many jewels—including brooches, bracelets, necklaces and earrings—to insist they leave.[15]

Not all of her adornments were the fruit of a collusion with a couturier. Idiosyncratic to her image, the audacious eye-flicks were her own.[16] Long before the leading ladies of tv would change their locks with every season the soprano was experimenting quarterly. By 1951 she had already tinted her brown hair so that it gleamed with auburn's shade; blonde was the hue in May of 1954. That December it was dark again—and yet the press employed the epithet "the redhead".[17] Depending on the tenor of event she could accessorize with wigs or hairpieces.[18]

Shopping was her blissful deviation from the chaos of the opera world. "I dress in Europe, but my—forgive me—my under things are real American because we really have wonderful things here," limned Maria.[19] Among her most beloved boutiques were Italy's department store Rinascente[20] and the British shop Marks and Spencer's: centers of bourgeois accouterment.[21] During outings on performance days she would exploit these escapades to saunter in serenity. Pals at the Galleria of Milan would watch Maria "stop at every counter and ask questions about almost everything. If she had something specific in mind, she'd stop at nothing to find it."[22]

Other times "specific" strayed far from her thoughts. Heading for the five-and-ten on every visit to New York, Maria would buy "kitchen gadgets and penny candy," in the words of Dorle Soria.[23] One of the gifts that awed her was a wicker basket rife with miniature perfume bottles a fan had purchased at a flea market. Each one was wrapped in tissue paper and she longed to strip them of their mystery.[24]

January 1954 marked the inaugural encounter of not so like minds. Herbert von Karajan had met Maria backstage at La Scala after his performance of *Der Rosenkavalier* on 31 January 1952.[25] Having listened to "a little spool of tape" that Walter Legge had brought to his hotel room—an excerpt from Maria's 1953 recording of *Lucia di Lammermoor*—the maestro had resolved to mount the work around her.

Stirring the ambience of the opera's source material in his head, Karajan began to study Donizetti's score and contemplate the Scottish Highlands of *The Bride of Lammermoor*; venturing to scribe Sir Walter Scott's hometown to scrutinize its "architecture, iron-work and light." Appointing himself both director and conductor of the imminent production, he was adamant to stop the opera's devolution into yet another dusty staging. Karajan wanted the sets to embody the frost of the wintery North.[26]

"It's not important," Maria responded when critic Lanfranco Rasponi asked why she hadn't read Walter Scott's novel. "It is the music that matters. The mad scene is a result of Donizetti's genius and not of the novel. These literary works are the springboard, but what really matters is what the composer does with them. There is nothing Scottish about the way Donizetti interprets her. She becomes a universal character. Try to translate 'Ardon gli incensi' into English, and much of the gripping drama is gone."[27]

With these contrarian conceits the pair embarked on their inaugural collaboration. Stepping onstage in rehearsal, the soprano was enshrouded in a swath of dismal white and gray; an "all-pervading gloom" drenched in "dust from old gauzes".[28]

"Could you tell me why I don't *see* anything?" Maria asked co-star Rolando Panerai. Her sight was bad enough; now it was suffering additional impairment.

"You can't see anything because there's a veil that's deflecting the light in the auditorium; it's opaque so you can't see anything."

"That's *it!*" Maria cried. "This is *not* possible—this veil's affecting the acoustics. The vocal vibrations lose their characteristics." Heading to confront the maestro, she found her argument did not gain steam: "Very well, then—*you* will be singing Lucia."[29]

After half an hour the stage manager alerted Karajan that she was sitting in her dressing room and crying. Understanding it was high time to surrender, Karajan determined to placate his singer. The veil was scrapped.[30]

Set in the eighteenth century, *Lucia di Lammermoor* revolves around the titular young woman, who is forced by her brother to wed Lord Arturo to salvage her family's fortune. Overcoming her love for Edgardo however becomes an impossible feat. Rather than confront her circumstances, fey Lucia descends swiftly into madness; first hallucinating that she sees a dead girl near the fountain—"the one stabbed by her jealous lover"—then marrying but murdering Arturo. The famous "mad scene" showcases Lucia's final bout of consciousness. During a fantasy about a wedding to Edgardo the soprano's voice pursues a fleeting flute's cadenza. Shortly afterward she dies.

Compelled to ditch a doom and gloom aesthetic, Karajan illuminated Callas' Lucia in the mad scene like a prima ballerina in a chasing spotlight.[31] Director Sandro Sequi witnessed the production and recalled, "She was extremely stylized and classic, yet at the same time human—but a humanity on a higher plane of existence, almost sublime."[32]

Although tradition mandates that Lucia come onstage after her husband's murder brandishing a dagger in a bloodied bridal gown, Callas and Karajan relied on audiences' imaginations to envisage gore. "I dislike violence, and I find it artistically inefficient," the former would articulate. "Where it is necessary to include the shedding of blood, the suggestion of the action is more moving than the exhibition of it. I always eliminated the knife when singing Lucia: I thought it was a useless and old-fashioned business, that the action could get in the way of the art, and realism interfere with the truth."[33]

When Ida Cook remarked that from the moment her Lucia surfaced at the steps, "everyone instinctively fell away from her, knowing that she had become a homicidal lunatic," whereas other Lucias "just come in, holding the dagger. You're just there, you poor thing," "in a chilling voice" Maria leaned in to answer: "Do you realise? I *don't need a dagger*."[34]

In this role she wanted to evoke, in her description: "a very melancholy world and a very sentimental one, and in the mad scene you realize there is a world above ordinary life; a nice world; a dream-like world."[35]

The little girl who would become a murderess.

A recording of this Milanese performance lays bare a Lucia very much enthralled in fairytales. When small, the voice is eerily curbed and disturbingly soured: the instrument of a Lucia so derailed, her world of make-believe has brainwashed her into defending killing as a logical resort. It's the state of someone strapped down to a bed between four padded walls. And yet it is an elegant, enticing mania; the visions of an adolescent who confuses dreams with life.

Charged with crescendi in the crazed cadenza, Lucia's mad scene isn't a delusionary thirteen-minute episode split by a blazing bolt of vexed lucidity. Instead it is a fluent daydream whose veneer begins to splinter with crude fissures of reality. The quasi-fractured tone on "Spargi d'amaro pianto" ("Sprinkle with bitter tears") is menacing not just for bystanders but for the lethal newlywed. If she retreats into real life . . . her death is imminent. The Callas version makes us wonder whether her demise occurs because of lunacy or its abrupt theft at the hands of sanity.

"A Rain of Red Carnations—Four Minutes of Applause for the Mad Scene" ran the headline in the Milanese *La Notte* the next day.[36] A contrast of eminent colors: Lucia's white wedding dress bestrewn with red streaks . . . where Maria had forfeited splotches of blood.

"Lucia is not a light role. It is a dramatic *coloratura*,"[37] she stressed. Yet such comments serve to go against Maria's school of thought. As we already know, in *her* mind there were no distinctions to be made between the various sopranos: "One must learn to perfection every musical role and be able to execute it—just like [Jascha] Heifetz, [Ignacy Jan] Paderewski and many other great artists learn all the musical works," read the dictum.[38]

Back in the nineteenth century, rules had been simple. "The soprano *then* was *soprano assoluto*; in other words with *all* the possibilities of bel canto, embellishment and so forth and so *on*. She had to be *soprano*, then there was the *contralto* and that was all . . ."[39] Maria educated. "*Today* there is a mania of saying, for instance, 'lyric soprano', 'coloratura soprano', 'dramatic soprano', 'lirico *spinto*'—that did not exist *once* because a soprano is a *soprano*, like a *tenor*, and that's *all*."[40]

Maria would insist, "I'm doing nothing special, you know," reminding her public that "all these operas"—such as *Il barbiere di Siviglia* and *La sonnambula*—had been performed by one type of soprano. Maria Malibran had sung *Norma* and Beethoven's *Fidelio*. Just like nineteenth-century soprano Giuditta Pasta, Maria sang Donizetti's *Anna Bolena* and Bellini's *La sonnambula* in the same month.[41] The problem wasn't in the works but other singers; those who "add empty fireworks for the sake of applause. This sets my work back a hundred years."[42]

On a quest to understand her predecessors, Maria treasured memorabilia associated with these prima donnas. When her friend Stelios Galatopoulos gave her the gift of a miniature portrait of Malibran for her birthday, she fawned. "I had been looking for one for a long time to put in a locket. When you gave it to me, I thought it dropped from heaven."[43] On her piano sat another portrait of the star.[44] Amongst her possessions were handwritten letters by Malibran from which she would quote all her life; citing how the latter's father scolded her for being too fat after childbirth. Because she worshipped them Maria was insistent to proclaim: "I make no claims to any innovations: my way of work has been practiced intermittently throughout opera history."[45]

Simultaneously she recognized the lofty heights to which she pressingly aspired. Despite pertaining to her "absolute soprano" ideology, Maria would concede: "It is always hard to compare singers one has heard with those one has not . . . the theatres in which they sang were not so large as those we use today, and their orchestras were small—thirty or forty, instead of perhaps twice as many today . . . Do you know the great well of violins and percussion you might sing across today to reach the first row of the stalls? It is like singing across a mighty river. In those days . . . it was not necessary to project the voice much more than in a salon . . . So I must not be hard on the concession which a modern singer must make to the demands of the theatre. And it is not good to assume that the great singers of the past were all that better—[Giuditta] Pasta frequently sang flat."[46]

In this way Maria never learned the destination of her summit: which exceptions were permissible and which were not. She likely didn't even know that Malibran had come backstage once after playing Desdemona in Rossini's *Otello* to catch violinist Ole Bull in tears from her poignancy . . . only to mock him and shatter his trance.[47]

But the singer did regard herself above the laity. In 1953 Meneghini had received an invitation for the couple to have an audience before Pope Pius XII; a suggestion his wife had dismissed. Maria termed the Pope "a nasty bishop" who had "elected himself the bishop of all bishops." Her attachment to the Greek Orthodox Church made her wary of Vatican antics. Only following a second invitation did the pair commit to an acquaintance with the leader of the Catholic Church.

The Pope told Maria he had listened to her as Kundry in *Parsifal* over the radio. "That's why I wanted to meet you," he explained. The ensuing conversation went like this:

POPE: That said, I don't like that you didn't sing the opera in German. Wagner loses a lot when the music is sung in Italian.

MC: It was being broadcast in Italy. If we had sung it in German, no one would have understood.

POPE: True. But it's not possible to think of Wagner's music detached from the words he himself wrote. It's a music born together with the words; one can't divide them.

MC: Well, actually, I don't agree. Of course the original version of the opera is more complete—but that doesn't diminish its worth in Italian.

In order to understand music fully, one must have a sense of the lyrics . . .

It wasn't in her plans to relent.[48]

After a few more *Lucia*s spread between La Scala and Venice's La Fenice that February, Maria assumed her first royal role at the theatre—albeit one mythological. Alceste, the heroine of Gluck's French opera of the same name, is the wife of Admetus (here in an Italian version, Admeto), King of Thebes. As her husband lies dying, Apollo announces Admeto can live if another is sacrificed. Alceste volunteers herself and dies. In a strange turn of events Apollo opts to suddenly rescind the martyrdom. He resurrects Alceste and returns her to the live Admeto.

Alceste was Maria's "favourite Greek heroine"[49]—the only other contender being Iphigenia in Gluck's *Ifigenia in Tauride*. Newly elegant and blonde, she "had the lightness of a dancer"[50] when the chorus carried dead Alceste on a funeral pyre. Witnessing director Alexis Minotis teaching "Greek chorus" gestures, she would acknowledge the mime as germane to her own: "I saw certain movements that I had never seen before, because in Greece I had not gone to see any play; I was too young and I didn't have the energy and time, and it was during the war. And I had never seen those movements, which were exactly the movements that I had used in *Iphigénie en Tauride*, er . . . *Alceste* [at] the Scala, and that really was a shock to me, because how could I have learnt gestures that Minotis taught to these girls? It must be something."[51]

Injecting life into this dusty score, Maria crafted an Alceste passion-fueled and stately; sometimes overly demure. A serene diminuendo ebbing like a stream along her servile prayers is undermined by low notes vibrating like stricken cymbals: mortal supplication stumbles on regality. In the aria "Divinità infernal" ("Infernal deities") Maria's soprano dives into the lowest of trenches to pulse with her potency—forging a fortress infrangible. Her harsh consonants are leaned on to secure the crispness of her words and fortify them with authority. The invincible Alceste is impermeable.

Why? Because like many other operatic heroines she has the Will to Die. The only difference is that in this work by Gluck it is presented in a more sophisticated guise. In her exclamation of "Ahimè!" we hear Alceste's top notes tremble in a purposeful, high-pitched vibrato. A snippet of the woman's vulnerability is visible. Callas will allow no more.

The studio recording of *Norma* that spring was accompanied by an unexpected addition. Likely not more than thirteen inches in its height, the creature's name was Tea and it was black and fluffy.[52] It wasn't long before this poodle and its playmate became part and parcel of Maria's image. The second inductee—a taller one—had to endure a complicated journey to Milan. In 1956 American journalist George de Carvalho—whom Maria would later come close to suing for libel—had promised a Callas fan he would deliver this gift to the singer.

It turned out to be a live one—so much so that de Carvalho was unable to transport it by himself.[53] The buck was passed to RAI broadcaster Mike Buongiorno, who conveyed the dog in a large paper bag through customs and a long-haul flight of some ten hours. Throughout this span it nestled stealthily behind his knees. A mysterious individual de Carvalho had appointed to collect it showed up at Rome's airport.[54] From the capital it made its way to the soprano's hometown[55]—where the animal immediately became Maria's center of attention: in her own words "the little monster of the house." Color-coordinating with his fellow poodle Tea, the misfit was named Toy. "Well—what name could you *give* a little thing like that?" she asked.[56]

Common knowledge had it that Maria treated her beloved poodles as Egyptians had their cats. Crowded by encircling paparazzi as she disembarked in Spain in 1959, she was asked if Toy liked opera. Eyeing the enquirers as though they were berserk, Maria pointedly corrected: "No. Toy likes to dance."[57]

Walter Legge was already at the end of his tether when Maria brought little Tea to the recording of *Norma* that April 1954. At two years old he offered yelps and outbursts of excitement scarcely serviceable to the record.[58]

The press was there to write up a report. They watched Maria reach to take Ebe Stignani's hand in "Mira, o Norma," the duet between the heroine and Adalgisa. Her and Meneghini's chauffeur "kept wandering in and out of the hall. Bored."[59]

Staying until 2 am to get the phrases right, Maria's stubbornness made EMI responsible for ordering the fifty taxis that her colleagues needed to get home.[60]

By this time she was the undisputed and resplendent prima donna of La Scala. Fans knew it, the administration knew it and she—gleefully—knew it. Closing the 1953–54 season with Verdi's *Don Carlo*, she found herself showered in gifts by that former foe, Ghiringhelli: the superintendent of La Scala who had vowed Callas would "never, never" be a regular. A silver bowl, a chandelier and a silver-backed mirror were some of the trophies he tendered her.[61] Superfluously honeyed notes were scribed by him: "Dear Maria, please accept my affection . . . What do you deserve, Maria? All the happiness in the world."[62]

Her glories at La Scala were "an electricity [that comes] from the electrician, from the stage designer . . . from the feeling of team work . . . from the *Maestro* . . . La Scala gave us the possibility to give the *best* of ourselves. And the public felt it and the public gave us fame; they gave us something they felt we had *deserved*. It was a happy marriage. A very, very happy marriage that is difficult to forget . . . That is the famous fever . . . the magical atmosphere."[63]

At the end of her final *Don Carlos* an audience member yelled "Regina della Scala!" ("Queen of La Scala"). Another wandered to the stage and shouted, "Arrivederci, Maria!"

"You know, we can hear them shouting, but we can't hear *what* they shout," was Maria's reaction when a reporter informed her. "I'm so happy to know it's so nice."

"They loved you in *Don Carlos*," the interviewer told. "But I don't think I'll ever hear anything like the reception they gave you after *Lucia*."

"What!" came the response. "Have you forgotten? I haven't done *Traviata* yet!" "This was three quarters a joke," concluded the journalist. "Almost exactly three quarters."[64]

Already emulated as a fashion icon, Maria composed other facets of her image with a like precision. The soprano wasn't one for tailoring her reputation: no hub of minions typed her future soundbites out around the clock. Nevertheless the person that Maria was in interviews was her most sharpened self.

First of all there was the accent. Having once proffered—according to Walter Legge—the parlance of G.I. American soldiers, Maria now spoke with a body of inflections that suggested "Bond Street rather than the Bronx."[65] Asked how her U.S. dialect had vanished by a Danish newspaper in 1963, she insisted: "I worked my way out of it, little by little."[66]

Yet every now and then across her glossary of interviews we hear an "off" that sounds a little "*awff*" à la the Rat Pack or a Katharine Hepburn, Bryn Mawr-crafted "*dawg*". Vowels are dappled all the while in tinges of Italian or Greek curves and there's a crunchy Spanish "k" resounding when she uses the word "scream".

Glasses weren't abhorrent to her; on occasion she would wear them to her interviews.[67] Contact lenses caused her irritation.[68]

Hoping to come off as upper crust, Maria made deft use of diplomatic cordialities like "Shall we say," "very possibly" and "with pleasure." She once even apologized for using the word "job" in a sentence "because it's so—*vulgar*."[69]

Occasionally she visited the Milanese salons: those quarters that housed cliques of the Italian aristocracy. Most of the time her company confined itself to singers, maestri and musicians who met almost daily at La Scala's Biffi restaurant.[70] Resenting being thought a haughty demon, Maria argued to an interviewer: "I live for all this, believe me. I live for my husband and our life together. For my piano, which I love. For my television, which I like to watch. I love parties but I adore my work still more, and my home and especially my privacy—which is why I am sometimes called a recluse."[71]

Efforts to appear relatable and down to earth were frequently aplenty. Behind closed doors Maria freely ate ice cream out of the carton.[72] Asked by interviewer Norman Ross to pronounce her full name [Kalogeropoulou], she slyly enquired: "You *ready?*"

Yet the preservation of her introvertedness was always a priority. "If people watch me when I'm working I get extremely shy," Maria would avow. "Especially in rehearsals I can't stand people looking at me. It makes me feel closed in."[73]

Day and night were separate entities cleft almost like a werewolf's meta-morphosis. "Nobody knew just how relaxed and easygoing Maria could be in everyday life, when she was picked up in the morning for a walk, to go shopping, to run errands, talking about this and that and mutual acquaint-ances," Giovanna Lomazzi would muse. "But when the time drew closer to when she had to go to the theatre for a rehearsal, she seemed to close up in her shell, and walking toward Via Filodrammatici [of La Scala] the expres-sion on her face would change, would develop graven lines."[74]

That June Maria recorded Leoncavallo's *Pagliacci*, which was eventually released together with Mascagni's *Cavalleria rusticana*. Nedda the heroine is married to Canio, enamored with Silvio, and coveted by the sleaze Tonio. Duplicitous and fanciful, she is an actress. The colors of Maria's voice in this recording are the differently shaped faces on an iridescent prism: dark flashes are emitted to reflect Nedda's derision of the lusty Tonio; sunrays limn the zeniths of her dreams.

In a crucial moment Nedda recollects the ditty about bird flight that her mother sang to her in childhood. The aria begins on a low note with Nedda newly terrified of her possessive husband Canio, a bestial man who will conclude their onstage spectacle by stabbing her to death declaring: "La commedia è finita" ("The show's over").

Nedda ponders the torturous flame in his gaze ("Qual fiamma avea nel guardo"). The voice for this role is initially designed with shades of tar; traits of Medea. And yet that stretchy limberness unwinds elastically until the timbre is twig-thin. With her propensity for flinging these staccati notes we learn that the trapped Nedda—who had come across as a repressed wife—is a woman frivolous and frolicsome; capricious and impressionably insecure.

Enraptured juvenility suffuses the vibrato in the soaring high notes through "Questi assetati d'azzurro e di splendor" ("Those birds thirsty for blue and splendor"); the instrument is not yet tattered by experience. Onomatopoeia is created: as the birds fly past the sea's abyss ("sugli abissi e i mar") the "mar" succumbs to slow diminuendo as we watch the lofty creatures shrink in flight.

Then there's the other Nedda: cruel and mindless. Her caustic tones crunch like a grinder in her coarse command: "Tell me, Tonio—does your back need a scratching today—or perhaps what your love needs is a good *ear*-pulling?" ("La schiena oggi vi prude, o una tirata d'orecchi è necessaria al vostro ardor?"). The sound is ruthless; so organic as to seem almost *parlando* (spoken singing). When Tonio threatens to alert the vicious Canio to her affair with Silvio, she dictatorially demands: "Orsù, parla!" ("Come on, speak out!"). Stripped of its sheen, the voice is shredded somewhat—yet its virulent vibrato ekes out eeriness.

It is a gallery of the mercurial Nedda's thoughts: psychologies amalgamated.

July 1954 saw Maria's last venture at the Arena di Verona: that once-prestigious site of her Italian debut. Singing the role of Margherita in

Arrigo Boito's *Mefistofele*, a work based upon on Goethe's *Faust*, Maria dismally discovered the Arena stopped short of her standards.

Rehearsing with conductor Fausto Cleva in the pit, she suddenly became enmeshed in an imbroglio that concerned their forthcoming *Aïda*. The maestro's attitude convinced her that he didn't know the music well enough[75] and suddenly she quit.[76]

Yet he wasn't the main reason that Maria never again sang at the Arena di Verona. "It's really becoming a genuine stadium," she professed to Lomazzi. "Young men sell drinks throughout the opera; people chat and sometimes even laugh."[77]

The lack of a recording of *Mefistofele* (just one aria from it features as part of the compilation album *Lyric and Coloratura Arias*) is a musical loss. Margherita kills her illegitimate baby, poisons her mother and goes mad in prison.

Yet her principal aria "L'altra notte al fondo al mare" has her convinced she did none of these things. In Maria's only published treatment of the character we hear a woman suffering hallucinosis: thoughts recur and recur and recur, resounding identically in her head every time. Margherita commands her soul to fly like a sparrow away: "Vola, vola, vola via!" Augmenting with these notes, the tentative crescendi are transfixing: proof the lost one has no path to follow but the grooves of her unwinding spiral. It's madness of a caliber Lucia couldn't rival.

Meanwhile Meneghini was doing his utmost to capitalize on his wife's newfound fame. RAI, Italy's premier broadcaster, proposed a televised *Traviata*.

Visconti was up in arms. "Have you ever seen a production on television? Not to mention—an *opera* production? My God! My God! To me it's the nastiest, most anti-artistic, counter-productive spectacle we have today—of all days ... a horrendous cinematographic output, a prison with no respite—with no life, no vigor," he bemoaned to Meneghini.[78]

Three days later Meneghini wrote back to allege his wife—for this "lousy" television project—was requiring five million lire.[79] But there was never any evidence for that. Maria never ceded to the concept. Recalling the discussions without having read her husband and Visconti's correspondence, she declared: "I can't see opera on the screen—I'm not convinced it would look right. My husband wanted me to make a film. I was thoroughly against it. I believe opera should stay in its own frame, otherwise it might look ridiculous."[80]

So she had been the scapegoat for her husband's falsified excuses.

*

Since summer was La Scala's designated period to make records, Maria spent two weeks of August working on Verdi's *La forza del destino*. Given its' dates' proximity to her *Pagliacci*, *Il turco in Italia* and the *Lyric and Coloratura Arias* and *Puccini Heroines* compilation albums, it's an ominous anomaly.

Donna Leonora is horrifically afflicted. A Spanish countess resident in eighteenth-century Seville, she is enamored with the enemy, Alvaro: an Inca. But in Maria's 1954 rendition Leonora is not suffering as much she is *strained* by an unfinished instrument. There is almost too much frailty in the slender timbre of "Me pellegrina ed orfana" ("I was an orphan, and they took me far away from my home"). The throbbing, shaking sound behind "dannato a eterno pianto" ("condemned to weep eternally") is not as much a reinforcement of the woman's pain as it is accidental. The romantic "Ah, per sempre!" duet is panic-ridden rather than passionate.

During the recording Walter Legge immediately discerned the shaky sound along the top and middle of Maria's voice. "I told her if we dared publish the records Angel and EMI would have to give away a seasickness pill with every side, which we could not afford." Disheartened, she began to work hard to eradicate this unexpected nuisance. Dining with Legge and his wife Elisabeth Schwarzkopf at a Milanese restaurant, she walked in, barely greeted them and called on the soprano's help: "Show me how you sing top A's and B's and make a diminuendo on them. Walter says mine make him seasick."

Amidst the patrons of the restaurant Maria struggled with the practice of her notes as Schwarzkopf pressed her diaphragm, her lower jaw, her ribs and throat to check if the right tremors were emerging. The student finally declared: "I think I've got it. I'll call you in the morning when I've tried it out."

The next day Maria claimed that it had worked.[81] But the recording still sounds like an incomplete and tense rendition.

Less than a month later magic seemed to have expunged the flaw. Tackling the most difficult pieces for the *Lyric and Coloratura Arias* compilation album, Maria sang Meyerbeer's "Ombra leggera" from his *Dinorah*. The composer is renowned for filling his interminable operas with the fussiest, most needless, long-winded coloratura. His music prompted Wagner's vehement anti-Semitic hate and a campaign against him. As Dinorah dances with her shadow, sprightly leaps across wide intervals and super-high notes symbolize her physical agility. With insurpassable insouciance Maria's voice pursues the flute-spawn melody by chasing it as though it *were* the shadow; scattering like a nomadic bumblebee.

The Bell Song from Delibes' *Lakmé* ("Dov'è l'indiana bruna?") features on the same album. In this opera about Hindus in the British Raj, Maria paints the notes of Lakmé (in Sanskrit "Lakshmi") with an oriental flavor; trills ring with the crystal-clear vibration of the trembling tambourines. When her character sings of a "squilla" or "squilletta"—the sound of a bell—it almost sounds as though her mouth is now half-closed: a muffled, artificial instrument. The feat is daring for a human voice—and works.

Mysteriously Maria's vocal shortcomings had slipped into oblivion.

Since 1953, Chicago-based young woman Carol Fox had hoped to found an opera company. Maria had dismissed this project with great ease; such plans had hit her ears before without fruition. This time however, Fox—together with her partners, impresario Lawrence Kelly and conductor Nicola Rescigno—wanted the soprano to be recognized as a co-founder. A mere formality, the title would require no investment on her part.[82]

In October 1954 Maria journeyed to the city to perform her long-awaited North American debut: *Norma* at the newly-founded Lyric Opera. A press delegation appointed by Kelly arrested her as she stepped down from the plane. Taken aback, she introduced her husband, accepted a bouquet from chorus members come to greet her and departed for Ambassador West Hotel.[83]

Bombarding Kelly with enquiries, Maria pressed on to unveil the full itinerary: where the other artists were, the schedule of rehearsals, what staging they would have, whether or not Maestro Rescigno would employ appropriate tempi . . . In one of *Norma*'s first rehearsals she performed "Casta diva" nine times.[84]

Adopting this young opera house as her first U.S. home was like escorting a new poodle to the vet for its first checks. Everyone had to be vetted. Maria had already tested Nicola Rescigno in Milan: "I'm *very* particular about certain things so would you mind that we go over certain things?" she had requested clumsily. "I knew that this was an examination," he remembered. "[But] from then on, we sort of spoke the same language."[85]

Together with Meneghini Maria had brought father George. And in between the crazy efforts at rehearsals, in between a frantic rainstorm that led Giulietta Simionato to fly in at the last minute after singing *La sonnambula* in Mexico and prompt Maria to exclaim, "Giulia—you make me so mad—you're a robot, not a singer!"[86] she shopped at supermarkets, cooked pasta for the family[87] and almost burned the kitchen of her suite down when she tried to bake a meat pie. Clotting clouds of smoke set off the drill and management was forced to call the fire department.[88]

When it came to that debut on 1 November 1954 Maria had a whole new public to bewitch.

It didn't take long. "I was glued in wonderment to my cheap seat in the upper balcony of the Chicago Civic Opera House for at least 10 minutes after the last curtain," one would-be journalist recalled.[89] "[The voice] is produced with such ease that at times it seemed to float in the air, an entity in itself, quite independent of any human agency. She has become extremely slender, a twenty-two-inch waist, and she is very girlish . . . with enormous, darkly outlined eyes, an archaic Greek profile . . ." was Leo Lerman's description.[90]

The *Chicago Tribune*'s music critic Claudia Cassidy—notoriously hard to please—was not impenetrable this time round: "Wand-slim, tragic mask of face, wonderful hands, and above all that voice. Formidable in range, dazzling in technique with the sound of the mourning dove." Later on she would remember, "Total strangers wrote me at *The Tribune*—'I see what you mean. I never really heard opera before.' "[91]

A couple of hours later the soprano was escorted to the Angel Ball at Hilton Hotel[92] "in a pale blue slightly bouffant gown, and magnificently diamonded." The sorcery was over and Maria was displaying—probably unwittingly—her other side. The kind that peered through gold-rimmed, jeweled harlequin glasses at the ball's ice show. "So antithetical to the glorious *Norma*," Leo Lerman related.[93] But it was the same spell. It merely liked to morph into another guise from time to time.

Attending the Lyric Opera's *La bohème* the next day, Maria was applauded in her role as Audience Member. "Nothing like that ever happened to me before," she remarked. "I was delayed getting there, and when I heard the clapping I thought the maestro must be entering the orchestra pit. When I realized they were applauding me, I didn't know what to do. I never heard of such a thing before, and it was wonderful."[94]

Predictably the headiness would meet with swift suspension. Maria's former "manager"—her onetime romantic interest and friend, Eddie Bagarozy—had heard of the soprano's not-so-overnight success. He wanted it made public that the product had been manufactured at his factory. Back in 1947 she had signed a contract with him he believed would prove her worldly goods were his.

Laying a contract breach lawsuit at the feet of the singer, Bagarozy caused a stir by spuriously alleging he had spent $85,000 on the part of his ex-client. Because the contract was a ten-year one and it was only 1954, this meant that Bagarozy—in his own words—was entitled to Maria's fortunes for the next three years, as well as ten per cent not just from fees of past performances but future profits from recordings.[95]

Dodging due process, he had someone break into Maria's hotel suite to hunt for blackmail bait.[96] Maria countered the false charges by responding that he owed *her* money: the five hundred dollars of her ship fare he had taken, promising to buy a ticket.[97] Circuit Court eventually ruled it was impossible for Bagarozy to sue Callas in Chicago: neither was a resident of Illinois.[98]

But that wasn't the end of that story.

The Callas hype was unabating nonetheless. About Maria's *Traviata* Claudia Cassidy wrote, "Its glittering brilliance spun into shadow play as feverish excitements sent feathery scales descending like falling leaves. She rivaled Garbo's Camille."[99] Her *Lucia* there elicited twenty-two curtain calls after her final Chicago performance on 17 November.[100]

For over three years now Maria and Visconti had been pals. Though often Meneghini had responded to the count's epistles on her part, she sustained this special kinship with affection. Vacationing in Venice that August she had written to ask, "Any chance you'll come by? I would be happy to have you here with me a little while. I'm doing well and have tanned nicely. Let me know your news."[101]

Despite his well-known homosexuality, Visconti relished courting prima donnas in the gallantly old-fashioned sense. His idol being Marcel Proust, he once hoped to transform *A la recherche du temps perdu* into a film with a script penned by Harold Pinter. The seven-volume novel devotes many pages to the fictional stage actress Berma, allegedly based on the iconic Sarah Bernhardt. As Proust had adulated Bernhardt, so Visconti played the same role in Maria's life; regaling the soprano with new earrings on the eve of a La Scala *Norma*. These would in turn be given by Maria to Montserrat Caballé when *she* debuted in *Norma*.[102]

When Visconti's assistant Beppe Menegatti delivered Maria a stack of her photographs, she signed one with the dedication: "To Luca, from your Maria." Their dinners would be long; Maria always being last to leave the restaurant. "If I'm the first to go, everyone who stays behind will later tear me to pieces," she once commented.[103]

Their embarkation on a lyrical collaboration was a mystifying choice: Spontini's 1805 Classical work, *La vestale*. Set in Ancient Rome in 269BC, it follows sacrilegious vestal virgin Giulia, who has betrayed her cause by falling hopelessly in love with warrior Licinio. When the sacred fire of Vesta—an eternal flame symbolic of the pledge of chastity—dies out as Giulia and Licinio declare love, the High Priest and Vestal Priestess vow to punish her by burying the girl alive. A thunderstorm provokes a change of heart and the spared Giulia is free to run into Licinio's arms.

Visconti's production at La Scala cost over $150,000 (a million, seven hundred fifty in today's terms).[104] Maria persuaded the director to consider young tenor Franco Corelli for the role of Licinio: "She was responsible for my debut at La Scala . . . I have to say that she rather protects me," he would note later.[105]

To shape Maria's movements in the role, Visconti studied paintings by Canova, David and Ingres. "Her gestures thrilled you," he would tell biographer John Ardoin. "Where did she learn them? On her own. But with *La vestale*, we began systematically to perfect them left and right. We selected some from the great French tragediennes, some from Greek drama, for this was the kind of actress she could be—classic."[106]

With a backdrop of "white marble, moon-struck marble"[107] the production was drenched in a dreamy façade. Its surreal nature was made more bewitching by Visconti's choice to stage this Ancient Roman drama's setting in Napoleonic times. In that era *La vestale* had been *all* the rage, prompting Napoleon II's noticeably pregnant wife, Queen Hortense, to appear at a society ball dressed as a vestal virgin.[108] The director's spectacle had ermine cloaks, laurel wreaths, feathered hats and Licinio clad in a velvet cape and a gold helmet: purportedly Napoleon himself.

Ten thousand carnations filled the auditorium on the opening night of 7 December 1954. Presented with a bounteous bouquet after Act II, Maria tossed one of the bunch to Toscanini, who was sat in the proscenium box.[109]

Difficult to place characteristically, the vestal virgin alternates between indignant, infantile impatience and a persevering piety throughout her diffident diminuendi. Her desire to nurture her lover—as heard in Maria's smooth, endeared portamento in "Ti vedrò" ("I will see you")—pours out despite a strained attempt to remain noble.

The opera's equivalent of a mad scene, "Tu che invoco con orrore" ("You whom I invoke with horror") is the only testament to Giulia's ire. Peppering the high notes with an agony-fueled, dense vibrato and a darkly scathing sound, Maria makes her bold plea to the heavens to "reject her prayers" ("Ricusa i voti miei") render a coarse timbre detrimental to her cause. While offering the servile supplication of apology the vestal virgin accidentally *dares* the deity.

Visconti's niece Cristina Gastel would recall Maria cowering behind her veil in shame; relating how the voice imparted "colors suggesting something fragile and childish that implied [Giulia]'s innocence before her salvation."[110]

Though critics did not warm to the director's risk-ridden experiment, their recognition of Maria's attitude to Classical composers turned a corner. One claimed, "Her prevalent moments were those of restraint; the lack of abrupt attacks, the way she permitted the music to breathe."[111]

New Year's Day 1955 was spent in the hearth of domestic simplicity at the house of Giovanna Lomazzi. "Around us she seemed like a little girl who was sensing, for the first time, the warmth of a familial atmosphere . . ." the hostess recollected. "It was a very bourgeois evening, so to speak."[112]

In the meantime the Meneghinis had officially moved to Milan—and were now living at 40 Via Buonarroti: a four-story home with wrought-iron staircases[113] furnished "splendidly in the seventeenth-century Venetian style," according to one journalist. "White walls, gold draperies, deep Oriental rugs, pink roses in crystal bowls everywhere, red and gray marble floors . . . Its occupant seems a myopic little girl in the midst of opulent splendor."[114]

Panic-plighted was the first month of the year when Mario Del Monaco—the notorious tenor scheduled to sing Manrico in *Il trovatore*—abruptly demanded the opera be swapped with fan-favorite *Andrea Chénier*. A twentieth-century classic, Giordano's opera is derided for its brassy outbursts of *verismo*.

When Ghiringhelli ceded to Del Monaco's request, Maria had five days to learn the role. The daughter of a countess in the French Revolution, Maddalena di Coigny is lusted after by her vile servant Gérard, who's on the cusp of rebellion. Andrea Chénier is a poet who writes of the woes of the poor and the derelict. An insouciant material girl, Maddalena is inspired through Chénier to seek redemption through love. Between acts the revolutionaries slay the countess; maid Bersi is forced to prostitute herself to care for Maddalena. Though the latter escapes death by condemnation, she trades places with a woman on the brink of execution—opting to be killed beside Chénier.

Something in *Andrea Chénier* sparks iridescent shimmers. Situated in a sphere of famine, guillotines and bloodshed, its immersive music paradoxically gleams with silvery and star-shaped rays of sunlight. Opera teaches us again that death is beauty.

Maria was allured by the spoilt rich kid-turned noblewoman "capable of the ultimate sacrifice."[115] Witnessing her in the role, Leonard Bernstein wrote his wife Felicia: "I heard her as Maddalena in *Andrea Chénier*, and she was a divine coquette of 17 or so, completely believable!"[116] Giordano's widow attended the opening night, praising Maria. It was the closest that she ever got to confirmation that she had fulfilled a dead composer's dreams.

Whilst her recording of the famous aria "La mamma morta"—which features prominently in the 1995 movie *Philadelphia*—is a part of the *Lyric and Coloratura Arias* compilation, in that rendition she is ceremonious. Applying cavernousness to her voice, she overlooks the woman's age and circumstance.

As a recording lays bare, all of Maddalena's colors were in evidence that January 8th: aristocratic, ostentatious, vulnerable and love-intoxicated. The role is secondary in the opera yet Maria makes it more about the chrysalis of Maddalena than Chénier's traumatic plight. Each moment is a shift in character. At first we're greeted with a nubile and derisive voice: high-pitched, bright, bouncing delicately in staccato as the prancing girl shares sordid anecdotes.

Following her life's destruction between acts, Maddalena's voice is bitterer; encompassing both trenchant tones and dire destitution. Begging Chénier to love her—"Son sola e minacciata! Son sola al mondo! Ed ho paura! . . . Proteggermi volete? Spero in voi!" ("I am alone and threatened! I am alone in this world! And I'm frightened! Do you want to protect me? I have faith in you!")—her urgency devolves into a shy enquiry; the tardy crescendo on "volete" ("Do you want . . .") suggesting a humbled advance.

When rebel-leader Gérard demands Maddalena prostitute herself to ensure Chénier's safety, desperation lends her voice a needle-like acuity. "Il mio corpo, ebbene, prendimi!" ("Then, take my body—take it!") she sings in surrender. Grave and dusky tones precede a bloodcurdling scream that stays strangely melodious. Those final words of "take me" ("prendimi") are uttered with such softness, shame is palpable in their diminuendo.

"La mamma morta"—Maddalena's monologue about her mother being killed before her eyes—is taken with a slower attitude than in the compilation album. No more a fanciful Shakespearean soliloquy, it blossoms into an epiphany.

Maddalena recollects her tortured past: how rebels burned her palace down and she was all alone. A gap of contemplation lingers in between the two halves of the word alone, "sola". Guilt percolates the line "Porto sventura a chi bene mi vuole!" ("I bring misfortune to anyone who loves me!") as she recalls how Bersi sold her body to feed both of them. Vibrato throbs all through "sventura" ("misfortune"): a human instrument so shame-riddled, it trembles.

For a while it almost seems as though we are transported to a higher realm: the gods must be in force. As Maddalena evokes the true bliss of her newly found love with the iron command, "Vivi ancora! Io son la vita!" ("Go on and live! I am life itself!") it resounds with fateful ecstasy caught even in the specially rolled "r"s of "Sorridi e spera" ("Smile and hope").

That rolled "r" hits our ears again when Maddalena comes to tell Chénier that she is dying with him in the "Vicino a te" duet ("Vengo a morire con te"): euphoria arises from her imminent expiry. With every instruction she gives to her lover before they are sentenced to perish—"Abbracciami! Baciami! Amante!" ("Embrace me! Kiss me! Lover!")—a novel, more potent crescendo expands. Upon being asked if she is Idia Le Gray—the woman she will substitute—her zealous outburst of "Son io!" ("That is I!") gleams sword-like with infrangible resolve. Death will bring her home.

Del Monaco did not regard the spectacle as a celestial chapter. Though a noisy claque strived hard to sabotage both their performances,[117] he charged Maria's husband with a plot to make La Scala's devotees believe his peak to be in peril. "Del Monaco—you're dreaming," Meneghini responded according to Giovanna Lomazzi. "Maria Callas doesn't need a claque."[118]

That wasn't the end of that argument. Eleven months later, during a Scala production of *Norma* that featured the pair, Meneghini would accuse the tenor of employing his own claque to vex Maria. He would even go so far as to complain to Ettore Parmeggiani, official "claque chief," to mourn the bygone days of comparably civil claques.[119] Assuming this to be Maria's personal vendetta, Del Monaco distributed a far-and-wide told fabrication: she had "kicked him in the shins."

"Can you imagine the picture of measly little me kicking a great big man like Mario Del Monaco in the shins, and he being so pain-stricken that he couldn't even get the curtain call?" was the rhetorical rejoinder that Maria offered to a question on the rumor. "You can imagine a tenor that would miss a curtain call; I still have to *see* him."[120]

Del Monaco would later admit, "Much has been said about the clamorous clash between us . . . no one talks about other aspects of our artistic coexistence in various parts of the globe, which denote sincere mutual respect. One has to look at both sides of the coin."[121] But the damage was done. In the eyes of many, Maria Callas was fast becoming the traditionally egotistic nineteenth century diva.

Another problem glossed this image. Though Maria had cemented a *La traviata* album only two years previously, in 1955 she planned a new edition. Since the latter had been a release for rival label, Cetra, EMI demanded that she wait until four years had passed. The muse hoped that the godly Serafin would join her in anticipation—and was startled when he opted to record the work with Antonietta Stella in her stead. She conceded later that she was "upset and annoyed."[122] *Time* magazine would mold the story into something sinister: insisting that Maria had attacked him publicly. "A devil with evil instincts," Serafin had allegedly labeled her.[123]

"Accusations of that kind are absurd . . ." Maria refuted. "It's not true that I eliminated Serafin from my records,"[124] although she elected to record a few operas with Antonino Votto. If an impasse came to pass it didn't last that long. By 1 January 1957 Serafin was sending her a New Year's telegram that told of his "eternal affection" and wished her "infinite luck."[125]

Many relish the conceit that fervid opera-singing can be spawned by crazy geniuses alone. It would be foolish to imply that Callas was a totally serene, completely reserved human being. There were moments that extracted silly or insensitive remarks; times that permitted rage to guide her thoughts.

"Hisses and yells do not frighten me, for I am not a stranger to the enmity of claques," she once professed. "They only make me furious, make me want to sing better than ever to drive the rudeness down their throats."[126] Another time she spilled: "When any of my colleagues can do in fifty years—no, make it a hundred—what I have done already with my 'Norma' or 'Sonnambula,' then maybe they can ride on the back of my publicity."[127] By her own admission it was true that "If one gives me a piece of advice in a brusque way, I can become *really* savage. But with kindness . . . you can get *anything* from me."[128]

Irrationality took place. In one particularly messy moment during the Chicago 1954 *La traviata*, technical impediments led Tito Gobbi to take endless curtain calls at Act II's culmination. Unaware that there were problems with the stage curtain, Maria feared that he was trying to steal her thunder—nearing him in spite to state: "You must understand that I will not allow anyone to interfere with the success of *my Traviata*. If you ever do such a thing again I will ruin your career." But following an explanation of the situation and her colleague's humbling point that *Traviata* was not *hers* but Verdi's, she enquired of him in a bashfully minute voice, "Tito, are you angry with me?" And the bass forgave her everything.[129]

Most of the time it was Maria's mantra to consider both sides of an argument. Her purpose, as she later explicated, was to "simplify" a situation. Partly on account of this she very frequently employed conjunctions in her speech to make it orderly: "however," "moreover," "as well as" were frequent additions.

The woman could defend a coherent opinion. "To simplify habitually you need not only the right kind of mind, but the right kind of temperament," she would expound. "You must be cool, capable of being cool, and want to be cool. Many people *want* to raise the temperature. Always. It is as though they had a kind of low emotional blood pressure—they feel they cannot do anything, cannot exist, cannot function unless they work themselves up."[130]

This was not Maria Callas.

"What I value most are normal reactions to anything."[131]

*

That February something quite abnormal left her bedridden. With a large boil on the back of her neck, Maria was unable to finish her series of

Andrea Chénier.[132] Young soprano Gigliola Frazzoni filled in for the final performance in February.[133]

In the meantime Bernstein had been called upon to lead Bellini's *La sonnambula*: an opera strange, old-fashioned and romantic. Simultaneously he was in the throes of composition with *Candide*[134] and *West Side Story*. After the cast and crew of the production discovered the postponement of *Sonnambula* on account of Maria's condition, one night ballerina Carla Fracci popped in to see Bernstein at the Hotel Duomo. A Steinway sat there. With Maria absent, that night Bernstein introduced a revelation—the song that he had scribed for a new Juliet who shared the singer's name.[135]

The former was hard-pressed to understand the title role of "Sleepwalker" in this incomprehensible bel canto work of the same name. Young Amina is a provincial Swiss resident in a small village in an unspecified era. Ecstatically engaged to her adoring beau Elvino, she is horrified to be accused by jealous Lisa of adultery. Why? Because Amina sleepwalks at night. When the villagers discover this unlucky ailment, she is finally acquitted. Happy Ending. That's the story.

After studying the score and listening to a recording by legendary soprano Toti dal Monte, Maria insisted the vocal lines resembled "a stupid bird."[136] Bernstein himself admitted that the orchestra "doesn't have too much more to do than a series of arpeggios."[137]

Eventually she ceded to the opera's innocuous trance. "It is an *intenseness* . . . it is a *smoothness* that . . . always *must* exist; but there are times when it's a—*purer* smoothness, it's . . . more of a *dreamy* or *poetic* . . ." she described elliptically.[138]

Under Visconti's direction Maria would rehearse in La Scala's hall of mirrors: its ballroom. In self-scrutiny she checked her gestures' elegance.[139]

Throughout these sessions she came close to stumbling at the summit of her self-exertion. While Visconti tried to calm her down she was compulsively insistent: "I couldn't continue—at a certain moment, I had to sit down. It was 3:30 in the morning."[140] Nevertheless she would go on. And *on*. "Her detractors think she is some sort of supernatural creature— half-woman, half-witch—who lives only for the theatre," an *Opera News* feature once stated.[141]

But—no. According to Maria, they just didn't get it. "It's not only *work*," she explained to an interviewer. "It's so much *love* . . . You discover new things, new expressions, new *legati*, new—*everything*, you know; each day you find something new and something wonderful. Of course, you put yourself up to a harder work and a more *strenuous* work, because you ask of *your* instrument, which is human, you ask . . . what another instrument which is *not* human but is guided *by* human nature—*does*. So, it's rather difficult."[142]

Visconti's staging was comprised of gentle pastel colors, silks and frills. Maria would be wearing moonstones. Bernstein was excited to be part of an integral whole: "I've never worked so close to a show: really into everything: painting the sets, & spending one hour arguing about the color of the cuff of a sleeve of one costume for one chorus-lady, and kind of co-directing with Luchino [Visconti], & planning out every second. I'm learning, learning," he wrote to his wife.[143]

In this surreal interpretation of an unrealistic opera, a waxing moon became a full moon overnight.[144] Maria was directed to have "steps like those of a ballerina, and when she stood still, she took a dancer's fifth position," in the words of costume designer Piero Tosi. "Neo-Gothic wood beams—the kind of wood that by night gives off the color of pale violet . . ." had been installed onstage. "When the Count touched her shoulder, she fell to the floor, but very softly, with her legs crossed like a Margot Fonteyn."[145] At one point Maria had to mimic almost falling off a bridge amidst her sleepwalk. Eyeing her closely, Tosi watched Maria's breathing simulate this perilous effect; her exhalation was so rapid that her shoulders sank.[146]

"She must have the *vibration* of her anxieties and her suffering," Maria observed. "But it's during *slumber*; she is 'La sonnambula' so—it's very difficult vocally."[147]

Indeed the voice one hears in the recording of the first *Sonnambula* on March 5th 1955 is so elastic, it comes close to self-endangerment. Breezy, light and harmless, Amina is a glow-in-the-dark damselfly. The accentuations in her dazed voice—such as her address to well-wishers with the stressed "PA" of "Care compagne" ("dear friends")—sound almost superfluous. But Amina is a sleepwalker in a mysterious and mystical time. She *is* superfluous.

Again we have the onomatopoeic traits: Amina sings of how she feels her heart palpating, leaping: "Palpitar, balzar lo senti." The "zar" of "balzar" shines with thick vibrato; quivers in Amina's voice invite us to her throbbing heart. So overcome is she with glee that the descent of a chromatic scale in "Non ha forza a sostener" ("It cannot sustain itself, this joy") escapes with airy, sweet exasperation.

The sleepwalking itself is furnished with an instrument that almost droops in frailty: floating, ebbing, struggling to sustain itself for abstinent alertness. At times it dissolves in crepuscular energy; somnolent semi-consciousness. When Amina refers to her desire to die ("more") each repeated pronouncement is feebler. Even the signature aria of lost love "Ah, non credea mirarti," is cautiously sung: wavering, slender. Her chance for love slips through her fingers in a long diminuendo on "amor." Bernstein found this pianissimo so insurpassably extraordinary that, according to director Franco Zeffirelli writing in the 1980s, "Today . . . when Lenny wants more pianissimo from an orchestra, he asks them for a 'Callas pianissimo.' "[148]

Amina suffers—in sleep.

Her celebratory cabaletta at the opera's end, "Ah, non giunge," was performed with house lights raised and flowers generously aflight.[149] When

Amina understands Elvino's love is persevering she commands "M'abbraccia!" ("Embrace me!") with a larger crescendo and emboldened vibrato; she is a *bride* after all. The broken arpeggios performed on staccato unfurl with the bounces of silk-enlaced bobbins.

These kinds of moments would be everlastingly engraved upon Maria's mind. "The most beautiful memories for me are when a public—when you manage to explain yourself to the *public* . . . it is under your *influence* . . . under your *magnetism*. *Those* are the most beautiful moments. When you have a piece that is one of *extreme* difficulty; even if it's just a melody— theirs is an extreme *poetry* that I love so much because—more than the difficulty, I love the *atmosphere*. The kind that the composers loved—the moment when you can hear the silence afterwards, when you can listen to it—hold your breath—just before the explosion."[150]

Ironically Maria's journey as an actress was still waiting for its passage to begin; seated at dawn and being cradled like a baby by Aurora's fingertips.

9.

"Chantilly"

Her fame eroded like old costumes shedding glitter, the once-cherished prima donna wasn't emulated in the twentieth century. Around mundane colloquialisms such as "It ain't over till the fat lady sings" prevailed a vulgar stereotype: a paunchy woman playing someone dying from consumption with a bulging stomach testing out her waistband. For all their vocal might, stars like Tebaldi weren't on course to substitute the glossy prints of James Dean or Grace Kelly on a teen's walls.

"An artist *develops* in *years*," Maria proclaimed. "Ah—shall we *say* that *now*, you *become* a tamed *animal*; before, you're just—you know, you just do things by *instinct*."[1] Circus troupes had stage presence—as did ventriloquists. The struggle of sustaining disbelief in opera was a battle with the art itself: those risible libretti. The kind that allows fugitives to cry *fortissimo*: "Andiam, andiam!" ("Let's go, let's go!") while they stand still like soldiers ready for inspection. "Sometimes they can be so nonsensical and so out of place that, try as you may, you just hate saying them," Maria said of her relationship with operatic text. "Sometimes when I first read the libretto I can't help laughing and I think: 'Well, I hope I can keep serious at this phrase— it's really the *most!*' "[2]

In this respect it's almost difficult to blame the other singers for *not* trying. With lofty notes enough to garner bullions of applause, heroines who die to rescue undeserving men, impersonators and mistaken identities, libretti often feel like shtick in a *commedia dell'arte* play. Only in this genre can a character convincingly recite a monologue whilst bleeding with a knife stuck in their heart. And only in this genre could a Tosca attempt suicide by jumping off a roof—then bounce back from a trampoline.[3]

"I would see singers acting with an old style, with ridiculous conventions— not at all adapted to our times," Maria recalled. "I would see them moving with very broad gestures—it was all a 'silent cinema' kind of acting . . . I always struggled to realize that our profession was very old-fashioned. Still *is*."[4]

For this reason she became one of the earliest operatic singers to assume a Stanislavky "method acting" approach to her character.

Let it be acknowledged that the vocalist was not the first. Bass Fyodor Chaliapin had attempted to sing *Don Quixote* with a thin, feeble voice back in the thirties;[5] director Wieland Wagner of the Wagner dynasty had founded a new school of thought with the productions of his operatic Regietheater.[6] Maria did not know of these—and, more surprisingly, was probably not curious enough to care. There was *her* work to be done. To our knowledge she had never read Stanislavsky. Her colloquies with actors had been sparse.

Branded innovative by the era's critics, Maria's attitude toward her roles was rooted more in intuition than the study of great acting masters or interpretive technique. "First, cold calculation. How would this person react?" was the start of her study. "Social class, nationality, period, individual. Then blend this with the libretto and the music in an approximate. . ." She mimed the gestures of a sculptor. "Later, start putting in the eyes, the nose . . .[7] if it's a *queen*, they'd mold, what *year* would it be, what *epoch*, and they would mold a crinoline or they would mold a class."[8]

At a time when *I Love Lucy*'s heroine was forbidden from saying the word "pregnant" on television, the demand for *performance* per se—good or bad—superseded a need for reality. While film directors Luchino Visconti, Federico Fellini and Roberto Rossellini emblazoned modern cinema with neorealist trails, opera straggled far behind. "Even if a libretto said: 'I'm killing you because I hate you,' the common style was to sing it with a clear, vibrant voice—a voice, ultimately completely inexpressive . . ." EMI France's Michel Glotz later stated. "It was even common to play the somber Chopin in a precocious way; with a kind of old-fashioned gallantry—precisely the opposite of his proud, wounded soul."[9]

Maria's undisclosed desire was to take much greater risks than was her wont—sometimes. On one occasion she performed Norma's "Casta diva" in a soft voice at a Covent Garden rehearsal, later telling Lord Harewood that she felt a reflective approach to the aria made more sense than a grandiose incarnation. At the same time she was certain audiences would shun any rendition of the piece short of "heroic".[10]

And it wasn't that Maria Callas *never* ceded to convention. But even in the scope of instantly familiar gestures she made room for much-needed experimentation. "She too frequently opens her arms as they all do," Milanese music critic Emilio Radius scribed after her 1953 Scala *Lucia*. "But with a meditated slow approach her hand can bear the weight of lead or the contrasting lightness of a falling petal."[11]

To a large extent Maria's faulty erudition convinced many she had merely been the puppet of conceptual directors; chiefly Luchino Visconti. And it was during La Scala's May 1955 production of *La traviata* that she most succumbed to the auteur's suggestions. Hellbent on showcasing the opera at most major theatres, Maria's every new rendition of her Violetta spotlit a new facet of her art.

A dreamy specter was this novel *Traviata*. In retrospect it almost seems to have emblematized the summit of Maria's onstage beauty.

During the rehearsal period Stelios Galatopoulos called on the singer to collect a parcel she was sending to de Hidalgo, who was still in Athens. At the threshold he found Toti dal Monte: Italy's premier soprano of the twenties and thirties. Despite apparent differences between the pair Maria had determined to extract impressions from the luminary just as she had studied Rosa Ponselle's records. She would take from everywhere; use very little.[12]

This Violetta Valéry was the fruit of a mutual craftsmanship. Who had the greater share in its conception is a separate argument. Visconti would approve the costumes—only for Maria to pause mid-rehearsal and alert him to the rustling fabric meddling with her hearing. Rather than changing the costume, he altered her movements.

Respect eventually cemented friendship. Maria got to know Visconti's six brothers and sisters and niece Cristina, daughter of Ida Visconti.[13] She would eventually send Christmas cards to him, requesting he pass on her greetings to "Lilla [*sic*], Gianni and all our other friends."[14]

Composer Hans Werner Henze spent a week lunching and dining with them at Biffi restaurant, discussing costumes with designer Lila de Nobili. Visconti would talk. Maria would listen, silent for the most part. Meneghini would fall asleep.[15]

Equality in friendship didn't signify equality in stage dominion. One of Visconti's "mishaps" in Maria's view was the inclusion of a bonnet in the final scene. The dying Violetta would hasten to church; she would throw a shawl over her nightdress, put a hat on; feel weak all of a sudden, sit and die.

Maria refused to die looking like Little Bo Peep. "Luca knows nothing about how women dress. The hat is the very last thing you put on before leaving the house. Violetta wouldn't have got that far," she insisted to William Weaver.[16] When the moment came the stage was hers. Slyly, Maria would position the bonnet. Mysteriously . . . it would fall off before she sat down. Every time.

In some instances Maria and Visconti seemed to wage war in a contest for her art; both being zealously possessive. Maria feared for her artistic liberty—freedom of movement; Visconti, the movie director, was accustomed to blocking his actors; arranging the cast like a painting's inhabitants.

His rehearsal notes for her demanded gestures overly specific:

1st Act

If possible on the words "È strano, È strano"—take off your gloves and throw them on the fireplace together with your jewels.

2nd Act

> *"Sarò là—in mezzo ai fior"—Turn your head to the right.*
> *"Donna son io signore" (abrupt jerk of the head to the left).*

Letter to Alfredo:

> *Write two words—then cross them out resolutely—cry—write them*
> *again—cross them out again—then write them again.*[17]

During the performance it was not uncommon for Visconti to be sitting in a box close to the stage and susurrating counsel to Maria like a prompter: "I would tell her, 'Do that, go a little to the left, come forward a bit'—I would tell her things like that," Visconti recollected.

"And I would tell *him* to hush!" she responded.[18]

On one hand he was owed a lot of credit. "He taught me something without his knowing it: that the less I move—without evident reason or profound reason—the more it is my own *personality*. It did me enormous good, of course," Maria would admit.[19] At the same time she was hard-pressed to ascribe her whole artistic physicality to one director. Later she insisted, "He knew better than to try to use me as a marionette."

It would have been impossible for him to funnel all his concepts through Maria: she was far too stubborn. Visconti's interests lay in the assemblage of a consummate creation. Despite her scrupulous review of a production's physiognomy, Maria had much better taste about its sound than its purported spectacle. "He would spend a whole day of precious rehearsal time deciding on the right handkerchief or the right parasol," she complained. "What perturbed me most at the time with Visconti was my inability to understand how a man of great intelligence could be excessively pedantic in matters of so little importance."[20]

An unrelenting and perennial worshipper, Visconti never stooped to taking credit for Maria's artistry. "Her gestures thrilled you. Where did she learn them? On her own," was his devout avowal.[21]

That didn't mean he wasn't going to make concessions out of self-aggrandizement. Maria was a goddess; yes—he had made opera "*for* her, not *because* of her."[22] Never would he have become one of the art's auteurs without her.

But was he relegated to the post of somebody backstage; a helpful figure who remained respectfully behind the scenes? Oh, no. Not in Visconti's eyes. For in Visconti's eyes Maria was in love with him.

He relished purveying the rumor in public: "It was a stupid thing, all in her mind," Visconti expressed in an interview. "But like so many Greeks, she has a possessive streak, and there were many terrible jealous scenes . . . Because of this crazy infatuation, she wanted to have me command her every step."[23] It was true Maria often asked Visconti what she ought to do onstage. She had also asked bass Nicola Rossi-Lemeni how best to open each act of *Norma* in January 1952 at La Scala.[24] Consulting with colleagues was part of her art.

Women's magazines spread stories that alleged that the director and Maria had been caught in passionate embraces in her dressing room.[25] All of Visconti's entourage knew of his sexuality—including Maria, whose puritanical nature preferred not to hear about *anyone's* sex life.

Like many artists idealistically inclined, Visconti didn't shy away from flowery expression of his adulation—plying Meneghini with elaborate missives: "Now I'm off to Venice . . . where I'll be a member of the Film Festival Jury. Ten days of uninterrupted film-viewing will, I'm sure, leave me disgusted with cinema forever. So I'll start planting flowers. Tell Maria that, if she wanted to employ me as a gardener, I would gladly step up to the job. That way I'd stand in her garden by the window, waiting to hear her sing."[26]

Similarly he begrudged her lack of correspondence: "It's obvious that you're having a tranquil, happy time of genuine rest . . . So you no longer write back to distant friends."[27]

Visconti's character did not prompt the soprano to solicit a close friendship with him outside work. Despite their chummy nature she was put off by his vulgar manner; the kind that could incite him to "scream, furious, like Jupiter in a rage." Explosions at rehearsal detonated into words such as: "This is a s**t theatre! *Basta!* Have you finished walking up and down the theatre?" This volatility was awkwardly at odds with the sophisticated, bourgeois manner of the count.

Maria wasn't one for swearing. Inextricably encrusted in her middle-class, good girl ways, she bemoaned to Meneghini that Visconti's language "turned her stomach".[28] Socializing with Richard Burton and Elizabeth Taylor in later years, she was astonished to hear Burton's niece exclaim "s**t" in the middle of a game.[29]

At loss to find the accusations of enamorment with her director entertaining, the soprano had a very serious response when asked about it decades later. "It is really too ridiculous even to talk about it . . . Decorum has always been fundamental in my life and I have never acted like a silly little girl who makes a fool of herself and thinks she is romantic."[30] While the verity of the last phrase is questionable, it's a fairytale to think Maria could have avidly been nurturing a fantasy about the count. She was too *busy*, married and uninterested.

All her daydreaming dwelled in another work of fiction: Violetta Valéry's sad tale. "Maria loves all romantic heroines," Visconti would declare in an interview together with her. "Well—*yes.* It is the basis of Woman," she would reply.[31]

The "self-sacrificing" nature of the character was once again what spoke so intimately to her. "She *does* become noble at the end because she sacrifices *herself*—for her *love* . . .[32] They [she and Norma] are both—can I say, *purified* at the end . . . noble enough to reach this *height*."[33]

In 1800s Paris ex-courtesan Violetta leaves lover Alfredo—despite dying of consumption—after his father pontificates on the risk of their union, which is disgracing Alfredo's young sister.

Visconti and costume designer Lila de Nobili brought the plot forward, setting the opera in 1875. The reasons—according to Visconti—were simply that "Maria would look wonderful in costumes of that era. She was tall and slender, and in a [scarlet] gown with a tight bodice, a bustle, and long train, she would be a vision . . . I sought to make her a little of Duse, a little of Rachel, a little of Bernhardt. But more than anyone, I thought of Duse."[34]

The day of the premiere, 19 May 1955, began with triviality: Maria's maid Edda Zoraide Casali made apple tart. Visconti came around. In the course of their exchange the three of them discovered "Zoraide" was a Russian name.[35]

A recording from 28 May guides listeners through a gallery of Violetta's switching sentiments: calling on her friends in the beginning ("Flora, amici"), she is perky and radiant: a voice light and limber. Notices of speculation about guest Alfredo's love are not a mere intrusion, they creep up on her like an intrepid insect. "*Nulla* son io per lui" ("I am *nothing* to him"), the flustered courtesan avers, her femininity enmeshed with embarrassment. The toast of the "Brindisi" is made powerful by evident denial: a voice that rises with such verve of a vibrato that it tremulously rings. Rolling every "r" with opulence, it crowns all top notes with crescendo. Violetta is living the unstoppable high life.

When she dismisses Alfredo's declarations of love, an insouciant playfulness pellets delightfully dropping arpeggios; notes plopping like delicate raindrops. Her enquiry "D'amarmi dite ancora?" ("You're still avowing that you love me?") is executed almost like a dare: so high-pitched, so thin, so riddled with vibrato is this instrument deflecting his avowals with mockery. Suddenly we're in a playground and she's nothing but a spiteful girl who pokes fun at a lovesick boy.

Then—silence. The guests have left. "The abandoned room looked like a cemetery—the great floral arrangements no longer fresh, the table a mess, napkins and fans on the floor, chairs in disorder," was the recollection of Carlo Maria Giulini.[36] Violetta's internality is now in disarray; that much is manifest. She is a dying party girl whose life is founded on the premise of being used for sex by rich men who reward her with the lap of luxury. Duplicitous in her designs, she is a fraud. Fooling others. Most of all— fooling *herself.*

Peering at clutter compiled by her profligate guests, Violetta feels something is wrong. "È strano! È strano!" she sings. ("This is strange, this is strange!") "In core scolpiti ho quegli accenti!" ("His expressions are engraved on my heart!"). The first inoculation has succeeded: the inception of intoxication. She acknowledges this fault—but only with a voice that tapers off into demure diminuendo. This isn't how she is *supposed* to feel, the headstrong hedonist. No one can take her on a path to love; love is ridiculous.

As she sings "O gioia ch'io non conobbi, esser amata amando!" ("Oh, the joy that I have never known—to love and to *be* loved!") we hear a thin, resentful, scathing voice. Violetta tosses that aside. It is pure fantasy.

The aria "Ah, fors è lui" ("Ah, maybe he's the one") is most frequently sung in a self-declaration: Violetta blissfully learning that yes, she's in love. But more than anything it is a monologue immersed in melancholy fear; a recognition of her illness and the reckoning that nothing—even the camellia given to her by Alfredo—lasts.

Maria's Violetta sits before the fireplace wrapped in a shawl as she performs the aria. Removing the jewels and the pins from her "Mélisande"-like long hair, she straightens it with a large hairbrush. Through this vapid bedtime ritual Violetta is left hopelessly to ponder.[37] "You can't very well speak of such intimate thoughts in an open *way*," Maria would describe this particular scene.[38]

She sings of "Croce e delizia": the "torture and ecstasy" love evokes. Elevating excitement and accelerating alarm each expand her crescendo. Her reaction is a child scared of the rollercoaster ride; fear and enticement crossing in the frazzled wires of her brain. Simultaneously she yearns for tenderness . . . slow-wilting notes in the contrasting "delizia" take a long while to ebb. This dream of hers is growing swollen and it *has* to be suppressed.

Glasses, plates and cutlery along the table are thrown brusquely off the surface on which Violetta sits to save her liberty: "Sempre libera" ("Always free").[39] In rehearsal Visconti had instructed Maria to fling her high heels off and rub her sore feet "like Filumena Marturano".[40] *Filumena Marturano* was a popular Italian play by Eduardo de Filippo in the forties. At one point the heroine complains of pain incurred from her high heels, swiping them off once she's home.

Apparently the gesture was considered scandalous. A year later, during the production's first revival, Maria found herself at the beloved Biffi restaurant accompanied by friends Giovanna Lomazzi, Eliana de Sabata (daughter of Victor) and Anna Veronese. Gnawing on a beef steak with her glasses on, she heard a much-revered industrialist cite Violetta's coarse shoe-throwing: "What Luchino, what Callas? If I were Ghiringhelli, I would ban all that stuff. La Scala is becoming the Togni circus."

Pretending not to hear, Maria finished her beef steak, paused and remained taciturn in thought. After a brief silent interval she flung her head beneath the table, sat up and announced so everybody heard: "Turns out I was right. Giovanna, Anna, Eliana: you're all sitting barefoot. And at a *restaurant*. You'd think we were at *home!*"[41]

Violetta's stance that opening night in May of 1955 was almost infantile: resistant against love like a toddler refusing to put on her hat in the cold. The "li" of the ebullient cabaletta "Sempre libera" sounds almost like a trill; so gleeful, so *unhinged* is the recalcitrant vibrato. Repeated cries of rapid roulades (quick series of notes stretched out over one syllable) on "gioir" ("to enjoy oneself") are let loose by rebellion. Splendidly sustained, the notes spring with such recklessness it dares the vocalizing to emerge as uncontrolled: a raving adolescent's manifesto.

When Violetta finally succumbed clad in a gown of scarlet taffeta, she stretched her arms behind her in complete submission, allowing Alfredo's camellias to drop to the ground.[42]

The ambience was altered. In the second act Germont—the villain of the piece—drops by to declare the heroine unfit for his respected son. "Donna son io, signore—ed in mia *casa!*" she defends herself. ("I am a woman, Signor—and in my *home*"). And suddenly we hear throughout Maria's previously limber instrument the toppled dignity of a belligerent Medea. Her epiphany of the impending doom is stunningly protracted; so much so, it almost slows down the conducting of her maestro. There is a tenuously perceptible and yet distinct pause as she learns Alfredo has a sister: "I . . . due figli?" ("Two . . . children?") she asks Germont.

The heroine's last ounce of strength is spent as she stays adamantine: she won't leave Alfredo. "Ah no! *Giammai!* No, no!" ("No, *never!* No, no!") she cries—the emphasis on "mai" four times the weight of its accompanying syllables.

Confiding in the father of her circumstances, Violetta doesn't plead for sympathy but is embarrassed yet again: "I don't have any friends or relatives," ("Che né amici, né parenti") she confesses to Germont in a stream of staccato. The first time that she dotes on the idea "That I should leave Alfredo" ("Ch'io mi separi da Alfredo"), the diminuendo struggles so much to emerge her voice seems to have sapped its potency: a bottleneck upturned to coax those final drops.

Germont expends not just her spirit but her health. Per the decrees of operatic heroines, Violetta's final force is salvaged for the Will to Die. When she insists, "Morrò! La mia memoria non fia ch'ei maledica!" ("I will die! But let the memory of me not be a curse to Alfredo!") that irresistibly rolled "r" on "morrò" reignites extinguished strength.

Alfredo comes home. Terror overrides the Callas voice as Violetta hastens to assure: "Perché tu m'ami, Alfredo, non è vero? Tu *m'ami?* Alfredo, tu *m'ami*, Alfredo—non è vero?" ("Because you love me, don't you, Alfredo? You *love* me, don't you? *Don't* you?"). The instrument is so high-pitched and scraping stridency its sheen has a metallic quality: here Violetta is a crying child. Briefly we wonder: does she truly doubt Alfredo's constancy? Could she be throwing her whole life away for *nothing?*

As Violetta pledges she will *always*, always be with him—"sempre, sempre, sempre presso a te"—Maria ignores Verdi's score, extending "te" into a long crescendo-portamento stretching from the C to the next phrase's F. The first note is feebly hesitant; the second forceful passion. When she reaches finally the climax of "Amami, Alfredo" ("Love me, Alfredo"), it is the insistence of *her* love for him she stresses: the "Io *t'amo*" ("I love you") palpates with the potent force of her vibrato. Her parting of "Addio" is so long we wonder if she'll leave at all—and can't believe Alfredo could be blind to the blunt urgency of her departure.

By the last act Violetta's resources are all depleted. "I had preferred *also* a er . . . sort of *useless* movement, like—trying to fetch *something*, whatever it was; a useless gesture like trying to get the mirror or—*something* on the dressing table and not being able to and always just—dropping the hand," Maria recalled. "She knows she's lost . . . So she immediately folds up and . . . *really* sacrifices herself because *also* she doesn't *have* the *strength*."

We hear her voice's color fade: it swerves, droops, wanes and wilts like that decayed camellia. Maria's breathing technique is intact in this scene: Violetta's errs *constantly*. How can she sustain her exclamation when she sees her pale self in the mirror: "Oh, come son mutata!" ("Oh, how I've changed!") she cries out—and the "oh" skids dangerously into "Oh-o-o-oh." Violetta isn't used to her defective voice and respiration. To that end her reflection on times past, "Addio del passato, bei sogni ridenti" ("Goodbye, beautiful, happy past dreams") is sung with almost no vibrato and no vigor.

Treacherous Germont at last reveals the bitter truth to his hurt son, prompting Alfredo to return. The lovers somberly renew their vows of unconditional devotion. Ready to resume life and suspend her illness, Violetta requests of Annina the maid, "dammi a vestire" ("hand me my clothes") . . . yet the command is almost scathing in its whisper. Violetta cannot regulate her intonations; she doesn't realize that her failing voice is now at odds with her intentions. Nothing obeys her anymore. Not her beauty, not her body, not her speech.

An electric current charges her: that urgent strength that thrills tuberculosis victims on the cusp of their extinction. She resents dying so young: "Gran Dio! Morir si giovine!" For a brief spell she is again a juvenile, enamored girl wistfully waiting to be whisked away by her beloved beau. Physical force revives her. "In me rinasce, m'agita . . . insolito vigor!" ("I feel . . . an unexpected vigor coming back to me") she sings. "It's coming back . . ." We hear that slow lifting of spirits and the voice in a struggling crescendo. "Oh, gioia!" ("Oh joy!") Violetta explodes—till her words ebb like finishing water.

It is a spectral sound; a shadow of a former self. Violetta died before she hit the floor. "That I learned from Visconti," Maria conceded.[43] "In fact, she never *did* hit the floor. Dying on the last phrase believing that she was *really* coming to life again, which is typical of that illness, and managing to *freeze* to death—*just* on the phrase." It was in that guise—performing that last "Oh, gioia"—that her spirit left her eyes.

Afterwards Visconti's niece Cristina Gastel paid a visit to Maria. "Sitting at her dressing room table still in that white nightdress—white like the fragrant gardenias that surrounded her; a gift from my uncle . . . Exhausted, sapped of her capacity to live . . . she couldn't manage to return yet to a world of words and contretemps."[44]

Critics were less inspired than the girl. Floored by the naturalistic incarnation, by a stationary dying Violetta, by her blatantly uncouth behavior in the first act, Teodoro Celli wrote that the director had "disfigured and defiled" the Verdi opera, turning it into "a villainous, vulgar *verismo* drama!"[45]

*

With the increasing expenditure of her vocal as well as emotional wealth, Maria's performances started to shrink in their number. She spent the greater part of summer 1955 recording a compilation album, *Aïda* and *Madama Butterfly*, and welcomed Elvira de Hidalgo to her Milanese home.[46] Her artistry was being saved for yet another debut—this time in Berlin: *Lucia di Lammermoor*.

With Karajan once again at the helm, it was no longer a question of occasional discord but livid imbroglios. Not all the tension was attributable to the maestro's obstinance, however. That opening night, 29 September, Maria felt vocally insecure. Certain people entertain the false impression that Maria Callas was infallible; that godly fire was enough to save her from the bane of mortal stagefright. This was not the case. Lord Harewood would remember her alerting him: "If you want to appreciate me, you must hear me often. I know I vary, that the voice varies, but I am always trying to *do* something and only sometimes will be successful. If you don't come often, you won't catch the good performances."[47]

Miracles were events. Maria could not always live up to "miracle" standards. "It has happened to me that I have made an entrance and felt that the public was not immediately sympathetic," she explained once. "To a singer this is paralyzing: it closes the throat. The tones are there, the sound is there, but confidence has gone. And there you are—beaten."[48]

Encrusted in humility, Maria shared her fears with Karajan, who recommended she skip *Lucia di Lammermoor's* high E flat [E flat 6] at the end of the mad scene. Reticently she obeyed.[49] Its recording bares scratchy B flats and tame shades when Lucia alludes to the ghost of the girl by the fountain ("l'ombra mostrarsi" etc.). She relies more on the dramatic voice—her former operatic staple—than the limber, lighter instrument she has elastically evolved. Maria's artistry regresses—only blossoming into fruition in the mad scene's second half where she contorts the heavy color to expel an echo stalker-like: "Alfin son tua, alfin sei miii . . . o" ("At last I'm yours; at last you're *miii . . . ine*").

Ever regal, she collected roses tossed by chivalrous spectators and flung one at a flautist. The critic for *Der Tagesspiegel* described her "pianissimo . . . sweet like a bell; she has a modulation for every sentimental vibration and the flighty lightness of birdsong . . ."[50]

But she was not happy. Coming offstage, Maria tearfully insisted that she was "no good".[51] "Well, my day was made of this and that and that," went Maria's post-performance ritual of contemplation. "Now, this and that happened, let's see what we can do *tomorrow*. The *good* things, we forget about—say, 'Well, that was *supposed* to happen, we *should* have done good. Now, what about the bad things? Well, let's see how we can *improve* those bad things.' "[52]

Otolaryngologist Dr. Alfred Tomatis alleged that Maria consulted him shortly thereafter—claiming there was "something wrong with her right ear" that left her "unable to control [her] tune."[53]

Whether or not this information is exact, the Berlin *Lucia* posed Maria multiple disturbances—including yet another conflict with her globally beloved maestro. Bowled over by the audience's reception, Karajan elected to repeat *Lucia*'s challenging sextet, leaving Maria more than just disgruntled.[54] So zealous was she about defending *her* music—or Donizetti's music, whichever way she might have put it—that when the time came for the mad scene Maria turned her back to the audience to throw Karajan's tempi off course. This would stop the conductor foreseeing her entrances. Was that smart? Probably not—but it lacked an effect. Or, shall we say—an *artistic* effect; Karajan was able to carry on normally.

The effect it *did* have was an on/off well-known duel between the pair—who thereafter referred to each other to Michel Glotz as "Votre chanteuse" and "Ton chef d'orchestre"—"Your singer" and "Your conductor."[55] Initially Maria had forgiven Karajan this trespass, writing in April 1956 to Walter Legge: "Karajan was not directing and I simply can't hear the opera [*Lucia*] without him. Tell him I miss him and it is a shame we don't work more together—don't you think?"[56]

But following another repetition of the sextet in a June 1956 Vienna staging,[57] in which—according to *New York Times* critic Harold C. Schonberg—Karajan had upped the volume of the orchestra so greatly that the singers had been forced to yell, and sped the tempo of the final scene up so intensely that the chorus had lagged woefully behind,[58] Maria grew embittered.

Her byplay in response to Karajan's artistic treason begs the question: did Maria Callas fight for the composer's or *her* favored version of the work? "Verdi is no longer here to explain his intentions, and today a personal moment must enter into interpretation . . ." she theorized. "You can't say Beethoven's Ninth should be played *this* way—who knows conclusively how it should be played? And, indeed, how dare we say it should be played *this* way? The most we can say is: I would like it this way."[59]

Scribed by her instincts, her artistic tastes did not consistently agree with the composers' scores. In *La traviata*: "What bothers me is the aria 'È strano . . .' in the first act. She says goodbye to her guests, and as soon as they go out she has this aria. But she hasn't had time to ponder. The timing is wrong."[60] In *Norma*: "I really don't like 'Casta diva' . . . It is a *straight* prayer to the [moon] goddess . . . she knows she can't stall for time . . . much longer . . . 'Casta diva' is only a consequence of, 'Well, I've *dominated* you [my people], and now we're doing what we . . . *believe* in.' "[61]

So this arrangement of Callas rules met with certain exceptions.

Thus Maria's kinships with conductors were determined mostly by their contribution to her art. Karajan was himself a notorious musical egotist; Visconti feared the clout he wielded would evoke "An Austrianized Scala, like Italy under the Occupation in 1848."[62] Despite having performed with Victor de Sabata, Leonard Bernstein, Erich Kleiber, Carlo Maria Giulini and others, Maria liberally averred: "I cannot in all sincerity and humility consider any of them in the same way as Tullio Serafin. This is not a case of comparison but of who has been the greatest influence for me."[63]

*

That October heralded her return to Chicago for a new season at the young Lyric Opera. Eddie Bagarozy was still hot on her heels. With his lawsuit dropped by Circuit Court because Maria hadn't been a resident of Illinois, the ex-lawyer had succeeded in Appellate Court, which had reversed the previous decision.[64] Knowing this to be the case, Maria had instilled a stipulation in her contract with the Lyric Opera. This imposed on its administration the responsibility of her protection for her stay's duration.[65] How such a clause could bear enactment or be recognized by law is an entirely other matter: the soprano deemed the promise ironclad.

At Carol Fox and Lawrence Kelly's insistence the Lyric Opera's publicist, Danny Newman, smuggled Maria into the U.S. through Canada to fend off authorities and "appealed to friends in high places" to encourage a "stay of execution." He was aware that Maria would be slapped with a lawsuit . . . but only *after* her performances' end.[66]

Elsewhere she continued burnishing her reputation. Having requested Fox and Kelly simultaneously recruit Tebaldi to cement a truce, Maria purposely attended both of the soprano's premieres on 1 and 7 November in *Aïda* and *La bohème*.[67]

At the same time Meneghini was involved in disputation with the Metropolitan's administrator Rudolf Bing. His wife's first grievance had involved her discontent with the selection of conductor Fausto Cleva—whose poor attitude had led her to abandon her Verona *Aïda*—for her Metropolitan debut to take place the following winter. Eventually, she gave in.[68]

Meneghini then demanded she receive two thousand dollars a performance: her salary at the Lyric for both the 1954–55 and 1955–56 seasons. Bing retorted with a scathing gibe alleging Meneghini was about to "ruin her career" for his own greed.[69] Eventually he caved, agreeing to deposit funds in a Swiss bank to guarantee that Bagarozy would have zero access to them if his lawsuit proved successful. He would later note that "Meneghini rejected all arrangements that did not involve payment to him *in cash*, before the curtain rose, of his wife's fee for each performance. Toward the end, I had him paid in five-dollar bills, to make a wad uncomfortably large for him to carry."[70]

Publicist Newman milked the situation to the utmost—ordering a swath of ravenous photographers to come into Maria's dressing room in time to witness Bing arrive and kiss her hand; hoping the press would capture what he called "the greatest surrender since [President Ulysses S.] Grant accepted [General Robert E.] Lee's sword at Appomattox Court House [during the American Civil War]."[71] Maria sang Elvira in *I puritani* then Leonora in *Il trovatore*, in which critic Claudia Cassidy referred to her as "a Spanish girl spinning traceries in the shadow of death."[72] It seemed her voice was on its best behavior, for another critic remarked, "It floated with effortless grace, swelled until it filled the whole block-long auditorium, tapered off sensuously into a decorative vocal arabesque . . . [it] went straight to the listener's solar plexus."[73]

The next challenge was her first live performance of *Madama Butterfly*. "I don't think the geisha is right for me," she had once told a music critic. "I'm too tall, and all those small, mincing, miniature gestures don't really suit my style. The music is lovely, but so sentimental."[74]

Sentiment had taken over. One night Meneghini had awoken to a half-bare mattress. Going downstairs, he had searched for his lost wife and found her kneeling and in tears, cradling the score of *Butterfly*.[75]

The epithet applies to Cio-Cio-san: a fifteen-year-old geisha who becomes the wife of egotistical Lieutenant Pinkerton, who uses his position in the navy to leave Nagasaki. While abroad he marries an American. Japanese soprano Hizi Koyke coached Maria to adapt her lanky body to the miniature gesticulation of the girl.[76] So much did she want the character to be innate to her, she strived to persuade tenor Giuseppe Di Stefano to carry her at the end of the first act when the new husband and wife are about to make love. "That would be too *long*," he insisted—clumsily referring to Maria's height.[77]

Although there is no document of the performance with the slight exception of a brief and silent video, the studio recording made in August 1955 with Maestro Karajan is maybe the most vivid paradigm of the soprano's malleability.

The instrument is close to being unidentifiable. Ethereal and slender like the timid grace of airborne leaves, its timbre isn't the sole property that's shaped. Though Maria cannot dress Italian words in Japanese intonements, certain stresses—such as Butterfly's reply when asked if she's from Nagasaki, "Veri-*tà*" ("It's true")—are tinged with oriental flair. Cio-Cio-san's nubile inexperience lines her treatment of the part in Act I. "Sono vecchia diggià" ("I'm already old") sings the bashful fifteen-year-old in a voice of superlative cuteness: blissfully blind to the brazen Lieutenant's insidious intentions.

The pudor that she proffers—casually informing him she can convert to Christianity, a sign that she is marriageable—percolates the skimpy sound until it slithers like crêpe paper. She is embarrassed for the statement ("Colla nuova mia vita posso adottare nuova religione"): in *her* culture people make no reference to relationships.

When finally she and Pinkerton are about to make love in the "Viene la sera" duet, the girl's excitement is such that it vocally cannot contain itself; thinning like a tapering braid on a high-pitched "e felice" ("and happy"). Onomatopoeically, when she sings of the "Little moon goddess who descends during nighttime from her bridge in the sky" ("La piccola Dea della luna che scende la notte dal ponte del ciel") the diminuendo is longer. We envisage a drizzle of moonlight the shape of a pyramid shrinking its gleam on a shimmering lake.

One almost fears her voice will shred itself to pieces as she pits her thinnest timbre forcefully against fortissimo dynamics in "Le sa. Forse dirle non vuole per tema d'averne a morir." ("She knows she is loved. Perhaps she doesn't want to admit it for fear she might die"). The squeal of a crescendo is a prescient warning signal threatening the modest girl's demureness. Carnally surrendering, she asks Pinkerton to "Vogliatemi bene" ("Love me well"); singing so softly in the midst of her decorum that her voice is almost hushed. So unaccustomed is she to refer to such ineffable details that shame seeps through her tone.

Yet when she sings, "The saying goes that if in your country a butterfly is caught, they'll pierce it and leave it to die" ("Ogni farfalla da uno spillo è trafitta ed in tavola infitta"), the phrase is rushed in a squelched voice of anguish: uncertainty trapped in the glimmering clasp of euphoria.

By the second act Cio-Cio-san's voice has surpassed recognition. Complete is the metamorphosis: she is a woman now; a mother of a three-year-old who's never met his father. No longer so inhibited, she almost scolds her maid Suzuki when she questions whether Pinkerton will come back with a scathingly hot "Tornerà." ("He will return"). An even harsher sound that vibrates with a piquant throb arrests her reprimands: "Piangi? Perché? Perché?" ("Suzuki, you're crying! Why? Why?").

"Un bel dì ti vedremo" ("One beautiful day, we will see you") begins with her sole ray of hope being cleft; lilac sky sliced by coal-colored twilight. The words contrast with Butterfly's intentions. Desiring to sing of hope, her staggering diminuendo suggests fear.

Butterfly contemplates what could transpire if her husband fails to surface: the notion of her panhandling around the city, scavenging for fodder. In the aria, "Che tua madre dovrà," the voice is significantly darker; bereft of all light, crisp like parchment.

Then Suzuki beholds the alighting ship, "Una nave da guerra." Cio-Cio-san's response harks back to her infatuated sapling self: her voice diminishing to its most girlish traits with tiny exclamations of "Bianca, Bianca . . . il vessillo americano delle stelle" ("It's white, it's white . . . with the American Star-Spangled Flag").

Upon Lieutenant Pinkerton's return Butterfly learns she must surrender her three-year-old son to her husband and Kate, his new wife. Unlike those operatic heroines who perish willfully for love, her suicidal resolution is deprived of vigor. So sharp and cutting is the vanquishing vibrato in the voice its sheen appears to self-excoriate as she calls out to her small boy, "Tu, tu, tu, piccolo Iddio" ("You, you, you, my little god"). Her death does not seem predetermined. Instead a mania envelops it; unhinged like the vibrato-riddled notes in the crescendo cry of "muor Butterfly!" ("Butterfly dies!"). "Gioca, gioca." ("Go, play"), Cio-Cio-san instructs her son so she can kill herself in private.

Unraveling the long pins nestled in her hair, Maria's Cio-Cio-san committed *hara-kiri* as the raven locks came floating down.[78]

The opera may be the sole one in which we hear Maria leaf through the entire catalogue of life's prevailing scenes: youth, first love, expunged excitement, terror, loss and death.

Sat in the audience that Friday night of November 11th was a young Leontyne Price—who would ascribe that performance to catching the "opera bug": "She *merged* the sound with the action . . ." Price summarized. "It was one of the most exciting experiences I have ever known."[79] One critic wrote, "[it was] as if she were a fully trained member of the Kabuki Theater."[80]

Beauty thrived beyond the wings. At an after-party she was welcomed with a standing ovation; a butterfly carved of ice was wheeled in.[81]

Only two performances were planned and yet the public yearned for one more *Butterfly*. Scheduled for November 17th, its three thousand tickets sold out in ninety-eight minutes.[82]

Meanwhile, banal concerns were pressing. Meneghini alerted Dorle and Dario Soria of Angel Records (a division of EMI) that he needed a place to meet Bagarozy's attorney in private. Seeking no interference from Maria, he asked Dorle to accompany his wife on a walk. The latter refused and sat down with the lawyer. All of a sudden Dorle heard "a piercing shriek." Maria burst through the door and yelled: "They want twenty thousand dollars!" Dorle's mother rushed to her. "Darling, have some cookies," she advised.[83]

It was on the night of her last *Butterfly* that U.S. marshal Stanley Pringle crowded her backstage and strived to thrust into her hands a brusque subpoena. "I refused to touch any paper," Maria later wrote in "My Defense," a document she opted not to publish. "I turned away of course—he and they—<u>10</u> of them—clawed at me and even scratched me and threw papers after me."[84]

That wasn't the worst part. The worst part was that a photographer had been on hand. The story the next day? Maria claimed to have the "voice of an angel," which equaled indemnity to United States courts' prosecution.

It took a long while for her entourage—which in this instance consisted of Dario Soria, Walter Legge, Lawrence Kelly and others—to "smuggle Maria out of a side door and bring her to Larry's brother's apartment where, egged on by Battista . . . she raged all night," as Dorle wrote.[85]

Maria believed somebody in the administration had conspired to exploit the moment to increase publicity; betraying their promise to shelter her. She herself admitted as much: "I wasn't angry at the poor sheriffs," she later wrote, "but at those who had set the trap in motion and ignobly betrayed me."[86]

To Dorle she exclaimed: "I couldn't have been betrayed worse. When I write you details you will freeze in horror."[87] She was adamant the truth be known. "How can I defend myself from such diffamation [*sic*] on the papers as the deputy saying that I refused to accept summons because I am the voice of an angel and no human being can touch me! Such preposterous lies from sworn officers of the Sheriff's office. I never said such things. It's not in my character and it's giving a very poor picture of me to the public that knows my modesty and serious character. And where did all the fotographs [*sic*] come from. All a setup I suppose from Bagarozy's lawyer."[88]

All kinds of claims ensued. Carol Fox and Lawrence Kelly blamed each other; they had been at odds now for a while. Kelly later left the opera house to found another theatre in the Dallas Civic Opera.[89] Maria would insist she didn't reproach any one: "When the three directors of Chicago's Lyric Theater—my friends Carol Fox, Lawrence Kelly and Nicola Rescigno—broke up in 1956, I did not want to take sides by working for one and not for the others. But this year I sang for Kelly in Dallas with Rescigno as my conductor, and each year Carol Fox and I try to agree on dates and other details for a program in Chicago," she scribed three years thence.[90]

The veritable source of chaos was a boring one. Doing his job of stirring hype, Danny Newman happily admitted in his memoir: "I, of course, just happened to be there with all the photographers to catch for posterity that scene more dramatic than even [Victorien] Sardou might have dreamed."

A publicity stunt forged by a publicist.

Ironically Maria didn't catch on. Over the years she and Newman would exchange "greetings . . . via mutual friends, and we had a warm reunion between the [1974 Verdi Congress] sessions."[91]

In Maria's never-published statement of defense she sought to clarify the facts: Bagarozy had been accused of mail fraud three times; she could not come to Chicago to attend the hearing because her performances took up her calendar; she "really [hasn't] calculated how much money this character owes [her] . . . it's not a large sum of course but back then I certainly needed it!"

Most of all she hated being deemed a craven fugitive. "They said in the papers that I fled. It's a lie. The Company Airlines can testify to that. I had already postponed my trip from the 15th to the 18th."[92]

Immediately Maria set about writing to Nelly Failoni—the woman for whom she had worked as a maid in New York, seeking from "the soul I know so well . . . a letter from you stating all the facts regarding Bagarotzy [*sic*] that you know as you lived through them with that unforgettable maestro—your husband."[93]

Back in Milan Maria met with other, even more mundane affairs. Meneghini's brother-in-law, Dr. Giovanni Cazzarolli—who had tended to the woman during her appendicitis back in 1948—was working with Gino Coen, the president of the Pastificio Pantanella Pasta Brand. Together they had mounted an advertising campaign claiming the "physiological pasta" had created the Great Callas Weight Loss.[94] The promotional endeavor had been spawned by her brief visit to the pasta factory. On that occasion

Cazzarolli had proposed that she exploit her slender figure for the sake of both her and the pasta brand's publicity.

Maria balked. "Why would you ask me, of all people, to do something like *that?*"[95]

After a long series of advertisements alleging that spaghetti was responsible for Callas' lost weight, she and Meneghini opted to take legal action. "It is damaging if, against such ideal spirituality, one finds behind the scenes a 'butterfly' who cures herself with macaroni," their lawyer declared at the court hearing.[96] The first round of the lawsuit would be won in March 1957. After the pasta brand appealed, the second victory would come about in August 1959.[97]

A stream of lawsuits seemingly was *everywhere*. Yet there was a naivety about it. Even Maria confessed: "Newspapers *have* to be written. Every day they have to *fill* those *hundreds* of pages . . . the truth sometimes is less sensational than the *lies* and sometimes—*most* times they are preposterous lies. What can I do? Sue them? Oh, how ridiculous. You can imagine how many lawsuits I'd just—spend all the money I gain or I have on . . . *lawyers*, and they *do* cost."[98] Somehow with her husband's goading and an urgent need to sanitize her reputation, there was legal action—and aplenty.

According to her friend Stelios Galatopoulos, her conclusion on the matter in 1977 was this: "I was terribly unhappy and hurt by the unkindness and the unfairness—in the paper I read nothing but insults. Eventually I did find justice and cleared my name. I do not mean the damages I received. That money went to charity immediately."[99]

The next new role was unexpected: Rosina in Rossini's *Il barbiere di Siviglia*. The production got off to a lackluster start. Conductor Carlo Maria Giulini was ill; director Carlo Piccinato "failed to appear."[100]

Critical reactions to Maria's Rosina were negative—and *adversely.* "Who the hell told her that Rosina is some café-concert singer who flirtatiously lifts up her skirt?" one demanded to know.[101] Even Maria's idol Elvira de Hidalgo would later aver, "In no way was Maria suited to this role," and Giulini himself would allege: "Her personality was wrong, her conception misguided. She made Rosina a kind of Carmen."[102] Tenor Luigi Alva remembered her interpretation as being "a sort of a kitten."[103]

For the most part the production saw Maria stick to the original mezzo-soprano key, performing "Una voce poco fa" in the prerequisite E major whilst embellishing Act I's "Dunquo io son" duet with soprano coloratura.

In recent years Rosina has acquired bite in her interpretations. A young girl trapped by her oppressive warden Doctor Bartolo in eighteenth-century Seville, she craftily conspires with her would-be lover Lindoro—who is actually Count Almaviva—to escape the guardian and marry him. Only after various shenanigans does she discover that Lindoro is a wealthy count and feels betrayed. The ending is a happy one . . . unless one counts the previously written Mozart's *The Marriage of Figaro* as a sequel (both were based on a series of plays by French dramatist Pierre de Beaumarchais).

"Perhaps I tried too hard," Maria would admit. "Afterwards, before I recorded the opera, Hidalgo, my teacher, helped me to put the role in a better perspective. Thinking back on it, perhaps I should have done it again . . . It was not the music—my interest in the character was ephemeral. Rosina was a passing fancy."[104]

Listening to the live recording of 16 February 1956, one learns the Callas incarnation of Rosina isn't a catastrophe. While her colors tend to alternate abruptly between very dark on some vindictive phrases such as "Se Lindoro mio sarà . . . Lo giurai—lo vincerò" ("If Lindoro will be mine—I swear it, I will win"), and specious cuteness on "Mi lascio reggere, mi lascio reggere" ("I let myself be ruled and guided"), the semblance suggests girlishness and cunning. Sprightly surges of coloratura come off hedonistically.

Yet when Rosina sings of how she can become a viper when provoked, we hear a thick vibrato on a viciously sepulchral tone: brash bloodlust in the voice.

More surprising, however, is the later February 1957 studio recording. In it the beguiling, nubile facet of Rosina's character sounds almost false. Hurling recitative curses such as "Crepa di rabbia, vecchio maledetto!" ("Choke on that, evil old man!") with comedic legerity, Maria relies on the ham of a caricature—not a full-bodied character.

March saw the soprano step into Tebaldi territory. Naples, home of the Teatro San Carlo, was so considered a fanbase of the rival soprano that the theatre's artistic director, Pasquale di Costanzo, had refused to accommodate Callas. Only after he advised admiring patron Antonietta Carrano, "Listen, if you can gather three thousand signatures from Neapolitan residents that demand the appearance of Callas, I'll get her to sing here," was the invitation reluctantly sent.[105]

Though scarcely covered by the press, this Lucia di Lammermoor was special to a pair of sopranos: Maria and Birgit Nilsson. The latter would remember: "She was booed in Act I and wildly cheered in the next—the gap between heaven and hell is very narrow in Italian opera."[106] A couple of weeks later Maria wrote to Walter Legge, "I'm sorry that you couldn't come to Naples because I even sang better than [in] Berlin . . . I'm most comfortable at home [Milan] even if every performance is a real bull fight! They all find my voice improving—I feel it too!"[107]

During Maria's reimmersion in a 1956 revival of Visconti's famed La traviata there was no pause from the bullfighting. "I have this presentiment that something will happen tonight," Maria told Giovanna Lomazzi with an aura of gravity.[108] It was 19 January, three months before the Naples Lucia. Maria warned Visconti: "The claques . . . You will see—just before I sing the 'gioir' [of "Sempre libera"]—someone will do something. It'll be an 'ooh' or an 'ahh' and it'll come from the gods."[109]

A holler of a moan arrived on point at the "gioir" exactly as Maria had foreseen. To the curtain call came a rainfall of gifts: flowers or jewels? No. Myopic Maria could scarcely distinguish them. Taking some into her hand, she offered an elegant curtsey; her arms draped in radishes.[110]

It was the Tebaldi claque. Had they been employed by Tebaldi herself, by her manager, or by an unknown representative? No one knew. And yet the war between these heated factions persevered.

Her next debut is a mystery. Giordano's *Fedora* is a fictional, late nineteenth-century story of nobles the "Romazovs". Heroine Fedora's fiancé Vladimir is murdered by Loris Ipanov; she swears revenge. The problem is that he's in love with her and openly admits it. Determined to stay true to the departed Vladimir, Fedora fights off her attraction to Loris. She pens a letter to the chief of the Imperial Police, accusing both Loris and his brother Valeriano. The latter perishes and dies. Meanwhile she learns that Vladimir died in a duel for sleeping with Loris' wife. Enamored with her former foe, she takes him as her lover.

Yet it's too late: Valeriano drowns after a river floods his prison; his and Loris' mother dies from shock. In her remorse Fedora swallows poison and expires in Loris' arms.

Officially no recording exists—although rumors abound.[ii] Directed by Russian director Tatiana Pavlova, the spectacle evoked an eerie ambience: Fedora "semi-spoke" in death. Before that her relationship with her ex-enemy grew dark and delved into an episode postmodern; emanating sado-masochistic lust.

Smitten with another caliber of fervor on the cusp of opening night, Maria suffered from a fever sparked by festering infection. The previous Saturday a fall had made her graze her left foot on a prop. Her fondness for rehearsal had discouraged her from seeking medical attention.[111]

The pain that night was real twofold. "I asked Maria if I could seize her by the hair during my anger," tenor Franco Corelli remembered. "She loved the idea and put a hundred pins in her beautiful chignon to hold it in place." When Fedora confessed she had reported Valeriano to the police, Maria fell to her knees. Denouncing her, Loris dragged the repentant woman by her hair along the ground. She drank poison she had kept sealed in a crucifix. As he finally forgave and cradled her, Maria sang those last words: "Loris, I feel cold. Warm me in your embrace. Give me a little of your love . . . your lips." Corelli cited how much she had made him work in order to perfect love born in death: "Maria had helped me so much during rehearsal that in performance we completely interlocked. That's the only word for it. Interlocked."[112]

That June heralded the Vienna *Lucia* under Karajan that would truncate their mutual respect—as well as a torturous thunder of panic. Having forgotten to transport the miniature of the Madonna Meneghini had once given her, Maria asked best friend Lomazzi to recover it and board the next flight to Vienna from Milan.[113] "I take it with me everywhere," Maria would enlighten the French press one day.[114] "Only twice have I forgotten to take it to my dress-

---

[i] Corelli's son told biographer René Seghers that he knew a magistrate who had a tape of it but had forgotten the latter's name. His wife Loretta insisted it didn't exist. (Seghers, 493, n. 24).

ing room and on both occasions I developed severe hoarseness and couldn't go on," she professed. "I don't think I'm superstitious. Such things have mystic implications in our lives. I am a fatalist and firm believer in destiny."[115]

As far as artists went, Maria's superstition inched toward extremism. One of her letters to Giulietta Simionato marveled at the fact that she had been reflecting on her moments with the mezzo when her missive had arrived. "Telepathy," Maria described. "It happens to me often, you know."[116]

Together with a fear of bad omens came a persistent belief in astrology: "I'm a Sagittarius: I throw arrows."[117] The older she got, the more often she referred to her horoscopes;[118] allegedly consulting a Parisian astrologer once.[119]

It seemed Maria's fears had saved the day. The journal *Kunst und Kultur* wrote about her Austrian debut: "the voice of La Callas is sometimes a bit cool and glazed . . . [but] she loosed all kinds of the most dangerous coloratura from the glimmering limbs of her flawless range!"[120]

Fate brought Maria and Karajan together again in the beach town of Ischia that July, where Maria and Meneghini vacationed for two weeks.[121] Whilst Karajan avoided cars by scootering, the couple tried to hire an amphibious aircraft. After their attempt to anchor it to a pier with a wire instead of a rope the plane sank. Its pilot was lucky enough to survive.[122]

Other amusements that summer involved Maria sitting on the jury of Miss Ischia: a modeling competition that took place at much-loved haunt Monkey Bar.[123] Shaded from the duty of performance, the soprano wandered round the beach in the company of the ever-present Giovanna Lomazzi, lightly performing or humming parts of *Norma* or *La sonnambula*.[124] Haphazardly she stumbled upon composer William Walton—who attempted, in vain, to persuade her to sing the part of Cressida in his *Troilus and Cressida*. Maria vowed she couldn't understand it and said no.[125]

Her rejection was deliberate. The soprano's animosity for modern music spanned the scope of many a composer's works—including Samuel Barber's. That fall he attempted ardently to have her sing the title role in his *Vanessa*.[126] Maria went so far as to visit the home Barber shared with his lover, composer Gian Carlo Menotti, in Mount Kisco, New York. Accompanying her were Meneghini and poodle Toy. Barber believed the magnitude of Erika, a mezzo role, was what deterred Maria.[127] The truth was closer to the contrary: "*I* would have preferred *not* the part of *Vanessa* but the part of the, er—other *girl* which was—I don't remember the *name*, whether she was 'Fricka' or something like that . . . the part of Vanessa had *nothing* to do absolutely with *my* spiritual world."[128]

Months later she would leave François Poulenc on tenterhooks after attending the premiere of the composer's *Dialogues des Carmélites*.[129] Imagining that she would play the heroine of his *La voix humaine*, he wrote excitedly to publisher Hervé Dugardin: "We await La Voix. It'll be Callas at La Scala, [Denise] Duval in Paris. Genius is ours!"[130]

It was never going to happen.

"I consider it some kind of noise—whereas music should do *good* to the ears, to the nervous system, to the heart,"[131] was her immoveable reaction to contemporary music. When on one occasion Georg Solti suggested she perform Alban Berg's *Lulu*, her response was: "*Lulu*? What *Lulu*?" Upon her learning who had written it, the swift dismissal was abrupt: "Berg? Terrible music! Why don't we do Bellini?"[132]

The next 1956 vacation transpired in Venice. On the Lido beach young men approached the sunbathing Maria and Lomazzi to invite them to a party.[133] Pointing to the sleeping Meneghini, Maria offered the response that she would "have to ask her father."[134]

By this period she was attempting to slow down with her engagements. Although Sander Gorlinsky pelted projects at her endlessly—including a Royal Opera concert to be held that 9 February 1957—Meneghini spurned a plethora of offers on his wife's behalf.[135] All her intentions purified, they were no longer quests for glory; the sole goal was art. Serving art did not mean serving art *x* times a year. Maria treasured having as much time as possible in order to prepare a role.

That summer registered two more recordings: *Il trovatore* and *La bohème*, the latter of which she had never performed on the stage. At the same time American artist Henry Koerner—who famously composed portraits of John F. Kennedy and others—arrived to paint Maria for an upcoming issue of *Time* magazine. Its release would coincide with her Metropolitan debut.

He remembered the *Bohème* recording: "The engineers and musicians, sweating and endlessly patient, were waiting for Callas' final approval. Callas, oblivious of her surroundings, her face transfigured with bliss, her wide lips spread open over her large teeth, repeated silently the tender phrase of Mimì '. . . ma quando vien lo sgelo, il primo sole è mio.' ('But when thaw comes the first sun is mine.')."[136] Twenty takes were made of her last scene and still Maria wasn't satisfied.[137]

Maria's approach to Mimì's character was quasi-patronizing: "She's so calm, she's *sick* . . ." she noted to Juilliard student Pamela Hebert in 1971. "That's why you're not interested in the part."[138] On another occasion she said, "If you were to ask me to sing *Bohème*, I'd have nothing to bite on."[139]

A large part of Mimì is spared vibrato through the course of this recording; Callas told a journalist much of her music "must be whispered over the microphone."[140] Mimì is innocent and dreamy; her stress on little details like the "si" in "poesia" when she sings of loving "things that seem poetic" symbolize her modesty's surrender to romanticism. Despite the consumption that will snatch her from life and the arms of failed playwright Rodolfo, in Maria's voice Mimì occasionally coruscates with vocal corpulence. When she sings of "il profumo d'un fior" ("the scent of a flower"), the vibrato embodies euphoric crescendo.

By the last act Mimì's voice is spent. In her dying days it's somber, slender; shier than it was in her first diffident encounter with Rodolfo. The aria

"Donde lieta uscì" presents a tone grown fuller and more resolute: she strives to save herself by clawing into love. Mimì's final arc of a crescendo ardently demands of her Rodolfo: "No, tu non mi lasci più" ("No, you won't leave me again"). A whisper of flirtatiousness insinuates her voice as she sings "Sono andati," admitting to Rodolfo she pretended to be sleeping "Perché volli con te sola restare" ("Because I wanted to stay here with you alone"). The last time she recalls their meeting by remembering her aria, "Mi chiamano Mimì . . . Il perché . . . non so . . ." ("They call me Mimì . . . Why . . . I don't know . . .") her voice drops off in feebleness. Or is she just coquetting still?

Maria's work in the opera is semi-inventive. Accused of the potential to do more, she might have blamed Mimì. It's difficult to know whether the singer or the character is more at fault for everything that *could* have been.

*

That fall the soprano prepared diligently for her Met debut in *Norma*.

Giovanna Lomazzi and her friend Anna Veronese were sent ahead together with Maria's wardrobe, which was carefully curated by the maestra Biki. Having instructed them not to iron the woolen garments—"Just expose them to vapor from hot water"—the two friends followed her suggestions, acting as assistants. Clothes were hung up on the rail above a running bath.

Later entering the bathroom, they found the thirty or so garments dunked in water: a black suit with mink cuffs, a camel coat, a cape, two velvet evening dresses.

Lomazzi didn't have the heart to tell their friend her clothes had all been ruined. So grand was the pressure of a Metropolitan debut, Maria scarcely referenced them. When she would ask about a piece Lomazzi, Veronese and the hotel maid had failed to save from shrinking, Lomazzi would avert her interest with: "Really? You want to wear *that*? It doesn't suit you very well . . ."[141]

By the time of her arrival on October 13th Bagarozy had started to blackmail Maria.[142] He had the letters she had written him in 1947: the kind that superficially implied they had been more than friends despite his marriage to her vocal coach.[143] Maria instructed her lawyer Walter J. Cummings to mention in court Bagarozy's efforts to market her letters for $30,000.[144] The ex-agent retaliated by taking his charges to New York's Supreme Court. This new lawsuit sought three hundred thousand from Maria.[145]

After a Chicago federal judge declined to let New York State poach the lawsuit, Judge Walter J. LaBuy of the U.S. District Court of Northern Illinois scheduled a trial date for November 18th, 1957.[146] Advised they would lose the case, Maria and Meneghini arrived at an out-of-court settlement only one day before.[147] Though the sum was never published, friend and biographer Stelios Galatopoulos surmised that Maria would have paid what constituted "a royalty on her earnings in the United States until 1957": around $40,000.[148]

Maria was accommodated at the Metropolitan with gallantry on Rudolf Bing's part but an abstinent decorum elsewhere. With old and barely maintained sets and a lethargic crew that often cited labor unions, the soprano was dissatisfied with the rigidity of such restrictions.[149] New York was so excited that its *Times* published an article announcing her arrival at the first day of rehearsal. "Metropolitan bystanders described Miss Callas as 'very charming,' " it read.[150]

One fan in particular was eager to pledge unconditional devotion: a lanky woman with a husky voice, blonde waves, and tweed, androgynous attire called Marlene Dietrich.[151]

Maria's friend Leo Lerman—a Bohemian contributing editor to *Mademoiselle*—set up the meeting. It was 21 October 1956. Maria was wearing a "beautifully cut black afternoon frock made by expert Italian hands. It was ornamented, in exactly the right spot, high on her left side, with an intricate diamond brooch." Those signature "white kid gloves" blanched her arms. Dietrich arrived in her tweed clothes looking very equestrian. They talked. Or rather—Dietrich talked; Maria mostly sat politely. Eventually Dietrich could not resist ceding a piece of advice: "But, *liebling*, you should really not have such hair . . . *Liebling*, I know exactly the right hair for you . . . And, *liebling*, I will make for you the most wonderful thing. It will preserve your voice. I will make for you beef tea."

Throughout this colloquy Maria was her awkward, good girl self. After she left, Dietrich remarked to Lerman: "She doesn't have much conversation, does she?"[152]

Some days later she arrived before Maria's suite at Hotel Sulgrave armed with her "beef tea". Though the legend had spent hours boiling "eight pounds of beef" for the broth, Maria asked: "Tell me, what brand of cubes do you use?"[153] Shortly after Dietrich's departure, she discarded the beverage.[154]

Meanwhile Evangelia was working hard to slash her daughter's reputation. Despite having commissioned a painter to work on her portrait that summer, *Time* magazine had scant interest in producing a verisimilitudinous Callas. The eventual feature by George de Carvalho read like a tabloid: accusing Maria of punching a colleague's nose, hating her classmates and advising her mother to kill herself.

Once again Maria worked on a defense. Once again—fearing the consequences—she elected not to publish it. "It's nonsense that I hated everyone at school . . . We rehearsed *Tosca* [in Athens] for three months— the bloody nose story . . . is nonsense . . . The story about my husband putting flowers on my bed is ridiculous."[155] Maria didn't have the fight to send it to an outlet. Her pluck was busy being channeled elsewhere.

Luckily for her, she and her father George were growing closer. That February he and Evangelia had finally divorced. In accordance with her lack of sympathy for Evangelia and Jackie, George would sarcastically refer to the inert two women as "great workers".[156]

He, Lomazzi, Meneghini and Maria would meet up and rove during her New York stay. George gave her a detergent to use on her eczema and was welcomed to the Met through a staff-only entrance. He attended every performance and Bing treated him with the utmost respect.[157] In 1958 he and Maria would appear on the tv show of Hy Gardner—who would reference Evangelia's mordant words to journalists. George would correct in half-honed English: "I believe this attitude of mother, somebody else is behind her, and does that."

Maria ignored the nefarious press for the sake of her training. In the future she would work full steam ahead to ensure a debut would be safe from a smeared reputation. "These are very personal and intimate problems or 'affairs' of the family and I feel it is my privilege and duty to keep them so,"[158] was her response to a reporter's probing about Evangelia. "All I can say is that, please, let's leave this in the four walls of the family because anything that happens only makes it worse for *any* reconciliation or anything."

A couple of years later Maria was being interviewed by Edward Murrow together with Sir Thomas Beecham. The elderly conductor declared, with regards to a colleague: "Madam Callas is supposed to have hit the gentleman on the head with a bottle of brandy, and I want to know if that's true or not," Maria laughed. "The newspapers have written *so* much and *so* much—God only knows . . . We remember to be ladies and we can't do that—and *then* . . . it would be a shame for the bottle you know, *really*."[159]

It looked like she was taking all these spurious anecdotes in stride.

She wasn't.

The day of Maria's Metropolitan debut in *Norma*—October 29, 1956— was marked with noxious augury. Badly congested, she was plagued synchronically by heat and air conditioning: singers' worst nightmare. "Battista," she alerted Meneghini in her dressing room as Lomazzi looked on, "I can't sing this evening."

"You can't *sing?*" came the brusque reply. "Goodness gracious, you are out of your mind, girl! You are out of your mind!"[160] His curtness hurt her. Maria started to weep. It was the first time in their five-year friendship that Lomazzi saw her friend cry.

Eleven curtain calls for the impaired performer.[161] Choreographer and ballet innovator Martha Graham was astounded. "Her sense of design, her never-failing animal-like absorption in the instant—that spiral of inner activity which is rare and devastating to watch . . ." she described in a letter.[162] A Chicago critic noted: "It was a nervous Maria Callas who took to the stage—a tremulous sound in the voice reminded one of Butterfly's entrance last November at Chicago . . . Then things, magical things, to Chicagoans familiar, but still and incomparably magical—began happening."[163]

The New York critics warmed to her with ease. Irving Kolodin limned "an organ made in the image of a sound in her ear which demands that it be flexible, far ranging, responsive to a wide variety of inflections and intensities . . . Miss Callas strikes me as possessed of the clarinet timbre, with the same kind of reedy fullness (and a trace of its vibrato), brilliant on top, misty at the bottom, and with the glossy agility of the black woodwind. And she works on it like a woodwind player fingering invisible keys."[164]

There followed a ball at the Ambassador Hotel in New York. It was one am when Maria came sauntering in clad in cherry-hued velvet and diamonds. A mysterious man followed close by. The next day Maria's friends learned jeweler Harry Winston had recruited the detective to protect one million dollars' worth of diamonds: all of them on loan.[165] By this point Maria had her own personal jeweler in Swarovski's Ennio Marangoni.[166]

The hype continued as Leo Lerman hosted a special "Attire mystical" gala for Callas with "pink tablecloths and napkins . . . and roses, and hysterics" and food catered by Pearl's, a Cantonese restaurant.[167] Gossip columnist Dorothy Kilgallen's headline read: "Long-Haired Darling Triumphs at the Met."[168]

That Saturday 3 November Maria's stamina began to shrink before her illness. A doctor was called to her dressing room shortly before her *Lucia* was due to begin. Bing was summoned to announce before the public that the lead was "indisposed" but would sing anyway.[169] Amidst the audience was Noël Coward, who would draw comparisons between Maria and renowned soprano Mary Garden that night in a journal entry full of exultation.[170]

Rehearsals for *Tosca* were mute on Maria's part. During one she slipped a note to conductor Dimitri Mitropoulos. She had last worked with him on the same opera as a teenager in Athens. It informed the maestro he had cued a certain section "two bars earlier than we had agreed on in the Athens performance."[171]

Among the dust-enrobed, decrepit, rusty sets, Maria was attempting to envisage something close to a production—especially when she and bass George London had to perform *Tosca*'s Act II for *The Ed Sullivan Show* on 26 November. "At one point, during the dress rehearsal, she couldn't pass to cross the stage and pick up the two candelabras and announced to the director, 'There are just too many legs around here.' "[172]

Maria's Met *Tosca* met with further elation from critics: "coldly beautiful and almost bonily slender . . . by turns a rather shrewish minx, a passionate Latin woman of mercurial temperament fully capable of the impulsive murder, and a tender young girl eager for Mario's love," scribed Richard Eyer in *Musical America*.[173]

Someone else was of a contrary opinion but did not express it to Maria. Unbeknownst to her, Rosa Ponselle was watching *The Ed Sullivan Show*. The soprano later referred to her *Tosca* as "a studied rather than spontaneous delivery . . . For instance, I kept being distracted by the way she took care of the train of her dress; she fussed with it, moved it around, as if to improve its line for some questionable visual reason."[174] Maria's Tosca had always been fussy; it had been her mantra to refer to the character's "nervousness".[175] Ponselle did not live up to understanding the artistic choices of the woman who still worshipped her. It was ironic.

Seemingly recovered, Maria attended the world premiere of Bernstein's *Candide* on 1 December 1956[176] whilst still struggling to accept the "awful" *Lucia* production: "I sang in cardboard," she would later recall. "It was *terrible*."[177]

Openly she declared two years afterward: "The Metropolitan has *not* got money—*unfortunately* because it *should* be—I *insist* upon this; that the government spends so much money *all* over—[it] could spend a *minimum* of money, which would be a *minimum* for the *stage* which would be an *enormous* thing for the Met . . . They [the public] *want* good opera and they pay whatever sum for *really* good opera . . . I hope it keeps on going. I hope it just doesn't fade out because today in the era of the Sputnik and so forth and so on, the public has become *wise*; they *want* lovely things and they must *have* it."[178]

On top of that the Met's acoustics made her anxious. "When you sing at the Metropolitan you lose control of your voice because you don't hear it at all so you force yourself. And that is very unfortunate for a voice 'cause *forcing* means that you use a muscle of the vocal cord and that is *very*, very bad. We should *never*, never use the vocal cords; we should only use *breath* and resonance . . . So at the Metropolitan, not hearing your voice, you get panicky, you force your voice and of course the whole—the whole picture of the music that you do is not just *it*."[179] Maria preferred La Scala's acoustics. What she especially enjoyed was singing in the shower. "Sometimes you wish in the theatre it had acoustics like that; it'd be easier!"[180]

Circumstances became triply trying when, during the performance of 8 December, baritone Enzo Sordello vulgarly held on to a high G in the second act duet of *Lucia*.[181] Walking offstage, Maria remarked: "Eh, Sordello—I think you may have overdone it somewhat!" The comment spawned Sordello's hissy fit: "You're not the boss around here! This is not La Scala. If you don't like the way I sing, then leave!"[182]

Headlines suggested that Maria had arranged to have Sordello fired: after all, she had been absent from the next performance on 11 December; substituted by Dolores Wilson. Surely she had given Bing an ultimatum?

Five years after the event Lomazzi insisted that wasn't the case. Maria's ailing health had been the reason for her non-appearance. Bing's press statement had cited Sordello's comportment as "uncooperative and insubordinate".[183] Three years afterward Sordello would wax lyrical about his much-discussed dismissal: "They gave me plenty of money and zumm!—I was on a plane to spend Christmas with my family in Italy. What could be nicer?" When the interviewer sought to know about the "tiger" Callas, Sordello responded: "She is not a tigress. She is a sheep."[184]

A recording from the performance of 3 December demonstrates both vocal insecurity and tension on Maria's part. "If, together, we [the artists] don't feel comfortable, the work is vinegar instead of Chantilly," she would explain.[185] This particular *Lucia* was the former.

That winter Maria finally got to spend Christmas at home in Milan. "The warm atmosphere of the Vigil with the painting of the Madonna [at the Duomo Cathedral], the streets of Milan packed with happy people hauling parcels underneath their arms . . . I had dreamt of that kind of Christmas," she would later recount.[186]

In the comfort of that space her haven was the nighttime. Wracked with nerves, she watched late-night talk shows or old films, avoiding cinemas for fear of catching colds.[187] Studying scores in bed was her ritual. "In the quiet of the evening it is possible to study. Not during the day. Then the phone is constantly ringing. So at night-time I like to go over a score, then I find I notice things which had escaped me before. I usually study when I am in bed with my husband sound asleep beside me, and my two poodles, Tea who is seven and Toy who is three, dozing away in a corner," she would write.[188]

The media was in a frenzy. It had been several decades since an opera singer had been profiled daily in the press. One journalist declared that popularity had swung in favor of the movie star over the diva—adding that the Metropolitan's metamorphosis was suggesting prima donnas would experience a renaissance of fame.[189]

To Maria "prima donna" had a single, very strict definition: "We are the first instrument of the orchestra. It's a whole orchestra, and the voices are the solo of this orchestra . . ."[190] It should have none of its present-day associations with caprice, with 'carrying on like a prima donna.' "[191]

A lost title had been resurrected. Unlike divas of the past who were alleged to have regarded their rehearsals as an inconvenience,[192] this singer was afraid to face one.

I do not know what makes me different, she wrote in an article once. *This may sound ridiculous, but it is true. I honestly have not fully realised what I have become. I cannot grasp it. I cannot see what I am. And the pity of it is that I shall never be able to see the total effect of what I produce.*

Then at other times when I feel I have really given of my best the audience's reaction is not the same. So the mystery remains. It haunts me . . . For just like a painting seemingly "finished" in every respect somehow looks cold, so too a truly great performance lacks the highest pitch if it is too perfect. That sort of perfection is not human, and I first of all am human, and also the roles I create.[193]

Branded a miracle, Maria was no longer interested in being held up as a god. Her miraculous repute was scheduled for a rewind.

1. *13-year-old Maria, 19-year-old Jackie, disapproving mother Evangelia. New York, c. 1937.*

2. *Adult-ish Maria drawing inspiration from canaries. Athens, c. 1940.*

3. *Maria on the S.S. Rossia on her way to Italy. June 1947.*

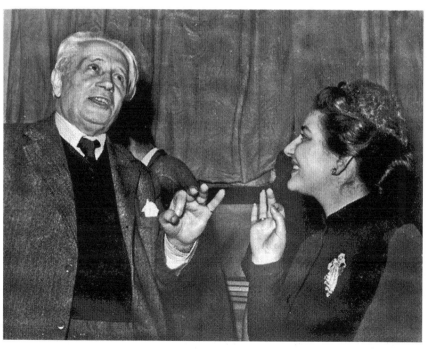

4. *Maria at the helm of Maestro Tullio Serafin, 1952.*

5. *Maria, Wally Toscanini, Meneghini, lawyer Teodoro Bubbio and director Tatiana Pavlova at the opening night of the La Scala 1953–54 season,* La Wally *starring Renata Tebaldi.*

6. *Already an actress. Still green. Maria as* I puritani's *Elvira in a promotional shot for the Palacio de Bellas Artes, Mexico May 1952 production.*

7. *Breaktime at the recording of* I pagliacci, *with Giuseppe Di Stefano, June 1954.*

8. *A pre-tearful Norma. Publicity shot for a La Scala production, 7 December 1955.*

9. *Maria and Lenny have tea. Callas and Bernstein during preparations for her* La Sonnambula *debut. Milan, early-mid February 1955.*

10. *Post-party, pre-enchaining love. Violetta wonders pensively. (Opening night of* La traviata, La Scala, 28 May 1955).

11. *Smug Maria and miffed Meneghini. Post the notorious Rome* Norma *in front of reporters on 14 January 1958.*

12. *This time with visible reporters. Unknown location, 1958.*

13. *Imogene not resigned to her destiny. A promotional shot for La Scala's* Il pirata *with Ettore Bastianini, 19 May 1958.*

14. *At Kingsway Hall recording* Lucia. *March 1959.*

15. *With father George after her Carnegie Hall concert performance of* Il pirata. *New York, 27 January 1959.*

16. *"With Germans, it's like a church. For them I'm like the Madonna." Maria onstage in Stuttgart, 19 May 1959.*

10.

"A human note"

Like an antique crystal vase, Maria Callas couldn't break. For she was too expensive an investment.

"Wherever I am, it is hectic," was her portentous avowal.[1] No wonder. Each of her appearances—at opera houses, ribbon-cuttings or society balls—was chaperoned by journalists as jealously as her most covetable diamonds by bodyguards. Always a person or a faction was appointed to keep tabs on any upcoming event. Chief of Police was none other than Man of the House, Meneghini himself. Such a commodity was his wife's name that there was no time for a fearful moment, let alone crisis of confidence.

Back in January 1957 they were growing in their number by the hour. "In such circumstances she wanted all those close to her to understand her," Giovanna Lomazzi reminisced four years later. "Battista Meneghini, despite having good intentions and hoping to bolster her morale, adopted a different approach: 'Goodness gracious, you are crazy!' he would yell at her. "You're perfectly fine—you've never been better. Come on—you've got to go onstage tonight!' "[2]

Maria did not always live up to her "unbreakable" image. In the words of Walter Legge, every recording session was met with: "Don't tell me what is good—tell me what you don't like and why you don't like it."[3] Despite "hating" to vocalize, she still spent hours at home practicing the exercises of composer-pedagogues Heinrich Panofka and Giuseppe Concone.[4]

Following a gospel that decreed a "singer, like an athlete, has to practice every day to stay in shape,"[5] Maria nonetheless was puzzled by her vocal qualms. "Mine is a capricious instrument," she claimed. "In other words, there are days when my voice refuses to sing certain registers—but the contract dictates that I must sing this or that opera on a particular day, at that particular hour, whatever my vocal 'mood' is. It's one of the hardest struggles that I must surmount. And so I adapt to the right approach and force my voice to do something it doesn't want to do."[6]

Chronic panic would invariably ensue. As a result Maria suffered irremediably from long bouts of insomnia. She had already been enduring them throughout her tours in South America, lying awake to watch the clock strike half past eight.[7]

In the weeks that bridged the end of 1956 and the New Year Maria called on a reporter for Italian weekly glossy *Oggi* to ghostwrite her memoirs. Journalist Anita Pensotti was instructed to arrive no earlier than 11:30 pm. "I have to go to bed very late," Maria explained. "Otherwise I just don't fall asleep and stay awake hour after hour." The memoirs—which are widely quoted here—were published in January 1957 in five separate installments.

After giving a benefit concert in Chicago for the Alliance Française in aid of Hungarian Relief[8] Maria landed in London to happily learn that her voice was behaving. For this incarnation of *Norma* on 2 February one critic referred to the "intense poetry and a poised beauty of line that recalled the Golden Age;" another cited "descending chromatic scales which are so characteristic of Norma's music, and which she weighs with a curious, highly individual melancholy that stabs at the heart."[9]

Thus 1957 started in good spirits: "This is the third *Norma* that I've performed here," she wrote to her friend, music critic Eugenio Gara. "And it was enormously liked . . . They found my voice better than ever; easier to listen to and more even. And I felt it too."[10]

Regarding the *La traviata* that she sang a few days later, French music critic Jacques Bourgeois would have like comments: "It must be said that Callas is in excellent voice. Of course, throughout the performance one could have counted half a dozen strident top notes but an American critic there that night who had witnessed her recent New York run told me that the ugliest note of the evening was still far more beautiful than the most glorious note in New York . . ."[11]

The instrument was a seesaw.

Similarly pleased was Maria with her next run of *La sonnambula*s at La Scala that March. "Here the Sonnambula goes beautifully, I'm sorry you miss them," she gleefully informed the British music critic Harold Rosenthal."[12]

It was thus with evident excitement that Maria boarded her next novel challenge: Donizetti's *Anna Bolena*. Termed "an old bore" by Rudolf Bing,[13] the 1830 opera struggled to elicit hype, premiering at the Metropolitan no earlier than in September 2011.[14]

Passing by her house in early April 1957, Lomazzi found Maria hidden by a horde of books on Tudor history.[15] On one occasion the soprano goaded her best friend to take her to a play about the hopelessly doomed British queen.[16]

Eventually Maria learned that Donizetti and librettist Felice Romani were fudging the truth. Though versions of the tale abound, in this romantic (and Romantic) story Anne Boleyn is torn between her love for the adulterous Henry VIII—by now romancing lady-in-waiting Jane

("Giovanna") Seymour—and her first love Henry Percy (known here as "Riccardo Percy"), who has recently been exiled by the king. After Henry frames her for adultery with court musician Smeton, she is taken to the gallows. The opera's core is censored when it comes to most historiography—some of which claims the king accused his wife of incest with her brother George.

Her conceit about the woman deromanticized, Maria suddenly lost interest in unearthing facts. Now she was reticent to even broach the subject of the queen behind the opera. "I didn't *want* to read about—I mean, I started reading about her, I saw that it was not at all—on the *contrary*, it was the *opposite* of what I—so I stopped. That was all," clumsily she explicated.[17] Music critic Lanfranco Rasponi, who once discussed *Anna Bolena* with her, even claimed: "Nor did she know how many other wives Henry VIII had had; they did not interest her."[18]

To emanate the ambience of Tudor London Luchino Visconti and designer Nicola Benois used "only black, white and gray" for the stage design. Relying on an optical illusion, the mostly two-dimensional décor had a deceptively voluminous veneer. Walls, staircases and hallways appeared oaken; roof beams lined the ceilings. The four-floor castle was luxuriously spacious. Inspired by portraits of the queen by Hans Holbein the Younger, every gown of Anne Boleyn's would be a novel shade of navy donning a gargantuan set of sparkling jewels; their shards of glimmer pierced a dusky backdrop.[19]

The Callas Anne Boleyn embodies discreet passion. Like a diamond brooch that glistens to attract attention to a woman in a bland black dress, her queen was poised and sometimes staid . . . yet purposely hypnotic. In her spectators witnessed a royal powerhouse with the impermeable dignity of a Greek pillar; simultaneously they watched "some lovely, terrified bird, unjustly pursued" in the description of Ida Cook.[20] Conductor Gianandrea Gavazzeni painted her in moments of acute fear as "wax-like, her hand damp and frozen."[21]

Every scene throughout this opera is a battle raging between Anna's outer image—noble, couth, demure, unflappable—and the innately wondrous woman reminiscing still about her courtship by the king.

Her expressions of turmoil barely hint at displeasure. The premiere's recording illustrates the persecuted Anna's bold determination to preserve respectability—at least, whatever lingers of it. After yielding to an agitated rush of notes when she admits to an "uneasy restlessness" ("Smania inquieta"), Anna immediately contains herself as she relates how it has snatched her peace away for days ("a me la pace da più giorni invola").

The arioso Anna sings about her court musician Smeton, "Come innocente giovane" ("What an innocent young man") is executed in a ceremonious fashion. Reflecting on her first love, Percy, she reluctantly unveils that if she didn't feel attachment to him she would be content in regal luxury. ("Ah! Non avessi il petto aperto ad altro affetto, io non sarei si misera nel vano mio splendor"). Pain is palpable through the crescendo of "si misera" ("so miserable") in which Maria accrues thick vibrato to hint at her heroine's anguish. The rest of it is sung at mezzo forte almost in tranquility: delivered like a sermon.

Confronted with the task of meeting her old love again she almost loses it. The frame of the façade that has enclosed young Anna comes abruptly off its hinges as she catches sight of Percy. "Eccolo! . . . io tremo! . . . io gelo!" ("There he is! . . . I'm trembling! . . . I'm shaking!") she exclaims with timidly awakening vibrato: the quickening pace of her heart. Her informal address of his first name Riccardo is performed with a delicate diminuendo. Anna can't resist her pathos. Or her tenderness.

Cue the onset of self-righteousness. "Non sai che moglie son, che son Regina?" she demands to know. ("Don't you know that I'm a wife, that I'm a queen?"). The voice accelerates and builds up more vibrato to accentuate the onetime sweethearts' differences in status. Stood before this exiled man, she must acknowledge her position and not stoop to pity.

At the same time she is loath but ready to admit the king detests her. It's a slow realization ("M'aborre è vero": "He abhors me, it is true") with an exceptionally tentative, unraveling roulade on "vero". If Percy loves her, she demands, he shall not speak to her of love ("Mai più, s'è ver che m'ami, non parlar con me d'amor"). Paradoxically as Anna issues this command her voice surrenders to diminuendo in compassion on the phrase, "if it is true that you love me" ("s'è ver che m'ami").

A volte-face has to ensue again. Anna's threat to Percy, "May a new dawn not find you still in England" ("In Inghilterra non ti trovi il nuovo albor"), exploits the cave-like Callas chest voice; echoing the Tower of London where Anna will meet with her harrowing fate.

So beholden is she to her regal status that she struggles to believe King Henry when he finally condemns her by accusing her of loving Smeton. "Giudici . . . ad Anna? Giudici . . . ad *Anna?* Ad *Anna* . . . Giudici?!" ("Judges . . . for Anna? Judges . . . for *Anna?* For *Anna* . . . there are judges?!"). The initial iteration isn't even exclamation—sounding almost like a stipulation on an academic thesis: it's possible Queen Anne could be arrested? *How?*

The second time is louder, quicker; shock pervades the tone. By the third time Anna understands her fate. Her cry for help is followed by an outburst of "ah-AH" performed with burgeoning anxiety; a stretched-out portamento rising through the pair of notes.

When she learns Giovanna is her rival for the king's heart ("Tu, tu, mia rivale!") an increasingly frenetic, venomous vibrato over "mia" rings with cruel astonishment. Anna doesn't merely grow indignant; she is danger-ously catatonic. It is with maternal sympathy that she forgives the young, impressionable woman: "Va, infelice, e teco reca il perdono di Bolena" ("Go on, you unhappy girl, and have the pardon of Boleyn"). It's not a ploy. A slow diminuendo on the word "perdono" lets us see that it is real: in Giovanna Anna sees a mirror image of her former self.

Her voice is slick with reverence as she supplicates the king: "A' piedi tuoi mi prostro" ("I prostrate myself at your feet"). But when Henry expounds further on the accusation Anna strips bare her impertinence. While the libretto has "Cessa, cessa!" ("Stop, stop!") Maria sings "Taci, taci!" ("Hush, hush!"). Unsealed once again are dark, defiant tones reminding the hubristic king that he is speaking to Queen Anne.

Like most bel canto heroines Anna is destined to depart her senses. Enwrapped in memories, she gazes at her servants unaware of her surroundings, wondering aloud: "Piangete voi? Donde tal pianto?" ("You're weeping? Why are you weeping?"). Here the voice has lost its stately clout—and bears a mere stain of the youthful lacquer it possessed before. With her hair loose, ready for the guillotine, Anna must stop her consciousness. Immersing her awareness in a hazy vortex of illusion, she recalls her wedding day and that sweet childhood with her first love, Percy.

"Maria, how great you are!" Giulietta Simionato marveled during a rehearsal of this mad scene.

"Baloney. I'm just in a trance."[22]

Stirring fluxes of this vision, Anna now commands her maid as she had on her wedding day: "Il crin m'ornate del mio serto di rose" ("Adorn my hair with my rose garland"): once more she is a wistful girl in love. No longer is the king responsible for her decreed beheading; he's a bridegroom who awaits her at the altar. "Il Re m'aspetta" ("The King expects me") she sings softly, deferentially; almost obsequiously.

Illusion cracks. Anna is jolted back into reality: "Ei viene . . . ei mi accusa . . . ei mi grida. Oh! mi perdona . . . mi perdona!" ("Percy is coming . . . He blames me . . . He decries me. Oh, forgive me, Percy! Forgive me!"). Broken-up by panicked pauses, every blow of her epiphany strikes one more nail into her coffin.

A retreat to the "sweet, castle of home" is her final resort. In a spell of nubile innocence Anna begs Percy to escort her back there in the mad scene's supplicating aria ("Al dolce guidami castel natio"). Behind the specious semblance of a happily enamored girl the acridly deranged diminuendo on "castel natio" demonstrates she is no longer just deluded . . . but insane. Anna's excitement as she limns the rivers that "still murmur with our sighs" ("Al queto rio che i nostri mormora sospiri ancor") peaks at a glistening roulade on the "cor" of "ancor" that unwinds in perturbed exultation.

A queen cannot die in such frailty. Cannon shots corrupt her dream. In a quick instant Maria's Anna searched for the crown on her head.[23] Circumstances are corrosive to her conscious.

Resuming the dominion of her status, she proclaims to everyone around: "Tacete, tacete, cessate, cessate!" ("Hush, hush, stop, stop!"). Explodent in her caustic speech, Anna calls Henry and his consort "Coppia iniqua!" ("False couple!"): for the first time we hear scathing rancor in the slender timbre of the elongated notes.

When she insists she now wreaks vengeance on them in her final hours ("Estrema vendetta non . . . non impreco, no! In quest'ora tremenda")— unfurling a crescendo on "non impreco" before a rattling rolled "r" in "tremenda"—a roused lioness comes uncaged. Anna wants her citizens to know that God will judge her mercifully: she has done no wrong. Yet her accented pleas of "tacete, tacete, cessate, cessate!" ("hush, hush, stop, stop!") and the descending scales that mark "estrema vendetta" ("extreme vengeance") are a tantrum rather than a royal indictment. The besotted bride has fused with the quixotic queen to foster a new frightful creature. Numbered are her seconds.

In Visconti's lugubrious staging hooded extras were supposed to enshroud her and lead her to death. An error on the part of the stage manager on opening night derailed their entrance. Alone, Maria improvised the final gestures of her spellbound heroine.[24]

"Would *Anna Bolena* enter the international repertory?" British critic Desmond Shawe-Taylor asked. "With Callas, yes; without her, or some comparable soprano of whom as yet there is no sign, no."[25]

The extolment left Maria happy for the sake of the composer. "I'm so sorry you couldn't be here to attend an opera such as *Anna Bolena*, which moved and amazed everyone," she wrote to Oscar and Carla Coltellacci, a couple of fans who later became pirate record collectors.[26]

May came together with the year's first tempest. Predictably its origin was Meneghini. On the 4th it was announced that Maria's appearance at the Vienna State Opera was cancelled. The engagement had been verbally determined: quite sufficient for Maria who disliked the very notion of a legally secure accord.[27] "I do not need to sign a contract if I agree to do a thing," she would avow in 1970. "In principle I do not like the idea of a contract, because a contract means your word is put in question."[28]

Unbeknownst to her, business manager Meneghini didn't reason this way. He and Herbert von Karajan, then the director of the Vienna Opera, had discussed the proposal of six *Traviatas* that season. Karajan had offered the same fee Maria had received for her *Lucia* less than a year earlier. Meneghini had informed him duly that her fees had risen.[29] The official statement of the Vienna Opera declared Meneghini and Callas had requested "$500" more.[30] Karajan's widow recalled in her memoirs that "Meneghini's exorbitant financial requests put an end to the project."[31]

Maria's memory of this alleged controversy cast on it a different shade. "It had only been *proposed* that I sing in Vienna, and I decided I needed rest instead."[32]

The hustling Meneghini may have taken this into consideration, may have not. By this point he was writing letters to administrators globally in his wife's name; signing her signature. Persuaded to defer to his decisions, sometimes Maria copied his text word for word. Other times she wouldn't know what she was signing but affixed her signature.[33]

Despite relatively smooth relations with La Scala Meneghini hadn't reined in his exigencies. Every year he would present a needle in a haystack. Every new season he would shun the concept of a new production or revival—penning blunt refusals in his wife's name that were nothing like her writing style.[34] He would stop at nothing to attain the sum of his desire.

In June La Scala was to stage Riccardo Zandonai's *Francesca da Rimini* with Maria as the titular heroine. Technical challenges compelled its substitution in the form of Gluck's *Ifigenia in Tauride* (based on Euripides' *Iphigenia in Tauris*), to be performed in Italian instead of the original French.[35]

Maria and this opera didn't get on well. Neither did she and Visconti when it came to this work. "He told me he envisaged it in oratorio style, with costumes designed by Coco Chanel. I said 'Me, in an oratorio, costumed by Chanel?' "[36] Maria was insistent on the opera having a dramatic, realistic genre: "It can be *very* still in movement and very *flowing* but then, I mean, if you do *oratorio*, that's a terribly easy way *out*."[37]

Visconti's concept for the staging was a "rococo version of mythical Greece."[38] While Mademoiselle Chanel was sadly not recruited for sartorial advice, he clad Maria in a long white silken gown with many folds, a lengthy train and loops of pearls around her neck. The filmmaker got ahead of the opera director. He wanted Maria to run down an extremely steep ramp with a wind machine behind her back; her more than twenty-meter red cloak "flying wildly in the wind."[39]

Running down the "extremely steep ramp" was an obstacle for myopic Maria: "I found it very difficult to do, and he became angry and told me that any of his artists would do it. So I said 'Then let any of your artists do it,' and then I left. The next morning when he picked me up to take me to rehearsal, before he could say anything, I said 'Do be reasonable Luchino, and don't throw at me about "any of my artists" . . . if your ramp were steps, I would do it for you.' He changed it. But I must say I never understood why, in this production, there were so many people popping in and out."[40]

"I conceived my production to make Maria look as glorious as possible. But she didn't understand my idea at all," Visconti would recall. Yet Maria realized his race down steep steps against awesome wind: "Every night she hit her high note on the eighth step, so extraordinarily coordinated was her music and movement. She was like a circus horse, conditioned to pull off any theatrical stunt she was taught." In Visconti's opinion, it was "the most beautiful production we did together."[41]

Perhaps because the set and costumes were at odds with the Greek myth, Maria struggled to decipher the psychology of Ifigenia. Although audiences responded warmly[42] the premiere on 1 June produced a singer somewhat monochrome.

The voice vacillates between extremes in a recording. As one critic later wrote, it yields "a single color throughout—forceful, dark and thick."[43] The result is that throughout the opera it seems constantly as though the ever-pious Ifigenia—who seeks to sacrifice her brother after he implores her to spare Pylades, his sidekick—is consumed with wrath and bloodlust.

Preferring to hurl rabid exclamations of alarm so endless they become psychotic, Maria's Ifigenia never stoops to desperation. She exudes not the grandeur of Greek tragedy but playwrights Racine or Corneille's takes on the genre: seventeenth-century monologues despoiled of all subtlety.

Four more *Ifigenia*s were followed by a concert performance of *Lucia di Lammermoor* in Rome on the 26th. Though the recording attests that Maria omitted the mad scene's E flat, it may be her superlative version.

With her Lucia having switched her incarnations like the changing creatures across Ovid's *Metamorphoses*, this figure strikes the perfect balance between little girl in love and lethal psychopath. The contrast is effulgent and yet fearsome. Beauty is perilous.

In the aria "Regnava nel silenzio" Lucia laments the dead girl by the fountain. She sings of a pale moon ray ("un pallido raggio di tetra luna"); her voice slims down to skimpy eeriness so stealthily, we hear her slow ensnarement by transfixion.

Phantasmagorically frightening diminuendi stretch into extending portamenti. Lucia notes the girl's "mano esanime" (her "lifeless hand") in an attenuated, strangely concentrated, harrowing crescendo of both horror and obsession.

The voice itself sounds spectral; like Lucia's ghostly stalker. Indulging in hallucination, she does not want to get better. Another memory ensues: "the waters of the fountain reddened with blood" ("l'onda pria si limpida di sangue rosseggiò") and suddenly the voice turns on itself, becoming jubilant in a succession of staccato arpeggios. Lucia relishes her fairytale-like world of make-believe.

In her stupefying daze the villainess' urge to be the leading lady in her horror story is a greater catalyst for murdering her husband than her love for the wrong man.

Onomatopoeia is included in this narrative. Through her amorous excitement in the famed duet "Verranno a te" Maria charges the word "l'eco" in "l'eco dei miei lamenti" ("the echo of my lovelorn laments") with a piquant vibrato; an embodying echo.

When Lucia believes she is surrendering herself to Edgardo at the start of the mad scene, "Edgardo, io ti son resa" ("Edgardo, I am yours again") the portamento on the two notes that split "gar" into "GA-AAR" emerge with feralness. Was Lucia ever actually in love? Or does she—like real maniacs— just get a thrill from the unordered frenzy of her thoughts; from the excessive dopamine being driven through her brain?

As Lucia hallucinates about marrying Edgardo ("Here's the minister! Take my hand—Oh, happy day! At last I am yours . . . at last you are mine . . ."): "Ecco il Ministro! Porgimi la destra . . . Oh, lieto giorno! Oh, lieto . . . Alfin son tua . . . Alfin sei mio . . ."), Maria sings the lines with an enjambment that convinces us that "lieto" and "alfin" ("happy" and "at last") unite to form a single word.

Deluded Lucia can no longer separate tales from reality—or, apparently, units of language.

With birdsong cleaner than the flute accompanying the cabaletta "Spargi d'amaro pianto," Lucia unspools. Two selves are constantly at strife. In modern terms Maria converts nineteenth-century bel canto opera into psychological thriller: she becomes a Hitchcockian heroine.

*

That summer Maria journeyed with the newly found La Scala touring company, "La Piccola Scala" ("Little Scala") to Cologne to perform *La sonnambula*. Arriving on 2 July together with Meneghini and Giovanna Lomazzi, she was enclothed in a heat of 102°F that ascended to 111 at noon. During breaks from rehearsal Giuseppe Di Stefano would take off his costume and wander around with a towel round his waist.[44]

Finished in 1955, the modern architecture of the opera house—whose vast array of long, protruding boxes look like rifles poking from a trench—threw visually conservative Maria off her guard. "It's sort of difficult to be used to seeing modern theatre this way . . ." she diplomatically confessed in a radio interview. "But I must say that it may not be beautiful to look at as our theatres [go]—but it has a *beautiful* acoustic. So that is—maybe the most important thing." Attempting to seduce her faithful German public ("Ich kann nicht spricht Deutsch," Maria later proclaimed wholly ungrammatically),[45] she was suffering the heat's effects on her impressionable voice. "You can *die* from it," she told an Italian journalist on 6 July. "I get very tired because I run out of breath."[46]

While one critic alluded to "melting sweetness in floating pianos, metallic brilliance in fortes,"[47] Maria was on newly poor terms with her instrument. The release of that summer's recording of Puccini's *Manon Lescaut* was delayed for three years at her urging.[48] She admitted she was not "very pleased with it."[49]

Another engagement was looming. Maria had agreed to return to the city of Athens for a recital at its open-air ancient theatre, the Odeon of Herodes Atticus. Its sequence of negotiations spun out of control. After offering to donate her salary to the annual Athens Festival of which her performance was part, Maria was spurned by its administration—who elected to forfeit her charity.[50] Meneghini's roiled response was to demand a hefty sum for his wife's fee. A public announcement was made that claimed Callas was making exigent demands on the land of her origin.[51]

Overcome with ponderous exhaustion and by now severely underweight, Maria underwent a battery of tests to find the reason for her tireless fatigue. After consulting a cardiologist, a neurologist and an otolaryngologist, she was referred to gynecologist Dr. Carlo Palmieri. Palmieri diagnosed the imminent onset of early menopause, prescribing a series of injections he insisted could postpone it for a year.[52] Oddly, however, Maria would still menstruate into her early fifties—when a vocal coach who worked with her would cite her gripes about its impact on her voice.[53]

Writing of his wife's condition, Meneghini didn't specify the reasons for the diagnosis; neither did the medical report in his possession he presented to Maria's friend and future biographer, Stelios Galatopoulos, less than a year after her death.[54] But another discovery by Dr. Palmieri was a congenital uterine malformation. Its type appeared unspecified in the report and remained unremembered by her husband.

Although it is possible to conceive with a uterine malformation, at the time in Italy it was believed that carrying a baby to full term would be impossible without surgical intervention to alter the state of the uterus. While research of the period suggests that pregnancy occurred in cases such as these, gestation often led to severe complications, miscarriages or breech births, endangering the health of the mother.[55]

Surgical procedures to repair the uterus were still in early stages of advancement.[56] According to Meneghini, Palmieri warned Maria that this kind of operation would be detrimental to her health and voice. Less than two decades afterward procedures to treat variants of uterine malformation were deemed safe and in large part successful.[57] Yet the suggestion by the doctor back in summer 1957 almost seemed to be an ultimatum.

Years later Meneghini wrote Maria didn't want to lend consideration to this kind of surgery.[58] Seven years before she had complained to a physician of a "problem in her nose" that caused her nasal sound but forfeited the option of an operation that might sabotage her voice.[59] Although Palmieri's diagnosis of impending menopause was incorrect, it is unlikely Meneghini could have fabricated a false tale about her uterine condition. He was thoroughly uneducated in these matters.

Despite doubting her fertility, Maria still proclaimed that family and children were a woman's monumental cause for living. "If Battista had wanted, I would have given up my career without any regret," she had written earlier that year. "Because in the life of a woman (and I mean to say—a real woman)—love is more important, there is no comparison—than any artistic triumph. And I sincerely hope that anyone who doesn't have it will one day have at least a quarter—or a tenth—of my marital happiness."[60]

For all her deviations from the period's housewifery, Maria very much subscribed to its beliefs. "Women have to make more concessions than men," she would avow later in life. "It shouldn't be so but—that *is* the way . . . They have the *responsibility*. The *major* responsibility of their *home*, of their *children*, and of their *husband* . . . their creatures."[61]

It would be typical of her to speculate about the future. So dependent was Maria on Battista that she didn't like their age gap. "Titta—think about it. You're twenty-eight years older than I am so it's very possible that I'll become a widow," Anita Pensotti, the ghost writer of her *Oggi* memoirs, heard her ponder aloud. She recalled how Maria liked to study all the possible outcomes by listing off people they knew. Among them were couples with children. "But that, for Maria," Pensotti wrote, "was an altogether insignificant detail."[62]

Between her moments as a newlywed when she had openly expressed a yearning to conceive until this gynecological appointment at the age of thirty-three Maria hadn't given motherhood much thought.

As well as learning of this she was diagnosed with clinical exhaustion by her general physician Dr. Arnaldo Semeraro, who ordered her to skip the Athenian concert.[63] Having accompanied her to the doctor, Lomazzi would later remember Maria's insistence that this was not possible: "You're free to sing whenever you like," Dr. Semeraro allegedly responded, "but I have to warn you: you're compromising your health."[64]

So Maria went to Athens—where, as she was wont to do, she paid a visit to a doctor. Three days after her arrival on 28 July, she felt hoarse. In her words, the heat was "more implacable than the Italian one."[65] Her old friend Dr. Ilias Papatestas—the tuberculosis specialist she had known during her years at Patission Street—took her to Solon Kotsaridas, an ENT doctor.[66] Kotsaridas informed Maria that her vocal cords were swollen but assured her the performance would go well.

The morning of the rehearsal on 1 August Maria felt intuitively that her throat and voice weren't responding "as usual". "The heat, the dryness, the wind, the dust must have had its effect on my vocal resources—for they were struggling to function," she recalled. Taking precautions, she alerted the administration of the festival she was unable to perform.[67]

National newspaper *Ta Nea* alleged Callas had balked at "frightening letters and phone calls . . . she was angered by the abstention of Royals and political leaders."[68] The real reason forfeited announcement till a mere half-hour prior to the concert. Then it was finally reported that the villain of the story was none other than Maria's larynx. On account of its misdeeds, however, she had called upon Athenian police to ward off protests . . . so imagined gossip columnists.[69]

So intense had the government's fear of a riot become that Evangelia and Jackie Callas were persuaded to leave Greece for the course of Maria's Athenian stay.[70]

Determined to placate her public, Maria gave an interview on 4 August:

I would like to say hello to my dear people, the people who heard me when I lived in Greece at the time when we all suffered together [through] the good years and the bad ones. I wish to tell you that nothing serious has happened. This concert is as important to me as it is to you, who wish to hear me. Unfortunately, I am not used to this climate with so much dry air and dry weather; maybe I was a bit tired or I might have caught a mild influenza. I can't think of everything, and I have strived very much [to do this]. Unfortunately, I did not inaugurate the festival due to slight hoarseness; this could have happened to anyone . . .

I would like to ask you for a favor on Monday [the second concert's date]. *The whole world says that I give only the best, that I am a miracle. Do not believe them . . . I can only sing. Do not expect from me I don't know what . . .*
If I please you on Monday, I will be the happiest woman in the world.[71]

It was characteristic of Maria to regard the public as an entity with which she fostered a relationship. The Queen of La Scala had subjects, not children.

Far from being "untouchable," Maria corresponded with fans either personally or through Meneghini, occasionally calling them. In one instance she invited the family of a twelve-year-old boy who had written her to her hotel suite in London.[72] To another she had Meneghini write on her behalf: "And best of luck for your exams tomorrow."[73]

Asked to grant the wish of an admiring group who wanted to establish an official fan club, she was humble. "Very often I have been asked for my permission for a club Callas—but I have always said that I personally cannot give me [sic] adhesion . . . if such clubs are to be founded I would love it but I find it quite embarrassing for me to give permission."[74]

Before a Met performance she had "500 fan photos of [her] in her Tosca costume produced, and another 500 in mufti," as her manager once requested to EMI Records' John Coveney.[75] Pictures to autograph had to be ready.

Alighting onstage in the Herodes Atticus that 5 August, the queen lost her trustworthy stateliness. "She was so nervous that her foot was shaking," recollected former accompanist Elli Nikolaidi, who had worked with Maria at the National Conservatory.[76] Elvira de Hidalgo was seated in front[77] and the country was not at her mercy: a war with a cohort of obstacles.

This time she lost. A recording demonstrates that her performance is by far not the most passionate or energetic; she forgets some words in "Pace, pace, o mio Dio" from *La forza del destino*.

Confronting the propulsive frenzy her initial cancellation had provoked, Maria sat down in her suite at the Hotel Grande Bretagne the next day and wrote up another "defense". As with the others, she never elected to publish it.[78]

By August 7th Maria and Meneghini were back in Milan, where they revisited Dr. Semeraro. "You need to take a rest," came the second command.

Maria couldn't *take* a rest. As well as exhaustion the patient was suffering from anemia.[79] Yet she was due to take an Edinburgh-bound tour for yet another series of *Sonnambulas*.

This time she wouldn't allow sudden illness or fatigue to prompt an ill-received last-minute cancellation. Armed with a medical certificate, on 8 August she and Meneghini marched to the office of Luigi Oldani, La Scala's General Secretary, to request he recruit an appropriate understudy. "Maria is capable of miracles," Oldani retorted insouciantly. "She can do anything."

Despite his sycophantic reassurance he enlisted young Renata Scotto—soon to be a popular soprano—as a substitute.[80]

To relieve tension Maria took a five-day vacation once again to Ischia.[81] Photographed clad in a bathing suit at Lake Ameno, on the 16th she was featured in Italian newspaper *La Notte* looking frustratingly healthy.[82]

The first *Sonnambula* in Edinburgh left the soprano spent. Having spent months stifled by the burning sun, she now had to resort to singing in a country which, in her words, "Is *so* dear but *so* cold . . . the kind of cold that's a little too *much* for me and from our—from the boiling warmth of our country; the blessed boiling warmth!" she told an Italian reporter.[83]

A British doctor was summoned to examine her after opening night. He recommended Maria withdraw. She did not.[84]

The second *Sonnambula* was a gift. Although the recording exposes occasional shortness of breath and instability in the high register, most of Maria's ornamentation, roulades and high notes are on point. Caution is apparent in the slower tempi and a tremulous E flat that caps the aria "Sovra il sen". Evidence of vocal wear appears in only vestiges.

Luigi Oldani's response to the dazzling success was to schedule a fifth *La sonnambula*. Maria was presented with a "marvelous bouquet of flowers" by Field Marshal Bernard Montgomery[85] and "had the honor of receiving the visit of the Lord Provost, which would be the Lord Mayor of the city. And er, I say 'honor' because usually er, the Lord Provost does not go and visit."[86] On the afternoon that she left Edinburgh the mayor and his wife arrived at her hotel to say goodbye.[87]

What of the fifth scheduled performance? The agreement surrounding it is enshrouded in mystery. While Maria had informed Luigi Oldani she would not sing more than four *Sonnambula*s, the contract stipulated five performances that ended on September 7th. With a pen someone had scribbled "30 August" over the typed date but failed to change the "five" into a "four".[88]

Everybody was confused. "That was some mix-up that my husband knew more about than I did," Maria remembered in 1962. "I still haven't understood exactly what happened . . . It seems that my husband had arranged a certain number of performances and they had understood differently. Who was right and who was wrong I still don't know . . . each one was telling me his side of the story and I paid the consequences. One becomes unwittingly a sandwich—I was sandwiched between two pieces of bread."[89]

Torrential media attacks immediately followed. By this period in her career Maria was receiving heaps of hatemail. One letter quoted Samuel Taylor Coleridge, "Swans sing before they die" and added, "But it wouldn't be so bad if certain people died before they chose to sing." Another read: "Dear Madam, it is my duty to inform you that on Wednesday you sang *like a dog*," while other missives contained copious expletives, scurrilous suggestions or pornography.

The source of obloquy was not confined to just one country. It derived from the United Kingdom, Italy, Greece, France, the U.S.A. and others. Maria never discarded it.[90]

Under this mounting pressure she elected to vacation briefly in her much-loved city, Venice. There it was that socialite Elsa Maxwell—a gossip columnist and longtime admirer of hers—had invited Maria to a party at the Hotel Danieli. Maxwell would later cause great inconvenience for Maria by bombarding her with love letters.[91] They were either lesbian or asexual in nature depending on the reader's interpretation of Maxwell's orientation, of which she herself was uncertain.[92]

The invitation was hardly a favor. Scarcely had Maria stepped foot on the island when the columnist ecstatically wrote: "I have had many presents in my life . . . but I have never had any star give up a performance in an opera because she felt she was breaking her word to a friend." Amidst her glitzy entourage rumors abounded that Callas was too busy living the "high life" to focus on singing.

At the event she met fellow Greek, shipping magnate Aristotle Onassis. The exchange was not seminal. "I was rather indifferent to him," Maria would later recall.[93]

Newspapers and tabloids hardly cared about her true intentions. They just knew that she was scheduled to perform another opera and yet partying. In Venice. With the glitterati.

It didn't look good.

Even Maria would later admit: "I simply believed that it would have done me good as I wanted, more than anyone else, to get over my ailments and carry out my contractual obligations. Well, the motive was right but the action was not."[94]

Little by little a new reputation was superimposed: apparently, she was a party girl. From that point on Maria sought to stump the spurious impression that she cared for high society. "Of course, whenever I go to a party or a dance to enjoy myself, the critics say, 'Why isn't Callas staying home and taking care of herself?' Well, I am only 35 years old, and I like relaxation with my friends. Must I stay home like a nun? If I stayed home all the time, I would be frustrated and nervous," she wrote in April 1959.[95]

To Hedda Hopper she bemoaned that week, "My nerves can stand just so much and not more."[96]

Given her insomnia and precarious health these weren't petty excuses. Giulietta Simionato would remember how Maria skipped a tea at Countess Crespi's glamorous salon to watch the extras of La Scala in rehearsal.[97] Headiness from crowds was something far beyond her social palate.

A little after the Venetian party Giovanna Lomazzi accompanied Maria to Doctor Semeraro again. Her debut at the San Francisco Opera House was imminent and she had never sung on the West Coast. Dr. Semeraro was counter-productively adamant: he was "prohibiting" this American voyage; the abrupt change in climate in Edinburgh and the energy she had exerted had taken a dangerous toll.[98] She would have to postpone her performances of *Lucia di Lammermoor* and *Macbeth*.

This wasn't enough. Meneghini called in another doctor: Professor Carlo Trabattoni, a clinical psychologist at the University of Milan.[99] Although Maria wasn't formally diagnosed with a nervous breakdown, a few weeks later she openly stated: "I'm amazed I haven't [had one]. I was on the verge of it about two or three months ago . . . I was run down, I was tired."[100] Trabattoni advised strongly against the American tour.

All of this provoked a greater panic in Maria who—according to Lomazzi's recollections four years later—now had a "psychotic fear of things going wrong. On the eve of every performance she would be very fussy about any draft, any minimal irritant that could cause her to have to cancel the upcoming performance. She would look for any possible means to avoid having to cancel."[101]

This time cancellation was out of the question. Having signed on to perform at San Francisco Opera on 3 January that year,[102] she was two weeks away from the premiere when she requested artistic director Kurt Adler postpone her debut to 15 October: the earliest date doctors allowed a return to artistic activity.[103]

Adler first responded by telegram that the "EXCELLENT CALIFORNIA CLIMATE" would cure her in no time (despite the theatre's location in draft-immersed San Francisco). Maria repeated her offer of a four-week postponement. Adler retorted by eliminating the prospected *Macbeth* and yet keeping *Lucia* for 27 September.[104] Maria proposed once again to delay her debut. Adler issued a press release claiming she had elected to cancel "only a few days" before opening night.[105]

Maria's request however hadn't entirely been hers. As always Meneghini was responsible for wiring Kurt Adler the explanatory telegram alluding to his wife's indisposition. He had neglected to enclose a medical certificate.

The lapse on Meneghini's part incited the first argument between the married couple that Lomazzi witnessed. Maria insisted that he had mishandled the situation and ought to have employed far more tact. Adler spoke Italian; Meneghini should have *called* the man instead of simply sending him a telegram.

The situation wasn't helped by the soprano's unavoidable commitments. Upon phoning Meneghini, Adler was informed by the unwitting maid: "Madam is at La Scala recording *Medea.*"

Meneghini then resolved to send a copy of the medical certificate to Adler.[106]

But the damage was done.

"I relied on my husband, who was obviously not a very good agent, to protect me," Maria would later express. "All artists need that. I am not trying to make excuses for the things I did wrong, but I will not be made a scapegoat either."[107]

Meanwhile, Maria's pool of detractors recruited a handful of colleagues. Baritone Robert Merrill raged to columnist Earl Wilson and accused her publicly of using "phony tricks" to further her career. He called upon the American Guild of Musical Artists to bar her. Because membership in this union was mandatory, this action would bring to a staggering halt all her U.S. performances.[108]

Simultaneously the San Francisco Opera took legal action—ordering a "formal hearing" at AGMA to expel Callas permanently from the national opera stage.[109]

"The situation created by your cancellation at San Francisco is full of danger for your future career in America . . ." Rudolf Bing wrote rancorously to Maria. "If they should terminate your membership or suspend you for any period of time, your Metropolitan appearances will probably be impossible. You must know that your appearances in this country depend upon your remaining an AGMA member in good standing."[110] Meneghini did his best to act as a press secretary. His efforts proved futile.

The *Medea* recording did not please Maria. "As she came to the control room to hear the playback, we greeted her with resounding *Bravas*," musical director Harold Lawrence would recall. "We replayed the scene, and liked what we heard even more. But Callas had some reservations. 'It was very well sung,' she agreed, 'and it was a moving plea [the moment Medea implores King Creon to allow her to part with her children]. But something was missing. You see, at that moment Medea already knows that she will utilize that one day to carry out her bloody revenge. Her mind is really on other things than pleading, and the music must bring out that ominous undertone. I must do it over.'

"So she went back, and did the scene over just as beautifully. But this time there was an almost imperceptible but nevertheless clearly menacing undertone to her singing. It was a spine-tingling experience."[111]

Ironically—perhaps appropriately—this recording molded in the heat of trying times is a superlative rendition of the anti-heroine. Surpassing the live 1953 Bernstein *Medea*, the incarnation is both more conniving and maternal; alternating between specious and authentic agony. What Maria wanted to achieve in this *Medea* was the portrait of a Machiavellian witch.

Plangently stressing the syllable "PLOR" in "Imploro, mio signor" ("I beg you, sir") is a bloodthirsty poser pretending to be a mere mother who fears for her children. As she begs Creon for an extra day before her exile to spend time with the small sons that she will kill, the command "Dei figli miei l'amor mi rendi" ("Return to me the love of my children") is fraught with excessive vibrato; charging a soul simultaneously desperate and ominous. The listener remains oblivious to whether she is earnestly or spuriously tender. And it *should* be that way.

Amidst an inner duel between Medea Mother and Medea Sorceress, the villainess staves off the former as she contemplates her children's murder.

"No, cari figli, no!" ("No, dear children, no!") she yelps. The last note wavers from *self*-fear.

Tradition vanquishes modernity. Feral instinct overcomes civilization. And yet with her declamatory stance she has inducted us into her tribe: Jason and Creon warranted their punishment.

By 25 September Maria was writing that she felt better to friend Oscar Coltellacci, despite having had little rest.[112] Five days later she adjusts her tone of correspondence—scribing to another friend, Charles Johnson: "I am rather ill now especially because I got the Asiatic fever. So I'm writing these few lines from bed with a temperature and all that goes with influenza."[113]

Butler Ferruccio Mezzadri began working for the Meneghinis that October.[114] Half of it was spent resting ... if one could call it that. Roiled by the impending Bagarozy trial, which would not be resolved out of court until 17 November,[115] Maria wrote incessantly to lawyer Walter Cummings. She was terrified of having to postpone rehearsals for her upcoming opening of La Scala's 1957–58 season, *Il trovatore*. "If I had to come to New York, when would the hearing take place? Could I postpone it and to when? Walter, I need to know about my future because I'm working and of course I don't live in the United States."[116]

At the same time she was trying desperately to "clear my name". Having requested that Antonio Ghiringhelli publicly announce that she had not absconded from the final *La sonnambula* in Edinburgh, Maria called upon Emilio Radius—her friend from the Italian weekly *Oggi*—to pay the general manager a visit. Radius waited. And waited. After two hours Ghiringhelli appeared and shooed him out of the office.[117]

This didn't embitter Maria against Ghiringhelli. Lomazzi recalled seeing him bump into Maria at the Biffi restaurant at that time: "Antonio," she said, "It's in our best interest to remain friends."[118] Ghiringhelli appeared courteous.[119]

Maria wasn't done yet. "I changed my strategy and succeeded in getting Ghiringhelli to the offices of the mayor of Milan," she later remembered. "There, before the mayor, Ghiringhelli and my husband finally agreed that I should write the story myself, at least in the first instance. I did so, praising La Scala for its excellence, explaining the confusion about the fifth performance and pointing out that in the previous six years I had postponed, because of illness, only two out of 157 performances and that I was not at all responsible for Edinburgh."[120]

After convalescing from the Asian flu[121] Maria's sole engagement in November was a concert honoring the founding of the Dallas Civic Opera. "I kept myself free for the whole month for the [Bagarozy] hearing—as well as April," she wrote to lawyer Cummings. "I can't miss out on contracts. Do you realize the scandal that arises every time I cancel for illness? My name and my career are at stake."[122]

Five days later came another panic in a letter to La Scala's whole administration. "Dear friends ... *Un ballo in maschera*, which you have chosen to replace

Il trovatore for the opening ... Although the available period of preparatory study was enough to allow me a brief review of the opera, it is nonetheless truncated by the following: the Chicago court has just now informed me by telegram that my hearing has been postponed—without further deliberation—from 12 to 18 November. Consequently ... I wouldn't be able to return to Italy before the 28 or 29 November. [*Un ballo* was opening on 7 December]."

Maria had no choice. It took her just three days to cave. "I will not be present at any rehearsal until the 30 November—given that I must study the opera with [assistant conductor] Maestro [Antonio] Tonini."[123]

Rehearsals for the Dallas concert had Maria in solicitous spirits. A recording of one shows her skipping several top notes and alternatively marking some; an exercise almost unheard of in her ritual. Also scheduled to perform, Joan Sutherland could not endure the work ethic. "At quarter to eleven I told Larry Kelly I was tired and going home. He said, 'Maria rehearsed until four in the morning.' I told him it was great for her but not for me—and that she wasn't singing too well now anyhow."[124]

With the concert a pronounced success, Maria's buzz persisted five days after it took place. She wrote to Leo Lerman—now "one if not the best friend of mine":

> *I hope to see much more next time and please bring me to eat Chop Suey, will you? I adore it ...*
>
> *What other news? About our fat friend? About my* <u>dear</u> *colleague? Please write me if anything is new.*
>
> *I am studying rather a lot for this "Ballo". It has to be a success. Why must I have to* <u>fight</u> *all the time?*
>
> *And please give Marlene* [Dietrich] *my very best and tell her that I'm sorry that the postal incident had to happen to her. But also I'm amazed she didn't receive my last Xmas telegram. Do you think I've the wrong address?*[125]

Ballo is a peculiar opera. Originally set in eighteenth-century Sweden—where it revolves around the assassination of King Gustave III at a masked ball—it was transferred by censorship in nineteenth-century Italy to colonial Boston; supplanting "Gustave" with "Riccardo": Governor of Boston and the Earl of Warwick. Today it is contrarily most often set in Sweden, sometimes even known as *Gustave III*.

Poor Riccardo is in love with Amelia, wife of his chief advisor, Renato. A fortune-teller named Ulrica prophesizes he will die at a friend's hands. She also tells Amelia a magic herb will cure her of her sinful love for doomed Riccardo. Subsequently she resolves to find the magic herb. Instead Amelia is exposed before Renato—who discovers that his wife pines for his master, doesn't know she *hasn't* been unfaithful and complots to have Riccardo killed.

It's a sad ending.

Down to fifty-three kilograms at a height of five foot eight and a half, Maria had to tolerate last-minute costume changes.

Amelia is not the most attractive role. A married mother who by chance becomes enamored with a king, her voice sticks to a milquetoast middle register.

Made in September 1956, Maria's studio recording of the part is not exactly special. Applying common accents to "Ecco l'orrido campo"—the aria in which Amelia comes to the field to seize the "magic herb" that will extinguish her illicit love—she mostly just sounds angry at herself. Vulnerability seeps through her proclamation to Riccardo, "io son d'altrui, dell'amico più fidato" ("I belong to another, to your closest friend"), but through a skimpy voice impaired by instability in high notes.

A live recording of this *Ballo*—for which Maria has done closer study—functions better. When Amelia demands her heart annihilate her sentiment ("T'annienta, mio povero cor!") a gentle pianissimo unravels to become the clamber of crescendo: a self-flagellating woman under the bewitching spell of a wrong love.

As she reminds Riccardo she is married to the man who risked his life to save him, soft diminuendo in the emphasis on "a te" ("for you") resounds with shame. Referring to the battles Renato has fought for Riccardo ("che il suo sangue ti diè": "who gave his blood for you") a horrified diminuendo is accompanied with ever greater shyness in a rallentando. Her confession of love is a reluctantly wrested expulsion. Urging Riccardo to defend her from it ("Me difendi dal mio cor"), fear-stricken Amelia sounds like a twittering fledgling.

In this potentially adulterous young wife there surfaces another Will to Die—this time for the honor of her husband and child. The rolled "r" in "Morrò, ma prima in grazia" ("I will die, but first, have mercy") wrestles with her resolution to become extinct. We hear humiliation in her voice as she implores Renato to permit her one last visit with her only son ("l'unico figlio mio"). She is steadier, more in control; afraid that sounding plaintive could be detrimental to her cause. "Che mai più vedrà"—her realization that she will never again see her child—is no shock but a slow rise to consciousness.

*

On 26 December Maria and Meneghini arrived in Rome, where she was scheduled to open a *Norma* and perform "Casta diva" as part of the televised Eurovision transmission.[126]

Following rehearsals that day the soprano was content with her achievement but unsettled by a mild sore throat. Mezzo Fedora Barbieri—who had been scheduled to sing Adalgisa—had withdrawn from the performance suffering from influenza. Miriam Pirazzini had replaced her.

Feeling well on both the 29 and 30 December, Maria performed at Eurovision on the 31st for a live broadcast to dozens of countries. She was wrapped up warmly in a shawl. It was also the day of *Norma's* general rehearsal. Previous rehearsals for the work had taken place at an unheated house in Piazza Esedra; "air currents came through the cracks" in its dressing room, in her words. With Italian opera seasons only opening in December—and this time, in January—the house had been in semi-permanent disuse. Maria felt "a chill—and the first symptoms of hoarseness."[127]

Coupled with that circumstance was the displeasing fact that she had once more caused offense—having allegedly "insisted that the general rehearsal be held on the condition that it *not* be open to the public."—"That happened without my knowing!" Maria responded. "I did not know that I was singing for an empty parterre and for empty boxes!"[128]

On New Year's Eve Maria went to a bar with Meneghini and a few friends, had some champagne and came home. She was in bed before one am. Fatigue led her to sleep until eleven in the morning.

The next day she opened her mouth to observe that no words could come out. "I was completely soundless, mute. My voice just wasn't there," Maria later recounted. "And *Norma* was to take place the following evening, and was completely sold out."[129] President Gronchi and his wife would be among those present.

Meneghini summoned a doctor who found a severe inflammation in the throat and recommended mustard plasters and poultices,[130] spraying it and prescribing some sedatives.[131] That day there was no one in the theatre. The artistic director of the Teatro dell'Opera, Guido Sampaoli, could only come by in the evening. Maria told him she was feeling better—and yet recommended that he find an understudy just in case. "An *understudy*. Brava. Who would that be?" was his question. "And then, people have paid to come hear Callas, you know—there's not much we can do. You need to sing." Maria took a sleeping pill and went to bed for twelve uninterrupted hours.

Rising afresh, she felt completely reinvigorated. "The voice was full and at my disposal!" she wrote. Jocundly jumping out of bed, she threw herself into self-preparation. After lunching and taking a rest, at two o'clock she realized her instrument "was not there after all". Poultices had mollified the inflammation—but provisionally.

Lomazzi called a while later. Not wishing to tire out Maria, she spoke to Meneghini, who insisted: "It'll all be fine ... Maria's been taking everything—cornmeal, fumigation, inhalations ... She'll be better come this evening, you'll see."

Come that evening Maria called Lomazzi herself. "Giovanna, could you do me a favor? In the Duomo, behind the main altar there's a little Madonna that's very dear to me. Light a candle and pray all will go well."[132]

Set to sing the role of Pollione that night, Franco Corelli remembered her entering the theatre "a little nervous, completely hoarse, and with barely the scratch of a sound coming out of her throat—but able to sing."[133] In her dressing room she "gulped down quinine and gave myself an injection—this stimulant which they say can bring the dead back to life."[134]

When it came to opera in Milan and Rome, in Maria's words, they were "two sisters that hated each other." Blasted by both boos and whistles as she came onstage, Maria was propelled into a horror movie.[135]

She began "Sediziose voci—voci di guerra," the lead-up to "Casta diva." "B Flat, A Flat and G, notes of the middle register: I heard the outcome and I thought to myself: 'My God. The middle's gone. Let's hope the rest can take it.'" Her "Casta diva" left her so ashamed that she regretted its applause. By the time of the curtain call at the end of the first act, "I felt I didn't deserve any applause."

So she shut herself up in her dressing room. A recording reveals that the voice has an echo-like resonance, sounding congested; certain high notes are scratchy. Would she have been able to continue? Probably. But it would not have made her proud.

"Just—sing the same way," the administration implored her.

"You can sing with a fever, sing with your legs hurting or with a blasting headache—I've done all those things many times. But you can't sing without your voice," Maria would scribe later.[136] "When they finally realized that I would not sing with a lost voice, they said, 'All right, don't sing. But you are an actress. At least go out and act.'"[137] Act . . . *Norma*?

An announcement was made: the performance would be discontinued on account of force majeure. In the refuge of Maria's dressing room her husband took the envelope of a good luck card from Visconti. On its surface Meneghini scribed a formal note of apology in his wife's eye pencil, intending for it to be read to the audience.[138] It went unacknowledged.

Riots ensued. Lomazzi called the Meneghinis' Roman friend, dentist Giuseppe De Tommasi. "Giovanna, you can't even imagine what is going on!" he exclaimed. "They want to *lynch* her. Maria's managed to get away to her hotel—and now the police are surrounding it, trying to bar access. It's the end of the world!"

Meneghini came to the phone. "What can you do?" was his resigned remark.

Listening on a portable radio during the intermission of *Adriana Lecouvreur* at La Scala, Lomazzi passed the receiver to Ghiringhelli. "Battista," he implored, "tell Maria to come back to Milan. Her theatre is La Scala; ours is a public that loves her and knows her worth."

But the good wishes were never relayed.[139]

Immediately another doctor was called, Umberto de Martini.[140] He diagnosed a fever of 102°F, bronchitis and an infection of the larynx.[141]

"Field day" would not suffice to capture the reaction. "There were heated demonstrations," a German journalist reminded her months later. "You, Signora, had to head toward the Hotel Quirinale through an underground passage—"

"There *is* none," Maria confirmed. "The Rome Opera and the Hotel Quirinale that stands behind it form a single building block together. There's a connecting door from the restaurant of the hotel to the foyer of the Opera. That's also the reason why we always stay at the Quirinale—we can walk to the theatre unnoticed."[142]

Maria sent a letter of apology to the Italian President. Before he had received it the first lady, Carla Gronchi, telephoned Maria to explain she had discerned her vocal struggles during the first act and sympathized.[143]

The next morning Meneghini called La Scala once every half-hour to assess the Milanese reaction.[144] The press enjoyed the incident's ramifications:

> *ROME, Jan. 3—Motorized policemen were called out today to quell demonstrations against Maria Callas . . . Hundreds of protesters, many of them middle-aged or elderly men, gathered in front of the New York-born soprano's hotel today. They whistled and booed. They shouted "Down with Callas!" . . .*
>
> *Policemen swinging truncheons charged the crowd repeatedly before order was restored. Old Roman music fans said with ill-concealed satisfaction that today's were the liveliest operatic riots since partisans of Verdi and Wagner fought more than half a century ago . . .*
>
> *The operatic scandal will be discussed also in Parliament. Questions to the Government introduced in the chamber by various deputies included one on why the management of the Rome Opera House had failed to adopt measures to prevent such "indecorous events" as those of last night. The implication was that a stand-in for Miss Callas should have been in readiness.*[i]

Reported *The New York Times*.[145] *The Washington Post* managed to quote Carlo Latini, superintendent of the Rome Opera, who suggested that Maria's illness could have been the consequences of her hedonistic New Year's celebrations.[146] *Il Giorno*, an Italian newspaper, labeled her a "second-class Greek artist."[147] In Bergamo, Lombardy—not far from Milan and thus considered Callas Territory—a one hundred-year-old Fife and Drum Corps suddenly broke rank over Maria's flaws and virtues. The pro-Callas ones were called "Callistas"—Italian for "chiropodist" or "corn-cutter"—by the anti-Callas brigade. They insisted they were not "callistas" but more aptly "Callasiani".[148]

"I have been literally lynched," came Maria's summary days later.

With the intensification of hate came the rousing of fandom. Though numbers vary, the most accurate estimate was a total of nine hundred and thirty-nine letters of support sent to Maria as a result of the Rome affair.[149] Gianandrea Gavazzeni, Giulietta Simionato, soprano Graziella Sciutti and Luchino Visconti all wrote letters of condolence—as though someone had died.[150]

Rome barred Maria. At least—that was the headline. "The order for the ban—a temporary one—came from the prefecture, the highest authority in

---

provincial Rome," reported *The Washington Post*. Carlo Latini promised a substitute, who turned out to be soprano Anita Cerquetti. Bedridden Maria urged her husband to propose a benefit performance for the Red Cross. They "reserved their reply."[151]

The sole explanation Maria received was a letter of request from the Prefecture warning "demonstrations" could spark if she chose to perform. "I as a disturber of peace!" Maria exclaimed in incredulousness.[152]

"I can say *one* thing: I may say I was *happy* it happened. *Because* you see, I had such a reaction from the public—the good public, the public that usually isn't heard—and they wrote to me; they sent me flowers, and I never have had so many flowers, so many letters when I *sing*. You see these people proved to me that I'm necessary to them, that my er . . . my reason of living—that is, music—isn't wasted. And in that way I knew that I'm very loved, I'm very needed and it gave me *courage* to go on—in fact, *new* faith in myself," were her thoughts in retrospect.[153]

Six days later Meneghini and a convalescent Maria departed the Hotel Quirinale.[154]

"You are divine and beautiful!" came the salute from some five hundred fans awaiting her arrival at Milano Centrale, her hometown's main train station. Leaving Meneghini to deal with reporters, she went home to bed.[155]

Maria went on to sue the Rome Opera in a lawsuit that spanned thirteen years. After she won the case in February 1968, earning the equivalent of thirty-two thousand dollars today,[156] it was appealed by the Rome Opera. In April 1971 the final decision was made in her favor.

By that time no one cared.[157]

Meneghini and Maria's closeness went untarnished. For his sixty-third birthday Maria would write:

> Dearest soul,
> I have nothing to give you as a gift because you have all of me. As a memento of the ten years we have passed together, I give you the infamous chain for the pieces of bread that always get taken away from you [by the waiters]. All you have to know is that you couldn't have done more for your wife because your woman is the happiest spouse in the whole world.[158]

Glitz followed gruel. On her second trip to Paris Maria stayed at the Hôtel de Crillon, was greeted at the airport by Jean-Claude Pascal with orchids, welcomed at Maxim's at 8:03 pm by Mademoiselle Marmiron, a renowned jeweler, and served an iced soufflé named after Maria Malibran: her adored nineteenth-century idol.[159]

American concerts came next. Arriving at the presidential suite of the Sheraton-Blackstone, Chicago, Maria exhausted manager Douglas Boone by demanding a piano be installed in the room. Also, the air was too dry. An engineer had to be summoned to correct that.[160] Spending only two or three days in Chicago to give another benefit for the Alliance Française, she managed in that period to lose a diamond brooch valued at five thousand dollars. She postponed alerting the police for a day because she was "busy with rehearsals and hoped to find the brooch herself."[161]

Returned to New York to stand trial before the American Guild of Musical Artists on 27 January, she was found guilty of breaching her San Francisco contract but given a "reprimand".[162]

Her performances in New York—*La traviata*, *Lucia di Lammermoor* and *Tosca*—allowed for a welcome diversion. Meeting with Greek designer Giannis Tsarouchis, she collaborated to choose the visual and vestmental palette for her upcoming *Medea* in Dallas. "Yes, yes," she would say, "the dark suit with the narrow red band gives the right dramatic tone . . ."[163]

In one of those Met *Traviatas* where the shabby costumes and trite sets were older than the theatre, one of Violetta's red-laced straps came loose. After being alerted to the indiscretion by her colleague, mezzo-soprano Helen Vanni, she instructed: "Tear the other one off, too."[164]

Wildness coursed through the spectators' veins. "Boy," a young man gasped, gulping down water from the drinking fountain after the first act on 6 February. "Only one act and I've already lost my voice," *The New York Post* reported. "He was not a featured tenor. He was a standee who had shouted 'Brava, Divina' at Maria Callas until he was hoarse. And at that he was only one of some 200 standees."[165]

Future chef Dolores Rivellino bribed a fellow admirer to toss her bouquet of camellias onstage. Such things were not permitted in the theatre but—"Oh my God, it landed at her feet!" the girl exclaimed during the curtain calls. Maria heard and smiled.

After the performance Rivellino and her friends snuck in backstage. "Callas was removing her make-up . . . We brushed ourselves off and stood in front . . . Face to face, we were staring at Maria Callas . . . I thought she'd throw us out." Maria laughed. "A huge, throaty laugh." She recognized Dolores as the girl she had heard yelping at the landing of the tossed bouquet. Dolores introduced herself and her friends. After taking a sip from a gargantuan bottle of orange soda, Maria extended the drink to the girl. Dolores politely declined. Maria gave her her telephone number and advised her to call her at 11:30 am the next day. They became friends.[166]

Such was the soprano's stage door etiquette. In those heady days it was a habit for her fans to go backstage. Meneghini would recall that if they clustered in Maria's dressing room she spent two hours signing autographs, eventually returning home at two or three at night.[167]

The admirers wouldn't go unnoticed. When one future recording executive showed up at several consecutive *Sonnambulas*, she enquired: "Didn't I see you at the premiere?"—"Yes," replied Jacques Leiser. "And you're back again?"[168]

Problems in her instrument persisted. *The New Yorker*'s music critic Douglas Watt wrote: "the high notes again wobbled very slightly now and then ... when one has become used to it, it seems to add intensity to her singing."[169] Another put it this way: "For all the disparagement of her 'ugly' sound ... I regard this observation to be on a par with the discovery that the Venus de Milo has no arms."[170]

At home relationships were turbulent. Pretending to await the provisional dates from Maria for La Scala's next season, Ghiringhelli was silent. Maria was compelled on March 11th to remind him to respond. The letter came six days later—with Ghiringhelli now using the formal Italian you, "Lei" as opposed to his usual "tu": "I asked your husband what period you wanted to reserve for your work with La Scala next season. That said, as we waited to be received by the mayor that 13 or 14 January, your husband informed me you had already received numerous and very lucrative requests and that you wouldn't be able to give me a response until after your return from New York."[171]

But Maria had *already* returned from New York. And supplied dates.

"There is a Callas-La Scala war" announced one headline in Italian weekly *Epoca*. "Commendatore Meneghini has been telling Ghiringhelli, 'Last year they threw a bouquet of radishes ... Ghiringhelli did not take any precautionary measures against that kind of behavior.' "[172] By April 10th Maria personally admitted there was a "cold war" between her and La Scala.[173]

After a series of *Traviata*s in Lisbon that fell short of perfection, Maria returned to her hometown anticipating a performance of *Anna Bolena* at the Milan Fair.

Except the work had suddenly been substituted with the premiere of a new opera, *Murder in the Cathedral*. And she didn't know why.[174]

In the run-up to the revival of *Anna Bolena* protesters obtrusively made themselves known. After one rehearsal Maria came home to find graffiti scrawled on the pavement outside; dirt and mud smeared on the porch.[175]

On opening night two hundred policemen mobilized to watch for violations of the law and maintain order.[176]

No entrance applause followed.[177] When Anna was seized by the guards Maria thrust herself to the front of the stage, addressing her audience: "Giudici? Ad Anna? *Giudici*, ad Anna? Ad *Anna* ... Giudici?!" ("Judges ... For Anna? *Judges* ... for Anna? For *Anna* ... there are judges?!").[178] They understood the metatextual gesture and exploded in a feverish ovation.

Twenty-one curtain calls revived her reputation.[179]

After signing autographs until three in the morning Maria was met by Meneghini and Lord Harewood outside the theatre, where she was zealously greeted by "hundreds of enthusiastic Milanese waiting to escort an enthusiastic prima donna to supper," in the words of the latter.[180] Armed police stood, stymied.[181]

Ecstasy around this homecoming was quickly stumped. Maria wrote a letter to the chief of police in the city, Fortunato Lo Castro: "I understand that you are very busy but I ask you to forgive my request ... I have been subjected to intolerable violations of dignity, propriety and tranquility. The most recent of these happened last night when I sang in a production of *Anna Bolena* at La Scala ... Thugs once again targeted my home. They dirtied and muddied the door, the gate and the pavement, and wrote numerous horrid things . . ." and so on.[182]

The police did nothing. Maria didn't realize that her enemy was not the public. It was one Antonio Ghiringhelli.

After failing to respond to her letters the superintendent of La Scala finally wrote on 27 April. He was leaving it to her discretion to settle on next season's dates. But she had already alerted him—numerous times—that it was *his* turn to tell her the dates that *he* wanted . . .

At the same time Maria had been learning a new opera in Bellini's *Il pirata*. Set in thirteenth-century Sicily, it focuses on nubile Imogene, who's enamored with pirate Gualtiero: the outlawed Count of Montalto. She is married however to the Duke of Caldora, Ernesto, who has fathered her son. Imogene has a vision of Gualtiero dying. When eventually the two men duel, her husband dies and she goes mad.

"Here I am at the 'Scala' studying like mad the 'Pirata' with rather a vague sense of let down," Maria had written to music critic Herbert Weinstock in March. "It really isn't a wonderful piece. It starts a lovely theme and then it always remains half way or no way at all. Well, anyway—we'll have to work even more for a success. As for my dates I'm afraid I can say nothing. The 'Scala' has a lousy habit of not knowing even ten days before a performance when it will take place. It is a most vexing habit . . ."[183]

La Scala's *Il pirata* was never recorded. A concert rendering performed at Carnegie Hall in January 1959 is holed by flaws and falls short of the Callas Imogene. Probably the most precise depictions of Maria in the role are live recordings from her 1959 concerts, of which one was televised.

Imogene is a bland but desperate character. Technically, she's Norma; characteristically she has no mordancy. In the mad scene for which the rare opera is known, "Oh, s'io potessi disspar le nubi che m'aggravan la fronte," ("Oh, if I could only clear the clouds that aggravate my head,") Imogene hallucinates about seeing her dead husband alive, confuses night and day and contemplates the sweet smile of her son.

Light diminuendi in the broadcast of the Hamburg concert indicate Maria saw the character of Imogene as a docile, inexperienced young woman. At the same time abrupt crescendi and staccati as the heroine envisages Gualtiero's corpse—before remembering Ernesto was the one who perished—serve to strengthen her self-loathing. So dismissive is she of her visions, she wants nothing more than death. Rapidly she recollects the harmless smile of her beloved son ("Col sorriso d'innocenza"). Her voice encounters tenderness; soothing diminuendi intent for a lullaby.

But quickly Imogene is restored to inner battle—realizing the condemned Gualtiero is about to die for having killed her husband. "Oh, sole, ti vela di tenebre oscure!" ("O, sun—may it veil you from the dark shadows!") she implores. The voice morphs to create another mood: "tenebre oscure" resonates in the chest voice with a bear-like, brusque growl. In the rabid coloratura behind the "rrò" of "morrò" as she yells "D'orrore morrò" ("I will die from the horror") we find someone lacking in reason yet consciously willing to die.

Frosty was La Scala's audience on the premiere that 19 May. Rumors about Maria's "feud" with Ghiringhelli glazed them with indifference.[184] "The masses: they can break you as easily as they can *make* you," she would one day observe. "You can't trust them; they are changing creatures. And they have the right to be. It's the law of the theatre; I accept it."[185]

A critic nonetheless praised "the extent of her legato, the richness, the continuity of the middle register and certain miraculous vocal descents."[186]

Exasperated by Ghiringhelli's sophistic reluctance to offer her dates or productions—together with the scrapping of her *Anna Bolena*—Maria could no longer stand the chicanery. "If it must be publicly announced," she wrote to Ghiringhelli, "or if the public remarks on my absence—it is not by my volition that I am compelled today to give up the pursuit of this ingenuine relationship."[187]

The press release arrived on 24 May. "I will not sing at La Scala next year even if I am offered a contract," she declared—with the emphatic caveat that she could someday happily return if Ghiringhelli could be substituted.[188]

"If the theater of which you are a guest adds to the tension by continual harassment and rudeness, art becomes physically and morally impossible. For my self-defense and dignity, I had no choice but to leave La Scala. La Scala did not dispense with my services. I resigned . . ." she would write a year later. "He might have come to me during that final season and said, 'Look, we have differences, but we need each other. Let us both try to work together again.' I would have said yes, but now it is too late, too much has been said."[189]

On the day of this announcement the soprano suffered a severe attack of hemorrhoids. Immediately hospitalized, she was forced to submit to emergency surgery.[190]

The doctor ordered a complete rest for five days. That was not possible; she had a *Pirata*. The next *day*. Maria took this in her stride. "For six days after the operation I was in pain, for I am allergic to narcotics and cannot have them," she wrote in 1959. "I had no sleep and almost nothing to eat. On Sunday, the day after the operation, I sang *Il pirata*. On Wednesday I sang it again."[191]

One week after that operation came Maria's final outing on the Scala stage. As Imogene watched a group of orderlies erect the fatal scaffold where her lover would be executed ("Il palco funesto") Maria gestured to the proscenium box where Ghiringhelli was sitting. In Italian the word "palco" ("scaffold") can additionally mean "theatre box".[192]

No flowers were permitted to be thrown that night: La Scala had reversed their policy about the practice. Fans ignored this. As the half-hour ovation thrived the iron curtain was abruptly lowered to the stage. "By order of the theatre, the stage must be cleared," yelled a hovering fireman.

Retreating to her dressing room, Maria wept as fans awaited her outside. Accompanied by Giovanna Lomazzi, she left the theatre and espied police attempting to disperse the flower-throwing crowd. "They had finally found a place where they could say goodby[e]," she remembered.[193] Officers attempted to restrain them. "Leave them alone!" Maria shouted. "These people are my friends; they are doing no harm!"[194]

Together with Meneghini Maria travelled to Sirmione, a resort town by Lake Garda and the home of Roman poet Catullus. Recently the pair had purchased a bright yellow villa there. They spent hours supervising its interior design.[195]

These eighteen months had unfurled tribulations unforeseen. In a moment of self-pity with a journalist in January 1958, Maria had remarked: "Put a human note into your story, please do ... Because I am rather human at times."[196]

The woman had a point.

But do we have to believe her?

11.

"Pure stage"

Inhaling torrid air, the slowly fearful, rising-falling chords cower and camouflage like animals in the Sahara desert scared of immolation by the sun.

Suffocation is inevitable in this opera's saffron mold. Another story of love versus luxury, Puccini's sensuous *Manon Lescaut* takes place in late eighteenth-century France and is based on the novel by Abbé Prévost. Twenty-year-old Manon falls in love for the first time with the Chevalier des Grieux. Shunning passion, she becomes the mistress of a tax collector in exchange for an existence of indulgent splendor.

When des Grieux resurfaces, Manon resorts to once again seducing him; the ravenous, rapacious creature hungers for excess. Caught *in flagrante delicto* by her keeper Geronte, the two lovers are dispatched to prison—where a botched escape plan sees them gallivanting through the desert, grinding the last ounces of their strength. Choking inch by inch on famine and infesting heat, the lapsed Manon spends thirteen minutes dying in her lover's arms.

Maria's recording of the work was made in July 1957—days before the cautionary Dr. Semeraro diagnosed her with exhaustion. Dissatisfied, she wouldn't let the vocal document be published till the end of 1959.[1]

And yet it harbors what is possibly her most explicit demonstration of the vocal contour of a character.

The opera is prophetically dark. While *Tosca*, *Madama Butterfly* and *Turandot* are underpinned by flagrantly conspicuous motifs, *Manon Lescaut* leans heavily on unexpected syncopations; juxtaposing ill-matched pairs of harmonies. The style is more symbolic of the turn opera would take throughout the twentieth century compared to the composer's much more popular and simpler works. A crucial theme that percolates throughout is the same melody that helmed an earlier Puccini work, "Crisantemi": a string quartet.

From Manon's introduction "Manon Lescaut mi chiamo" ("My name is Manon Lescaut") we hear a girlish, tender voice made taut and almost soured by deliberate harshness. This is not an inexperienced fledgling suddenly exposed to city life but a voracious woman eager to explore urbanity.

In repeated coquetry with des Grieux, she's a manipulative minx: "Vedete? Io son fedele alla parola mia," ("You see, I keep my word"), she points out when she meets with him again. And yet the voice possesses an emphatically unfinished tone; its timbre crunched, a little perforated: far too playful for the audience to trust Manon.

Foreboding blackens her words' supplication: "Una fanciulla povera son io . . . regna tristezza sul destino mio" ("I'm a poor young girl . . . sadness reigns over my destiny"). For the first time we hear prescience in the attitude of the apparently insouciant woman. Throughout the growling underbelly of the languorous, erotic cellos, premonition lingers.

The second act sets off an anxious waiting game in which Manon—now kept by old Geronte—asks her brother if there's any news of des Grieux. Its music stretches playfully into a syncopated series of swift bursts of unforeseen flats, sharps and naturals: "Volevo dimandar" ("I wanted to ask . . .") Manon begins—"Risponderò" ("I will reply") Lescaut confirms. "*Risponderai?!*" ("You *will?*") she asks, bemused. In this zappy prognostication of twentieth-century rhythms Maria lets Manon's insatiable curiosity slip through the notes, stressing "Risponder-AI" with an anxious alarm.

Eventually we learn Manon is somber. Her life is not a cavalcade of careless dreams; in spite of newfound opulence she pines for her forsaken past. The aria "In quelle trine morbide" ("In those silky curtains") is the first example of vocality that serves to humanize Manon. The ambience of her abode is chilling: "v'è un silenzio, un gelido mortal" ("there is silence, a deathly cold"), observes the dreamer. "Gelido mortal" ("deathly cold") grows reticently fearsome in vibrato.

As she contemplates how she exchanged those "zealous lips" and "fiery arms" for these surroundings, which are "tutt'altra cosa" ("a completely different thing"), the diminuendo on "cosa" makes the note almost mute for her anguish and shame. We espy a brief glimpse of the little girl Manon Lescaut when she compares her former "humble dwelling" ("dimora umile") to a "gentle dream of peace and love" ("un sogno gentil e di pace e d'amor").

"D'amor" attenuates so tenderly it goes beyond the reach of even an inhuman instrument.

Seized by panicky excitement as she meets with des Grieux again ("Tu, tu, amore, tu?!"), the febrile duo is embroiled in a licentious contretemps. Manon accuses her ex-lover: "Tu non m'ami *dunque* più? M'amavi tanto! M'amavi *tanto!*" ("Then you no longer love me? But you used to love me *so* much! So *much!*").

Enter exuberant techniques of emotional blackmail: a harsh accent on the "dun" of "dunque" ("then") that makes the accusation cutting. This is the same woman who just bars before had looked into the mirror and exclaimed: "Oh—sarò la più bella!" ("Oh—I shall be the most beautiful!"); Maria leaning on the luscious double "l" of "bella" to express Manon's enjoyment of herself.

As the accusations cross like gunfire Manon's devolve into a toddler tantrum: "Ah, è vero? Non m'ami dunque più? M'amavi *tanto!*" ("It's true then—that you no longer *love* me? You loved me *so* much! *So* much!"). That grating "t" of "*tanto*" ("*so* much") gives us the impression this is more beguilement: bait.

When she confesses that she favored riches over their illicit love ("T'ho tradito, è ver!": "It's true, I betrayed you!"), it is no mature admission of remorse but an impulsive exclamation meant to rouse his rogue affection. "Cedi . . . cedi, son *tua*," ("Give in . . . give in, I'm y*ours*"), she reassures him carnally—effusing those prolonged notes with the thrall of a bewitching spell.

Finally her cries are beastly mating calls: "Ah-ah *vieni*, ah *vien* . . ." ("Ah . . . *come* to me, come to me . . ."); the growing crescendo on Maria's prolonged portamenti ignites with the lovers' abandon.

Yet when Manon decides to leave cantankerous Geronte, she is hard-pressed to desert her lavishness. "Tutti questi splendori! Tutti questi tesori!" ("All these splendors . . . All these treasures!") she laments. Maria gives the accents on "splendori" and "tesori" equal measure, making them symmetrical: unwittingly Manon has sunk into their trance. Again.

By the fourth act the imprisoned Manon's voice has grown much darker and much older: racked by genuine despair. She tells of how "the breeze roams over the great plain" ("Erra la brezza nella gran pianura") with a timbre as thin as the tip of a paintbrush. The fragile voice emits diminuendi whose allure begins to wither; weakening from her expiring strength. Echoing the slow melodic pattern that begins "Crisantemi," Manon begs des Grieux to come to her ("a me t'appressa, a me . . ."). Faltering in the desert, she demands that he find them a refuge: "Oltre ti *spingi* . . ." ("Go on, make haste"). Her once-enticing voice is turning out a set of matronly commands.

des Grieux vanishes to embark on this vacuous search. Manon ponders her destiny: "Sola, perduta, abbandonata" ("Alone, lost and abandoned"). Maria stays the second syllable of "desolata" ("desolate") to show Manon is slow to comprehend her destitution. Rancorous, she finally becomes enraged: "strazio crudel, ah, sola, abbandonata, io la deserta donna!" ("cruel torment—ah, I am an alone, abandoned and deserted woman!").

We meet her cavernous, almost contralto voice. Her plea to the heavens, "Ah, non voglio morir! Non voglio *morir!*" ("I do not want to die! I do not want to *die!*") is executed with a rugged, anguish-gulped vibrato. Hampered by Maria's insecurity in an intrusive wobble, its erroneous veneer reflects the desperation of Manon before her Judgment Day. In one of her last implorations the "rir" of "morir" ("to die") emerges especially long; by now violently urgent. Manon exploits her final strength to seek forgiveness from a higher power.

Even in death it is the girl's prerogative to stay seductive. Her lover surfaces—equally helpless. "Fra le tue braccia, amore, l'ultima volta!" ("In your arms again, my love, the final time!") she tells des Grieux. That final time ("l'ultima volta") is embodied in a tender, slick diminuendo that implies the last drops of her vigor have been saved to charm him. Uninhibited swings of vibrato atop of crescendi convey a lugubrious pledge: "Ma posso dirti che t'amo tanto … che t'amo tanto!" ("But I can tell you that I love you so much … so much!"). Manon insists that des Grieux not weep for her: this is the hour of kisses ("ora di baci è questa"). Her voice becomes as airy as a breeze as she instructs him with a torpid sensuality to kiss her: "il tempo vola—baciami!"

The heat dies. "Cupa è la notte—ho freddo;" "It's getting dark—I'm cold," she tells des Grieux, the word "cold" ("freddo") shaking in her frost. "Oblivion will sweep away my wrongs" ("Le mie colpe—travolgerà l'oblio"). Manon fights off encroaching death. "Ma l'amor mio—non … muor." ("But my love—doesn't … die"). The instrument delays its expiration till she reaches that last note of "muor".

Erotic is the eerie death.

Certain critics took issue with some of *Manon Lescaut*'s wavering notes. While at the time of the recording in September 1957 they were relatively scarce, by summer 1958 they were beginning to abound.

One writer cites Maria's recording of the aria "Senza mamma" from *Suor Angelica*—performed in September 1954 for the *Lyric and Coloratura Arias* compilation—as the first sign of her later chronic vocal problems. "It has also been termed a 'tremolo,' an 'undulation,' and even erroneously—a 'vibrato.' " he writes. "Just where vibrato ends, or becomes excessive, and a wobble begins depends on the individual listener."[2]

A wobble is discernible in the A flat [A flat 5] of "mie" in the word "mieto" that concludes the recitative "Sediziose voci" in Maria's first *Norma* recording, made in April–May 1954.

"What a singer has to have is the support of <u>breathing</u>. The diaphragm—am I right?" Maria had written to Elvira de Hidalgo in January 1946. "When the breath support is strong the voice no longer trembles."[3] From this quote one can speculate Maria had been struggling with the wobble from the onset of her training.

What is stranger is the unpredicted cruelty of this instability: a relapsing-remitting disease. Chronologically the ill-fated *La forza del destino* made in August 1954 might be the halfway point. Yet *Madama Butterfly*, the live March 1955 *La sonnambula* with its unsparing and high-pitched coloratura and a plethora of other pristine records followed.

A problem had arisen in June 1956 in the Vienna *Lucia di Lammermoor*: "At one point in the pyrotechnics of the Mad Scene her voice just simply doesn't respond," the *Chicago Tribune*'s Claudia Cassidy had written.[4] In

January 1957 Maria's Chicago concert performance of "In questa reggia" from *Turandot* had led to the same critic scribing: "It got them cheering, but at what cost? It meant that a superb singer . . . sang that cold, cruelly beautiful aria with every ounce of strength she could summon, driving it like nails into the consciousness of the audience."[5]

It was in *Turandot*—recorded at the same time as *Manon Lescaut*—that grating notes now reared their ugly heads again. "Perhaps it's possible to argue that her interpretation . . . exudes a certain lack of vocal potency," French music critic René Leibowitz remarked. "But on the other hand, the voice was able to find an extremely penetrating timbre; a piercing emission that compensates for this lack of potency a great deal, conveying to the character an aspect especially cruel: one that possesses extraordinary dramatic verisimilitude."[6]

Merciless Chinese princess Turandot will watch anyone perish to preserve her rule. To her interpretation of the anti-heroine Maria lends a stately, slender voice of steel; commencing the aria "In questa reggia" ("In this kingdom")—with the shrill blast of a cymbal. "Un grido disperato risuonò" ("a desperate cry resounded"), she relates before her people, harshly rolling that first "r" to startle them. Turandot's principal purpose is avenging the death of her ancestress Princess Lou-Ling: a slain hostage in an earlier war. Her design is to remain impenetrably independent. Maria's emphasis as she describes how Lou-Ling's cry echoed from generation to generation ("traverso stirpe e stirpe") caustically leans on the harsh "st" of "stirpe": Turandot can tame her subjects without giving them directives.

Only a man able to decrypt her torturous three riddles can defeat the emptiness of the princess. A description of one captures her ambivalence: in "candida, ed oscura" ("white and dark") Maria oscillates between the ceremonious "candida" and the doubt-ridden, dwindling "oscu . . . ra".

After Calaf is successful in his guesses love works to unhinge her iron gates. Suddenly—albeit in a different guise—that "little girl" voice surfaces: "con angoscia ho sentito il brivido fatale di questo mal supremo" ("I felt with anguish the fatal shudder of this great ailment") is how she professes her love. A slimming voice in "supremo" suggests a solicitous bride. The princess unveils a paradoxical admission: love and hate for Calaf ("E ti ho odiato per quella . . . e per quella t'ho amato") emerge equal in their passion.

The work is nevertheless plagued by intermittent vocal insecurity; some of it in favor of the slayer's stridency. "When I got thin they said I was dying, that I had lost my voice," Maria told a reporter in November 1954.[7] Music critic Eugenio Gara was already writing that the public feared her newfound beauty would curtail the Callas instrument.[8]

Repeatedly Maria would insist that weight loss hadn't been a factor in her vocal struggles. "My great career *began* when I lost weight," she told a journalist in 1963.[9]

Nonetheless by 1958 she was acknowledging her need for rest. Opinion is divided among singers when it comes to how much they should actively "preserve". It was Maria's dictum *not* to save the voice. With the best technique it was unconquerable—or so she doggedly insisted.

Despite her obstinate avowals she had started paying more attention to the concept of time off. "My rest will be of course more—more than three months this year," she told Harry Fleetwood in March 1958. "No recordings or at least, maybe one or two that's all. But erm . . . I intend to rest—*really* rest."[10]

For summer 1958 Lord Harewood had been hoping to recruit Maria for a trio of productions at the Royal Opera House. She agreed to only one.

On top of that was an occasion that Maria couldn't miss: a celebratory performance in honor of the Royal Opera House's centenary Queen Elizabeth II was due to attend. While Maria was to sing "Qui la voce" from *I puritani*, other singers would perform the final scene from *Aïda* and Margot Fonteyn would dance to Glazunov's *Birthday Offering*.

Joan Sutherland was also featuring. Led through the theatre that June by Lord Harewood, Maria happened to catch her rehearsing. "She has learnt very well how to copy me!" the soprano exulted. Sutherland was performing "I dreamt that I dwelt in the marble halls" from Michael William Balfe's *The Bohemian Girl*.[11] In the presence of Giovanna Lomazzi, who as usual had accompanied her, Maria stepped up to where Sutherland was standing. "You are really very good," she lauded. "You have everything that it takes to become a great soprano."[12]

Faced with her first encounter with the queen, who praised her "wonderful performance,"[13] Maria was hard-pressed to curtsey properly: her black, floor-length, tight backless gown could only compromise the gesture.[14] "She isn't an opera fan," she would allegedly tell somebody at Covent Garden. "I could tell by looking at her in the Royal box."[15]

When *La traviata* opened at the House that June, Maria had a doctor backstage every night of the performance to administer her vitamin injections.[16] Interpolating aspects of Visconti's *Traviata* into Tyrone Guthrie's "run-down" staging,[17] her remodeled Violetta shocked the London public by removing her high heels to rub her feet; eliciting a swath of gasps.[18]

Contrary to the 1955 *La traviata*, a recording of the live performance on the 20th displays a somewhat anxious singer. Struggling to sustain the necessary breath support, Maria rushes parts of the first act. The action sounds a great deal more like the soprano than the coughing Violetta.

Afflicted by impediments, her vocal state allows us paradoxically to hear the ailing Violetta running out of strength. Her reaction to Germont's insistence that she leave Alfredo, "Ch'io mi separi da Alfredo?" ("That I should leave Alfredo?") exits in a tentative diminuendo; attenuating symbiotically with life. When she instructs Germont to tell Alfredo's younger sister of his lover's sacrifice in "Dite alla giovine" the phrase is so impetuous, according to one critic it emerged "suspended in mid-air."[19]

Violetta calls this unseen sister "si bella e pura" ("so beautiful and pure"). Before she enunciates the word "pura" we hear a deliberate omission; a tiny gap described by Lord Harewood as "a perceptible comma".[20] It's supposed to denote shame: Violetta is a former prostitute, Alfredo's younger sister an angelic bride. Leaning into "pura'"s "p", Maria makes it plosive—as though struggling to pronounce the syllable.

Upon Alfredo's rush to Violetta's deathbed in the final act Maria quickly tried to fix her hair and appear fresh and comely.[21] Exasperated by the thought of dying at this moment in "Ah . . . Gran Dio morir si giovine!" ("Oh . . . great God, to die so young!"), she takes the phrase in just a single breath. At the end of her aria "Addio del passato" the final note of "tutto finì" ("everything has ended") is not finished but scraped messily away. Conductor Nicola Rescigno recalled advising her to "sing it just that little bit louder, then she could diminish it." But she elected not to—and the note would crack.[22]

The tragedy is palpable as she and Alfredo envision their life in "Parigi, o cara." In the phrase "la vita uniti trascorreremo" ("We will pass through life together") the last word is barely—and deliberately—an echo from Maria's throat. Some deemed this deliberate timbre controversial. Calling the role "a trapeze part filled with sick pianissimo,"[23] Maria stressed: "I had striven for years to create a sickly quality in the voice for Violetta; after all, she is a sick woman. It's all a question of breath, and you need a very clear throat to sustain this tired way of talking, or singing, in this case . . . And in the last act they [critics] even said: 'Callas is having trouble with her breath.' "[24]

Violetta has a final surge of strength before her sudden death. Maria sings—or almost speaks—in a hallucination: "in me . . . rinasce . . . rinasce . . . m'agita . . . insolito vigor!" ("In me . . . I feel again . . . it shakes me . . . an unusual vigor!"). She accelerates her voice in a crescendo that plummets . . . floating away like a scarf snatched by winter's cruel gales.

"Violetta rose from her chair to greet what she thought was a new life," critic Harold Rosenthal wrote. "A glaze came over her eyes, and [she] literally became a standing corpse."[25]

Following this performance an English nurse sent Maria a letter. She had attended one of her *La traviata*s and was stunned by how much the soprano could embody "an actual sufferer or one who had studied tuberculosis in the wards."[26]

Returned to her haven of Sirmione that July, Maria busied herself with light, trivial activities. "I *know* what you're going to ask—'What do I do?' " She once followed up on a journalist's question. "*Nothing. Nothing*, I just *live* a human . . . *life*. I have lots of fresh air; I just er . . . when it rains I go out and I don't care if I get wet, you know—just to relax the nerves."

Meneghini had bought them a motorboat. Maria wanted to learn how to use it.[27]

Her cooking attempts were disastrous. Inviting both Lomazzi and her other friends to degustate these culinary works, Maria channeled efforts into baking sweet Greek pastries.[28] "Unimaginable things would come out of the oven," Meneghini would later remember. "But she wouldn't get offended—she would just start over the following day."[29]

Even in the balm of this resplendent otiosity Maria was still mentally half-steeped in work. On 16 July American impresario Sol Hurok booked her for a series of concerts across the U.S.[30] Later on director Franco Zeffirelli came with Nicola Rescigno to discuss designs for the upcoming Dallas production of *La traviata*. Rifling through the sketches, she extended comments on each one.[31]

"I'm here resting in my new home at Lake Garda," Maria wrote to Leo Lerman. "It is peaceful and thank Heavens people have stayed away a bit . . . I really <u>intent</u> [*sic*] to rest!"[32]

In the bosom of her new abode Maria had a twin distraction: masons and workers chronically making noise—"When you're at home, they come and make a mess in the place and over the walls, etc. I feel like killing them!" she wrote to her American lawyer, Walter Cummings[33]—and the hobby of matchmaking. During Stelios Galatopoulos' visit that summer, she gossiped of various courtships, lamenting: "I am not a successful matchmaker, am I."[34]

Maritally speaking Maria was still fostering bliss. It had become her tradition to offer Meneghini either three bouquets of flowers or three roses for each anniversary. "It's seven years of tradition and I don't feel like changing the habit," she had written to him back in April 1956.[35]

"I'd like to dedicate all my life to my husband. And, er . . . to *art*, which is really so great that it frightens me sometimes. That's what eats my heart and that's what keeps my weight down, I suppose," she had told reporter Norman Ross in 1957.[36]

The problem with this dual existence was that even in hiatuses her mind was often elsewhere. Habitually taking scores to bed as Meneghini slept beside her, Maria would acknowledge her career was not confined entirely to the workplace. "Singing or being an actress or things like that—takes *so* much time, you know—your *subconscious*, your conscious, *everything*, it—even when you *relax*, actually the *mind*, I think the subconscious doesn't even *relax*. It works."[37]

While most couples close off their bedroom, Maria made it look as though she and Meneghini had nothing to hide. She once perused the score of *Lucrezia Borgia* lying in bed as he slept and Leo Lerman—her gay, music critic friend—trailed her studious eyes.[38] On another occasion Walter Legge paid a visit to Maria and Meneghini's hotel room in Berlin in September 1956 to find them "sitting up in their beds, woolen undervests visibly projecting above their nightwear (very Italian!) reading Italian illustrateds while they waited for an inquest on the performance."[39]

"If you love your work you willingly accept the discipline that governs it—these standards become ingrained and naturally colour your private life too," she confessed to a journalist.[40] This was the same Maria who had prior to her marriage entertained a handful of romantic yet unconsummated dalliances with men. In later years she would admit she lacked a "sex education;"[41] we already know that she professed not to have known "how babies are born" till the age of eighteen. "I can't have sex with anyone unless I love with both my head and my heart," she would tell Lerman in 1971.[42]

In Maria's early onstage love scenes manifesting romance with small, subtle gestures was a must. When one tenor held her closely in rehearsal she abruptly stormed out. A bouquet of flowers and a note of apology later appeased her.[43]

Even when he met Maria in 1970, by which time she was forty-six, author Alberto Moravia referred to her as a "prude".[44]

"You have a saying that diamonds are a girl's best friend," she addressed a U.S. press corps once. "It is not true. A good husband is a girl's best friend. A woman needs to be loved; to have a husband's protection whether she has a career or not."[45]

Carnal needs did not exactly figure in her repertoire.

For that reason it is not surprising that Callas biographer Michael Scott once heard from an assistant of impresario Sol Hurok that Meneghini "would pay him to procure girls."[46] Although this claim is speculative, his wife's priorities suggest that Meneghini didn't have an enviable sex life.

Assistant Elly Schotte—who was hired as a temporary secretary for Maria during her performance at the Holland Festival in 1959—recalled him as a man who "looked gloomy and seemed more or less lost. At loss for things to do, he would pop into my room for chats. On one occasion he put his hand on my knee and asked in broken English if I wanted to be Chief Secretary of the three he had already back in Italy. A strange proposition considering I had little or no command of Italian. Perhaps it was his boredom; he was just shooting the breeze."[47]

Her respite sated, in September 1958 Maria journeyed back to the recording studio. On the 19th she began work on her first Verdi compilation, *Callas Portrays Verdi Heroines*. Comprising arias from *Macbeth, Don Carlo, Nabucco* and *Ernani*, the album manifests Maria's acute vocal problems. Skimpy high notes haplessly abound in "Una macchia": Lady Macbeth's illusion of being smeared in the blood of her victims. Abigaille's coloratura-ridden, regal demonstration of strength from *Nabucco* ("Anch'io dischiuso un giorno") concludes with a squeak.

Ironically, after her first take of "Una macchia" Maria was most pleased with herself: "I was in quite good voice *then*. That *day*—because, you *know*, we all have our ups and downs," she later told John Ardoin. "I was kind of very *proud*, as soon as I stepped down to listen to the playback. And I told our then artistic director, Walter Legge, 'Well, Walter, that was—I *think* some good singing, don't you *think?*' He said, 'Oh, *extraordinary*,' and he says, 'Well, you'll *hear* it now and then you'll understand that you'll have to *redo* it the proper *way*.' I was—you know, *shocked*. I said, 'What do you mean by that?'—'Well,' he says, 'you'll listen to it, you'll see.' In fact, I *did* listen. It was astonishing as perfection—*vocal* ... it was *perfect* vocally. Nobody could say *anything* about it. *But* the *main* idea of this 'Sleepwalking' scene was not *underlined*."[48]

Recording it the "proper way" laid bare Maria's faults. Perhaps it was that day. Perhaps the earlier take had sounded better . . . if less convincing. Such was the hopscotch of Maria's voice.

Arriving in London to perform a concert on the 23rd for the television broadcast, *Chelsea at Eight*, Maria shocked listeners with a BBC interview she gave the same night. Asked whether she would "go away for two years and not sing at all," she announced: "I'm afraid that will happen in about a year. After that I will give up singing . . . [or sing] very rarely, and on occasions that will be worth my while. I really feel I am wasting my energy, wasting my own young life just for the sake of celebrity, which I feel I have obtained."[49]

This was hardly the first time Maria had alluded to her growing disillusionment with all things operatic. Asked whether she liked singing following her period of exhaustion, Asian flu and chronic "scandals" in the fall of 1957, Maria had replied: "Well, I used to; I'm afraid I don't *now* because it scares me so. You see Norman, music—singing isn't only vocal display; it's serving music."[50]

Her statement in September spawned a swath of rumors. Maria debunked them: "It has been put into my mouth that I intend to retire. But I have not yet reached my peak—I hope. If I don't sing so frequently now it is because that can ruin an artist."[51] Yet she became diligently cautious in selections for her repertoire. Giovanna Lomazzi recalled in 1961 that by November 1958 Maria "was lacking the confidence in herself."[52]

Her manager Gorlinsky proposed many engagements: a concert tour in Australia for summer 1959;[53] a concert at London's Royal Albert Hall for early December 1958[54] which then became an offer for March 18th, 1959.[55]

These projects were rejected.

Though at the time Maria never openly admitted there were problems with her voice, she regularly cited its capricious nature and her need to rest.

Her instrument was not the only problem. There was the art of *opera* in its half-dilapidated state—at least, according to Maria:

"I'm not accusing anyone but unfortunately, nowadays, too many opera houses are in the hands of people who don't know music well . . . They think that opera is created from grandiose, flashy, seemingly spectacular scenery. They don't realize that this method is dated and no longer acceptable today. Pure art must be presented on a pure stage, the emphasis being on the artists and not on useless, overwhelming stage décor," she wrote for French newspaper *Arts* in December 1958.[56] The statement came out sounding like Zola's *J'Accuse!*.

She was not the sole detractor. Visconti had written to Meneghini back in 1954: "The lack of professional seriousness [in opera] astounds me."[57]

Opera was difficult enough to execute without a shoddy attitude. Frequently Maria would refer to it as "dead" and "old-fashioned". Singing was not a natural way of saying things. Repeating phrases adamantly was no natural means of self-expression. "So we *give* it a breath of life . . ." she explained to Lord Harewood. "*Even* if the composer *maybe* didn't feel it *then* because as *life* goes on, time *has* changed, life has become more *modern*, people are less *patient*, I *feel*. They're less *naïve*, I think. We must *grant* them that. If you see a picture which is . . . twenty years older, it was *easier*, it was more . . . *credible*, you took things . . . you *believed* things easier. A hundred years ago things were—even *jokes* were more easy. *Today*, people are more *serious*, you can't fool them *that* much."[58]

And while Maria spent a while delivering "an expert treatise on Bellinian phrasing and *fioriture*" as she recorded an album of mad scenes that fall,[59] others failed to breathe life into opera.

*

With a round of concerts looming the soprano spent a great deal of October corresponding back and forth with Rudolf Bing about her future Met dates. As she arrived in New York on the seventh she discovered it was in Bing's plans to have her perform *Tosca* in the early months of 1959 and alternate it with *Macbeth* and *Traviata*.[60]

This did not suit *her* plans.

After giving a series of concerts in Atlanta, Montreal and Toronto, Maria came to New York once again on 22 October. The Metropolitan's assistant general manager Francis Robinson personally ventured to Idlewild Airport to urge her to sign Bing's proposed contract.

It was met with refusal.[61] She and the Metropolitan had been experiencing domestic problems for a while now. During the November 1956 *Tosca*s Maria had been outraged to discover that rehearsals were both minimal and not prioritized. Expecting to view all her castmates and an orchestra, she had arrived to spot a pianist and vocal substitutes. "Of course, she blew her stack," remembered director José Quintero, who witnessed the subsequent argument.[62]

"[The Met] rehearses an opera on stage only for its first performance of the season," Maria later explained. "This would be satisfactory except that then the Met makes major changes in the cast without having a new rehearsal. It is the only opera house I know where this is done."

Then there were its boring, bland productions; famed worldwide for lack of luster and their matte monotony. The one for *Lucia* she had performed a year earlier had in Maria's words highlighted, "in the famous well scene, a monstrous well that covers half the stage and looks no more romantic than an oil tank."

Traviata was one step ahead of *Lucia*. For the series of performances that she had sung in February 1958 Maria hadn't been permitted an acquaintance with the stage. Instead she had been relegated to rehearsing on the stage roof "with a chair and table for scenery and a few marks on the floor to indicate the limits of the stage. This is not art," Maria explained. "In Italy it is called *botteghino*, or 'shop.'"[63]

Designed by Tyrone Guthrie, this particular *Traviata* had been set in a rustic expanse of swaths, tufts of grass, slippery foliage and quagmires.

With no contact lenses and just one onstage rehearsal, Maria had feared tripping up at every step.

And she had never even met the baritone who was to sing Germont and ruin Violetta's life forever.[64]

The grievances were not just hers. "Many great singers have never appeared there at all, and many others were cast in the wrong roles or in cheap productions with inadequate rehearsal," soprano Eileen Farrell would note in her memoir.[65] Maria cited the Met's inability to recruit Giuseppe Di Stefano, Ettore Bastianini, Elisabeth Schwarzkopf, Nicola Rossi-Lemeni and others.[66]

Her next step—taken on 23 October—was to write to Bing with an inarguable rebuff. "Too much work and too much trouble . . . for instance I do not want ever—and I mean ever—to see the repetition of one of those things such as the Traviata of last season." If he could mount a production "new and interesting to your public," she would "co-operate modestly in attaining the good results we all desire."[67]

Believing that Maria was engaged in cat and mouse, Bing was nevertheless sure that she would yield. Her other concern was a lack of time between *Macbeth* and *La traviata*; she needed a period in which to remodel her voice for the latter. Bing was giving her eight days between the two performances. *La traviata*'s instrument could not be the same voice used for *Macbeth*.[68]

Bing pressed harder. Maria responded on the 27th with a harsher letter written in Italian by Meneghini on her behalf: according to Bing, Tebaldi had "demanded" that Maria not usurp her *Traviata*. Bing had responded by telling Tebaldi to desist from her tantrums. Tebaldi had relented—then held fast again: if the *Traviata* would be Callas' she wasn't going to sing it. "You also told me, a few days ago . . ." Maria wrote, "that you, for the sake of peace, have accepted this [Tebaldi's decision]. It is therefore logical that I should not perform this role either . . . Last spring, after my engagement at the Met, we talked about the next season. I said that among the roles you suggested for me, I would have liked to add Butterfly. Why did you not do it?"[69]

When Maria opened the Dallas *La traviata* on 31 October 1958, she received a telegram of "good wishes" from Bing that read: "But why in Dallas?"[70]

Suffice to say that Bing had also roiled Maria other times. "Please, don't launch any more opera companies," he had begged her after her co-founding of the Dallas Civic Opera.[71] The man's hostile stance of ignorance embittered her. "You wouldn't believe it . . ." she later reported. "One day . . . we were talking about [Gabriele] D'Annunzio's play *Francesca da Rimini* and the opera by Zandonai. Bing immediately asked his secretary, 'Who is this Madame Francesca?' He thought that d'Annunzio was a cyclist and Zandonai, a boxer! And he didn't even know that *Fedora, Armida, Medea* existed!"[72]

This did not bode well for Bing.

Franco Zeffirelli's *Traviata* offered an interpretation then deemed novel. With the opera staged as a flashback, Maria's Violetta was already dying in bed in her nightgown at the start of the prelude. "If you listen to the prelude *and* the fourth act prelude—it is *really* the same in another *key*," she would explain. "So in other words it *gives* us an impression that . . . she's on her deathbed, and thinks back to her three crucial moments: before she met Alfredo . . . when she had to give him up, and in the third act . . . tragedy *bursts* upon her. It is her spirit *thinking* back."[73]

Hazy gauze served as the stage's scrim. In Franco Zeffirelli's description, lighting designer Jean Rosenthal illumined the bedridden courtesan in the first scene till she "lay in a sepulchral glow with her eyes in shadow like a corpse. Yet when the party begins, she is able to jump to her feet already dressed in what is no longer a shroud but a beautiful white brocade dress."[74] In a controversial move for the time Violetta retreated from the party to her bedroom to succumb to her coughing and Alfredo—who was not yet her lover—immediately followed. Dallas music critic John Rosenfield merely remarked: "This is not, of course, the first time she has had a man in what might be euphemistically called her workshop."[75]

It was not the first and wouldn't be the last occasion on which Callas would assume the unnamed role of Co-Director.

Having deferred habitually to Visconti when it came to choices about sets and lighting, props and costumes, Maria fostered a new tenor of collaboration with Greek film and theatre director Alexis Minotis. Its foundations had begun with the following telephone call:

"She asked me to sign up for *Medea* in Dallas," he remembered. "I told her no: I didn't know the work, I didn't know anything about opera and apart from that I didn't like the genre.—'So much the better!' Maria replied. 'A thousand times better! I am not asking for an opera director. I'm asking for someone whose heart will bring life to the work—the way it does with Visconti, Jean Vilar, Zeffirelli . . .' "[76]

Singing and acting weren't sufficient anymore. When it came to mounting new productions she no longer wanted to be just a puppet or a pupil. She was an *accomplice*.

Too many times Maria's wishes had conflicted with directors'. Even in the spectacularly successful production of *Fedora* she had opposed the conceit of director Tatiana Pavlova. Whereas Pavlova had staged the opera—which takes place in 1881—in 1900, Maria had preferred the costumes of the earlier period. In that instance she had counted on designer Nicola Benois to craft a bevy of them. Benois' prior commitments had derailed the dream. Pavlova's turn-of-the-century suggestion didn't sit well with the singer: "I dislike that period for *that* particular opera because this *should* live in its frills."[77]

Preparations for the Dallas *Medea* gave Maria a semi-autonomy. "Now . . . I went to Milan and saw Maria," Nicola Rescigno reported to Alexis Minotis in September 1958.

I have already sent you a telegram à propos of the costumes. Please tell Jean [Rosenthal] that Callas did not dislike them, but she couldn't under-

stand what it was all about, because the sketches aren't sufficiently detailed. She desires to see finished sketches and please tell Jean to send them to me, air mail, as soon as possible, so that I can send them on to her . . .

She would also like a cape, which she says she needs for the numerous asides that there are in the opera; with the use of the cape, she can seclude herself from the other personages on the stage, and this is of great help to her . . .

About the scenery . . . [For the third act] *She would like more sky in the background to have a play of clouds, lightning, and fire. She likes your idea of the chariot in the end, but doesn't want it to come out of the temple door, but rather desires the temple to crumble, at which point she is standing on the chariot with the children slain. She approves very much the idea of the Deus ex machina; as a matter of fact she would like the chariot to take off in the finale, while the chorus is singing the fuggiamo.*[78]

An equal footing now sustained the artists. When Minotis later told Maria the Royal Opera wasn't granting him the dancers he required for their 1959 *Medea*, she stormed into the office of its general manager to speak out for her ally.[79]

It was logical. Fighting for art is harder in some instances than fighting for a social cause.

Caution seemed to be her first priority this time. Maria cited onstage dirt Medea's cape was sweeping up; she feared that it would ruin her performance. Henry Miller, Founding President of the Dallas Opera, and William Reed, Chairman of the Company's Information Committee, mopped the stage floor in a break from rehearsal.[80]

At this time Maria met another ally. Tenor Jon Vickers' impressions about the soprano had not been auspicious. "That Dallas day when Vickers met Callas, he began by metaphorically strapping on his sword," biographer Jeanne Williams recalled. "Bliss Hebert, the assistant to musical director Nicola Rescigno . . . had the job of driving Vickers to rehearsal . . . On the half-hour ride, 'He was mutter, mutter, mutter. "I've heard about her, her reputation, I won't let her get away with anything with me." ' "

Relying on an opera board member to drive her, Maria happened to be late that day: the only episode of tardiness in her career. "This is terrible," she told Bliss Hebert. "My first rehearsal with Jon and I'm late. I feel terrible about this. Where is he?" As she alighted at his feet Maria let out a superfluous apology: "Mr. Vickers, I can't tell you how sorry I am, but I had no control over arriving here. I've been waiting . . . and so looking forward to working with you. I've done this with several tenors and you're the first that has the voice that is appropriate and wonderful."

According to Hebert, "He looked up at her and melted. Absolutely melted." Though he and Maria were the same height, Vickers took to calling her "little Maria".

When she began to challenge his compliance by commanding him onstage, Vickers straightforwardly made it be known: "Madame Callas, Alexis Minotis has already put me through the production. You show me what you are going to do." Maria respected his moxie.[81]

Another cooperative comrade was then twenty-three-year-old mezzo-soprano Teresa Berganza, who was performing the role of Neris. Taking the unknown vocalist onboard, Maria commanded her to call her "Maria"—not "Signora Callas"—and called her "Teresina". Berganza urged Maria to highlight which qualities she liked in her performance, which she ought to improve. "Nothing, nothing; you're divine," Maria responded. With a thirty-step-long ramp along the stage, Maria had to make her entrance as Medea running down the slope as rapid as "a bolt of lightning". So she took off her glasses and arrived a while before rehearsal every morning for a period of fifteen days; descending dangerously in her quasi-sightless state to get accustomed to them.[82]

Along with this came frantic late-night phone calls to Minotis. At three or four in the morning the telephone would unfailingly sound. "What exactly did you say this afternoon when I come out and climb the steps—from the left or from the right?"[83] And it would go on and on.

Now Maria's Medea had fully changed. Though she could hardly portray the personage as a wronged woman, she was less vicious, more prudent: "She kills her children because she feels she has no other choice, and because being a goddess she can remove them from this bitter and bloody world, and enable them to join her in everlasting Life; she kills so that they may live in peace and dignity. She knows there will be no hope of that for them in this world, so she commits them to the next," was her thesis.[84]

While Maria mused on the poetic ramblings of an unreal outcast, in the dreary world of actuality the stubborn Rudolf Bing refused to budge. In lieu of compromise, his answer to her latest letter *wasn't* a desire to capitulate: "I feel your refusal to do *Traviata* to be unnecessary and deliberate unfriendliness which I deeply regret; but if you insist on it I will accept it."[85] In place of *Traviata* he proposed the preposterous *Lucia* whose vices he himself would admit some years later: "The *Lucia* in which Miss Callas had been appearing was one of our oldest and poorest productions still on the boards . . . Lily Pons . . . had also complained bitterly about it."[86]

Concluding his response, Bing wrote: "Your letter . . . sounds more the Maria Callas of whom I have been warned than the Maria Callas I know, like and respect."[87]

The comment touched a nerve. Specious smiles were out of the soprano's shooting range. "I have to *feel* what I do. I have to *like* people to be with them," she would explain. "I just . . . *cannot* learn the art of being a hypocrite. I wish I *could*."[88]

Falsehood or stepping on tiptoe was out of the question: "I cannot hide from you my disgust that you should have dared to write me a sentence such as this," she wrote. "There arises a question and that is do you make your judgments with the brain of some little fool or rather with your own brain, basing yourself on the facts and not on gossip? That I am the one, according to you, who wants to make things difficult is another judgment that has no validity . . . Give me a period of rest and that will [be] the best that you can do for me . . . Your important organization and I do *not* work by the same principle and thus it will be just as well that each should go his own road while the honest friendship that has united us exists and will surely always exist, at least on my part."[89]

On 5 November, the day before Maria's opening *Medea*, Bing sent her an ultimatum in the form of a telegram: she would either accept three performances of *La traviata* or *Lucia* accompanied by *Macbeth*—or have nothing at all.[90]

Hectic was the day. Leo Lerman came to her dressing room to find her "in a rage such as I never had seen. She was clutching a telegram from Bing."[91]

The final rehearsal began at 5 pm. During the course of it one of the onstage pillars almost fell on her.[92] It finished at two am.[93]

The following morning Maria replied to Bing's telegram—once again accenting her unwillingness to alternate "so heavy an opera as *Macbeth* with such a light opera" [as either *Lucia* or *La traviata*].[94] She proposed to switch the second opera with another.

The telegram arrived in New York at ten am. Prior to receiving the notice, Bing had dispatched his own message:[95]

SINCE YOU HAVE NOT SEEN FIT REPLY MY TELEGRAM NOVEMBER THREE AND NOVEMBER FIVE OR FURNISH CONFIRMATION AS REQUESTED PLEASE CONSIDER YOUR CONTRACT FOR METROPOLITAN 58–59 CANCELED.[96]

Along with this notification came an immediate press release: Maria Callas had been "released" from the Metropolitan Opera. There followed a barrage of quotes—among which Bing's assertion: "I do not propose to enter into a public feud with Mme. Callas since I am well aware that she has considerably greater competence and experience at that kind of thing than I have."[97]

"Again and again she came into difficulties," Peter Diamand, director of the Holland Festival, recalled seven years later. "Everything about her is super-dimensional, extra-large, including her intuition and even her less attractive characteristics . . . And I wondered whether the people there begrudged that she was more intelligent than they. Especially if the interlocutor was a man."[98]

Before Rescigno cued the orchestra that night Maria was sufficiently ablaze.

What ensued was a dark voice so petrifying it pealed almost like a gong. A recording illustrates that even "Io . . . Medea" ("I . . . Medea") is varnished with ridges of vicious vibrato.

As she asks Giasone if his old and new loves war inside him ("il nuovo e il vecchio amore in te fan guerra") the brazen instrument diminishes its texture into a derogatory squeal. Superficially endearing are the words with which she probes Giasone to remember the first time he saw her ("la prima volta quando m'hai veduta?") as they drop into the honeyed drizzle of a specious girlishness.

Detecting whether love still lingers in her devious denunciation is a difficult affair. Only when we hear an even longer, more attenuated diminuendo through "in sacro eterno amor" ("in [those days] of our sacred, eternal love") can we surmise Medea pines for these elusive hours.

And yet her newfound tenderness is swapped immediately for a vociferous inflammability.

As she turns to re-accuse him: "Non io veg-LIAI allor a tua difesa? Non io spez-ZAI de tuoi nemici il vanto?!" ("Did I not look OUT to defend you? Did I not CRACK your enemies' pride?") her voice is so coarse and the accents on the second syllables of both "vegliai" ("look out") and "spezzai" ("crack") so sudden they embody flowerheads cut down by tractor tires.

Pseudo-desperate in her plea as she asks Jason how he tolerates the sight of her "iting the hour when she woul vinta e afflitta" ("vanquished and suffering"), Maria leans on the vibration of the "vvv" sound till it's dental.

When she alleges spuriously that she still wants him ("Io non voglio che te, non voglio che te solo. Medea t'implora qui"), the sound is thinned little by little till the words possess a semi-sexual allure.

Reverting to her mother self, the sorceress pleads with her psyche not to pulverize her children—*this* time for real. The words "Mai più vi avrò con me" ("You will never be with me again") emerge through a peculiar shaping of the mouth that willingly constricts the oral palette; eking out a pain-stricken emission.

In the final act Medea beckons the infernal gods to come to her: "Numi, venite a me, inferni dei . . ." The timbre purposely sounds fragmented. With a condensed voice and her mouth in a strange shape Maria renders her voice scabrous: splintered wood painful to touch.

Pristine chromatic scales, fine trills and clean coloratura are aplenty through the whole performance.

"From the moment of her entrance, cape raised to face, until she materialized from the bowels of a crumbling temple astride a chariot whose frame was coiled serpents, Maria Callas was a creature possessed and driven, a Eumenid come to life on the stage," wrote Roger Dettmer for the *Chicago American*—citing several facets of the production's direction Maria herself had conceived.[99]

Backstage after the performance she invited a procession of reporters to her dressing room, desiring to enlighten them on where she stood with Bing.

Clasping his telegrams, Maria read each one aloud: " 'Why in *Dallas* and not *here*?' That's something I'd like to tell *him*. Why doesn't he *do* these performances at the Met? And I would be there with pleasure." Desperate was the press to learn what Bing had offered. Maria informed them—together with: "I said, 'No, I'm sorry—I cannot do *routine*. I want *new* performances—staged *well*. You know, like here—a little *young*—like what Dallas are doing, my *God*.' And I suppose that made him angry—*I* don't know. I mean, I can't explain it *otherwise*."[100]

At the after-party Maria walked around with a bouquet of long-stemmed roses, handing one to every member of the chorus. "I am not good at words, but I want to thank you for your support, your love of music, and your personal affection, which I feel," she expressed.[101]

It was four am when Leo Lerman finally escorted sleeping beauty home. Sitting by the knowledgeable critic, she enquired in a soft voice: "Who is this Rachel of yours?"—"She was one of the very greatest French tragediennes," replied Lerman. "She began by singing in the streets, a poor Jewish girl, and she became the greatest actress of her day, before Bernhardt." "Oh," Maria wearily responded. "Before Bernhardt . . . hmmm."[102]

Next there began a press campaign on her part fought as zealously as any presidential one. (Ironically it was early November in the midst of the United States midterm elections). She called for a conference, insisting: "My voice is not like an elevator going up and down. My seriousness as an artist does not permit it."[103] She wanted everyone to know that she was not the only singer fazed by Rudolf Bing's incompetent productions and unthinking managerial choices—why was *she* being picked on? "When Mario Del Monaco refused to do any more 'Aidas' or when Tebaldi refused this same 'Traviata' recently, Bing said nothing. So why me?"

"If the ear of the world will hear," she professed, "then the world will know that great art can be created outside of New York."[104]

Residents of the world reacted. *The Washington Post*'s Paul Hume argued the Met should fire Rudolf Bing unless he could recover Callas.[105] John Rosenfield of *The Dallas Morning News* called Bing "more top sergeant than artistic salesman."[106]

Delivered in an article she penned in April 1959, Maria's final statement on the incident was solemn. "I will miss the Met public, which is among the finest in the world, eager to hear and appreciate something new on the rare occasions when it is offered. But I will not miss the Met performances with their scenery and costumes from the Middle Ages."[107]

The crisis with the Met abruptly opened up the managerial flaws of Meneghini in his loving wife's rose-tinted lens. Blaming Bing for the debacle, Meneghini stressed: "It was necessary to exasperate him to such a degree that he would cancel the contract himself. Bing could not stand the sight of me. He had described me as greedy and grasping and that only money was important to me."[108]

Unbeknownst to his wife, Meneghini had requested that Gorlinsky funnel his wife's future funds into a bank account in Switzerland.[109]

At around this time she suddenly discovered that her husband had been bankrolling investments in his name with large sums of her money.

Meneghini heatedly contended that his deeds were in the interests of the couple's finances. Maria forgave him. Nonetheless she now resolved to circumvent her husband when it came to companies' deposits of her salary; goading managers of opera houses either to transfer the money to their joint account or at the very least not pay the man in cash as Bing had done.[110]

Maria's U.S. concert tour continued with performances in Detroit and Washington D.C. Attired for the latter in white silk with scarlet, full-length gloves that ran up almost to her shoulder,[111] she additionally wore a "crimson satin stole draped around her slender shoulders [that] served Callas as a torch, a mantle, a scarf: a brilliant device with which she toyed as she reveled in the flood of easy, stupendous sounds that poured out of her throat," limned Paul Hume.[112]

The typical repertoire for this series of concerts included "L'altra notte in fondo al mare" from *Mefistofele*, "Nel dì della vittoria" from *Macbeth*, "Una voce poco fa" from *Il barbiere di Siviglia*, "À vos yeux, mes amis . . . Partagez vous mes fleurs" (Ophelia's mad scene from Ambroise Thomas' *Hamlet*) and Musetta's "Quando m'en vo" from *La bohème*.

Offering her sole interpretation of the maneater Musetta, the lattermost embodies a coquette's insatiable radiance. Maria plays with it a great deal from the rhythmic point of view; delaying words and syllables such as the "ta" on "La gente so*sta* e mira" ("People stop to admire me"). Similarly she suggestively withholds both "tutta" and "m'aggira" when Musetta describes how the "scent of desire *enwraps* her *entirely*": "Così l'efflucio del desio tu-*tta* . . . m'a-GGIR . . . a". The image of Musetta slipping snippets of herself to men then snatching them away is palpable.

In Washington all hell broke loose—as critic Paul Hume vividly described: "Grown men and women, making their way to the front of the floor, reached up to the stage to hand her flowers—two red roses, a bunch of flowers, hand-written notes, to touch her hand, and to tell her, or try and tell her, what her singing had meant to them."[113]

Dolores Rivellino—the admirer who had met Maria at her *Traviata* seven months before—was on hand to respond to George Callas' question, "Is she doing good?" with "Oh yes, sir. She is doing VERY good."[114]

After celebrating her birthday in Milan, Maria retreated to Sirmione for a few days that December.[115] Two weeks thence she was set to make her long-awaited Parisian debut in the Légion d'Honneur Gala to take place at the Opéra Garnier.[116] In preparation she spent hours testing out a gamut of resplendent gowns at Biki's atelier.[117]

She came by train on 16 December to the Gare de Lyon. National paper *Le Figaro* reported her every migration. Greeted by photographers at 8:30 am, she told them she was weary and accepted a bouquet of scarlet roses. With her were eight trunks and numberless hat boxes.

At 9:10 am she was received with plaudits at the Ritz Hotel. Browsing jewelry on display, Maria gaspily enthused: "Look at those diamonds!"

Only in the afternoon would she permit herself to be subjected to a press conference: three hundred reporters in her hotel apartment, which was "enshrouded in white lilies, gardenias and black roses."[118]

"You have shown so much love and respect for this singer who has never sung for you that I feel—as I said earlier—so small and so human," she told them. "One never knows how the 19th will go . . ."[119]

The gala would include arias from *Norma*, *Il trovatore* and *Il barbiere di Siviglia* together with the second act of *Tosca*, which was costumed with a dress of beige satin and a border of sable. The first act concert dress would be red velvet with a lengthy train: a gown Yves Saint Laurent admired. Both garments were designs of Biki.[120]

Rehearsals appeared almost ominous. With no director present both the chorus and the actors loitered aimlessly onstage. This dystopia so vexed Maria that she rose and suddenly demanded everyone's attention. In search of a solution to the chaos, she appointed Tito Gobbi—the insuperable bass who had sung Scarpia beside her *Tosca* several times—Director. He advised Maria not to raise her knife so high before she stabbed him. "I can see what is coming and would take evasive action," he explained.[121]

Meanwhile she accepted future performances of *La traviata* and *Medea* in Paris for May 1959; informing Alexis Minotis their Dallas production would ignite the French capital.[122]

The night of Maria's Parisian debut was aglitter with glints, minks, chinchillas and sequins. Meneghini would drink up the glory—later recalling who sat in the audience: "The French president, René Coty; the president of the Assemblée Nationale; ambassadors from Great Britain, Italy, the U.S. and the Soviet Union . . . Paul-Henri Spaak, the general secretary of NATO; the Dukes of Windsor . . . the Rothschilds . . . Juliette Gréco . . . Brigitte Bardot . . . Charlie Chaplin, Françoise Sagan . . ." and it went on.[123] Olivia de Havilland was also present.[124]

The event was being broadcast to eleven countries. Audience member Jean Cocteau declared: "This woman is inhabited by fire."[125]

For all the hype, a tape of the event informs us this is not among the most iconic Callas feats. She begins "Sediziose voci"—the recitative that precedes *Norma*'s "Casta diva"—with her hands crossed on her chest almost protectively. Technically the voice is crystal-clear. Artistically it's lacking in audacity.

Her high notes are on-and-off strident. Though "Casta diva" is the heroine's command to pray, a portion of it is performed with eyes half-closed; enshrouded in a daze. Uneven coloratura scales stabilize—but not perfectly. Georges Sébastian conducts the orchestra ineptly.

Only when Maria launches into *Il trovatore*'s "D'amor sull'ali rosee" do we hear stylization: diminuendi that radiate shameful love. Yet they precede an unstable cadenza.

"Una voce poco fa," Rosina's teasing aria from *Il barbiere di Siviglia*, is possibly Maria's best example of it. This time, as Michel Glotz described it, "Her 'ma' emerges like a bursting soap bubble."[126]

The coloratura in "Sì, Lindoro mio sarà" ("Yes, Lindoro will be mine") is tentative and girlish; reeling in the audience to wonder what Rosina shall be plotting in the bars to come.

Her embodiment of Tosca as a fussy prima donna isn't consummate. In this staging of the second act her head shifts left and right and spins inelegantly as she wonders how to save her lover Mario—who's being tortured to spill information by the henchmen of Scarpia, Chief of Police. After betraying her boyfriend by revealing his secret, Maria's Tosca takes the staggering, bleeding man and observes to the *audience*: "Quanto hai penato, anima mia!" ("How much you have suffered, my love!") without looking at Mario.

A beautiful moment arises when "Vissi d'arte" begins. Stood upstage, Maria leans her hand along a cabinet and casts her head down. Contemplation douses notes laced in diminuendo as she recollects the pains that she has known: "quante miserie conobbi."

Sadly she understands the public demands something showier than Tosca singing with her head bowed. By "Sempre con fe sincera . . ." ("Always with sincere faith"), her arms are outstretched.

As she ends the aria kneeling with "Perché me ne rimuneri così?" ("Why do You pay me back like this?") Maria's fingers cross like swords on "co" and clench on "sì". The rhythmic gesture is pure theatre—and makes sense for both Maria *and* her Tosca.

Standing over Scarpia after stabbing him and screaming, "Muori dannato! Muori! Muori! Muori!" ("Die, damned one! Die! Die! Die!"), Tosca lords over Scarpia like a skyscraper. The vicious mien she hopes to stamp on his last memory is ripe in smugness.

Setting candles at his side, the singer shirks when her gown's train comes close to tangling with the corpse—immediately swinging it behind her. Maria times the dropping of the crucifix on Scarpia's chest with the orchestral timpani's last rumble. Hurrying together with its drumbeats, Tosca flees.

"A Father Christmas Named Callas Has Sent Thirty Million Europeans Dreaming," was the headline of *Arts*.[127] Despite customarily refraining from comments about her performance, Maria was happy enough to tell the ever-present Lomazzi: "Can you imagine, they heard me in Italy. Who knows what Ghiringhelli had to say . . . Giovanna, can you imagine what they're talking about now at La Scala?" Every now and then she interrupted her excitement to enquire: "How did I sing?"

"You sang very well," Lomazzi responded.

"But don't you think the chorus were out of sync?"[128]

A few months earlier Maria had enlisted a new maid: Bruna Lupoli. This woman would eventually become her figurative next of kin. "She is unique in this world," Maria raved about her.[129]

That New Year's Eve Maria wrote to Walter Cummings: "I'm doing well. I couldn't be happier."[130]

Lord Harewood paid Maria a visit that January, intent on persuading her to sing another role at Covent Garden besides the perennial *Medea*. She cited the Royal Opera's willingness to mount *Lucia di Lammermoor* for Joan Sutherland rather than her. Harewood insisted they were trying to persuade her to sing it that summer. Maria smiled, "eventually saying she did not want lunch but we would have coffee together in the Via Monte Napoleone on her way to try on a dress at Biki's . . ." The conversation reverted to Alexis Minotis' *Medea*.[131]

Picking up where she had left off on her American tour, Maria performed in St. Louis and Philadelphia. In New York she wrote to music critic Irving Kolodin:

> *I had called quite a few times but always without luck. Herbert Weinstock even gave a number that usually finds you in the afternoon but still I had no luck . . .*
>
> *Anyway now I do wish to thank you for publishing the articles of late. You always were a friend and I do appreciate it.*
>
> *I will try to thank you for your respect in my artistic capacities by the only way I think I should and can—and that is to sing as best as I can so you all will be proud of me.*[132]

Being friends with music critics was among Maria's many specialties. Her secretary Teresa d'Addato would be sure to keep her up to date.[133] Among those she befriended were Eugenio Gara, who wrote a tiny book about her in 1957; Emilio Radius of *Oggi*, who had interviewed Ghiringhelli on her behalf after the Edinburgh scandal; Claudia Cassidy of the *Chicago Tribune*, whom she had telephoned after her first U.S. performance to ask: "You think I have improved?;"[134] Renzo Rossellini, a writer for Roman newspaper *Il Messaggero* and cousin of movie director, Roberto;[135] musicologist Eduardo Arnosi,[136] French music critic Jacques Bourgeois, Dallas music critic John Ardoin, *Washington Post* music critic Paul Hume, musicologist William Weaver, Emily Coleman of *Newsweek* and Herbert Weinstock of *Opera News*. The latter later told his boss—editor Gerald Fitzgerald, who would himself write a Callas biography—that he would not pen a feature about her without her consent.[137]

Then there was British critic Harold Rosenthal of *Opera* magazine, to whom Maria once wrote, "Every now and then we write to each other, or rather every now and then you remember me . . . have you all missed me? Have other singers stolen me your admiration and love!"[138] She had attended his book party the previous summer.[139]

The list continues. To some it may appear as though Maria was enticing critics into friendship to secure their positive reviews. While it couldn't have been detrimental to her cause, it wasn't in the interest of careerism. Frequently Maria found in critics constant allies in her staunch campaign to "restore opera to what I believe it must have been during the Golden Age of the last century."[140] Camaraderie between the on- and offstage players had been rampant in that era; unified as they all were by the pursuit of beauty.

For this reason Maria even maintained friendships with critics who wrote of her faults. "Every now and then, some of them do *not* understand," she freely admitted to Edward R. Murrow. "Eventually with time you can prove your point of your way of singing."[141]

Rehearsing for a concert performance of *Il pirata* in which Maria would make her Carnegie Hall debut on 27 January, Rescigno took the tempo of the first-act finale at so swift a pace "[it] required a machine gun rather than a singer." As he recalled, "Maria looked at me a bit frightened when her solo passage was coming up, and she didn't make it. I told her next time around I would put on the brakes just before her entry. 'No, don't do that,' she countered. 'I like the tempo very much; it is very valid, and I don't want you to help me.'

" 'Well,' I said, 'what if you don't make it in the performance?' 'That's my business, not yours,' she answered."[142]

For all the visual splendor of her *Il pirata*—including the use of "a thirteen-foot raspberry red silk stole with which she draped and shrouded and shielded herself, and around which she moved with the grace and agility of a Manolete [a famous Spanish bullfighter]", in George Jellinek's words[143]—the voice fell short of her desires. Describing the performance he had witnessed in his journal, writer Glenway Wescott quipped: "She sang as loud as possible almost all the time, like a buzz-saw, with a slow tremolo."[144] Despite her obvious vocal problems, the soprano was still singing certain passages transposed a few tones *higher*.[145]

A recording demonstrates the common Callasian vocal defects: a skimpy high register, sudden crescendi of panic with withering breath, coloratura top notes at the end of their tether.

In October 1958 critic Noel Goodwin had put forward a bold prophecy: "I predict that if international opera queen Maria Callas, now 34, goes on performing at her present rate she will have no professional singing voice left by the time she is 40."[146]

Not coincidentally, Maria now began to take even *more* caution with regard to the engagements she selected. In an article she wrote in April 1959 she notified her readers: "Of course I will not sing as frequently as I used to . . . I am now choosing my performances with extreme care, singing only when I believe that the high standards of operatic art will be fulfilled in every respect."[147]

The Paris *Medea* previously announced for May 1959 was then postponed until October.[148] By July 3rd, it was being postponed to a period from 27 November—5 December.[149]

That April Maria would have no performances or recordings at all.

In February she took rest in Sirmione.[150] "How much I have cherished these two weeks at home, you have no idea," she wrote to one friend. "I rested, I went shopping and I tried to tidy up the house—I did everything except think about singing or anything to do with it. Almost every evening I spend at home in my <u>study drinking</u> all the happiness that comes from freedom and lack of responsibility."[151]

More passively she was engaging in another legal battle—this time against libelous critic Beniamino Dal Fabbro of the Milanese daily *Il Giorno*. Fabbro had called Maria's *Traviata* "a great disaster for opera and for the public"[152] and written a manifesto about her *Anna Bolena*:

> The administration of La Scala must rid this production, and, further—rid our theatre altogether—of Maria Meneghini Callas . . . Her acting is nothing but camp, she reduces graceful pages of music to a sluggish grievance in the middle register, transforms romantic, exalted parts into irrational vociferations, corrupts the taste of the public, and reduces the standards of our theatre to contests between stadium hooligans.[153]

On 5 February 1959 she lost the suit when the court ruled Dal Fabbro's words did not constitute libel.[154]

In the second half of February Maria planned to attend Joan Sutherland's *Lucia* rehearsal at the Royal Opera House. "I think she will do it well," she wrote to music critic Herbert Weinstock. "She has studied after my way of singing . . . I go to see it also because they want me to do it in June and if I like the production and, between us, the soprano is not better than me, I will."[155]

After the rehearsal on 16 February Maria slipped backstage to congratulate the Australian singer. As they were photographed together by the press she reassured, "I sort of feel very all-for-her."[156]

At lunch with Walter Legge some hours later she unveiled her thoughts. "She will have a great success tomorrow and make a big career if she can keep it up. But only we know how much greater I am."[157]

The altruistic, art-devoted side of Maria was inarguably happy for Sutherland. After all, she had bemoaned for years the lack of true sopranos, tenors and conductors. "I am attributed of having rivals. I'm afraid I haven't. It's not being immodest that I say this. But my rivals cannot be considered *such* if they sing certain operas of Puccini and very few other composers who did not require the *virtuosismo* . . . Forgive my immodesty, we *could* use more singers. For instance, I cannot go everywhere and show *Medea, Norma, Anna Bolena*; and *this* is music, this is precious music," she had stressed in 1957.[158]

But it was 1959. Little by little opera houses were beginning to expand their repertoire *because* of her. Certain performers were daring to try out new roles. At last this revolution of Maria's had borne fruit. And yet her own was waning.

"The greater I grow," she told an interviewer that June, "the more doubts I have, the less I feel sure. Each time there are new gestures. Years of love go into the search for perfection. Someone may write: 'Callas sang well.' But millions of details are ignored. You feel as if you have worked for nothing because it isn't noticed."[159]

Though she could badmouth colleagues in her private conversations she could equally ask critics—as she did once William Weaver—"Oh, why did you have to come tonight?" because she was sure that she hadn't done well.[160]

That March Maria tackled what could easily be thought her greatest vocal challenge; one that superficially seemed simple. Recording *Lucia di Lammermoor* once again, tenor Ferruccio Tagliavini witnessed Maria applying "superhuman efforts" to finish the mad scene with a high note that "her vocal cords could no longer yield. She tried and restarted dozens of times."[161]

The result is almost frightening to hear. In what is thus far her worst studio performance, Maria's notes possess an almost nasal quality. Episodes of shrinking volume aren't diminuendi but exhibits of a fast-expiring instrument.

In certain moments her delivery is commonplace and void of character; in others rashly rushed. Attempting to lend potency to her strained voice, she darkens it and makes Lucia's timbre heavier and matronly. The mad scene is emptied of eeriness.

"I was expecting Maria and you in London this week for your planned gramophone recordings, but I hear from the Savoy that you had cancelled reservations and consequently I assume recordings do not take place," Gorlinsky wrote to Meneghini on 20 April.[162] The sessions had been called off at short notice. Maria retreated yet again to Sirmione, from where she sought to know how the feature she had written in *Life* magazine—whose lawyers had strongly advised against publication[163]—was faring among the elite. "How did you like my 'Life' article?" she scribed to Leo Lerman. "What do people say? Or don't they care any more?!!"

Pedantically she was insistent that her break take precedence: "You must know that I've been so busy <u>resting</u> and being, as near as possible, a human, normal person that time slipped up and here I am practically leaving (in 10 days) for a concert tour and really I hate the idea! Whoever said that I couldn't live without my work!!!" she repined.[164]

That 21 April the Meneghinis celebrated their tenth wedding anniversary at Maxim's in Paris. Maria emphasized Meneghini's devotion to her to reporters.[165] In private she was harboring doubts.

"Callas gave, without a doubt, the best and worst of her art," wrote Antonio Fernández-Cid of her Spanish concert debut in Madrid on May 2nd. "... A descending chromatic scale that resounded like an anthology ... instrumental purity and human emotion. The counterpart of all this is the imperfection of several high notes ... the wavering sound of the voice in the long notes, the inequality across the voice's color."[166]

Meneghini failed to notice this. Instead, a new idea excited him: would Maria be willing to perform in a cabaret act in Las Vegas? They would be paying a hell of a lot. Walter Legge was hard-pressed to explain to him that opera singers did not sing at cabaret shows ... much less in Las Vegas.[167]

The trip to Spain had left Maria with a horrid cold. Returned to Milan, she took straight to bed. But Meneghini was insistent. The German tour was coming up: they needed to depart for Wiesbaden. Maria insisted there was no way she could sing in Wiesbaden. The impresario who had organized the concert was furious—commanding that Maria's doctor, Arnaldo Semeraro, recite the note exonerating her aloud on television. Maria found this luridly offensive.[168]

Rather than release the news a few days in advance, a spokesperson for the impresario from the Hoffmeister Concert Agency announced that Maria had cancelled the concert at the last minute.[169]

Meanwhile, Sander Gorlinsky was pressing Maria for future dates: 23 September at the Royal Festival Hall in London and a concert to be televised at the same venue days later. "Could you be an angel and make a decision on it quickly."[170]

More rejections. Grounded at home by her cold, Maria asked Lomazzi to report back on the happenings at La Scala. How had Margherita Roberti fared as Leonora in *Il trovatore*? she hankered to know. Learning backstage gossip only saddened her.

Lomazzi was in their living room one day when Meneghini abruptly stood up. "Where are you going?" Maria asked. "To Dr. Semeraro. I'm going to ask him to read your medical certificate aloud for German television."

Maria blew a fuse. "You are my *husband*—how could you agree to hold me up to such ridicule? Don't you care about my pride—about my dignity as an artist? How could you *do* such a thing?" She stormed off to her bedroom and shut herself in. Ten minutes later she was calm. "I'm sorry," she told Meneghini somberly. "Do what you think is best."

Maria's first German concert was in Hamburg on 15 May. Broadcast and preserved, it went better than she likely had expected. Performing "Tu che invoco con orrore" from Spontini's *La vestale*, she used infrequent swivels of the head and those expressive eyes to extricate her heroine's emotional evolvement. When Giulia hallucinates that her lover Licinio is close by ("Ma Licinio è cola . . . posso mirarlo"), her curling hand clasps her face. She nestles tenderly against it; eyes aglow in adoration. Removing it, she gestures slowly and deictically at what's before her in a luminous, proud smile. Eventually she interlocks her fingers as she muses on the fact that she can listen to him ("ascoltarlo").

Suddenly she has to switch back to her vestal virgin piety and fury freezes her. Placing her right hand along her chest, Giulia must pledge allegiance to her cause. "No, non più . . . non più" ("No, no more, no more") she sings. It's a singular moment of artistry in a concert where Maria takes many safe detours—omitting the high Cs [C6] in both this aria and the mad scene of *Il pirata*, where she supplants it with a lower G.

After concerts in Stuttgart, Munich and the delayed Wiesbaden, Maria journeyed homeward to Milan. Lomazzi now observed she seemed impatient with her husband.[171]

Scheduled to perform Minotis' *Medea* in London, she arrived on 11 June[172] together with Meneghini and Lomazzi—exhausted and, in the latter's words, "awaiting the hour when she would go home."[173]

"Callas appears to have profited from a period of relative idleness . . ." Irving Kolodin reported in the *Saturday Review*. "The sound was fresh, responsive, endlessly expressive in her veiled, *chalumeau* manner. But the range continues to contract, with a lunge for a C in Act II that came out merely as a shriek."[174] A recording of June 30th's performance shows us she is still relying on that sinister intonement from her Dallas 1958 *Medea*. Although she appears breathless in some phrases and relies more on abrupt shifts in dynamics, Maria is more stable vocally than she has been in the preceding months.

In an effort to revitalize relations between Great Britain and Cyprus, shipping magnate Aristotle Onassis had organized a lavish ball after the premiere of *Medea* at The Dorchester Hotel.[175] Across a hall drenched with pink curtains, roses, tablecloths, champagne and plinths,[176] one hundred and seventy guests appeared; among them Margot Fonteyn and Cecil Beaton. Loath to attend the party, Maria went only at Meneghini's insistence and stayed for a little while. Onassis and his wife Athina ("Tina") extended the same offer they had made at Wally Toscanini's ball in April: a cruise on their yacht in July. It wasn't long before Maria left and went to her hotel.[177]

Stelios Galatopoulos watched the final London *Medea* from the wings on 30 June 1959. He witnessed Maria awaiting her first entrance, hurriedly praying and crossing herself several times. Prior to entering the stage she knocked on wood. When it came to threatening to kill her children, Maria picked the knife up, changed her mind and tossed it. Somewhere onstage it camouflaged. Galatopoulos feared myopic Maria wouldn't catch sight of it. At last she located it.[178]

A few days later Galatopoulos teased Maria; joking that she had looked "like a blind woman" in her search for the knife. Failing to appreciate his humor, she insisted: "Because I am 'blind' my hearing is very good. I only had to hear the knife fall to know exactly where it was."[179]

After the performance Maria dined with the Queen Mother at Clarence House. Philosopher Isaiah Berlin watched the difference between the two figures: "They were like two prima donnas, one emitting white and [the] other black magic. Each tried to engage the attention of the table, Miss Callas crudely and violently, the Queen Mother with infinite gracefulness and charm of a slightly watery and impersonal kind . . . I see that she is the strongest musical personality on the opera stage since [Fyodor] Chaliapin."[180]

Needless to say Maria didn't merely act on whims. Courting all the different peoples before whom she took the stage, she sustained the semblance of a gracious princess. Asked where she most liked to sing by a reporter, she responded: "That's a . . . a very difficult question to answer because, you see, whatever I *do* say, I always offend *someone*."[181]

An almost political diplomacy would at times enter her discourse. She greeted Lisbon on the radio before her *Traviata* in March 1958 with, "I send you a most affectionate greeting;"[182] she charmed Athens with the statement: "I belong first and foremost to the Greek people. I am married to an Italian, the whole world praises me, but my blood is Greek, and no one can nullify that."[183] Four weeks later she addressed her American audience: "I have the great, great pleasure of saying a hearty 'hello' to my fellow countrymen."[184]

Then there were the British, whose understanding of her work—despite not knowing the Italian language—"made me respect you all the *more*;"[185] and the French, who had a "very special courtesy of loving, of respecting artists;"[186] and the Germans, who loved you "as though you were the Madonna."[187]

Thus she became almost regal.

But she also knew her audience. Self-adjustment didn't come so naturally to her. When the humorous William Weaver told Maria he had journeyed to Verona for the express purpose of hearing her sing *Mefistofele*—only for the performance to be cancelled by rain—she replied slyly: "Oh yes I remember that night: easiest money I ever made."[188]

On account of such remarks a handful of acquaintances deemed the soprano shallow, trivial or boring. With an inherently shy nature and a lack of erudition when it came to lofty topics, she attended a party where photographer Diana Vreeland was present and lengthily spoke of the chicken.[189] Lost for words with gregarious socialite Wally Toscanini—a woman who adored glamour and gossip—Maria made her think she was "devoid of personality in real life."[190] Franco Zeffirelli marveled once that her "conversation was silly, superficial even."[191]

Some of it was genuine; Maria needed to unwind between performances. But sometimes it was just a cover. Appearing simple was an easy way to lessen her responsibility in others' eyes. Friend Carla Nani Mocenigo had a contrasting vision of her. "She was like a sponge, she took in everything. She hadn't been able to study and get an education, but she had a natural talent for observation. She watched others and took note. She was incredibly attentive."[192]

At times nevertheless Maria's faulty insight into her collocutor submerged her in hot water; casting an irreparable impression.

The penultimate concert that season in Amsterdam was a near-total disaster. Terrified of seeing the audience, Maria requested that the house lights be dimmed.[193] She also conferred privately with Peter Diamand—Artistic Director of the Holland Festival—advising him not to deposit her performance fee to her and Meneghini's bank account.[194] Maria feared her husband might end up misusing it. "I did in fact try to confide in a friend," she later told Stelios Galatopoulos—referring either to Diamand or someone else—"hoping that he might help me, not to get rid of my husband but take away my financial arrangements from his absolute control. I am not sure whether it was this friend's inability or unwillingness to be involved in other people's affairs, but he evaded my call for help by trivializing my problem and trying to persuade me not to worry too much."[195]

In the concert the soprano sounded hopelessly congested, began "Tu che invoco" with the wrong line and was late to start a verse in the *Don Carlos* aria.

Three days later she performed the tour's final concert in Brussels. Sixteen months before she had been passing through the city and ornately laid a wreath before the mausoleum of Maria Malibran. A reception had been given in her honor by the Mayor of Ixelles, Charles Janssens. During the occasion Maria had dropped her champagne glass; splitting it into splinters all over the floor. "Your glass has broken, Madame," Mayor Janssens had observed. "It'll bring you luck."[196]

The prophecy was not entirely accurate.

12.

"Being conscientious"

Blacklisted at most of the world's major opera houses, Maria's name was not as smeared as that of Senator McCarthy's targets. Similarly to the witch-hunt nonetheless, it did restrict her options work-wise.

Early July 1959 saw her being courted by two theatres only: the Opéra de Paris, which wanted badly to stage her in Alexis Minotis' much-hyped *Medea*,[1] and Dallas Civic Opera where her old pal Lawrence Kelly held the role of General Manager. The Texan press reported that the impresario was "dangling two Donizetti rarities, 'Lucrezia Borgia' (1833) and 'Maria di Rohan' (1843), and Rossini's 'Elisabetta, Regina d'Inghilterra' (1815) . . . Still in the running too for 1960–61 are Offenbach's 'Tales of Hoffman' [*sic*] (with Callas doing all three soprano roles), a connoisseur revival of Meyerbeer's 'Les Huguenots' or Donizetti's 1824 success, 'Emilia di Liverpool.'"[2]

Flaring with the zeal of blazing coal effulgent in a fireplace, the revolution of bel canto thus pursued its restless war on opera's stagnant repertoire.

Far from its scarlet flags the golden goose Maria chased was fresh repose. Following her Brussels concert she and Meneghini swiftly ventured back to Sirmione. A bounty of rest and a bowlful of sea air were her doctor's prescription.[3] Conducive to this counsel was a proposition Lawrence Kelly and his partner David Stickelber had made in London at the time of the *Medea*s: they were hoping that the pair would join them on a cruise of the Caribbean that summer.

Instinctively Maria had invited Giovanna Lomazzi to tag along. Some days later she had telephoned her to announce that they were calling off the trip: Meneghini wasn't satisfied with the idea of going on a cruise with Lawrence Kelly. His preference rested with another bidder for their summertime excursion: billionaire shipping magnate Aristotle Onassis and his wife Tina.[4] They could mingle with celebrities on *that* kind of a cruise, he contended; make connections and score profitable business ventures. "Although I was very run down and unhappy at the time, I primarily went on the *Christina* cruise in order to please my husband who was very keen to go," Maria later remembered.[5] Had the choice been left to her she would have gone with Kelly—but she lacked the strength to argue.[6]

When Lomazzi visited Maria in the middle of July she found the couple struggling further in their marital relations. Loath to confide in anyone about her problems, Maria couldn't hide the weary aftermath of Meneghini's slow-to-surface secrets. Investments he had put in motion with Maria's hard-earned money and imbroglios stirred by his demands at opera houses had aggrieved his wife.

There was a novel cause for argument this time. Meneghini was considering an offer for Maria to be leading lady in *The Prima Donna*: a German film to be produced by the renowned distributor Gloria Filmverleih.[7] What could be easier? Her fee would be two hundred million lire: around three hundred twenty thousand dollars at the time and the equivalent of some three million, two hundred thousand today.

But Maria had never intended to star in a movie—she couldn't *act*. She didn't want to act. Asked if a speaking role would interest her in 1961, she openly responded: "Sometimes I'm very tempted, and I have had lots of offers. But I feel I should have to learn a new enunciation, a new kind of voice-control, a whole new technique. And perhaps I should find that it wasn't my world."[8]

An industrious type like Meneghini wasn't one for hearing out these sentimental manifestos. "Could you imagine how much land and how many businesses we could buy with that money?!" he demanded to know. Maria heatedly contested this. "It beats the hell out of art!" yelled Meneghini according to Giovanna Lomazzi. "Land—land is what matters!"[9]

A cautious wife, Maria opted to postpone the discord. On 21 July she and Meneghini flew from Milan to Nice to board Onassis' luxury yacht, the *Christina*, named for his daughter. Despite its manifold descriptions as a fairytale-like vessel, the small boat was three hundred and twenty-five feet long and had miniature cabins. Sir Winston and Lady Churchill, his daughter Diana and his secretary Anthony Montague Browne would be spending their summer there. This news tickled social climber Meneghini.[10]

Maria had a score of Bellini's *La straniera* with her. Appearing at the docks to see off the departing passengers, Prince Rainier asked if a performance at the newly-founded, scarcely-finished Monte Carlo Opera House might be of interest. "Possible," was her alleged response.[11]

Onboard Maria struggled to impress the other guests. When the yacht sailed in to Capri on the 26th to pick up music hall performer Gracie Fields, the passengers convinced the latter to sing ditties like "Volare". "There was something incongruous about the sight of Maria Callas pretending to enjoy singing along to 'Daisy, Daisy,'" Churchill's granddaughter Celia Sandys remembered. She and her mother Diana deemed Maria haughty; misinterpreting her urgent need to switch off air conditioning and put up stabilizers as blunt signs of starry arrogance.[12] They didn't know that air conditioning is any opera singer's nightmare—and the rocky waves of her career could not permit Maria a pernicious cold.

Sea air replenished her. The "really magnificent Capri" was her description in a letter to Bruna the maid. "Even if I'm better off at home it would be a shame to miss such a beautiful cruise," she pondered in writing. Bruna was also on vacation. "Make the most of it and come back relaxed and refreshed for the peripatetic adventures that deep down we love. We are so used to being in motion, aren't we Bruna?"[13]

Almost fifteen years had passed since she had last seen Churchill in the flesh: in 1944 the Greeks had welcomed the prime minister to Athens. Sir Winston was a hero in her eyes. Maria was at loss to know how to behave with heroes. Witnessing the frailty of the wheelchair-bound octogenarian, she would address him tenderly, liberally touching his hand;[14] never once assuming her behavior could be seen as superficial. Very soon both Celia and Diana were aghast by the distinctly European ways of her tactility and fussing; Maria "spoon-fed" Churchill ice cream and her manners far transcended what was "proper" among English ladies.[15]

Some days later the unpleasant subject of a movie arose yet again—and not at Meneghini's bidding. Film producer Carl Foreman was on the island of Rhodes, when he intercepted the *Christina* and paid Maria a visit. His hope was to convince her to play a Greek partisan in the war epic *Guns of Navarone*. The picture would eventually be made in 1961 with Gregory Peck, David Niven and Irene Papas. Foreman left the boat in good spirits[16]—sure that Maria would consider the part despite her insisting years later, "Parts such as what they had in *Guns of Navarone* . . . don't interest me."[17] Her ambiguity with the producer may have been a circumventive effort to appease her husband.

Already bored—Meneghini only spoke Italian and was hard-pressed to communicate with other passengers—he turned against the party altogether. Later he would fabricate fallacious tales about the cruise; insisting that the clan had turned into an orgy in which people had bathed nude and swapped their sexual partners.[18] In his rendition of events Gianni Agnelli, the founder of Ford, his wife, and more "Greek, American and English personalities" had all huddled together in intimacy.

This allegation angered Churchill's secretary Montague Browne—who wrote a letter to *The Times* decrying the alleged moments of "gross impropriety" described in Meneghini's memoir. He also clarified that Gianni Agnelli hadn't been present—and neither had anyone else but the Churchills, the Onassises and their staffs.[19]

As Browne would later scribe, if anyone had overstepped the threshold of decorum it had been the man himself. Meneghini was a character repellent to the female guests. The pipe-clayed white shoes that he wore would stain their skirts each time he tried to play a game of footsie with them.

Not all of Meneghini's rage was thoroughly unjustified. A notorious ladykiller, Onassis was bestowing copious attention on the irremediably naïve Maria; ensnaring the insomniac in conversation on the deck at night and serving Greek hors d'oeuvres to her at any hour.[20] A runty fellow of some five foot five,[21] he was fifty-three years old with an ungainly figure and projecting belly. From almost anyone's perspective he was unattractive: wrinkles on his sagging cheeks carved deep into his countenance to make it look like a sultana.

Maria had no interest in his billions—or his face. What she witnessed in her host on the *Christina* was a penchant to be warmly welcoming and generous. Whether or not this constituted a façade or his true nature can be left to the discretion of the reader. Likely it was both.

Idolizing Churchill, Onassis tended scrupulously to the living legend and his family and went so far as to request the ex-prime minister's sign "W.S.C." on every copy of his books aboard.[22] To one of Sir Winston's nurses, Sister Thomson, he gave a Swiss travelling clock.[23] Though some accused the man of sycophancy, Churchill's daughter Sarah expressed gratitude for the attention he bestowed on her old father. "My parents' affection for him, and indeed my own, extended beyond his and Tina's impeccable hospitality. Onassis never expected any favors in return or used this friendship in any way for his own ends. Now that he is dead some people run him down. This is no more than groundless gossip and perhaps jealousy," she told Callas biographer Stelios Galatopoulos in the nineties.[24]

Witnessing Onassis' venerable hospitality as Meneghini whined and browbeat her about unwanted film deals, Maria fostered admiration for this self-made businessman.[25] Despite possessing altogether different interests they could fill exchanges with a host of subjects. Both had left Athens very young and struggled through horrific conflicts: Maria in the battles waged throughout the civil war in Greece; Onassis Turkey's capture of his homeland Smyrna in September 1922.

With his father Socrates incarcerated in a Turkish prison, Onassis had bribed an official to let him inside. After being caught the sixteen-year-old boy had turned into a target for the Turkish Army. Subsequently he had sought asylum at the office of the U.S. vice-counsel, whose officials hid him in a rolltop desk. The subterfuge allowed the teenager to finally escape and wrest his sisters and his other female relatives from Lesbos Island's refugee camp.

One release would not suffice. Onassis had conspired afterward with long-held British, Turkish and Italian acquaintances in Smyrna to plot an escape route for his father from prison.[26] "My life has been—and still is—a battle, and every phase ends up either as a gigantic victory, or else formidable defeat," he allegedly told Italian newspaper *La Stampa* in 1966.[27] The creed bore similarity to how Maria saw her life and dealings on the opera stage. Four years later she would tell a British daily: "Life is a battlefield. There is a novel, isn't there? By Graham Greene. 'Life is a Battlefield.'"[28]

With nothing but the shirt on his back—or so goes the legend—Onassis had moved south to Buenos Aires late in 1923. Working at a telephone company at night and scouting for business by day, his acumen had started shaping the tobacco industry; eventually expanding it. By the age of twenty-three he had become the owner of a factory. At twenty-five he had been unexpectedly appointed Greece's Consul General to Argentina.

Apparently he worked twenty-four/seven.[29]

By the time of this *Christina* cruise Onassis owned a seaside villa in Athens and a Paris apartment on the Avenue Foch among multiple other properties.[30]

What Maria found refreshing was his honesty. Their discourse extended to "philosophizing" about struggles in life, sacrifices one makes for success and the bitter fight for survival. Meneghini—whom Browne described as epitomizing "the very worst traits of a greedy and selfish Milanese bourgeois"[31]—spent excess time self-praising. Unlike Onassis, he concealed his vulnerability. He had never responded to Maria's musings on abstract ideas. What interested him most was material.

"In Monte Carlo, where the cruise began, I was very impressed by his [Onassis'] charm but above all by his powerful personality and the way he would hold everybody's attention," Maria would later recall. "Not only was he full of life, he was a source of life . . . I began to feel strangely relaxed. I had found a friend, the kind that I'd never had before and so urgently needed at the time. As the days went by I felt that Ari was a man who would listen to other people's problems in a positive way."[32]

Indeed Onassis possessed widespread popularity for being an attentive listener. British diplomat Sir John Russell once commented, "He loved hearing other people talk about something they knew about, and he never forgot anything . . . He used to ask me a lot about British policies in the days when I was with the foreign office, not for his own purposes but just because he liked to hear me discussing it."[33] Unlike Meneghini—who was prone to drifting off at dinners with Maria's colleagues—Onassis had a zealous zest and curiosity.

Little by little their enlightening discussions grew in number. Maria's entourage consisted mostly of young women who went shopping with her and accompanied her on her operatic tours and to the beach. Thus in a strange coincidence the power-hungry shipping magnate now assumed the role of her first confidant in years. "I saw in Ari the type of friend I was looking for," she would clarify. "Not a lover (a thought that never even crossed my mind in all the years I was married), but somebody powerful and sincere whom I could depend on to help me deal with the problems I had had for some time with my husband. I knew no one else capable or willing to give me this support."[34]

She hoped a similar kinship would evolve between him and her husband.

A colloquy between the trio brought up the unwelcome subject of the latter's failed investment in expensive paintings. Though Maria was reluctant to explain the situation, her accommodating host enquired what had happened to the works. The silly tale unfolded: together with another investor Meneghini had purchased "original" paintings for a huge sum of money, only to discover they were frauds. Now the hapless pair was arguing about their ownership. It was something that Maria found especially amusing. Still under the impression that their funds were inexhaustible, she likely found her husband's error quite endearing. Onassis also laughed—and Meneghini flew into a rage.[35]

The friction grew between the couple as they plunged into another "lengthy and rather irritating argument," in Maria's words. "[He] went on and on about my future engagements, I got up and went on deck for some air and also to be by myself ... Ever since my disagreements with the big theatres which began roughly eighteen months previously, Battista talked of nothing else but engagements—more of the exceptionally high remuneration than their artistic level—and what a fantastic businessman he was." On account of her discovery that Meneghini had misused her funds, "My confidence in him was all but lost. All I needed was somebody to help me handle my situation."

That night on the deck Maria pondered in a tranquil silence. Staring into space, Onassis doted on the vista; he was achingly enamored with the sea. The magnate pointed to Mytilene, the capital of Lesbos. Gradually he and Maria recommenced their existential discourse. Onassis had a confession to make. He was satisfied; content—but something was amiss from his luxurious life. The truth was he had always wanted to become a sailor.[36]

The admission made him highly sympathetic in Maria's eyes. His words were hardly total fabrications: the Christina seldom carried sailors since Onassis relished steering his beloved vessel. To guests he would insist he was a "man of the sea" and loved kayaking.[37]

His allusion to a sentimental outlet that was lacking in his life stirred something in Maria. "I am sure our friendship began on that occasion," she recollected. "Suddenly my hopelessness and that terrible irritability, which I had had for several months, all but vanished. My quarrels with the theatres had given me no elation but disillusioned and distressed me because they could have been avoided. Even though my conscience was clear and I had never acted on whims, Battista should have handled the situations with more diplomacy ... When I told my husband on the Christina that I had found in Onassis a great spiritual friend he did not pass any direct comment, though I sensed that he was simply furious; not so much with me but with the idea that I had found the spiritual support that had been lacking in my life for some time."[38]

Meneghini's ire scarcely went unnoticed. Soon Churchill's daughter and granddaughter began to speculate that something was suspicious in the Callas-Onassis relationship. Christian Cafarkis, the magnate's "man-Friday" (or one of them) would insist that Meneghini's wrath had been uncalled for: "Onassis and Maria were indulging in a perfectly harmless flirtation and never once said or did anything that could be interpreted the wrong way . . . [one day] things became very uncomfortable when Meneghini, who had been in bed for forty-eight hours, finally felt well enough to get up. He immediately sensed what had been going on and the two men had a terrible scene in Onassis' office."[39]

Either before or after that Meneghini confronted his reticent wife on the film deal again: "Hollywood is *calling* you," came the command. "But I haven't changed my mind."[40] Once again the conversation wound itself into a wiry impasse. "Maria—you realize that you have to work if we want to continue living the way we do," he insisted. "What do you mean?" she demanded to know. "Look at the amount of money I've already made!"

He grunted. "Well, it may not be as much as you think."

What did Meneghini *mean* by this? The suggestion was astounding.

On board was a man who knew a little about money: Maria's newfound friend. Having no one else to turn to and increasingly solicitous about her finances, she asked for his advice. Onassis counseled her to ask her husband to produce a statement listing all of his investments; one that specified the stock and businesses, when and how much.

Meneghini refused the request.[41] "Very well. In that case, from now on I'm going to manage my own business affairs," Maria conceded.

This he couldn't handle. Insisting they leave the cruise early, he wouldn't hear of his wife's inexplicable requests. "After some beating about the bush, Battista showed his true colors in no uncertain terms: he adamantly demanded complete financial control over me, or nothing,"[42] Maria would remember. They disembarked at Venice on 11 August,[43] using the pretext of Meneghini's mother's illness as a reason to leave prematurely.[44] Instead of returning to Milan with Maria, Meneghini sought refuge in Sirmione— where he telephoned his lawyer and demanded he prepare the documents required for a legal separation.[45] Divorce was still illegal in Italy—and would be until late 1970.

"Nobody is happy to be appreciated, even loved, only for their 'investment' potential. It became impossible for me to go on in that way. On the other hand I needed the security of a real friend—and, I must repeat, not a lover," Maria later emphasized.[46]

All hope was not lost. Dumbfounded by Meneghini's reaction, Maria headed to Sirmione to mollify him. She insisted they forget their recent quarrel, the projected film deal and his financial faux pas. All she wanted was the reparation of her marriage: a vacation alone would do both of them good. Meneghini's reaction was to accuse her of betraying him with Onassis; her shenanigans with the billionaire had made him a laughingstock.

He went to bed. Maria was in shock. By the time he awoke she had left. Meneghini dashed to the telephone and immediately called a friend: "You have to come here," he cried out. "Maria wants to *leave* me!"

Still she was determined to salvage her marriage. Onassis just happened to be in Milan—coincidentally or not coincidentally. Maria called on her dependable new friend for help; he needed to precise to Meneghini the pure nature of their innocent relationship. That evening Maria and Onassis arrived at Sirmione together with the best of intentions. Meneghini wouldn't listen to reason.[47]

On 25 August Meneghini petitioned for a legal separation. Through a letter from her lawyer Augusto Caldi Scalcini, Maria made it clear she was determined to resolve the marriage. Her proposal was denied: the head-strong Meneghini adamantly sought a split.[48]

Too much had happened in too brief an interval. Bombarded by these ruthless revelations, Maria struggled bitterly to reconcile herself to the idea that she had loved an unreality. They hadn't grown apart or fallen unexpec-tedly in love with others. He was simply someone else.

She didn't relish self-reflection. Asked about therapy on one occasion, her response was "Psychoanalysis? I don't believe in it. I perform my own psychoanalysis all the time."[49] Yet she was also wary of her arable imagina-tion; in later years implying that she might have studied psychology or psychiatry if she had not been a singer. "There are so many people in the world—and what things we invent in our mind!—what fantasies!" she remarked to a colleague.[50]

This bleak and dreary plot twist was one typical of neorealist cinema: an affable and gentlemanly Veronese man who had tended to and treasured this young woman suddenly turned out to be a vicious swindler. "The moment I stop *respecting*, I don't *love*. I might have *affection*. But love goes with *respect* so it's a . . . *strange* combination," Maria would tell a reporter.[51] The loss of Meneghini didn't only represent the loss of a rapport, it doggedly encouraged her self-doubt.

Realizing her marriage had been detonated, Maria wrote to her American lawyer Walter Cummings on 28 August, advising him not to tell anyone of her circumstances. "Battista and I are separating. When it comes to the reasons, I can only say that they are personal and that we have our differences. Later on, I will be able to explain. Don't be alarmed by the newspapers when they come out. There will be gossip." She asked him if it would be possible to obtain a quick divorce in America.[52]

"For me, it was a terrible step to take. I consider a marriage break-up one of the greatest admissions of failure," Maria would tell journalist Derek Prouse two years later—adding that her parents' divorce had provoked her aversion to it.[53]

In shock, her thoughts veered far from the desire for a new relationship.

Contrarily it's hard to think Onassis' designs were no more than platonic.

Having wed the seventeen-year-old Athina "Tina" Livanos at the ripe age of forty, Onassis had a marriage of convenience. Tina had been given to him by her father Stavros Livanos, a shipowner descended from an affluent dynasty. Respectful of each other, neither had envisaged the arrangement as romantic. Nonetheless it had produced two children: Alexander, born in 1948, and Christina, born in 1950.

When it came to them Onassis wasn't absent-minded. Despite sending them to boarding school, he pondered on their futures with minutious detail. A 1956 epistle to acquaintance Spyros Skouras specifies that his intention was to keep his children in European schools till the age of eleven or twelve with the purpose of making them multilingual. Following that they would return to American schools.[54]

That said, Onassis had compulsively been interested in business matters: spending nights discussing acquisitions and investments with affiliates. Tina was a party girl. Onassis had devoted endless time to his potentially illegal operation of a fleet of U.S. tankers—which had prompted a perennial investigation by the U.S. Department of Justice.[55]

His appetite for business wasn't entertaining to his hedonistic wife. It likewise didn't help that his insatiable skirt-chasing had enticed Jeanne Rhinelander, a friend of Tina's.

But the latter was no victim. Ranting to the press about her husband's purchases of properties in Monte Carlo, she expressed exasperatedly: "Buying up the place! . . . I can't tell you how much I dislike Monte Carlo . . ." In the meantime she was keeping company with Reinaldo Herrera, Spanish aristocracy who would eventually become the 5th Marquis of Torre Casa and marry designer Carolina. This embittered chauvinist Onassis—who most likely deemed his infidelity more pardonable than his wife's. He spent a drunken night badmouthing the treacherous Tina to friend Basil Mavroleon. By 1958 the spouses' lives were so detached that there was nothing left but legal action to cement their obvious estrangement.[56]

With this in mind Onassis now began to pay Maria frequent visits. Back in circulation and determined to attain control of all her assets, she became extremely busy.

On 1 September—just three days after notifying her American lawyer of her desire to attain a divorce in the States—she met with Sander Gorlinsky, now her sole manager. They discussed potential future appearances.[57] The following day she appeared at La Scala for the first rehearsal of her second studio recording of Ponchielli's La Gioconda.

With the Christina docked in Venice, Onassis paid Maria a visit at her Milanese home the next day. Reporters camped outside the building— spying on the pair as they sat in the garden and listened to records. To escape the craze Maria and Onassis fled to a nightclub called Rendez-vous in Monte Merlo, staying the night in separate rooms at the Hotel Principe e Savoia. On 4 September they met together with Maria's lawyer Caldi Scalcini before Onassis had to leave Italy and Maria attended the final rehearsal of La Gioconda.[58]

Enough grounds to imagine an affair? Of course. But all of this was happening to Maria: a near-asexual woman reeling after the discovery that Meneghini was a monster; already under the impression that her mother and her sister were both monsters and that life had thrown her far too many lemons. "If you can't trust your husband or your mother, to whom do you turn?" she would ask a friend many years later.[59] In the company of her new chum Onassis, carnal notions didn't enter her imagination. "I have been brought up on Greek moral principles of the 1920s and 1930s and sexual freedom, or the lack of it, had never been one of my problems," she would explain. "Besides, I have always been an old-fashioned romantic."[60]

Where reporters saw an opportunity to elaborate on a Callas-Onassis affair Maria was flummoxed and caught unaware.

*

5 September saw the start of the *Gioconda* recording and an unexpected new pledge of allegiance. During her session at La Scala Antonio Ghiringhelli came by with his secretary Luigi Oldani and Maria's friend Francisco Siciliani.[61] That night she went out for a midnight dinner with the trio to discuss future engagements. By pinpointing Meneghini as the principal cause for Maria's divide with La Scala, they finally came to a truce.[62]

La Gioconda is a peculiar four-act opera. Although Maria insulted Ponchielli by declaring that his work "just about touches the bel canto line," the piece drifts from *verismo* lyricism into Verdi-like, brisk agitation. "Gioconda" means "the joyous one". This juvenile heroine is a street singer in eighteenth-century Venice living with her blind mother, "La Cieca" ("The blind one"). Enzo Grimaldo—the subject of Gioconda's affections—is in love with young Laura: the wife of Alvise, Leader of the Inquisition. Alvise's sidekick Barnaba frames Laura for adultery with Enzo. This infuriates Gioconda, who discovers her enamorment is unrequited.

Amidst her festering contempt Gioconda learns that Laura saved the life of her blind mother after Barnaba alleged she was a sorceress. Fearing Alvise will murder his wife, Gioconda extends a sleeping potion to Laura so she can play possum. When Enzo is caught alive Alvise hastens to have him arrested. Gioconda—in true operatic fashion—offers herself instead, vowing to die in the aria "Suicidio".

In contrast to Maria's earlier 1952 recording, this 1959 *Gioconda* is a multi-layered psychological investigation.

When Alvise accuses her mother of witchcraft Gioconda begs with the voice of a boor: "Pietà . . . ch'io parli attendete . . . ora infrango il gel che m'impietrava" ("Have mercy . . . Wait for me to speak . . . Now I can break the ice that chilled me"). The voice reflects the situation rather than the character: Gioconda is a menace when she ought to be disarmed in desperation. Why isn't there a prominent diminuendo? Where is her vulnerability? Or is she simply young and stupid?

Perhaps she is. For when she declares: "Mi chiaman . . . La Gioconda, Viviam cantando ed io canto a chi vuol le mie liete canzoni" ("They call me 'The Joyous One'; we make our living by singing to everyone who wants to hear happy melodies"), her voice is docile and high-pitched; endearing and despoiled of fear. Toward Laura she feels only deference: a steady diminuendo on "salvatrice" ("savior") implies this when she asks for her name to pronounce it in prayer.

Gioconda's love for Enzo is a symbol of her adolescent dreaminess. In the declaration "Enzo adorato! Ah, come t'amo!" ("Beloved Enzo! Ah, how I love you!"), the "t'a" of "t'amo" is a high B flat sent flying down in delicate diminuendo; swooping like a bluebird to a branch amidst the maiden's flighty wanderings.

All this changes when Gioconda understands that Enzo loves another. Anchored in the chest register, the voice loses its sheen and emerges unfinished. Her experience on the streets is palpable in an unpolished instrument so scabrous.

This is the moment she turns on her axis. Gioconda's epiphany that her destiny is either love or death is no mad scene. As she addresses God in church with sedulous solemnity the corrugations of her voice surrender to composure in her prayer; her vocal cave begins to stream a gushing molten gold.

To the accompaniment of the organ the pious Gioconda speaks of the "fatal gift" of her love ("Cuore! Dono funesto!") with repressed sentiments of injustice. "Retaggio di dolore" ("a heritage of pain") is her almost ironic remark. From "mor" to "te" the voice endures a mountainous descent as the young woman confronts death ("O mor . . . te"); a pattern repeated across different notes to conflict with its foe, "O amor". Love versus death. Serenity foresees Gioconda's resignation to the latter. Pain has provoked a change of character; catharsis lets her know the world is greater than her qualms.

Her resolve to suffer suicide in the last act is rigidly sustained by an emboldened chest voice—a gnarly monster targeting her *self*: "In questi fieri momenti, tu sol mi resti" ("In these awful moments, you alone are left to me"), professes La Gioconda. Tremulous vibrato creeps into her terrified avowal: "Tu sol mi tenti" ("You are all that tempts me").

Like Norma who will haul herself along the pyre, Gioconda is desperate to die. It is "Ultima croce del mio cammin:" the last stop of her path. Embodying Gioconda's desperation, Maria's crescendo cuts into "cro" like a knife hacking into a wall. Having surmounted the fever of jealousy she falls into darkness, exhausted ("Or piombo esausta fra le tenebre . . . fra le tenebre"). "Tenebre" ("darkness") shudders like an echo in an empty marble hall.

Preparing to perish, Gioconda collects her composure. She begs the heavens to sleep quietly inside her grave ("Di dormir queta dentro l'avel") in a fashion that is slow and almost purposely delayed. Her gradual and cautious acquaintance with death is made palpable by Maria withholding "within the grave" ("den . . . tro . . . l'a . . . a . . . vel"); unraveling the syllables slowly to cement her lugubrious sacrifice.

"It's all there for anyone who cares to understand or wishes to know what I was about," Maria told music critic John Ardoin, referring to the recording's last two acts. It was one of few performances that pleased her.[63]

By 8 September too many gallons of ink had been wasted on rumors about Maria and Onassis' growing relationship. To set the record straight she let a statement loose: "I confirm that my separation from my husband is complete and final. It has been in the air for some time and the fact that it has actually happened during the cruise on the *Christina* is purely coincidental. The lawyers are now working on the case and will make an announcement in due course . . . I am now my own manager. I ask for understanding in this painful personal situation. Only a genuine friendship exists between myself and Mr Onassis."[64]

Newspapers reported the statement with different quotations. One referred to a potential business partnership between Maria and Onassis borne out of her interest in the Monte Carlo Opera House; as the principal shareholder of Monaco's Société des Bains de Mer, he controlled it.[65]

Allegedly a journalist had conducted a conversation with Maria by telephone during a break from recording *Gioconda*: "The idea crystallised in his yacht Christina while we were cruising. Now we are getting down to details. Aristotle suggests that I should have my own opera company. No theatre in Italy would be available for that. At least, not the sort of theatre that would be suitable. So we are planning something for Monte Carlo. No, I cannot say what it is. You know what people are. It must remain a secret for a while, but not for long . . . He is just a very, very good friend. Don't ever describe him as anything else for me."[66]

In the meantime Meneghini applied zealous efforts to evoke the "tigress" image of his wife he had spent years discrediting. "Maria has lost her head," he told one paper.[67] To others he proclaimed, "I bear no bitterness towards Maria, who has been honest and truthful, but I cannot forgive Onassis. The laws of hospitality were sacred for ancient Greeks . . . It was I who made Callas what she is, and she showed her appreciation by stabbing me in the back. She was fat and drably dressed, more like a penniless gypsy refugee without career prospects, when she came into my life."[68]

This drove the dagger further into his estranged wife's wounds. Maria had anticipated that her husband would bear rancor. Launching a smear campaign against her was another matter. In the years to come she would express to friends the unexpectedly abhorrent shock that she experienced as a result of Meneghini's "mania" for publicity.[69]

In the middle of September Onassis and his endless resources became her easiest refuge from the persecuting press. On her own she would be chased and hounded; everybody in Milan knew where she lived. Onassis had a crew of dozens. Unstalkable on the *Christina*, she made the yacht her sanctuary in these paparazzi-ridden days. Following the recording she sailed with Onassis to Athens[70] to meet with Alexis Minotis and discuss their now imminent Paris *Medea*.[71] Plagued by reservations when it came to their rehearsal time and various specifics, she phoned Lawrence Kelly—who wrote to Minotis the following day: "Maria will not accept the Paris engagement unless both yours and Rescigno's rehearsal wishes are satisfied."[72]

It was with Onassis' airline Olympic Airways that Maria journeyed to Spain without him for a concert in Bilbao. Accompanying her was one of his secretaries, Jenny Rocca-Serra. To stave off harassment Onassis instructed the airport officials to keep her arrival a secret.[73]

By the time Maria entered her hotel at 8:15 am on 17 September two police agents had been posted at the building in case of disturbance.[74] Fearing the hazardous breezes, she was wearing a headscarf.[75] With the omission of the "Meneghini" name her billing would be just "Maria Callas".[76]

Her live performance for the first time in three months was not auspicious. Prior to the evening she had cited the impending concert as a "test" to the enquiring reporters due to what she called a "sentimental crisis".[77] Spanish critics weren't accommodating. "Frankly her recital was unfortunate," one scribed. "She stumbled lamentably in various moments in the mad scene from *Hamlet*, especially in the final coda, which she cut off so abruptly that you could feel throughout the auditorium an air of discontent."[78]

A few months later she would cite the aria's "stratospheric heights" as the main reason for this concert being the "most difficult stage" of the tour. It was a factor that colluded with Maria's struggle to create a "voice-room liaison." "It is a hard thing to explain," she alerted a journalist. "When we singers find ourselves in a new environment we need to adapt the sound to the particular acoustic of that particular room. A mutual agreement must be established. This explains why any given singer is more successful in one environment than in another. It is an aspect of elective phonology that has yet to be studied."[79]

Eschewing the press, Maria boarded an Athens-bound flight to rejoin the *Christina*. When she arrived in Greece police had to surround her car to guard it from reporters.[80] She met with Kostas Bastias, an old acquaintance from her days at the Athens Conservatory and former General Manager of Greece's Royal Theatre. He was considering operas for the upcoming festival at Epidaurus, an ancient arena five hours from Athens.[81] They deliberated about staging *Norma* and *Medea*.[82]

Sailing on the *Christina* to Messinia—where she would fly to London for her concert at the Royal Festival Hall[83]—Maria cabled Gorlinsky aboard:

ARRIVING BEA FLIGHT 131 18.30 PLEASE CALL DOCTOR GRIFFITHS THROAT SPECIALIST FOR APPOINTMENT FROM 2000 to 2100 HOURS TOMORROW EVENING REGARDS = MARIA[84]

"I wanted to stay on holiday," began her public admission. "My husband and I quarreled over these engagements. But I shall keep them." Laryngologist James Ivor Griffiths, whom Maria had consulted several times throughout her Royal Opera engagements, declared her "one hundred per cent fit."[85]

This didn't stifle her fear. Afraid the air conditioner would plague her with a cold, Maria wouldn't linger in a hotel hall where fifty guests were coming to salute her after a rehearsal. Standing in that area was a safety hazard. As they ascended in one elevator she descended in another.[86]

Although only select arias from the 23 September concert were preserved on recording, its examples are likely superior to Maria's Bilbao fiasco. Singing Lady Macbeth's obsessive "bloodstain" aria ("Una macchia, è qui tuttora") her voice is both dark and premeditative. Although the top notes are occasionally shaky they embody the dominion of the villainess.

At the piece's end Maria cut the orchestra in half by walking through its middle to display her character mid-trance.[87]

Brief silent video footage from the concert shows us an effulgent singer: hair in a chignon and attired in a shiny, pale green gown with an expanding a-skirt and thick straps. Delectably ashine with a seductive smile, she kisses two joint fingertips and floats them elegantly to her fawning audience. In 1997 this short clip was used in an advertisement for Apple's "Think Different" commercial campaign, featuring in a montage of geniuses that included Albert Einstein and Pablo Picasso.

A woman handed her a couple of carnations; Maria turned and gave one to Hugh Maguire, the leader of the London Symphony Orchestra.[88] She yelled "I love you" to the audience before declaring with a laugh: "I don't know if such a reception is good for one or not. But for me . . . tonight . . . it is good."[89]

Reviews were mixed. Though some enthused as warmly as her spectators, occasional critics channeled disillusionment: "There were moments of beauty, yes, even magic," Clive Barnes of the *Daily Express* wrote. "But the gaps between them were too widely spaced for comfort. Sadly this was not the voice that first floored me in Rome six years ago."[90]

For the first time in a while a new production was announced: Maria would open *Macbeth* at the Royal Opera House in spring 1960.[91] Gorlinsky simultaneously proposed a series of concerts that could make her two hundred and fifty thousand pounds over the course of a year (over five million dollars today). "Her personal and private affairs are weighing heavily on her," he told the press. "We talked about all sorts of things in the last two days . . . She said she would like to think about it, and there was plenty of time for that."[92]

The next concert—a recording made for television scheduled to take place in London on September 29th—had to be deferred when maestro Nicola Rescigno's hands mysteriously grew swollen.[93] Still insecure about her voice, Maria wouldn't work with a replacement:

APPEARANCE ON TELEVISION AFTER TOMORROW IMPOSSIBLE DUE TO LACK OF TIME FOR REHEARSING SERIOUSLY WITH SUBSTITUTE THEREFORE MAKE THE NECESSARY ARRANGEMENTS FOR THE POSTPONEMENT AND SUGGEST DATE TO BE AGREED UPON[94] she immediately cabled Gorlinsky. On the same day she fell ill with fever—an event the press would speculate was the result of her discovery that Meneghini planned to cite a reprehensible "third party" in their legal separation hearing.[95]

Wrestling with her multiple responsibilities, Maria spent a great deal of her time soliloquizing on the phone to Lawrence Kelly. He in turn began relaying some of their discussions to Rual Askew of *The Dallas Morning News*: "Kelly talked by phone with Maria Callas in Milan Thursday and everybody—ticket buyers as well as Dallas Civic Opera supporters—can relax ... The soprano made it clear in her opening remarks, implying a healthy weariness with incessant headlines and distorted stories sensationalizing her domestic affairs, that she had had more than enough and would not discuss the matter of her estranged husband's recent legal action set for an Oct. 24 court hearing in Brescia ..."[96] But she was still coming to perform in *Medea*, *Lucia di Lammermoor* and *Il barbiere di Siviglia*. That was what mattered.

At home in Milan Maria radically changed her hairstyle, adopting the "bombe" look. While in London for the postponed concert on 3 October, she made sure to send a bouquet to Joan Sutherland, who was singing Donna Anna in a concert performance of *Don Giovanni* at Royal Festival Hall. The latter telephoned her and arranged to meet. Maria then had to call back and cancel their planned tea: all her bank assets had been frozen and she needed urgently to fly back to Milan and hide her jewels. Meneghini likely wanted to abscond with them before the hearing. Only after it would she recover access to her funds.[97]

On 18 October Maria travelled to Paris to discuss her and Minotis' *Medea* with the artistic director of the Opéra de Paris, A.-M. Julien.[98] Foreseeing frenzy, she requested that the pilot in command convey a message to the airport that instructed press to disappear before her landing. He refused to heed to her instruction.[99]

After a concert in Berlin on the 23rd Maria flew to Milan for the first of her separation court hearings.[100] Two days later she was at Idlewild Airport in New York en route to Kansas City for another concert at Loew's Midland Theatre.[101] Somebody telephoned the venue to inform its staff a bomb would go off any minute. Police rummaged through the premises. "I will sing my first aria," was Maria's reaction. As the press wrote at the time, "She said she wanted to resume the concert so that the audience would not think that she had quit the show in a display of temperament."

Maria sang "Non mi dir" from *Don Giovanni* before making space on the stage for Governor James Blair of Missouri, who announced without disclosing the reason that the theatre would have to be emptied indefinitely.[102]

As Giovanna Lomazzi awaited the concert's resumption thieves broke into her and Maria's hotel room and stole all her jewels. Maria's gems were unavailable: back in Milan they had been locked inside a vault to stop her husband finding them.[103]

Half an hour later the concert continued. Among the patrons that night was former president Harry Truman, attending the concert in the company of Maria's friend, *Washington Post* critic Paul Hume. Bumping into the soprano on the street as she was heading to her car, Mr. President became ecstatic: "You know, she remembered me!" he exulted to Hume.[104]

Everyone expected Maria to fly from Kansas City to Dallas for her impending engagements. Instead she had no choice but to postpone her second separation hearing to make time for *those* engagements. Her flight took her to New York together with an old male friend. Their eyes perked-up again, the press was hungering to know: who *is* this man? It was David McElroy, a television producer and an old friend of Lawrence Kelly's partner, David Stickelber.[105]

As dozens if not hundreds of reporters crowded to receive Maria back at Dallas Love Field Airport, they watched unfamiliar faces disembark together with a plaid bag bearing Toy the poodle. Rual Askew—music critic for *The Dallas Morning News*—was mistaken for Maria's manager. Lomazzi was there, together with her maid Bruna and Toy. Herself in Paris, Maria was attempting to take measures to postpone the hearing.

That didn't work out.[106]

Meneghini's vengeful scheme involved convincing Brescia's court Maria was entirely to blame for their failed marriage; citing "grave injury" to him as its sole cause. She would not accept that.[107] It took days for him to finally surrender and agree to the statement of separation "by mutual agreement." Rumors circulated that Maria planned to get divorced in the U.S.[108]

Exhaustion led her finally to cancel the planned Dallas *Il barbiere di Siviglia*—to which she had consented only after the withdrawal of its initial star.[109] Following the mixed reception to her onstage incarnation of the role in 1956, her attitude was unequivocally ambivalent: "The necessary enthusiasm, the commitment, was not there," Maria later admitted.[110]

Entrapped by court hearings in Brescia, the soprano arrived punctually at the first rehearsal for Franco Zeffirelli's *Lucia di Lammermoor*—a staging that had grown popular with Joan Sutherland at the Royal Opera House—by landing in Dallas at five am. Charily cautious, Maria was loath to sing in full voice in rehearsal; preferring to mark.[111]

Artistic discrepancies flared yet again. The blood-stained gown was excessive; Maria sought something purer.[112] Then her costumes failed to arrive altogether. Zeffirelli and Giovanna Lomazzi labored to transfer the pearls from costumes of the chorus to a plain dress to fabricate a wedding gown.[113]

Lack of rehearsal hours meant there was no time to stage the fountain scene. Addressing Ruth Kobert who was singing the role of Alisa, Maria alerted the soprano on opening night: "I will direct you with my eyes."[114]

The audience was in rapture: a "long, standing ovation" followed.[115]

Maria was not so entranced. For the first time in five years she had opted to finish her mad scene with a high E flat [E flat 6]. After this note Lucia dies offstage. It cracked. "I had the note. I had the note. I don't know what happened," she was allegedly heard telling a couple of chorus members.[116]

Back in her dressing room she summoned the *maestro sostituto*, Assistant Conductor Vasco Naldini, together with Nicola Rescigno and Zeffirelli to hear her. "I have the note . . . I know what happened tonight. All this damn press on to me. They make me so nervous . . . I've got the note." Maria played it on her dressing room piano. She tried a few other notes, embarked on the same aria and once again missed the E flat. After several more attempts she gave up.[117]

That night at the Sheraton Dallas Lomazzi lay awake in their hotel suite as Maria spent the whole night stifling tears in bed.[118]

Five days after her second *Lucia* Maria once again had to voyage to Italy. Stopping by New York, she used an airport telephone to place an urgent call to Rudolf Bing. "The return of a prodigal daughter is as welcome as the return of a prodigal son," was the way the press phrased it.[119] Having concluded that their conflict had been largely the result of Meneghini's maladroitness, she proclaimed: "That was misguided, and Rudolf Bing now accepts that it should never have happened, and we're perfectly good friends again."[120] To the crowd of reporters enquiring about a potential imbroglio, she answered: "No more fights—I'm sorry for you, gentlemen."[121] She clarified that she would sing "not this season but perhaps next year" at the Met.[122]

The armistice was genuine. Bing had nothing but kind words to offer following her death. "She was a professional to her fingertips—and they were beautiful fingertips."[123]

Since productions were planned eighteen months ahead, Bing expressed to Maria that he would be unable to secure anything "interesting" in the near future. "Now please don't shoot at me but I think I could, shortly before Christmas with one rehearsal, revive *Traviata* . . ." was his incendiary proposition.

To that she wouldn't heed—insisting that she wanted something *new* that would "make news".[124]

*

On 14 November Lomazzi accompanied Maria to her final court hearing before Justice Cesare Andreotti, President of the Brescia Tribunal. At the six-hour session it was decided that Meneghini would keep the villa in Sirmione, Maria the Milanese townhouse. Her income would be split between them but Maria would receive all future royalties and keep her jewelry. Poodles Tea and Toy would live with her. Presumably, however, she allowed her husband to keep Tea; Toy was the only dog who featured in her travels later on.[125]

Although the court affirmed Maria's earnings would be split in half, determining which spouse had earned what sum was harder than expected. Meneghini's thirst to register so many of their funds in just his name meant many of Maria's fees would be regarded as *his* revenue. As a result she would refer in later correspondence to her husband having taken "two thirds" or "three quarters" of her fortune; Meneghini had declared dishonestly that a great portion of their income were the profits of his former business.[126] Despite being bitter about this, Maria was relieved the separation was over. "I was ready to leave him everything," she confessed to Lomazzi.[127]

Her respite was unduly premature.

So exhausted was Maria that the Dallas press began to doubt she would return for her last opera scheduled that year: a revival of Alexis Minotis' *Medea*. Four days after the hearing she arrived. Kelly introduced her to a "member of the company": a woman who was actually her understudy. The subtext was apparent and as soon as she was gone Maria pointedly advised, "Tell her she won't be needed."[128]

The following day on 19 November she opened the *Medea* revival. In contrast to her earlier negative critiques *The Dallas Morning News*' review was almost an extolment: "In exceptionally good voice . . . Madame Callas sang . . . with some tonal velvet and positively mezzo-soprano richness and variety in middle and lower register . . . We left 'Medea' more with the sense of having experience [*sic*] a Greek tragedy than of hearing an opera composed in the last years of the eighteenth century . . . It was a Callas vehicle full of Callas opportunities. She made the most of them and we can thank her for one of the most electrifying last acts that may be encountered within a lifetime on operatic or dramatic stage."[129]

The result was another standing ovation.

Overwhelmed, Maria cancelled the upcoming Paris *Medea*s.[130] Four months later she wrote to Secretary General of the Opéra de Paris, Robert Favre Le Bret, to request a postponement to January 1961. No one replied.[131]

Days later something stirred the buzzing paparazzi yet again: Tina Onassis had filed for divorce against Aristotle Onassis, citing another woman in the break-up of their relationship, her old pal Jeanne Rhinelander.[132]

Lacking juicy fodder, the Italian press jumped on another bandwagon: Maria was pregnant, weekly magazine *Annabella* alleged on 30 November. A frequent reader of the magazine, she seethed upon discovering the rumor. "The interference with my privacy has now reached an unprecedented point," Maria told United Press International. "The report of my pregnancy is completely groundless. The purpose which those who spread it want to attain is just a full-fledged defamation. I am now considering a legal action against the persons responsible for the publication of this false report."[133]

That day Maria anxiously wrote to her American lawyer Walter Cummings. Would it not be possible to get a divorce in America fairly quickly? The law insisted she would have to stay there for six weeks. "What would I do there? I'd die of boredom!" she bemoaned in her letter. "I don't have any other news except that for the first half of next year I will probably rest. I owe it to myself and to my voice. For the moment, I'm tired, I've really lost my instinct for my art with all the blows that my husband has dealt me and my work. I want to love my art by wanting it."[134]

That did not suspend negotiations. A prolonged telephone conversation with Gorlinsky transpired the next day. Would she be willing to give a concert for American television on 31 December, January 28 or February 3rd? How about an evening with Sir Malcolm Sargent at the Royal Festival Hall in May? And a Scandinavian tour: Maria had never performed in that part of the world.[135]

She would think about it. She would think about everything despite writing to several music critics to alert them she was taking "a nice long rest" and planning to "avoid any thinking and work until next season."[136]

"I don't know what I'm going to do yet," she elaborated to Emily Coleman of *Newsweek*. "I may stay in Milano or go to St Moritz. I [am] resting trying to get over the blow of having a <u>dear</u> like my husband ... Well, you can't say I tried to do my best to resist a break-up. But when I found out that he had all in his name and God or he only knows what he did with so much money that he couldn't justify where it was or what he had done with [it]."[137]

Her attempts at self-justification were endless. In the ski resort of Saint Moritz was located Onassis' villa on 12 Via Clavadatsch.[138] As Gorlinsky publicly announced Maria would "not appear in any opera house until after May ... I think she feels that she is not up to the strain of the rehearsals necessary for any full-length operatic engagement," and cancelled her Royal Opera *Macbeth* planned for that March, Maria spent the second half of December in Saint Moritz with Onassis. She didn't return to Milan until 2 January.[139]

After a hectic time juggling engagements and lawyers, Maria embarked on a period of rest in which she and Onassis grew closer.

The man had many amiable qualities. He adored his nine-year-old daughter Christina to whom he refused nothing,[140] and was generally affectionate to young people and children.[141] Ostensibly supportive, he was generous to all his staff. When Captain of the *Christina* George Zacharias went on a two-year military leave, his boss sent sixty drachmas to his family a week.[142] The yacht's head chef was taken to Parisian specialists to solve his stomach problems while another cook was sent to a Miami dermatologist to treat a skin condition.[143]

Well-versed in the art of making an impression, Onassis spoke seven languages including Italian.[144] The *Christina*'s shelves were lined with novels by Émile Zola and Balzac, as well as *The Diary of Samuel Pepys*, classical works by Euripides, Herodotus and Plato, and many tomes on ships, the arts and Greece.[145]

His most attractive quality was a rebellious nature not at odds with the conventions of good manners. "Our system of life outlaws individualism today," he told a reporter in 1957. "Everything is done through public corporations, associations, groups of people. If an individual is mediocre today, he can get away with it. If he's outstandingly successful, he becomes suspect. Outstanding individualism aggravates and disturbs the rest of society. A pity, perhaps, but it is so."[146]

Christina caterer George Koutis recollected that the host skipped some of his own parties—which were mostly held for business purposes. Describing him as someone who dressed casually, Koutis averred: "He was never known for being showy. He was a very plain man."[147]

Striving to seem humble, Onassis once greeted Maria's hairdresser on the *Christina* by offering him two hundred-year-old rum. The stylist had thought him a waiter.

He relished trivial entertainment such as slot machines and his "most prized possession": a jade Buddha from the Ming dynasty that stood on a white marble pedestal in a glass dome. If you pressed a button Buddha would respond by sticking out his tongue. Onassis found this funny.[148]

Delectably endearing were these traits for vulnerable Maria. At the beginning of their closeness he displayed his softest side. She didn't find him sexually appealing but in her words: "adorable, straight and fearless, and his boyish mischievousness made him irresistible and only occasionally difficult and uncompromising. Unlike some of his friends, he could be generous (and I do not mean only materialistically) to a fault and never petty. Obstinate he was, and quite argumentative like most Greeks, but even then he would eventually come round and see the other person's point of view."[149]

For him rejection and antagonism were the greatest turn-ons. Refused use of a Monaco building for office space, Onassis had slowly acquired the Casino de Monte Carlo by secretly purchasing stock in the Société des Bains de Mer and then selling it at a huge profit.[150] Maria was a globally respected, prudish, principled soprano. To obtain her was a challenge. And Onassis thrived on challenges.

Ingratiating himself with Maria's nearest and dearest, such an impression did he make on Elvira de Hidalgo when they eventually met that she wrote to Maria, "Aristo is always so nice. I think of him with so much affection. Kiss him for me."[151] If one of Maria's guests aboard the *Christina* sought to be flown to any city in the world, he would arrange it. At dinnertime he would distribute gifts.[152] Assuming the role of Protector Against Paparazzi, Onassis would chasten reporters—commanding a handful of Las Palmas newshounds who followed them during a cruise: "You can follow me all you want—but *la señora*, no."[153]

Despite having separated with rancor from Tina, Onassis for the large part bore no grudges against women. Having always been close to his sisters and stepsisters, he was the first to pay Tina a visit in June 1960 when she suffered a horseriding accident.[154] Nine months later when she broke her leg in Saint Moritz he also came.[155]

Self-reportedly his first sexual encounter had transpired at fifteen—when the precocious adolescent had apparently seduced his twenty-five-year-old French teacher.[156] He also liked to boast of having courted Anna Pavlova[157] and made sure to report this to a visiting Margot Fonteyn. The latter found him "very intelligent and civilized".[158]

For her part, Maria deemed him a good man—as well as "*charming*, very *sincere . . . spontaneous.*" Her emotions for him gradually evolved into what she called "something even stronger than love: friendship, which is inalterable."[159] If she had any doubts about him it was rooted in his work's integrity.[160] Nevertheless she once described him as "a solid businessman who, when he gives his word, will keep it even at the cost of a great fortune."[161]

Only after Tina announced her divorce from the man did Maria and Onassis' friendship intensify. The relationship would likely not have turned romantic till the early months of 1960.

He was far from perfect—and Maria would eventually discern his vices, which included sometimes sounding brusque or using literal, broken English in an uncouth manner. Defying people's predilection for formality, his parlance was at times alarming in its forwardness.[162]

Yet flaws like these seemed meaningless for now.

Returned to Milan in January 1960, Maria was a gratefully refreshed soprano finally at ease. "She had lost that stern and closed-off aura of a wicked man," Giovanna Lomazzi remembered. "In the months that followed, Maria became calmer, more serene, far less nervous . . . 'I still can't believe all this happened,' she would tell me. Other times she strived to explain how little her husband had understood her: 'Do you remember the concerts in Germany? Battista couldn't understand that he was already losing me then, with his absurd insistence to make me sing at all costs. Even if I was ill—even if I was exhausted.' "[163]

Gorlinsky gave more statements to the press on 20 January: "I have never seen her so contented and radiant. All her personal problems have been resolved and she is quite reconciled to the separation from her husband."[164] Galatopoulos gleaned that her "rather limited sense of humour developed . . . She was more fun and even a little outspoken about herself, but not about Onassis."[165]

Maria openly avowed: "When I return, it shall be to La Scala. That's my post."[166]

Being her own manager was complimentary to the soprano's independent nature.

About this break from singing she was frank. "It often happens that the first essential to one's best work becomes the hardest thing to achieve— freedom of mind . . . It's a capricious voice. So my psychological situation must be perfect, otherwise I don't find certain passages easy to execute," she would tell journalist Derek Prouse a year later.[167]

Her time off wasn't limited to cruising on the yacht; she and Onassis weren't a unit indivisible. He had several businesses to run—a great deal of the shipping industry, Olympic Airways and a host of other enterprises— and she was now responsible for running her career. During the first weeks of 1960 she hopped back and forth between Milan and Paris while Onassis entertained the doted-upon Winston Churchill at his Monte Carlo home.[168]

That February 3rd she took the opportunity to watch French ballerina Yvette Chauviré in a ballet of *La Dame aux Camélias*, the novel that had inspired *La traviata*.[169]

Her outing at the Opéra de Paris produced an "interview" with French reporter Marlyse Schaeffer published in *France-Soir*. Evoking an entirely fabricated dialogue, it quoted a soprano who now hoped to give up singing and desired "nothing more than to get married and live with her husband and dog."[170]

Taking Schaeffer's word as gospel, the insatiable press provoked Maria's feral fury—prompting her to rapidly refute the made-up comments to Italian magazine *Settimo Giorno* and Greek newspaper *Eleftheria*. Once more she was waging war against the fictional Maria they preferred.[171]

There came a long-awaited announcement: Maria would return to La Scala in Donizetti's rare opera *Poliuto* in early December. To accompany this she commanded Italian news agency ANSA to distribute her statement: "I will sing next November at the Opera in Paris and at La Scala in December, for the traditional opening of the Sant'Ambrogio festival . . . I hope this shall serve to refute, once and for all, the statement that certain newspapers attribute to me, saying that I would never again have the intention to sing."[172]

In fact she had great plans in store—intending now to train "with greater energy than before," as she told one reporter. "And I count on the collaboration of Maestro Tonini at La Scala. A guy I like because he is relentless: an unforgiving torturer. A kind of Dominican Order of music." Musical musing was meticulously being undertaken. "I have been thinking about Isolde and Brünnhilde for a long time and, to be able to sing them in their original language, I continue to study German . . ." Maria told the same journalist. "Other projects? Almost certainly Bellini's *Beatrice di Tenda* and Donizetti's *Lucrezia Borgia* or *Maria de Rohan* . . . and also *Gli Ugonotti* by Meyerbeer."[173]

Still considering the Met, she wrote to let Bing know she would consider *Tosca* for next season if Corelli could be present next to a "good baritone".

"Surely you know that our planning is always much further ahead than just a few weeks," arrived Bing's terse response.[174]

On 22 February she replied to a letter from Gorlinsky. "I received your telegram, and must say that the offer you made me to sing for the Television in London two or three arias for ten thousand pounds interests me. If you could postpone it to the beginning of May or even to the middle of May, it would be better, as in April I intend to leave for the Easter Holidays on a nice trip."[175]

Lawrence Kelly wrote to Alexis Minotis on 4 March that Maria would be interested in singing the trouser role of Gluck's *Orfeo ed Euridice* with Elisabeth Schwarzkopf as Euridice. "We are prepared to go on receiving an okay from Maria. This will never come by cable or telephone. She requires a personal visit and a great deal of discussion about details. I believe that she will accept this work but I cannot know definitely until I arrive in Italy at the end of this month."[176] She went back and forth on the subject. Eventually the destiny of Callas in a male role remained unfulfilled.

That 12 March she wrote to her friend, music critic Herbert Weinstock:

> One day rather soon I will decide to write my book—biography. But I need someone to make some research—in Greece of pictures—declarations (true) and information that my memory can fail. You know how I'm precise in everything. At least I try my best to be . . .
>
> Well, my friend, the hope is that I manage to handle my future as I wish. Of course I need the so called rest—but I call [it] licking of wounds. Wounds that were caused by my husband and not by <u>any</u> third party as so said in these rattish newspapers, where they invent just anything they wish.
>
> Of course you must confess that I didn't have a very happy face before, can you [sic]. Even certain articles had referred to that saying why—what was the matter with me.
>
> So Herbert—pray for me—and write, they will forward the letters to me and I will probably return around the first ten days of April.
>
> Love, Maria
>
> (P.S. I'm leaving again for the mountains).[177]

Her resort was Saint Moritz, where Maria would be reunited with Onassis. He had spent the greater part of March with Winston Churchill on the yacht.[178]

Alternating between warding off and pondering engagements, on 21 March she wrote personally to Australian composer Peggy Glanville-Hicks to turn down the role of Nausicaa in her work *Sappho*, an opera about the renowned poetess: "I'm afraid I cannot accept your offer, for I probably am going to Greece to sing Norma at the Epidaurus Theater."[179]

She was back by 11 April.[180] The Epidaurus *Norma* was announced only on May 21st. Alongside it came the news that Maria was going to donate all her fees from the performance to Greece's National Opera "in reciprocity" for what they had done for her early career.[181] Alerting Lomazzi of the upcoming engagement, "She was radiant."[182]

Still fighting with the problem of a possible divorce, Maria was determined, but: "I can't simply spend six weeks in Nevada, so don't try to persuade me," she wrote to her American lawyer.[183]

On 12 June she was announced to open Dallas Civic Opera's 1960–1961 season with *Il pirata* on 4 November.[184] Back in Milan Maria studied *Poliuto*; striving simultaneously to relax as much as Callas-ly possible. In attendance at an Issac Stern recital with Lomazzi on June 27th, she proclaimed to the enquiring press: "In the future I will devote myself solely to art."[185]

Maria counted Stern among her comrades. Despite not being erudite in the domains of chamber or symphonic music, she possessed recordings of works by Sibelius, Chopin and Saint-Saëns.[186] Inasmuch as she was snobby when it came to her internal hierarchy of sopranos, tenors and conductors, she expressed the same elitism toward orchestras and instrumentalists. Listening to a performance of Beethoven's Eighth Symphony conducted by George Szell in 1968, Maria mourned: "Well, see what we have been reduced to. We are now in a time when a Szell is considered a master. How small he was next to Furtwängler."[187]

In the concert hall she adored Jascha Heifetz,[188] disliked Artur Schnabel and defended Vladimir Horowitz when a radio host criticized his performance.[189]

After socializing a little with Margot Fonteyn on the *Christina*,[190] Maria was in Milan by 10 July discussing potential costumes for that August's *Norma* with Alexis Minotis and Greek costumier Antonis Phocas.[191]

Three days later she arrived in London to cement another compilation album. What ensued was not as much a fully-fledged recording as a miserable attempt. Performing "Bel raggio lusinghier" from Rossini's *Semiramide*, the soprano barely scraped the top notes. "Arrigo! Ah, parli a un core" from Verdi's *I vespri siciliani* exemplified her at her worst: inviting blunt crescendo to disguise her vocal faults. Maria's reaction was to put the recording aside and delay its release.

Permission was never *given* for its release.[192]

On 20 July she landed in Ostend: a Belgian town where she was due to give a concert. Accommodated with Lomazzi at "a squalid hotel that had once been a train station . . . Every day it rained," in the words of the latter, Maria was forced to confess she was fighting the flu. And a sore throat. It would turn out to be a bacterial infection. Though she attended the concert's rehearsal, Maria had no choice but to cancel.[193]

"Newspapers write a lot of junk, as usual!" she wrote to Leo Lerman ten days later.

> I had this idiotic tracheitis that made me miss the concert in Ostende and it really was a pity. But as you see everything went well. No scandal—I no [sic] better how to take care of myself.
> Dear, I wish I had dropped this blackmailer of a husband before! When I see you I'll tell you all! It's a pity all that I wasted 12 years of my life for nothing but a smeared name & not even one third of my fortune gained! . . .
> You would of [sic] never believed it from that numb-face would you!
> Now I'm preparing to go to Greece for Norma at the Epidauros. I hope everything goes well! I wish it and desire it as you can never imagine![194]

By now Maria was resolved to have her husband sign American divorce papers. Meneghini, on the other hand, would not relent. Though the legal separation papers would declare Maria a free woman everywhere but Italy,[195] he was unmovable. In fact his solution was blackmail—as Maria advised her Italian lawyer:

Please could you send these documents yourself to Meneghini's lawyer who's being rude and threatening to get out his claws. You know that he's been swindling me, asking me to pay off half his debts—as in, from the court settlement—and then admitting he requested that you get a million dollars for him from Onassis. So tell him that I had a recorder on me at the time, and that if I come forward with that and with the truth about how he dispensed with my money and how he left everything for himself, etc!

And then, he still has all my things except for [Elsa] Maxwell's letters and my contracts. I don't have my [bootleg] recordings from Mexico, papers concerning my engagements, my reviews, etc.—all my activity in the course of twelve years he had nothing to do with.

I want him to give all that back to me. I'll give him his letters back and he should give me mine back . . .

According to our settlement he is supposed to divorce me, and he is swindling me for the umpteenth time. And he still has my things. He won't let me go to retrieve them because he's threatening to write as well about the made-up story about Onassis. He says he's written a word for word account of what we said to him and that he'll publish it! And then I know that he called United Press—Signor [Aldo] Trippini (a good person—really, believe me) offering to write articles, that London rejected him saying he's old news and nobody's interested!

Threaten him by saying we'll come forward with the truth if he doesn't act justly and put on a muzzle! Do it in the toughest way you think— don't take the high road. He's taking us for fools and thinks we're going to give in from necessity!

I don't know how you'll go about it but you need to shut him up and make him give me the things that belong to me.[196]

The "made-up" story cited is the one that slowly became "common knowledge": Meneghini's fable of her fervid fling with the irreverent billionaire under his nose; the falsehood that alleged she had betrayed him.

Taking paper from the Savoy Hotel, London and dating it 28 May 1959, Meneghini wrote a note in Maria's name declaring her undying love for him. By this time their relationship had likely become fraught. Situated in Milan that day, both Meneghini and Maria hadn't come to London till 10 June. The note would serve to "prove" Maria had adored him without respite till the fated voyage with the rogue had snatched her from his arms.[197]

That tale would grow into his book, *My Wife Maria Callas*. To lend his narrative more credence, Meneghini drafted an alleged diary he purported to have written during the *Christina* cruise: several sheets of paper head-lined with their old address, 40 Via Buonarroti. Numbering the pages, he crossed the original dates out and swapped them for others. For every day reporting on the so-called facts of August 1959 there was another seedy story.[198]

The "diary" had amounted to the kind of trashy soap opera too bad for television. But Meneghini wouldn't cede to his estranged wife's ultimatums. He kept her correspondence and her pirate recordings. He refused to sign the American divorce papers. By October of that year he was still threaten-ing to write a "novel" about the events of their marriage. "When we obtained our separation last November, we both promised the court in Brescia we would never write articles or books on our married life," Maria would tell ravenous reporters.[199] It was in vain: the damage had been done.

*

Arriving in Athens to begin rehearsals at the Ancient Theatre of Epidaurus on August 9th, Maria was housed in an apartment deliberately built for her near the arena.[200] According to *The New York Times*, the arena's acoustics were "generally acknowledged to be almost perfect."[201]

Onassis was nearby. Crunching peanuts, he looked on as his companion tested her corrupted voice onstage. "Every time she tried to execute a note in rehearsals she would abruptly withdraw from it—producing not more than a hint of the sound," Mirto Picchi, who was singing the role of Pollione, recalled. "She gave the impression of somebody wanting to dip in their toes just to test out the water. And the water was always too cold."[202]

Plagued with a literal cold, Maria turned to her young colleague, twenty-four-year-old mezzo-soprano Kiki Morfoniou, for help. "When you have a sore throat, what do you do?" she asked the fledgling. Morfoniou told her she drank chamomile tea in a thermos, extending the drink to her stagemate. Maria took sips.[203]

A miracle transpired on 21 August. *Norma* was cancelled for unforeseen circumstances. There was a storm that night; it routed the fourteen (or twenty, depending on the source) thousand spectators. Learning of the opening night's postponement, Maria lingered in her colleague Picchi's dressing room, resting her head along his shoulder; serene.

Three days later came the real opening night. The unsatisfied soprano wanted someone to announce that she would not continue. Maestro Tullio Serafin reminded her thousands of people had journeyed to hear her sing from all over Greece; she was *obliged*.[204] Giovanna Lomazzi was there among other friends—as was her father, George, who had come from America,[205] and Maria's never-seen maternal cousin, Ninon Dimitriadou.[206] Onassis sat beside Lomazzi with his teenage step-niece, Marilena Patronicolas.[207] He asked Lomazzi to point out Maria's entrances. Unfamiliar with her voice, Onassis couldn't recognize her underneath her wig.[208]

It's difficult to understand Maria's own evaluation of the night. She received a wreath of laurel from the Greek earth that was reverently placed before her feet,[209] as well as a bronze medal chiseled with her face as Norma. The latter she eventually gave to Onassis' step-niece, Marilena.[210] Reviews were once again mixed; pinpointing impoverished vocality and simultaneously describing how she had sung "Casta diva" with "eyes half-closed, static, ecstatic."[211]

After the performance Maria invited Lomazzi aboard the *Christina*. Tranquil in her stance, she barely mentioned the event—merely citing the civility of spectators compared to the shenanigans at the Arena di Verona. The yacht advanced toward Piraeus as Maria sat squeezed in between Onassis and Lomazzi, whispering the name of every island the boat passed.[212]

Stumbling upon Maria and Onassis—who were making a pilgrimage at the island of Tinos—the next day,[213] Stelios Galatopoulos espied her wearing her protective headscarf, "dressed simply in black and white" and in good spirits. "It is wonderful to be happy and know it right at the time you are," was her remark.[214]

Then a flu epidemic broke out. A feverish Maria performed the second *Norma*. By the 27th she was bedridden and advised by a doctor to cancel the final performance. On the 29th she moved back to Athens where she stayed with Onassis' brother-in-law, Dr. Theodore Garoufalidis. There she issued a statement to the Greek press regretting her indisposition and thanking them for their hearty reception.[215]

Six days later came another *Norma*—this time in the stuffy theatre of La Scala, where Maria was imprinting it in history the second time around. Displeased with her unheeding instrument, she struggled with select parts on the first day of recording. After assuring Walter Legge and EMI engineer Robert Gooch she had a plan to improve it, Maria returned the next morning with a new vocal veneer. Gooch asked Legge what had concealed its imperfections. Legge revealed Maria had consumed a tumbler full of castor oil; an old trick that allegedly assisted with the vocal tract.[216]

It was something the singer in no way come close to admitting. Vocalists did not need either teas or aliments to help the voice; *technique* was indisputably enough. "It's a matter of being *conscientious*," was her favorite thing to say. Asked by David Frost whether she did anything to "keep the voice—" she cut the journalist off. "*No . . .* It's the brain that molds the voice *too*."—"But it's the *brain* that *commands*," Frost averred. "You don't take honey—" "*No*," Maria adamantly stressed. "No, no, no, no."[217]

The 1954 *Norma* recording had unmasked a domineering but self-regulated heroine; frequently suppressed by that unfinished tone that relished obfuscating her expression. Every now and then in listening to it we hear prophetic presages of those prolonged diminuendi: superhuman ones developing as gradually as photos in a lab.

Especially expressive they are *not*.

With rhythms, tempi and dynamics that sound neither craftily creative nor adventurous, the outcome is a more or less banal result: the stereotype of Norma's devil versus Norma's angel.

Her performer knew something about the angel-devil dichotomy. "I am not an angel and do not pretend to be," she had declared to *Life* in 1959. "That is not one of my roles. But I am not a devil, either. I am a woman and a serious artist, and I would like to be so judged."[218]

Such a description bore something in common with *Norma*. A woman torn between contrasting states of mind, she is the neglected wife who wishes to wreak havoc on her cheating lover Pollione—also a Roman and enemy of the state; the disloyal druidess who failed her people when she fell in love with him, and the devoted friend who hopes to have the strength to pardon Adalgisa's crime of sleeping with her lover . . . and her foe. Only Bellini's music can do justice to the character's psychology.

In this September 1960 effort there emerges the regality of a red-blooded, fully-fledged, despotic ruler. The leader who addresses her people in the recitative "Sediziose voci . . . voci di guerra" ("Seditious voices— voices of war") is both potent and collapsible. Her voice's timbre is made thinner now: more flexible, more feminine. Demanding to discover of the populace how they can dare to raise "seditious voices" to her, ("dettar responsi alla veggente Norma"), her voice rises on a rushed and almost menacing crescendo: she desires most of all to tame her people into vener-ant submission.

This "Casta diva" is the first symbolic of the attitude Maria later cited: Norma's surreptitious means of stalling for more time. The priestess may be "praying" to the Moon goddess—"Chaste goddess, who bathes those ancient, hallowed trees in silver light, Turn Your radiant face to us . . . Disperse over our Earth the peace with which you rule the sky," ("Casta diva, che inargenti queste sacre antiche piante, a noi volgi il bel sembiante . . . Spargi in terra quella pace . . . che regnar tu fai nel ciel")—and yet her thoughts are those of an enamored woman. She is contemplative; her approach is wistful. When she sings of the Moon goddess' "bel sembiante" (her "radiant face"), the mellifluous diminuendo hints that Norma may be thinking of the mien of both her nemesis and lover, Pollione.

Pleading with the Moon goddess to temper the crowd's raging hearts, Norma reignites her ruler self: "Tempra, o Diva, tempra tu de' cori ardenti" is sung with deferent diminuendi scattered through the words. Her second plea, "Temper once again their audacious zeal" ("Tempra ancora lo zelo audace"), comes across subdued. What right does Norma have, after all, to be *asking* for something from the Moon goddess? She hasn't even managed to be faithful to her people. In her imploration there are vestiges of shame.

This may be the sole performance where the aria emerges as an intro-spective study. Outwardly it is a prayer almost hypnotic in its calm. And yet beneath the subtle chords beats the ferocity of inner conflict—as we hear in that repeated high B flat [B flat 5] over the "pa" of "pace" in its final incarnation. Norma must insist on something for *herself*: peace for her people's sake; peace for her soul.

As we now learn, she lacks the strength to punish Pollione. "Ma . . . punirlo . . . il cor . . . non *sa*." ("But . . . my heart . . . doesn't *know* . . . how to punish him"). Suddenly the primal warrior of a woman has regressed to wear the guise of an infatuated girl with the curvaceous, long roulade on "sa". It's a perfect prelude to a girlish cabaletta: "Ah! bello a me ritorna!" ("Ah! Come back to me, you handsome man!").

We lose faith in this Norma as a dependable woman. She is too quickly changing.

Adalgisa shares her suffering with Norma. Unaware the former's bout of lovesickness originates in the same man as hers, Norma assures her: "M'abbraccia e parla" ("Give me a hug and speak to me"). Its delivery is lined with deft diminuendo showcasing their similarity. As Adalgisa tells her story Norma slowly sees herself: "Io fui così rapita al sol mirarlo in volto!" ("I too was taken with him the first time I saw his face!"). The comparison is performed with a slow entrance into "sol mirarlo . . ." the memory of first seeing Pollione. Norma is nostalgic for those times of negligence when she renounced her people for this treacherous liaison. She insists to Adalgisa: "Vivrai felice ancor" ("You will live happy once again") with a chromatic descent of impassioned auspiciousness.

As she slowly realizes her best friend stole her love, Norma is inconsolable. Her commands to Pollione, "Vanne, sì, mi lascia, indegno," emerge in four brusque separate phrases: "Go—yes—leave me—you ingrate." Each contrasts with the next: "Vanne" ("go") is a straightforward command; "sì" is more emboldened; "mi lascia" ("leave me") presents a paradoxical diminuendo of distress and "indegno" ("ingrate") is a resolute epithet. Norma is not only vexed but must abandon this man; must force her wrathful self to hate him.

Her next determination: killing her children to avenge his affair. She will not let them be the "schiavi d'una matrigna"—the "slaves of a stepmother" like Adalgisa. The voice is made expressly strident with the cutting accent on the 'sch' of "schiavi": scathing with her devious denunciation.

"Muoiano, sì.": "They *must* die." The mother refrains from approaching them; "Non posso avvicinarmi" ("I can't come close"), she commands herself, Maria's voice withering into near-silence. But then: "Un gel mi prende" ("A chill is taking hold of me") unfurls into a gradual discovery. "I figli uccido!" ("To kill my *children?!*") Norma panics in a clamorous crescendo—waking from a nightmare.

Suddenly she is enamored with her children; with their smiles that let people believe in the mercy of heaven: "nel cui sorriso il perdono del ciel mirar credei." Gentle diminuendi with which they are sung reflect tender endearment.

No, no—they *must* die; they are Pollione's progeny. "*Feriam*," she resolves, "I must *strike*." Raising the dagger, Norma shirks all of a sudden in

Maria's near-shriek: "Ah! No! Son miei *figli!* . . . miei figli!" ("Ah, no! They are my *children!* . . . my children!").

Switching schemes, Norma resolves instead to kill herself and leave her children to Clotilde, a close friend. "Questi infelici a te li affido" ("These miserable beings . . . I entrust them to you"), she sings with solemnity in a soft, humble tone. Adalgisa's pathos melts her. In their duet "Mira, o Norma" she demands to know: "Why do you strive to weaken my resolve with your sweet sentiments?" ("Perché, perché la mia costanza vuoi scemar con molli affetti?"). The phrase comes out with shriveling diminuendo notes: the final drops of Norma's pride are being drained.

Scaling the pernicious pyre to spare Pollione, Norma ventures on her last duet with her unfaithful lover—who extols her piety and now falls back in love with her as a result. "In mia man, alfin tu sei" ("You are in my hands at last"), is proffered with a paradoxically submissive Will to Die.

When she announces to her people that she plans to sacrifice herself in place of Adalgisa and Pollione, "Son io" ("It is I") rises and falls in the vast arc of a crescendo-turned-diminuendo; declaring her supremacy by stressing Norma's selflessness. She addresses Pollione ("Crudel Romano, tu sei con me": "Cruel Roman, you are with me at last"), with a purposely savage crescendo on "Crudel Romano" contrasting an amorous "tu sei con me" ("You are with me").

Describing how the pair will be united in their deaths ("Sottera ancora sarò con te"), Maria finishes the phrase with a roulade on "te". Shy diminuendo displays her still-lingering love. Pollione elects to join Norma in fatal surrender.

The past year's chaos of real life had been too much for her. "I've always fought to be a normal human being," she would tell an interviewer six months later. "But I've been unfortunate in having people around me who have done everything to prevent me from being that. I have frequently found myself in inflated situations where I have looked around and asked myself: 'What is all this about? What and where is the true reality of the situation?' "[219]

Music was still her safest sanctuary. On its good days.

13.

"Little checking machines"

Days after the completion of her *Norma* recording Maria returned to her refuge from ponderous thought: crowded leisure. Having promised her best friend a cruise with David Stickelber and Lawrence Kelly fifteen months before, she now invited Giovanna Lomazzi aboard the *Christina*.[1]

On its Mediterranean course it crossed another yacht: Prince Rainier of Monaco's *Deo Juvante II*.[2] The relationship between Maria and his wife Princess Grace, formerly known as actress Grace Kelly, was easy. In the latter's words Maria was a "very honest, forthright person. She says what she thinks and what she feels, which is a quality I admire very much."[3]

Pseudo-biographers and screenwriters enjoy describing these *Christina* sojourns as epitomes of opulence and grandeur. For Maria they were closer to a day spent on the beach without the buzz of tourists or mosquitoes or— as the Sicilians call them—"paparazzi". Hers was the cabin "Ithaca;" each was named for a Greek island.[4] Termed by her a "little boat,"[5] on this humble yacht there were no lavish balls or six-course dinners. Guests would rise at any hour, take a swim in the small pool and saunter back to solitude.

Throughout Lomazzi's stay Maria spent much time preparing for her comeback at La Scala with the scrutiny of *Poliuto*'s score. The production was being directed by Luchino Visconti. Evening conversations would center on music, her and Onassis' early years in Greece and the luminous balm of the moonlight.[6]

It was Onassis' intention to facilitate Maria's life as much as possible. According to one guest, the *Christina* would be decked with "white pedestals with huge bouquets of long-stemmed American Beauty roses":[7] a pink flower that in 1965 would earn the name "Maria Callas Rose" when it was bred anew by one Madame Antoine Meilland.[8] Together with gardenias[9] and orchids[10] it was Maria's preferred floral specimen.[11]

"Not very meticulous" when it came to her business affairs in the words of EMI's Dorle Soria,[12] the soprano was relieved of certain duties when Onassis helped her by enlisting diplomat Roberto Arias—Panama's Ambassador to the United Kingdom and husband of Margot Fonteyn—to take care of her finances. Following Arias' advice, Sander Gorlinsky would commit himself to the protection of Maria's funds: "As requested, I herewith submit a proposition for a solution for the channeling of Madame Callas' earnings through a Swiss company for tax purposes," he wrote to Arias in summer 1960.[13]

Discussions on Onassis' involvement in Maria's work are often tinged with melodrama; among them one biographer's assertion: "He wanted a slave—and a new career is not conducive to slavery."[14]

A "new career" was actually Onassis' objective. According to EMI France producer Michel Glotz, after witnessing the stress and badgering fatigue that plagued her before each performance he suggested that Maria guard her art an easier way. The resulting proposition was the rental of a television studio in her name together with an orchestra under contractual obligation. This would let Maria record any time she wanted.[15]

On 26 June 1960 Gorlinsky had written to Arias a letter concerning a "Maria Callas Television Production Company." It would "produce a television spectacular with an opera of her choice which could be taped in London. Madame Callas would be the head of the company and be able to profit greatly with the capital gains situation."[16]

But with Maria's non-negotiable proclivity to favor live events the project never neared fruition.

Back in Milan by 20 October, Maria surfaced at La Scala on the 26th for the beginning of rehearsals.[17] Her old friend Francisco Siciliani was at loss to understand the opera's strange selection.[18]

Donizetti's *Poliuto*—which revolves around the martyr Saint Polyeuctus and is based on Corneille's play *Polyeucte*—is focused not on one but *two* men: the titular hero and his nemesis Severo. Three arias make up the soprano part. Yet it wasn't in Maria's interests to return with a grand "showcase" role; her frayed and hole-punched nervous system sought a sanctuary: one afforded her through brief appearances onstage.

Accompanying the anticipation of *Poliuto* were more noxious rumors: now that Joan Sutherland "surpassed" Maria Callas as the *prima donna assoluta* of the opera world, the latter spent rehearsals throwing temper tantrums. In an attempt to rectify her public image once again Maria published a denial of these accounts in the *Rome Daily American*: "[it is] the most ridiculous and silliest stunt I ever saw in my life ... I have expressed a highly favorable opinion of that young Australian soprano and several newspapers printed my remarks about her. It is only regrettable, to put it mildly, that someone literally invented a story and published it."[19]

Days later came another blow. Following persistent problems with Italian censors—who had shut down his production of a play that had a homosexual character and edited his neorealist masterpiece, *Rocco e i suoi fratelli*—Visconti suspended his domestic artistic engagements. *Poliuto* was stranded.[20]

On 16 November he wrote Maria a painful apology. She took it in her stride, lamenting that she had been "counting the hours" till their first rehearsals for *Poliuto*, expressing her hope that his conflicts would end but admitting she doubted he or she "would ever be free of troubles." Astounded was Maria to discover that the government could censor art but let the gossip rags produce "obscene, inexact and defamatory" tales of celebrities' private lives. To her it was an "incongruity so absurd, so contrary to common sense." She struggled to believe "it could exist in the world of today".[21]

With every passing day the opening of *Poliuto* grew more imminent and equally more hallowed; an ornate cathedral that intimidates when finally in reach. "You also pray for me, Maestro," Maria instructed Tullio Serafin in a letter on the 26th. "Because this return is very important for me, or rather— decisive ... Write to me, dear Maestro, because I need moral support as always. Here [at La Scala] everyone is very dear to me; they want only my triumph and are doing everything to ease the expectation. But the responsibility's only becoming heavier—and making itself heard more loudly. Let's hope for the best."[22]

Prior to rehearsals she had spent two months determining which cuts to make in *Poliuto*, where to apply vocal accents and the markings that would best evoke doomed Paolina.

With Austrian director Herbert Graf now at the helm of the production, the endeavor was disrupted when La Scala's stage-hands suddenly announced a strike.[23] In the closed, emptied theatre Maria requested that she and Graf go through her paces alone.[24] Urban operatic legend also has it that she taught the role of Poliuto to her stagemate, tenor Franco Corelli, "phrase by phrase".[25]

With eight days to go before the opening of *Poliuto*, Meneghini filed a new lawsuit against his estranged wife on 29 November. Appealing the first verdict—which had held the couple equally accountable for their disunion—he now wanted it declared she was entirely at fault, having "ruined" him financially and damaged both his "dignity and respectability".

Ten months had passed since they had seen each other last. "He filed the suit in court on 29 November, hoping that I would be summoned to appear in the days right before the opening of the season, probably to ruin my nerves just before the performance or something like that. How can people be born so cruel?" Maria wrote to her American lawyer Walter Cummings. Again she sought to know: was there any way that she could snag a quick divorce in the U.S.? She understood there was the option of a six-week stay in Reno. But she couldn't do that. She would "die of boredom."[26]

Four months later little would have changed: "Dear Meneghini has lost his head. He continues to pursue me in court and he couldn't be crueler." She was willing to divorce in Alabama. As for the necessity of having to remain there for a while: "We will see and I will reconsider the situation in a few months' time."[27]

Over two years after that in summer 1963 Cummings suggested that his client venture to the state of Idaho for her divorce. "How does one get there and what can one do there? Is it very hot in July-August?" Maria responded. "Can I be at peace and practice there?"[28] Meneghini was still causing reckless havoc.

Back in Milan that December 16,000 carnations were arriving by plane; all of them bound for La Scala. Three days before the opening Maria wrote a letter to a clan of La Scala subscribers who had gifted her with a gold medal.[29] "I don't know you," she began, "but I am infinitely grateful for the locket that I shall keep among my most precious gifts. I hope to live up to your expectations on 7 December, so that your affection is justified."[30]

Onassis had booked a suite at the Hotel Principe di Savoia.[31] That night he would be sitting in a box supporting his new consort. Maria would have butterflies in hindsight: "It was a very emotional time for me and in some ways difficult . . . You see, spiritually I never left La Scala but, physically, I was returning there as an estranged artist. Would the public accept me on these terms? I was very nervous about this as it had really nothing to do with my artistic capabilities. But people are influenced. Also my voice had undergone rather significant changes since I had last sung at La Scala. Nevertheless, I was happy during that period, and the relative tranquility I had found gave me the strength to return 'home.'"[32]

That "relative tranquility" was due in large part to the thus far well-behaved Onassis. His support of her career was no *de facto* social demonstration: Onassis' affection and attraction for Maria stemmed from veneration. "What always impressed me was the story of her early struggles as a poor girl in her 'teens when she sailed through unusually rough and merciless waters," he would tell biographer Willi Frischauer. "At the age of fourteen, this girl earned a scholarship to the Greek National Theatre, but was so poor that she could only pursue her studies with borrowed music and borrowed books. During the German occupation her family was starving, literally starving, and while studying she did not only have to run the house as well but help to find food, which was very hard to come by . . . For her as a dedicated performer to assert herself in the tough and competitive world of the stage was a great achievement."[33]

Designated a domain of ruthless rifts with general managers, salacious speculation and the pests of press, Maria found a prime escape in the *Christina*. "What our friendship means to her," Onassis would elaborate, "is that it gets her absolutely outside the world of opera houses . . . away from professional matters and preoccupation with her career."[34]

After a period of escalating tension she elected to acknowledge life had several sides. "For some time at the beginning of our relationship we were blissfully happy," Maria would later remember. "I also felt secure and even unperturbed about my vocal problems—well, for the moment . . . I was learning, for the first time in my life, how to relax and live for myself and even began to question my belief that there was no life beyond art."[35]

Accosted was Maria by more rumors of a stumbling voice just before opening night. They demanded to know if it was true that a) "her voice is not as good as it was," and b) "she wants to marry Greek shipping million-aire Aristotle Onassis. When asked about the first she gently shakes her head and says she has no comment to make," reported the *Daily Express*. "When asked about the second she replies, enigmatically: "I *am* married— to Giovanni Meneghini . . ."[36]

Maria had been captured by her heroine. Wife of Roman Christian convert Poliuto in 259 A.D., Paolina stands by her afflicted consort as he wages war for his religion. The problem? Her first love Severo leads the enemy: Armenian pagans. Rather than abandon her endangered husband, Paolina chooses to convert to Christianity and die with Poliuto as a feast for lions while her former lover Severo looks on.

A recording of the opening night unveils a petrified soprano charged with panic. The characterization emerges in haphazard leaks of crazed coloratura, strident notes and boisterous outbursts of crescendo; pillaging the opera of its nuance. Haplessly Maria's own hysteria becomes a hybrid with her heroine's: "Un dubbio, un fero dubbio è sorto nel mio pensier" ("A doubt, a wild doubt has emerged from my thoughts"), Paolina alerts us in the aria "Ove m'intoltro." Racked by nerves, Maria rushes it.

There are tender moments—such as Paolina urging Poliuto not to openly express his love of God: "Taci, se m'ami! Taci . . . Taci, se m'ami!" ("Hush, hush if you love me!") she implores, following the phrase with "o di spavento, o di spavento morrò" ("or else I will perish, I will perish from terror!"). The words are performed in an ominous diminuendo.

But the first act finishes with a high D [D6] that wavers wantonly as well as senseless, extra-loud coloratura.

Only in the second act when Paolina gives herself to Christianity ("Nazareno, a te mi volgo"—"Nazareth, I turn to you") do decorous diminu-endi surface; inviting a dazzling crescendo of hope as she begs, "tu soccorri il mio consorte" ("Succor my spouse").

Then the last note of the act cracks.

Embraced by Ghiringhelli after *Poliuto*, Maria appeared overwhelmed by the crowd; vigilant of the press: "I am very moved; I'm too emotional to even talk to you," she told a RAI reporter.[37] To another journalist she helplessly confessed: "I am upset to such an extent that I do not know if I am still alive in this world. I have silently suffered a lot. But there is always God's hand to protect His creatures. I am elated to see that the La Scala public is still mine."[38] Patrons were engulfing her to manifest their awe. Among them was Giulietta Simionato, to whom Maria allegedly said: "Giulia, all these people are making me nauseous: I know very well that I did terribly."[39]

Simionato may have misheard. Six days later she wrote happily to Serafin: "With God's help, everything went well . . . I am happy that you liked the premiere; the second performance went even better because I was calmer."[40]

The press was more interested in the presence of Onassis—"a short, middle-aged man, with bushy eyebrows and tortoiseshell spectacles, who wore a blue dinner jacket that looked rather shabby and was a bit shiny at the elbows, like that of a Monte Carlo croupier"—than the performance itself.[41]

Before he caught hold of Maria and escorted her to the Ristorante Savini, where oysters and turkey were gobbled till dawn,[42] she was greeted by her old friends the Cook sisters. Ida remarked on a gesture of hers: selecting between two religions and two men, Maria would put her hands to her face to express indecision. This had been purposely done, she replied. Ida then noted that after making her choice Paolina desisted from touching her face. "*That* I didn't know!" Maria cried out.[43]

The visual acting couldn't mask the vocal flaws. While old friend, French critic Jacques Bourgeois referred to "captivating beauty" and a "miracle of expression", he confessed: "Callas' voice, according to conventional stand-ards of music criticism, appeared ugly with an emphatic metallic sheen that is unusual—as well as a very pronounced *vibrato* in her top notes."[44]

By the third performance on the 21st she was completely spent. "There had been too much tension, and one started to pay the price. This is too much of an artist. All I want is the chance to give what I can. I confess there are times when a part of me is flattered by the high emotional climate, but generally I don't like any moment of it. You start to feel condemned."[45]

Two days after the last performance French newspaper *Le Figaro* claimed La Callas was quitting.[46] The next day heralded her curt dismissal: the news had been a "silly rumor" that "did not even deserve a denial".[47] Bruna the maid told wire service UPI she would be singing *Medea* at Epidaurus that summer.[48]

Her note to Walter Cummings on the 27th found Maria dismal. "I ask myself if there is really anyone who is happy and content. I doubt it a great deal . . . My performances went well. Thank you. I had the most wonderful reception I've ever had . . . The American and London newspapers referred to 'praise and whistles for Callas'. I assure you that I wasn't the one being whistled at. Why do they always invent these untruths? I'm so fed up with them!"[49]

Receding to a period of relaxation once again, Maria spent New Year's Day 1961 in Monte Carlo with Onassis at a ball; remaining in the city for the greater part of January.[50] When the hounded pair went to a local nightclub in the early days of February, the announcer introduced its enter-tainer as "the Callas of stripteasers". Maria walked out and the press insinu-ated that Onassis was behind the prank. Still irked, a few weeks later she negated the report: "The truth was that at the end of the number I'd asked to be taken home simply because I'd found it rather boring. But the news-papers of the world found that incident more newsworthy than the first night of 'Poliuto', for instance. That seems to indicate to me that some-where along the lines values have become ridiculously distorted."[51]

Although Onassis and Maria were both stubborn, independent characters, the former didn't suffer an aversion to the art of opera as select reporters would allege. His physiotherapist, Korinna Spanidou, as well as his step-niece Marilena Patronicolas, remembered him as a casual consumer of classical music; one who enjoyed Bach's "Ave Maria" and the aria "Casta diva" without caring to know what they were.[52]

It was he who reconciled the ever-feuding pair of Karajan and Callas. According to both Eliette von Karajan and EMI's Michel Glotz he persuaded them to dine together at Maxim's in Paris.[53] Recalling the trick she had played on him during their Berlin *Lucia*s, Maria now needed to know: "What was it you did when I was so itchy and turned my back on you in the mad scene? I knew you were clever. But the accompaniment was so perfect, I decided you were not only a genius; you were also a witch."—"It was very simple," came Karajan's rejoinder. "I watched your shoulders. When they went up, I knew you were inhaling and that was my cue for attack."[54]

An armistice was born. Though they were never reunited in the realm of art the maestro would still cruise on the *Christina* and consider projects with Maria.

As she juggled various propositions back in February 1961—including negotiations with La Scala about Bellini's *Beatrice di Tenda*,[55] Maria dealt with an unprecedented insult: Giovanna Lomazzi had written a tell-all series of features about her best friend for the magazine *La Settimana Incom*. Though not incendiary, some reports about Maria—as well as details of their intimate exchanges about Meneghini and Onassis—were too personal and fresh to become public knowledge. "I cannot feel *hate* and all that, but I can ignore a person completely," Maria responded when asked how she handled betrayal. "Sometimes I have to ask myself if I ever really *knew* this person."[56]

Such was the case in this instance.[57] Though Maria forgave Lomazzi and remained civil to her,[58] she struggled to imagine why her best friend of a decade would have marketed her story. "How can I trust anybody when even a close friend as well as my own family sold me for money?" she asked Stelios Galatopoulos at around the same time.[59] Just a few months earlier Evangelia had published a biography, *My Daughter Maria Callas*. So riddled had the book been with untruths that it had highlighted the idiocy of Evangelia more than her cruelty.

Yet the press had been hot on her heels.

With more time on her hands, Maria strived to cultivate a better friend in her persona. It was nonetheless still not unheard of for a chum to write: "You didn't, of course, say a word about our invitation to spend an evening or a Sunday afternoon with us while you are here." A besieged mind made her negligent.[60] And yet she also had a thoroughly accommodating nature that accepted many. When her Italian lawyer's daughter, Alba Cinzia Caldi Scalcini, locked herself out of her Monte Carlo hotel room at the Hotel Hermitage, Maria bade the near-stranger sleep in her own.[61]

A new acquaintance she had made months earlier was Marguerite van Zuylen, wife of Belgian diplomat Egmont van Zuylen. Known as Maggie, she was of Egyptian origin and twenty-two years older than Maria; an aspiring novel mother figure in her life.[62] Little by little Maggie would become the first port of call: a respondent Gorlinsky would contact when hard-pressed to reach his itinerant client.[63]

Slowly Maria settled down in Paris—taking frequent trips between her Milanese abode and the metropolis that was Onassis' hometown. Renting an apartment at the Hôtel Lancaster, 7 rue de Berri,[64] she hopped peripatetically between the cities.

Fastidiously loyal to Biki,[65] Maria craved the 1960s Saint Laurent collections ("It's such a shame that this style doesn't suit me," she confessed) and adored Pucci.[66] Now that garments were much looser and their colors flagrant and flamboyant, the soprano could be seen in strapless dresses, halter-neck gowns, jumpsuits, waistless frocks and floral patterns. Her wigs embraced the range of "big hair" vibrancy: thick bob-dos, bouffants, flips and beehives. Topped with tortoiseshell glasses, the looks made for a humorous sight.

Without the services of La Scala's *maestro sostituto* Antonio Tonini at her helm, Maria heard of vocal coach Janine Reiss through their mutual friend Michel Glotz. Preparations for a compilation album of French arias propelled her to arrive at the instructor's decorous apartment on the rue de Courcelles. In retrospect the latter would recall, "I would say that Maria had lost—not her top notes—but her ease of reaching the top register: it had lost its stability."[67]

Maria's first move was to ask if Reiss had any neighbors. There was an old general at the Hôtel Lancaster who hated the sound of her practice; resorting to banging his cane on the ground when she vocalized. The answer came in the negative: only a deaf lady lived on the story above. Maria opened the score she had brought—Bizet's *Les pêcheurs de perles*—and performed several arias. Upon completion she demanded Reiss dissect one of the piece's tough cadenzas and explain the right way to interpret it.[68]

In a similar fashion Maria would bring along all sorts of scores—including her well-known *Medea*—and solicit advice: "Can you give me some ideas?" she would request.[69] The women would spend hours going over the same page. It riled Maria when her coach did not immediately call out her mistakes. "But, Maria—I was waiting for you to finish the phrase before pointing it out!"

Reiss was later eager to aver that the soprano had possessed "an excellent technique: she knew how to breathe, to lift the soft palate at the right moment, and she herself could hear perfectly the sound she produced."[70]

When one day fellow student Michel Hamel arrived to get a notebook he had left behind,[71] he spotted the bespectacled soprano midway through her lesson. She greeted him politely. During his next visit he exclaimed agog to

Reiss: "You know, Janine, that woman that I saw—she looks *extraordinarily* like Maria Callas!"

Never did the man discover her identity.[72]

While Onassis toured with Winston Churchill once again on the *Christina*[73] Maria prepared to record the French arias disc, beginning rehearsals on March 24th, 1961.[74] For this endeavor she had carefully recruited a new favorite among maestri: young Georges Prêtre, who was almost her age.

Like her compatibility with Serafin, the pair's alliance never risked divergence in creative styles. "Sitting eye to eye, something clicked, something that has never ceased to exist . . ." Prêtre recalled. "From the word 'go' we understood how similar we were in our ways of being musicians . . . there were never any exasperating debates or preliminary rehearsals: 'Maria, don't you think . . .' 'Georges, perhaps here we could . . .' and that was enough."[75]

To him Maria turned for reassurance during these rehearsals: "Maestro—could I do that at that point? Does it adhere to the French tradition? Maestro, do you think that I could slow down here?" French opera was a quasi-virgin territory for Maria.[76]

Upon Onassis' return from the *Christina* the couple spent Sunday browsing a chateau in Châteaudun, one and a half hours from Paris. Its owner, Fernand Pouillon, was in prison for swindling his company's shareholders. The ever-observant press alleged Callas was retiring to live with Onassis in one hundred and sixty acres of forest.[77]

Three days later he was back aboard the yacht[78] and she was in recording sessions at the Salle Wagram. It was perhaps not accidentally-on-purpose that Nicole Hirsch—a reporter for French music magazine *Chaix Musica*—had been dispatched to write about the work.[79] Later Maria was denied admission to the studio when its unwitting guards would not accept her absence of ID. The appearance of Michel Glotz finally saved her.[80]

Walter Legge was also present. Hirsch captured Maria's recording etiquette: mounting the podium, removing her shoes, crossing her arms. Rehearsing in full voice as always, she informed the journalist: "I'm warming up."

The orchestra was "stupefied", according to Walter Legge. "While other singers rarely stop in a recording session—preferring to then re-record and have the prior recording 'retouched' with the edits to avoid making the orchestra start again—Maria can sometimes restart an aria ten times consecutively . . . because a note didn't seem to go well," he explained to the hawk-eyed reporter.[81]

"Tell me if I make a mistake in the French," Maria had implored Janine Reiss.[82] To Pamela Hebert—a student Maria would coach ten years later—she explained it this way: "There's a difference between French music and Italian music; I've learned that on my own experience. In Italian you have to be *very* clear on the words. In French, the whole phrase passes through more smoothly. If it were Italian music, they would say, 'Qui m'aurait dit la *pla*-ce que dans mon *cœur'*—you're chopping it up. Whereas in French music, it has to be more of a whole *phrase*."[83]

The musical document—originally known as *Callas Sings Great Opera from French Arias*, later *Callas à Paris I*—is perhaps the greatest testament to her artistic malleability.

It is not perfect. In this first example of her *Carmen* "Habanera" acute vocal insecurity is palpable on phrases such as "c'est l'autre que je préfère" ("it's the other one that I prefer"). Watered down to tones recalling her Rosina in *The Barber of Seville*, the oddly molded voice transforms what ought to be a *femme fatale* into a cute coquette.

Paradoxically another track unmasks her exploration of a more erotically calculating character: Delilah from Saint-Saëns' *Samson et Dalila*. In this take on the biblical tale that sees the High Priest of Dagon use Delilah to distract Hebrew leader Samson from his charge on the Philistines, the woman wallows in sexual dominion. Languid, wistful, sensuously slothful music crafts a carnal creature who exploits not just her assets but the aphrodisiac of the surrounding climate and her primal environs to get exactly what she wants.

"Printemps qui commence, portant l'espérance, aux cœurs amoureux . . ." ("Spring that dawns and brings hope to the amorous hearts . . .") limns Delilah. For the first time we hear Maria use sequential notes contrastingly: "PRIN-*temps*," she sings, leaning on the "*temps*" with a pleadingly desperate, deliberately vulnerable pressure. The sound is as soft as a pedal being freed from a pianist's grasp.

In each of these instances there is a lean-on: "En vain, je suis BE-*lle* . . ." ("In vain, am I *beau*-tiful . . ."), "A la nuit TOM-*ban* . . . te" ("As night *falls* . . ."). Select diminuendi employ a small mouth to connive; evoking a sight of the heroine fanning herself in the sweltering heat; her breath ebbing from torrid fatigue.

Contesting snares of these diminuendi are the antithetically contralto, brazenly conspiratorial tones. It is the voice she uses to accuse Samson of treachery: "Pleurant l'infidèle" ("Weeping for the infidel"), she describes him. The aria ends with a contrast to both of these paradigms as we hear a subtler, more nubile Delilah; one who can only be "saved" by his lovemaking: "A lui ma TEN-*dre* . . . sse . . . Et la douce . . . iv-RE . . . sse . . ." ("To him belongs my TEN-derness . . . And my sweet ECS-tasy . . ."). The final words, "Qu'un brûlant amour . . . garde à son retour" ("That a burning love can keep for his return") fizzle: a wavering flame in the night wind.

In another aria Delilah reflects on her plan with Maria's despotic, vibrato-strewn voice: "Samson, recherchant ma présence, ce soir doit venir en ces lieux" ("Looking for me tonight, Samson will come to this place"). Portents percolate these dark tones; diminuendo lends enigma to the slow-to-surface "en . . . ces lieux" ("in this place"). She commands love—as though love is Cupid—to come "help her weakness . . . pour poison into his heart!" ("Amour! Viens aider ma faiblesse! Verse le poison dans son sein!").

Her voice is so perversely curved around these words, they peter out in sly diminuendo: she becomes a succubus. A cutting, onomatopoeic "k" sound in the word "es-*clave*" ("slave") resounds as harshly as a smacking whip. Delilah is a dominatrix.

It is an ugly voice that sings of Samson's fears: "He who breaks the chains of a people will succumb to my efforts" ("Lui, qui d'un peuple rompt la chaîne, succombera sous mes efforts"). In its deviation from a natural-sounding timbre the insatiable instrument approximates the bent voice of an unreal beast; descending to the growly pit of an A flat below the middle C.

In "Mon cœur s'ouvre à ta voix" ("My heart opens up to your voice") the instrument is thinned to forge the spurious impression of Delilah's innocence. A sensual diminuendo percolates "Redis . . . à ma tendresse les serments . . . d'autrefois . . ." ("Tell . . . my love again . . . all that you used to tell me in the past . . ."). "D'autrefois" ("in the past") is so soft it suggests a dangerous proximity; Delilah inching closer to her prey.

Over the lengthy legato that makes up "A . . . ah ré . . . é . . . ponds . . . à . . . à ma . . . a . . . a ten-en-dre . . . *sse*" ("Ah . . . respond to my tenderness"), the sound writhes like a lilypad stirred by a ripple. When Delilah finally bursts through the small talk—dictating the same in a crescendo—it is a euphoric cry; almost climactic.

In comparison the other arias scarcely qualify as musical exhibits. Maria's Juliet in "Je veux vivre" from Gounod's *Roméo et Juliette* is so derailed by vocal insecurity the character falls through. In "Je suis Titania" from Ambroise Thomas' *Mignon* she is too screechy to suggest a personage. Across "Depuis le jour" from Charpentier's *Louise* too many high notes come out as a squeak.

*

Possessing an identity card in the "tax-free Principality of Monaco," Maria now began to travel regularly between Paris, Monte Carlo and Milan.[84] In the interest of her reputation's tailorship, that March she gave *The Sunday Times* a three-part interview.

Its cultivation began when she greeted journalist Derek Prouse. "One encounters a friendly, bespectacled American girl mixing a whisky and soda. 'I'm fixing you a drink. Is Scotch all right?' " By this time Maria's accent had reverted somewhat to its earlier American proclivities: "off" could be pronounced as "orf" while "past" would lose its British "ar".

What was the purpose of this exposé? To tell the world that she was never satisfied because the kind of perfection she desired was "not of this world."[85] Maria had insisted on one truth for years: "We always have our little checking machines."[86] And it was this reason—and not any other— that accounted for increasing caution when selecting her engagements.

Later she would phrase it similarly—enlightening a French journalist about her crisis of confidence: "I no longer wanted to [perform] because my instrument wasn't giving me—it wasn't responding to me the way I would've *wanted* . . . I would sing when I did not *want* to sing."[87]

Though these were not the words she used with Mr. Prouse, one thing was clear: "Now, first of all, I must find my joy in music again. I feel I am already well on the way to this; in the last few months I have found serenity and good friends. And one thing I am immensely gratified to discover in my own character is the fact that these stormy years have not left me embittered; on the contrary, I find I have a new tolerance, a new willingness to understand other people's point of view and not to form too hasty judgments."

Two months earlier, in a piece for *Newsweek*, the soprano had been asked about the plight of loneliness in being an opera singer: a fate Leontyne Price had mourned to the reporter. "Loneliness is emptiness and that is nothing," she avowed. "It is worse than nothing: it is being misunderstood, and it can happen when you are not alone, but even with people. Maybe it happens most then. It can happen with your wife or husband. I'm afraid most people are lonely in that sense. No, I'm speaking of isolating myself with my work. That is a thrilling challenge and then you are never lonely."[88]

Reminded that she had the range of both Giuditta Pasta and Maria Malibran, Maria contradicted her old self: "One should not get into the habit of always singing light operas like 'I puritani' and 'La sonnambula.' They are considered light today, even though they were sung then by Pasta, Grisi and Malibran, who had heavy voices like mine."[89] Her abrupt *volte-face* suggests she might have been attributing some of her vocal faults to challenges she had performed years earlier.

And that was something she had never done before.

In that vein it was taking her too long to make decisions. That October Gorlinsky would write about a concert he had proposed at the Royal Festival Hall: "You will remember that we have already talked about this when you were in London, and at the time you said you wanted a week to think about it, and it is now nearly a month."[90] Frequently she would respond concerning future operas to Michel Glotz with: "How can I know today whether or not, one or two years from now, I will be capable of singing or identifying myself with this or that role?"[91] Glotz now found in her a woman who was "fatigued—physically, mentally and when it came to the nerves."[92]

Efforts were being exerted to take care of herself. On April 9th she emphasized to Walter Cummings: "I am well as I have never been before—vocally, morally and health-wise."[93]

The problem was that these impressions mutated—and almost daily. On 12 April she was finally able to consent to a recital to be held at St. James Palace, London in late May.[94]

After three weeks apart she rejoined Onassis aboard the *Christina* in New York's Hudson River.[95] Close by was old pal Leo Lerman, who scribed later in his journal: "She came off the [Onassis] yacht, having telephoned Dario and Dorle [Soria] . . . Maria is leading the life any woman lives, her timetable being totally controlled by the whims of her man who is apparently more loved than loving. 'I'm an Oriental,' she said. But there is so much more of this: Her new smile—very young, sweet, hurt; her softness; her vulnerability . . . She went up the steps of [the restaurant] El Morocco going to meet Onassis. This person is the center of her life, not music."[96]

Many of Maria's friends regarded the old-fashioned shipping magnate's character as patriarchal. They imagined that Onassis had been raised in an environment that saw men as the dictators of women.

To an extent he did purport to have such qualities. Following the "honeymoon" stage, when Onassis stopped sending her flowers, Maria asked why. "You belong to me. Why would I send myself flowers?" responded the chauvinist.[97]

This was Maria's implication when she later told some friends—including music critic John Ardoin and accompanist Robert Sutherland—that Onassis regarded himself as a "pasha": a high-ranking Turkish lord in the Ottoman Empire. Possessing a boorish bravado, Onassis would relish this image. What many failed to understand was that Maria bolstered his pathetic ego quite deliberately.

"Being a woman, most of all, is being intelligent," she would later relate in an interview. "It's giving the man the impression that . . . that he is the one who *commands*, even when it's entirely the other way around . . . I find that *delicious*."

The interviewer would reply: "It's a little Machiavellian, nonetheless."— "Well, yes," Maria conceded. "And I am rather persuaded that since you are *men*, you enjoy that. You don't want a woman who tells you—'You, get up, move'—or whatever—you don't want the woman to wear the pants in the relationship."[98] Another interview elicited the nutshell: "You give the man to believe that he is a leader. But don't go too far."[99]

Likely Maria was referring to this when she later told Stelios Galatopoulos that Onassis "made me feel liberated, a very feminine woman, and I came to love him very much."[100]

The magnate might have thought himself a "pasha" but he didn't live with her. Unlike Meneghini, Onassis didn't schedule Maria's itinerary. Throughout their relationship they maintained separate apartments, separate staff and entirely separate careers. Evidently Maria did *give* him to believe he was the leader—some of the time; likely enjoying an orthodox male-female interplay.

Compared to her conservative Italian marriage, she and Onassis had a more egalitarian rapport. The former referenced this when later stating that a relationship required "good companionship . . . you have to be—*strangely*, you have to be a good *pal* of your—lover, husband—call it whatever."[101] Onassis rarely felt emasculated. "All his life he trusted them [women] more and preferred to confide in them rather than in men," Maria would explain to Galatopoulos.[102] Onassis' aide Christian Cafarkis recollected that he "listened to Maria, who told him her opinion on virtually every subject."[103]

The *Christina*'s owner had a special Steinway manufactured to withstand the damp aboard the yacht.[104] On this piano the soprano ritualistically practiced—often when Onassis was asleep, often up to five hours a day regardless of whether or not an engagement was imminent. His teenage step-niece Marilena Patronicolas absorbed this replenishment.[105]

In their evasion of the press the couple purposely selected different lodgings during trips abroad. On the occasion of their London sojourn in May 1961 Maria stayed at the Savoy; Onassis preferred Claridge's. To fend reporters off he promised he would double money spent on tips of the pair's whereabouts.[106]

"I have learned not to allow myself to be hurried into a haphazard schedule of work which turns your life into a mad scramble across the world at the mercy of financial planners,"[107] was Maria's new axiom. "Nowadays the stress on us [singers] is great. We scarcely have the advantages which our great predecessors had and we travel too much—constantly on the move with planes; never the calm, lengthy train journeys, where in the old days, one could recollect one's strength from time to time."[108]

As for her entourage of Princess Grace and other stars, the singer held resentment for her reputation as a socialite. Philanthropists and patrons had supported opera since its nascence; why were journalists surprised that she associated with these people? "I live among the bourgeoisie because the artist needs it," she would write in a letter to socialist friend Pier Paolo Pasolini in 1971.[109] "I did not want this . . . *kind* of notoriety; they placed me among the jet-setters and all that and I had *nothing* to do with that at the time," was how she remembered the period many years later.[110]

When friend and media mogul Christos Lambrakis asked her how she could pass time "with people of this ilk," her response was philosophical: "You're right, my world is music. When I'm alone with the score, that's where I find my true self. But how can one bring paradise to Earth? That's why I'm also obligated to live another life."[111]

Maria encouraged her critic friends to disperse the right rumors. Irving Kolodin announced on 28 May that "for the foreseeable future her appearances will be under highly selective circumstances and auspices so that she can prepare herself well, concentrate on a particular task to ensure an ultimate success beyond doubt."[112] She made sure that French journalist Nicole Hirsch was aware that Maria always "goes to bed at a good hour, and consumes nothing but steaks and mineral water when she's singing."[113]

Her poetic internality was safe. "I cling to this musical world of mine. It's a—no, I won't say superior—it's a very nice, good world. No envy, no gossip, no nonsense, everything is so pure and serene," she related that April to Mr. Prouse. "But there is great passion, great love there too. In operas so many times I've played heroines who die for love—and that's something I can understand. I would surely have done the same in their place."[114]

The backstage prose was a completely different matter. Opera house managers worldwide were struggling to capitulate with a soprano almost overcautious.

"Only two weeks ago impresario Lawrence Kelly was assured vis-à-vis the diva in New York that if she performs at all in this country next season 'It will be for you, in Dallas,'" *The Dallas Morning News* reported on 28 May. "She has expressed interest in either 'Norma' or, from the French repertory, 'Carmen', 'Samson et Dalila' and, of all things, Massenet's 'Le Cid.'"[115]

In April Maria had written to her friend *Washington Post* music critic Paul Hume to tell him she wanted to perform in Washington either before the end of the year or the start of the next: "I promise I will do everything possible [to ensure it]."[116]

None of that happened. None of it even came close.

On May 30th she performed her London concert at St. James Palace after a regular check-up with her ENT doctor, James Ivor Griffiths.[117] Detesting the piano accompaniment of Sir Malcolm Sargent—which she later referred to as "terrible"[118]—Maria didn't even manage to impress music connoisseur (later British Prime Minister) Edward Heath. "On the night she arrived with a very heavy cold," he recalled. "She gamely struggled through her arias."[119]

Performing "Pleurez mes yeux" from Massenet's *Le Cid*—one of the most melancholy arias in the entire operatic repertoire—the soprano spewed a series of precarious notes. Sudden outbursts of crescendo constituted little but a crude attempt to prove she still possessed a voice.

Hellbent on resting to improve it, off she was again on the *Christina*; to Greece and Monte Carlo[120] and eventually Majorca, at whose Hotel Son Vida she stumbled upon notorious columnist Hedda Hopper. "Had a long talk with Callas and I believe she'd like to wipe out the bad impression she made in San Francisco by opening the 1962 opera season there," the latter reported. "I feel certain the Rainiers and Aristotle Onassis would go along—in fact Onassis told me he'd been talking with Bob Miller, president of the opera, whom he knows quite well."[121]

It sounded swell in theory but reality was fear. July was spent aboard the *Christina* with Margot Fonteyn and Roberto Arias,[122] the former of whom became a friend to Maria.[123] In relaxation mode Maria listened to beloved dance records: cha-cha-cha, some Afro-Cuban rhythms,[124] in her words: "sometimes even rumbas and things like that."[125] She liked Frank Sinatra and popular songs like "Stormy Weather" and "Hernando's Hideaway".[126]

Meneghini was still raging. "We shall tell everything, if it is necessary. It will be a bomb shell," was his response to an Associated Press reporter's enquiry.[127] Entrenched in preparations for *Medea*, Maria was in disbelief—still: "I've read about the lawsuit of my dear consort in Milan," she wrote to music critic Renzo Rossellini. "You'd think that I'd be used to it by now but

I'm afraid that I'll always be a fool who deludes herself into thinking she'll find a little bit of peace, justice etc. I still live in the atmosphere of those silly libretti full of foolish innocence and naïve idealism!"[128]

Arriving on the *Christina* in Epidaurus in early August, Maria took to the stage on the 6th and was warmly received.[129] As he was coming off the boards *Medea*'s Giasone Jon Vickers wrapped his arm around her: "You know, Maria, I've sung quite a few performances with you now—but tonight you were absolutely phenomenal."—"Oh! Don't be silly! I am just a big fat girl with an ugly voice."[130]

The reviews were mostly plaudits—with the exception of a reference to "a steely edge [that] more than once robbed Mme. Callas' otherwise masterly singing of some of its tonal beauty."[131] Eleven days later she exulted in writing to Herbert Weinstock: "You would've been so happy to hear the performances of this *Medea* . . . I don't have any news except that I sang very well. I haven't been so relaxed in a performance for a very, very long time."[132]

An unexpected visit from her sister proved an obstacle. Resolved to reunite the pair, George brought a wary Jackie to *Medea* one night. "No significant development in my relationship with my sister followed," Maria later recalled to Stelios Galatopoulos. "We were really back to square one. Maybe I did not play my part well or perhaps I played it too well. In an effort to be natural and not at all condescending, like we were in our teens, I may have appeared somewhat belligerent."[133]

Confusing her two meetings with Maria in the 1960s, Jackie remembered their impasse as having taken place shortly after *Medea*—but it may have transpired in Rhodes ten months earlier.[134] At first she seemed to relish being in her sister's company—later writing in her book, "She was really good fun and kept the conversation going . . . [she] introduced me to Onassis and he seemed genuinely interested to meet the sister at last." Then a wrong turn of phrase changed her perception. She related that their father had beheld Maria "with a look of pity on his face as if to say here is someone who has forgotten how to feel for another and that is a terrible thing." The assertion was embellished with a "moment" in a taxi in which George had taken Jackie's hand and solemnly averred: "She cannot change now. It's too late."[135]

Whatever sparked the sour episode, Jackie stayed acrimonious. Since, in Maria's mind, her sister had "at no time in the past [shown] any sign of solidarity towards me and she must have known I badly needed it," she likewise made no effort to revive the lost relationship.[136] Exchanges between them continued sporadically; mostly when Maria needed a bank account number to know where to send Evangelia and Jackie their money.[137] By now she was supporting both Jackie and George on a regular basis.[138]

The end of this *Medea* run meant more *Christina* touring and a whirlwind of fraught possibilities. On 21 September 1961 Maria met with Gorlinsky in Milan to discuss future engagements. No outcome emerged.[139]

Six days later she was in London dining with Lord George Harewood and his wife to discuss potential productions at the Royal Opera House.

Again nothing exact was cemented.[140] Three weeks passed and she was contemplating yet another concert: this time at the London Palladium for the popular BBC television series, "Sunday Night at the London Palladium." Maria toyed with the idea before returning to Gorlinsky four days later with the proposition that she do it at a later date.[141]

Meanwhile, the forthcoming La Scala *Medea* was looming. Anxiously she wrote to Alexis Minotis: "I am here in Milan these days and will come back again in a few weeks' time for two or three days, and then finally will be here for the last provas [rehearsals]. Please prepare everything perfectly well, be exigent with your rehearsals, do not be too ~~acquiescent~~ accordiscent [*sic*], because they always promise, but sometimes do not maintain."[142]

Together with that burden she was set for a recording of bel canto arias in London from 13 to 16 November. Released only in 1972,[143] the album mostly displays endless struggle. In "Selva opaca"—a coloratura-ridden aria from Rossini's *Guglielmo Tell*—Maria's breathing falters. It sounds as though she lacks the muscular support required for the harder lines.

The stridency was far too palpable for her absorbent ears. Abruptly terminating the ordeal, Maria forbade the release of her work. Conductor Antonio Tonini recalled her "weeping" at the prospect of being unable to finish the record.[144]

Averse to performance, she felt forced to keep up appearances. A little later she met up with Gorlinsky again—conducting a meeting in which they agreed she would tour Europe the following year with a series of concerts:

January 27th—Copenhagen
January 31st—Hamburg
February 4th—Berlin
February 8th—London, Festival Hall
February 11th—London, possibly television[145]

"This would give you sufficient time after Christmas to do something about your sinus trouble, if necessary," Gorlinsky wrote to her after their meeting.[146]

The "sinus trouble" in question may have been one of her luckier moments. Finally Maria could ascribe her vocal problems to a recognizable condition. Suffering from sinusitis, she would later explain, "my sinus was full of pus and my resonance chambers were not working."[147]

Unsurprisingly Maria sounds congested in a tape of the La Scala *Medea* from December 11th that year. She relies on the chest voice throughout. With the instrument kept relatively homogeneous, Medea haplessly regresses to the incarnations of her youth: bombastic, grouchy, barbarous. Her attempt to mask her vocal struggle has Maria overuse vibrato to portray her villainy. Too many notes yield to a wobble; flapping like a flag at half-mast.

After hissing from the gallery attempted to deflect her concentration on the opening night, Maria took her character's denunciation of foul Jason—

"Crudel, crudel!"—("Cruel man, Cruel man!") and hurled its second epithet toward her spectators. In conductor Thomas Schippers' recollections, the action was "as if to say, 'Now, look! This has been my stage and will be mine as long as I want it.' "[148]

Surrounded by Onassis, Walter Legge, Elisabeth Schwarzkopf and friends Marie-Luise von Criegern and her husband Adolf Westphal at dinner that night, Maria launched a tirade of enquiries: "What did you think of such and such a passage in the second act? Did I hold that note long enough? Why did they start to whistle?"

It persisted for over two hours.[149]

Four days later she wrote to Emily Coleman. "Thank Heaven my performance went beautifully; they say it was my best. I wish you were here, you would have enjoyed it."[150] Possibly she wanted to convince herself of this. Possibly she *did*. Yet previous remarks of doubt suggest she couldn't fully yield to this belief.

The next day Maria underwent surgery for her sinusitis and caught the flu. Eventually—reluctantly—she postponed her final *Medea*, intended for 17 December, to the 20th.[151] The day before she wrote to Eugenio Gara, "These days I try to relax a little, because I'm still feeling that nervous tension which, as usual, accompanies every opening night of mine, and, I confess, I'm still not used to these wrong-doers, those paid claques that are everywhere; they dishearten me to the extreme."[152]

The third performance went even worse. Confronting the audience with a theatrical entrance in which Medea would be, in the words of friend Fabrizio Melano, "upstage center between two massive columns, a tall figure completely shrouded by a somber mantle, held up in front of her face by her right hand so that all you could see were two burning dark eyes," Maria opened her mouth to announce herself: "Io? Medea" ("I? Medea"). Her voice cracked on the "de" of "Medea". Those in the gallery gasped. The note—an E5—was no challenge. Now even charier, she "scaled her gestures down to match the reduced dynamic level of her singing," as Melano recollected.

Intermission stretched beyond its limits. Half an hour turned into thirty-five and eventually forty-five minutes and the houselights still hadn't been dimmed. People anticipated it was just "another Rome". They were mistaken: Maria returned onstage and continued to sing; albeit in tremulous fear. Acclimatizing her voice to that of her colleague, the loyal Giulietta Simionato shrank her volume. Her appreciation of the gesture gave Maria strength to sing more loudly. By the third act she had ceded to the character and was exploring different traits of the insidious woman: "terror, pity, tenderness, desperation, murderous rage, steely resolution," wrote Melano.

Melano went to greet her backstage. As usual she was copiously crowded by ferocious fans bombarding her with "brava"s and "divina"s. Discerning her concern, the friend could not express himself. "But when I reached her she seemed relieved and just looked right into me with those huge eyes. As

I pressed her hand I realized that I didn't have to say anything—Simionato had already sung for me, for everybody."[153]

According to Maria's recollection of this "sinusitis" period in 1964, "I started to force my voice because when the pus drops onto the cords and blocks the sound chambers, it's like a deaf man who shouts because he cannot hear himself any more . . . It took a lot of courage to go on singing and to have the humility to stop and start all over again . . . I had to completely forget expression and art for two years and cope with purely technical problems."

What had started out as a remediable fault had led apparently to unintentional abuse of her decrepit instrument: "My biggest mistake was trying to intellectualize my voice," she observed. "It set me back years. Everyone thought I was finished. I tried to control an animal instinct instead of leaving it as it was—just a God-given gift. I admit to having a terrible vocal crisis two or three years ago . . . I had tried to place my voice so well that I just couldn't sing anymore. I also developed a terrible sinus trouble in my right jaw and continued singing with this trouble so that nobody could say I had walked out on performances . . . I got complexes for the first time and lost my audacity. My vocal cords have always been and are perfect, thank God. It's nonsense to say that my cords are ruined. But I got so many complexes from continual negative criticism which contributed to what I admit was a vocal crisis."[154]

In January 1962 Maria didn't stop convening with Gorlinsky—signing up to perform Verdi's *Requiem* that fall.[155] On 26 February she was at Royal Festival Hall for the start of her scheduled concert tour, performing in English the aria with which she had auditioned for the Athens Conservatory, "Ocean, thou mighty monster," from Carl Maria von Weber's *Oberon*. The complicated, choppy nature of its verbiage left her so addled she was forced to stop and start anew.[156] Six weeks had been spent attempting to perfect the text. "English words are not at all easy to sing," she confessed.[157]

Wearing—in the words of Neville Cardus—"a spotlighted cerise jacket over a black dress so tight that she looked at times to be encased in slacks," Maria appeared humble when she issued her apology.[158]

Written in 1826 in a Romantic, grandiose tradition, the aria is a Homeric, bard-like narrative that spans twelve minutes. "Ocean, thou mighty monster, that lies curled like a green serpent, round about the world!" Reiza begins. In a studio recording from December 1963 an American twang would unmistakably ring the word "art". Consonantal clusters crunch throughout Maria's mushy diction.

What she accurately executed in the piece was an increasing aura of momentum; clambering crescendi that arouse the same anticipation as the ship that Reiza hopes will save her.

The live performance of this concert magnifies the virtues of the later studio recording. In this fairytale-like opera the soprano stresses the word "serpent" with a startled horror. Every new face of the ocean is another wave of terror slowly surfacing: "But . . . when thou risest in thy wrath . . . as now . . . and fling'st . . . thy folds . . . around some fated *prow* . . ." Forceful, cutting breaks split the words "folds" and "around" and a fear-layered "prow".

That aura of intensity increases with roulades throughout the line, "Through the gloom their white foam flinging," in which "gloo-oo-oo" and "fli-i-i" are serial notes that swell like sea crests.

A swift shift from excitement to suspense is suddenly pronounced in the *piano* that pervades "But lo! Methinks a light is breaking." The music slows down and is steadied by the time she sings, "Slowly . . . over the distant deep." Rhythm and dynamics contrast as she limns the changing landscape, "And now—the Sun bursts forth—the wind is lulling fast," through a long-held crescendo and a trill on "lull".

The aria goes on to mount a steep ascent along delirious ecstasy. In a role that had eluded her onstage she morphs into a narrator omniscient. A critic for *The Observer* wrote, "On Tuesday she was in fact in better voice than when I last heard her in Milan some fifteen months ago [during *Poliuto*]. At any rate that wide, throbbing vibrato which invades her top notes in full voice was less in evidence."[159]

To Gerardo De Marco, a doctor who had once treated her, she complained: "The London concert was marvelous but a disaster for the critics. They were, I think, annoyed with its success and with my beauty. And then they hate Donizetti (the horror!) . . . In any case I go my way and they go theirs. It's a shame about [Joan] Sutherland; I wanted her to follow my path but she herself admits she can't."[160]

*

Far more than any other year, 1962 became acquainted with Callas the Concert Singer—one who detested the genre: "I have nothing to express there," she sorely repined.[161]

In the gallery of her recitals there are radiant moments. Maria thanks her public by extending a raised half-cupped hand: split so that the third and fourth fingers curl up, the fore- and second remain slack. Sophistication crowns her artistry.

Yet mid-performance it seemed sparse. In the May 1959 Hamburg concert Maria spends a great deal of time resting her hand on the bar that encloses conductor Rescigno's gold podium. One critic would later address "all her characteristic mannerisms . . . her way of singing, head down as though to herself, in the more meditative passages and thus throwing out in full contrast the soaring top notes when she opens up securely and confidently."[162]

It was not her natural habitat. "More and more I realize I am not a concert singer," was a 1964 avowal.[163] Maria told Michel Glotz she felt "naked" in it—without stage make-up, her colleagues, a set.[164] Obstinately folded, the soprano's arms suggested she had stomach pain or was in hiding. Sadly the latter was the truth. Folding or crossing them was a defense mechanism; a gesture designed to protect her from spectators possibly out for her blood. Intermittently there were intriguing moments— mostly when she used the stole or shawl that she was wearing for effect.

That March she informed Walter Cummings that her "sinus trouble" had been "perfectly cured;" she was preparing for the European concerts.

Yet ten months later in January 1963 she was writing to Elvira de Hidalgo that she had "almost conquered" her sinusitis, which had belea- guered her with "so many complexes."[165]

"You may be unhappy with a phrase you have just sung, and immediately you're conscience-stricken," Maria had told Derek Prouse. "You think: 'Oh, I could kill myself, I want to go away, I don't want to sing anymore.' And already the next phrase has suffered."[166]

Nowhere is this more apparent than throughout the Hamburg concert of 16 March 1962. Ending Massenet's aria "Pleurez mes yeux" by crossing her arms over her shoulders, Maria emits strident tones, thrusts forth her torso to force out the high notes and sounds sour still. Demoted to a comic piece in which she manages to muddle up the words not once but twice, Carmen's seductive "Habanera" is a mother fed up with her child.

Only "O don fatale"—a mezzo-soprano aria from Verdi's *Don Carlos*—is performed with some scant strokes of character. In the opera, Eboli—an aristocrat in King Philip's sixteenth-century Spain—curses the terrible gift of her beauty. Maria performs the aria with bloodlust in the word "beltà" ("beauty"); propelling it to palpate with self-loathing. The hurled denunci- ations of "ti maledico . . . ti maledico!" ("I curse you, I curse you!") are thrown boisterously like epithets.

Six days afterward Maria was in tears aboard a plane. The reason wasn't psychological. In her attempt to take off contact lenses during landing she had managed to detach her retina.[167] From the airport in Bonn, the location of her next concert, an ambulance arrived to escort her to hospital, where a doctor extracted a speck of dust trapped in the lens.[168]

The European tour paused to make room for recording sessions in London that April: another endeavor that was eventually scrapped because of Maria's pronounced "sinus trouble".[169] Elsewhere she was serving her art silently by guaranteeing young soprano Kiki Morfoniou—the Adalgisa to her Norma in Epidaurus—an audition for the Royal Opera. "I told them that you're unable to travel at your own cost, so they're going to send you the plane tickets . . ." she wrote. "It will probably be for the role of Azucena in *Trovatore* but also maybe for work there in general."[170]

When Gorlinsky arrived to pay Maria a visit in Milan in late April she was unable to discuss any forthcoming project. Evangelia had just attemp- ted suicide and been hospitalized in New York.[171] She had been discovered by a neighbor in the building after taking too many barbiturates; to doctors Evangelia claimed she had ingested poison.[172] A friend of hers—named by

Maria in her correspondence as a "Mr. Kalminoff"—had written to her seemingly on Evangelia's behalf. He threatened to sell dirty stories to the press unless Maria sent them both a bulky sum. "The usual blackmail," was Maria's term for it.[173]

Calling the suicide attempt a "strictly personal affair," she had no comment for the media. Evangelia recovered quickly.[174]

"The doctor from the Hospital wrote to me saying she is an unstable personality," Maria scribed ten months later to her godfather Leonidas Lantzounis.[175] She had delegated him to take care of the matter and update her. When in December 1962 the Welfare Department instructed Maria to support her financially, she agreed to accord Evangelia two hundred dollars a month through Lantzounis. Maria promised to increase the sum on the condition that her mother wouldn't blabber to the press.[176]

The press could fill her pockets with more speed—together with her new job as a nightclub entertainer.[177] Scarcely had a few months passed when Evangelia fed a story to Italian weekly *Gente*.[178] Soon after she was making Maria Callas dolls to earn money.[179] Her fearful daughter however continued to pay all her hospital bills,[180] as well as her debts.[181]

"God has given me two crosses to carry, one my mother who is not quite sane . . . and second my dear husband who has eaten nearly three quarters of my money . . ." Maria wrote to her friend Edward Konrad two weeks later. "Of course singing under such circumstances are quite hard [sic]. (Unhappy birds cannot sing, do they?)".[182]

Five days after that she faced Meneghini in court again. If the judge could place the blame for their failed marriage squarely on Maria's shoulders, he would be entitled to around a million dollars' worth of common property. Justice Mario Usai set the date of June 18th for the interrogation of witnesses.[183] With Maria absent on that day, Meneghini used five reporters to give testimony.[184] The lawsuit was still active by December 1962, when Italian journalist Giancarlo Fusco was fined for his absence.[185]

Summoned by the president, Maria travelled to New York. It was JFK's birthday: an event better known as Marilyn Monroe's coquettish rendering of "Happy Birthday, Mr. President."

Almost nobody remembered that Maria Callas sang that night, May 19th, 1962. A nervous wreck as always, she immediately expressed her horror at the air conditioning astir in Madison Square Garden. "I can't sit in here," she urgently alerted the event's organizer, Clive David. "I won't have a voice. Can you find me somewhere that's not so cold?"

Maria spent an hour in the broom closet. She was very grateful to Mr. David.[186]

Not only was her voice almost inaudible across the auditorium (she had refused a microphone)[187]—President Kennedy mistakenly reported that Maria hailed "from Brooklyn".[188]

20-30 June had been reserved for a recording of *Tosca*[189] with Lorin Maazel.[190] In the meantime she was adamant to stop reporters: "I am not 'crazy' about Onassis," Maria alerted her correspondent at United Press International. So enraged was she at magazines intent on speculating, she declared that she would sue them if the fabricated tales continued. "It is clear that someone wants to hurt me at the expense of my reputation, and probably at the expense of his own."[191]

Two weeks later Onassis descended the trenches to help his companion. "Maria Callas and I have never discussed marriage . . ." he precised to the press. "But people who do not know us talk about us as though we are teen-agers who youthfully hold hands declaring their love . . . Madame Callas is still in litigation with her former husband; the case is once again in court. She does not want to marry before the case is settled one way or another. She does not want to run the risk, accused of bigamy, of ending up in jail. She told me she would not want to marry before the case is resolved in her favor. How therefore, can anyone claim that she is angry with me because I don't want to marry her, when she does not want to do it herself? This is nonsense . . ."[192]

There was always that option of spending six weeks in Reno to procure a divorce; the one she had cited so frequently. Yet for fear of having to be bored—away from art, away from her relationship—she didn't want to sacrifice the time. Other thoughts were coruscating on her mind's canals.

29 May saw another La Scala *Medea*. "Her voice, now smaller in scope and distinctly nasal in quality, sounded even and steady after a few warm-up measures; dramatically she left no doubt who remains the outstanding figure on the operatic stage," Gerald Fitzgerald wrote in *Opera News*.[193]

It was evident Maria once again was suffering from "sinus troubles". At *Medea*'s second outing on 3 June, the audience threw flowers at the end as they awaited Callas' unending curtain calls.

Nobody surfaced.[194] The performance had been such a vocal struggle that Maria probably surmised she didn't merit it.[195] "Lots of times I think that what I have done is so disgraceful that I should just vanish and never come back, never open my mouth again," she had told Derek Prouse a year earlier.[196]

And so she left the theatre that night. And she never trod its boards again.

*

Three weeks later she and Gorlinsky were exchanging opinions about the proposed 1963 concert tour. It turned out she wasn't able to record *Tosca* in London: her sinuses were at fault.[197] Snapping shots of the soprano window-browsing in Milan with Toy, surrounding journalists were well aware that she was suffering from sinusitis.[198] The dog died shortly after-ward.[199]

By August it was still a problem—with Grace of Monaco writing to her: "Sorry to know your sinuses condition is still bothering you—what a nuis-sance [sic]. I have a lot of hay fever trouble myself . . ."[200]

Interlacing work and leisure, Maria spent most of the summer aboard the *Christina* as the yacht crossed the Mediterranean. In Athens she stopped by with the objective of discussing a performance at the 1964 Winter Olympics and another run at Epidaurus.[201]

Il trovatore had been booked for the Royal Opera House for somewhere between 21 March and 6 or 7 April 1963 with Carlo Maria Giulini conducting.[202] The theatre's manager David Webster was no short of ecstatic.

Out of the blue Gorlinsky wrote to notify the latter some months later: "Madame Callas has pointed out to me that until now her fee at Covent Garden has been very low." The production never materialized.[203]

Exigent salary demands were out of character for her; most likely they were just a cover-up. With Franco Corelli unavailable to sing the role of Manrico,[204] Maria had the perfect reason for abandoning the project.[205] "We lost the tenor—a great tenor," she told a Danish newspaper in summer 1963. "Performances on my level of interest must be prepared very thoroughly in advance. I suppose I have become a little difficult."[206]

The U.S. concert tour—originally planned by New York impresario Frederick Schang to be a huge and multi-state affair—was shrunk down at Maria's bidding to just "four locations in the East" to take place in July.[207]

Too many roles were still unsung. Studying Debussy's *Pelléas et Mélisande*, Maria would even "wake up at night and think about it." The role would not be realized.[208] Neither would *Orfeo*, which she had wanted to sing, or melodies by Fauré and Duparc that she likewise explored.[209]

Staying on the *Christina* for most of August, September and October that year, Maria kept postponing her resumption of engagements. She was due to perform a televised concert at the Royal Opera House on 4 November entitled *A Golden Hour from the Royal Opera House*.

Flying in from Athens a day previously,[210] she was alarmed to witness chaos hours prior to the concert: Giuseppe Di Stefano, her scheduled vocal partner, was unwell and refusing to leave his hotel room. Nauseous from nerves, Maria demanded a B12 injection. Roiled was the administration— who now had to find a doctor late that Sunday evening. Only at the last minute was John Tooley, General Administrator of the Royal Opera House, successful in persuading Di Stefano to perform his duet with Maria.[211]

Appearing in a broadcast with a somewhat ridiculous bob of a wig, Maria performed Verdi's "Tu che le vanità" with a series of wavering high notes that make one imagine a quivering zipline. Nostalgic moments in the work were constantly devivified by wobbles.

A passage of reflection by Elisabeth de Valois—who knows her lover Carlos will be sentenced to death by her fiancé, his father King Philip of Spain—the work is one of opera's most majestic arias.

Only the recordings of her German concert tours in 1959 can paint a picture of Elisabeth as she despairs and pines for her extinction. In her finest exposition of the work at the Hamburg recital, Maria makes use of her cavernous chest voice to nourish the opening lines: "Tu che le vanità conoscesti del mondo" ("You, who have known the vanities of the world"), Elisabeth addresses God. Quickly she grows desperate: "Porta il pianto mio al trono del Signor" ("Carry my tears to the throne of the Lord"), she sings with a soft whisper of diminuendo on the "gnor" of "signor". When she imagines the arrival of Don Carlo: "Carlo qui verrà . . . sì . . . che parta . . . e scordi omai" ("Carlo will come here . . . yes . . . that he may leave . . . and forget me forever"), Maria splits the phrase into succinctly distinct sections; turning her head left and right to look for him.

A delicate flute paves a path for naïve reverie as the princess remembers her youth. Aglow with patriotic love, Maria sings the portamento-held, diminuendo-softened notes of "Fran . . . cia" ("France"). A reverent gesture sneaks into her carriage as she solemnly begins to raise her hand to touch her chest. "There I swore eternal love," she remembers, "but it lasted only a day" ("un giorno . . . sol . . . durò"). Sweetly her diminuendo withers like her years. Releasing that idyllic memory, she lets it slip from her frail grasp.

But Elisabeth yields to her love—for a moment. She pledges that, should Carlo cross her path again, "May the earth, the streams, the founts, the woods and flowers with their harmonies sing of our love" ("Che le zol . . . le . . . i rusce . . . lli, i fonti, i boschi, i fior . . . con le lor armonie . . . cantino il nostro . . . amor"). Softly tugging at the vocal line, the singer lavishes the words with tender tremulations of vibrato; growing the saplings of "fonti" and "boschi" into burgeoning notes of emboldening hope.

Immediately—as always—the heroine changes her mind. She has a sole desire: "la pace dell'avel" ("the peace of the tomb"). Embarking on a quicker and more urgent repetition of the first line, "Tu che le vanità conoscesti del mondo," Maria spouts panicked crescendi in Elisabeth's cries. As she pleads for her tears to be brought to the throne of the Lord, she raises her curled hand abashedly. It travels to her face at the same pace as her diminuendo shrinks the note . . . alighting at her cheek with grace.

It was her greatest concert performance on film. November 1962's rendition suffered from the shakes of high notes. As Elisabeth implored the Lord to take her tears Maria's bangle slipped down from her wrist and tumbled to the stage floor with a thud.

It was a marvel nonetheless compared to a comedic "Habanera." This Maria performed with one hand on her hip and the exaggerative expressions of a kindergarten teacher reciting a story. Confusing the libretto yet again, she spawned nonsensical and almost made-up French.

The only partially ill-fated evening was a great improvement on the Hamburg concert given earlier that year. For this reason Maria left London pleased—urging Gorlinsky to pass on the following message to the team of the broadcast's producer, Bill Ward:

I would like you to thank them and tell them that I am most grateful and touched by all the respect and collaboration I have had from them—the gentleman also with the earphones on stage (the television man, not the Covent Garden—though they are all to be thanked, they were so nice.)

I would like also a special thanks to the girl who made me up. Apart from knowing her job well, she contributed in calming me down with her lovely manner, and the extra trouble she took with me. I don't know her name, but I wish them to know what a wonderful staff they have.[212]

Following a cruise on the *Christina* to Capri,[213] Maria found another reason for her vocal instability: a hernia located on a stomach muscle close to the location of her now removed appendix. Referring to it almost two years later, she would assert that it had "knocked me out so much I damaged the muscles of my abdomen, which naturally drained my strength and affected my singing apparatus to which the abdomen and diaphragm are as much a part as the vocal cords."[214]

Though the finding doesn't account fully for her stridency, it may explain why the soprano had experienced struggles with her breath control. A rendition of "Bel raggio lusinghier"—an aria from Rossini's *Semiramide*—was pillaged by poor respiration in a concert in June 1963. Performing *Oberon*'s long showpiece back in February 1962, Maria had raced clumsily to catch up with the maestro.

"The proper *breathing* . . . It's not as *easy* as one *thinks*; it had even made *me* mixed *up*," she would relate ten years later. "At a certain point of my life—'cause I had forgotten to *use* certain *muscles*. I'd forgotten to use the diaphragm. I had tried to, er . . . *exactly*, what you said—*place* the voice. I had placed it *perfectly—before. That's* how I got into trouble and I didn't use my muscles for a long time . . . I was not comfortable. I was not *comfortable*. I felt that, er . . . no matter *how* much for instance a critic could've . . . said beautiful things about me—*I* knew very well I *was* doing something that was not *right*."[215]

It's difficult to understand to what extent the hernia and the soprano's subsequent misuse of her felled voice contribute to its defects. Any "damage" to the stomach muscles was entirely speculative. So anxiously did the soprano want to strengthen them, her and Onassis' physiotherapist Korinna Spanidou would be astonished when she ordered: "Punch me in the stomach, as hard as you can!"

After the blow she wasn't satisfied—urging Spanidou to punch harder. "By doing breathing and diaphragm exercises she had made her stomach muscles unbelievably tough," the physiotherapist observed. "I was amazed! . . . The muscles of her stomach and abdomen were like steel."[216]

Maria underwent surgery for her hernia that 15 January 1963 at Columbus Clinic, Milan. Her surgeon, R. Felice Parravicini, notified reporters that she would be able to depart the hospital in four or five days.[217] Commissioning a bouquet of a dozen red roses to be brought to her daily, Onassis came every evening to visit. Maria spent hours singing into her tape recorder, desperately attempting to discern any difference in sound.[218]

Recovery took longer than expected—with Maria only being discharged eight days following the operation on the 23rd. "I would prefer to say nothing about it," she informed her correspondent at UPI. "The fact that such a small operation should provoke such a reaction really does amaze me. In the last twelve hours, the clinic has been flooded with telegrams from all parts of the world."[219]

It may have been a comfort for Maria to believe that with the regulation of her sinus problems and the hernia her voice would swiftly be restored to its defiant self. Examination of her records nonetheless exposes faults apparent back in August 1954. Since then they had grown incrementally prolific. Remedying novel ailments wouldn't guarantee their reparation.

After the surgery she was compelled to wait a few weeks before practicing again.[220]

Embraced by the support of many in the operatic sphere, Maria continued her correspondence with bass Giacomo Lauri Volpi. He was urging her to return to the Teatro dell'Opera in Rome. "My dear friend," she wrote on 25 January, "I don't have the physical strength to confront the arena of lions. Everyone promises me something, everyone gives me a lot of assurance—you, the Maestro [Serafin], critics, but I will never be able to forget that night at the Rome Opera and how much I suffered. Perhaps, if I were twenty or thirty years old, my attitude might be different . . . But I no longer feel I want to take risks, especially to take the risks of eventual new, cruel blows to the soul that nothing could really hope to heal."[221]

Still juggling offers, she considered the Chicago Opera the next day and wrote to Walter Cummings that she was in touch with Carol Fox again. Nothing ensued.[222]

After convalescing in Milan and Monte Carlo Maria spent most of that March aboard the yacht. There she followed a ritual she had recently launched: calling people late at night and conversing . . . for long periods of time. She would telephone to await news; telephone to tell a friend the color of a new hat; to describe a piece of furniture that she had seen in an antique shop; something that had happened on the street.[223] Anything to seek the most banal distraction. That St. Patrick's Day she was babbling with Dolores Rivellino, simultaneously eating Greek meatballs and drinking Ouzo. "When you feel passionate about something, anything, like how I feel about my music and the way it should be performed, don't settle for less . . ." and it would go on and on and on in anxious spillages.[224]

That April, as Onassis entertained Lee Radziwill—the sister of First Lady Jacqueline Kennedy—in Capri, Maria stayed aboard the yacht with laryngitis.[225] A week later she was back at her latest Parisian abode at the Ritz Hotel, preparing for Volume II of her French arias album. At her behest the management had furnished her apartment with three radios, a grand piano and a record player.[226] Television host Merv Griffin came to the hotel in the wee hours of the morning one night and immediately went to sleep. Two hours thence "an earthly wailing" roused him. Telephoning the reception desk to grouse, he was informed that Madame Callas was rehearsing in her suite—as she did every day.[227]

The recording of this other set of arias endured impediments. As Maria started to warm up, an engineer in the control room accidentally pressed the loudspeaker; she heard a burst of laughter. Imagining the worker had been laughing at her voice, she got upset and stormed out of the building.[228]

On a different day Maria spent three hours repeating the last dozen bars of the "Jewel Song" from *Faust*.[229]

Callas à Paris II is a selection that invites more mezzo arias to her register. In Marguerite's piece from *La damnation de Faust* by Berlioz, "D'amour l'ardente flamme," Maria taps into the smoothest and most velvety compartment of her cavernous contralto. A diminuendo strives to tender wistfulness to "Son départ, son absence . . ." ("His departure, his absence") but results in stridency.

Yet when she sings of "Sa marche que j'admire, son port si gracieux" ("The steps of his that I admire; his gracious carriage,") the notes swell with those lingering lean-ons ("MAR-*che*"), and a dwindling roulade on the "ci" of "gracieux". Languid accents on "l'ar-DEN-te flamme" and "a . . . mou-REU-se flamme" ("ardent flame" and "enamored flame") gleam with a gentleness not heard elsewhere amidst her repertoire.

In the "Air du miroir" (better known as the "Jewel Song") from Gounod's *Faust*, we hear sly diminuendi and exuberant self-adoration: "Comment . . . n'être-pas co-QUE-tte?" ("How could I *not* be a coquette?") asks Marguerite. For a moment it appears Maria recedes easily to her contriving "little girl", Fiorilla in *Il turco in Italia* mode; espousing smooth arpeggios that ascend in cleanliness.

Yet as Marguerite looks in the mirror she is vanquished by her singer's wobble.

Following a modestly successful concert in Berlin on 17 May, critic Werner Oehlmann wrote in *Der Tagesspiegel*: "What is Maria Callas, the artist, today? What is achievement, what is myth? The evening could not provide an answer to the questions. What is the magic that she exerts based on? Suffice it to say that it is still there; she is the mistress of the evening."[230]

The next day an announcement was made: Maria would be performing *Norma* at the Paris Opera in May 1964.[231] Stopped at Dusseldorf Airport en route to the following concert, Maria was pelted with questions: was she a mezzo now? Many of the arias of her recent compilations had been parts of the low-medium register. The *Chicago American*'s Roger Dettmer had scribed: "If she pursues this course her mezzo colleagues one and all will flee to the wings where Maria Callas stands ready."[232]

"Not at all, not at all," came Maria's response. "In fact, the only mezzo-soprano piece [in her concert tour] is not *originally* a mezzo-soprano piece because Eboli of *Don Carlos* is also sung in Italy *quite* frequently by *sopranos*. So you see, it's a *mistake*."[233]

Pride accounted largely for her blatant lack of interest in these roles: in her view, mezzos were inferior. Proposed *Carmen* under the baton of Sir Thomas Beecham in the late fifties, she had responded to Walter Legge: "I don't think my French is good enough yet and I won't take the risk of some damn fool critic saying that I've lost my top—which I haven't—and that now I'm only a mezzo."[234] Years later she would explain her school of thought to Chicago-based publicist Danny Newman: "What kind of a writer would you be if you could only type A, B, C, D, and E on your typewriter, and not F, G, H, I, J, K, and all the other letters of the alphabet?"[235] That—for Maria—defined the term "mezzo".

After concerts in Dusseldorf, Stuttgart and the Royal Festival Hall that were warmly received, Maria grew slightly in confidence: "I hope you liked the concert," she wrote to one fan in a note to thank him for her flowers. "I'm coming back don't you think?"[236]

Prior to her Paris concert on 5 June at the Théâtre des Champs-Élysées, Maria's blood pressure plummeted.[237] Terrified to go onstage, she surfaced in a long red dress of shantung[238] with a drooping a-skirt, her head topped with a beehive hairdo.

There was more abandon from her in this program; one work in particular suspended spectators mid-breath. "There should be a great presentiment of disaster in this aria . . . with colors of nostalgic memories . . ." was how Maria would describe it. "Her whole soul is poured into that one single name."[239]

Werther—the agonizing hero of Massenet's eponymous opera—is the young poet of Goethe's *The Sorrows of Young Werther*: a mourner in love with Charlotte, who has married his best friend.

The "Air des lettres" ("Werther, Werther . . . Qui m'aurait dit la place . . .") symbolizes opera's sinister persona: omens are everywhere. Cellos storm seditiously until the music embodies frenetic foreboding. Charlotte is reading Werther's letters; too aware of his forbidden love for her. It's Christmas. Outside snow is raining down and children squeal in mirth. Werther will eventually kill himself. Charlotte does not know this. Yet at this point her presentiment seems almost greater than her love.

In this recorded concert Charlotte treads into the aria in torment: a diminuendo lingers through "qui m'aurait dit la place . . . Que dans mon cœur il occupe aujourd'hui . . ." ("Who could have told me . . . the place he would occupy in my heart"). That softening of "aujourd'hui" carries portentous sympathy for him: Charlotte prognosticates his suicide from the beginning of this contemplative episode.

By the time she sings of her fatigue the weariness is palpable: a whisper is the texture around the word "*la* . . . sse" ("fatigues"). Spookiness seeps through its phantasmagorical nature. She reflects on herself slowly: "Et mon â . . . me est plei . . . ne de lui" ("And my soul . . . is full . . . of him"). The slow diminuendo forestalls her remorse. A transfixed state of love.

The pronouncement of "Ces lettres! . . . ces lettres!" ("These letters! . . . These letters!") is at first a cry of alarm—then another diffident diminuendo.

Even more engrossed is she in her reflection as she wonders, "Je les relis sans *ce* . . . sse" ("I re-read them incessantly") . . . "cesse" is delayed to impart her entrancement. She wants to destroy them. "Je ne puis!"—she can't. Mouse-like is Maria's little voice in Charlotte's shame.

Finally she chooses to surrender: "I'm writing to you from my little room," Charlotte explains. "Je vous écris . . . de ma pe-ti-te *cham* . . . bre." The diminuendo tapers off as naturally as petals of a daffodil receding to their tips. December's gray sky weighs down on her like a shroud: "pè . . . se sur moi . . . comme un lin-*ceul* . . ." Afflicted by her presage, she leans into that "ceul" with static terror. Hypnosis holds fast as Charlotte performs in exactly the same volume and timbre: "Et je suis seule . . . Seule . . . toujours seule . . ." ("And I'm alone . . . alone . . . always alone . . .").

She must snap out of it. "Ah! No one is near him!" ("Ah! Personne auprès de lui!") she exclaims in a forte, quickfire realization. She asks how she summoned the courage; the sorrowful one that demanded he leave her alone. It so provokes Charlotte to quake that her interpreter chops up her staggering   syllables—oddly   placing   the   quivering   accents: "Comment—m'est ve*nue*—ce triste cou-*rage*—d'ordonner cet e-*xil*—et cet iso-le . . . *ment?*"

Suddenly she is awakened to contemporary events: children's cries of joy are climbing to her window. She recalls how Werther caught her taking care of them. "Ils m'oublieront peut-être . . ." ("Perhaps they will forget me . . .") she sings eerily.

No, no—Werther will surely return: "Et quand vous reviendrez . . . mais doit-il revenir?" ("And when you return . . . but must he *return?!*"). His last letter chills and terrifies her: "Ce dernier billet me glace . . . et m'épou-*van*-te!" Maria splits the words "glace"—"chills" and "m'épouvante' "—"terrifies"—by the means of poetic caesura. The crescendo-strewn epiphany abruptly prompts the sections of the orchestra to collapse into split fragments.

Her voice is almost audacious—perhaps even ruthless as she challenges fate to respond. Charlotte demands to find out in a semi-strangled tone: "Tu m'as dit . . . à Noël . . . Et j'ai crié . . . jamais! On va bientôt connaître qui de nous . . . disait vrai." ("You told me you would come at Christmas . . . and I cried, 'Never!' Soon we shall learn which one of us . . . was telling the truth").

She slows down in thought. "Mais si je ne dois reparaître . . . au jour fixé . . . devant toi . . . ne m'accuse pas—pleure moi!" ("But if I don't reappear on the decided day . . . before you . . . don't curse me, weep for me!"). Her plea of Werther not to curse her is so rapid and vibrato-fueled, Charlotte seems hopelessly ashamed.

She mustn't cede to love's prevailing hazards. "Oh, Charlotte!" Embitteredly she reprimands herself. "Et tu frémiras!" ("You will tremble!"). The command is as brusque as a caw in its cry of crescendo. Charlotte repeats it more lengthily: "Tu fré-mi-*ras* . . ." but then coarsely abandons the phrase; scared of the imminent horror. And then—one final time—"Tu ... fré ... mi ... ras." The cavernous instrument echoes like footsteps in catacombs.

Paris' public was stunned. "As Pascal would have said—although he applied his reflection to higher matters—this is of another order," critic Marcel Schneider wrote.[240] "Nothing is more moving than this struggle of one of the greatest singers of all time against Nature, which seems to want to rob her of the voice it has given her."[241]

Not yet. Not on that night.

14.

"Like a signature"

Judging by her serial migrations, one of Maria's aphorisms may have been the title of an old Cole Porter song, "There's No Cure Like Travel". In June of 1963 that axiom stretched further by advancing to the permanent exchange of one home for another.

"It almost killed me to work as I did before my separation," she wrote to Walter Cummings on the 17th. "I'm leaving Milano. I've sold the house."[1] Most of her work was now being conducted in Paris and London in any case. "I thought I had a good offer and wanted to leave bad memories," Maria specified to Leonidas Lantzounis.[2]

As a symbol of her new life—and the new career that might go with it—Maria engaged in an auto-da-fé. "You told me," French music critic Bernard Gavoty reminded her during a 1964 interview, "that you once burned or threw out the dresses you'd worn ... your old theatre costumes?"—"Oh—yes. Because that's a past—that I didn't like; that is to say—it was the *birth* ... my birth artistically, and so, one's tastes change, the body changes; one changes artistically—the *base* of it all doesn't change, obviously—because whether you have black or brown eyes, that stays the same—but during fifteen, twenty years, evidently one's own art—if one is conscientious—*changes*."[3]

Accompanying this statement were more rumors of potential landmark projects: she had reconciled with San Francisco Opera's manager Kurt Adler; they were now considering the new work *Sappho* previously proposed to her in 1960. Its avant-garde modernity predictably repelled her.[4]

But she kept Adler leaping to her bait. Other plans went unfulfilled: from 26–28 June and 1–2 July Maria hoped to resume work on the suspended compilation album of bel canto arias she had begun back in November 1961. Her plan was to come to London and stay at the Savoy during the sessions.[5]

That never surfaced.

After a concert in Copenhagen on 9 June Maria's next confirmed engagement was as last announced: she would be returning to the opera house as Tosca at the start of 1964.[6] Following negotiations with the Royal Opera's David Webster, he emerged at a production meeting with Maria's signature in hand. Franco Zeffirelli would be staging *Rigoletto* in that period; he could undertake Maria's *Tosca* simultaneously.[7]

She also discussed plans with Gorlinsky for another American concert tour[8] and a second "Golden Hour" recital to take place that November.[9] Her escape from Italy was a more jagged flight than she expected. Struggles to select a permanent Parisian dwelling kept her in Milan for several weeks that summer. "Only I haven't found a home I like yet so maybe that's why I'm depressed," she wondered in writing to Leonidas Lantzounis.[10]

From there she answered a request made to her personally by the U.S. first lady, Jacqueline Kennedy.

I would love to sing for you at the State dinner in honor of the Emperor Haile Salassie [sic] of Ethiopia on October first, but I'm afraid I will be occupied at that period with recordings. Therefore, if you could submit to me some other dates, I will be more than happy to consider them.

As for the accompaniment wouldn't it be wonderful if we had Leonard Bernstein accompany me either on the piano or with a small orchestra and have him participate.[11]

But a recital at the White House never came to pass: the president was shot before it could.

Juggling her domestic affairs, a recalcitrant Meneghini—who was refusing still to sign any American divorce papers she extended to him[12]—and her largely self-managed career, Maria was struck with a novel offense. Having promised to record Verdi's *Requiem* with her a year earlier, Legge had adjourned the engagement after technical difficulties. That summer nonetheless he reinstated it—enlisting wife Elisabeth Schwarzkopf to perform the soprano part.

The affair could not go without comment. "The news of your doing the Messa di Requiem without even consulting me about it comes to me as quite a shock," Maria wrote to David Bicknell of EMI. "The only thing that consoles me and makes the hurt less is that my role in the Messa di Requiem has been given to a very dear friend of mine, Madame Schwarzkopf, whom I admire immensely. But this does not change the present situation."[13]

Nourishing her solacing proximity with Michel Glotz of Pathé Marconi, Maria saw her ties with EMI UK begin to curdle. It is believed that she abandoned the company immediately after the *Requiem* conflict—about which she didn't endeavor to hide her sore feelings. "If your wife can sing my repertoire then I can sing hers. I intend to record a recital of Mozart arias. Please recommend to me a good Mozart repetiteur," she allegedly told

Legge.[14] As late as November 1963, however, Gorlinsky was still writing to Legge to ask for an annual renewal of contract.[15]

It was only during 1964 and Legge's retirement from EMI[16] that she suspended her affiliation with it—bitter at him seemingly for the renunciation of his post. In later years she would resume their contact nonetheless.[17]

Toppled by exhaustion from her tumulus of troubles, Maria was like a post-operative patient who could scarcely come to. "I was very tired the end of June [1963] and had a light nervous breakdown. I overworked myself this winter and just collapsed at the end," she wrote to Leonidas Lantzounis a day after reviling EMI for her loss of the *Requiem*. "But, thank God, everything went well . . . I have a wonderful friendship with the person you know [Onassis], but I think I have gone through too much and started working too early in life not to feel tired and with no enthusiasm left for anything. Even my personal life. After the experience with my husband!"[18]

In early August Maria ventured from Nice to Athens, where she boarded the *Christina* for another vacation.[19] The previous year Onassis had purchased a private, five hundred-acre island he had named Skorpios,[20] to where the couple retreated for some of their cruises. Having surpassed the stage of blind infatuation, they began to catch repellent glimpses of each other's characters.

Attempting to defuse one of their many arguments, Maria would draw closer to a public place aboard the yacht where staff were easily in earshot. Onassis was unlikely to display the full force of his temper with the crew around. At times she vanished for a while and chose to hide on the *Christina*.[21] In instances like these she wrote notes to her butler in the vein of: "Ferruccio, I am sleeping below. Don't make a fuss. Jeddah [her next poodle] is with me."[22] Sometimes the offense would be so bad, Onassis would enlist the services of a bouzouki band to serenade his scorned inamorata outside her apartment. Parisian press caught sight of it.[23]

Now he was hosting a new, irksome passenger on the *Christina*. Lee Radziwill—the sister of Jacqueline Kennedy and wife of Prince Stanisław Albrecht Radziwiłł—was once again aboard. Unbeknownst to the soprano, Radziwill had over time become the casual mistress of Onassis. Shortly after she embarked that summer, Radziwill found out her prematurely born nephew, Patrick Kennedy, had died two days after his birth. Cutting her vacation short, she flew to Massachusetts to attend his funeral.[24]

On account of this Maria didn't right away catch wind of her experienced partner's infidelities. During the third week of August 1963 she stopped in London to discuss details of her upcoming U.S. tour with manager Gorlinsky.

"The only stipulation Madame Callas has made is that she does not want to open the tour in New York," he wrote to American impresario Frederick Schang. "She would prefer to do Philadelphia or Washington, or some similar location first, and do New York say as the third concert of the tour.

The reason for this makes sense—to have the first concert in New York involves a lot of nervous tension and publicity . . ."[25]

A few days later Maria was back on the *Christina*; as was Lee Radziwill. On an excursion to the Meteora monastery in Thessaly, the latter was denied admission for her inappropriate attire.[26]

Forty-eight hours had not passed when the small incident evolved into a story: "Onassis is in Love with Princess Radziwill" read one headline in Brazilian newspaper *Folha de São Paulo*.[27] And soon enough Maria couldn't overlook the obvious relationship. Soon she stumbled upon love notes that implied Onassis and the married woman shared a bond more intimate than friendship.[28]

"How can a man who really loves you at the same time have affairs with other women?" Maria asked her friend Stelios Galatopoulos many years later. "He couldn't possibly love them all. For some time it was only a suspicion, which I tried to dismiss, but evidently I could not and it was out of the question to accept it into my moral code in any circumstances." Oblivious to the culture of casual sex, Maria saw the faux pas as an outright betrayal.

Too private and old-fashioned to discuss the fling, she was eventually persuaded to reveal her fears and insecurities to Maggie van Zuylen. "Being the genuine person she was, [she] made it easier for me to open up," she confided to Galatopoulos. "Like a mother, sister, friend, she explained to me that there are men who find it impossible to be physically faithful to one woman, especially to their wives. Nearly always, a man like that genuinely loves his wife or the woman in his life. To his way of thinking these extra-marital affairs are no more than biological infidelities . . . A man does not, cannot change some of his ways."[29]

It was an outmoded theorem but one that somewhat eased her anxiousness. Eventually she would resent the Radziwill affair; describing disbelief in her nocturnal conversations with some friends.[30] For now it was easier to imagine Onassis was simply like other men. In spite of this Maria didn't get accustomed to his nature. "I could not then accept this," she continued to relate to Galatopoulos, "my reasoning being that I was neither French [a people who could tolerate this in her view] nor Ari's lawful wife; the role of the betrayed wife was not in my repertoire."[31]

And yet it was no dealbreaker. Why not? Maria was a prudish and in some ways puritanically moral woman. But she was also busy and in need of kinship and without a family. If compulsive male lechery was simply "biology," it was an error forgivable. And she herself was hardly irreproachable relationship material.

On one evening later related by both Maria and one of its witnesses, dinner guest Taki Theodoracopulos, the couple was dining with Maggie van Zuylen at Maxim's in Paris. Endearingly van Zuylen tossed a playful observation: "You lovebirds, I am sure you make love often." Maria winked at Onassis flirtatiously: "We never do."[32] For reasons difficult to comprehend he snapped. The magnate began yelling in Greek, "Με εσένα ποτέ, με άλλες πολύ." ("Me esena pote, me alles poly."): "With you, never, with others—a *lot.*"

The caustic bite devolved into a rant. Embarrassed for herself, Maria's horror doubled when she realized there were other people at the table who spoke Greek. She implored Onassis to stop but he only continued. To lessen her tension Greek native Taki Theodoracopulos left the table.[33]

She was at loss to understand her partner's rancor. When she explained the next day that her understatement had implied the contrary, he tossed off the excuse: "Right, and mine was a normal overstatement which also conveys, even more effectively than yours, the opposite meaning."[34]

The non-apology was charred with bitterness. A coy remark made at a restaurant could surely not have brought the popular Lothario humiliation. Maria's phrase "We never do" had likely hit a nerve she didn't know about.

It was a relationship of many imperfections.

She immersed herself in plans for the upcoming tour—dates ranging from 31 March to April 21st across Connecticut, Philadelphia, New York, Dallas, Chicago and Los Angeles; arranging the terms with Gorlinsky at her unwanted home in Milan.[35] No sooner had she soothed her sentiments after discovering the Radziwill affair than a brusque blow resounded: Onassis had invited Jacqueline Kennedy for a two-week cruise on the *Christina* that October.[36] For the duration of her stay his consort couldn't be aboard.[37]

Despite having no urge to join America's First Lady on the yacht, Maria saw this caveat as a denouncement and a sign of disrespect. Later she would admit to several people—including acquaintance Aileen Mehle—that his treatment of her as the "mistress" in these situations denigrated the soprano: "I never wanted to meet Jackie. Or see Jackie. Whenever she was going to be on the yacht, I was out of the picture. Whenever some grand person was going to be on the yacht, I was out of the picture," Maria bemoaned. "He never included me. That hurt me so terribly."[38]

It was a flaw familiar to his entourage: Onassis relished being encircled by revered and celebrated people. Whether among the royalty of Monte Carlo, French aristocrats, Manhattan socialites or British stockbrokers, he would assuage his self-loathing as a foreigner and self-made businessman among the quote-unquote "elite". It was not fashionable to be Greek—even a billionaire Greek—and he *needed* to be. "The thing to remember about Onassis is that he liked to collect fabulous people around him," a journalist who knew him once remembered. "But I think Maria finally belonged to herself and to no one else."[39]

Confronted after Onassis' death with the idea that he "always wanted to be seen in the company of famous people and beautiful women," Maria conceded, "This observation was partly true."[40]

Ultimately he had far more insecurities than did Maria. This cluster of complexes led Onassis to visit the White House and pay his respects to the first lady with Lee Radziwill after the assassination of John F. Kennedy that November.[41]

In the meantime Maria practiced and lamented times past. Switching between Paris and Monte Carlo, she was still looking for a new apartment when she called Leo Lerman on the night of 21 October. "Don't believe newspapers," came the command. "She's working hard—she will do the *Tosca* if everything is perfect," Lerman wrote in his diary. "Should she come to America for the concerts? She seems in good spirits, but she does get down. 'Twenty-six years . . . and they take away my confidence . . .' "[42]

The end of that month saw Maria "disposing, packing, storing and transferring the contents of something one has accumulated in a life time," as Gorlinsky wrote to Frederick Schang. "At the same time she has been unable to find a new suitable residence in Paris and, under the circumstances, she will take some temporary apartment in Paris until she has settled something definite. In view of all this you will appreciate that she is at the moment in no mood and I was unable to settle with her the details of locations for the American tour."[43]

Parting with Milan was no sweet sorrow. Still suffering bouts of nostalgia for her "Regina del Mondo" years at La Scala, she lamented to Georges Prêtre: "There was no opera house quite like it, [she said] and . . . when she came in from Via Filodrammatici she felt she was at home."[44]

As she elaborated to La Scala's *maestro sostituto* Antonio Tonini, nobody wanted her on its illustrious stage. "La Scala isn't offering me anything interesting. It is no longer the place for me! The people that sit up in the gods told me my middle register has a wobble—but it already had a wobble during the first *Norma* I did at La Scala. *Now*, they're telling me about it. So I'm going to try to 'reconstruct' myself because [Giulietta] Simionato, who is older than me, is still singing well. I have to leave and look for peace."[45]

The sold 40 Via Buonarroti would be totally demolished by its new owner—a real estate company—within several months.[46] A week later Maria was finally settled. Her new home was an apartment rented from her friend Countess Anna Andreoli-Brusadelli at 44 Avenue Foch,[47] not far from Onassis' lodgings at 88. Despite renting the abode and planning to spend just six months there,[48] she spent time buying "romantique Espagnol" antiques to decorate it.[49] The French lifestyle was much easier on her nerves: "I've been very well since I left Milan. Here they respect your peace and kiss (for now) the ground I tread," she wrote to Augusto Caldi Scalcini.[50]

Doing her best to pass as a Frenchwoman, Maria worked on her language.[51] Her pronunciation strived to sound authentic in its intonations and yet faltered sometimes with Italian "r"s.

Ahead of her Royal Opera *Tosca* and recordings to take place that December, Maria's fear rockily clambered: a gawky gorilla ascending a tree. She was quick to reply to a letter from her old friend Giulietta Simionato.

You can't know how much emotion your letter brought me.

I have so much affection for you, we spent so many hours together before I became La Callas, this Callas who is so extolled and thus unhappy on account of her responsibilities . . .

I'm going to act as you did: work—admittedly, not as you did. I'm not that strong; completely the opposite of what they say of me. I've never been strong enough to work the way you do. Maybe turning forty will make me stronger. What do you think? Should I have hope? My sinusitis . . . You remember Medea, *with its relentless hospital procedures? It shook me so much that it made me lose confidence in myself.*

I have remained physically vulnerable. I can't sustain battles in these conditions. They would be lost from the start. I ask that you not speak to anyone about this; it's a battle I must win without anyone knowing about it. I want to be as strong as I was ten years ago; I will do my best, and life continues.[52]

Less than two weeks after that she cancelled her long-pondered U.S. tour.[53] "Maria is returning to opera this season, singing TOSCA . . ." came Gorlinsky's new excuse, this time to Nicola Rescigno. "Consequently she needs all the time which is not booked for appearances for recordings, and so she feels that she would prefer to return to America and do some operas first, before doing a concert tour."[54] An official from the Athens Festival administration met with her to plan a *Tosca* for that year's event.[55] It never came to be.

It seemed her image as a miracle-maker had been growing more famous than Maria herself. That shadow of perfection in the press persuaded her that only the divine was good enough. "In fact, I could say that in this present phase of my life I am in the process of rediscovering myself, trying to disassociate myself from the spurious image of me which other people tried to impose," Maria had told Derek Prouse in April 1961.[56]

"We *need* idols," Bernard Gavoty would later alert her. "I'm frightened," would be her response. "You *destroy* them; these idols—very easily. Just as you *create* your idols, the moment that this poor idol is either sick, or else—deals with a very difficult episode in their life—the moment the idol needs help, he is . . . *ruined*. There you go."[57]

Yet these insufferable impositions, these exigent and implacable demands the "public" forced on her collided with the strenuous commands she blasted at *herself*. They weren't at odds.

Relaying her responsibility was a much simpler detour. Following her establishment of a scholarship fund to subsidize the studies and auditions of Greek singers abroad, in September 1963 Maria appointed her old friend Christos Lambrakis to manage it. "He is an excellent musician, I trust him and I am sure he will do things objectively," she wrote to Organizer of the Athens Festival, Kostas Bastias. On 30 November 1963 the scholarship committee announced the first round of auditions to take place that December. The program bankrolled singers' excursions and studies for years.[58]

At the same time she was roiled at Lawrence Kelly for his failure to propose a *Norma* for the Dallas Civic Opera's 1963-64 season: "I'm really sorry that you didn't have the courage to insist on my doing *Norma* this year," she wrote. "Remember, a great impresario like you . . . should always insist even if you receive ten thousand 'no's in response."[59]

*

That December Maria leant her voice to two compilations: one with arias by Rossini and Donizetti, the other, Mozart, Beethoven and Weber. Undertaking the tough feat she had erroneously executed in recital, "Nacqui all'affanno" from Rossini's *La Cenerentola* ("Cinderella"), she was at loss to refashion the role. It came out as a showpiece laden with extravagant coloratura; the use of her "little girl" molding considerably sparse. Switching from a growling chest voice on "baleno rapido" ("a quick flash") to a tender sweetness on "la sorte mia cangiò" ("my destiny changed"), she abruptly changed timbre.

It's one thing when the voice begins to undermine technique. It is another when it hinders artistry.

The most successful work recorded in this period was a standalone concert aria by Beethoven. Spanning fifteen minutes, "Ah! perfido" ("Ah! traitor") is a bombastically crescendo-fueled excoriation. With its unrestrained expulsions of blunt ire through "Ah—*perfido!* Spergiuro! Barbaro traditor—tu *parti?*" ("Ah, *traitor!* Liar! Barbarous betrayer—you're *leaving* me?"), the ragged nature of Maria's upper register becomes her.

Unforgiving is she in this aria. "E son questi gl'ultimi tu-oi . . . con-*ge*-di?!" ("And are these your last farewells?!") she demands to know, scathingly rushing "congedi" ("farewells"); mockingly emasculating her ex-lover.

Toward the quieter passage of the piece her heroine has an abrupt volte-face: "Per pietà, non dirmi addio!" ("I beg you, do not say goodbye to me!"). The wobble rears its ugly head again to fracture what could easily have been a smooth legato. While the changing rhythms illustrate the character's vast sentimental spectrum, erosion in the higher timbre stops this being the tour de force it could have been.

That didn't halt her manifest excitement. After her first day of recording Maria wrote exultedly to Giovanna Lomazzi—whom she likely hadn't seen in well over a year: "I've already done the *Guillaume Tell* aria very well and Beethoven's 'Ah Perfido!' extremely well . . . I have regained my former courage. It's obvious when I see that the voice is good and I let myself go like before."[60]

Her endeavors to embrace the Mozartian repertoire struck hurdles. Donna Anna's "Non mi dir . . . Or sai chi l'onore" from *Don Giovanni* is executed without regal potency; her efforts with *Così fan tutte* and *Le nozze di Figaro* are scarcely worth mentioning.

Maria knew that there were days she couldn't function vocally. "At those times she would just pick up her bag and say 'Ciao!' " EMI's Jacques Leiser would recall. "It was not a matter of temperament. We knew she couldn't perform, so we simply worked on some other section of the recording."[61]

These arias left Maria satisfied—for *now*. "I've recorded quite well the following," Maria wrote to Leo Lerman on 15 December, listing the pieces:

"The two Don Anna [*sic*] Arias—think—hope you'll like them. In any case the voice is quite healthy."[62]

The bolster to her confidence led her to field fresh offers from Chicago Lyric Opera and Dallas Civic Opera. Rumors began once again to abound.[63]

A few days later she was struggling in the studio to execute a high B flat: the end of "O Cielo! Dove son io," from Verdi's *Aroldo*. Journalist Suzy Patterson watched her repeatedly cracking the note, shrugging her shoulders, saying "I'm sorry" and grabbing the white phone beside her to call the technicians. By the end of the sessions a record that spanned forty minutes had taken around forty hours.[64]

Probably because her voice persistently reminded her that it was not in shape, Maria began trivially to contemplate a film career. "She doesn't want to be the female version of Mario Lanza," Sander Gorlinsky emphasized to press on 3 January 1964.[65] If Maria planned to be an actress she would be a *speaking* one.

Some days thence there came another caliber of rumor: Hollywood producer Dino De Laurentis wanted Maria for his film version of *The Bible* that would star John Huston and, potentially, Marlon Brando and Paul Newman.[66] She could play Sarah.

Possessing a peculiar relationship with actors and the spoken theatre, Maria had been offered musicals but almost suffered an aversion to them: "I do not like music with prose . . . I like—you know, the straight way: either *all* prose, or *all* singing."[67] Upon seeing Julie Andrews headline *My Fair Lady* in the West End, she had been astounded to discover that the genre's actors starred in eight performances a week. "How do you survive?" she had probed Andrews.[68]

When it came to movie stars she wasn't interested enough to scrutinize the art of acting. Asked who her favorite actors were, she cited Laurence Olivier (who had written her a laudatory letter[69] and massaged her ankle), and her good friend Greta Garbo. She loved the 1939 *Wuthering Heights* for its romantic quality.[70]

Being for the most part an instinctive actress, the singer took scant interest in the method actors of her time like Vivien Leigh or Marlon Brando but allegedly revered the art of thespian Paul Scofield.[71]

As Maria began preparations for her London *Tosca* Huston paid a visit to encourage her participation in the film. "Do you sing?" Maria asked him at dinner. "Only when I'm drunk," responded Huston.[72]

Gorlinsky later wrote to producer Walter Wanger: "He had a long talk with Madame Callas . . . they both seemed to like each other very much."[73]

Once again what seemed like a new venture was the victim of tremendous indecision. "I have been offered parts," Maria would admit in 1965. "There's only one thing: that I would have to study a lot the projection of the voice which is not like singing of course—it's completely different. The projection, the pronunciation, and then—I mean *completely* starting anew.

Well, I mean—why should I? Maybe risk everything for nothing whereas I'm quite pleased, even overwhelmed by what I have had."[74]

The next day her thoughts would be different.

Among the cinematic projects offered to Maria through the years were a screen adaptation of Edgar Allan Poe's *Extraordinary Tales* and several parts in movies by director Joseph Losey. One of these would grow into Elizabeth Taylor's starring vehicle in the 1968 movie *Boom!* based on Tennessee Williams' little-known play. Asked to play the damaged and brash woman at its core, Maria turned it down. "I preferred not to start off a film career with a difficult role, that of a woman of a certain age, who speaks in slang, who swears . . ." was her justification.[75]

One of the problems was Maria's ignorance. Her tastes in cinema were quite restricted; almost totally confined to comedies and westerns. "I like to watch tv, I like to watch pretty films . . . detective stories, westerns . . ." she would explain to Micheline Banzet in 1965. "Because it *relaxes* me, because the infantile side each person has—I don't *hide* mine. I have even remained very young, in that respect. Our profession is very serious. That kind of thing helps us. It's funny."[76]

Her entourage sprung forth with other propositions. When it came to popular songs the answer was simple: "I don't know any," she once told an accompanist.[77] Despite being familiar with several Greek folk songs, she refused to record a compilation of them "on account of her personal ethics," according to EMI's Michel Glotz.[78]

Maria's approach to her *Tosca*s resounded with ominous prophecies: "Janine," she alerted her vocal coach, extending complimentary tickets. "In our work, I know that I give you much pain. I hope that in London, I will be able to give you a little pleasure!"[79]

It was no longer enough to give a great *Tosca*: that had been Maria in the fifties—at her heyday's peak. This time—as with every role Maria studied—it would have to be a new and *different* Tosca.

Following an evolution into a more cerebral artist in the early sixties, the forty-something singer sought to harness her generic gestures. "Good tradition is a blessing as it brings to life subtly and convincingly what is often beneath the surface," she would explain. "Bad tradition, on the other hand, is a curse as it only treats music superficially achieving little more than exhibitionist effects. It is in the same way that irrelevant clichés can ruin a well-written story."[80]

Perhaps because her voice was growing noticeably tarnished, Maria was determined to beget multiple paradigms of any operatic personage. "There's always an elasticity about music and about art—I feel," she affirmed. "But of *course*—up to a certain limit . . . you cannot make two steps up front, one step behind—it'd be like a . . . robot. You *can't* do that—*then* it's not art. But *within this* . . . er . . . shall we say, 'square box', you can't move *out* of this 'square box' but in the meantime you can go *around*, in the *room*—but it has to be that particular *room* which means—square or round or *oval*—the capacity of a *composer* . . . I cannot do the same gesture the *same* way . . . it's like a signature. Two signatures cannot be alike."[81]

During one rehearsal of *Tosca* that January 1964 Maria's Tosca stabbed Scarpia so much in the moment, she failed to observe the retractable knife not receding but *stabbing* her co-star.[82]

Luckily the man in question was Maria's old friend Tito Gobbi: an artist who could rival her intensity onstage if ever one existed. "When I find another singer, or shall we say, actor, that really can *act* back, it's a *most* enjoyable experience because there's nothing more monotonous and stupid than repeating the *same* gesture over and over again, which is not natural from time to time, or from gesture to gesture," she would relate in allusion to him.[83]

"We would bow down to each other before every performance," Gobbi added.[84]

This *Tosca* saw Maria being once again entrepreneurial. She spent the breaks of her rehearsals serving opera in a score of other ways: instructing her colleague, young tenor Renato Cioni, where to breathe and how to perform certain sections;[85] discussing *Il trovatore* with assistant director John Copley and breaking up the cadenza of "D'amor sull'ali rosee" to show him its layout.[86]

Nevertheless the "little checking machines" persisted. Prior to rehearsals the soprano had scribed Carlo Felice Cillario a letter that warned of her plentiful difficulties. Cillario subsequently had his friends Fiorella Mariani and Pia Lindström—the niece of Roberto Rossellini and daughter of Ingrid Bergman respectively—record a rehearsal. Listening to it, Maria became luminous: "Yes, I was in voice. Not bad! I've never sung so well!" Despite the Royal Opera being against bootleg recordings, she insisted on keeping it—advising Cillario: "Tell them you offered it to me. They'll never have the courage to ask for it back."[87]

As she had done in the past with directors Visconti and Alexis Minotis, Maria surrendered a share of her scenic decisions to Franco Zeffirelli. He commanded her to run into the church with flowers Tosca had just picked and toss them in insouciance. She would fidget with a six-foot-long stole Zeffirelli had found in an Indian shop.[88]

Together they envisioned nineteenth-century opera singer Tosca as a flighty and theatrical, impulsive woman. It was not a character Maria liked but, "When I don't care for a role I try to do it even *better* because I *must* do my job!"[89]

Rehearsals were sacred. Visconti's teenage niece Cristina Gastel attended the last one on 18 January. She watched as Maria stood dangerously close to a candelabra; igniting her wig on its flame. Gobbi clapped his hands to snuff the fire.[90] Reluctant to disrupt the action, Maria merely whispered: "*Grazie, Tito.*"[91]

Opening night was another experience of torment. Maria clung to somebody—anybody who was present—with the full force of her anxious nails; digging into dresser Gertie Stelzel to leave bruises on her hand.[92]

"The first act of *Tosca* is quite ridiculous," haughtily she stated. "I mean, one phrase, she's angry, the next phrase, she's this way—changeable, very changeable. My logic does not accept that."[93] Yet this is what Maria scrupulously captured in this opening night performance. A recording shows us Tosca's browbeating of her beloved Mario: "Perché chiuso? A chi *parlavi?*" ("Why was the door closed? Who were you speaking to?") emerge as blatant accusations and exigencies. Maria's voice is coarse; unsympathetic.

Melting soon into a high-pitched, nervous register when Mario attempts to kiss her in the church before the Virgin Mary, she rebukes him, "Oh! Innanzi alla Madonna!" ("Not before the Madonna!"). Tosca is suddenly coy and coquettish. How can Mario *fear* this woman?

His terror is nonetheless just. Tosca doesn't know that Mario, a painter, is hiding the political prisoner Cesare Angelotti, brother of the Marquess d'Attavanti. Discovering his portrait of the latter, she demands that Mario recolor the blue eyes to make them dark like hers: "Sia treccia BIONDA o bruna" ("Whether she's a BLONDE or a brunette"). Maria's menacing crescendo on "BIONDA" hammers home Tosca's resentment of the blonde in the portrait; she is wildly possessive.

When Chief of Police Scarpia—who hungers both for Angelotti's blood and Tosca's body—finds a fan belonging to the marquess in the church where Mario paints, he can't help but flaunt it under Tosca's nose. A gullible idiot, she immediately falls for it: "Oh, mio bel nido insozzato di fango!" ("Oh, my beautiful lovenest is smeared with mud!") she exclaims stridently.

Critic Philip Hope-Wallace would write: "There was the uncanny suggestion of the ex-convent child in her acting and of her origins in her frenzy and desperation."[94] In this live recording it is easy to imagine an Italian matron at the market bellicosely bargaining.

Though the first act went well Maria approached Cillario during intermission to alert him she didn't feel she was in voice and was thinking of calling it off. He persuaded her otherwise.[95]

The second act is trickier. Following Mario's arrest he is being tortured to reveal Angelotti's location by Scarpia's men at his home, the Palazzo Farnese. Tosca arrives and tries to be sophisticated. Her hair is long, black, curly and bedraggled. In the televised recording of the opera's second act on 9 February, we watch Maria rush in with those gapingly suspicious, foolish-looking eyes. She's almost gawky.

Fumbling with that lengthy Indian stole (a bothersome accessory), Maria spends excessive time removing her long gloves. Scarpia interrogates her: when she last saw Mario, was he alone? He needs to know where Angelotti is. Tosca thinks only of her supposed rival, the marquess: "No, egli era *solo.*" ("No, he was *alone*"), she insists, nodding to herself to confirm it. When Scarpia asks again, the claim is almost bat-like: "*Solo, sì!*" she yells.

Here is Scarpia: sadistic tormentor. And yet in other circumstances Tosca's reprimands would almost seem comedic. Abruptly she jumps up: "The sneer of a *demon!*" she remarks to herself in an uneven rhythm: "So-*ghig*-no di *de*-mo-ne!" Tosca should be scared of lethal Scarpia. Instead—according both to the libretto and Maria's accurate interpretation—she's a woman yelling at the boss dismissing her. "So—in order to please you, one has to *lie?*" she asks upon entering the study of the chief of police ("Si dovrebbe ... mentir?"). Both orchestrally and vocally it is performed with patronizing slowness: Scarpia is a little boy who ate too many cookies.

Tosca lacks in self-awareness: her vulgarity and her stupidity are almost even. Raising her hand in this performance, Maria's Tosca points at Scarpia's torture chamber: the location of her lover's lashings. "Che avviene in quella stanza?" ("What's going on in that room?"). As if she doesn't know. It's a brash gesture; more akin to a bad actress than a woman fervently in love. Then again—Tosca is, as far as we can tell—a *bad* actress.

As though pointing out a happening unknown to Scarpia, she panics: "You're hurting him! You're killing him!" ("Lo strazi, lo uccidi!") she hurls out. "Più non posso! Ah! Che orror! Cessate il martir! È troppo soffrir!" ("I can't take it any longer! Ah! What horror! Stop the torture! It's too much to suffer!"). The "tir" of "martir" and the "ffrir" of "soffrir" emerge in symmetrical squeaks: Tosca's vulnerability now surfaces at last; perhaps she understands it's not an onstage game. She beats at Scarpia with her fists and throws her head back in unbridled fury. Gobbi exploits the moment to grab Tosca's wrists and wrench open her arms: in the bass' words, "literally crucifying her".[96]

She pleads with Mario: "Consenti ch'io parli?" ("Mario, let me speak ...."). By now she has discovered Angelotti's whereabouts. "As-COL-ta ... non posso più ... non posso più ...." ("Listen, I can't take this ... I can't *take* this ...."). Her pleading is ironic: Mario is being tortured; Tosca's begging *him*. Stressing that "col" of "As-*col*-ta" ("Listen"), Maria is a superlative prima donna: one in the gaudy and tawdry, Floria Tosca sense of the word.

"Che v'ho fatto in vita mia?" ("But what have I done to *you?*") she asks Scarpia with a dwindling instrument. "Torturate l'anima, sì, l'anima, mi torturate ...." ("You're torturing my soul, yes; my soul is what you're torturing ...."). But in those grave, bombastic sounds of "l'an" in "l'anima" and "ra" of "torturate," Tosca still appears unbroken. She is panicking—yes. Simultaneously she is indulging in her trade: the theatre.

When Tosca surrenders—she can't handle it anymore and fails to understand Mario's political cause—she divulges the prisoner's hideout. The victim grabs Scarpia to supplicate: "Nel pozzo—nel giardino" ("He's in the well—in the garden"). In real life someone in her situation—more or less, a hostage—would be loath to grab the arm of her tormentor to confess. Tosca hates Scarpia; experiencing bitter aversion to him. In classically hammy opera, almost every gesture is illogical: even Maria would submit to them from time to time.

But is this an artistic fluke—or simply Tosca's inbred actress ways?

The tortured, bleeding Mario is finally brought in. In one performance when the henchmen dragged him, one of them pushed Tosca down. Maria stumbled on a step and fell. After seeing that she wasn't injured, Gobbi neared her and his Scarpia stretched out a hand. Maria seized on the moment: her Tosca elected to "claw her way up" Gobbi's arm on the pleading word, "Salvatelo!"—"Save him!" to which Scarpia responds, "Io? Voi."—"I? You must." Gobbi recklessly released Maria's Tosca. She fell back aground.[97]

The opera star determines to be clever: she can bargain with Scarpia in exchange for her lover's lost liberty. "Quanto?" ("How much?"), she demands to know in a voice that is more yelled than sung; it's a parlando (spoken) phrase. Once again it appears Tosca's at a flea market rather than being held hostage. Scarpia informs her there's no price: he doesn't "sell himself to beautiful women." She scowls in displeasure—as if to ask, "What do you mean—there is no price?!"

Tosca needs to calm down before she can make a decision—and pray.

For all the drama of the second act, "Vissi d'arte" is Tosca's sole vulnerable moment. In one of the performances Maria internalized the beginning so much that she sang with her back to the audience.[98] "I lived for art, I lived for love" ("Vissi d'arte, vissi d'amore"), she sings with a tender diminuendo on the "d'amore". "Non feci mai male ad anima viva" ("I've never caused harm to a living soul") is sung with even greater diminuendo; pure shock at her circumstances. Yet thinking of the suffering she has endured ("Quante miserie connobi, aiutai!": "How many miseries I have known—help!"), Tosca slips into her hammy ways: a crescendo of flagrant self-pity.

When she recalls the goodwill she has exercised, "Sempre con fé sincera diedi fiori agli altar" ("Always, with sincere faith, I brought flowers to church altars"), Maria chooses a commonly used, vulgar "choking" sound as she begins "agli" ("to the"). In desperation she extends her arm. Both these gestures are well-known examples of poor operatic tradition. Again . . . is it Maria's flaw or Tosca's questionable taste?

There is no elegant gesture to finish the aria as there was in the Paris opera gala of 1958. Her earlier Tosca was more composed; almost demure. This one heeds to grandiose gesticulation. The somewhat lazy, self-important stereotype of the soprano diva is Maria's foe. Her Tosca is the woman the media wants her to be.

Grabbing Scarpia's arms, Tosca pleads: "Vedi . . . le man giunte io stendo a te . . . e" ("Look at me! I'm clasping my hands before you") in a voice made especially humble.

But it's not long before she's riled—repeating that phrase with a venomous vibrato and crisp, cutting consonants. Can Tosca actually be humble? In extreme circumstances, does the actress remember she's mortal?

Who knows.

Reflecting to herself, Tosca resolves to accept Scarpia's offer: he will issue a permit of passage for her and instruct his subordinates to let Mario go in a mock execution . . . if she gives him one night. Fine. But she continues to command him; she cannot *stand* it being the other way around. "Ma libero all'istante lo voglio" ("But I want him freed this *instant*.") she demands—again with Maria exigently accenting various syllables.

To brace herself for rape she wanders to the table to collect a glass of wine. Her eyes fall on a glistening blade. "[There is] a glint in the eye practically, that lets the audience know that she's seen the knife, and then, she doesn't pick up the knife until the very last minute," William Weaver would recall. Maria related that she and Zeffirelli had plotted the action together. "Everybody knows the banality of this scene—taking the knife, how do you do it without seeming too hammy, as they say, and all that—so it's the first thing that comes into your mind to discuss. And this really was his idea, a very good idea of er, just *looking* with a stare and using it at the last minute."[99]

Her hand is on her midriff. With the orchestra underpinning the moment with slow, eerie strings, Tosca casts her eyes down and thinks. And thinks.

Scarpia is about to seize her; Tosca seizes the knife—"Questo è il bacio di *Tosca!*" ("Here is Tosca's *kiss!*")—and stabs him with urgency—again with theatrical flair. Terrified by her action, she drops it.

In the recording from the opening night her voice grates as the murderess demands to know: "Ti *soffoca* il sangue?!" ("Is your own blood *choking* you?!"). She almost relishes her mockery of Scarpia with the sadistic observation, "E ucciso da una donna!" ("and killed by a *woman!*"), belittling him in a contemptuous voice. She orders him to look at her as he expires: "Guardami! Son *Tosca!* O SCARPIA!" ("Look at me—I'm *Tosca*, O SCARPIA!"). Denigratingly Maria stresses their respective statuses: he—the great Scarpia, Chief of Police—is being killed by a locally famous soprano. Look at him *now*—and look where *she* is now; about to run off with his permit to leave town.

"Muori dannato! Muori! Muori! Muori!" ("Die cursed! Die! Die! Die!"). The ponderous commands expire in Maria's dying breath; emerging like an invocation of the gods. With Scarpia dead she considers, "E avvanti a *lui* . . . tremava . . . TUTTA *Roma* . . ." ("And before *him* . . . trembled . . . ALL of Rome . . ."): the slow, fearful realization of what she has done.

Frantically she rummages through his pockets for the safe-conduct—jerking away upon finding it. Now that he's a corpse, she fears him; when he was alive, she didn't. The Catholic Tosca understands she must be reverent toward the dead. Taking the candles on the table, she sets one beside each flank of Scarpia. Each of Maria's hands slides on the floor as they take turns to set the tapers. Psychologically it is uncalled for. Stagewise it's delicious.

In the third act Mario awaits his execution. Sure that Scarpia's directive would ensure a "mock" one, Tosca fails to understand what lies in store for her beloved—rejoicing as she teaches Mario to fake his death: "Simulato supplizio. Al colpo, cadi" ("You pretend to beg. Then, once the shot is fired—fall"), she instructs him in a high-pitched, almost cutesy voice. As she watches Mario be killed under the false impression he is merely—just like her—a good performer, Tosca smugly comments: "È una commedia, lo so" ("It's a performance, I know").

Then Tosca discovers that Mario's death wasn't faked. Realizing she's the target of a manhunt by the despot's henchmen, she immediately runs to stand atop a roof. The singer hasn't finished acting: "O Scarpia, avanti a Dio!" ("O Scarpia—I shall see you before God!") she yells before her suicidal jump. The scream emerges resolute: in part a promise, in part cursing God. Even in death, Tosca must have the last word. She's an *actress*.

"No matter *how* much and how *well* you've sung in the very few one or two or three or four first acts, if the last act is *not* superior to all the rest, well—you might as well *not* sing it," was Maria's stage policy—one that must have extended to Tosca's worldview. "We *have* sung, frequently, roles that do not have the *best* last act but I *essentially* choose an opera where at the end, the *last* impression is the best."[100]

Too exhausted was Maria to socialize after that opening night. Leaving Zeffirelli and Renato Cioni to dine at a restaurant, she later invited them up to her suite.[101]

"There will be every Oscar for the new *Tosca*," touted *The Guardian* the next day.[102] Another critic, David Cairns, summed it up thus: "There will always be a tendency to flawed tone and excessive vibrato on sustained high notes ... but she, and we, will surely now take it in the stride of her tremendous and total mastery of every other aspect of the opera singer's art . . . she can still ride the pit and dominate."[103]

Gobbi's phone kept ringing. On the eve of every other *Tosca* she would call to say she couldn't sing—her voice was AWOL or she had to change her acting. A long time would be spent consoling her until he finally conceded: "All right. You don't sing. It is enough for you to appear. You just act and I'll do the singing."[104]

There was no question: Maria *would* sing, Maria sang all the planned *Tosca*s and *Norma* in Paris was not far ahead.

After their run she wrote to dear friend Eugenio Gara: "I've worked a lot to remove the faults that remained after having to sing with sinusitis. I told you before that I hadn't had my last word yet. But I meant as a soprano. I am and I always will be a soprano and I'm stubborn . . . I think you underestimated me."[105]

A month later she was still pleased with her work—a great improvement over her most recent studio efforts: "Admirers of London made a tape from the Broadcast of Tosca in London—so I finally heard it with my own ears!" she wrote to Harold Rosenthal. "I loved it and damn it I'm difficult to please, you know-!"[106]

At around that time her godfather Leonidas Lantzounis wrote to inform her that George had just married his longtime companion, Alexandra Papajohn. Owing to conflicts that Maria had experienced with the woman, she could not conceal her feelings of betrayal at George's failure to report it to her.

At the same time he was critically ill and awaiting treatment in hospital.[107] "My father gave my address to the Lenox Hospital and consequently I received the bill," she explained to Lantzounis. "I authorize you to take over on my behalf this situation as if I was there."

It seemed that George's indiscretion had encouraged his bride's family the Papajohns to write to and solicit money from Maria. They had also told her sister he was dying "in an awful hospital".[108] "Tell my father not to give my address to people . . ." Maria wrote. "Moneywise let me know and I will send you directly the money . . . Tell him to tell <u>you personally</u> anything he needs for if I receive other letters my maid has orders to hide them from me. Before my opening [*Norma*] I must not have worries of any sort and usually even the theatre does not give me telegrams."[109]

The relationship between her and George had been sorely precarious. Though not much is known about him as a father, his insouciance is easily believable when one considers that he didn't know the date of either daughter's birthday.[110]

In February 1957 George had written to Maria complaining: "It's been 50 days and I still haven't heard any news from you, not even a few words to know how you've been. You can't find any excuse that you are busy all the time because it wouldn't take more than five minutes to write me something . . . I read in the papers, the Greek papers, that you've signed up for the Festival, the Athens Festival from the 1 to 5 August, and that made me really upset, because if you do that you will regret it I'm afraid, because of that crazy woman [Evangelia]—who will create troubles and even harm you."[111] Perhaps George's attempt to interfere with her career had vexed her.

Now there was also Maria's mistrust of the Papajohns.

"If my father was crazy enough to remarry—sick, old and dependable on me without having the decision of informing me—all he has to do is keep on that way. And not bother me any more," she bemoaned to Lantzounis. "My duty is to do what he really needs and from there on I want no more relationship."[112]

Eight days later she elaborated: "I still cannot digest my father's immense egoism and stupidity. Anyway I hope he's better but I would like to know exactly what he has . . . If he is very bad off let me know by cable or telephone. And if he is at the end one day. Take care that he dies well taken care of because of course if he dies in bad hands or things like that I alone will be blamed . . . I'm sending you from now on $200 also [a month] for him. But remember I'm not maintaining any wife."

Aligning George's longtime monetary exploitation of her with the unashamed venality of Evangelia, Maria felt deceived. "I'm very dissapointed [*sic*] in him. Maybe worse than my mother," she wrote.[113] Despite receiving regular funds from her, when George recovered "he came <u>storming</u> to many friends in Athens saying he <u>demands</u> to see me—he has no money, etc." Maria told. Silently she took care of this by employing an intermediary to send him two hundred more dollars.[114]

Evading the dolorous subject, Maria never saw George again. Simultaneously she managed to discover a new father figure in the form of Onassis' old friend, London-based shipowner Panaghis Vergottis.

The latter had advised her to invest some of her money in a vessel; convincing her to purchase twenty-five shares of the *Artemision* for sixty thousand pounds. During her *Tosca*s in March 1964 he, Maria and Onassis had assembled at a restaurant to toast the acquisition.[115]

Speaking later of their kinship, she would state: "I had great joy in considering him as more than my father, because I never had a father or mother virtually. I was very happy with that. He knew it. He considered me as a great joy in his late years. He was pleased to travel around and participate in my glory."[116]

*

Engrossed in work that April, Maria recorded another selection of Verdi arias. *Aïda*'s "Ritorna Vincitor" was an accidental addition. "She was nervous, everybody was nervous," conductor Nicola Rescigno recalled. "So [Michel] Glotz called a break to calm us down. During the break, he played a tape of "Ritorna vincitor" which had been recorded for EMI the day before by Régine Crespin. Maria became highly indignant. 'This is not Verdi or *Aïda*,' she said. 'I remember when I prepared this with Maestro Serafin he wanted such agitation that I could hardly get the words in; this is like a funeral march.' Turning to Glotz she said, 'Are the parts still here?' He answered 'Yes,' and she said, 'Come on, Nicola, let's sing it!' " It took a single take.[117]

An Ethiopian princess in Ancient Egypt, Aïda surrenders both her homeland and her father Amonasro's love to perish with Radamès: leader of the Egyptian army: Ethiopia's foe.

"Ritorna vincitor" sees the doomed woman struggling to decide whose side to take: her father's or that of her lover. By this time the Egyptians have seized her and made her their hostage. She commands "Ritorna vincitor!" ("Come back victorious!") in a blackened voice of scorching rage. Ignited with ire, Aïda summons her people to conquer their nemesis. The music quickens while the voice takes flight in a belligerent crescendo: the Ethiopians must win in order to restore to her "Una patria, una reggia, e il nome illustre che qui celar m'è forza!" ("A homeland, a kingdom, and the illustrious name that I'm here forced to hide"). Maria chops the trio up to render a tricolon of directives as though Aïda is a *queen* and not a princess; as though she is commanding troops.

Swiftly she changes her mind. It is Radamès who must return felicitous; her father must be captured in chains.

The music softens. Aïda suddenly addresses her internal schism: "Sventurata . . . che *dissi?!*" ("Oh, how miserable am I . . . what did I *say?!*"):

the diminuendo of realization. Across the aria Maria highlights the contrast between Aïda's father and her injurious lover, emphasizing the gap as she cites, "I sacri nomi di padre—e d'amante" ("The sacred names of my father—and of my lover"). Each of these arouses fright. Her only choice? The usual one: "E nell'ansia crudel vorrei . . . *morir*" ("And in this cruel anxiety I want . . . to *die*"). Accumulating speed, Maria pursues Aïda's desire to perish, accenting the "rir" of "morir" ("to die").

In June 1964 she and Aïda would cross paths again—this time for a proposed album of duets with tenor Franco Corelli. Though Corelli had agreed to record with Maria's beloved conductor Georges Prêtre, he harbored ill will against him for having enlisted Nicolai Gedda to sing Don José in her recording of *Carmen*.

Thus when the sessions finally began Corelli wasn't in the best of moods. As Michel Glotz instructed the recording crew to switch on their machines, an insecure Maria only "marked" her part while her bold colleague sang in full voice. The duet "Pur ti riveggo"—in which Aïda resents Radamès for having married Princess Amneris, the Egyptian who's holding her hostage, and tries to persuade him to flee with her—unwinds a vulnerable woman. Maria's timbre is more cunning than the lioness she spawned before.

After tensions rose between Corelli and Prêtre the former stormed out of the studio.[118] Maria forbade the release of the recording—which was released posthumously—but eventually reconciled with Corelli.[119]

Glimpses of what could have happened if Maria had sustained her interest in the role are laid bare in the studio recording made in 1955. Aïda is not barbarous to her captor Amneris. Rather than treating her like an inferior rival and the enemy's daughter, she extends a reverent supplication: "Pietà ti prenda del mio dolore . . . È vero . . . io l'amo . . . d'immenso amor" ("May you have mercy on my pain . . . It's true that I love him . . . with a great love"). Maria's Aïda is almost reserved in her plea. She tries to praise Amneris with the phrase, "Tu sei felice—tu sei *possente*" ("You are happy— you are *powerful*"), accentuating the "ssen" of "possente" ("powerful") with a palpitant force. When she sings of her own circumstances, "Io vivo solo . . . per questo . . . amor" ("I live only . . . for this love"), her voice is deliberately shorn of vibrato. So enfeebled is she by her feelings that she doesn't have the strength to fight them anymore.

Her resignation to the notion that she'll never again see her homeland has a solacing, nostalgic odor to it: dog-eared, yellowed pages of book. Simultaneously she marvels at the beauty of the Nile, in whose dark eddies she might find at last oblivion in her tomb ("Del Nilo i cupi vortici mi daran tomba, e pace forse, e oblio") before expressing wonder at the valleys where she used to wander as a girl ("O fresche valli . . . o queto asil beato"). It comes out in a voice so tiny she sounds prepubescent; channeling the child she recollects.

Parting with her homeland, Aïda is urgent. She rises in a steady but resolved crescendo in the final "O patria mia, o patria MI . . . a . . ." before swooping to sobriety: "Non più ti rivedrò" ("I shall never again see you"). The final syllable of "drò" extends into a languorously rising, long arpeggio. We hear fragility and delicateness. We also hear sagacity and prescience: young Aïda understands the measures she must take.

Expiring together with Radamès, Aïda is complacent. In the duet "O terra addio," which describes how their "wandering souls fly to the light of eternal day" ("l'alme erranti . . . volano al raggio dell eterno . . . dì"), Maria lines her voice with light diminuendo lilts of hope to boost her dying lover's lost morale.

30 April brought with it a cue for supplementary panic: the start of rehearsals for Maria's Parisian series of Normas.[120] Having never performed a full opera at Paris' Opéra Garnier, her fear was irreparably frantic. "I'm studying a lot—as if I were a student at the conservatoire!" she wrote to Augusto Caldi Scalcini on 1 May.[121] With her vocal difficulties mounting, the production's director Franco Zeffirelli urged her to bring the entire score down a tone. She refused.[122]

Prêtre offered another alternative: Maria was in conflict with a strenuous cadenza he could change; spectators would be none the wiser. Yes—but *she* would. The cadenza stayed.[123]

"I like challenge," Maria would reflect in 1968. "And after twenty years, more or less, of *Norma*—it certainly *still* is a challenge."[124]

Riots broke out at the first night on 22 May—inciting newspaper reporters to keep score of pro- and anti-Callas factions' (literal and figurative) throws and punches. Critic Harold Schonberg cited the soprano's fluctuating force; referring to an aced high C but unreliability above a G.[125]

Many were blissfully blind to her faults. French writer Georges Conchon composed a "Lettre d'amour à Maria Callas," a "Love Letter to Maria Callas" which he published in the newspaper *Arts*: "Madame . . . I am nothing but a melomane . . ." it began. "If you danced, you would be Dance. A tragedienne, you would be Duse. But in everything and for everything, you are La Callas! When the performance ended, I wandered around the Opéra for a long time . . . I wanted to hear people who love you speak of you."[126]

Having declared a year previously that 1964 would reveal whether Callas could weather her technical problems, Jacques Bourgeois ventured to claim: "La Callas has conquered Nature! The voice has returned. Fuller, rounder, more stable than it has been all these years . . . The famous prayer *Casta diva* . . . began with a pianissimo of air-like purity in a climate of ceremonious ecstasy."[127]

On the reverse side of the coin was Andrew Porter of *Musical Times*: "True the ugly notes were uglier than before. But there was also a new sort of vocal ease and happiness in the performance, as if Callas had accepted the fact that some parts would never come right."[128]

It wasn't that Maria's voice had been restored. She had merely managed to convince herself of an improvement—or would do so intermittently. In moments such as these the panic plaguing her performances could loose its clasp.

On the performance of 6 June she cracked the high C of "Sangue romano". "A brawl broke out," wrote Parisian journalist Sylvie de Nussac. "We saw the most elegant ladies and gentlemen in tuxedos rise up against each other in a manner unheard of anywhere but at a fish market . . . 'This is shameful!' yelled one gentleman, his fist pointing at Callas. 'It's shameful that you're here!' his neighbor responded. Box 38 was threatening Box 37: 'You know nothing about singing. What are you doing here?'—'I love opera! I'm here all year round!' "[129]

While a great deal of this journalism may be ornamental, members of the press were hard-pressed to restrain their zeal. "Yves Saint Laurent dealt his neighbor a smart kick in the shins," *Time* magazine claimed quite dubitably—adding that Onassis and Princess Grace "fled" for the exit.[130]

The show must go on.

Six days later Maria received old friends Ida and Louise Cook at her apartment on Avenue Foch. Together with fifteen "near strangers from Britain who have come over to hear her at every possible concert," Maria had cherry cake.[131]

Her solace was these visions of ubiquitous rose-tinted spectacles. Maria's own were jarringly transparent.

15.

"Consciously watching"

For too many years now Maria's excuses for dodging her genre's most popular work—Bizet's *Carmen*—had bordered on petty. Walking back to her hotel one snowy New York night in 1956, she had met Leo Lerman's suggestion by lifting her skirt: "Look at these legs! Are they legs for Carmen?"[1]

Then there was her fear of being labeled a mezzo. Even after finishing the studio recording, she wished to clarify to music critic Paul Hume that she "will not sing the part on any stage."[2]

In June 1964 "she threw herself into the work . . . the tiniest details of Mérimée's [novel] *Carmen*, the story of the Carmens who had sung the work before, the musical aspects, the pronunciation of the French language, the dramatic intention . . ." Michel Glotz reflected. While other guests on the *Christina* went swimming in Corfu[3] Maria toiled at the Steinway with Maestro Georges Prêtre. "It was a wonderful period," he recalled. "I also have very pleasant memories of Onassis . . . He was charming and affectionate with Maria as well. She was like a young girl at that time, always smiling, ready to joke around, always moving about, so much so that she aroused concern. Onassis never stopped warning her, 'Watch out, if you're not careful you'll fall overboard!' It was all care and attention. But when we started studying, all of a sudden she switched into the artist that she was: serious, intelligent, focused."[4]

If there was any opera in the world on which Maria *didn't* want to focus it was *Carmen*. "Carmen is one of the greatest characters in the world," Visconti would proclaim in her presence on the French television program *L'invité du dimanche*.

"Oh . . . *Pfw*." Maria replied.[5]

She even complained to Janine Reiss that it was "scandalous," the way the early nineteenth-century Spanish cigarette girl used her men.[6] "It doesn't really *interest* me, it's against my principles," was how she summarized it to

Lord Harewood. "A woman *should* be completely *for* one person or . . . nothing at *all* . . . she [Carmen] *takes* things, she takes *men*, rather more like a *man* would *feel* about a woman. Don't you think?"[7]

In earlier recordings of the "Habanera" Maria had relied on the vixen's comedic side—later insisting to accompanist Robert Sutherland that "Carmen's not just a *femme fatale* as they all sing her. If you look back to the book you'll see she also has humor."[8] That approach had startlingly detracted from the layers that she *should* have granted her: sedition and sagacity and stealth and sexuality. All of which would be amiss till this recording.

Maria never understood Carmen profoundly. Rather than citing the ominous way in which Bizet's ebullient and sensuous music depicts the seductress' danger, she looked for its defects. "The voice, first of all, I find too *dark* for a Spaniard; for a gypsy . . ." the soprano insisted. "They're *usually* rather . . . er . . . you know, very *intense* and very *nervous*. Have you ever heard Spaniards talk? It's quite a . . . *nervous* voice; a high-pitched voice. They talk very quickly. It's *extraordinary* but—*also* I could see it more in a *film* than on*stage*. Because er . . . *Carmen* is very *virile*—to *my* impression."

Nonetheless she gauged one crucial point: Carmen's first sight of Don José ought to involve "the *least* movement possible. 'Cause I think it's more an *animal* when it sees its prey. She wouldn't *move* because it's the sort of intensity . . . hypnotism, or rather intense *feeling* between Don José and Carmen. She knows exactly that he feels *exactly* what he feels about her, and she doesn't even *care* so long as *she* feels what she feels about *him*."[9]

The *Carmen* recording—which was so hyped that Paris was plastered with posters declaring "CALLAS est CARMEN"[10]—is for the most part successful. Catching Don José for the first time, Carmen asks, "Quand je vous aimerai?" ("When will I love you?"), teasing the man with "Peut-*être* jamais . . . Peut-*être* . . . demain. Mais pas aujourd'hui—c'est *certain*." ("Maybe never . . . Maybe . . . tomorrow. But not today—that's for *sure*"). Maria's contralto melts languorously into diminuendi along the contrasting "ja . . . *mais*" ("never") and "de . . . *main*" ("tomorrow"). Her insistence that the sorcery won't happen today ("Pas aujourd'hui") is tossed off dismissively: she has lost interest and shifted her focus elsewhere.

A crowd has gathered in Seville. Carmen is a gypsy; a natural performer. She must tell them about love with her rendition of the Habanera. "L'amour est un oiseau *rebelle*": a brusque accent strikes the "belle" of "rebelle". What is this thing called love? A flighty bird, apparently. Nothing but a flighty bird.

Explaining love's mercurial ways, Maria relies on enjambment—leading one line to the next without stopping for breath: "s'il lui convient de refuser . . . ER—*rien* n'y fait, menace ou prière . . ." ("No point calling on love if it doesn't feel like it; threats and prayers are useless"). Continuing to use the same device along the other phrases, she endows the aria with a circus-like and showpiece feel. Perhaps Maria overestimates her anti-heroine's humor—*again*.

Thankfully we come to the subject at hand—Don José: "Il n'a rien dit . . . mais il me *plaît*" ("He hasn't said anything . . . but I *like* him"). Maria's Carmen sings in a dark, almost threatening tone; daring the man to approach her.

The first time Carmen openly addresses Don José—in speech, not song—she asks, "Eh! compère, que fais-tu là?" ("Hey, comrade—whatcha doing there?")—"I'm making a chain to fix my priming-pin," is his response. "Ton *épinglette?*" ("Your *priming-pin?*") comes Carmen's swift denunciation. "Épinglier de mon *âme!*" ("Pin-maker of my *heart!*"). The phrase emerges with the mocking chortle of a bully.

Following her conflict with a fellow cigarette girl, Don José drags her away to imprison her. Carmen is certain his love will release her: "Tu feras tout ce que je veux . . . et cela parce que tu *m'aimes!*" Maria leans on the "m'aimes" of "tu m'aimes" ("you love me") in a way almost patronizing. Carmen must imagine Don José's Achilles' heel is his desire for her; an emasculating flaw. Knowing full well that he'll give in before nightfall, she makes fun of it: a fearless misandrist.

Enchained, Carmen uses her feminine wiles as a tactic—alluring Don José with a song about visiting the bar of her friend Lillas Pastia to drink manzanilla and dance: "Près des remparts de Séville, chez mon ami Lillas Pastia . . . j'irai danser la Séguedille et boire du manzanilla . . ." Unexpected words are lent emphasis: the sly diminuendo of "nil" of "manzanilla", a Spanish wine; the racy execution of Carmen's determination to dance "la Séguedille". Through subtle applications of faint pressure on the syllables, Carmen can seduce Don José without touching or pillow talk.

It's not enough. She must become more intimate than that. "Donc, pour me tenir compagne—j'emmenèrai mon amoureux!" ("So, to keep myself company [at Lillas Pastia's], I'll bring my lover!") she hints, charging "com-PA-gne" with a crafty, excited crescendo. But no: "Mon amoureux? Il est au *diable*—je l'ai mis à la porte hier!" ("My lover? He's with the devil—I threw him out yesterday!"), the demoness boasts with a laugh of dominion.

"Who wants to love me?" she clamors to know—even offering brazenly: "Qui veut mon â-*âme*—elle est à *prendre*" ("Who wants my soul? It's *available*"). Carmen is impatient. She will never appear vulnerable before Don José or anyone else. As she launches into "Je n'ai guère le temps d'*attendre*—car avec mon nouvel amant . . ." ("I hardly have the time to *wait* because . . . with my new lover . . ."). Maria splits the syllables distinctly: "a-TTEN-dre—car a-*vec* mon nou-*vel* a-*mant*." They emerge in an iambic but robotic verse: Carmen is fed up.

When Carmen must at last confess, "Je pense à certain officier . . . je pense à certain officier . . . qui *m'aime*—et qui à mon *tour*, oui—à mon to-ur . . . je pourrais bien . . . *aimer*." ("I'm thinking of a certain officer . . . who loves me and who—in turn—yes, in *turn* . . . I may just *love*"), there is a seductive rallentando on "aimer". We can envisage Carmen slyly inching toward Don José.

She knows well how to amuse herself. During Act II's Gypsy Song ("Les tringles des sistres tintaient") Maria's Carmen leads and then indulges in a frenzied choreography. Her emphasis on certain syllables—such as the "llique" of "métallique" ("metallic") when she sings of the sistrums' rods that jangle with "metallic bursts"—make her soprano effervescent. When in another stanza she refers to the song's rhythms in "ar-DEN-tes, fo-LLES, en-fiev-RÉES" ("burning, crazy, febrile"), the tricolon is compulsive and accumulative; granting Carmen greater power in her gypsy clan.

Discovering her imminent death in the third act, the woman is stoic. Before her friends Mercédès and Frasquita she must constantly assert her potency. At her side they have beheld the verdict of her fate. Panic rises in crescendo as she reads the cautionary cards, "Carreau . . . pique . . . la mort!" ("Diamond . . . spade . . . death!") and yet she simultaneously sustains her strength.

Carmen's reaction is to praise the cards: "Les cartes sont sincères . . . et ne mentiront pas . . ." ("The cards are genuine . . . they will not lie . . .") warily she sings. Death-bound Carmen seems instead to warn her fellow cigarette girls of their unpredicted perishments. When she arrives at the end of the aria and turns the cards up again: "Encor! Encor! Toujours . . . la mort!" ("Again! Again—always . . . Death!"), Maria's booming chest voice strives to stress unebbing might.

After her attraction shifts to Escamillo the bullfighter, Don José comes equipped with an ultimatum: she can choose him or choose death. Carmen is frustrated; bored. "C'est toi!" ("It's you!") she chides in her exasperation; the accent on "toi" brutally belittling. "L'on m'avait même dit de craindre pour ma vi-e . . ." ("They even told me to fear death at your hands"), she explains—her voice lined with propulsive vibrato: mock-terror. "Mais je suis brave et n'ai pas voulu fuir." ("But I am courageous—and refused to run away"). The diminuendo on "n'ai pas voulu fuir" ("refused to run away") is so derisive it is manifestly hinting at what Don José's reaction would have been to such a threat.

He demands a declaration of love. "Tu demandes l'impossible—Carmen jamais n'a menti," ("You ask for the impossible; Carmen has never lied"). Maria's chest voice stamps its prints on the stressed syllables: "si" of "impossible"; "ja" of "jamais" ("never"); "men" of "menti" ("lied"). Again her emphases suggest belittlement: to let the small boy understand her words she must pronounce the syllables with clarity.

The ones that finally provoke him—"Non, je ne t'aime plus" ("No, I no longer love you")—emerge with noxious insolence; "plus" is pronounced with denigration. Finally she must command, "Stab me then—or let me pass!" ("Fra-ppe-moi donc—ou laisse-moi passer!") and the demand sounds almost barbarous and vulgar. Beside the helpless Don José the line lends Carmen masculinity.

Where some elect to showcase Carmen's sexuality Maria channels her cupidity for power. In this more innovative incarnation Carmen is seductive nonetheless. The treatment of the role led music critic Howard Klein to liken "Callasmania" to "Beatlemania" in his review.[11]

Fresh off this success, talks were embarked upon with Rudolf Bing for a potential comeback to the Met. He was offering Maria a new opera: Marvin David Levy's *Mourning Becomes Electra*, based on Eugene O'Neill's play.[12] This would evidently not transpire—but at that time the Met's treasurer, George Moore, had dinner with her and his old friend Onassis. *Tosca* was selected for the coming season.[13]

After sailing aboard the *Christina* that August—on which she fell, sprained her foot and alighted at Capri to hobble around[14]—Maria presented an impromptu recital of *Cavalleria rusticana*'s "Voi lo sapete, o Mamma" as well as an aria from Norma at the Lefkada Festival.[15] Next she pondered on a possible *Macbeth* in Paris for October.[16]

Despite Maria having pledged never to sing Carmen onstage, Rudolf Bing and Luchino Visconti were soon in an avid exchange: "I am delighted to hear that you feel you may be willing to commit yourself to a new CARMEN production in the 1966–1967 season. I am indeed very much thinking of Maria Callas—indeed I doubt whether I could do the production without her. I talked to her only two or three days ago on the telephone in Paris, and she promised me a decision by the end of this month,"[17] Bing wrote. He planned to stage this *Carmen* in November 1966.[18]

On October 30th *Life* magazine published a piece on Maria in the form of a signed article in her name. Among the quotations were several phrases ascribed to her that would interest reporters: "You said to a journalist—or at least he wrote—that life begins at forty," Micheline Banzet alerted her some months thence.

"No . . . that's stupid," Maria negated. "Life doesn't begin at forty; that's stupid . . . You know, journalists say *anything*. Like when they said that I bought an apartment—that I bought a house in Paris on rue Albéric Magnard—and evidently now I get all of my mail there."[19] Another statement made allegedly on her part was the claim that she had been "kept in a cage" until Onassis' relieving liberation: something she denied to have expressed.[20]

Maria eventually commenced legal proceedings against *Life* magazine—going so far as to have Gorlinsky provide cables exchanged between her and *Life*'s representatives, as well as correspondence between them and EMI's John Coveney, who had made the arrangements.[21] Although no suit was filed, Gorlinsky and his colleagues sent letters of accusations and threats—as per Maria's instructions—for months.

Yet while certain paragraphs were misconstrued or obviously exaggerated, a great deal of the interview made sense—including parts about Maria's vocal crisis she confirmed were true.[22] One of the other veritable sections was the statement: "I'm in a stinking situation because of the Italian divorce law. I have no real freedom because Battista watches me constantly . . . If I marry tomorrow and have a child—and like all women I want to have lots of children—I could go to prison for two years according to Italian law."[23]

At forty—an age at which few women bore their first child at the time—the question of a family occasionally crossed Maria's mind. In February 1961 she had experienced a melancholy moment in the company of vocal coach Janine Reiss. "I meant to ask you a few days ago—who are those two little boys I keep seeing at your apartment?" she had enquired.

Taken aback, Reiss had responded: "But, Maria—those are my children!"

Following a pause of shock her student had expressed bewilderment: Reiss had secured the real deal. "But how do you manage to have it all?"— "Oh, it's nothing; you know—it's a question of organization," the coach had thrown off in response. Some moments later she'd adjusted it: "Don't make any comparison between the career of Maria Callas and that of Janine Reiss. The career of Maria Callas is a lot more difficult to carry out than mine is. Dedicate yourself to your art: no one can do it as well as you do."[24]

While Maria channeled all her energy into her work and its ensuing panic, her maternal instincts found their targets. Her cousin, Helen Arfaras, had borne a daughter, Mary, who had been fifteen in 1960 when Maria and Onassis had met up with them in Rhodes.[25] Mary would frequently recall Maria's loveliness with children.[26]

Then there was Taki Theodoracopulos, the son of one of Onassis' friends. Maria had espied the young man in his twenties looking bored one evening at a shipping conference. By convincing his father to give him a hundred dollars to spend, she had saved him.[27]

Onassis' step-niece, Marilena Patronicolas, deemed Maria her mentor. From the ages of twelve to sixteen the girl would spend summers aboard the *Christina*. Maria let the adolescent style her tresses in her cabin; Patronicolas later worked as a hairdresser. When the shy sapling finally admitted she could sing, Maria found a vocal coach for her. Aboard the yacht she frequently absorbed her tales of teenage heartache.[28]

Another niece kept popping up on the horizon: Visconti's. Cristina Gastel was around seventeen. "We would always meet at her apartment in Paris with a dear friend of mine [Monika Wiards] . . ." she remembered. "In the evening we would go to the cinema or to the theatre . . . she would want to know at what time we'd be back at our hotel. Since we were never there, Monika and I told her we'd been to a nightclub . . . I had some local brochure in my hand flipped open to the last page. I saw an advertisement on it for a nightclub called 'Le chat noir'. So we told her that we had been to 'Le chat noir'. Her eyes grew wide in terror! But just as she was telling us that we should never do something like that again, I showed her the brochure I had. She got the joke and we all burst out laughing."[29]

Maria's thoughts about her life in February 1965 were soberer than her enchanted juvenile meanderings: "I have no illusions . . . After you turn forty, you don't have many illusions. Overall . . . I have a side that is *very* poetic. Obviously I hide it—everybody has it, I think. A little world all to ourselves, a little *corner* where everything is beautiful, everything is loyal, wonderful. And so … previously you thought that it *existed* somewhere … Now, you know it's been invented in the *brain*. It doesn't exist."[30]

November 1964 entailed another cruise. Once again Michel Glotz was graciously received by Onassis, relishing what he considered a "fairytale vacation—not only because the tours of Greek islands were enchanting, but because every day I got to accompany Maria at the piano—one can imagine with what fear and emotion! Those vacations, that intimate life of the couple and our closeness transformed my friendship with Maria into a quasi-fraternal relationship."[31]

Not all of Maria's colleagues warmed to the Greek magnate. Nicola Rescigno was affirmative in the assertion that Onassis "ruined Maria … unfortunately!",[32] basing his impression on an episode that had transpired during a Parisian dinner. Received late by Maria—who had spent too long deciding on her outfit—the conductor watched as she attempted to wrest compliments for her attire. Its top was a headdress embroidered with ribbons and veils. When she finally asked outright, "How do you like Biki's latest creation?" Onassis' response was curt: "Either you cut your nose off to match the hat, or you get a bigger hat to match your nose."[33]

Other displays of Onassis' brazen bravado were risible. "Greek men feel they must dominate the woman," Maria would gripe to Dorle and Dario Soria years later. "It is alright 50/50, 60/40, 70/30 but not 100%! He always tried to destroy me—belittle me—if I bought a sofa he would say, 'Why did you buy it? It's not right.'—'It's my taste,' I would say."[34]

While there was tension in their bond, Onassis' infidelities and public humiliations were not solely responsible. Years later Maria confessed that his "craving to conquer" was "basically the cause of our arguments. Of course I tried to change him but I realized that this was not possible, any more than he could change me. We were two independent people with minds of our own and different outlooks on some basic aspects of life."[35]

Neither party could adopt this attitude in 1964. While outspoken Maria might have criticized Onassis' actions, he publicly rankled her. On another occasion in July 1961 one of Maria's friends Marie-Luise von Criegern had been shocked at his reaction upon seeing her in one of his companion's borrowed gowns. "Oh Marie-Luise … You look beautiful in that dress! Don't you think it's nice on her, Maria? Look at her bust. Look at how beautifully her bust fills out that dress of yours!" von Criegern had described this commentary as "brutal".[36]

These kinds of actions were interpreted by several of Maria's friends as systematic psychological abuse—and Maria herself would complain to Alberto Moravia: "You see, Alberto, a man can say whatever he wants to a woman in private, but not in public. Onassis had the habit of saying degrading things to me in front of everyone."[37]

Yet whilst Maria's etiquette and private nature largely stopped her lynching him amid their cliques, behind closed doors she gave as good as she got—and didn't take most of his insults that seriously. "Obstinate he was, and quite argumentative like most Greeks," she would later recall. "He liked to tease, but if you dared pull his leg in an effort to fish for compliments he would sometimes retaliate like a tiresome schoolboy."[38]

And she herself was not the *easiest* partner. Onassis often did his best to make her friends feel comfortable. "And Lord knows putting me at ease—the young and shy man that I was—was not an easy thing!" Michel Glotz explained. He didn't care however if these people overheard their arguments. One imbroglio transpired when Onassis took a business trip to Saudi Arabia during this *Christina* cruise on which Glotz and Maggie van Zuylen were present.

The magnate was to meet the newly crowned King Faisal of Saudi Arabia: he thus resolved to organize the expedition by himself. So the *Christina* set sail to Port-Saïd in north east Egypt; "a veritable habitat for dolphins" in Glotz's words. It was forecast suddenly that Egypt would be plunged into 122°F. Maria asked Glotz for a favor: could he point out to Onassis that the temperature was going to spike? That way it wouldn't be coming from *her*; she was hoping he might cancel the trip. With low blood pressure and changes in weather afflicting her voice, her relationship with hot climates was rocky.

Onassis was roiled. "I would do anything for my friends, but I will never yield to that kind of caprice because of the *weather!*"

So the foursome set sail from Port-Saïd to Cairo—where the heat was worse—and crossed the Suez Canal.

For a while all was beautiful. Gazing at the landscapes' luminosity, Glotz and Maria envisaged *Aïda*. "We were so taken aback by this mysterious atmosphere—aglow with moonlight that would make it seem like day at night—that we remained on the [Suez Canal] Bridge; petrified by a summit of beauty till the sun rose on the Great Bitter Lake," he would scribe.

After crossing the Red Sea they finally arrived at their awaited destination: the capital city of Jeddah. The Minister of the Court had arranged for a lavish reception in Onassis' honor. Men could wear anything they wanted. Women had to display modesty by covering their legs. Thus began the row between Maria and Onassis—at first in French, then English, and at last in Greek: "It's very simple—either you put on stockings or you don't come . . . In any case, I can't understand your stubbornness, the *Christina* has air conditioning, as well as the cars waiting for us at the palace where we're going," Onassis yelled. "I will not put on those stockings," Maria yelled back. "After all—I am Maria Callas!" It was the first time Glotz had heard her use her name in combat.

This reminder of her status vexed Onassis to the point of fury. "What do you think it means to them—that you're Maria Callas? Here, in Arabia, Maria Callas is worth less than s**t because with s**t they can at least grow a palm tree!"

Maria cried, raged, and finally put on the stockings.

Not long after that came another dramatic upheaval: King Faisal had invited them to join him for a Méchoui at his Shubra palace; they were going to see Mecca. To reach the palace they would have to fly on the king's plane. It took off with ease before plummeting down to the runway—boosting Maria, Onassis, Glotz and Maggie all out of their seats. After taking a wrong lane the pilot had been forced to skirt a palm tree.[39]

The experience wasn't entirely traumatic. Either Onassis or King Faisal himself—depending on the source—gave Maria a new black poodle she named after the city of Jeddah.[40]

Did Onassis envy Callas? Not her fame—but its accompanying reverence. While Maria couldn't understand her lover's ruthless tactics in the business world, he held resentment for what he perceived to be an easily attained attention. Never had he nurtured great respect for the performing arts; literature was an entirely different matter. A daring avowal made by one of his colleagues aggrieved him: "In fifty years' time no one will remember Onassis, but Maria's name will live forever."[41]

Having imagined her attachment to her art to be the drive of an entrepreneurial, Greek female counterpart, Onassis was surprised to learn it was a pledge untouchable: an alien phenomenon to him. He would demand to know why she lived "like a gypsy"—bouncing from one country to another when her finances allowed her to suspend a traveling career.[42] He would be vexed, in times of bitterness, to hear her vocalizing in her cabin: "Oh my God! Here we go again!" he bemoaned to EMI's Jacques Leiser on the yacht.[43]

The principal difference between Maria and Onassis was easy. While both were obviously determined to be No. 1 in their professions, Maria's confidence in her superiority was never swayed. Knowing that her gift was a unique one, she did not feel threatened seriously by a Joan Sutherland or a Beverly Sills.

Onassis was no artist; his domain was ever-wavering. The world's most pioneering businessman could not forever stay the world's most pioneering businessman. Economic changes would defy his status; politics would trammel it. With the exception of her voice the hurdles that Maria met in her career were uncooperative colleagues. Obstacles along Onassis' path were borne of almost anything: ratifications by royals, presidents; new laws or bills; the stock market. He lacked the confidence Maria could sustain at her *worst* self.

"I really had only one thing against him," she would remember. "It was impossible for me to come to terms with his insatiable thirst for conquering everything. I appreciate achievement immensely (at one time I considered it the only reason for living but then I was young and unwise) but with him this developed into something else. It was not money—he had plenty and lived like the richest man in the world."[44]

The arguments that stumbled out of this were plenty—and the varying impressions of Maria's friends and colleagues never-ending. Hélène

Rochas, a French businesswoman and Maria's sometime friend, would be astonished at how "difficult and cruel" he was, and how his language "even made the sailors blush."[45] Georges Prêtre would speak of "a charming man—authentic and simple . . . He was truly lovely . . . We had a beautiful friendship . . . They made him out to be a vulgar man, whereas Aristotle was always elegant—whether he was dressed in a tuxedo, a suit or in shorts, as he was on the boat. He had a way of wanting to please everyone he liked . . . And I was lucky enough to be part of that circle." When Onassis' son Alexander later died he and Georges Prêtre had an intimate telephone conversation, "father to father."[46]

The tycoon's resentment of Maria's career was not as tyrannical as some individuals imagined. He himself told Maria that she ought to have been a conductor—[47] and would turn their disputes into jokes. When on one occasion Maria left his business associates to go for a swim, Onassis responded by wheeling her Steinway to the edge of the deck. "Come out, or this goes in with you," he warned humorously. Maria found it hilarious.[48]

According to the memories of Glotz, at times Onassis even wanted her to sing.[49] "Monsieur Onassis cared a great deal about Callas' career," he told EMI archivist Réal La Rochelle.[50]

Despite her lover's infidelities their closeness remained stalwart. "Whenever they were together, they spoke sort of conspiratorially in Greek," columnist Aileen Mehle recalled. "There was this badinage, lots of laughter—they were so absorbed in each other that sometimes you felt as though you were intruding."[51] In the words of Onassis' man-Friday Christian Cafarkis, Maria's "feminine intuition" and "great intelligence" would venture to offer him business advice.[52]

In no way was he responsible for her avoidance of the stage. "He never interfered with my art except in telling me that I should not feel any obligation to continue my singing career," Maria specified to Galatopoulos. "Obviously, he maintained, the stress had come to be too great and as I had more than done my duty (his words, not mine) I was entitled to relax and enjoy my well-earned money. He would have liked me to make films as he believed the strain wouldn't have been excessive. Anyway as far as my artistic career is concerned I always took the decisions. Neither Ari nor anybody else could have influenced me during that stage of my career."[53]

By 19 November Maria was in Paris preparing for her second studio recording of *Tosca*.[54] Having examined her vocal condition, she had remarked in the *Life* interview weeks before: "I had a big wobble in my voice two years ago but now it's out. I couldn't control my ears anymore, so I pushed and pushed and opened my mouth too much. The sound just poured out without control. I had to face the world again, so I forgot who I was and went back to being a pupil again after 28 years of career . . . For the last two years I have lived really for my voice—I studied myself for seven or eight hours daily. I studied again in spite of the fact of knowing full well that the musical world had dug my grave and was waiting for me to throw myself into it."[55]

Nonetheless she was aware that faults were chipping at her instrument—even if they seemed less magnified. "If your middle voice is weak, you make up for it on the top; but when you build a more solid middle voice, something gives on the top. What can you do?" she asked critic John Ardoin.[56]

During the London *Tosca*s Carlo Felice Cillario had enquired: "Donna Maria, you who incarnate perfection—explain to me why your voice wobbles in the high notes?" She had wrapped a cushion round her ears. "Stop stop—don't say that to me; I know it—I know it all too *well!*" After contemplating this, Maria had explained: "I've sung too many super-high notes and since then my diaphragm has been shifting." No one could know what that technically meant. "I'm trying to control it but it keeps getting the best of me."[57]

For this reason Maria had spent a great deal of time corresponding with her old surrogate-mother, Elvira de Hidalgo. "You must abandon the New York [*Tosca*] performance, as well as all other engagements, to rest at home in Paris," the teacher advised. "One month of absolute peace and then you should slowly work on preparing *Norma* . . . I am addressing you as if you were my daughter . . . You must do something very important: put yourself in the hands of a doctor, a very conscientious one, who will not see the famous Callas in you, but a fragile person who suffered and suffers."[58]

Cornered by Réal La Rochelle at her recording sessions for *Tosca* that December, she was asked: "Is the work going to your satisfaction?" Maria was troubled by this. "It's going . . . You came yesterday, I hope? *Yesterday*, it was going well. Today . . ." Maria brought her hand to her throat. "Today, the voice . . . but weren't you supposed to be here for *Carmen*?"[59]

This *Tosca* was a pale and struggling imitation of that year's spectacular accomplishments.

*

Christmas and the New Year were spent with Onassis at his villa in Athenian suburb Glyfada.[60] After recording more Verdi arias that January Maria began rehearsals for her Paris *Tosca* the following month. The night before the premiere she responded to another missive from her mentor de Hidalgo: "You know me. I'm timid and rather strange. But you love me as I am. The rehearsal went magnificently with two high notes as they were in the past-! In the third act I had a moment of panic and fatigue but vocally I managed the C of 'lama'! well and even the last note splendidly. If I know how to control myself tomorrow I will do everything well—I'm always studying—and I think of you with so much love and await your coming."[61]

Reviews for her *Tosca* were much like the London ones: waxing lyrical about her artistry but noticing the "voice that is becoming darker, the timbre that is thinning and vibrating like the arch of a wind instrument."[62] Five days later Maria declared to her old friend Herbert Weinstock, "I had a check-up from my old and only teacher Elvira De Hidalgo and she found my trouble. I've been singing extremely well these days. As the best good old times-! Happy."[63]

Later in New York Maria would also work on the voice with the Met's longtime coach Walter Taussig, who suggested select breaths and pauses. "They shared this wonderful musical agreement, he really loved her," his daughter remembered.[64]

As she concluded her series of *Toscas* in Paris, the line for tickets for Maria's return to the Met formed too long in advance. A *New York Times* report described the pilgrimage of Mary Swezy and Eleanor Kraft: both nurses from Mount Sinai Hospital who spent their sole off-duty weekend that month waiting to buy tickets for the Callas *Tosca*. At 5:30 am they had arrived armed with the guts and gall to brave Manhattan's bristly end of winter.

Six and a half hours later an employee at the theatre had seen fit to notify them they had come a whole week early . . . tickets wouldn't be on sale for seven days.[65]

"50 Shouting Youths Greet Maria Callas" ran the headline when she came on March 15th. Disembarking her Air France aircraft at the now named John F. Kennedy International Airport, Maria was greeted by "fifty screaming youngsters" who "loosed streamers from the observation deck and waved signs that said, 'Welcome Home, Callas' and 'Regina del Mondo'."[66]

"Of course I felt very uneasy because you never know what happens in minds after an absence of seven years; probably people remember all the beautiful things I used to do and not my faults . . ." Maria shared with interviewer William Weaver some weeks later. "I was *told* that they loved me. I was told that they wanted me back. Before I went back, I really, sincerely tell you—I was terrified. I didn't want to and I was trying to find excuses *not* to go." Rehearsals—as per the tradition at the Met—were scant.

But once she stepped onstage on the 19th euphoria broke out before she even sang a note: "As soon as I came out and applause started *enormously*, one thing I was happy about it, but . . ." Maria mused. "The first thing I *wasn't* because it stops the entrance of *Tosca* which could be a very nice part of music; though I knew it *would* happen but to such an extent . . . I never thought."

"I had to . . . freeze the position that you don't know how—what to do about," she continued. "But especially, the great emotion because . . . I wish we *weren't* emotion[al], I mean I really was crying and I had to sing, and that kept on for about ten minutes during my singing."[67]

Critics were warmer than expected. "She is concerned not with the production of a flawless stream of pearl-like tones," asserted Paul Hume almost matter-of-factly, "but with the vital business of depicting a human being full of caprice, a woman at once tenderly loving, jealous, disdainful or willing to do violent battle against anyone who attempts to harm her lover."[68]

Her extremely ardent welcome—including "the letters, the presents, the flowers, the . . . *adoration* that I have had . . . that was really unique,"[69]—revived her confidence so much she considered more *Tosca*s in Dallas for the following year.[70]

Departing on the *Christina* again after the final *Tosca* on 25 March, Maria came back home to Paris in late April.[71] Keeping her options open, the singer was considering a film version of *Carmen* that would feature her recent recording. For the first time she would star on celluloid. A contract had already been drawn up between her and Walter Wanger Pictures. It asserted that the shoot would occupy a "180 day period" and that "Miss Callas will receive star credits on the film of the Photoplay and paid advertising."[72] Zeffirelli was to direct it.[73]

May 2nd saw Maria pre-record a televised recital with Georges Prêtre. Among the arias featured were Duparc's *chanson*, "Invitation au voyage," whose recording, for some reason, was lost.[74]

On her trail this time was *France-Soir* journalist Marlyse Schaeffer. Schaeffer had slipped into hot water five years earlier with her insinuation that Maria wanted nothing but Onassis and a dog—compelling the enraged soprano to refute her comments in a magazine. Not that Maria remembered—for she never cared to keep track of such minor details . . . as the names of reporters who tainted her image. The scribe espied Maria as she sat in her dressing room, took a pill—"It's for breathing," she explained—and watched Prêtre jokingly enter her room: "Hey, Maria—does this remind you of anything?" He began to twist to *La sonnambula*. She burst out laughing.

Once onstage, Maria's face was grave as always. About to perform "Ah, non credea mirarti" from *La sonnambula*, she waved her hand in dismissal. "Not yet." Murmuring the words in whisper, she compelled the crew to wait.

Filming commenced. A note slipped and the orchestra stopped suddenly. "Maria, Maria—you don't need to take the whole aria again. Just pick up from where you left off."—"*Non.*"—"Why?"—"Because the Maestro wants it this way."

She recommenced. Fragility became Amina twofold as Maria's frail voice symbolized the fey girl's vulnerability. Her vocal feebleness could be interpreted mistakenly as artistry. The aria emerged aglow for the most part together with "Adieu, notre petite table" from Massenet's *Manon*: the only visible examples of Maria playing naïve, nubile women.

Suddenly a blackout plunged the whole Parisian studio into darkness—together with Avenue du Président Kennedy. Maria's reaction: "Why did they stop filming? Was I not good? Was I not doing well?"

The soprano didn't want to hear the broadcast after the recording. "I want to keep my illusions! If not, I won't sleep tonight!"[75]

Could Maria still dissolve so fully into character—or did her mature artistry necessitate a distance? "You seem to be so *concentrated* in everything you do," musicologist Edward Downes would tell her, recalling her 1956 Metropolitan *Lucia di Lammermoor*. "Some of the moments that

stuck in my mind were moments when you *yourself*, officially in your role—
you had nothing to sing, you had no prescribed pantomime—you were
watching . . . And you *watched* with such participation, such intensity, that
I felt the whole drama was going on *in your mind*."[76]

But Maria wasn't going to let herself be swept away by such romanticism:
"One must be wary of becoming obsessed by the beauty of a performance.
If you relax too much, you lose control. There must always be a small part
of one which is consciously watching and controlling."[77] This meant Maria
could never lose her "lucidity": "If I did, how could I be an artist? I must
guard it to be able to give you my best."[78]

To a degree this was true. To another it was overblown talk.

Nine days later Maria's blood pressure suddenly dropped. She began to
suffer from pharyngitis.[79] Three days were left until the opening of *Norma*.
That was *one* opera she could *never* cancel.

And so it was that scions of the media reported Callas had performed
against her medical advice.[80] Cracking at multiple points, her voice failed
her.[81] "The Callas miracle is now almost an anti-voice miracle," wrote
Joachim Kaiser of the *Süddeutsche Zeitung*.[82]

"Your heart is beating, you are like an animal, you feel ill at ease in your
own skin, you want to leave," was how Maria later described stagefright. "I
am in such a state of nervous tension that I don't want to see anyone."[83]

The next performance went even worse. Having heard a rumor that
Meneghini was coming with two of his friends, Maria feared her estranged
husband would cause an eye-catching scene. Her blood pressure dipped to
an all-time low: seventy over fifty.[84] Upon receipt of Coramine (nikethamide) injections, she insisted on going onstage. The medication's side effects
included nausea and disorientation.

"She could hardly walk straight," audience member Stelios Galatopoulos
wrote. "The first two acts were barely passable, but in the third and fourth
acts . . . After a slight vocal mishap, she gathered her strength and with a
superhuman effort saved her reputation."[85]

Her next *Norma* four days afterward was an improvement.[86] The fourth
provoked another fall in blood pressure. Baritone Claude Calès—who was
portraying Flavio—lent her medication that contained caffeine and
ephedrine; it made her feel better.[87]

The performance was a testy one however. Mezzo-soprano Fiorenza
Cossotto—who had performed with Maria on several occasions and benefitted from her help during the 1959 London *Medea*s—[88] decided this time
to upstage her in Norma and Adalgisa's famed "Mira, o Norma" duet.
According to soprano Shirley Verrett, "Cossotto didn't like me or anyone
else who appeared on the scene whom she considered a threat."[89]

Her modus operandi was holding on to long notes without respite. This
was her way of outperforming Maria.

The following day a London fan club sent Maria another gift: a three-
month-old white poodle bred by Dorothy Brauer of Hampstead. Later

christened "Pixie" by his new owner, the dog boarded a Paris-bound plane.[90]

It made no difference to the present challenge. In the final *Norma* on 29 May Maria's blood pressure dropped to another new low just before the last act. "I was at the pulpit and waiting," Prêtre would remember. "I thought for around five minutes . . . Then I made a decision. I left the orchestra and the public and ran to Maria's dressing room. She was ill. Very ill. She couldn't finish the performance."[91]

Not only does a pirate record of the truncated performance show a strident and unstable singer, it includes a "Casta diva" that begins with lyrics from its second line. In the cabaletta "Ah, bello, a me ritorna," Maria takes a phrase a tone lower.

When a doctor tended to Maria he commanded absolutely that she discontinue the performance.[92] Finally persuaded by her colleagues to stop singing, "she was white, really white," tenor Gianfranco Cecchele remembered.[93] At the stage door Maria beheld a warm, welcoming crowd: "Come back, we're with you, we love you . . ."[94] Bursting into tears, she begged the throng for mercy granted her already: "Please forgive me, I will come back to earn your pardon."[95]

The next day Maria apologized over and over again: to Stelios Galatopoulos, to whom she explained, "It was not I who was singing, I could not hear myself but I thought I was hearing somebody else, a stranger to my ears,"[96] and to Cristina Gastel, whom she asked for forgiveness when none was required.[97]

Embarking on another period of mandatory rest, she boarded the *Christina*—making sure to write a letter to Georges Auric, the director of the Opéra de Paris: "I would like to thank from the bottom of my heart all the people with whom I've worked for this past month, who have shown me such kindness for which I am deeply grateful."[98]

The *Christina* sailed to Naples, where Onassis and Maria climbed Mount Vesuvius. An elderly couple spotted her. They lavished praise on Maria but failed to recognize Onassis, who didn't seem to mind considering the circumstances. Both were invited to lunch. Accepting on Maria's behalf, Onassis ordered champagne to be brought from the yacht.[99]

"As I ought to have understood by now—and you would say it to me—I was tired," Maria wrote to Elvira de Hidalgo. "Working on the voice anew, changing my technique during the performances did not bode well for my nerves, which have been tense for so many years now . . . As you said, one can't do everything in three months. Now I'm on the cruise . . . I hope to sustain myself for the London *Toscas*—of which I've four in July . . . In Paris I will go to a doctor and come to a decision."[100]

Arriving home on 21 June, Maria told reporters: "The three-week cruise permitted me to have complete rest and I am now perfectly well. I am now going to have a complete medical examination and if all goes well, I will sing as scheduled July 4 in London."[101]

Gorlinsky telephoned the next day. They talked for "about an hour, and you seemed to be in a very good mood, and optimistic, and advised me that you would see your specialist later during the week, and that I should ring you again," he reminded Maria.

The next call came on June 24th, "when you told me that you would have your X-ray on Monday and would then decide [about London]." On June 29th Maria informed Gorlinsky that doctors had advised her against any performance—but she would concede to the first two. Two turned into one on the condition that Gorlinsky promise to release a statement prior to her hyped arrival.

But that same day Maria was in doubt. Bruna told Gorlinsky she was unsure Maria would travel to London.[102]

Finally Royal Opera House manager David Webster flew to Paris. He showed up at her door to implore her to sing.[103] To avoid scandal she agreed to perform before the queen for the Royal Gala Performance.[104]

In the meantime conductor Georg Solti—then music director at the Royal Opera—threatened to quit. "I found her attitude intolerable . . . 'Either she is in or she is out,' I told David. I was so upset that I sent David a letter of resignation." Lord Drogheda persuaded him to reconsider. Solti deliberately skipped her performance.[105]

More of a wreck than usual backstage, Maria came close to hysterics. "Georges, could we go to the cinema?" she half-joked to Prêtre as she paced in her hotel room.[106]

On 5 July Maria sang her final *Tosca*. She was passionate, irritable, girlish; striving to convert her vocal weakness into Tosca's tenderness for Mario. Blasting Scarpia in the second act, a throat-breaking yell emerged: "As-sas-*SI*-no!"—"Murderer!"

"Vissi d'arte" had more pathos to it. It relied on soft diminuendi and was more reserved. Tosca's theatricality had dimmed somewhat.

Her last notes on "O Scarpia, avanti a Dio!" wavered a little. "In the middle range the voice was almost lovely as of old in tone and texture— steel wrapped in velvet—and the phrasing and delivery were beyond compare," Frank Giles wrote for *The Sunday Times*. "What a woman, what an artist."[107]

After a bombardment of bouquets and twelve curtain calls[108] General Charles Guthrie—an SAS soldier on duty for this Royal Command Performance—watched Maria exit and collapse on a sofa backstage. A stage-hand flapped a towel before her. In his words she was "rather like a boxer."[109]

"I assure you, one is in such a state of agitation before the curtain goes up and in such a state of exhaustion when it has dropped, that you have no real notions of how the whole thing went," Maria had described her onstage fears in 1963. "Everything is remembered as one crazy effort and it has not become easier over the years."[110]

Critic Harold Rosenthal could not enthuse the way he had in days of yore. "I had the feeling that we might well be witnessing her last London

stage performance. I hope I am wrong, for she still has the power to illuminate the part she is singing as no other singer can."[111]

Maria was not happy with herself. "When people look at me with
obvious affection, that makes me twice as angry. You think: 'These people
are looking at you in admiration. Why should they? I don't deserve it!' . . .
When you are working well, life can be sublime, but when you are not it can
be a torture," she had years before opined.[112]

It was only the beginning.

16.

"Redimensioning"

The day after Maria's final *Tosca* Sander Gorlinsky advanced a much-needed rumor: she was considering a *Norma* at the Royal Opera for the 1965–66 season. "It is now just a question of fitting it into her programme," was the official statement, together with the stipulation that the dates "may be announced today."[1]

There came no announcement.

Thirty-eight-year-old Australian soprano Marie Collier had been chosen to stand in for her at the remaining *Tosca*s. Despite the substitution being prompted by Maria, it made for a sore subject for the indisposed soprano. "You asked me what kind of a performance Miss Collier gave, and I told you that she had a very nice personality and very good high notes, but that her middle register was not very developed, and that her phrasing was certainly wrong and needed adjusting," Gorlinsky wrote to her three days after her 5 July *Tosca*. "And I finished by saying that in two years she could become a great Tosca if she worked on this role very hard." But Maria had read certain "press reports" alleging that Gorlinsky was particularly interested in Collier.

For all her aversion to hearsay the gossip had kindled her envy and served humble pie to her not-at-fault manager: "I sincerely hope that any doubts you have entertained, through hearsay or press reports, have been dispelled, and I finish up by confirming my devotion and loyalty at all times," he concluded the epistle.[2]

The needless upset was symbolic of Maria's state of mind. A month later she was on the *Christina*—still apologizing in her correspondence to Cristina Gastel:

I was tired, exhausted from the effort I exerted with these performances that were too close to each other, with my poor low, low blood pressure, and they took me away to force me to rest. They still haven't understood what happened to me [the doctors], *that is, they said that I forced my system too much and for too long a time and I can no longer carry on working so much. I knew that at the end of 1957 I was irremediably tired, but I didn't want to surrender. Now I must dose everything. My darling, life is hard, now even you understand this, and yet it carries on perhaps for the best, perhaps for the worst, but you have to keep defending yourself. I started at the age of thirteen—now I'm 41! I'm not sorry. But it's a lot of years. The soul eats itself up; as does energy.*[3]

As usual Maria's home remedy against the exhaustion was leisure; mostly bathing in the Mediterranean off Monaco's shores.[4] "On the *Christina*," Georges Prêtre would reminisce, "she was very different from the singer . . . She loved to have fun. And I preserved this image of her as a woman who would burst out laughing and liked sliding into the sea from the emergency slide on the boat . . .[5] She would climb onto it over and over again and let herself go . . . She wasn't scared, in spite of her short-sightedness, and would laugh like a child!"[6]

This kind of Maria came as a surprise to many people—likely even to herself. Yet her actions weren't entirely targeted to the sole purpose of distraction. Displaying herself in this way, she had something to prove: her humanity, relatability or simplicity . . . whatever one calls it.

In the company of fourteen-year-old Josephine Chaplin three years earlier she had eased the girl's nerves by diluting her image: "You've written me piles of letters, and now that I'm in front of you, you don't say a word!" she rebuked her. "Everybody should have an idol. You are lucky to have me; at least you can be with me, not only admire me but have fun with me too. Look," Maria descended the slide and crashed into the ocean. "Look at the prima donna now!"[7]

In the aquatic realm she was no amateur. An avid fan of snorkeling,[8] Maria also counted on these moments to give evidence of her banality. "I believe that, as a *woman*, I'm completely *normal*," she had explained to interviewer Bernard Gavoty in 1964.[9]

The comment seems entirely credible. And yet its utterance was only the beginning of an ardent quest to demonstrate the face of her conventionality: "It's a little hard to *believe* because people have given a completely different impression of me as *Callas*. The *woman*, she is simple; she likes watching tv, reading nonsense, she likes—naturally sometimes she likes to listen to pretty things, read and . . . pretend to be an intellectual which I am *not* because I've never had the time for it."

If her behavior could conform enough to other people's she could easily convince her audience that she was *not* a goddess. By extension the soprano would demand less of *herself*.

Therein lay the miscalculation.

People who met Maria socially in the mid-sixties were exposed to someone silly at times almost to the point of being nauseating. When Maria's poodles Jeddah and Pixie accompanied her on the *Christina* a butler would bring little swimming mattresses to let them float beside her in the pool.[10] If company were present an enthused Maria would persuade her poodles to perform; singing half-heartedly while Pixie raised her chin and wailed in an attempt to imitate her.[11] Or else Jeddah would yowl "because her eardrums had nearly burst," according to photographer and princess, Marianne Sayn-Wittgenstein-Sayn, and Maria would point out, "You see, Djedda [sic] can sing."[12]

The less work Maria had, the more a need to frivolously entertain became pedantic and compulsive . . . leading us to question its veracity.

That summer she engaged in more diverting thoughts: the planned film of *Tosca* that would feature her recent recording. In 1958 Franco Zeffirelli had strived hard to persuade Maria to film a *Traviata* under the baton of Victor de Sabata.[13] When a wealthy oil tycoon had offered to invest two and a half million dollars in the project (the equivalent of twenty-three today), Zeffirelli had won over Meneghini. Maria had turned down the offer.[14]

"I don't think that taking away opera from its place would be good," she told Harry Fleetwood. "Because that is the *thrilling* part of opera; it's . . . on the spur of the moment, whatever happens, whatever you do, there it is—*that's* the excitement. But just put it on . . . celluloid, well I don't know, I don't think I'd like it."[15]

Yet now her attitude was wavering again—conveniently synchronically with the apparent degradation of her voice. Zeffirelli was proposing to shoot *Tosca* in Rome that October, a period convenient for both Maria and her would-be co-star Tito Gobbi.

At the same time the music publishing company that owned the rights to Tosca, Ricordi, had sold exclusive European television rights to Herbert von Karajan. The maestro was also envisaging the work as a movie.[16]

What followed was a convoluted series of confusions. Eager to announce his starry vehicle, zealous Zeffirelli shunned Maria's sensitive request not to disclose it to the press. One month later he announced that the world's greatest singer would immortalize her art in cinema: "It will be a marvellous film. The sound track has already been made," the director alerted *The Guardian*.[17]

In September 1965 Maria did a screen-test and was ready to start shooting.[18] Interceding at Maria's resolute request, Onassis postponed its production—expressing dismay at "what he perceived as the miserly conditions offered" contractually speaking.[19]

Negotiations between Maria, Zeffirelli, their film company, Gorlinsky, Onassis, Ricordi, Karajan and his producers broke down when the lattermost refused to relinquish the rights. Zeffirelli pursued his new role as the leaking insider.

"Well, our friend Zeffirelli certainly can't stop talking, and although we have asked him many times to keep his mouth shut, he just goes on," Gorlinsky wrote to Maria on 21 October. "From the [press] cuttings, you will see that he makes a big song and dance about the 'Callas film crisis' and the rescuing of the film. All this information comes from Rome, and I shudder to think what is going to happen during the shooting of the film if he is going to carry on like this . . . there was no necessity to publicise it to the world . . ."[20]

Zeffirelli's crew consisted of producers from British Home Entertainment, a government-backed enterprise.[21] Karajan was working with Beta Films, a small German production company.[22]

Eventually the two teams came to an agreement. After agreeing to finance Karajan's *Tosca*, Leo Kirch of Beta Films signed on to produce Zeffirelli's. The British and German companies decided to make a joint venture including both Zeffirelli *and* Karajan.[23] Onassis likewise enlisted the help of Jack Warner of Warner Bros.—cabling him on 22 September:

DEAR JACK A FEW WEEKS AGO YOU SENT ME A LETTER WITH SOME MESSAGE FOR MARIA CALLAS STOP I PASSED THE LETTER TO HER IMMEDIATELY STOP IT APPEARS NOW BECAUSE OF HER ILLNESS SHE FORGOT TO ANSWER YOU AND AS THE LETTER HAS BEEN MISPLACED PLEASE SEND HER A COPY IF YOU WISH TO 44 AVENUE FOCH STOP PLEASE ACCEPT MY AND HER APOLOGIES CORDIALLY ARISTO ONASSIS[24]

In December 1965 the movie seemed unrealizable.[25]

Then something changed. By 26 January 1966 the distribution of the film's potential profits had been set: all income above $3,000,000 would be shared 60% by Warner Bros. and 40% by the "original producers": Maria, Onassis, British Home Entertainment, Leo Kirch and Sander Gorlinsky together with his company Interart.

Maria and her envoy Onassis "were up in arms that this was a bad percentage," despite the former being about to receive $250,000 (over two million today) for four weeks of work without singing a note. Together they began to complicate Gorlinsky's life increasingly, accusing him of having been "bribed" by the Germans in secret "against [his] better judgment and against the interests of the artists," or of having a "personal interest in the Warner Bros. deal."[26]

Negotiations persisted into May, at which time Onassis sought counsel from Spyros P. Skouras, president of 20th Century Fox. Maria was to first receive a tenth of the first $3,300,000 of the film producer's share of film rentals. She would be likewise guaranteed $250,000 after the completion of the movie and a quarter of the share of profits borne of film rentals surpassing $3,300,000.[27]

The project was scrapped. In June 1966 Zeffirelli took a cruise aboard the *Christina* together with Lord Brabourne and Tony Havelock-Allan of British Home Entertainment. The director would recall Maria telling him: "I was just telling John and Tony that I'm only doing this because Ari insists

I should go into movies . . . You know, Franco, I've been through hell all my life, worked like a slave and look what happened—Meneghini stole everything. So is it really worth it?"

According to him their exchange was interrupted by Onassis, who counseled Maria to "save your voice for when you go on stage, because that's when you certainly need every bit of it." Since the motion picture seemed increasingly unlikely, she began to scapegoat: "If Karajan is involved then I'm not interested." Upon Onassis' suggestion to "buy him out" the pair became embroiled in a dispute in which the former lost his temper by referring to Maria as a "night-club singer". The next morning he promised to give Zeffirelli production money: ten thousand dollars. In the movie business it was just a token.[28]

The hesitance and arguments were not authentic. To Stelios Galatopoulos Maria would later recall: "Ari wanted to deal with that film contract himself and, with his tongue in his cheek, made that grossly exaggerated remark in order to give me the excuse of walking out and leaving him to handle the situation. We did rehearse it but he surprised me when he mentioned night-clubs. Afterwards we laughed about it, especially when he said that he only tried to imitate me—that is in the way I improvise in my stage movements."

Understanding full well that the sum of ten thousand dollars would get Zeffirelli nowhere, they offered an investment picayune because of the soprano's indecision. "Film business people, including producers, naturally preferred to deal with me," Maria would relate. "They took it for granted that if I were involved Ari would put up any amount of money. And he would, provided it was a sound investment. It was I who withdrew."[29]

To Zeffirelli Maria allegedly claimed Onassis requested a return of the money because of her reluctance to work with Karajan, who wouldn't relinquish the rights.[30] To Michel Glotz Maria said her hesitation stemmed from fear that Zeffirelli would exploit her reputation to augment his own success. She also feared that in a context that involved no live performance the director would have the final say "without her artistic approval."[31]

Despite Maria's later admission that she "did not really like the idea" of the Tosca film[32] Zeffirelli believed that Onassis had severed the project.

The latter and Gorlinsky were investigating how to buy the rights from Karajan as late as July 1967. But, as Gorlinsky wrote to Onassis back then: "the main point is really to come to a conclusion in principle whether you wish to go ahead with it and whether we can talk Maria into it . . . I have no doubts that it would be an enormous success and bring to Maria a terrific amount of money."[33]

Her resolve could not be rustled.

On 16 August 1965 she turned down a proposition from Leonard Bernstein to engage in a new project. "You know how much I would have loved to come and taken pleasure in making marvelous music, as you say. I will be very busy in this period. Probably shooting a film of *Tosca*. But don't forget me in the future."[34]

This kind of stalwart stalling symbolized the two years following her final *Tosca*: she would grasp at any straws to shun the burden of consideration. On 28 August Maria learned Panaghis Vergottis' elderly father George had died in London. Her immediate reaction was to rush to the city from her location on the *Christina* to be by his side.[35]

At this time Maria and Onassis had a "row" that prompted a brief rift. Each of them separately enlisted the help of Vergottis. According to the latter's recollections of the argument—whose derivation is unknown— Maria telephoned Vergottis from her London hotel to reveal that Onassis had called from the *Christina* and left her implacably "furious". "She would not tell me anything at all," Vergottis would recall. "The following day we had lunch at the Savoy and I tried to extract from her what had happened but it was impossible for me. On the third day she told me that she had given instructions to the telephone operator at the Savoy that if Mr. Onassis telephoned not to put him through and she did not want to see him anymore."

Upon visiting Onassis, Vergottis allegedly found him "distraught" and was swiftly persuaded to beg her to see him. "He asked me what was wrong with Maria and why he couldn't get through to her. He asked me to ask her if she would see him for just five minutes. Before I left London he wrote to her asking her for five minutes . . . I said, 'He loves you.' She said she would see him for five minutes with me." They finally reunited in Paris.[36]

Whatever the grounds for the quarrel, it led to a maudlin Maria. In the early days of September she "had a long heart to heart" with Gorlinsky during dinner in which she implored him to "treat [her] as a sister, to look after [her], and to ignore any upset which [she] may create on some occasion."[37]

Despite leaving the city allegedly broken-hearted, Maria stopped to weigh herself at the airport. The scales displayed a number strangely high until she saw three feet atop them—one of which extended from an airport employee. "As a matter of fact she has been trying to put weight on," Gorlinsky was forced to explain to the press. "If anything she is underweight."[38]

With her and Onassis on friendly terms again, by 17 September she was back on the *Christina*—this time with Greta Garbo as a guest.[39] That day the icon turned sixty. Hearing of the possibility of the then relevant *Tosca*, Garbo assured Maria she would offer her help with the movie. The latter had retired at forty, having last acted in 1941. "I asked her—how did it turn out that you just quit?" Maria remembered. "And she said, 'I quit because it was destiny.'—'What do you mean "destiny"? You were responsible for your own destiny.'—'No. It was destiny—and then it was also *hormones*.' She told me precisely *that* and I said, 'But what do you mean by that?' She said: 'Oh, there were films that—they didn't go the way I wanted them to.'—'Well,' I said, 'You can't quit on the basis of one failure or even another . . . Me—I would *never* have quit right after a failure. I would've quit well *after* that.' "[40]

Yet at the time Maria couldn't easily explain why there were no professional engagements in her calendar. Asked in 1958 what other instrument she would have liked to play, Maria had responded with "The carillon. There's one trouble: that I have too good an ear, and I hear them, you know—doing something I don't like; I get angry but I do *love* carillons."[41]

Now her ear made her enraged at her own instrument.

"I was not quite happy with my *self*," she would later aver. "And, er . . . I decided to *retire*, shall we say, and *re-dimension* my whole situation and start . . . if one can say, 'start', 'cause we never *stop* studying—but start *eliminating* bad habits that had, little by little, come into *myself* as a singer. So I *retired* and *restudied* like the early days of the conservatoire . . . Taking time *out*, by *yourself*, and . . . looking *back*, sincerely, with an open mind, object- ively *weighing* everything . . . This means *redimensioning*."[42]

Still on the *Christina* in late October 1965,[43] Maria returned to Paris the following month.[44] Remaining in the city, she attended some performances including that of Margot Fonteyn and Rudolf Nureyev in *Raymonda* at the Théâtre des Champs-Élysées.[45] Her message was something she touted ubiquitously: opera was dying.

"Young singers are *broken* 'cause they're easily *applauded*," she would tell a radio host one year later. "[They think] 'Well—why should we work *harder?* Look—we have a wonderful success.' And they stop working. They go around performing, they sing just *anything* under the sun—heavy roles, light roles."[46] Maria abhorred what she perceived as an absence of "team work . . . during the war we would spend six months preparing a produc- tion."[47] She lamented the shortage of conductors and by extension "too little competition. A beautiful voice is an immediate success because the public *likes* it immediately, they don't bother about other things; *so*, when you're an *immediate* success, it is *rare* that you *last* long."[48]

The advances that had overseen tremendous progress in technology, communication and air travel had hacked into opera's entrails. She blamed their expediency for a "quantity over quality" approach to the art.

What emerged as an excuse was actually a wide-held notion among many. In 1975 tenor Richard Tucker told George Jellinek on the radio program "The Vocal Scene": "We're living in a different era now George . . . that of the fast buck."[49]

Still in Paris in January 1966, Maria welcomed Cristina Gastel to her home. Once again she sought to analyze her situation from a distance, often speaking of herself in the third person.[50] Then another proposition came her way: a film of *La traviata* to be directed by Visconti with a new recording conducted by Karajan. Onassis wrote to Jack Warner again and arranged a dinner for himself, Maria, Herbert and Eliette von Karajan and Michel Glotz. Once again he was willing to finance the film.

Maria's hesitation defused the excitement. Karajan inanely tried to placate her: "I know that you're scared to death of recording *Traviata*, but I'll always be at your disposal in Berlin. Come when you want; do the first act whenever you want—all you have to do is give me a call. Once you've got the first [most difficult] act 'in the can'—it's smooth sailing after that." But she would postpone and postpone the telephone call till it didn't happen at all.[51]

The vision of a novel *Traviata* haunted her. Closing all the doors in her apartment, she practiced the opera for up to three hours a day.[52]

*

On 20 January a herd of fans led by young Jacqueline Pétiard was lingering outside her home. They had spent a few days loitering around the quarters and eventually befriended Bruna and Ferruccio. That afternoon Maria invited them in. Upon learning their names she began citing quotes from their letters—much to their astoundment and pleasure. With too much time at her disposal, she would re-invite them to her house six times in future weeks.[53]

"Occasionally I receive them when I'm there," Maria scribed to a fan three months later. "Even at times in my bathrobe and without any make-up."[54]

Her relationships with other fan-friends thrived. She was still in touch with Olive and May Haddock—to whom she had on two occasions given complimentary tickets for performances of hers.[55] "I must say that I *want* to thank them because it's the only way I *can*; of course one can't sit and write and thank *all* the people, especially so many people that wrote without addresses, anonymous people," Maria had told William Weaver back in April 1965. Yet there was a shocking number of admirers with whom she *did* exchange epistles.[56]

Gorlinsky was concerned about Maria's lack of presence. "It is upsetting to me that for many months I have hardly received a single enquiry or request for you, and my personal feelings are that unless you go back into circulation with something in the very near future, it will be very hard to get back again and re-start all this business of a 'comeback,' " he warned her in a letter on the 22nd of that month.[57]

She bade her time. That February 1966 Maria returned to the *Christina* and spent a great deal of unproductive hours in the company of Gina Lollobrigida,[58] whose films the pair would watch in the yacht's cinema. Preferring to stay aboard most of the time, she probably practiced. During her free hours they played backgammon and visited Cairo's museums. Onassis escorted them by car to Luxor, where the pair explored temples in Karnak and trekked through the Valley of the Kings to behold pharaohs' tombs.[59] Lollobrigida would speak fondly of Maria decades later and remark, "I loved her a lot."[60]

Some weeks thence Maria's lawyers found a loophole to uproot her from her marriage. A recent law had declared marriages of Greek citizens not performed in the Orthodox Church after 1945 to be void. Attributing no value to the question of her nationality, on 18 March Maria surrendered her American passport at the U.S. Embassy in Paris, leaving only her Greek citizenship. This action would invalidate her marriage in all countries except Italy.[61] With proceedings at the U.S. Embassy in Paris finalized on 6 April, she had Gorlinsky draft a press release reflecting her desire to become a single woman—nothing else.[62]

Reporters outside the embassy were scarcely content with the answer. Asked whether this meant she intended to marry Onassis, Maria was almost naïvely coy: "Oh . . . I don't *know* . . . Right now I'm very happy to be a free woman."[63]

If she wanted to perform in Italy again she couldn't marry elsewhere for the fear of being charged with bigamy. The Italian laws vexed Maria—who would later aver: "Religion *is* a *must* in life—but I think that as life becomes *modern*, religion *also* must modernize itself. Because, er . . . I mean look at the *velocity*, the way things *change*: *style, mentality*, er . . . You *have* to be up to *date* but in the *right* sense. So religion cannot *really* stay at what it used to be once upon a *time*. Because people are more *intelligent* now. They study *more*."[64]

Meanwhile she and Onassis were getting on splendidly. Early in April they took a private plane to Crete. Throughout the journey Maria sat in the cockpit, flinging "very sharp and pointed questions" at the captain, Paul Ioannidis, and being "very polite, self-confident and glowing with happiness."[65]

Because the pair lived separately, annoyances like teenage Alexander and Christina's mistrust of Maria rarely posed a hindrance. Believing her to be the source behind his parents' split, Alexander balked at the idea of conversation with Maria though she made considerable efforts to communicate with him aboard the yacht.[66] During one of his imbroglios with Onassis she had even sided with the boy and told his father he was paying him too little heed.[67]

Onassis' sister Artemis Garoufalidis also bore a grudge against his mistress. Their physiotherapist Korinna Spanidou feared "being friends with Maria in case Artemis would find out."[68] Among most couples such familial problems posed a hurdle. For the adamantly independent individuals they were, neither Maria nor Onassis paid a great deal of attention to these qualms.

"Onassis *needs* me as a *friend* because I would tell him the *truth*. Not that *you* men *like* the truth," Maria would enlighten David Frost. "I'm quite sure though that Mr. Onassis would *always* come to me—*with* his problems knowing that I would *never* repeat and—he would find an objective *mind*."

She understood that "You have to make a lot of *concessions*, and it has to go—*mainly*, both ways. Your man—companion . . . you have to be *pals* with him. You have to share *everything* with him. You have to *share* . . . his sex life, his *problems*; you have to share *everything*. It's hard work and it's lovely."[69]

Maria didn't make concessions easily. Onassis gave her grievances—but they were just a handful among dozens in her repertoire of quandaries.

Though marriage may have been discussed at intervals it was no deal-breaker. "I am sure he was aware of my inability to come to terms with any infidelity a husband of mine might commit," Maria later reflected. "Being more practical than I was in such matters, and more experienced, Ari . . . did love me but also knew that sooner or later we would have been at daggers drawn had we married . . .[70] my intuition, or whatever you call it, told me that I would have lost him the moment I married him—he would then have turned his interest to some other younger woman. I also sensed that he too knew I could not change my outlook on life to fit in with his and our marriage would probably have become, before long, a squalid argument."[71]

As early as October 1964 Maria had made clear that she was not possessed by a desire to remarry. "I don't know if I would even consider marriage even if I was free to do so," she told an interviewer. "Once you're married, the man takes you for granted and I do not want to be told what to do. My own instinct and convictions tell me what I should or should not to. These convictions may be right or wrong but they are mine, and I have the courage to stand up for what I believe."[72]

Certain biographers have enjoyed the assertion that during this period Maria allegedly became "pregnant" with Onassis' child: a tale unsupported by evidence.[73] Although the question of rearing a family entered her mind, she spoke with relative ease about childlessness. Before the birth of Mary Annexy's daughter Lydia in April 1971 Maria had been "fascinated when I was pregnant," in her words.[74]

"To deal with human *lives*, even if they are your own children is . . . something that is *extremely* difficult and delicate. And . . . the mother has the responsibility of her creatures," Maria would tell David Frost in 1970. "If I hadn't had an interest in the life of singing and my work, I would've found something *else*; I would've been a mother of—I would've had *children* and I would've been the same thing in my family, I think. Or else I would've played the piano—I don't know what."[75]

A year before her death she spoke of it with calm. "Today, having children is considered nothing at all . . . Young people are the future of the world. And we *mothers*—I say 'we' because I am a woman, even though I never had children—these young people are our responsibility: our future."[76]

Back in April 1966 Maria was still rummaging for clues to find her missing voice. Writing to the fixer of all problems, Elvira de Hidalgo, she explained: "I was tired, I'm better now; I'm still tired but I'm much better, I only exert myself when it's worth it." She had found a new apartment that was being furbished to her taste at 36 Avenue Georges Mandel. "I'm dedicating myself to it for the moment, that way I won't get tired too much by having vocal and apartment-related engagements at the same time!" Maria expressed her wish to come to Milan soon to work with de Hidalgo. "I'm a lot more tranquil. Tranquility has nothing to do with happiness, but it's managing nevertheless to restore my nervous system, which was really to blame for everything, as you once said."[77]

Despite Maria apologizing for not writing to her for a time, de Hidalgo was bitter. "Your silence was excruciating for me," she responded. "I felt jealously neglected and I suffered in silence without being able to explain to myself this behavior of yours toward me."[78] Though the pedagogue did not admit it, her impressions had been tainted by a tinge of jealousy. Following the death of Maria she responded to a critic's request for an interview by enquiring "what fee" he would pay "for the privilege of conversing with her."[79]

Ambivalence does not suffice as a descriptor of Maria's sentiments in these days. On one hand she wrote to a New York music critic to alert him she was weary of cruising on the *Christina* and desired to resume her work soon.[80] On the other she scribed to Eugenio Gara: "You can't imagine what sadness opera today is for me, or rather you yourself would know because you see it frequently, maybe even every night. I'm not saying that what they used to do was perfection, but at the very least it was performed with so much sincerity, seriousness; humility and devotion; today there's so much vanity, presumption and let's leave it at that."[81]

Later that month Gorlinsky wrote to Bernard Gavoty, one of Maria's old critic-friends. He was organizing a musical gala on behalf of newspaper *Le Figaro* in which she had hoped to participate. The concert was to be held on 17 November that year.

A week later she was holding on to this proposal[82] but another issue had arisen: radio station Europe 1 had mentioned her name prior to a broadcast of the hit parody song, Juanita Banana.[83] Written by Tash Howard and Murray Kenton, the spoof describes a Mexican banana grower's daughter yearning to succeed in opera. As a showcase of her (very poor) ability she feebly makes a stab at *Rigoletto*'s "Caro Nome". After hearing the show's hosts joke "Callas liked 'Juanita Banana' so much she's decided to record it herself," Maria was disquieted. Such was her state of sensitivity she asked Gorlinsky to explore the possibility of legal action.[84]

More time was spent at leisure. In mid-May Maria traveled to Geneva, informing a standby reporter she planned to go shopping for one day then come back to Paris.[85] Two weeks later she caused a stir simply by attending the Met's touring production of *The Barber of Seville* at the Théâtre Odéon. When some of the public were disappointed by Roberta Peters' Rosina, someone cried out "Vive Callas!" ("Long Live Callas!").[86]

After the performance Maria dined with Glotz and Onassis. "An evening like that is wonderful for me," she told them. "I had the whole of Paris at my feet and didn't even have to sing or suffer butterflies."[87]

Two days later she was attending a concert of Juliette Gréco.[88] Maria's liaison with *chansons* and cabaret colored in part her artistic approach. She never underestimated what proponents of contrasting genres brought to music's legacy. "Great dancers in theatre can do many things but they sometimes cannot do what a cabaret dancer can. In other words, you can always learn," was her principle.[89]

One popular singer she met at an Athenian nightclub was Nana Mouskouri. Having requested a Greek song, Maria listened to the young woman sing "I amygdalie" ("The Almond Tree"), coming back on several occasions to hear her perform. After a few such evenings she sent Mouskouri a note: "Would you like to join me for a moment at the intermission?"

Mouskouri sat at her table. Maria assured the young woman, "I've heard good things about you. For instance, I've been told that you're very versatile: that you can do every kind of music there is. Where did you learn to sing?" Her interlocutor explained that she had taught herself and then attended a conservatory. "Really? So you wanted to sing opera?"—"That was my goal at one time, yes. But my teacher refused to allow me to earn my living by singing in nightclubs, and he expelled me."—"I see." Following a moment's pause Maria took Mouskouri's hand and started to philosophize: "You know, life may have given you a gift that day. There are many of us who want to sing *Norma*, *Tosca* and *Traviata*, but ours is a very cruel art, and in the end very few make it . . . It's better to be a great popular entertainer than an unknown opera singer. The important thing is not what you do but *how well* you do it."[90]

In other words Maria maladroitly put it this way: "There is no place for racism in music."[91]

By 11 June Maria was having issues with the proposed *Le Figaro* gala concert. As it was going to be conducted by Igor Markévitch and would be largely orchestral in scope, his ensemble was performing *onstage*. Fearing it might drown out her voice, Maria requested the orchestra play in the pit—if only for the span of her arias.

Despite Gorlinsky's countless pleas to Gavoty it was impractical to have the orchestra switch places several times throughout the concert.[92] On 1 April Maria had been proposed a series of concerts at Manhattan's newly built Lincoln Center.[93] After postponing the decision for two months she finally declined on 21 June. "She is not very keen on [it]," Gorlinsky wrote to Vice President for Programming, Schuyler Chapin. "When she was last year in New York she attended a concert there, and did not like the acoustics, which were, as you know, generally criticised, and Madame Callas feels that if she returns to New York she would prefer to appear at Carnegie Hall."[94]

Receiving Italian journalist Emilio Pozzi of RAI at her home a few weeks later, Maria addressed her public in an interview for the first time in almost a year.

Asked why she was not performing at La Scala, she replied: "When I come back, I want to come back when I have peace—not the peace of the public which I know I'll have but . . . an *interior* peace . . . not with *myself* because I *know* I will have it even if third parties won't leave me alone; little *enemies* such as—as I was saying before; people taking sides, useless disturbances such as claques, which I think shouldn't exist—but peace from a personal perspective; if my husband could leave me alone; could let me return almost to my country because Italy *is* my country, musically, even more than that; sacred peace to be able to work at La Scala which is the *only* theatre in the world—the *only* theatre that has truly *seen* me, suffered with me, heard the bad and the good—and can have the best of me."[95]

On 20 June Maria wrote to Giulietta Simionato: "I am tranquil, and for now happy not to be singing. I've worked so much that frankly, if one works today, it's not really worth it—don't you think? You remember how we used to work—when it was worth it. Not now. I don't know what I will do."[96]

Some people have marital problems, relationship problems, parental problems. Maria had problems with her *self*.

By the time of her attendance at that summer's Athens Festival in the company of Margot Fonteyn,[97] Maria had personally cancelled her stint at the *Figaro* gala. "I had a rather disturbing telephone call . . ." Gorlinsky wrote to her. "As I did not have any indication officially from you I told them that I would discuss the matter with you upon your return . . ."[98] For two weeks he waited for a change of heart. Maria kept citing the orchestra's placement. By 4 July he had no choice but to write an official apology.[99]

That summer afforded Maria more company than expected. With the *Christina* circling Lefkada,[100] she bumped into Cristina Gastel, who was touring the island together with her friend Monika Wiards. Recognizing the yacht, they telephoned her and were immediately invited aboard.

As the two twenty-somethings were departing for a trip of the Greek islands, Maria asked them to stop by at every office of Onassis' airline they passed to call and assure her the duo was safe.[101]

Endeavoring to find new ways to occupy herself, she attempted to embroider cushions and tried Swedish exercise.[102] Onassis' step-niece Marilena Patronicolas was purchased a gift for her wedding: a diamond ring so dear Patronicolas had it locked in a vault still in 2012.[103]

Herbert von Karajan and his wife Eliette had been summoned aboard by Onassis. "I didn't know him at the time but later we became great friends," Maestro von Karajan recalled.[104] The journey gradually unwound into discussions of their past. "[Maria] had an *enormous* nostalgia. She *liked* to talk about the past. I proposed everything to her—perhaps she had the feeling in herself that she could no longer do it; I was ready to do *everything*."[105] This included the *Tosca* film—still on the cards. "She was afraid. She had left the thing and felt out of it."[106]

Still aboard the yacht that summer, Maria fielded unrelenting threats from Meneghini—who continued his obsessive quest to overturn the judge's verdict that held husband and wife equally responsible for their failed marriage. On 18 June 1966 yet another appeal of his was rejected.[107]

By 22 August he was back to making personal threats. "Of course Meneghini is the worst and the lowest of all blackmailers. I don't know what to say," Maria lamented to her Italian lawyer Augusto Caldi Scalcini.[108]

With Maria still aboard the *Christina* as late as 19 September,[109] her new apartment designed by decorator Victor Grandpierre—who would later work for Dior—was fast approaching completion.

The abode—comprised of six bedrooms, both a large and a small living room, a dining room with a veranda, an office, the staff's rooms and several bathrooms—[110] was "a sophisticated mixture of Persian rugs, Venetian lacquer ... mannerist paintings, Regency furniture, and Qianlong porcelain," according to Grandpierre's biographers.[111] In her bathroom he installed a pink and white marble bath with cherry-colored dolphins for faucets,[112] a large sofa with a telephone opposite it and a phonograph.[113]

Converting this into the ultimate distraction from herself, Maria troubled others with her worries about furnishings: "As for books, I don't know if you remember which ones I've had . . ." she wrote to her now part-time secretary from the Milanese years, Teresa d'Addato. "I've been offered Hemingway and Shakespeare recently, the complete works, two huge books on Michelangelo (excuse the handwriting, I'm distracted by Wagner's music on the turntable) . . . I can buy the French authors here if you tell me which ones apart from the usual."[114]

Four months later she requested that Gorlinsky use some of his leisure time when on vacation in Berlin to buy specific cushions for her pillow cases. He purchased twelve altogether.[115]

"I don't know what your plans are—do you propose to work in the near future and/or do some recordings?" the latter wrote to her on 8 September. "Peter Andry [of EMI] has asked me a couple of times, and I understand you recently had a discussion with Michel Glotz about certain possibilities. Also, what about public appearances?"[116]

A month later she was still considering an offer to perform a television concert that would never come to life.[117] By early November Maria continued to battle her ex-husband's "Pay up or else" threats: he planned to take even *more* legal action against her. "What has taken hold of him?" she wrote to her lawyer on the 1st. "I'm a little better—these abrupt changes in my blood pressure, which switches from normal to extremely low with terrible crises of fatigue, are still bothering me. I'm going to go for a check-up this month in London—because there's no reason that it should be this way."[118]

A couple of weeks later Maria was considering a return to the Met, which was facing the threat of immediate demolition. On the condition of its preservation she agreed to perform four *Medeas* there. Lawrence Kelly promised to exert his efforts for its rescue.[119] She also entertained a proposition by Dino Yannopoulos—who had directed eighteen-year-old Callas in her premiere *Tosca*—to sing at the next Athens Festival.[120]

*

After spending December's first weeks with Onassis in St. Moritz,[121] Maria returned home to Paris.[122] Another bother vexed her: the release of a record by a young girl named "Nina Foresti" performing "Un bel dì" from *Madama Butterfly* in 1937.[123] The album was peddling the child as the pubescent Maria. Not long after, she wrote to her fan, Olive Haddock: "The Butterfly piece is not true. I always called myself my own name."[124]

Decades later Dallas music critic John Ardoin—the man responsible for touting such a tale—confessed that it had been a fabrication.[125]

By January 1967 one plan had been ratified: "Maria has unequivocally agreed that in the event the old [Metropolitan Opera] house is saved that she would perform five performances of 'Medea' as the re-opening production of that house," Kelly wrote to director Alexis Minotis.[126] She continued to be onboard with this idea into February, with most people presuming this "re-opening" would take place in November.[127] But the Old Met would never be salvaged.

And that wasn't even her fault.

The soprano hovered near Onassis in Las Palmas and some other parts of the Caribbean where she spent several weeks in February and March 1967.[128] Practicing remote control interior design by writing to maid Bruna on the yacht, the restless Maria arranged her apartment's development: "I hope really to find the living room <u>better</u> lit. Remind [Monsieur Grandpierre] to change the Chinese lamps ... And ask the gardeners to hurry up with the balconies ... Ask Hanlet [the piano-tuner] to tune the piano half a tone higher." Likely she desired to challenge herself with the newly raised pitch.[129]

March marked her and Onassis' arrival in Nassau.[130] Cruising on their speedboat, Bianca and Paul Cole were among those who spotted her: an ivory-clothed figure sat on the yacht's stern, waving frantically and pointing to a poodle's toy afloat across the straits. To her delight the friendly couple let her board their boat so that Maria could retrieve it.[131] From there she sailed to Miami and eventually on to New York.[132]

On 4 April Maria informed Walter Cummings she was fully intent on retraining her voice to conserve all her energies.[133] EMI producer Peter Andry had seen rising tenor Plácido Domingo perform in *Madama Butterfly* with the New York City Opera at Lincoln Center. Immediately he called Maria and suggested him for their proposed recording of *La traviata*: "Tell him to make a test of the 'Brindisi', 'Lunge da lei' and 'De' miei bollenti spiriti,' " she advised,[134] despite having heard Domingo in Carnegie Hall's concert staging of *Anna Bolena* the previous year.[135]

Back in Paris, Maria was not entirely impressed with Domingo's test record. "Not experienced enough, though the voice is nice," came her response. "What is the name of the other man?"—"Pavarotti," replied replied Andry. "Well, he might do."[136]

Vergottis had promised to make Maria a majority shareholder in Overseas Bulk Carriers, the company that owned her ship, *Artemision II*. Unfortunately this had slipped his mind and now Maria and Onassis struggled to persuade him of it.[137] Vergottis now alleged the £60,000 Maria had bestowed on him had merely been a loan. In fact they had been payment for her twenty-five shares in the vessel. Onassis had bought twenty-six, intending to convey them to Maria as a gift and thereby make her the ship's biggest shareholder.[138]

Chronically denying that the deal had ever taken place, Vergottis' dissension had left both Maria and Onassis no resort but legal action. "This thing has compelled me to drag to court a friend I have loved and known for more than 30 years," Onassis told the press at the time. "I am unhappy and miserable that this friend has pushed me to this stage."[139]

Initial discussions for Maria's investment in the ship had taken place in September 1964 on the *Christina*. On 25 November 1965 Maria had sent a telegram to Vergottis:

THIS IS TO NOTIFY YOU THAT I HAVE TODAY DECIDED TO REQUEST YOU TO CONVERT MY UNSECURED LOAN TO YOU OF 60.000 POUNDS INTO 25/100 SHARES OF THE M/S ARTEMISION IN ACCORDANCE WITH THE OPTION GIVEN TO ME VERBALLY BY YOUR PRESIDENT MR. P. VERGOTIS IN CONSIDERATION OF GRANTING YOU THIS LOAN STOP PLEASE ISSUE THE CORRESPONDING CERTIFICATE OF THESE TWENTYFIVE SHARES AND MAIL IT TO ME 44 AVENUE FOCH PARIS-MARIA CALLAS[140]

Interrogated over this in court, Maria spoke about her father-daughter-like relationship with Vergottis and how "she did not expect a receipt" for the investment at all; so inflexible had been her trust.[141] Each of them more than two decades older than Maria, Onassis and Vergottis had believed it wise to give the woman something to protect her finances in the event of either dying.[142]

Maggie van Zuylen was likewise called in to give evidence.[143] Despite having entrusted Maria with the bearer certificate confirming Onassis' own twenty-six shares of the ship,[144] Vergottis argued that the lawsuit was a foul conspiracy against him and preferred to shift the focus to Maria and Onassis' ubiquitously hyped relationship.

Onassis was cross-examined: did he regard Miss Callas as the equivalent of his wife? "No. If that were the case I have no problem marrying her, neither has she any problem marrying me."[145] What was the nature of his relationship with Miss Callas? Did he feel any obligations beyond friendship? "None whatsoever."[146]

Years later Maria reflected on it. "What Ari said in court was absolutely correct. He was referring to the case and as far as that was concerned he had no other obligations ... It was quite clear that Vergottis thought that he would win his case by exposing my relationship with Ari and create a scandal. How misguided! And besides, why should Ari have had any obligations? We were both independent and responsible people. He was not my legal husband."[147] Accused of turning Maria against Vergottis, Onassis replied: "Madame Callas is not a vehicle for me to drive; she has her own brakes and her own brains."[148]

19 April saw Maria forced to spend three hours and fifty minutes sitting still in the witness box.[149] Judging by her change in headgear—first an orange caftan, then a white one—and the frequent application of her humor, she appeared profoundly bored. To accusations of lies she smiled sardonically and responded: "I am here to answer all questions. Ask anything you want. But please speak louder. I am short-sighted and cannot see what you say."[150]

That evening she escaped from the legal harangue to watch Visconti's La traviata at the Royal Opera House: Mirella Freni was starring. She and Onassis then stayed until two am at the director's after-party in a Kensington basement.[151]

A few hours later she called Carlo Maria Giulini—who had been set to conduct the recording of this new Traviata. "Our Traviata mustn't die," was her plea. Giulini promised to give her a year and a half to work on the music, assuring her that his assistant conductor resided in Paris and would prove a great help. Maria agreed. A tentative recording date was set for September 1968 and eventually brought forward to June.[152]

Maria's last professional alliance with the popular composer had transpired back in January 1964 with the recording of the second volume of her Verdi compilation record, Callas Sings Verdi Arias from Don Carlo, Otello and Aroldo. Documenting her in decent voice, arias from the little-known opera Aroldo, "Ciel, ch'io respiri!" and "O Cielo! Dove son io?" present conventional examples of the Callas-Verdi pairing: sudden blustery crescendi, delicate diminuendi and abundant reverence.

A testimony to her genius is the album's Desdemona. Performing the heroine's monologue before the dangerous Otello's imminent return, Maria's voice embodies the wronged newlywed with an alarming combination of naivety and premonition. "Emilia, te ne prego" ("Emilia, I implore you"), she addresses her maid. "Lay my bridal gown over the bed" ("Distendi sul mio letto la mia candida veste nuziale"). The music is almost orchestrally minimal: a motif climbs from an ominous cor anglais. Extending orders to her maid, Maria's Desdemona cedes to fearful, serial diminuendi: every line ebbs like her hope. Suddenly she tells Emilia when she dies she wishes to be laid to rest in one of the gown's veils.

As Desdemona reflects on her misery ("Son mesta tanto ... tanto ... tanto ...": "I am sad so much ... So much ... so much"), Maria's voice slows down to become graver: almost miniscule. She is more contemplative. Desdemona harks back to her youthful days: her mother had a young maid, Barbara. Barbara fell in love with a man who eventually left her. "Era il suo nome Barbara ... Amava un uom ... che poi l'abbandonò ..." her tone alternates between a bard-like narration and petrified presages. We learn that Barbara used to sing the Willow Song: "Cantava una canzone

... la canzon del Salice." Again a soft diminuendo percolates the somber
thought.

As she imitates doomed Barbara's singing to the willow: "O Salce ...
salce ... salce ..." ("O willow ... willow ... willow"), the words are a
contrasting trio: each diminished to grow cautiousness. When she mimics
Barbara's cries ("Cantiamo! Cantia-amo . . ."), "Let's sing! Let's ... sing ..."
the first is declamatory, in the style of a bard; the second is frightened ... as
if someone might hear her. As if Otello were present.

Barbara's repeated phrase is: "Il salce funebre sarà la mia ghirlanda"
("The funereal willow tree will be my garland"). Desdemona attempts once
again to mirror Barbara's voice—but falls short; succumbing instead to
crepuscular sentiments.

When the violins stir disarray with frantic tones and Desdemona hears an
unexpected knock she rouses suddenly: "Taci—chi batte quella *porta?*"
("Hush—who's knocking at the *door?*") she demands to know of Emilia. The
abrupt crescendo is unjustified: no one is there. But Desdemona knows her
destiny. Maria illustrates it for her.

She has no choice except to pray. "Ave Maria, piena di grazia ..." ("Hail
Mary, full of grace . . ."): Maria instills forced calm in her voice; breaking up
the words to give each syllable of the repeated note—an E flat after middle
C—pronounced composure. Throughout the execution Desdemona must
restrain herself. Applying tentative diminuendo in her glacial stasis, she begs
the Virgin Mary to pray for the sinner, the innocent. Only in one line, "Prega
per chi sotto l'oltraggio piega la fronte e sotto la malvagia sorte" ("Pray for
him who bows to injustice and abides by the blows of cruel fate"), does she
release her voice into the bold, despairing flight of crazed crescendo ...
eventually shrinking it into a wary *piano*. Pronouncing her last "Ave Maria"s,
Desdemona is fixated: congealed by the visceral prescience of death.

The court hearing continued and Maria fled.[153] Though her presence was
further required, British authorities could do little if she failed to attend.

28 April witnessed her victory: Maria was made a majority shareholder
in the ship.[154] Upon appeal in 1968, Vergottis was again unsuccessful.[155] She
spent some time in Cannes at the film festival[156] and later journeyed to
Florida on the *Christina*.[157]

That summer Luchino Visconti had been invited to Skorpios together
with one of his most used stars, Helmut Berger: an actor later known for his
performances in *The Damned* and *The Godfather Part III*. Though the
former had declined, the latter came aboard together with Maria's friend,
film producer Franco Rossellini (nephew of director Roberto), his friend
producer Marina Cicogna and her lesbian partner model-actress Florinda
Bolkan. While Onassis entertained the guests—escorting them to a new
island every day—his manifest flirtation with young Bolkan roiled Maria.
Conflicts grew more and more proliferate.[158]

A heyday of debauchery was taking place before her eyes: the skinny-
dipping, openly homosexual and hedonistic foursome of Bolkan, Cicogna,

Berger and Rossellini were raucous. Marina Cicogna remembered Maria as "a boring woman, very bourgeois . . . [she] had a problem with the two boys being noisy and gay . . . it was the end of his [Onassis'] relationship with Maria, and they were screaming and yelling at each other in Greek."[159] For Bolkan the soprano was a "very closed off" woman.[160] Berger remembered her probing old pal Rossellini for gossip.[161]

From there she retreated to Karajan's villa in Saint Tropez, where Maria tried on various outfits to tailor her wardrobe.[162]

On 4 August she attended the Menton Festival in France with Princess Grace during her stay at her palace, where she witnessed performances by pianists Sviatoslav Richter[163] and Byron Janis.[164]

This fresh immersion in the world of music led her to reach out to her old mentor, Tullio Serafin. "How are you? You are so often in my mind," she wrote. "I'd like to come to Rome and see you this autumn. I am recommencing my work but with calm—I don't have the physical strength that I did as a young girl. I have never been as strong as I was then. I had such willpower and faith, as you wrote in your dedication to me. But life wears out."[165]

From the middle of August she was back in Paris, now working with British accompanist Richard Nunn.[166] Onassis remained on the *Christina*, where he began once again to entertain Jacqueline Kennedy.[167]

"Here in Paris, studying is so hard," Maria wrote to Giulietta Simionato in the meantime. "But, God willing, I will pick myself up spiritually and physically, I hope."[168] In an effort to strengthen her diaphragm she was frequently wearing a corset.[169]

And yet already the soprano had vacation plans. "I love life, but I'm the kind of woman who asks herself, 'If I don't have my work, what do I do from morning till night?'" Maria had told Derek Prouse six years before. "I've always been active in my life, and I have no children. Now, more or less, I haven't even got a family. What do I do if I don't have my career? I can't just sit and play cards or gossip. I'm not the type."[170]

Now she was resting at Haar Castle in Holland, the home of Maggie van Zuylen. A reporter followed her there. "I'll give you two minutes," she conceded—sitting down to offer soundbites. "You know, two years ago I became ill. I could not sing against the advice of my doctor. I needed to unwind. Slowly I began to train again and I do so fairly regularly now. I'm currently working on just making some records. Then I'll see what happens. Naturally, I shall sing in public again. When? Maybe in December. I must prepare and train." Sensing Maria was overwhelmed, the journalist reported that she wanted "to return to the pool table to play cochonnet with her friends: a billiards game without a cue."

Instead she continued to lounge on the couch. "I gave concerts in 1959 at the Concertgebouw in Amsterdam," she made a point of reminding him. "It was fantastic."[171]

Maria's fear had led her to an unexpected destination: boredom. Boredom and billiards surpassed truth.

Peter Andry began calling Maria to uncover details on her everyday training. "Madame's not here, Monsieur," Bruna often informed him—till the day she herself picked up the phone: "Can you come round for a chat?"[172]

An ensemble was enlisted for the *La traviata* recording: the RAI Orchestra of Rome. Greek baritone Kostas Paskalis would sing the role of Germont. For Alfredo Maria and Andry reflected on Carlo Bergonzi and Franco Corelli. She remained undecided.[173]

Maria reverted to Elvira de Hidalgo—eager to inform fans in an interview that November: "I had Elvira de Hidalgo again *now*, a month ago at my home—she *will* come back again, by the way, so's I'll *train* again . . ." When asked why she still trained, her response emerged almost resigned: "Well, you know . . . You say I'm famous, but the more famous I become, the more I have to *train*. Hmm."[174]

After spending weeks in Paris with de Hidalgo, Maria's anxieties returned to distraction. "Sometimes I say, 'I would like to go and see X or Y', and I get on a plane and go," she would later express to a journalist.[175] This was characteristic of Maria the Fugitive: the one at odds with reality. On 24 October she and Onassis stopped by London to attend Tito Gobbi's birthday party at the Savoy.[176] When on the next day Gobbi sought to send her flowers to express his gratitude, he was informed she had flown home to Paris.[177]

Maria supported de Hidalgo financially.[178] Now almost seventy-six years old, the elderly soprano marveled at Onassis: "There were great emotions during the days that we spent together. It was like a dream!" she wrote to Maria on 10 November. "As it suits you, I will come back to yours, whenever you like, and you will be able to tranquilly think of your voice in your home . . . In any case, I was very happy that you left [with Onassis for New York], because from what I could tell in both your voices, I understood that you were very happy to leave together. God bless you both! Thank Aristo for his exquisite hospitality."[179]

Apparently content, Maria and Onassis spent their time frequenting restaurants, allegedly recruiting a French chef to teach them to cook "delicate crêpes".[180] A week later she replied to de Hidalgo: "Dear Elvira . . . Did I not tell you I've been crazy? Look what love does to a person . . . Aristo is my love. He sends you his love and thanks you for being so understanding and dear with me . . . Don't you think Aristo has changed for the better?"[181]

The ecstasy was short-lived. As is frequently the case between two headstrong individuals, the wrong kind of sparks began to fly. One night when Maria bumped into Byron Janis at Luchow's restaurant, the pair threw themselves into musical discourse: "talking artist to artist, passion to passion," in the words of the latter. "And Onassis became more and more annoyed by our artistic liaison. Eventually, shouting broke out between them. 'Why are you doing this?' she snapped. 'I have a right to speak with anyone the way I want to.' But he grabbed her arm and pulled her away to the waiting limousine."[182]

Relatability had turned to rancor. "It is true that I had quite a few arguments with Ari," Maria recollected later. "For some time I simply couldn't take it and felt angry and unhappy. The situation was getting worse because I became touchy and a little haughty, and probably misconstrued some things as a sign of rejection. The old saying familiarity breeds contempt was very much at the back of my mind. You see, before I met Ari I had not really experienced lovers' tiffs and being by nature rather shy and introverted (when I am not on the stage), I was losing my sense of humour, not that I have much. When you can't laugh at yourself life becomes dreary. It took time, but once I understood this other side of his character, by and large I accepted it, even though in part I still disapproved of it."[183]

While Maria continued to resent Onassis' hunger to own almost everything, he took it out on her sore spot. In May 1966 he and Maria had been dining at Le Pavillon in New York one night when she had pointed out to their friend: "He made rose-petaled cigarettes for Claudia Muzio." Muzio had been a soprano Maria ironically hated.[184] Onassis had commanded a waiter to bring him a rose; he wanted to display his cigarette-making technique. "Claudia Muzio and Maria were the only sopranos who could do lyric, dramatic coloratura . . ." he had announced. "Rosa Ponselle also could do it," Maria had argued. Perhaps drunkenly, Onassis had insisted: "Only two . . . I started with the first, Claudia Muzio in Buenos Aires long ago. And now I wind up here in Le Pavillon with the other."[185]

The magnate's foray into the terrain of Muses had been wearily ephemeral. In the early sixties his and Maria's good friend, director Alexis Minotis, had dangled bait at what he liked to call Onassis' "manie de grandeur". After suggesting that Onassis fund the restoration of the legendary ancient Theatre of Dionysus, Minotis stressed that if he did this he could "achieve immortality". Racing to this like a dog to a bone, the businessman smacked himself into a hurdle: Greek law forbade the restoration of antiquities unless they were at least one quarter Greek—unlike this theatre. He lobbied bureaucrats to change the law and made progress with sitting Prime Minister Konstantinos Karamanlis. Following Prime Minister George Papandreou's appointment the project was nixed.

By 1967 Onassis was a sixty-one-year-old shipping magnate whose businesses were not always afloat. Having fulfilled his dream of founding a non-government-operated Greek airline, Olympic Airways, he struggled with its endless delays, cancellations and plummeting ticket sales. "Onassis never created a modern, streamlined business corporation with a clean chain of command or effective intercommunication among employees," his biographers would write. "He never had a private secretary to handle his airline affairs. His 'office' was a tattered old notebook wrapped in rubber bands and filled with phone numbers."[186]

In August 1967 former head of the Greek Civil Aviation Authority, Air Marshal George Doukas, had submitted a report on Olympic to the Greek government citing its failures. Calling Onassis "a cancerous growth on

Greek society," Doukas claimed he would buy "people and favors by the classic method of corrupting consciences" and alluded to his "brigand-like hunger". For the first and only time, Onassis sued for defamation of character.

Compelled to take the witness stand again, he managed to unmask the fact that profits from the airline had amounted to a mere "few drachmas". "Then why do you keep Olympic?" the judge demanded to know. "What should I do? Throw it in the sea?" quipped Onassis. "These things are not logical. If it is not making progress, why is it continuously expanding?"— "We are trying to lose less," disputed the founder.[187]

Several months previously he had at last hung up his spurs after a series of fraught legal contests had resulted in him losing his last shares in Monte Carlo's Société des Bains de Mer to Prince Rainier.[188] "We lost," he admitted the following year. "When a government says 'I'm taking over,' there's nothing you can do to stop them. Those shares were worth six or seven times what they paid me."[189]

Less than two years afterward Maria would describe him to the Sorias as "mad, unstable, fragile—my Mister O. He is an unhappy man. He would sit, sulk on [the] floor. I would say, 'What more do you want? You are rich, powerful, famous, I am famous.' He said, 'You don't understand.' I couldn't understand him. He had a destructer [sic] logic. I see things straight. When his nerves were going I begged him to go to a doctor. He did. [He] said 'my liver, blood pressure, heart [are] all right.'—'Did you tell him about your nerves?'—'No, it was not the business of a doctor.' "[190]

"Oh, those Orientals!" she would vent to Leo Lerman in 1971. "He's Greek, but born in Turkey. They can't let anything out. It's in the head, and they can't let it out. They can't go to a doctor and say, 'Help me. I can't sleep. I have anxiety. I am nervous.' I am born in America, so I know these things. You have something wrong in the head, you go to a doctor, and he helps you—like with a broken toe. The first duty is to cure the brain."[191]

It was this Onassis who was altercating with Maria in late 1967. Acquaintances were starting to observe the woman made him tense. Actress Elsa Martinelli remembered her evenings on Onassis' island of Skorpios were magical "when Maria Callas wasn't there . . . he would be transformed . . . And he would invite me to dance the sirtaki with him."[192]

At the culmination of their arguments Maria would fly back to Paris and unplug the telephone. Endeavoring to counter the chagrin with the unfailing antidotes of drink and dance, Onassis would head straight for a Glyfada nightclub or stop by at Paris' Maxim's.[193]

Maria's celebrated yet impaired voice didn't help. "Her singing exercises disturbed him [on the *Christina*] just like they did us," Helmut Berger would recall. "Especially," he added, "when he concentrated on difficult business negotiations."[194]

In Onassis' eyes it was a contest.

In Maria's eyes his work could *never* surpass hers.

For this reason the man's denigration of her art became more frequent. "To him an opera career was nothing," Maria would tell Dorle Soria. "He spoke of me as 'an entertainer.'"[195]

On 9 November Maria attended Elena Suliotis' concert *Norma* at Carnegie Hall, visited her backstage and congratulated her with a "Brava, brava, brava."[196] Seven months later she wrote to John Ardoin: "Suliotis' *Norma* wasn't bad at all but I was terrified by the way she uses the capital instead of the interest—and her near-total lack of technique. A shame, because the voice is sublime."[197]

Tenaciously nevertheless Maria fueled this novel reputation: that of a fragile, complex-ridden woman.

Naturally girlish, she adjusted her image to appear almost helpless. Maria cited constantly her problem with articulation—even begging David Frost in 1970 before their interview, "If I have trouble with my English, you'll help me, won't you?"[198] Frequently she made allusions to its faults: "Thank you for understanding me so much and giving me the possibility of expressing a few phrases—though they're . . . very badly expressed," the soprano repined in another discussion.[199]

The public Maria was no longer the world's greatest singer who chastened sopranos for not singing *Norma*—and eloquently. She was an uneducated, unfortunate creature of destiny who—apparently—knew almost nothing: "I'm an animal, I can't say that I'm very, very intellectual," she would tell Lord Harewood for the BBC in 1968. "But this is to a *disadvantage*, and an *advantage*."[200]

Her melancholy likewise made her spoilt. Hellbent on concealing it, she morphed into the worst rendition of a singer she could be: the diva. A disguise that prompted her to act on whims a gossip columnist would die to see.

An example of these surfaced during this Manhattan sojourn. Maria was scheduled to have a meeting with Peter Andry on November 11th. Yet she insisted—evidently to deflect attention from the imminent *Traviata* recording—that she needed another mink coat. "But you already have six hanging in the wardrobe," Andry responded. "Yes, but I think a need a new one."

It was a Saturday. Most of New York's furriers were religious Jews. Maria coerced them to open up shop and defy the commands of the Torah. Rummaging through all the coats, she tried them on and took them off exhaustively. Each left her unimpressed.

At the end of the day came another idea: "Could you get me a radio at a discount?" she asked Andry.[201]

Four days later she was at her old friend Leo Lerman's house from 12:30 am to 4:30 am: "the new, very young girl, loving, funny Maria," he wrote in his diary. "I am a better man," she professed, "than most of you know."[202]

Thus emerged Maria's worst nightmare: a prima donna incarnate. Who couldn't *sing*.

For this reason many who first met Maria in her later years encountered someone very contrary to her original persona.

It depended on their character nevertheless. If Maria deemed them cosmopolitan, open, Bohemian—much like Leo Lerman—she would unravel a relationship-obsessed, "hip" image; imagining this was the act they sought to see.

It was a process. Maria's letters to Leo Lerman had always been skewed to an audience: he was an intellectual, New York aesthete. Despite almost never using the word "damn" in real life, Maria had once written to him in a missive: "I never was a strong horse even fat. I'm a race horse. Rather delicat [sic] and sensitive! Damn it!"[203]

In front of her hairdresser, Frédéric Simogli of Alexandre de Paris' salon in Paris, she would roll on the floor with her poodles.[204]

Yes, it was the sixties. But Maria's sense of elegant decorum hadn't vanished; she had simply shredded it. Oppressed by torturous anxieties, she couldn't deal with anyone believing her a goddess. She resolved to prove the opposite.

During that visit Rudolf Bing gave Maria a guided tour of Lincoln Center's new Metropolitan Opera House. He had another proposition for her—Richard Strauss' *The Legend of Joseph* in English—and finally sent her the score. Maria politely rejected the offer.[205]

One of Maria's last New York activities was paying a visit to her old friend Fabrizio Melano. She asked him to locate her birth certificate.

Hoping this would ascertain her date of birth, Maria asked Melano to deliver the found document to an astrologer.[206]

"I hate to know what is going to happen tomorrow. And no one would ever persuade me to go to a fortune teller," she had told journalist John Cruesemann eight years earlier.[207]

That was the past.

One of Maria's greatest grievances was suffering from "amour-propre": a French term that denotes a stronger word for "self-respect". "It's very accentuated in my character," she told Micheline Banzet in 1965. "One should never touch it. It's a . . . a very vulnerable side. Stricken, I can become nasty, sometimes . . . They call me crazy. I am not at all; on the contrary, I see things very—*too* closely. And too *clearly*."[208]

"Careful Maria," old friend Eugenio Gara had warned several times throughout her glory. "Remember the Chinese proverb that says: 'He who mounts the tiger won't be able to dismount.' "—"No, no, dear Eugenio," was the reassuring answer. "Don't fear for me; I will do everything I can, not to dismount from my tiger."[209]

Now the tiger had thrown off Maria.

17. *"I began directing opera for Callas, not because of her." In the embrace of Luchino Visconti during her second studio Norma recording. 5 September 1960.*

18. *In deep conversation with Onassis. Monte Carlo, 22 July 1959.*

19. *The height difference is unmissable. Maria and Onassis, 1962.*

20. *A little too romantic for Carmen, but she's still fleshing her out. At the Salle Wagram for the studio recording, July 1964.*

21. *Pure disdain. Maria as Tosca with Tito Gobbi as Scarpia. January 1964.*

22. *In a still from Pasolini's* Medea. *Summer 1969.*

23. *Maria and PPP (Pier Paolo Pasolini) accompany Jeddah and Pixie on their morning walk. Monaco, 1971.*

24. *Maria and PPP present* Medea *at Paris' Cinéma Bonaparte, 31 January 1970.*

25. *Bittersweet bows in Toronto during Maria and Di Stefano's concert tour. Massey Hall, 21 February 1974.*

26. *Less than self-pleased. Maria and "Pippo" Di Stefano in Spain, post-curtain call, Madrid, 20 November 1973.*

27. *Amused by Jacques Chazot at a Les Halles restaurant. Paris, 13 December 1974.*

17.

"The 'intangible' "

It was the Age of Aquarius. Amidst the hazy days of paper flowers, "Lucy in the Sky with Diamonds," spirals of bedraggled hair and denizens in denim fences, opera had devolved into a fusty haunt for grandparents. If rock 'n' roll and Elvis were outmoded, opera was an attic's ghostly spiderwebs.

Spectral also was the voice that held its scepter.

Maria's refuge had lost both its sites: the venerated opera houses she had entered as a pious devotee and her defected inner world. "An intermediary of the spirits impossible to resist," she had once called it.[1]

"I have studied for myself with the pianist [Richard Nunn] . . . and just a week ago I embarked on a new route, or rather—I found my old one," she wrote to Elvira de Hidalgo on 20 January 1968.

> I am rebuilding everything. We'll see—in any case before it wasn't working out so I have nothing to lose at this point.
>
> It's a long work but I have so much patience. I'm tranquil here at home. I have my records that teach me about what I used to do and my tape recorder that plays back what I'm doing and what I shouldn't do . . .
>
> I am taking myself to pieces as I've always done up to now. If it works out, great; if not, I'll give up everything.
>
> After all, I have Aristo—what else could I ask for?[2]

It was easy—or rather, *easier*—for Maria to tell herself that.

Now a philosophical woman with a "Que Sera, Sera" attitude, Maria toyed with the components of her fractious image. She met with Chief Assistant of Music Television for the BBC, Desmond Osland, to arrange a series of opera-centric interviews with her for late April.[3] Inane exchanges persevered with Rudolf Bing: "Thank you for your letter . . ." he wrote on the 31st. "If you say, 'It would have to be together with something to sing,' do you mean something to sing at the same evening or an opera in the repertory? . . . Do you know Cocteau's play *La voix humaine* with music by Poulenc?"[4]

The offers were so tentative, the dialogues so tenuous that it was little more than courteous bluster.

On the 20th Onassis turned sixty-two. Over ten years earlier Maria had written a birthday message to Meneghini:

> *Dearest soul,*
> *I have nothing to give to you as a present because you have all of me . . .*
> *Know only that you couldn't have done more for your mate because your woman is the happiest wife in the world.*[5]

That day heralded Onassis' gift:

> *Aristo my love—*
> *I know this is a meager birthday present but I must tell you that I am after 8 and a half years with—with so much we went through, happy to tell you from the depths of my heart—proud of you, I love you body and soul and only wish that you feel the same.*
> *I feel priviledged* [sic] *to have reached the highest level in a tough career and to be graced by God to have found you who went through hell also—reached the heights and to have us together as we are.*
> *Try, o please do, to keep us united always for I do need your love and respect forever.*
> *I am too proud to admit it but know that you are my very breath, brain, pride, and tenderness—that if you could see into my feelings for you, you would feel the strongest & richest man in the entire world.*
> *This is not a child's letter. This is a hurt, tired, proved woman that gives you the most <u>fresh</u> and youthful sentiments ever felt.*
> *Never forget that and be always as tender with me as these days and you make me the Queen of the World—my love. I need affection and tenderness.*
> *I am yours—do as you will with me.*[6]

The sentiments are similar: a letter as a gift without the need of a material accompaniment; avowals of incomparable belonging. Maria likely didn't draw the parallel. Her self-reflection could incorporate comparisons between her past and present onstage gestures . . . but it didn't always touch her private life.

Gorlinsky wrote notes on Maria's plans: concerts in Dallas, San Francisco, Seattle, and a production at the Paris Opera.[7] On 2 February she invited Leontyne Price over for dinner after her debut in Paris as *Norma*.[8] Price later recalled Maria receiving her in her salon and remarking how "voices were an expression of one's own personality . . . she heard a lot of love in mine."[9] That Christmas Price penned her a tender message—reassuring her potential castmate that she often said a prayer for her health and happiness and found her graciousness toward her unforgettable.[10]

That same day Tullio Serafin died. Maria sent her homage to her friend Irving Kolodin at the *Saturday Review*: " 'When I am in the pit I am there to serve you because I have to save my performance,' he would say. We would look down and feel we had a friend there, in the pit."[11]

Another relic of the past was swiftly swept away.

A little later a nostalgic urge caught flame: a prospective return to the Royal Opera. She conversed with Gorlinsky, who conversed with David Webster. The project would involve five or six concerts to take place from May to June of 1968.[12]

Postponing grave decisions as per usual, Maria embarked on another tour of Las Palmas and eventually the Caribbean.[13] "I don't know when I'm coming back," she wrote to Bruna on March 4th. She was considering going to New York, to where Onassis hoped to sail. "That way I can study with the excellent pianist of the Metropolitan and Dallas Civic Opera [Alberta Masiello]. I haven't decided yet."[14]

Enshrouded by the company of entrepreneur Francis Fabre, Hélène Rochas, her partner Kim d'Estainville, Maggie van Zuylen and others, Maria and Onassis stirred the gossip of Port-au-Prince, Haiti—where Dictator President François Duvalier had commissioned a quatrain for the "voice that makes sound preferable to silence."[15]

Welcomed at Sans Souci Palace, Maria gave the despot a signed copy of her *La Gioconda*.[16] A grandiose reception featuring ballet was given in her and Onassis' honor at the Hotel El Rancho. In it flautist Alupcion Cadet unveiled a musical mosaic of enchantment. After demanding to meet the man, Maria alerted Director General of Tourism, Luc Albert Foucard: "In the course of the last two years, we've visited all the Caribbean islands aboard the *Christina*, but we've always avoided Haiti for fear of not finding the peace and the atmosphere we were looking for. Now we regret greatly having taken so much time to reach this Eden."

Advising him on propaganda slogans the soprano counseled: " 'Lands of the Sun'—one encounters them everywhere from Africa to America. You should call your country the 'Land of the Smile', appealing not to traditional Haitian hospitality but to the smiles surfacing on locals' lips that make one's heart sing."[17]

Progressively her closeness to Onassis putrefied. After continuing their cruise in Nassau in late March Maria left for Paris while the former ventured to New York. It was there that he revisited his latest accessory Jacqueline Kennedy, and was spotted dining with her in a Manhattan Greek restaurant, Mykonos.[18] When Kennedy then travelled to Florida Onassis flew from New York to collect and escort her to Nassau, where she spent Easter weekend aboard the *Christina* with him.[19]

Kennedy and Onassis had first met in 1954 amidst her husband's Massachusetts senatorial campaign. Throughout her days of mourning following the president's assassination he was one of the few visitors she comfortably received.[20]

In Paris Maria busied herself with accompanist Richard Nunn once again. She was still corresponding with Peter Andry about the proposed *Traviata* recording.[21]

On 24 April Maria sat down with old friend Lord Harewood to record her BBC extensive interviews. For a refreshing interval she tapped into her roles, expounded on bel canto and alluded to opera being "old-fashioned" and the need to "breathe life into it". Following the discourse she served plates heaped with spaghetti to the drained crew.[22] The next day Onassis returned to Paris following his cruise with the former first lady.[23]

Hairdresser Frédéric Simogli recalled Maria's disgust when her friends told her tales of their intimate lives.[24] Yet the tension coursing through her veins now prompted her to publicize a daily column of her own.

The insomniac compulsion to call anyone at almost any time swelled like infected skin about to dribble pus. "At around three or four [am] I take the phone and ring my friends," Maria proudly told Marlyse Schaeffer, forgetting the latter's fabrication of an interview with her nine years previously. "In Rome, in London, in New York, through the whole world . . . They don't complain, they are delighted!"[25]

What gossip fodder did these calls solicit. At times it seemed that all her entourage—from music critics to accompanists to make-up artists— beamed with pride for being treated in this special fashion. Most of them relished laying bare this side of her once she was dead. "She would tell me, 'I love you a lot, my dear,' which meant, as I understood later, that she was feeling blue," her hairdresser reported.[26]

On another night the target was an eager Jacques Bourgeois. Maria was complaining of Italian film director Pier Paolo Pasolini's new film, *Teorema*: a dark allegory centered on a young god who ingratiates himself with a mysterious family. Subsequently he seduces first the maid and then the mother, son, daughter and father before suddenly deserting them.[27]

Other times Bourgeois would be subjected to her rants about Onassis: "We're not made for each other. Me—I'm a creature of destiny; he is incapable of understanding me." Or else: "He is a total idiot! He doesn't *deserve* me!"[28] Sometimes the topic would surround the vocal lesson she had learnt that day: "I've re-discovered it," she would inform him. Then, next day: "What I re-discovered *yesterday*—it's gone *today*, and I don't understand *why*." A week later, more news: Maria had regained "control of certain things."[29]

Hoping to discuss future engagements, Gorlinsky would receive an earful of Maria being "depressed last night about the world political situation."[30]

Customarily a telephone call would be elongated by "glissades and diminuendos of ciao," according to Leo Lerman.[31]

Maria didn't care about the nature of her interlocutor, how closely they had known her, or at times how trustworthy they were. She cared about not being by herself. With a destructive lack of sleep and a barrage of tumbling thoughts, there were too many questions left to conquer. What had happened to her voice? Why couldn't she just marry and have children like most "normal" women? What would she do if singing were not possible? The obstacles were endless. Phone calls couldn't make them obsolete—but they would *stay* them. For a while.

Her letter-writing contest with the testy Bing continued: *Lucia* wouldn't work out—Maria needed "another opera 'less perilous'."[32]

In mid-May she remained in Paris to work with Richard Nunn on *La traviata*, its recording having been scheduled for June.[33]

Across the Atlantic brewing rumors had come to the boil. On May 6th Rudolf Nureyev and his assistant Joan Thring threw a dinner party in an apartment lent them by Lee Radziwill—inviting Jacqueline Kennedy, Onassis, Robert F. "Bobby" Kennedy and his wife Ethel. It was the season of the primary elections; Bobby Kennedy was far and wide expected to become the Democratic Party's candidate. Talk began to stir about the plans of Mrs. Kennedy: she was considering a marriage to Onassis to acquire privacy, protection and financial gains for both her children and herself. In the interest of preserving the pristine Kennedy image, discussion of the subject was embargoed for the period of Bobby's run for president.[34]

From 21 to 28 May Jacqueline Kennedy boarded the *Christina* again, this time to cruise the Virgin Islands.[35] Tagging along was Joan Thring. Herself engaging in a fling with the Lothario Onassis, Thring would watch him toss Maria's records in the ocean as he discharged grievances about the way she practiced scales and sang aboard the ship. "He said it was awful, he hated it."[36]

It was precisely the kind of impetuous, childish behavior Maria was slighting at home. That month hailed the Paris protests. Students and professors fused into a homogeneous brigade to fight against materialism, capitalism and the bourgeoisie; workers on strike hurled furniture across the street; stores stagnated. For two months the media asked if the 20th century French Revolution was imminent.

This celebrated decade of looseness espoused an inferior approach to the arts in Maria's eyes. Baby-boomers were more focused on societal ideals and freedom: one corruptive to the cause of pure perfectionism.

"There are no longer any great men," Maria had told Micheline Banzet in 1965. "*Why?* They're scared. Scared of losing their position. Scared of dying of hunger. Scared of being crushed or else defeat; scared of *everything*."[37] "Youngsters think that if they wear their hair long or if they wear—I don't know, they're *hippies* or things like that [that they seem strong]. That is *not* a way of showing themselves strong. I think they have to *think*, take *time* to think *sanely, healthily*—even if the others will say, 'Oh, how *stupid* you are, how ridiculous, how old-fashioned.' "[38]

Academics were determining what was in vogue in music; melody had morphed into the sacrificial lamb of themes experimental and atonal. "As soon as a composer *comes* along with a lovely *melody*, what will the *public* say?" Maria asked. " 'Oh, he is imitating Verdi,' or 'This reminds me of Puccini' or 'This reminds me of Bellini.' "[39]

Her affiliation with the present world began to shrink. Terrified of pursuing the *Traviata*, she rescheduled the recording in June to September. After a while Maria called Peter Andry to tell him that September would be "too hot to record in Rome. We had better postpone things a little longer."[40] Informed of this proposal, Carlo Maria Giulini advised Peter Andry that October "would be too cold" for him.[41] That response scrapped the planned *Traviata* recording for good.

At the end of May Maria voyaged to Milan, where she selected among Biki's new designs and on the phone discussed a possible Royal Opera House recital with Gorlinsky.[42] It was time for her to schedule summer cruises on the *Christina*. Then a dire conflict between her and the Greek magnate seemed to rupture the relationship.

While the reason for this quarrel didn't come to light it probably involved Onassis' most recent cruise with Jacqueline Kennedy.[43] Maria's presence was unwarranted while Kennedy was on the yacht. As his mistress she did not possess the necessary status to accommodate an ex-first lady.

Oblivious to the ongoing courtship between Onassis and Kennedy, Maria wrote to Elvira de Hidalgo on 16 June:

I'm rather well considering the circumstances but I feel as though I've had a huge blow and I'm not able to breathe yet. He rang three times. On one occasion, I didn't pick up. Twice I did and it was disastrous both times. As I told him, he's an irresponsible man, which is a disgusting thing for me. I'm in Paris and I will try to impose a little order in my head—which is still so much in pain. I'm trying to survive these months. I'm not exerting myself too much because I don't have the mental strength and, subsequently, the psychological strength. I don't know where I should go to have a little rest. I feel so lost because of so many years of work and then because of this man I'm finding that I don't know where to go; this is the last drop.[44]

Following this burdensome dispute with his contentious lover, Onassis renewed his suggestion of marriage to Kennedy. She promised her answer would be shortly forthcoming.[45]

A few days later unexpected circumstances lent it extra urgency: Senator Robert F. Kennedy—the man predicted to become the next U.S. president— was shot dead at the Ambassador Hotel in New York during a televised press conference. Immediately Onassis flew to the United States to comfort sister-in-law Jacqueline.[46]

In Paris still, Maria was discussing the idea of a *Medea* at the Met with Rudolf Bing—who was so confident that he commanded his assistant Robert Herman to commence its preparations. By 23 June it seemed impossible because of the Met's shortcomings: "I'm afraid this season it may not work with *Medea* ... If you can still see your way to accepting

Lucia or *Traviata*—please send me another cable, which would make me very happy. It was lovely seeing you again."[47]

A few weeks thence Maria mended fences with her former lover. Onassis invited her to spend most of July aboard the *Christina* in the Mediterranean.[48] Having heard rumors that Maria was in circulation, Lawrence Kelly came to Paris on 4 July and caught her on the verge of her departure.[49] Maria advised him it would be better to discuss future work on the yacht; Kelly followed.

Across the oceanic straits the couple's acrimony grew acute. Lawrence Kelly would later refer to there being "something . . . terribly wrong with the Callas-Onassis relationship."[50] Maria was due to return from the *Christina* on 25 July according to Gorlinsky's correspondence with her.[51] In conversation with Onassis she discovered Jacqueline Kennedy, as well as Senator Edward "Ted" Kennedy, had been invited to the yacht for a mid-August cruise.[52]

The subject of her not being permitted to meet Jacqueline Kennedy incensed her yet again. Once more Maria couldn't stand Onassis' gluttony for power; once more Onassis couldn't stand her confidence.

In operatic terms she would explain the rift to Leo Lerman three years later—albeit citing an event in "Nassau" when the straw that broke the camel's back had taken place in the Mediterranean: "I finished with him in Nassau. He's sick, destructive. He brainwashed me. 'You with that whistle in your throat, on your high horse . . .' If I had stayed with him, he would have killed me or I would have killed him: 'You can't break me,' I told him. 'You can kill me, but you can't break me.' "[53]

Her grievances against him would be overdramaticized in other ways. On 29 April 1969 she had told Dario and Dorle Soria: "The people on the *Christina* were always *his* friends—not mine."[54] Had she forgotten the multiple stays of Giovanna Lomazzi, Michel Glotz, Georges Prêtre, Franco Zeffirelli and Herbert von Karajan among others? Or that she and Princess Grace had been friends?

At war again, Maria and Onassis jabbed each other's sore spots. This exercise was too fatiguing for the worn-out singer. Asking Lawrence Kelly to accompany her, she abandoned both Onassis and the cruise in mid- or late July and flew straight to New York.[55]

As the Kennedys were entertained aboard the yacht that August[56] she transformed her boredom into restless travelling. Following Lawrence Kelly around like a fast-panting puppy, Maria was a woman hopelessly at loss for what to do with either others or herself. On the 28th they went to see the musical *Hair*: a romp of rock and nudity featuring then little-known Diane Keaton. Maria's shock was such that she absconded prior to the end of the performance—hastening to send the cast a cordial telegram:

SINCERELY ENJOYED ALL YOUR PERFORMANCE [sic] THIS EVENING I AM TERRIBLY SORRY THAT I HAD TO LEAVE THE THEATER EARLIER AND COULD NOT COME BACK STAGE TO

VISIT YOU NEVER THE LESS THANK YOU FOR SUCH A VIVACIUS [sic] PERFORMANCE WHICH I ENJOYED A LOT SINCERELY[57]

The emphasis remained on "having fun" . . . whatever *that* was. During a television interview with Pierre Desgraupes months later, she would joke with fellow guests Visconti and Francesco Siciliani: "You see how we have fun sometimes?"[58]

Dumbing down the self was necessary. "What do you *do* if you do not work? I do not understand. Perhaps people who do not work pass the time in talking of themselves. I do not want to talk about myself. I find me boring. It is what I do that interests me, not what I say. How can you exist if you do not do things, and how can you exist with self-respect if you do not do things as well as lies in you?" she would ask a journalist rhetorically in 1970.[59]

Yet Maria spent these months engaged in everything she pledged to ardently despise—and *did*: playing card games, talking of herself a *lot*; discussing matters that were far beyond her interests.

Back in 1965 she had met John Ardoin, a critic for *The Dallas Morning News*. "Did you like my voice when you first heard it?" she had asked. "No."—"Generally, I upset people the first time they hear me, but I am usually able to convince them of what I am doing," had been her response.[60]

Ardoin was a relatively cosmopolitan, opera-loving, gay music critic; Maria likely pigeon-holed him as another Leo Lerman. For this reason Ardoin was exposed to a similar character: playful, down to earth and trying too hard to acclimatize. "Your problem is that you're still thinking too much about Callas and you really don't know Maria," she alerted the man. "Well, don't worry dear, we'll take the time to get to know Maria."[61]

In her he found someone who had "no intellect . . . I didn't mean she wasn't smart—she was a different kind of smart. What I meant was, she didn't read books; she didn't talk about intellectual issues or matter. She loved cartoons on television . . . You know, conversations with Maria were very mundane—very mundane."[62]

Bent on deflecting everyone's attention from the shadow of the goddess, Maria was hard-pressed to understand that she was not convincing in the role of Average Woman. Rather than sympathizing with her vocal or romantic plights, her entourage regarded her as a strange creature; a bête noire about whom they could gossip and share sordid anecdotes. That same John Ardoin—with whom Maria had strived hard to seem outgoing—later wrote a tell-all book that splintered their relationship.

In Kansas City Lawrence Kelly took her to the house of their friend David Stickelber, the heir to a bread-slicing machine fortune. He would later tell *The Washington Post* how "Maria insisted on my creating the illusion that time was passing rapidly . . . So each day I would go into her bedroom and say 'This is December. Tomorrow it will be January. Thursday will be Valentine's Day'—and so on."[63]

Next she moved to Santa Fe, where she stayed at the Rancho Encantado Four Seasons resort[64] and "strolled about good-humoredly in Levi's, her dark hair hanging loose," as one hotel employee told. "When two men were celebrating their birthday in the dining room, she even sang happy birthday."[65]

For a couple of days she stayed in Las Vegas,[66] attending comedy shows by Merv Griffin and Shecky Greene.[67] By 9 August she was at the Bel Air Hotel in Los Angeles, refusing to let photographers take her picture. Accompanying her were Lawrence Kelly and her old friends, Robert and Mary Mead of Dallas.[68] Everyone among her posse—including her Milan-based part-time secretary—was enlightened of her separation from Onassis.[69] By August 25th the gossip columns had caught wind of it.[70]

Days had scarcely passed when she met old foe, San Francisco Opera's manager Kurt Adler at the city's popular Charles Restaurant.[71] They talked about the possibility of *Norma*.[72] Gorlinsky wrote to tell her Adler had enquired of potential dates for a Los Angeles engagement after 28th February, 1969.[73] To Bruna Maria wrote that she hoped to return in early September to resume work on her unfinished compilation of Verdi.[74] Sleepless at six o'clock in the morning, she wrote a brief letter to Lawrence Kelly to apologize for a faux pas she had made.[75]

The site of her vacationing then moved to Cuernavaca, Mexico,[76] where Mary and Robert Mead rented a house. The former would recall how she would spend her hours watching westerns and then "talking, talking, talking."[77] What she likely didn't know was that Maria didn't think too highly of her either—having written once to Lawrence Kelly, "I'm happy to hear that she is more mature, etc."[78]

There she consulted EMI's John Coveney. He advised Maria to enlist the services of La Scala's chorus master Norberto Mola, who was then working in Dallas. Frightened by the prospect of this reimmersion, the soprano turned down the proposal. She channeled her ambition into a desire to perform *Norma* in Dallas from October to November and *Medea* at the Met immediately afterward—and finally determined to record *La traviata* in the spring of 1969.[79]

It was in this Mexican metropolis that she slipped on the bathroom floor, fell down and cracked her ribs.[80]

Only following her arrival in Dallas over a week later on 3 September[81] did Maria at last see a doctor. During her stay at Lawrence Kelly's house Onassis called incessantly. According to his housekeeper, Georgia Vetta, he struggled both to eat and sleep after her sudden flight. His phone calls went unanswered.[82] The gargantuan bouquet he had dispatched went unacknowledged.

Her visit to the doctor afforded Maria an awkward experience she could mince into anecdotes: "Larry would pick the one doctor in town who loves opera!" she exulted to John Ardoin. "He loves all my records. When I took my blouse off, his hands started to shake so badly, he couldn't strap my ribs. He could barely touch me!"

"Do you know any card games?" was her enquiry one night. Maria attempted to take part in one—which involved having to lie—then stood up and demanded to know: "How can you ask me to do that? How can you ask me to lie?" and stormed off. It was easier to express unfounded moral outrage than to state the obvious.[83]

Much like the voice that she had exercised unstoppably, her boredom never took a rest. She practiced her reactions to it endlessly—insisting John Ardoin accompany her to a cinema. They sat and watched *The Graduate*. Maria tossed comments at the screen, asking Mrs. Robinson: "How can you let him treat you like that? Never mind, I understand. I have been treated like that too." Ardoin later took great pleasure in asking a journalist, "Who would have believed that the woman sitting at a mall table eating a hot dog and guzzling an Orange Julius could be the great Callas?"[84]

"Many people want me to be an 'actress' at all costs—to be making an exhibition of myself. And nothing I can ever do will change that," Maria had scribed back in 1959.[85] Nine years later—with no voice and no activities— the star was making gossip-mongers' wish come true.

Her success with friendship had been tentative. In Maria's words in 1970, a friend was "Someone you can *count* on . . . *any* moment of your *life*. Ah . . . *good* friends, I suppose, I *will* find out—and I hope I never *do*—if I, *tomorrow*, have no *money*, no *fame*, and am very *sick*. The ones that are *near* you for a *long* time are the *ones* that are good *friends*."[86] Asked how one could lose her friendship, she responded: "By taking advantage of me . . . There are friends whom I've completely lost touch with and they don't understand at all why. Because they never see what they have done that could have upset me . . . I lead a very isolated life because of that, because sooner or later someone will do me harm . . ."[87] "Opportunism makes me sad."[88]

Yet she was giving opportunists *so* much ammunition. Was it blind trust? To some extent. To another, she appeared indifferent to being viewed a shallow or a stupid woman. "Shallow" or "stupid" was better than "victim" or "has-been". These adjustments in her character became a fine mode of escapism.

Contrarily the context of an interview provoked her to be self-aware, composed, well-mannered and premeditated: in retention of her reason and not trying hard to please.

In Dallas Maria formally announced she would be making her operatic return. "I think the Met, San Francisco and Dallas is a good enough begin- ning, and these depend on a decision regarding repertory and other matters," she informed the press.[89]

While in the city she recorded a one-hour interview with John Ardoin. In it she spent almost thirty minutes dissecting Lady Macbeth's "Sleepwalking Scene".[90] The president of the Dallas Civic Opera held a luncheon on the 12th in her honor with a champagne reception.[91] Maria succumbed to the genre by offering to submit a recipe for the cookbook being prepared by the junior group of the Dallas Symphony Orchestra.[92] Adapting herself socially was second instinct to her. She just wasn't very good at it.

From Dallas Maria traversed the Midwestern states to land finally in New York, where she stayed at the Sherry Netherland Hotel. Catching wind of her arrival, Met treasurer George Moore resolved to bring her to Renata Tebaldi's opening night of *Adriana Lecouvreur* at the start of the season.[93]

Sat beside him that evening of 16 September, she confirmed the status of her relationship with Bing to the press: "definitely friends . . . we are talking, of course, we're talking."[94]

In accordance with theatrical tradition Maria asked to see Tebaldi at the end of the performance. "When they told me, I was quite taken aback," the latter would tell a biographer.[95]

The two were photographed embracing backstage. Four days later Tebaldi wrote to Maria:

Dear Maria,

Thank you for your telegram, which I received with pleasure, despite the fact that it was delivered—who knows why—the day after the performance. I was happy to see you after so many years and thank you, once again, for coming to hear me sing. I wish you everything you desire and, again, best wishes, Renata.[96]

Rumors were swirling that Maria and Onassis had split—along with the forecast that she would star in *La traviata* in Paris.[97] Upon returning to her hometown on the 17th she hastily resumed her talks with Rudolf Bing,[98] advising him that he should "try a little harder" to facilitate her comeback at the Met.[99] On 27 September she visited a lung specialist to consult him about her vocal support. He advised her to be careful owing to her broken ribs, and to postpone the recommencement of her training for a period of "ten-twelve days".[100]

That 3 October she wrote to de Hidalgo:

It's going to be a while before I heal—it's very burdensome—inconvenient for a singer.

But you have to take life as it comes—I'm very well and of good humor—I'm liberated from a horrible nightmare that came in the form of a love that was destructive from all points of view . . .

I'm going out every evening with friends and a week from now will be able to recommence study little by little.[101]

So she raced between friends old and new; seeing Richard Burton and Elizabeth Taylor on the 6th and informing them of her and Onassis' rupture. The former noted in his diary, "I think she's a bit of a bore," and described how she plied him with compliments: "She told me how beautiful my eyes were and that they demonstrated a good soul!"[102] Two days later she accompanied them to the racetrack at Longchamps—as though she were one for equestrian matters.[103] She went to the première of *Phèdre* at the Opéra with her friend Hélène Rochas on the 14th.[104]

The following day as Maria's stylist was preparing her hair for a photoshoot, the French radio reported former U.S. First Lady Jacqueline Kennedy was set to marry Aristotle Onassis. Maria burst into tears. Eventually she resumed preparations and started the shoot.[105]

Because neither had announced their separation, the abrupt turn of events made it appear as though Onassis had abandoned her when it had actually been vice versa.

She had ignored his calls and pleas and gifts. At the time of their parting his engagement to Jacqueline Kennedy had neither been formalized nor confirmed. The courtship had been undertaken largely for political expediency on his behalf—and at a time when the litigious couple had been constantly at strife.

Bereft of subjects to converse about and things to do, Maria was regaled with an extremely useful scapegoat. At Onassis she could fling all of her grievances; the much-maligned Greek magnate she could blame for everything. "It's cruel, isn't it, but they're both paying the price—and they will pay—you'll see," she wrote theatrically to Elvira de Hidalgo. "I think he was at least obliged after the nine years that I spent with him not to let me learn of it from the newspapers. But I consider him a crazy man and as such there is liquid in my mind. I'm rather well given the circumstances and I thank you for the great affection that you have for me."[106]

Eventually Maria came to terms with his decision—telling Stelios Galatopoulos in 1977: "No, he did not marry for love and I do not think that his wife did either. It was more a marriage of business convenience. I have already told you that he was afflicted with a predilection for conquering everything. Once he set his mind on something he was determined to achieve it. I really could never come to terms with this philosophy."[107]

At the time she determined to prove herself twofold: firstly to the press as a durable woman; secondly, to her friends to detract from her atrophied voice. The night before the Kennedy-Onassis wedding Maria attended the 75th anniversary of Maxim's, the restaurant;[108] the previous evening she had gone to the movie premiere of *A Flea in Her Ear* at the Théâtre Marigny.[109] There she sat next to a then thirty-one-year-old Warren Beatty and doled out her vocal philosophy.[110]

That same night she received Franco Rossellini at her apartment for dinner. He was about to helm a movie version of the story of Medea under the direction of Pier Paolo Pasolini. Maria had of late rejected several film propositions—including an idea for *Macbeth* with Michelangelo Antonioni directing.[111] This conceit sparked something in her.

She shunned the fearful chance to be alone. When French television aired the Onassis-Kennedy wedding on 20 October, she invited both Janine Reiss[112] and EMI France's Thérèse Darras[113] to sit with her and watch.

In Dallas John Ardoin had taped some of their private conversations. Though he would insist that he had done this following their interview at her request, the change in room acoustics and the sound of chinking glasses don't suggest a studio recording. He had likely caught Maria's words without consent.

Probably oblivious to their exchanges being immortalized, she ranted for a long time about almost everything: "For nine years you've been living a humiliating life. And you're not *cured* in two months," began the tirade of her sentiments about the marriage. "For eight years, nine years, we did our best to be happy—'Oh, ain't that sweet?' as they say vulgarly. So easy to say, 'No resentment.' Sure, Christianity says, 'You must forgive, you must have no resentment.' I don't have resentment, but I have hurt—how do I get rid of that?"

"I have so much good sense—that it hurts. But on the other hand, when you work, it would be so nice to be able to have some honest shoulder to lean on. I had hoped that of my husband. I was so wrong. Because glory went to his head. Glory goes to people's heads. Not my head. Glory terrifies me. You are quite uncomfortable up there. But people around you get drunk."[114]

Syncopated by the beats of indignation, her extended diatribe resounded with defensiveness and wrath. "My religion is that, integrity, no matter what the price. You can't breathe otherwise. But there are people around you who are not like that, and that is what hurts. You feel like a strange animal that is out of place and misunderstood."[115]

To the press she refused comments—insisting she had "never allowed interviews on issues outside her profession" and never would.[116] To those who wrote with condolences she replied cordially. "I am proud that so many people and friends appreciate my qualities, if any—and your letter will remain deeply engraved in my mind & soul forever—dear friend," reads a missive to Irving Kolodin. "I will write of future plans or decisions later. Now I'm trying to hold myself and heal my broken cartiladge [*sic*]—amongst other things."[117]

Speaking one and a half years later she would tell Sylvie de Nussac of *L'Express*: "I choose one suffering as opposed to another. Even if one is, as they say, a great interpreter, we all go through the same problems. I'm no exception."[118]

Suffering because of her perfidious ex-lover was a solacing retreat for now. Meanwhile, Maria and Kurt Adler couldn't manage to concur on dates of imminent engagements at the San Francisco Opera; or such was her excuse for the ensuing impasse.[119] To Leo Lerman she explained that Adler wanted her "to do eight *Traviata*s over two months—too long."[120]

In early November Maria received some divertissement: Onassis announced his impending arrival by phone. Commanding him not to approach her door, she wouldn't let him in when he came knocking later. According to the recollections of butler Ferruccio almost five decades afterward, his first bid to enter resulted in night-long entreaties outside her apartment.

They were met with indifference.[121]

In a successive bid Onassis proceeded to whistle "as young men used to do in Greece fifty years ago—they wooed their sweethearts with song," Maria would tell Galatopoulos. "So I had to let him in before the press realized what was going on in avenue Georges Mandel. With his return, so soon after his marriage, my confusion changed into a mixture of elation and frustration."[122]

Readers may imagine that Maria was a perfect pushover. Living solely to survive, she could no longer think about the right or wrong way to behave. Though she didn't take Onassis back, Maria resumed tentative communication with him for *her* sake. Speaking to him was better than hearing her voice. "The woman—you can spit on her, and I'd still be the nicest person in the world," she would tell a journalist in 1970. "But the artist—you mustn't shake her; mustn't do her harm."[123]

Soon Onassis' attempts to infiltrate himself into Maria's life became the nightly entertainment of *le Tout-Paris*. Maria would call Jacques Bourgeois and rave: "He's here! What should I do now?"[124] On 22 November, the fifth anniversary of John F. Kennedy's death, she conceded to dinner with him at her apartment. Having excused himself to use the lavatory, Onassis disappeared for a long time until Maria asked her maid to look for him. Bruna entered her mistress' bedroom to discover a naked Onassis. Maria threw him out.

Incidents like these were juicy anecdotes for her. Events that she would never have confided to a soul years earlier now fed her dinner guests.[125]

*

Meanwhile Maria hunted for material that could restore her to her former self. Spontaneously, she wrote to tenor Max Lorenz—a colleague whom she likely hadn't seen in twenty years—on 14 November. "I hope you remember me since the old days we sang together. I will never forget our performances together . . . I wonder if it is true that you have a tape of our 'Tristan' together. I was told that you have one—and I would be so happy if I could have a copy for my personal pleasure—could you write to me if so—and anyway I would so like to hear from you."[126]

From one of her collector fans she requested "a favor? I need some copies of the Dallas 'Traviata.'"[127]

Simultaneously the concept of a film about Medea kept being catapulted in her mind. That week she received Pier Paolo Pasolini at her home. Despite having confounded her with his film *Teorema*, the artist—a young, gaunt, reserved, extremely communist, gay intellectual—was much to her liking. "He's a humble man, who speaks little, who lets me express myself, tell him my little philosophies," she would later aver. "He listened to me a lot, and he understood me on the human level."[128]

Pasolini wasn't taken with Maria Callas the soprano. His cousin Guido Mazzon once remarked to him: "You don't like opera that much; it's a thing of the bourgeoisie."[129] As for Callas, the actress, she was likewise of scant interest to him. In fact, using actors *per se* was a concept foreign: "If I want to speak of a tree, I show a tree, not something that represents a tree . . . The same goes for people," he described to a journalist. "The idea of an actor being someone other than himself is alien to me . . . It's from personal qualities in Callas that I realized I could make *Medea*. Here is a woman, in one sense the most modern of women, but there lives in her an ancient woman—mysterious, magic—whose sensibilities create a tremendous inner conflict for her."[130]

Maria wallowed in the peace of their artistic comprehension. "He is an introvert, and I am an introvert, and we did not know each other before the film: I wondered if we would be like two Great Walls of China, facing each other, staring at each other, and saying nothing. But no. There was the maximum communication between us."

At that dinner in Maria's apartment she made sure to insist, "If I do this film, and at any time my treatment of the role or my performance in general causes problems for you, do not go to anybody else—come right away and tell *me*. I shall try to do what you want."[131] And a spiritual liaison was born.

On 30 November Gorlinsky cabled Franco Rossellini to inform him that Maria was "TO STAR IN PASOLINI'S MEDEA FILM SUBJECT TO ACCEPTABLE TERMS AND CONTRACT BEING SUBMITTED TO ME LATEST DECEMBER 22nd." Production was scheduled to begin that April 1969.[132]

Simultaneously another concept took wing in her mind: that of producing an autobiography. Resources that she might find useful were requested from old friend Eliana de Sabata, daughter of conductor Victor.[133] Four months later she asked of Elvira de Hidalgo: "When you have nothing to do, write me what you remember, and send it to me."[134] Dorle Soria got a similar message: "Some day I will put down my biography. I want to write it myself, to set the truth straight. There have been so many lies."[135]

Gorlinsky was busy investigating how to maintain complete rights over an autobiography[136] by corresponding with Doubleday and other interested British publishers.[137]

Christmas 1968 was blighted by more trauma when Maria had the sacks beneath her eyes removed in hospital.[138] "If somebody tells you it's nothing at all I give you permission to slap them," Maria wrote to Teresa d'Addato. "It's a horrible bother. I spent Christmas and New Year's Day sad and annoyed, naturally the main reason being my eyes. Patience."[139]

Since the soprano now intended to perform *La traviata* at the Opéra de Paris,[140] in early 1969 Gorlinsky had her down for possible recitals in "Berlin, Hamburg, Aachen, Copenhagen, Boston, Amsterdam, Brussels, Japan, Korea, Australia, Barcelona, Russia."[141] Together they endeavored to recruit Leonard Bernstein to conduct the upcoming *Traviata* but the maestro was unavailable.[142] André Chabaud, the Paris Opéra's interim director, wrote to Luchino Visconti to confirm that he would direct the production to take place in February 1970.[143]

Now that her life was overflowing with distractions, Maria committed her voice to recording for the first time in four years that winter. Resuming her interpretation of the Verdi arias she had left unfinished back in January 1965, she returned to the guidance of Nicola Rescigno's baton in a nervous, at times unprofessional state. Audio footage of the sessions lay bare a Maria in denial of herself. "I'm getting tired, eh?" follows an awful attempt at a section. On one occasion she stops mid-note and insists "No, I'm tired." Having failed to launch into the phrase, "Io muoio" ("I'm dying") in the aria "Te vergin santa" from *I Lombardi*, she laughs girlishly. At another time Maria tells the orchestra: "I don't feel like it, *stop*."

While there are squeaks of high notes in the final version of the arias from *I Lombardi*—which splices the 1965 and 1969 attempts together— among works new to the soprano's repertoire *Attila*'s "Liberamente or piangi" is the only refugee from vocal plight. Her scales, though somewhat strident, surface in a smooth legato and wrap Oldabella's mournful ode in languid resignation.

Renditions of old favorites such as "Tacea la notte placida" from *Il trovatore* and the two pieces from *Un ballo in maschera* emerge more in the chest voice: gloomier and darker than their earlier reprises. Vulnerability is scraped out of the roles.

Maria openly expressed her discontent. "I am not happy with it yet; it isn't *there* yet," she would announce in a French interview.[144] Attempting to make light of the experience, she stated, "At the studio, everyone was swept away: the artistic director, the technicians—everyone. But me—I took it apart piece by piece, page by page: 'There, the recitative should be stronger. Here, my intention doesn't come out. There, the cadence. There, the cello.' It's crazy! I destroy myself."[145]

Habitually she summoned EMI producer Peter Andry back to her apartment. Lifting the old bootleg records from her plentiful collection, Maria listened to them in his presence. "It became something of a ritual," he would later remember. Following a brief dinner they would adjourn to the living room and continue the exercise.[146]

"We of the theatre—we cannot think of what we did before because we do not have the time for it," Maria had asserted to a journalist in 1964.[147] Previously a friend's suggestion of absorbing one of her old records had incited the reaction of her covering her ears and threatening to leave his house.[148] Now nostalgia became inescapable.

Resuming her contact with EMI's Walter Legge, Maria wrote to him on March 18th: "Did you have to hear the *Tosca* recording with De Sabata to understand that it is and was ridiculous that two highly intelligent people (as you say you and me) who have together made immortal contribution through records to the artistic history of our time, should have broken off all communications and relations."[149]

Following a request from composer Nicolas Nabokov (cousin of Vladimir) to perform at the biennial music festival of Tehran that October, she declined reverently.[150] On 24 March she wrote to former colleague Giacomo Lauri-Volpi and told him she was considering Bizet's *Les pêcheurs de perles*.[151] Other plans were ahead—namely Verdi's *Requiem* in Dallas with Shirley Verrett in the mezzo role scheduled for 26 and 29 November.[152]

A month later the idea was scrapped. "In seeing all this hype, I took the phone one night and made a long distance call across the Atlantic. I told the director of the Dallas Opera [her friend Lawrence Kelly] everything I thought! . . . I hate it when people create publicity at my expense," was the reason she gave to a journalist.[153] On 29 April 1969 her official press release read: "The announcement that I would appear in the Verdi Requiem in Dallas was unfortunately premature, for when it was made, I had not as yet signed a contract. The announcement also stated that this would be my only engagement for 1969-70, which is not the case. These factors, combined with other circumstances, convinced my manager that it was best for me not to sign the contract and not to accept the Dallas engagement. I have had, with great sadness, to agree with him."[154]

Maria prepared to become a non-singing actress in *Medea*. "In the meantime I have a hernia in my stomach (salami's fault!)," she wrote to Elvira de Hidalgo. It was a new one. "And naturally it doesn't help my physical state because I have a low white blood cell count . . . I hope to God that it [*Medea*] gives me satisfaction. I'm taking it as a diversion and a new door (perhaps) that will open for me, except for my singing which I'm always keeping alive."[155]

Perhaps on account of this foray Maria was eager to divulge to the public her struggle to temper the voice. For her participation in the French talk show, *L'invité du dimanche*, she invited Visconti, Francesco Siciliani and Jacques Bourgeois as her guests. Here the soprano openly expressed her confrontation with her long-term vocal problems; how she had been weary, how she had demanded of herself: "Now, that's enough Maria—you must take everything under control and eat a little humble pie." Her sole wish was "to be able, at least for a few years, to conclude [my career] in beauty. That's all that I ask."[156]

Pleased with her reception, Maria wrote to Elvira de Hidalgo, who had agreed to be interviewed as part of the program. "It was a success. I had so many compliments . . . Of course at the end after two and a half hours they asked me why I had stopped singing, and I responded in all honesty that I was not happy with myself and that I've taken up work again to take care of that."[157]

She spent the weeks before *Medea*'s filming sauntering in Switzerland, where she attended a jewelry auction in Geneva[158] before venturing to Vevey for a brief stay with the Chaplins.[159]

Her contract for the movie—which was being produced by the San Marco Financial Company in association with Franco Rossellini, Marina Cicogna and others—stipulated that Maria work for a period of eight weeks, be invited to watch dailies, dub the film into Italian, French and

English and be equipped with a dressmaker, make-up artist, hairdresser and secretary.[160]

Despite the press' furor the idea of Callas ceding to this kind of cinema was not met with acclaim. As well as his tale of a "God" who seduced a whole family, Pasolini's other movies made for masochistic exploits: his 1975 film *Salò, or the 120 Days of Sodom*, would center on hundreds of adolescent children being physically, psychologically and sexually tortured by World War II fascists for almost two hours. It would feature graphic presentations of both heterosexual and homosexual rape, physical mutilation, amputation and deviant sexual acts.

The cinematic style of the auteur almost dehumanized its subjects— making movies so intensely focused on a theme or concept they occasionally obscured them.

For this reason Visconti—a director whose embroidered masterpieces designed portraits of his personalities, elaborate set décors and backdrops dripping opulence—opposed the coupling. "I'm not sure you have chosen *well* your debut in the cinema," he openly told her during *L'invité du dimanche*. "You see, Pasolini's cinema is not made for great *actors*. Do you understand what I'm saying? It's a completely different thing."

Too enamored was Maria with the concept to withstand this. "There is something between Pasolini and me," she avowed. "We understand each other. When I don't have those kinds of 'electromagnetic waves' with a colleague, I can't *be* there. Pasolini and I studied the *mise-en-scène* together, as well as the costumes, but he also let me improvise . . . He would always ask for my opinion."[161]

About the film Maria would accentuate the visual and conceptual: "We have taken much of the sound and fury out of the original story, by what I would call significant silences. There are comparatively long passages in which no words are spoken . . . He is concerned only with the purity of the artistic product, and he will sacrifice everything to get it."[162]

Although Maria wanted—as she had in *Lucia di Lammermoor*—to keep the action as "bloodless as possible,"[163] Pasolini spends the first half-hour of the film depicting the cannibalistic ritual of Medea's people, the Colchians. They sacrifice a little boy, burn him at a pyre and distribute portions of his blood and guts in bowls.

While Maria's face reminded Pasolini of "an Etruscan vase,"[164] his references to Euripides' play were largely oblique. For him the venture symbolized the exploration of a greater concept: "*Medea* is a conflict between the archaic, hieratic, clerical world of her own with Jason's world: one that is rational and pragmatic."[165]

The infanticide—which takes place in a bath and isn't seen directly— precedes two variations on the ending juxtaposed. In one Medea sends incendiary gifts to Jason's wife Glauce to immolate her. In the other the gifts are benign and conveyed in good faith. Glauce leaps off a cliff to take her life voluntarily.

While Pasolini's focus remained ethnographic, Maria channeled themes familiar to her from the world of opera: "She's—a *woman*. With all the experiences of a woman . . . even more *so*. Everything is *bigger*. Bigger sacrifice . . . everything is *bigger*, the scenery is *bigger*. But the hurt is just there, just the *same* as *any* other woman. Even *more* so. So I find the same problems of *today's* life in a *bigger* schedule because she *was* a bigger woman and it was *mythology*," she told the BBC.[166]

"You must remember that in Medea's religion the killing of her children meant that they would become immortal," was her description of the plot to *The New Yorker* two years after shooting. "She does go mad, of course, but it's a kind of static, internal madness—no yelling or screaming until the absolute end. The emotional scenes were not particularly difficult, it took me perhaps one minute to get into the proper mood. Then I just looked past the cameras and played to the stagehands and the extras. They were my public."[167]

Maria arrived in Rome on 15 May for a first week of screen tests, costume fittings and pre-production arrangements.[168] Filming would eventually span a gamut of locations: Göreme, Turkey and then later on Aleppo, Syria then Pisa, Venice and the town of Anzio.[169] On the first evening Rossellini and Pasolini held a champagne party for Maria the Roman press flooded. She soon recruited publicist Nadia Stancioff to act as her secretary since the film's press agent, Matteo Spinola, wouldn't be able to join them in Turkey.

When Maria flew to Göreme via Paris, the arrival of her suitcase—packed with sheet music as well as her belongings—was delayed. She loitered through the airport and read horoscopes.[170]

Hair and make-up would begin at 12 pm with filming ending close to midnight every day but Sunday.[171] Immediately Maria exercised a manifest amenity around her colleagues. Pasolini had chosen another non-actor—Italian athletic jumper Giuseppe Gentile, bronze medalist at the 1968 Summer Olympics—to play Jason. "He was seized by panic at the start when I arrived," Maria would recall. "Everyone was impressed by the 'monster' they believed I was. I understand that people are scared the first time they see me, and there is in me, shall we say, a devil that enjoys this. But on the other hand, there's kindness: I should empty these people of the block they face and put them at ease, or else we won't be able to work together."[172]

"So I immediately tried to create a kind of camaraderie; to approach them as a young boy would another—shall we say—as much as I could because I am a *woman* . . . So much so that at the end, we were all very sad to leave each other. If I can just say—you see, it was really an ensemble piece," she told a Belgian journalist.[173]

About Gentile she possessed no qualms. "He's young, athletic and tall. He's handsome. God bless him. He's good for me."[174]

The jumper relished time spent with Maria. "Though we belonged to two different worlds . . . we had many things in common . . ." he wrote in his memoir. "Together we had sought to have the greatest mental concentration [in our work]: she in order to control the diaphragm, I in order to engage all my muscular force for a fraction of time . . . we took great pleasure in telling each other about our experiences and discovering how beautiful it was to share our practices . . . She really managed to conquer her timidity when she took my hand and placed it on her stomach to make me feel how her diaphragm moved in her training: 'Do you know what I'm capable of? The diaphragm has a mind of its own—but I dominate it.' "[175]

With Ninetto Davoli—Pasolini's nineteen-year-old lover who paid them a visit in Rome—Maria pursued an identical ritual: persuading him to place his hands along her back and "feel" her sing.[176]

Two hours long, *Medea* doesn't offer many scenes of its conniving villainess; preferring in their stead to show her environs. Romanian chants and Iranian classical music Pasolini employs to embody the disparate cultures of Colchians and Argonauts play a great role.

Dialogue would be regularly substituted or adjusted.[177] No rehearsals took place. Maria would stop after certain takes to ask, "Now, is that gesture too big? Too operatic?"

The camera caught her glares more often than it did her voice. In the words of one film critic, when Medea first sees him "it is Jason's virility that prevails. Medea has lost her dazed manner of a disoriented animal. Suddenly she finds in love (which humanizes her) a substitute for her lost religious sense. In the sensual experience she finds the lost rapport, the sacred identification with reality."[178]

Staying at the Hotel Konya in Ürgüp, Göreme that June,[179] Maria was hounded by calls from Onassis. In a cloak and dagger act the man announced himself to anyone who asked as "Mr. Lupoli": a fictional relative of Bruna the maid. A wary Maria didn't come to the phone.[180]

As they continued shooting in the stifling Cappadocia, Maria turned to almost anyone to check: "How did I do? Was that gesture too much? Was my make-up all right?"[181] Learning her role's text became a struggle. Words with music were a challenge in itself; without it she endured a poor lexical memory. Archival footage shows a crewman prompting every line as her Medea crosses back and forth and chants.[182]

In spite of this Maria surveyed filming of all scenes to chart the work's progression.[183] Medea had to spend a great deal of the movie running across hills and plains. One afternoon her incarnator fainted in a hundred-degree heat; losing consciousness for a brief moment. Upon regaining it Maria hastily began to supplicate the crew: "Please forgive me! I'm so stupid. I shouldn't have done that. It's cost everyone so much time and money."[184]

It was a struggle for the non-professionals to seal the kiss in Jason and Medea's love scene. Tilting their heads awkwardly, they were hard-pressed to fuse. "Do you two want to kiss or not?" Pasolini commanded. "We were so embarrassed that we had to shoot the scene six or seven times—and even then didn't manage to make lip contact," Gentile remembered.[185]

In another instant the stuntwoman standing in for Maria caught fire—propelling the actress to feature herself in the hazardous scene. Then unexpected wind blew flames onto her dress' hem. Climbing up her costume, they engulfed it in a hellish torrent. Rossellini had to interfere to quench the blaze.[186]

The final product unfurled a Maria who preferred to simulate a great deal of the action. She is not irreparably smitten when she first sees Jason; neither is she hopelessly infatuated as she stares down at his naked body. While there is drama in Maria's physiognomy, her intonations mostly sound affected and at times even pretentious: a bad audiobook reading.

When Medea is confronted for the first time with the lifestyle of these foreign Argonauts she traipses up and down their raft to study them in vexed suspicion. Maria's vicious shouts are breathy, panicked, operatic. Though vocally she conjures some of her protagonist's contempt and xenophobia, she strains to replicate them in her eyes' expression.

Her best acting moment comes a decade after the conspiratorial villainess has killed her brother and bestowed on Jason the prized Golden Fleece. When a maid instructs her to continue to "work magic," she blinks ponderously in nostalgia. "I have been far from my land for more than ten years ... I've become someone else now; I've forgotten everything. What used to be reality no longer is." The words surface subtly in reflection.

Episodes that showcase the complotting of the sorceress are stilted moments overridden by exaggeration. When she begs Creon not to banish her, the intonations mirror the affected placements of the voice employed in 1930s radio dramas. At other times they retreat homeward to Maria's clichéd acting in scarce dialogues of opera: Violetta's phrases before "Addio del passato" in the last act of La traviata or the words that introduce Macbeth's "Vieni t'affretta".

Because of her Veneto accent Pasolini was reluctant to apply his star's Italian dubbing to the film[187] and had experienced dubber Rita Savagnone fill in vocally.[188] Since Savagnone's version was exposed to both Italian and U.S. audiences, Maria's textual performance remained scarcely heard until a DVD release more than three decades later.[189]

When in July French journalists caught up with her in Anzio, Italy to register her exploits, the new actress was accommodating and expressly affable. Casting her eyes at her gargantuan, jewel-laden costume, she released a smile. "It's rather silly," she remarked before taking a sip of orangeade. The reporter watched Maria bring the scene in which Medea kills her children to a halt when "suddenly she burst out laughing." Accidentally, Maria would refer to the script as "my score" and to Jason, or Giuseppe Gentile, as "the tenor". A piano had been stationed in her Grand Hotel room so that she could practice.[190]

Despite her immersion the usual distractions were needed. Walking around between takes with a portable radio, Maria listened avidly to an

Italian soap opera, responding to the drama with: "What's that? What did you say! Go! Go!"[191]

She managed to convince new friend, young publicist Nadia Stancioff, that she actually was "one of them": "With your friends, I neither have to explain myself nor feel I am jeopardizing my image."[192]

Under the tension of this new profession Maria even engaged in some smoking. Having dabbled once or twice in the pernicious habit in the forties[193]—at a time when few had understood the harm it brought to singers—she had taken great precautions to eschew smoke in her life. Ritually she had persuaded former friend Vergottis not to enter her apartment since he was an avid cigar smoker.[194]

Now she was photographed taking a puff. It was as though there was no point avoiding it. If her endeavors failed to mend her voice, how could a little smoking further damage it?

The relationship was a brief dalliance and infrequently pursued. Meanwhile, having accustomed herself to this new field of film-acting, Maria retreated to comfortable hobbies. She subjected Giuseppe Gentile—who barely knew her—to long rants about Meneghini and Onassis and compelled him to listen to old records of hers in her Grand Hotel suite.[195]

When Ninetto Davoli was called upon to "entertain her in Rome," he cluelessly escorted the soprano to a seedy bar. Realizing the potential consequences of his actions, Davoli took fright. Maria knew how to loosen the tension. "She was exceptional," he remembered. "She had an incredible internal strength . . . I was bowled over by her, and the owner of the bar was bowled over by her."[196]

The bond between the unexpected allies Pasolini and Maria grew. He instructed his old friend, painter Giuseppe Zigaina, to take care of the newcomer. She in turn plied Zigaina with questions about Pasolini's childhood, teenage years, character and beliefs. The painter-director drew sketches of Maria he decorated with "drops of wine, rose petals or crushed poppies, squeezed grapes or coffee." Since they were staying near the Roman city Aquileia, he gave her the gift of a ring with an Aquileian carnelian gemstone.[197]

In their nightly conversations Pasolini would enlighten Maria on the difference between theatre and cinema, later writing her letters:

Dear Maria,

Tonight, no sooner had we finished working on that path of pink rose dust, than I felt with my antenna the same anguish in you that you yesterday picked up with your antenna in me. An anguish that was so, so slight—not more than a shadow—yet invincible . . .

This tightening of the muscles of the heart, I've felt it often through the process of our work: and I will likewise feel it in your presence. It's terrible to feel used, but also to use. But cinema is made this way: we need to fragment it; break up a "whole" reality and then rebuild it in its synthetic and

absolute truth in order to make it more "whole". You are like a precious
stone that is violently shattered into one thousand pieces to be rebuilt
into a material that lasts longer than life; the eternal material of poetry.[198]

Maria for her part became a mother figure to the boyish film director eighteen months her senior. Following his break-up from Ninetto Davoli in
1971, she would counsel in a matronly approach: "Ninetto has the right to
live his own life. Let him do so—try to be strong—you must. All of us have
had to cross from one way of living to another; I know what immense
suffering it is—perhaps disillusionment more than anything else. Some
words don't work at all to solace you—I know."[199]

But at the time the Italian media—whose censorship was such that it was
loath to reference Pasolini's homosexuality—was anxious to portray an
amorous affair between the colleagues; or at least obsessive love on *her* part.
Having befriended numerous artistic, homosexual and at times outlandish
men, Maria readily acknowledged their disparities despite her awe. "I know
that Pasolini is a man of very strong political views. But I never mix myself
in politics . . . We artists should only be artists. We have enough to do just
being artists without also being politicians. But Pasolini is one of my very
best friends. It's just that he has his beliefs and I have my beliefs."[200]

Suffused with an array of orthodox traditions, Maria's courtesy was
nonetheless accepting of her queer compatriots. In a letter to J. Warren
Perry in 1958, she had enquired about the professor's "father & mother,
brother & escort?"[201] It was her custom to send letters to the couple Herbert
Weinstock and his partner, Ben Meiselman, as well as warm wishes to Leo
Lerman's significant other, Gray Foy.

Though certain writers have alleged Maria hungered to "convert" gay
Pasolini, such a notion couldn't have been further from her thoughts. "If you
did not like a person his homosexuality would be a disgusting and unforgiv-
able sin," she acknowledged in retrospect to Stelios Galatopoulos in 1977.
"On the other hand, if you liked the person you could well consider his
homosexuality to be an unfortunate phase, hopefully a passing one. But I
must come to the point . . . Fortunately, I did get over my prejudices and not
too late in life."[202]

Maria felt at ease describing her and Pasolini's kinship in an interview
that summer. "He feels my mind and er . . . the way I *feel*—he's like a . . . an
eagle that *looks* straight into the *mind* and the *soul*; this is his . . . great
quality . . . I call it '*quicksilver*'. *I'm* quicksilver and *he* is . . . the same *kind*."[203]

He took Maria to visit his mother Susanna in Casarsa, where she met
with several members of his family and signed autographs for local
townspeople.[204]

Adamant was she in her resolve to let the press know she adored this
venture. "I am like a general who studies very carefully the plan for battle
and in his strategy keeps in mind future moves to win, of course," Maria
told one journalist.[205]

The outcome of the film? *"Bellissima!"* was her reaction to a set of stills. "Look at this one here, when they're bringing me on to the boat—I really look like a beast . . . I'm quite astonished, aren't you?" she asked an interviewer.[206]

On the surface it appeared to have created a near-consummate experience. "There's no music that *blocks* you. There's more *liberty*, here you have a . . . a vast—*conception* . . . depth, and possibilities . . . You have a *freedom* that you don't have in *opera*," Maria concluded.[207] "In the theater you project something that is not true but is effective. On the screen you can reach deeper to what is more profound and real. Consequently, you must subdue your gestures for the screen . . . Most of all, I think what I liked best about the film was the challenge. I thrive on the difficult."[208]

As for future roles, she agreed she would "accept everything that excites me in the good sense of the word. On stage, I've played all kinds of different roles; if I could do the same in cinema, I'd be delighted."[209]

Charismatically calculating, Maria sat down with American network NBC toward the end of filming—alerting them beforehand that she "would not answer *any* questions about . . . Greek shipowners." Asked "What makes a person like yourself?" Maria slowly shook her head and offered a forced, enigmatic smile. "I wouldn't *know*."[210]

Throughout the press tour for *Medea* she was endlessly effusive when it came to her descriptions of the joy of acting. "One might say that making a film after singing opera is like leaving one man for another . . . For me, the problem is very simple: in creating cinema, I changed my means of expression, yet I remained exactly the same."[211] "If one likes the role, and is well guided, you can be completely spontaneous. That is the "intangible" of which I spoke to you—it's poetry."[212]

Her private musings were a different matter. Following the Rome *Medea* premiere in February 1970 Giulietta Simionato told Maria she was "not at all herself without Cherubini." In response the singer thanked her and admitted, "I was only able to *be* Medea on account of Cherubini's music: in doing the film, I felt like my wings had been taken away from me, along with my teeth and my nails."[213] Similarly she admitted to Thérèse Darras that it had left her ill at ease.[214]

Stationed at a mountain of spaghetti alle vongole a week after *Medea* finished, the soprano expressed satisfaction. "Now that the film is done—at least in what concerns me—I can finally go back to my everyday life," she replied to a journalist. "Listening, as I always do, to my old records, and to my new recordings on my tape recorder. Yes, I can say it: I am genuinely happy. Happy that everything is finished. Happy it went well. Happy to relax a little bit."[215]

26 July heralded the *Medea* wrap party hosted in Grado at the home of Giuseppe Zigaina. A hundred and fifty came to mingle in the sweltering Italian heat. Maria was all-smiles.[216]

18.

"Espèce de vapeur"

Freud would have interpreted Maria's thirst to be among the echelons of the elite that summer as a deep-seated rebellion against Woodstock.

After spending early August 1969 in Paris[1] she took shelter in faraway opulence; attending the Red Cross Gala in the company of Princess Grace and Prince Rainier in Monte Carlo.[2] Two days later she inaugurated the Menton Festival in the company of twelve-year-old Princess Caroline.[3] Since her old pal pianist Byron Janis was performing there again she loitered at his side.[4]

Following a brief return to Paris the new nomad's next site of repose was Venice, where a reporter eyed her walking along Lido beach in blue jeans with her hair tied in a ponytail. She stayed at the palace of Countess Nathalie "Lily" Volpi, the island's doyenne, and told a journalist that she was yet to see *Medea*. "I still don't know what kind of face I have on screen, the way I move, the effect I create, how Pasolini inspired me. But I do know one thing for sure: I hope that this is not my last and only film!"[5]

Pasolini's next film *Porcile*—described by one critic as "an allegory of contemporary society as seen through the eyes of a groundless pessimist, ex-anarchist, and ex-Marxist"[6]—premiered at the Venice Film Festival.[7] Maria graced the arch director's own premiere in Grado; later spending several days with him in this small town where Pasolini owned an island.[8]

Stewing in the sun did not accord sufficient alienation from the real world. In mid-September Maria embarked on another journey to Haar Castle—the home of her friend Maggie van Zuylen—where she took walks in the woods, greeted villagers in Utrecht[9] and sat on the jury of a children's parade.[10]

Flitting hither-thither customarily, at home Maria attended the premiere of *Battle of Britain*[11] and spent hours on the phone begrudging a fictitious report in the *News of the World* to Gorlinsky.[12] Early October took her back to Rome, where in the company of Marina Cicogna she went to the premiere of *The Lion in Winter* and socialized with her chum Gina Lollobrigida. Still she was one of the scant few who left the party early.[13]

Franco Rossellini and Pasolini visited her in Paris to discuss dubbing plans for the film.[14] Her *Medea* secretary and assistant Nadia Stancioff dropped by and accompanied her to screenings of *Midnight Cowboy* and *Easy Rider*.[15] To make peace with Onassis and display that she had no desire for the role of Concubine, Maria summoned him to a small dinner party to take place on 25 October. He was in town for business.[16]

Bereft of caring confidants, she labored to preserve the charred remains of their combusted kinship through a bond strictly platonic. Apropos of their relationship she had no reason to regret.

That said, she would concede to Galatopoulos years later, "I was not so philosophical about [it] as I am now—when human emotions simmer down it is easier to see more clearly other points of view and one can put the whole affair (saga is a better word) in a rational perspective. If only one could do this from the beginning! Make no mistake, when he married I felt betrayed, as any woman would, though I was more perplexed than angry, because I could not understand for the life of me why, after so many years together, he married another."

Asked if she bore bitterness against him, she was quick to answer: "None whatsoever. I could have, if I were inclined to such feelings. In life everybody can find a reason to be bitter about friends, family, even parents. But there are two kinds of people: those who remain bitter and those who do not. I am happy that I belong to the second category."[17]

For this reason she had no qualms when it came to speaking to the press about their closeness. "Honestly, I think I'm Onassis' best friend and he's mine," Maria told Angela Cuccio of *Women's Wear Daily* in 1970.[18] To *The New York Times* she was a little more explicit: "When two people have been together as we have, there are many things that tie you together. He knows he will always find cheerfulness, mutual friends and honesty when he sees me."[19]

But in the fall of 1969 the cultivation of this new attachment was a steep mount. Friends had to be stationed as a buffer to suppress the paparazzi's wagging tongues. Hélène Rochas was invited together with her partner, Kim d'Estainville. François Valéry—an old friend of Onassis' and French Ambassador to UNESCO—was present, together with Maggie van Zuylen.[20]

As Maria discussed opera and showed guests the pictures from *Medea*'s shoot[21] reporters camped out in the rain before 36 Avenue Georges Mandel. They scribbled down the entrance times of every guest, the movement of the swinging door, the changing brightness in Maria's dining room and who sat where around the table. Their espionage determined that the dinner finished at eleven thirty, Onassis exited the building with François Valéry and Maggie van Zuylen, and the trio advanced to the latter's apartment.[22]

During his business trip Maria and Onassis dined together on another three occasions, alternating between hosts and hostesses: their mutual friend, Perry Embiricos on one evening, Herbert von Karajan the next; Hélène Rochas and François Valéry the final time. The press exulted in these social gatherings conducted partly to deflect their interest: if Maria and Onassis were dining with friends, they had nothing to hide.

Paparazzi didn't agree.

The hawks kept track of all Maria's daily rituals: watching her rise late each day at 12 pm, have breakfast, read her mail and train with Gordon Mackie, an English accompanist, three times a week.[23] In the second half of November she travelled to Rome to finish dubbing *Medea* in English and French.[24] Struggling to identify a new pursuit, she paid a visit to an ailing Nadia Stancioff—at whose home Maria cooked, burnt meals and posed as an unwitting maid before a none the wiser doctor.[25]

Giulietta Simionato was invited to stop by to see her at the Grand Hotel. To her Maria likewise showed the photo album of *Medea* whilst admitting that it hadn't been her finest hour.[26] Days later she was stressing how superior the film was to the play and opera of *Medea* to Giacomo Gambetti for Italian tv guide, *Radiocorriere*.[27]

After months of endless correspondence and exchanges, Paris' *La traviata* was cancelled. "The Opéra couldn't guarantee me a certain number of rehearsals—I asked for at least a month of rehearsals—as well as a great conductor," Maria bemoaned. "They had Visconti as the director, but just Visconti and I—that's not enough. Mounting *La traviata* is like using a razor-thin blade: you have to be very careful."[28]

At the premiere of the Bolshoi Opera's *Eugene Onegin* at the Opéra de Paris[29] on 23 December she met legendary Soviet soprano Galina Vishnevskaya, wife of cellist Mstislav Rostropovich, who was singing the role of Tatyana. Mezzo-soprano Elena Obraztsova sat next to her in the audience.

After speaking with Obraztsova during intermission—along with several members of the cast and her friend, semi-successful Greek pianist Vasso Devetzi—Maria invited the mezzo to have dinner with her at Maxim's. "I like to be with myself every now and then because otherwise I get—my mind gets *confused*. So I have to *recharge* my batteries," she would tell David Frost eleven months later.[30] This had been a primary axiom.

The adage wasn't fully operable in this period. At a dinner of oysters and white wine with Obraztsova, she subjected the singer to hours of talk: discussing her voice, how she had just called off the *Traviata*, how she hated the press referring to her as "the dumped girlfriend of wealthy Onassis". At five am she let her go.[31]

Two weeks later Maria was in Abidjan on the Ivory Coast.[32] Accompanying her was her new best friend Pasolini and his old pals, writers Dacia Maraini and Alberto Moravia. The trio scouted for locations the director could exploit for his next venture—as well as extras among natives living in the huts. The movie, inspired by Aeschylus' *Oresteia*, would never materialize.[33]

Together with Maria they moved on to Dakar, Senegal,[34] Bamako and Timbuktu in Mali[35] and finally Niamey, Niger.[36]

Clad in blue elastic jeans, Maria listened to the radio by the Bandama River. Later in Bamako, Maraini knocked on her hotel door to announce dinner was ready. Maria's eyes and ears were fixated: a popular song by Italian star Claudio Villa was playing. "I thought you'd be listening to opera," Maraini remarked. Maria responded with a "mysterious smile".

Being the only women in the company, Maria and Maraini spent a lot of time together, on one occasion sharing a room in a hostel.[37] Whenever the troupe found themselves near a metropolis the former would be met by heads of state who offered private airplanes, limousines and personal services. Resistant to these luxuries, she trailed her herd quite happily on a Land Rover through the African jungles, sleeping wherever was comfortable. Only one alarming thought disturbed her momentarily: "Could we be attacked by tigers?" she asked Maraini.[38]

Intellectual Alberto Moravia was repulsed by her almost immediately. Maria tended to observe some of the tribesmen's rituals, point them out and find them funny. Pasolini corrected the fish out of water. Embarrassed, she confessed with delicateness: "You're right—I'm sorry."[39] At the dinner table she sang capitalism's praises as Pasolini denounced it; on other occasions she would slavishly melt at the sight of bedazzling rare jewels. Moravia referred to her as a "Greek bourgeois woman . . . naïve, with a remarkable predilection for luxury in its most conventional forms."[40]

An aversion to the novelist likewise arose in her. Later she instructed Pasolini to "try to be patient with those weak types like Moravia."[41] After the pair fell out she wrote, "Alberto didn't really convince me, you know—forgive me. But I don't like that you are suffering so much—he was your friend."[42]

With Maraini she was cautiously reserved. Then little by little Maria began opening up. Once again there came an outpour on her childhood and Onassis and lost chances. "I'd like someone to be near me, who could help me make decisions. I've always had to make decisions by myself, to rely on my own strength. It's not a nice thing, living alone. I'd like a family, children," the forty-six-year-old stated. "I've given a great deal to the theatre, but not to family because I've never had one."

Contrarily she would tell David Frost that year: "I don't think there are very many men that would *like* to be with *me* because they're *afraid* of me, ah . . . I'm a fast *thinker*, they're afraid of being *exposed* with me—it's not easy to be a . . . a good friend of *Callas*, I must say. I find it—I *found* it very painful but now I'm sort of . . . *resigned* to the fact."[43]

Crisscross in its wanderings, her mind was inexhaustible. Stressing to *Elle* magazine that February that she "doesn't show either her highs or lows. It's good manners," Maria was making a habit of unveiling her sorrows. Asked if she was happy, she responded: "What does that mean? I'm happy to have you here, to speak with you, I'm flattered to still be so appreciated at my age . . . Happiness lasts three, five minutes: what does that even mean—being happy?" Did she fear others? Her response diverged somewhat: "Well, maybe, yes. Maybe because I fear myself—that's the same thing. The fear of living. It's not pretty."

Without any prompt on the reporter's part she suddenly averred: "When I die, I will breathe a sigh of relief telling myself, 'I did my work well.' I often think about death because I'm not scared—provided that I don't suffer. What would I be scared of? Of leaving what behind—glory? I don't trust glory. It can be given and snatched away so quickly. You have to earn it every day—glory. Give one hundred per cent of yourself to obtain one per cent. Glory astonishes me. Art? I've done so little in comparison with what I would've wanted to do . . . I can say, in all honesty, that the moment when I finish living, I'll be very happy. I don't want to die, but I wouldn't want to live forever."[44]

In Africa Dacia Maraini asked Maria if she believed there was a heaven. "I don't know," Maria pondered. "There's no proof for it. I'm very, very grounded, Dacia. I think the most important thing is to try to find ways not to make trouble for yourself, here, on this earth—than to occupy your mind with those kinds of thoughts."[45]

*

Newly immersed in cosmopolitan Paris, Maria screened *Medea* for the first time on 25 January in the company of Franco Rossellini and Onassis.[46] Her invitation to Jacqueline to tag along to the film gala's premiere was rebuffed.

The social obligation had been exercised—and now Maria could use Kennedy Onassis' reluctance to explain the women's distance to the press. "Frankly, I don't understand why she doesn't come into my life. If we did meet, it would certainly stop all the gossip in the newspapers," she told *The New York Times* ten months later.[47] To Barbara Walters on NBC's *Today* show she explained: "When I invite Mr. Onassis to a party or a gala like the *Medea* film, or an *opera*, when they [my friends] invite *him*, they must invite his *wife*. And many friends of mine *then* had said, 'Well, we will *not* invite her,' I said: 'Well, you *will*, I'm *sorry* because she *is* his wife and you *must*.' And we talked about that with Mr. Onassis . . . and, *er* . . . she did *not* want to *come*. So you see therefore there's no *problem*. But it is not—I hold no *grudges*."[48]

Unsurprisingly Maria's references to her in private conversations were a little different. Jacqueline Kennedy became a gambit in a great deal of her talks; almost a source of fun Maria could exploit to shift the focus from herself. She would call her "the gold-digger"[49] to some friends; alluding to her and Onassis' sometime mistress Lee Radziwill as "the sisters".[50] Many listeners reaped relish from these epithets.

Rumors of the Kennedy 'curse' may have started with her. "[After] The first time Jacqueline Kennedy was on the ship [*Christina*] her husband was assassinated. But after the second time Bobby K. was killed. Twice brought disaster," Maria informed Dario and Dorle Soria.[51]

Adopting an approach far less theatrical in retrospect, she would reflect, "The only thing that I can say on the subject of my life with Onassis is that when one person tries to change the other, then it's time to go. And *that* cuts a long story short. I cannot be changed, and neither would I have liked to change him."[52]

When she wanted the soprano could attend to her sagacity. Andreas Paridis—an accompanist and old acquaintance from her youth in Athens— heard her speak of Kennedy's relationship with her ex-lover with "no bitter words . . . She deals with this fact with a logical temperament, with self-control and pride."[53]

The *Medea* premiere—a benefit that raised eighteen million francs for medical research in France—was a glamorous affair attended by France's First Lady, Mme. Claude Pompidou.[54] Screams of "Brava, brava" struck Maria afterward: she would surmise the film had garnered "the best notices that year."[55]

Wary of the dangers of appearing without Jacqueline present, Maria and Onassis skipped the after-party by attending a supper hosted by Maggie van Zuylen.[56] *The Washington Post* carried the scoop: "Mrs. Onassis had sent formal regrets (she's in New York)."[57]

In the United States the Italian-language version premiered later in 1971. "I only wish they had used the English language version of the film, which we also made. I hate all those English subtitles cutting across my face. At any rate, it's the kind of film people will either love or hate," Maria told John Gruen of *The New York Times*.[58]

Reviews were favorable but split between the pans and panegyrics. While Jean Gênet of *The New Yorker* described Maria's acting as "a virtuoso corporeal and psychological triumph . . . which will rank the film as a rare work of cinematographic art"[59] and Kevin Kelly of the *Boston Globe* called it "[a] performance of static grace and, as counterpoint, sweeping madness,"[60] Richard Roud of *The Guardian* expressed discontent. "Without her voice, Callas is not all that extraordinary an actress. She looks impressive, but somehow, diminished."[61]

The European press was more elated. "Only Maria Callas could make for such a furious *Medea*," Filippo Sacchi wrote in the Italian weekly *Epoca*.[62] Henri Chapier of French newspaper *Combat* stressed that "Callas . . . perfectly integrates herself in the poetic symbolism of the film and transforms into an unforgettable Medea."[63]

Overall the film was not a commercial success.[64] Especially displeased was Callas fan, auteur Luchino Visconti. "I don't like this movie," he told a *New York Times* reporter. "The great moment of Maria is finished. It was finished when she stopped singing. That was the real talent of Maria. I don't think she's a movie actress. I advised her not to do the film, but she is . . ." *Visconti heaves a sigh and taps his head with his knuckles*, scribed the journalist. "Maria is, you know, so stubborn."[65]

Four days after the premiere, Maria arrived at Cinéma Bonaparte in Paris for a Q&A session with university students. Engaged hotly in the film's promotion, she was on hand to take enquiries from the strangers. Her nonchalant, sophisticated outfit was intent on mirroring their intellectual clique: black pants and a long jersey chasuble dress made smart by giant spectacles.

Sadly for her, these upper-crust Bohemians catapulted questions not dissimilar to those cast by the paparazzi. "Does this excellent cinematic debut mean an unhappy ending at the opera's in store?" asked one questioner. Maria consulted privately with Pierre Kalfon, one of *Medea*'s producers, before pivoting back. "No—an unhappy ending is in store for *opera*. Let me explain: it's an art that's in decline; me—I'm not! I'm waiting for it to be reborn so I can come back and sing!"[66]

By these early 1970s her fashion tastes had undergone another metamorphosis. Florals, frills, a-skirts and petticoats had fled her wardrobe. Some of Maria's casual clothes emblematized the modern woman. Finally attuned to wearing trousers, she would be accoutered in white pantsuits,[67] navy blue pantsuits[68] and on one occasion a black pantsuit with a black cloak and black suede boots.[69]

The latter became rampant in her repertoire: there were "beige boots"[70] and "knee length black leather boots".[71] With freedom's fountain finally unleashing its effusive spurts, Maria let her long dark waves hang loose. She began experimenting with cosmetics—on one occasion wearing white eye make-up.[72] Her favorite perfume was the 1961 fragrance Hermès Calèche.[73]

At the same time she was loath to rid herself of more extravagant accessories. "How about those gold chandelier earrings that almost touched her shoulders?"[74] a gossip columnist discerned. Another noted "immense sapphire and diamond earrings"[75] while one reporter limned a "long green, red and brown paisley dress."[76]

"What stands out in my wardrobe," Maria told a French interviewer, "is indoor outfits, caftans, Moroccan djellebas embroidered with gold; I have around fifty of each . . ."[77] And they would come in luxurious colors of dark scarlet, gold or maroon.

After spending most of February in Paris giving countless television interviews,[78] the movie's actress and director flew to Argentina to present *Medea* at the Mar Del Plata Film Festival.[79]

Their stopover was Rio de Janeiro—where the two conducted restless tourist-like activities for four days. Maria warded off Brazilian press rumors of their impending marriage, addressing journalists in the scant Portuguese that she had learnt between performances there in the early fifties.[80] As they were boarding the plane bound for Buenos Aires, it abruptly burst a tire and departure was delayed for several hours.[81]

Arrived in Argentina, Maria and Pasolini hosted a press conference: "Do you identify with Pasolini the director from ideological and aesthetic perspectives?"—"I don't identify with him," she disclosed bluntly. "I identify with the version that Pasolini gives of 'Medea'.—"You don't think your make-up in

Medea is excessive?"—"No, I think my make-up was 'Hollywood-like'. My God! Could we talk about *real* things, please?"—"To what in general would you attribute the dehumanization of art?"—"A person is either human or not."[82]

After spending two days in the capital and visiting amusement parks with Robertino Rossellini—son of Ingrid Bergman and Roberto—[83] the misfits halted at a ranch for a brief sojourn. Maria managed to fall off a horse and sustain a bad back injury.[84] Perseverance was persistent nonetheless and she tailed Pasolini for a few days in Bahia, Brazil.[85]

Ten days later on 30 March she was in Lausanne for *Medea's* Swiss premiere—from where she journeyed to Geneva to spend time with friends. At one of their chalets Maria ventured finally to test the icy waters. In a small recital viewed by forty she performed some Schubert Lieder, "Mi tradì" from *Don Giovanni* and a few arias by Donizetti and Verdi. Her accompanist remained anonymous. Also present was a critic from the *Journal de Genève*:

There was something rather moving in hearing again—or rather rediscovering—what was once the world's most famous voice. Maria Callas has lost none of her dramatic expression, which is always moving, even in the less interesting Schubert Lieder. Her timbre, on the other hand, has not survived these years of inactivity. Perversely hoarse, it doesn't always avoid hardness or vulgarity, which is further accentuated by an ill-controlled vibrato ... La Callas, admittedly, was not at ease in any of these works. Overly emphatic in the classical pieces, striving to accentuate her elastic virtuosity in the Italian arias, she couldn't find a way to stop bad taste from creeping into her performance.[86]

Though her practice continued Maria resumed her inane tasks that April. After giving an interview for a BBC *Omnibus* program celebrating David Webster[87] she partook in a marketing campaign for mink coats. Her image graced advertisements of American furrier Blackgama, captioned with the slogan: "What becomes a legend most?"[88] Rudolf Nureyev, Margot Fonteyn and Leontyne Price were among other stars who lent the fur their frames.[89]

During other shoots at her apartment it became her custom to interrogate photographers on call. "She was not egocentric," Christian Steiner remembered. "She wanted to know all about me, about the fact that I had stopped playing the piano. She compared my experience to hers, because I had what she had been searching for, something else to do with life."[90]

At a social function she swapped woes with Margot Fonteyn. The latter's husband Roberto Arias—Maria's one-time financial adviser and former Panamanian ambassador to the U.K.—was quadriplegic as the result of an assassination attempt. When the fifty-one-year-old Fonteyn lamented being forced to dance to fund his care, repining: "The more I dance, the more debts I seem to have!", Maria quipped, "For all your miseries, I envy you!"[91]

"What is there in life if you do not work?" Maria asked Kenneth Harris of *The Times* during *Medea's* press junket. "If you do not work there is only sensation, and there are only a few sensations—you cannot live on them. You can only live on work, by work, through work . . ."—"Do you think that music is the only thing that matters in life?" he retorted. "No, not at all. Communication is the most important thing in life. It is what makes the human predicament bearable. And art is the most profound way in which one person can communicate with another. Music is the highest way of saying things. But it is not the only way. As for me, I could easily have moved into another field when I was young. And I would have worked at it."[92]

Still she was quick to emphasize she was preparing—*always* preparing. "I work physically, mentally, I work all the time. I continue to sing in order to see how I'm doing, in order to keep the instrument agile. You have to keep singing, even if you don't plan on singing again. It's also because we have inside ourselves this need to give, this kind of vapor ["espèce de vapeur" in the original French] that you have to release by and by. Even if you're alone, even if there's no public."[93]

In the same month she remarked to another reporter: "You see the piano over there. You see the music. And here am I, more critical of myself than ever. But there are relaxations in the life I know here in Paris which I have never had before. And I am grateful for them."[94]

Accompanying the series of self-contradictions was a self-awareness that was shrinking—or stepping out onto the balcony to take a breather. After the 1961 death of journalist Edward R. Murrow—whom she had met only twice—Maria had been quick to convey her condolences to his wife through a mutual acquaintance.[95]

Now she learned abruptly that her thirty-one-year-old accompanist, Gordon Mackie, had been killed in a bizarre and violent car crash.[96] Rather than reacting with the proper etiquette when she first heard the news from Peter Andry, she enquired: "Who will play for us now?"[97]

Onassis came to visit her toward the end of May. Unbeknownst to her his public socializing with Maria may have harbored an ulterior motive: intimate letters between Jacqueline Kennedy and her once-alleged lover, Roswell Gilpatric, had been leaked to the press. In the media's eyes they served to compromise the status of the Kennedy-Onassis marriage.[98] By appearing with Maria publicly he could embarrass Jacqueline Kennedy the way she had humiliated him.

In the company of Maggie van Zuylen Maria and Onassis dined together at Maxim's on 21 May. The photographs of them would scarcely have been newsworthy if the ensuing days had not been so dramatic. Maria invited Carlo Maria Giulini and his wife Marcella for dinner, insisting that she sought to resume her career. Discussions of the ill-fated *La traviata* studio recording lingered; there was hope of its revival.

Two days later a representative from EMI flew in from New York to have dinner with them. He told Carlo Maria Giulini that Maria had called earlier to excuse herself; she was feeling unwell. Prior to leaving the restaurant he alerted Giulini that Ferruccio the butler had found her unconscious; his turn of phrase insinuating that Maria had attempted suicide and been saved "at the last minute."[99]

"I didn't try to kill myself—I'm too full of life," she told U.S. press a year later.[100] The rumors became a fiasco—and it was partly Maria's own ignorant fault. Since barbiturates had only recently gained popularity as sleeping aids, Maria took them as she might have vitamins. In her complete lack of education she imagined that ingesting several extra could result in nothing but a deeper sleep. That night she had consumed too many. Finding her unconscious at seven o'clock in the morning, Ferruccio had escorted her to Neuilly's American Hospital.[101]

Released just hours later, Maria was astounded to discover Radio Luxembourg had issued a report about her so-called "suicide attempt". Tabloid *Noir et Blanc* attributed the singer's "desperation" to the evenings that Onassis had spent with Jacqueline at Maxim's.[102] "Some of the French newspapers printed that, and now I'm suing them," she told a journalist the following year. "They've given me some guarantees that they will never print anything about my private life again."[103]

Her cases against both Radio Luxembourg and *Noir et Blanc* were won with ease. Still she insisted the reports were "embarrassing and untrue".[104] All copies of the magazine were subject to a seizure order and Maria was eventually awarded ten thousand francs in damages: around four thousand dollars at the time.[105]

Partly on account of this she would express regret for not attempting to deal better with the press. Personal efforts had been exercised: "Once or twice in the past I have called a newspaper editor on the telephone, or sometimes I have written a letter to him, and I have told him what was wrong and asked him to withdraw what he has printed because it was untrue."[106]

But she had pointedly avoided the full entourage expected of celebrities. "It may be my fault *also* because I have *not* communicated a lot with them in the past because I didn't feel it *necessary* . . ." Maria told David Frost six months later. "I did *not* feel it necessary to *explain* myself or my feelings; I thought it was enough just to *sing* and, er . . . do my job *conscientiously* and—that's *all* but I suppose—I was wrong *there* . . . But I *should've* had, as they *say*—public *relations*."[107]

It didn't help Maria's case when, as she was returning from the hospital, she spotted a photographer nearby and tried to swat him with her purse.[108]

At around that time Ekaterina Furtseva—the Soviet Union's Minister of Culture—invited Maria to be received at the Kremlin and sit on the jury of the well-known Tchaikovsky Competition.[109] From 21 to 27 June Maria spent a lot of time with Furtseva, passing some days at her dacha in the village of Bakovka.[110] The latter later sent her a note telling her, "You are enchanting, polite, and I have a sincere affection for you."[111]

The event hosted two hundred and fifty-eight candidates in piano, violin, cello and voice hailing from thirty-five countries.[112] Joining Maria in the panel was her good friend Tito Gobbi.[113] During her time in the Soviet Union Maria attended the Bolshoi Ballet's performance of *Raymonda*[114] and visited Leningrad.[115] Among the vocalists she chose mezzo-soprano Elena Obraztsova—whom she had ironically encountered months before, but who would go on to pursue a glittering career—and soprano Tamara Sinyavskaya as the joint winners.[116]

At the Gala concert held to crown the competition's end, Sinyavskaya sang *Carmen's* "Séguedille". In the course of it she caught sight of Maria sitting in the audience's sixth row, mouthing the words to "Près des remparts de Séville, chez mon ami Lillas Pastia . . ."[117]

Three weeks later she received John Ardoin at her Paris apartment. It was the day of an opening *Norma* that would showcase the talents of both Montserrat Caballé in the title role and Shirley Verrett as Adalgisa. Maria offered Ardoin lunch and then conveyed him to her bedroom, where she proceeded to play a tape of the unfinished Verdi arias recording. "You see, I've been working," she smiled, relaying her hope that she could finally finish it that October. "Did this mean that Callas would finally return to the opera stage?" he asked in his article. "I'm afraid not . . . I guess I am too concerned with art, and I see few others who are. I've worked hard. Why now should I have to battle to make my art?"

When Ardoin returned to his hotel room the phone rang. Maria told him Caballé and Verrett's *Norma* had been cancelled owing to a chorus strike.[118]

That night she received both singers at dinner together with John Ardoin and pianist Ivan Davis. Verrett would later describe her as "very gracious that evening . . . I remember her asking if I had an issue about my age. The question seemed a little odd, but when she asked how old I was, I responded, 'How old do you think I am?' We both laughed . . . Callas had never performed with a black singer and was fascinated by me."[119]

"Pay close attention to Norma. Don't oversing it," Maria counseled Caballé that evening[120]—tergiversating from her earlier doctrine of soprano omnipotence.

Later she would likewise instruct Caballé not to sing Verdi's *Nabucco*: "*Your* voice in that? It's like putting a Baccarat glass inside a very shaking box. It will break! . . . Remember, it's not proper for your voice. Not only today—*always!*"[121] The following year she would advise a Juilliard student against singing Verdi's *Ernani*. "I might be wrong . . . It's too heavy for a voice like yours. And instead of doing you *good*, it might do you *harm*."[122]

A few months earlier Maria had enquired of Giulietta Simionato: "How do you explain the fact that my voice has this problem, about which I have already asked de Hidalgo and others? Why do my A-natural and A-flat always wobble? . . . but you know why that happened. My mother used to say, 'you must! Since you've got a voice, go on, sing!' And I obeyed."[123]

This concept of excessive singing was a new one in Maria's repertoire. She strived very hard to exercise a principle derived from celebrated tenor Beniamino Gigli: "A singer should *always* [sing] on his interest—not on the

capital. Now, what he meant by this *was* that we work on *technique*—
mainly, rather than ... Mother *Nature* because, you see, Mother *Nature*
with *singers*, finishes like an *athlete*—very *young*. Very young *career*, shall
we say, so you—you sing on *youth*. After a certain *age* it depends on how
strong you are or—I don't *know*. Twenty-*two*, twenty-*four*, twenty-*five* is the
limit for a singer if you sing on sheer *strength* ... From then on you *really*
last on your own technique," she had espoused.[124]

It turned out technique was not enough: now "overdoing" it could pose a
peril. In 1965 Maria had begun rewriting her career: she had sung—so she
alleged—because "They made me sing."[125] "They" had meant her mother
and eventually Meneghini.

She chose to cast a new light on her history. Her whole career could be
accredited to other people—so she claimed. "I would've preferred to have a
happy family and have children; I think *that* is the main vocation of a
woman. But destiny brought me into this career, I couldn't get out and, er
... I was forced into it quite frequently. First by my *mother*, then by my
husband ... I would've given it up—with *pleasure* ... Other people were
more ambitious than I *was*," Maria would tell David Frost.

It became her quest to prove that she had almost been oppressed;
compelled to act against her will at the behest of others. She would admit
that she believed it near-impossible to run a family and a career in tandem.
"It doesn't work together. I doubt whether being a good mother at *home* can
make you *also* a wonderful career woman. Not *my* job. It doesn't work. It's a
full-time job—my career."[126] Yet simultaneously Maria also wanted everyone
to know that the creation of a family was what she wanted most of all.

"I think the program was set not by myself in life in the very beginning.
It was set by my family, my mother *mainly*, [who] was commanding the
family *then*, so er, I had to act accordingly. Of course, I again repeat it was
no *trouble* for me because I didn't really enjoy myself playing around as
children *then*," had been the 1968 avowal.[127]

A year later she alluded to "a double personality: the woman, or the
person, who *guides*—that's the critic—there are always critics in creators,
aren't there? There's the one who performs, the instrument, the reflexes,
and then the other person in you who says, 'Well, that—that wasn't good;
that could've been better.' I don't know. There are *two* people." In response
to this Pierre Desgraupes retorted, "It's as though one of the two people is
forced to accomplish this duty to be *worthy* of the other."—"It's not—no, no;
I'm not *forced*. It's a *love*. I *have* to do it ... It's not a sacrifice for one who
loves his profession. Tolerating the nonsense of others is a sacrifice. And
also your own nonsense—because we do all kinds of stupid things. But our
duty, with love—that's not a sacrifice. What else am I supposed to do?"[128]

Certain writers have enjoyed describing Callas—on account of her self-
contradictions—as "schizophrenic."[129] There are phrases of hers—such as
the oft quoted, "There are two people in me; I would like to be *Maria* but
there *is* the Callas that I have to live *up* to. So I'm—coping with *both*, as

much as I *can*," that fall prey to that tenor of argument. In the same interview she nonetheless concedes, "I like to think that they both go together because *Callas* has been *Maria* in my singing and in my work; my own self has been [there] every second . . . If somebody really *tries* to listen to me, *seriously*, one will find *all* of myself in there. So probably you *can't* detach. Only that, er . . . Callas is sort of a celebrity. I've been mixing you up, I'm afraid, there."[130]

Instability did not encroach upon the woman's wavering reactions. Habitually straightforward, orderly and cogent, Maria didn't come across as someone mentally imbalanced. By insisting that her mother or her husband had directed her career she merely reassigned the blame for her persistent problems.

What she was loath to openly admit was that the "Callas" she was fleeing—these oppressive labels of "divina", "icon", "legend" pelted by the media; the miracle that everybody wanted her to be—was the same person that she emulated studying a score in bed. "I receive letters from people who tell me that they leave my performances feeling stronger," she said in 1970—using the present tense when she was giving no performances. "Being Callas, it's a religion that I carry in myself. It's *my* religion."[131]

Moments of denial continued. Questioned on her voice by Dacia Maraini in Africa, the response was, "When the voice is there, it's there. It doesn't change and it doesn't get ruined. The only thing that I can do is dominate it."[132]

But Maria went even further in her contortions of truth. That November she responded to David Frost's on-air question, "Which would you say has been the *happiest* period of your life—now? Or would you pick—" with the curt answer: "*Now.*" Upon further probing, she elaborated: "I'm at *peace* with myself. I was too *busy* before. And then I was persecuted *after* . . . Now I've *defined* peace. I've eliminated the most problems *possible* . . . When you *try* to eliminate problems from your life . . . private life and things like that, automatically you're at *peace* with yourself. I've made the right decisions and I'm taking care of myself, my *career* and my *voice*."[133]

That summer Maria took a long vacation to Tragonisi, a private island owned by her and Onassis' friend, Perry Embiricos.[134] Ironically he was a relative of Milton, Jackie's former lover.[135] At her behest both Pasolini and her friend Nadia Stancioff came to join her. They went on a visit to Meligala, once the hometown of Maria's father George.[136] Pasolini spent ephemeral episodes on the beach sketching Maria; his opus grew to comprise fourteen portraits.[137]

After learning of her presence on the island of his longtime friend, Onassis flew in on a private helicopter and greeted Maria—who was celebrating the Greek Orthodox tradition of her name day that 15 August—with a kiss on the lips. Not being one to grant a great deal of significance to kissing, she accepted it as paparazzi snapped nearby. Another scandal followed.[138]

Less than two weeks later sixty-three-year-old Maggie van Zuylen unexpectedly died in Biarritz of a heart attack.[139] Maria curtailed her vacation to fly to Amsterdam, where she attended the funeral of the baroness at Haar Castle.[140]

Reports circulated in September that she was in talks with French actress Marie Bell, the director of the Théâtre du Gymnase, to star in a stage play.[141] Maria found another way to pass the time by wandering through Capri in the company of Franco Rossellini and Pasolini as the latter filmed scenes for his 1971 movie, The Decameron.[142] By early October she was back in Paris, browsing antiques at the Biennale festival.[143] Ten days later she meandered around Rossellini and Pasolini again—this time during shooting in Naples.[144] Her activities also involved having lunch with Pablo Manzoni, creative director of Elizabeth Arden, on a boat at the Seine. "Why can't someone invent an invisible shield that protects skin?" she demanded to know.[145]

That November Rossellini accompanied her to New York when Maria flew in to record her stint on The David Frost Show, joining her at a party at Trader Vic's.[146] Simultaneously she was striving to work on her autobiography—or rather, delegating others to do the work for her. Maria wrote to her former maid, Matilde Stagnoli, informing her that she was sending her part-time secretary and "dear friend" Teresa d'Addato,[147] "so that you can relate to her something true and interesting about our life together . . . Naturally I can't talk about myself—that would be lacking modesty."[148]

Another maelstrom of winged gossip flew around as she prepared to take another shot at her suspended Verdi arias compilation. That 2 December the French press announced her return in an imminent concert at the Théâtre des Champs-Élysées. Maria was training hard with Vasso Devetzi, who was now working as her accompanist.[149]

Back in New York she telephoned Seattle Opera's Glynn Ross to discuss a possible La traviata—yet again. This left Sander Gorlinsky disgruntled. "[He said] that you agreed to do an opera in Seattle if Giulini would conduct it. I wrote to Mr. Ross telling him that Giulini has no desire to conduct opera in the near future. I enclose photocopy of a letter I received from Mr. Ross enquiring about an alternative conductor you would accept and if you want me to pursue this perhaps you will advise me."[150]

She wasn't limiting her options: Maria had also elected to be one of the chief organizers of 1971's Gala de l'Union des Artistes—an annual charity circus performance to take place that April in Paris.[151]

Then the hottest piece of news was finally unsheathed. In New York Maria had accepted an invitation to host a series of masterclasses at the Curtis School of Music in Philadelphia. The accord was inconclusive—but negotiations were in full swing.

She left the city for Milan on 29 November.[152] Attending La Scala's opening night of I vespri siciliani on 7 December, Maria paid homage to soprano Renata Scotto: her substitute in the unlucky fifth performance of the

1957 Edinburgh *Sonnambula*s. After slipping backstage to wish Scotto "In bocca al lupo," the Italian equivalent of "break a leg," Maria entered the auditorium to be swept up by such a reception, spectators almost forgot who was singing. They failed to identify Franco Corelli when he also appeared in their midst.[153] "It's a painful memory," Scotto would later admit. "Callas ... applauded and sent flowers to my dressing room."[154]

*

In 1971 *The New Yorker* reported Maria's records were selling as rapidly as they had thirteen years previously.[155] She spent January alternating between Richard Nunn, her new accompanist,[156] and Janine Reiss. The latter would tutor her at the Théâtre des Champs-Élysées. She had demanded that the theatre be completely empty during practice. The moment that she heard unwelcome steps Maria would unleash the mighty power of her speaking voice: "Is someone there? Say something!"[157]

It was a comfort for the homesick singer to be back in this untarnishable haven. Referring to her work weeks later at a press conference, she shared, "We singers like the feel of a theater. We suffocate in small rooms."[158]

The plans on the cards were abundant: Gorlinsky scribbled notes about that yet-to-be recorded *Traviata*, a possible *Anna Bolena* at the Met in fall 1971 then *Medea* in 1972.[159] Since Giulini no longer conducted opera they were counting on Georges Prêtre, who notified Maria of his forthcoming availability: the last week of October that year, then between 1 and 22 November and from the 5 to 10 December.[160]

A fleeting notion was a studio recording with the London Philharmonia and Lorin Maazel. Hearing that she wanted to record in Monte Carlo spurred Gorlinsky to investigate *that* city's orchestra.[161] By June Maazel was still an option—having supplied Gorlinsky available dates. The latter envisioned that "half an LP" could be made in three sessions.

"I am trying to get some dates for you in May/June 1971 to appear as a solo artist in an orchestral concert with a top conductor and for you to sing one single item of approximately twenty minutes of a big piece out of 'Traviata', 'Anna Bolena' or 'Pirata,' " read Gorlinsky's missive dated January 26th.[162]

Maria's mind was luckily elsewhere. Since 1961 she had been offered master classes.[163] Having caught wind of her imminent engagement at The Curtis Institute, in December 1970 the president of New York's Juilliard School, Peter Mennin, had proposed a longer span of classes at his own conservatory.[164]

Her first reaction was a gelid fear. She telephoned Walter Legge "begging me, after years of non-communication, to share her Juilliard master classes with her, 'because we are the only two people who know what bel canto is, and you can talk.' "[165]

Already there was talk about the lessons being open to the public—for up to two hours' duration, as Irving Kolodin scribed in an epistle to Maria following her meeting with Mennin and him.[166]

That 3 February she invited reporters to attend a press conference with her at the Juilliard Opera Theater. One thousand people huddled in a throng including Rudolf Bing. In reference to her Curtis Institute tuition, the soprano shared, "I feel I have something to give, and if you're too old you can't do it. I have been taught many things, but I have taught myself more. I don't want what I know to die with me."

Declining to announce when she would next perform, she made sure the discussion was on point: "I don't have the patience to give instruction on breathing, proper registration, things like that . . . But I can advise: if a phrase is not as it should be, I can show the right way." A little later—somewhat out of context—came the statement: "Thank heavens, I haven't lost my voice," along with the emphatic claim, "I'm dearly loved by conductors, colleagues, everybody."[167]

The Q&A ended with an enquiry on Rudolf Bing's part: "Will you have lunch with me on Friday?" Maria chose not to reply to it in public.[168]

Ascending in the elevator with his pal some minutes later, Leo Lerman accidentally touched her bosom. In her hip, cosmopolitan self, Maria seized on the moment to joke to the *Mademoiselle* editor: "Oh, oh, you're exciting me."[169]

That was very much the tenor of her 1970s New York persona.

"Maybe I am Victorian," she had told Kenneth Harris a year earlier. "I believe in self-discipline and a degree of self-restraint. We live in such a complex, small and intimate relationship, all of us in so-called civilised society, that we must not shock one another too much. We have to live with one another—we need to be a little, shall we say, strait-laced?"[170]

Her principles were flying out the window.

The "openness" devolved into defensiveness. Having vowed not to discuss her private life, Maria told a *New York Times* reporter: "I would never make up with my mother, and I have very good reasons. She did many wrong things to me, and blood is just not that strong a tie." About Meneghini—on whose subject she had mostly publicly stayed tacit—she remarked, "He had a bad case of the bla-blas. He told lies and tried to take credit for everything in my success."[171]

It did not occur to her that she was coming off melodramatic—just as it did not occur to her that she was tending to misjudge her audience. Purported friends would cite peculiar anecdotes about the star to take pride in their poise. Gratifying was it for the pack to learn their "genius" was little more than the facetious, backwards kind of woman they disdained. "Maria says Onassis was sleeping with Mrs. Onassis's sister [Lee Radziwill] before Mrs. O grabbed him," Lerman had scribed in his diary. "All very Greek classical."[172]

Her humor misfired. In a classic case of overcompensation, Maria wound up looking silly every time she notified a journalist, "I like to wear pretty dresses, talk gibberish—just a woman like any other!"[173] or, "I'm just like any other normal woman who goes shopping, goes to the movies, and shames her friends, because she comments on a lot of things, or screams with laughter, or cries like an idiot."[174] Speaking of another upcoming vacation to Tragonisi, she fantasized aloud of "swimming, snorkeling, nonsense. When I play, it is so nice to be a child."[175]

An inhabitant of opera's bubble for the greater part of her existence, Maria had been loath to venture too profoundly into people's psyches. When it came to playing one in real life she was lacking research to portray the part. Believing she was stupid, many held contempt for her. The supposedly devoted Mary Mead would describe her as "self-centered and unimaginative"[176] while Lawrence Kelly termed her "extremely careless and extremely selfish."[177]

Thus many of the friendships that she entertained throughout this period were false . . . completely unbeknownst to her. Still a performer, she had stumbled onto the wrong stage.

Peter Mennin attempted and failed to convince Maria to teach opera acting in Juilliard's drama department.[178] By 8 February she was staying at the Barclay Hotel, Philadelphia—primed to engage in her first lessons with the Curtis vocalists.

The visit was brief. "When I arrived there I found eighteen students who were simply not prepared for advanced training. So I asked them to sing for me one by one and made some suggestions about vocal technique," Maria described.[179] Three days were endured before she bolted—venturing to take a long weekend of leisure at a chalet by the Magic Mountain ski resort in snowy Vermont. Needless to say, Maria couldn't ski.[180]

Left to give an explanation to the students, director of the opera and conducting department Max Rudolf averred: "She definitely plans to return, but we don't know when . . . She told me and Curtis director Rudolph Serkin that she will definitely keep in touch."[181]

Later on he sat them down to give a thorough explanation: "[He] called us together and explained that part of the problem was emotional, the frustration that Callas feels in her own career," one student told *Opera News*. "Remember she stopped singing at 42, when most sopranos are in full bloom."[182]

Days later Maria was at Juilliard receiving a fresh batch of auditionees. These included bass Willard W. White and soprano Barbara Hendricks, who would go on to have fruitful careers.[183] Lincoln Kirstein—art connoisseur, impresario and co-founder of the New York City Ballet—had enlisted Leo Lerman to enquire if Maria would perform *La voix humaine* at the New York State Theater the following season. "No, no, no . . ." came the response one day. "I'm going to Juilliard to do a little research on my own . . . You have your police everywhere."—"Like Scarpia," Lerman retorted. "But you are kind and good and sweet," Maria pointed out. "That's the worst kind of Scarpia," Lerman quipped.[184]

That same evening she was scheduled to attend Franco Corelli's *Werther* at the Metropolitan Opera.[185] Plagued by sentiments of vocal insecurity, the tantrum-inclined tenor was refusing to appear and had already locked himself inside his dressing room.

Rushing from the Regency Hotel in a black evening gown and coat, the soprano was saluted by Onassis' chauffeur. Throughout her New York trips Maria counted on his limousine service for privacy. It also facilitated their now secret meetings as friends, which almost always occurred in the presence and at the apartment of longtime pals Costa and Anastasia Gratsos.

What Maria *didn't* know—and neither did Onassis—was that the driver at the wheel was budding tenor Marko Lámpas: student of the Juilliard School. Lámpas in turn had no idea Maria Callas was auditioning his classmates and intent on working there.

Stepping out to head toward the stage door of the Met, Maria tripped up on the curb; the chauffeur steadied her. "Thank you, young man. I'm blind as a bat," she replied. The ensuing conversation led her to decipher his Greek accent. "Με σωσεις. (mhé sosses),"—"You saved me," she informed him. "Tell your office to charge this to Mr. Onassis and to give you a handsome gratuity."[186]

Unsuccessful in her implorations that night, Maria watched the role of Werther being sung by understudy Enrico Di Giuseppe.[187]

Over the next few days Lámpas frequently found himself fetching or dropping Maria off. During their rides he would listen to New York's classical music radio station, WQXR. Swiftly noticing his penchant for the genre, Maria began plying him with questions on his family, his children and his marriage. Several trips convinced her he was reticent to talk about his spouse. Unbeknownst to his enquiring passenger, Lámpas was engaging in an extramarital affair. "You're not happy with your wife," Maria observed bluntly. "Why is that?" Despite Lámpas' insistence all was well back at the homestead, he eventually caved and confessed her suspicions were justified. "You love your children and you are sentimental. Most Greeks are," Maria conceded. "But you must find happiness in your life, Marko. It is very important."[188]

It was one of many ventures into lecturing at that time of her life. Unafraid to lay bare her opinion, she converted her merciless boredom into merciless preaching: most of it warmly maternal.

Similar words targeted a disillusioned Pasolini in their correspondence. Following his break-up with lover Ninetto Davoli, Maria wrote: "The reality is what you <u>must</u> confront but you cannot as you don't <u>want</u> to. You will succeed—I did—a woman with such sensibility—I have nonetheless learned that we can rely only on <u>ourselves</u> . . . I don't mean to sound like a mother, sweetheart—neither did I look at you as my father. Pier Paolo, books contain a great deal of wisdom, yes—but not the harsh reality—and they don't teach what I <u>believe</u> and will die believing. That man <u>alone</u> can make his life—from pure will. From *amour propre* and pride . . . Of course words are only words—easy to write etc. But when are you going to grow up, P.P.P? Isn't it time for you to be richer and more mature? I know you're going to hate me for writing this."[189]

Maria returned to Paris in the early days of March. In Italy divorce was slowly being legalized. Fast on the heels of its inevitable nascence, Meneghini was already working hard to stop his and Maria's final separation. He had managed to suspend proceedings for two weeks proclaiming that the new law was "unconstitutional".[190]

From the comfort of her home on 9 March Maria wrote three letters in contrasting tones. One of these was to the Metropolitan's coach Alberta Masiello. Having coached Maria intermittently throughout her prime, she was now tutoring the would be coach at Juilliard:

> *I want once again to thank you—if I can, because I can never thank you enough—for all your affection and the precious time you gave to me. The years in America, as I told you, represent for me perhaps the most beautiful moments in my artistic life, and working with you is like a tonic . . . I will be eternally happy and grateful for it.*[191]

To Leo Lerman came the letter of schoolgirl:

> *Dearest heart, (!!!)*
> *How can you ever forgive me, but you always do, don't you? You love me and you understand. I was very busy singing; moreover, I had a sort of a rash on the face, probably due to some indigestion. So now you owe me two dinners instead of one next time I come, hoping you* [she means "I"] *will have a clean face by then, please me, love.*[192]

And to longtime friend, music critic Irving Kolodin:

> *I was quite unhappy to leave without saying at least au revoir, because good bye* [sic] *it is not, but I was hoping to stay more; instead I had to come back as my time was running out.*[193]

The three are adequate examples of how hard Maria worked in order not to misconstrue her audience. Advertisers skew to a specific demographic; the soprano tried the same.

A week later she also wrote a most formal letter to Peter Mennin, thanking him "most sincerely for having facilitated my practising at any time allowing me the use of your halls at any hour."[194] It was agreed upon that Maria would return to Juilliard at the "end of April or beginning of May."[195]

On 23 March Maria attended Marilyn Horne's Parisian debut in the company of Janine Reiss at the Théâtre des Champs-Élysées. After hearing Horne accord her version of Rossini arias "a lot of coloratura, cadences and fioritura," Reiss was left dumbfounded. Maria smiled, began to clap and whispered in her ear: "Applaud, *chérie*. They are looking at us."[196]

The following day Maria composed a letter to Roland Bourdin, Director of the Orchestre de Paris:

Three months ago, with your amicable vows, you expressed the desire to one day see me perform with the Orchestre de Paris. I was very touched by this . . . But how could I realize such a desire after the concert I heard yesterday at the Théâtre des Champs-Élysées? I told you this after the concert, and I promised to write it to you. This morning, I still could not believe my ears.

How can around one hundred musicians present themselves so poorly onstage, and not take music seriously at all, or rather, treat it as a joke . . .

I ask you to excuse my bluntness, but all of them played "like pigs". Please believe that it is with immense sadness that I wrote these lines to you, because, as you already knew, I was going to record a disc of Verdi arias with the Orchestre de Paris. A date had already been tentatively chosen: the month of September.

This recording will now not take place, thus depriving your musicians of a month of work—and me the joy of returning to the studio with what ought to have been one of the world's most illustrious orchestras.[197]

"Just to give you a pale idea of how awful they played, the Orchestre de l'Opéra in my protested record were angels in comparison," Maria insisted to Gorlinsky three days later.[198]

In the company of French actor Jean-Pierre Cassel Maria attended Jerry Lewis' comedic show at the Olympia on 16 April. The two were there with an ulterior motive: as the principal organizers of that year's Gala de l'Union des Artistes, they were enlisting Lewis to take part in the events. Cassel recalled Maria's eagerness to oversee the entertainment: "She accepted interviews, attended rehearsals at the Cirque d'Hiver, gave her opinion about the sequence of performances, the style of the costumes. A great, great professional . . . We paid [Lewis] a visit backstage before the perform-ance, and I remember the emotion and pride he felt at meeting her."[199] Lewis' show that night involved a parody of opera.[200] "During the perform-ance, she laughed like a child," Cassel wrote.

At dinner at the latter's house one night Maria laughed again when she was greeted by an overzealous Basset Hound who hid beneath her dress. Speaking of her hopes for the impending Juilliard classes, she was cut off unceremoniously by two intensely staring bleary infant eyes. It was Cassel's son Vincent, who would likewise pursue a screen acting career. Awoken from his sleep, he stood and fixedly beheld his onlooker. Breathily Vincent exulted: *"Comme elle est belle!"* ("How beautiful she is!").[201]

Another artist she attempted to invite was Marlon Brando. Whether or not he made sure to R.S.V.P. is unknown.[202]

Maria opened the 38th Gala de l'Union des Artistes on 23 April with the words "Que le manège commence!" ("May the festivities begin!"). Clad in a floor-length, sparkling red, glittery gown with hoop earrings to match, the star rivaled the shades of the circus. Juliette Gréco took part in a number about training tigers, Catherine Deneuve—training elephants; Omar Sharif made do with horses.[203] At the sight of Maria's provocative red, a baby elephant hungrily dashed at her—sending her running for cover. Relenting, he surrendered the frail human. Maria laughed but took her stage revenge by slapping him.[204]

It was not the prettiest of moments. And while Maria chortled all throughout the evening, it is somehow difficult inspecting the brief footage that remains to think that she took pleasure in the role of hostess.

By the beginning of May it had been agreed that Maria would not receive payment for her Juilliard classes—requiring solely that "all travelling and living expenses for me and my secretary during the periods of my visit and works will be the responsibility of the Juilliard."[205] The school responded with the offer of a suite at the prestigious Plaza Hotel.[206]

"Marko, wonderful to see you again!" she greeted her chauffeur upon returning to Manhattan in late April. "Take me to the Juilliard School, please. You know where it is?"[207] Lámpas was still oblivious to her now pressing pedagogical pursuits.

The second round of auditions was held on 7 May; the third on the 9th. This didn't serve to be distracting enough for Maria—who found herself calling Leo Lerman at night on the first of these dates: "I'm finished . . . Last March was too much. He [Onassis] almost had me again—but he's such a pig. And what for? . . . I'm doing Juilliard for nothing. I have enough. Not as much as before. They can't pay much—so I do it for nothing."[208] Ten days later came another one am disruption on the phone. "Let him have his two whores. I'll never forgive him for humiliating me in public and taking me away from my music. 'What d'ya wanna work for?' he asks me . . . So adolescent." Maria's latest "realization" had her share with Lerman that she should probably have an affair "with a married man"—it would be "safest."[209]

Now that more people had suffused her life, Maria packed her nights with extra talk. A while was spent on the telephone advising her incipient student, Luba Tcheresky. The latter was so shocked that she immediately wrote to her: "I know I did not sing nearly as well the 3rd time as in the previous two . . . but I HATED to complain about being ill, and was most overwhelmingly grateful that your intuition picked that up. I really did feel awful . . . my throat was still not well from that cold I had had, plus it was a bad time . . . and that TINY room!"[210]

By 10 May Maria had narrowed the shortlist to twenty-five students. They were invited to come to converse with her on 16 May in Juilliard's Room 535.[211]

Those she rejected were accorded first priority for access to the classes.[212]

A final round of auditions was heard on May 23rd. By this time chauffeur-tenor Marko Lámpas had heard of Maria's projected adventures in teaching. He had prepared three arias with his teacher Gibner King and Juilliard's accompanist Viola Peters.

After dropping off Maria in his after-hours role, Marko returned to studenthood at Juilliard. He had deliberately enlisted with the name "Lamas" at the audition to preclude suspicion. Growing puzzled as he surfaced in the theater, she approached the stage. "Marko? What are you doing here?"

"I would like to audition for you, Miss Callas."

Peter Mennin intervened—insisting Lámpas was a longtime member of the opera school who had performed the lead role in their recent staging of *Il giuramento*. Momentarily subdued, Maria climbed the steps that led up to the stage. Lámpas immediately offered his hand. "What is this? All this time you've been with me, and you never told me you were an opera singer! Aren't you ashamed?" She slapped his face jokingly—a Greek custom—and returned down the same steps taking Mennin's stretched hand. "I did not know, he never told me," she told the Juilliard dean. "He's been my chauffeur for all this time, and he never mentioned it once!"

Terrified of being accused of picking students for improper reasons, she addressed the young man sternly. But his performance of *Lucia*'s "Tu che o Dio spiegasti l'ali" sealed the deal.

Entering Lámpas' limousine after 7 pm that night, she said nothing about the audition's results—merely stating: "You sang beautifully, Marko. I am proud of you. Now, let's go to the hotel. I am very tired." That night he drove her to dinner with Onassis at Costa Gratsos' apartment. Two hours later he was stunned to see Onassis leave his driver to accompany Maria. The former lover sat beside her in the back of the limo as Lámpas looked on in contempt. He heard the pair whispering and occasionally laughing.

Fearing that Onassis would escort Maria to her Plaza Hotel suite, Lámpas was relieved to see her bid the man goodnight and issue him a caveat: "Ari, this young man is my protégé and a very talented opera singer. I want you to help him. I don't want him to work so many hours driving a limousine."

After their parting Onassis returned to the limousine, instructing Marko to take him to one of the city's most popular restaurants, El Morocco. Later he gave the young man ten dollars and patted him on the back: "Here, there isn't much of a future in singing classical music, keep your job." Lámpas soon learned he had been accepted in Maria's Juilliard classes.[213] It was no favor, though: recordings of the lessons prove that he possessed a weighty and commanding tenor voice still raw.

Of the three hundred and fifty singers Maria heard she finally chose twenty-eight.[214] Privately she met with each of them on 27 May for a five-minute talk; advising which operas to work on, urging them to prepare vocal exercises and even—when it came to the twenty-two-year-old Barbara Hendricks—discussing their weight.[215]

Returned to her Parisian home by June, Maria was the first person granted a divorce by Brescia Civil Court on the 16th.[216] She continued her pursuit of interesting material for her memoirs, writing to Cristina Gastel's old friend, Monika Wiards.[217]

After spending much of June training with Vasso Devetzi, that July she took another trip to Tragonisi: "Anastasia [Gratsos] was so down that I thought I'd go with her to cheer her up," Maria wrote to Pasolini. "I think that through contact with young people—lost in the fog—without being able to have faith, without exemplary guides—I'll do some good."[218]

Continuously in search of her old self, Maria wrote to Antonio Caraza Campos, once the artistic director of the Palacio de Bellas Artes in Mexico. "I will never forget our glorious years together. This has became [sic] history, forgive my immodesty but you had great faith in the then Callas that became later the great!"[219]

It was on 20 August that Maria boarded an Air France plane to New York to begin the first six-week session of Juilliard classes.[220] She telephoned her student Luba Tcheresky again to discuss repertoire,[221] as well as Walter Legge, who then wrote: "I was deeply touched that you had telephoned to enquire into my state of health . . . I am sorry you are already in America; I had made my mind up to cut Salzburg short and fly to Paris for the [purpose of] seeing you."[222]

Like police scouring a range of areas in an exhaustive manhunt, she was adamant to cover all and any bases in her search for answers. "I am a simplifier," Maria had told a journalist the previous year. "Some people were born complicated, born to complicate. I was born simple, born to simplify. I like to reduce a problem to its elements, so I can see clearly what I have to do. Simplifying your problem is halfway to solving it. It is with life as it is with art. To simplify a problem is not to solve it, not even to make it easier, but it enables you to concentrate your energies on a real solution. Of course, if you are going to simplify, you must face up to what you find. Some people complicate in order to veil."[223]

It seemed Maria's life had turned into a helter-skelter of deliberately crafted complications.

19.

"Inside is your mirror"

In the screwball that was 1970s New York the shades were bolder than the pastel hues of flower power. Tourists had been banished from Times Square: an effervescent hub not just for prostitution but the swelling pornographic market; peep shows sold at less than thirty cents a pop. In more upmarket districts disco balls and flared palazzo pants were swiveling to Bee Gees songs and little Michael Jackson singing "ABC"; coiffed hair had long become a bygone trend. While the Supreme Court had ruled in favor of desegregation busing, opera was still stranded at a highway stop.

The sixties had dethroned high culture; merging the artistic interests of the rich and poor, the disenfranchised and the spoiled. Events such as the opening of the Salzburg Festival no longer had the draw to be a headline in themselves; their clout usurped by raucous incidents at Madison Square Garden or the bar brawls triggered by Muhammad Ali's boxing matches. Classicists and modernists waged war. "Democracy is fatal for the arts," Walter Legge stated. "It leads only to chaos or the achievement of new and lower common denominators of quality."[1]

Maria had assumed a harder role: attempting in this atmosphere to draw a middle line between the so-called high- and lowbrow.

It was the end of August 1971. As Tennessee Williams spied on the next table in the Oak Room at the Plaza Hotel, "dazzled by Maria", she once again cursed her predicament. "I have the hernia, in my diaphragm," she informed Leo Lerman. It was likely the same one that she had mentioned to de Hidalgo two years earlier. "But I don't do anything, since the doctor told me that if I had an operation, I couldn't sing. I will sing. I must show myself that I can do it—and I will do it."[2]

She was using a studio at Juilliard for two hours a day[3] to continue her work with Alberta Masiello, who would later insist that she "only played for her—not coached—and learned from her."[4] "I'm in my own little enclave, a big, beautiful room which has huge bay windows," Maria wrote to Teresa d'Addato. "I'm the only one who has a key—it belongs to housekeeping—and I go there whenever I want to study."[5]

A gamut of distractions granted her relief. One day that week a strange man surfaced at the door of her hotel suite bearing a bouquet of roses. Admitting him without much thought, Maria eyed him with suspicion till the unexpected guest explained that he was Robert Ross, President of the Muscular Dystrophy Association, come to persuade her to partake in its Labor Day telethon hosted by Jerry Lewis.

Knowing the comedian well, that 6 September Maria stunned the presenter by appearing on live television a few hours into his annual fundraiser.

"You must be shocked." Settling down on the couch, she ignited a radiant smile.

The man's mind was wandering.

"I'm very happy but I'm . . . shocked."

Maria laughed.

"That was—that was my *intention!* . . . I happened to be here and I made the point of coming here and thanking you, with all my heart."

"Just from Paris."

"Just from *Paris.*" Maria fudged the truth.

She was wearing an extravagant striped dress with an expanding skirt; it looked like a balloon.

"By the way this gown . . . seems *funny,*" Maria acknowledged before the live audience and some fifty million viewers at home. "I don't know if you recall—the ceiling of the *circus.* It has these kinds of *stripes*—it just *happened* to be, so I thought I'd wear it for the [event]."

Maria was a presentational star that night; assuring Lewis she was "optimistic—I've seen it; I've been under heavy *gunfire,*" and urging him to be "prouder and prouder" of the pledges he raised. At the same time she was down to earth and lacking grandiosity: "Shoot me off when you don't want me," she assured him. "You stay right *there,* Maria," Lewis countered.

After the show she sat down on the floor of an Americana Hotel conference room to speak to an enthusiastic clan of volunteers who had been taking donors' pledges through the night. Addressing them as comrades, Maria took off her shoes.

Following their meetings, Robert Ross became a newcomer among her late-night telephone call bullseyes; being targeted for talk about what she should wear and her poor eyesight. He goaded her to have an eye examination[6] to which John Ardoin escorted her. Maria was diagnosed with glaucoma. Shortly afterward she phoned Ross to lament being forced to insert eye drops every two hours for the rest of her life.[7] At first this was a handicap: Maria had to wear a watch with an alarm to signal when to take them. Eventually she got used to the ritual and was able to do it in front of acquaintances.[8]

Two weeks later on the 20th Maria attended the opening night of the Met's 1971-2 season: *Don Carlos* with Plácido Domingo. Having spent several evenings of late in the company of Juilliard president Peter Mennin and Georganne, his painter-photographer wife, Maria had been introduced to a possible beau in sixty-one-year-old Bernard Lasker,[9] a former chairman of the New York Stock Exchange and friend of George Moore, President of the Metropolitan Opera Association.[10]

Sharing a box with her that evening, Lasker later dabbled in a tentative, brief courtship of her. Together they attempted to attend the famous 21 Club—where Maria was denied admission as a woman wearing pants.[11] The press would spot and speculate about them at this venue several times.[12]

Casually Maria tried to bond with Lasker's daughter Joan. Owing to her tepid interest in her father, she was clumsy when it came to socializing. Joan's admission that she never went to the opera was met with the feeble suggestion, "Maybe you're a loner like me." At one point she asked Joan if she believed her father would be going out with her if she weren't famous.[13]

Young singers were a different matter altogether. A few days after his *Don Carlos* Maria bumped into Domingo at a restaurant. "Only you were good, Plácido," she let him know. "But you're singing too much."—"The more I sing, the better I sound," he insisted.[14]

Disgusted with most aspects of the opera house's standards, the soprano felt her rancor fester. "I hear you've been offered some sort of situation at the Met, Larry," she wrote to Lawrence Kelly that October. "And for heaven's sake, please do not. This is my good, sound advice, if you want to take it."[15] The only artist for whom she held tremendous respect at the time was a young James Levine.[16]

Now opera's fate fell to Maria once again; this time backstage at Lincoln Center. A podium of ivory exhibiting the marble trio of the Metropolitan, New York State Theater and the Philharmonic Hall, the spotlight of the square and its effulgent fountain were the mother of pearl luster in Manhattan's matte gray oyster.[i] Drenched in a dim illumination under twilight, the expanse of white and gold extended grounds on which to wander mentally removed from the chameleonic city's switching slides.

Behind the final building of its stately triad stands a silver triangle that looks a little like a Toblerone. This is Juilliard.

Sessions would begin on 11 October. Before that spell Maria held a last round of auditions on the 6th.[17] Ranging in age from around twenty-three to thirty-seven, most of the twenty-eight selected students didn't know each other well and were at different stages of their training.[18]

"I will be playing it by ear. Each singer is an individual and must be treated differently," went Maria's doctrine.[19] A memo was distributed to all the students taking part informing them the classes would be free of charge and emphasize artistic tailorship. It likewise notified they wouldn't constitute a series of ancillary voice lessons.[20]

---

[i] New York State Theater and Philharmonic Hall have since then been renamed David H. Koch Theater and Avery Fisher Hall (today David Geffen Hall) respectively.

Though what the public witnessed was four weekly teaching hours—two every Monday and Thursday for a span of six weeks throughout fall 1971, then another six weeks from February to March of the following year—Maria conversed with and counseled her students beyond what was visible. Her advice extended into extra one-to-one discussions. Prior to February 1972's student production of *La bohème* she reserved a rehearsal room to consult with the cast.[21]

When Peter Mennin stepped onto the Juilliard stage to introduce Maria and implore the audience neither to laugh nor to applaud, she was immediately stunned to find a gaping public. Cries of "Brava" and "Divina" struck her ears. Flowers had been laid across the stage like wreaths along a casket. Stymied, Maria turned to her students: "I'm sorry. This is wrong. These people are not supposed to be here." Despite Irving Kolodin's earlier suggestion of the concept, she appeared not to have known.

A talk with Peter Mennin led her to discover it was indispensable to have an audience present: though tickets only cost five dollars, each class was oversubscribed and the funds would prove useful for Juilliard. Maria ceded but told spectators: "This is a working class. You must allow us to do our work."[22]

"I'm sure you must be nervous," she addressed the reticent Juilliard crew. "I know all that but . . . I'd like you to calm down. Who would rather . . . stand up and sing?"[23]

The imposition of a public meant Maria would feel obligated to perform in every session. A cross between formal and casual, her outfits were semi-elegant. For the first class she arrived wearing a "full-sleeved jersey blouse" and "black palazzo pajamas of impeccable cut;" her hair dangling loose round her shoulders but raised by a black velvet clasp," in the words of scribe Francis Rizzo.[24] Another time she wore brown slacks with a black belt, a seventies-style silver cross and generous pearl earrings.[25] Occasionally a dress could boast a multi-colored, glimmering brocade; its girlishness diluted by a pair of knee-length leather boots.[26] Always her glasses would perch studiously on her nose.

Half sitting and half leaning on a stool, Maria would be stationed next to the accompanist. In the first weeks this was Viola Peters, an elderly member of staff.

The soprano's accent had become a richer panoply of lilts. A typically New York and almost Brooklyn curve would lend a crude effect to her pronunciation of "girl", "chance", "job", "can't" and "off" (*"awff"*); the British "a" would creep into her utterance of "talk" but words like "stage" expelled Italian vowels.

Staving off the fabled image of a stuffy and old-fashioned, patronizing prima donna, Maria would appear theatrical and playful, juvenile and understanding; perpetually displaying camaraderie. Sometimes this persona would be welcomed: certain students grew to love her. Other times the efforts she exerted became palpable and pupils noticed something forced about her presentation.

The press was hungry for a taste of this new Callas paradigm. "Now tossing her hair impetuously or inclining her head against the wicked world, fingers aflutter with geisha delicacy, she does produce an uncanny simulacrum of girlishness," Jack Hiemenz wrote for *The Washington Post*.[27] Although audio recordings of the classes don't permit us visual insight, a reporter discerned: "when the kids hit their high notes squarely, her face breaks out into a truly radiant smile."[28]

It was her ambition to project her polished discipline on the impressionable students. Each had been designated summer homework in the guise of nineteenth-century vocal exercises by Heinrich Panofka and Giuseppe Concone; Mennin's assistant Wriston Locklair had sent copies to them.[29]

Yet the pedagogue was also keen—especially before an audience—to appear an equal ally rather than a dictatorial instructor. "Are you impatient to sing?" she asked her student-cum-chauffeur Marko Lámpas.[30] The young tenor was still driving Onassis and Jacqueline back and forth whilst receiving the latter's complaints. According to Lámpas Mrs. Onassis had an issue with the "smell" of Orthodox Jews on the flights of her husband's airline, Olympic Airways.[31]

"Not actually, no," came the tenor's rejoinder that Monday evening. "Not actually? *Good*," Maria replied matter-of-factly. Lámpas felt he was in terrible voice. He would later remember: "I couldn't reach the high notes comfortably, and no one could tell me what the hell was wrong ... My coach Gibner King said one afternoon, after looking in my throat with a flashlight, that my tonsils were very large, and he assumed that was the reason I was having so many frequent colds. 'You have to take them out, my boy. I think they're infected.' "

When he embarked on "Che gelida manina" from *La bohème*, Maria intuited his insecurity instantly. Approaching him, she whispered in Greek, "Are you nervous? What is the matter? Here, let us start again. Come, take my hand." She was referring to the aria's words: Rodolfo's first encounter with Mimì. "Feel what you are saying. Feel the coldness of my hand." Lámpas struggled to complete the aria. Upon discovering his coach believed that he was suffering from tonsillitis, she offered to find him a specialist doctor.[32]

While the core of her instruction was artistic stylization, there were technical faux pas Maria couldn't overlook. "A note must *always* be hit in the middle," she would stress—disputing many singers' practice of anticipating high notes in advance. "One rule for *all* of you—*never* slur on a note ... Colleagues of mine, famous singers do it—it's a bad *habit* ... If a composer wants a slur, he *writes* it. If he wants a glissando, he writes it. A glissando would be 'Ah-ah-ah-ah-ah,' A legato would be 'Ahhh . . . ah.'"[33]

Much of the technical advice Maria doled out during Juilliard classes was the dictums cited in her interviews. At the same time there was exposition of some concepts left unveiled. Tutoring soprano Syble Young about "Der Hölle Rache" from *The Magic Flute*, she observed: "Lately I have a vague idea— now, I hate to say something that'll probably jump up on my back—the

German is too *harsh.*" (According to Walter Legge, Maria believed the language "hounds the voice").[34] "You should be *easier* on the accent, and more with the *voice.*"[35]

As for the use of various muscles for vocal projection, she didn't touch upon the matter in great detail. Scarcely able to discuss the pharynx let alone the intercostals muscles, Maria simply heard her sound and felt inside where it was resonating; lacking a specific method to convey. For this reason she was quick to highlight an achievement of her student Barbara Hendricks when the latter noticed, "I've been using some muscles I did not use before."—"Did you *hear?*" Maria alerted her audience. "Miss Hendricks has been using some muscles that she did not use before. That is *very* important because singing is based on *within:* it's the *inner* breathing that controls the sound."[36]

Testing with a show of hands, she was disheartened to discover many of her students hadn't studied the compulsory Panofka and Concone exercises. Loath to suffer fools, Maria sought immediate explanations. "My teacher does not like me to do them," one inanely justified.

"I don't like to mix up with teachers, of course it's not my job but these are very necessary—exactly for the registration of the voice, and also to *exercise* the voice . . . It's not just a *display* that I'm trying to put you on Panofka and Concone; it is because I will not have any further questions like, for instance, 'How is the trill?' or 'Which is the trill?' like Miss [Barbara] Shuttleworth asked me last time . . . All your solutions are in those *books.* I insist on your Panofkas and Concones—that was your homework for this summer. You should've done it—*period,* as they say."[37]

Between the six-week periods of sessions she assigned another set of exercises set to words by Nicola Vaccai.[38] To enhance vocal agility among her female students the new pedagogue asked five sopranos to inspect the twelve-minute Beethoven aria, "Ah! perfido."[39] Thus while Maria stressed that she was no instructor, her restricted tutelage seemed like an after-hours clinic while her students saw the Juilliard staff as full-time doctors.

Celebrities were far too spottable. Throughout that twelve week-spell innumerable luminaries dropped in on the classes: Plácido Domingo; pianists Alexis Weissenberg and Gina Bachauer; sopranos Alice Tully, Elisabeth Schwarzkopf, Grace Bumbry, Bidu Sayão and Licia Albanese; conductors Sir John Pritchard and Michael Tilson Thomas; basses Tito Gobbi and George London; Italian actor Ben Gazzara and legend Lillian Gish; drama teacher Stella Adler; Maria's old friends John Coveney of Angel, Carol Fox of the Chicago Lyric Opera, Michel Glotz, Franco Zeffirelli; many, many critics and the list goes on.[40]

"*Please* refrain from laughing, eh? If you were here—you wouldn't like it," she beseeched the public.[41] The context prescribed Maria a Catch-22: it was her duty to perform yet simultaneously construct the false illusion of a fourth wall to ensure that students took her seriously. "I remember my first class teaching at Juilliard. All the students applauded each other's efforts. I say, 'What is this? Did they come to applaud or to learn?' " she would later recount.[42]

So she assumed the role of mediator. "If one gets applause and the other does not, it might hurt the other's feelings. This is supposed to be again, I *repeat*, an intimate class."[43]

No guidelines dictated which student sang and when. Some were selected to perform with noticeable regularity; thirteen times in the case of superlatively talented tenor Mario Fusco. Others were called upon just once or twice. Some were expelled for lack of progress; even lack of attendance. "I hope none of you—each and every one of you should *not* feel neglected," stressed Maria. "I have a way of working that—if I work with any one of you, it should be a lesson for each and *every* one," she explained one evening.[44]

For them Maria aspired to be a team member; even fellow soldier in combat. Of the aria "Quante volte come un dono" from Verdi's little-known *La battaglia di Legnano* we hear Maria tell soprano Zenaida Luz: "I wanted to record it and I still haven't managed because—I mean I was *supposed* to so—we *both* have problems with this aria." The audience laughs. Maria doesn't chasten them. "Next time both you and *I* will prepare this piece. It is *very* difficult."[45]

"Which one of my girls knows *Puritani*?" is how Maria saccharinely starts another session.[46] To Marko Lámpas—who is suffering from a cold—she bashfully advises: "Please do not sniffle that much onstage; we're not supposed to *do* that onstage."[47]

"Mr. Fusco—how do you feel?" she asks the tenor in a February class.

"Well."

"*Well?* I never heard you say *that* before," Maria quips in mock-astonishment. "*Good.*" Shedding humor's sheen, she reassumes her teacher-self: "No—are you all *right?*"

As he launches into the bombastic, volatile crescendi of "Guardate, pazzo io son" ("Look—I'm crazy!") from Puccini's *Manon Lescaut*, Maria beholds him unplugging a tempest of might.

Once he is finished they start backtracking—dissecting different sections under her incisive operatic microscope. He resumes the aria. The slender murmur of a harsh, corrupt soprano voice inevitably tags along: Maria can't resist accompanying him—a little bit. Shyly. And it's not even to reel in the audience: it's *just one of those things*.[48]

"[Here] comes the *very* impossible next phrase," mezzo-soprano Sheila Nadler says of Aïda's duet, "L'aborrita rivale".

"There's *nothing* impossible. Don't give me that!" Maria laughs. "*Nothing* is impossible; not for *you*, Sheila. If you think *positive* . . . if you just would *think* of the beautiful phrases you're singing, *nothing* would be impossible."

Later on, Nadler remarks:

"The excitement comes very easily to me—"

"That's good—that's very *good!* That means *life* if you're excited, thank *heavens*—that's what I'm *looking* for. You've got to breathe *life* into these things 'cause they were *born* with life."

Toward the end of the duet Maria counsels, "As you will have a tenor there—don't worry, he'll scream his head off there—" The audience explodes in laughter. "*Excuse* me," Maria acknowledges, "There are tenors here . . ." It's a non-apology apology. "*Always* save a little breath—in fact, the tenor will do the same."

Sometimes Maria was anxious to prove she was just "one of them".

"I don't like it either—which is why you must love it even *more*," she tells Barbara Shuttleworth about Micaëla's aria "Je dis que rien ne m'épouvante" from *Carmen*.

"You're a bit hoarse," Maria alerts Barrie Smith as she tackles *La forza del destino*'s "Me pellegrina ad orfana". "But are you well today?"

"No," the juvenile soprano stresses. "There's certain spots—like, three notes in my voice that I can't sing today."

"Yeah, I know," Maria acknowledges—her mind on other things. A pause. "Likewise."

The crowd unleashes cackles once again. Maria doesn't begrudge them. If the part of lyrical performer has escaped her repertoire, she might as well . . .

Advising soprano Pamela Hebert on "Ernani, Ernani, involami," she remarks, "You can hear Rosa Ponselle in this aria—it would be a much better example." A slight pause of hesitation on Maria's part. "And you can hear me *too*—not that I'm such a good example but . . ." Applause cuts off her speech.[49] Relating an anecdote to Barrie Smith, she recalls how back in 1951 a theatre employee had told Maestro Serafin, " 'It's for Miss Callas'— 'cause I was 'Miss Callas' *then* . . ." Maria sniggers, weakly attempting to hold back her laughter. "I am 'Miss Callas' *now* . . ."[50]

Thus it isn't possible for her to be—exclusively—a *teacher*. Yet she rebuffs attempts of fans to have their pictures taken and their photos signed—harshly rejecting an imploring tourist's plea. "Untamed audience today, eh?" Maria asks the public. "What are we gonna *do* about it?"[51]

At the same time the soprano doesn't struggle to observe a group of fans that has attended every session. "Nobody could be more faithful than you people!" she exclaims.[52]

That's not to say the students pose a lesser interest to her, for they don't. Boasting of them where appropriate, Maria tells the audience soprano Jacquelyn Benson has made progress with her "Caro Nome": "My compliments in front of all of us: she's worked on her trills. *Brava*."[53]

Callas is entertainer, guide and mentor all rolled into one. Peter Mennin was increasingly impressed with her magnetic easiness: "Don't call me a teacher," she insisted to him. "I hate that!"—"You illuminate . . ."—"Eh!" came her Italian peasant-like response. "Yes—anything—not a teacher. I don't teach. I advise."[54] He and his wife Georganne had only seen her perform once: the 1965 Met *Tosca*. To enlighten them of her significance, she had EMI supply a full set of her records for free.[55]

There were certain principles to which she wanted all her students to adhere. The virtue of image curation was one of them. Maria kept an especially scrupulous eye on "her girls": "The first *Traviata* was a fiasco in Venice," she would later explain to an interviewer, "because of a prima donna who was too fat. And . . . in the last act when she started to cough, everyone started to laugh and mess around so . . . it was a *fiasco*."[56]

Rumors circulated that Maria had said no to a plump female singer during the auditions even before *hearing* her.[57] In that vein she advised Sheila Nadler to "dress better", dye her red hair blonde and lose weight.[58] With the Women's Liberation Movement gaining steam, Maria hastened to elucidate: "I don't like any movement, or any rebellious sort of thing. I'm a rebel myself, and I do what I want to do, and I don't blabber about it . . .[59] Women's Lib is going a bit too far. Women will never be the same as men. They have other qualities—better qualities sometimes—but they should not have that banging-through quality."[60]

For this reason her approaches to the men and women of her group were different. "I wish every one of you—I hate to say it but you should wear longer skirts or *slacks*," she pled onstage as she beheld soprano Syble Young. "Because—during daytime it's all right but you must remember—I'm sorry I'm bringing it up but this is *general*: the public who looks at you from down there sees a little *more*—" Ms. Young reacted by pulling her skirt down. "No, well it's no use *now*, you should've thought of it *before*! Or *slacks* . . . Forgive me, eh? But I've sort of been patient all these months. You *should* wear onstage, for auditions, you should wear shorter skirts." Ferocious audience laughter. "Oh—*excuse* me—longer skirts. Or *pants*."[61]

Most of the female singers had no problem with her somewhat motherly approach. It would elicit onstage comments such as, "Gee, you look quite elegant—all of you *today*,"[62] and "My compliments on your *appearance*, Ms. Schmidt. You've cut your hair. You look very *well*." Maria faced the audience. "Doesn't she?"[63]

Toward the end of October Eugene Kohn—a nineteen-year-old pianist who had worked as an accompanist to his great idol, Renata Tebaldi—wrote to Wriston Locklair at Juilliard "on the recommendation of my friend, Mr. Gideon Waldrop," a former dean at the school. "My occupation is an opera coach. I work at my studio with many young singers . . . I could furnish letters of recommendation to you from the following people: Maestro Fausto Cleva . . ." etc.[64]

At the further behest of Maria's old friend and colleague, George London, she considered Kohn as a replacement for her Juilliard accompanist, Viola Peters. "Eugene is so young that he's not going to tell you anything. He'll just do what you say," London was said to have insisted to her.[65] So she happily recruited him.

Despite not having quite warmed to the Callas artistry,[66] Kohn adulated it when he became another student taking her advice: "Please don't be offended," he wrote shortly after the completion of the classes. "But I love you, I miss you and I am <u>personally lonely</u> for your <u>person</u>. I wish I could speak to you and see you."[67] That December he wrote a memo to all of her students inviting them to partake in a recording as a sign of their progress; the pedagogue's Christmas gift.[68]

The greatest gift Maria gave to *them* was her command that every student tinge tradition in the opera world with a uniquely individual style. "Tradition in the theatre is not something to be respected unquestionably," she stressed. "Sometimes it can foster vulgarity when a singer slavishly imitates the so-called traditional way."[69]

To students enquiring whether it would be correct to add or remove a particular ornament or accentuate a particular syllable, Maria neither confirmed nor denied. Her prerogative was to allow each artist to apply their subjectivity. During Sheila Nadler's treatment of *Il trovatore*'s "Stride la vampa" the latter asks which word to highlight in a phrase. "That's up to *you* to solve. Try one; try the other, see which one is better. You can go to your *coach*. Very fine coach. She'll tell you which. 'Cause—sometimes *we* cannot hear what we do, but another ear *can*."[70]

There were unbreakable rules. "Don't *pull* the rhythm," she advises bass Sung Kil Kim after his performance of *La traviata*'s "Di Provenza al mar." "You must always keep rhythm rolling. If you *slacken* it a little bit you *have* to give it back. This is the secret of *all* music; especially the famous "rubato" [which means "robbed"]. If you *steal* a little bit from *here* you've *got* to give it back elsewhere."[71]

Barrie Smith sings *Cavalleria rusticana*'s "Tu qui, Santuzza" duet with Mario Fusco and ends the phrase "La tua Santuzza . . . piange e t'implora" with an extra note on the "ra" syllable; much like Maria had done before Violetta's outburst of "Amami Alfredo" on the phrase "sempre, sempre, sempre presso a te-*EH*". The tutor reprimands her: "No—don't do that."[72] At the same time she praises Sheila Nadler's decision to add an extra sixteenth-note before "morire" in "L'aborrita rivale," calling it "Good tradition" but insisting it has to be a "last-minute portamento—otherwise you *cannot* do it."[73]

Thus Maria acknowledged that taste—even the name of her classes, the "Lyric Tradition"—relied on the nature of every interpreter. Components of her artistry were not to be conveyed; each singer was entitled to their own approach. Quality was measurable by listeners' and critics' tastes but passing time appraised it best.

Her relationships with the students were abundant and varying. Perhaps the most salient one was her kinship with Barrie Smith. "This young girl sang very beautifully [at the audition]," Maria introduced her at the second Juilliard class. "But I had the impression that she was a soprano instead of a mezzo. Now—I'd like to hear *what* she has done. Miss Barrie Smith did *not* want to—but I don't want her to go on *singing* because I want to see whether she's *on* the right *path* . . . So you must not *criticize* her."[74]

South Carolinian Clifford Barrington "Barrie" Smith was now twenty-eight. After earning a bachelor's degree in music from Converse College she had spent a year studying at the American Opera Center at Juilliard.[75] Maria warmed to the young woman instantly—treasuring what Smith would describe as her own "strict self-discipline . . . Even as a third grader I would get up at 5:30 am to practice the piano. And I've always made myself go to bed at a certain hour, knowing that it would pay off when I had to perform the next day."

A dreamer, Smith confessed a few months prior to the classes that she "[didn't] have much social life . . . Besides, most guys, when they hear I'm an opera singer, stand back four paces and then run like mad!"[76]

This frankness aligned the two different sopranos. Following stints with the Texas Opera Theatre and Houston Grand Opera as soprano-in-residence, Smith would change course and eventually become a psycho-therapist.[77]

Amidst the twosome's mischievous shenanigans the lessons' majesty made room for zany repartee. It called to mind a couple of contemporary rolemodels: Mary Richards and her sidekick Rhoda Morgenstern.

"How are you doing, Miss Barrie?" Maria asked her one November evening. "Not that I want you to sing . . ."

"*Terrible.*"

"Oh—you *can't* feel terrible; you've got to feel *well.*"

"I *don't* have to feel well; everybody keeps telling me I *have* to and I—"

"Of *course* you do . . . Well, so do I but I came to the *class*; I felt pretty lousy," Maria conceded.

"We're not helping each other, are we—"

"Of *course* we are. Of course I am helping you."

"But you *asked,* so . . ."

"If you have that reaction, that means *already* you're all right. So long as you have that *nerve* to react, then you're all right."

"Well—I've *always* got that."[78]

On that occasion Barrie was excused. The next time, she approached Maria closely.

"Ooh, you're coming *near* me."

"Yes, I *am.* I need all the help I can *get,*" Barrie professed.

"Well—I'll come *near* you."

"So I'll stand, and—look like I'm singing and you *sing,*" the student offered. "D'you *want* to? I've got three copies."

"You've got *three?* Gee, that's *awful,* eh?"

"I've come *prepared.*"

"This is yours, too."

"Yes."

"Well—you've got plenty of things *coming* to you."

Barrie presented her with some kind of amplifier; possibly a ventrilo-quist's dummy.

Maria burst into the waves of tuneful girlish laughter—her voice rising by about an octave as she spoke:

"Are you hoping to get my lousy voice outta *that?*"

"Yes. And I'm gonna ask Santa Claus for a trill for Christmas *too!*"

Maria struggled not to chortle.

"Well, I'm gonna *answer* that. If you think Santa Claus is gonna give you your trill—you're *wrong!*" The audience applauded. Maria came to the conclusion: "So there's no Santa Claus, Barrie."

"*No!*" Barrie mock-lamented. "How can I *sing* now?!"

"No—you can sing; you're gonna *make* it. Without Santa Claus, too. If *I* can make it, *you* can make it."

Kohn began playing *I puritani*'s tough nut of an aria, "Qui la voce."

"D'you want to start from the beginning?" Maria was referring to the aria's prelude "Oh, rendetemi la speme."

"I don't wanna do that," Barrie insisted.

"All right." There was silence. Then—all of a sudden—Maria cried out in a near-melodic voice that made her sound like someone half her age: "But it's good warming *up!*"

"I'd rather warm up somewhere *else.*"

"*All* right." Another pause. A puzzled Maria remarked to her audience, "I'm being *had* today."

"You *know* I'd never do that to you!" exclaimed Barrie. "Don't you *trust* me?!"

"You watch until you *sing* and I'll get *even.*"

"I *know!* God . . ." Barrie groaned. "My voice keeps going to sleep and I can feel it just . . . *leaving.*"

"No, no, no—now, no *tragedy*; come back to earth. To earth and to *work.* No more joking—*please.*"[79]

The two kept in regular contact after Maria left Juilliard. Barrie wrote to her a Christmas card that quoted Henry Thoreau: "If a man does not keep pace with his companions, perhaps it is because he hears a different drummer. Let him step to the music which he hears, however measured or far away."[80] In her sixties Barrie began to write a book about her relationship with Maria. She passed before the memoir was completed.[81]

Mezzo-soprano Sheila Nadler had a different story. One of the older singers, Nadler had been training with Maria's idol Rosa Ponselle for a few years[82] and would go on to have a successful international operatic career.[83] During her time at Juilliard she underwent a crisis of confidence. Maria's abrupt order to change her appearance didn't help to relieve it.

Nevertheless the two at one point had a tête-à-tête—and Nadler found behind a more controlled façade a softer person. "Looking back I think she gave me the courage to continue," she would recall decades later. "I was so concerned about my nervousness. I told her I had to make a comeback. She said, 'So do I—we're both in the same boat.' "[84] Nadler thanked her in writing:

You are beautiful and kind. You have given me courage and made me very happy.

I promise you that I will work very hard. I'll also try not to be gloomy!
Do you know that your eyes sing too—like your beautiful voice! They sing
deep eternal songs.

Love,
Sheila[85]

While many of the Juilliard students were in rapture and the audiences were lavishing affection on Maria, the profession was unsatisfying.

Greeting Maria in his limousine after a session, Marko Lámpas often found her utterly depleted.[86] Eager to rid herself of the persistent praising mob, she depended on the occasional presence of John Ardoin to excuse herself after the classes: "I would like to stay and talk with you, but Mr. Ardoin and I have an appointment, and I really must not keep Mr. Ardoin waiting."

Back in her hotel room she would avidly watch *I Love Lucy* reruns.[87] Before her friends Maria once again propounded novel theories: "I hate opera—so old-fashioned. I detest it," was her insistence one night to Leo Lerman. "I'm a very literal woman,"[88] was another epiphany. Three months before, she had endeavored in a letter to enlighten Lawrence Kelly: "By the way, I am very literal."[89]

No one could aspire to know what she meant.

Her compulsion to have company around her was exacerbated. One night after Tito and Tilde Gobbi dined with her at the Plaza, Maria deliberately stayed their departure by babbling about her potential engagements. When they accompanied her to the hotel elevator she implored, "I feel so lonely. I haven't even my little dog with me here. Wouldn't you like to offer me just another ice cream?"[90]

Eugene Kohn would wonder later if she didn't drink somewhat excessively in those days;[91] Georganne Mennin denied Maria drank at all, stressing she never had appetizers.[92] Asked about her alcoholic habits a few months earlier, Maria had insisted she was "practically a non-drinker" because "My friends provide all the spirit I need."[93]

Indefatigable worries fused together with Maria's terror of insomnia to shrink her courtesy. Entrapping many friends in unsolicited discussions at the dead of night, she even telephoned nineteen-year-old's Eugene Kohn's girlfriend Connie Barnett to discuss the weather.[94]

One aspect of this wanton, diva-ish behavior was apparent when John Gruen, an openly gay reporter for *The New York Times*, dined with Maria to interview her at the Plaza. Though wary of speaking to him and almost defensive at first, Maria discovered his harmlessness. This reassurance led her to invite him to her suite and fervently pursue her monologue into the night. Parting later on, she kissed him on the lips.

Gruen reacted to this with tremendous shock: his memoir is named for the incident.[95] But for Maria kissing didn't have the intimacy that it does for the majority of people. She had smooched Pasolini in public despite treating him like a son.[96] Three months later she would lightly kiss her student-chauffeur Marko Lámpas on the lips to say goodnight.[97] It likely stemmed from lack of sexual interest and a growingly diminishing decorum. Asked about embracing Pasolini by a journalist years later, she retorted: "What's the harm in an affectionate kiss?"[98]

On a daily basis she was working hard with her own coach at Juilliard.[99] Together with Masiello they studied *Lucia*, *La forza del destino*, *Macbeth* and many others.[100] Whenever Maria saw her opera critic pal Irving Kolodin at parties, she supplied updates on her vocal condition. Adamantly she insisted she had never "lost her voice". The problem remained unrelated to her vocal cords—there was "no functional failure due to nodes or polyps, or even partial paralysis," Kolodin wrote. In his words, Maria "had lost poise and control as the result of a muscular mishap, she declared, which cost her the all-important breath support from the diaphragm. That shortcoming, she contended, was now behind her: 'All' she had to do was realign the internal mechanism and make it do her bidding . . . As the weeks and months passed, she would repeat that she was well on the way to her goal—half the way, two thirds of the way, finally 'almost' all the way."

Eventually Maria alerted Kolodin that she was "singing much better than when I did those last *Tosca*s at the Met." Inoculated with the media's asser-tion that Maria had abandoned art for luxury aboard a yacht, a great deal of her colleagues were still skeptical. When Kolodin told Nicola Rescigno that at Maria's "last estimate, she was 'ninety-five percent of what she had been,'" the maestro's response was, "Not good enough. If she's not a hundred percent, she shouldn't sing again."[101]

Every time the Mennins and Maria came into a restaurant a band of viol-inists ventured into *Tosca*'s "Vissi d'arte" or another showpiece. "We would find her an escort when we were together . . . if she was single, we would complete the party with a man," Georganne Mennin would relate. That had previously been Bernard Lasker and would later be one of John Coveney or Irving Kolodin, Maria's old friends.

Also a composer, Mennin had unwavering respect for his new Juilliard pedagogue. Together with Georganne the trio went to *Carmen* at the Met.[102] One night at their apartment they determined to acquaint Maria with her childhood idol on the telephone. Rosa Ponselle was at her home, Villa Pace, in Baltimore. Interrupting her as she watched television, Mennin informed her that "someone" wanted to speak to her, passing the receiver to timid Maria. The latter began "heaping praises" on Ponselle and mentioning their mutual friends Louise and Ida Cook. Ponselle in turn expressed her admir-ation for Maria and began to discuss *Norma*. Maria sorrily admitted having failed to heed to Serafin's advice when he had counseled her to seek Ponselle's advice before embarking on the role.

Not known for tact, Ponselle responded with a brusque "It's too late now, dear!"—prompting her hurt listener to pass the telephone to Mennin.[103]

Meandering thoughts about the idea of a memoir were aswirl in her head yet again. She had told her old friend Joan Crawford that she intended to write one; editor Peter Schwed of Simon & Schuster had expressed interest.[104] For a little while she also considered the possibility of contributing to a book about singing.[105]

The plans were dismissed. "If I did [write one] I would have to tell the truth," Maria would tell critic Alan Sievewright six years later. "And that would hurt too many people. As I am a woman who cannot invent the truth, it has to be, and therefore it is better for me to be silent."[106]

Film producer Joseph Wishy surfaced with the idea of a film of the Czech play, Karel Čapek's *The Makropulus Secret*. He entertained Maria at the Plaza's restaurant with the details. Wishy later told Gorlinsky that the weeks that followed their exchanges at the Plaza saw Maria staying mutely enigmatic on the matter.[107]

That December she tacitly turned down an offer from La Fenice, urging Juilliard's secretary Lorna Levant to type up the rejection.[108]

On the last day of her fall Juilliard classes the stage was bestrewn with bouquets.[109] Maria returned to Paris on 26 November.[110] Throughout December she continued her ritual of telephone-calling: "Someone's been in town," she advised Leo Lerman toward the end of that year. "He's awful . . . sad . . . in a bad time. And who wasn't even touched? Me! He needs a shoulder to cry on, so he came to me. He's not so young anymore."[111]

Ironically, if anything was stable in Maria's life it was her kinship with Onassis. "After his marriage we never quarrelled," she would remember to Stelios Galatopoulos, more sober-minded in retrospect. "We discussed things constructively. He stopped being argumentative. There was no longer the need to prove anything either to ourselves or to one another."[112]

*

Returning to New York that January, she immersed herself in the societal scene, in the words of Aileen Mehle, "in a glamorous black jersey . . . [and] huge, gold, dingle-dangle earrings," attending a party hosted by shipowner John Goulandris' wife at their Fifth Avenue apartment. By her side was longtime friend, Maggie's daughter Gabrielle van Zuylen.[113]

For their second round of classes Maria's approach to the Juilliard students was stricter. She had emphasized before "the courage to say 'no' to contracts—also to *starve* yourself a little bit—of course, you know I did quite a bit of *that* and I'm quite sure . . . if you read the history of *composers*, they certainly went *hungry*. So we *cannot* have our cake and eat it."[114] After certain singers failed to live up to her expectations or missed classes, several were dismissed.[115] Wriston Locklair informed them in writing that Miss Callas had been given the right to expel and enlist vocalists at the start.[116] Additional auditions were held to find others.[117]

"The *experience* you cannot obtain by starting *off* with the Metropolitan or the Scala," Maria had told a reporter before. "Our experience was *obtained* by starting in little theatres and coming up the *hard* way—which is not something that people *like* to do but it makes you or it *breaks* you."[118]

There were exceptions. Maria made that clear as she lectured her class at the end of February 1972, alluding to having granted soprano Anita Terzian permission to partake in a concert. Nevertheless she advised: "If I were you, I would sit here and learn, and audition later when I've known a little *more*. Don't you *think?*"[119]

Bass Willard W. White—who would sustain a sterling international career—auditioned on 21 January.[120] A scholarship student,[121] the Jamaican-born British singer encountered Maria only once outside class: "There was one time I remember being in the lift, and there walked in the great Maria Callas with the president of the school at the time. And she was so beautiful, so powerful, this aura that she carried, and everything, and she was smiling at me, and the president [Mennin] was there, both smiling at me, and I just went: 'Er ... urm ...' and before I could get something out, we reached our destination, the lift doors opened, and we never spoke."[122]

With the student production of *La bohème* imminent, the soprano restressed her commands. "I want each and every one of you to become an *individual*. By that, I don't mean you go *crazy*—you start doing whatever you *want*, because *first* of all you have the composer to serve; then you have the style of each composer *in* each opera ... You must *really* respect the style *of* this composer—and *of* each opera; *Forza del destino* has one attitude; *Ballo in maschera* has another attitude because he [Verdi] has grown *older, then* he was younger. Things move *on*. But—it is *always* within our good taste. And that we *must*—this is the *must* of my being. It always *has* and I want to instill [it] *in* you—who will carry on—*must* carry on ... This applies *also* to drama and also to instrumentalists."[123]

To a new recruit, bass Lenus Carlson, Maria cautioned about Iago in Verdi's *Otello*: "You have to sing the notes *precisely* ... like hammers ... You have to have it more ... *savage*. Savage expression."[124]

Rigoletto was described to Sung Kil Kim as "a real animal that's *trying* to dominate himself"[125] while Jacquelyn Benson learned his daughter Gilda was "*desperate* but ... not *really*."

Mario Fusco—a tenor endowed with an incomparably luxurious, colossal voice not unlike Mario Del Monaco's—was asked: "Do you feel like *singing?*" Having observed his penchant for the art, Maria coyly laughed. "You *always* feel like singing."

"Even when I shouldn't," Fusco responded.

"Mmm—you *know*, if we sang when we felt like it ..." Maria told him and the audience, "Oh, that'd be twice a year." The audience spluttered into laughter. "It's true, eh?"

As he launched into *Turandot*'s "Non piangere Liù" a desire to gesture got hold of him. Maria instinctively seized his hand. "I'll put your hand in your pocket?" she offered, sticking it inside.[126]

"I have a bit of, er . . ." he attempted to excuse himself.

"*Yeah,*" she acknowledged.

"I'm *Italian.*"

"Ah—but *onstage,* the hands *should* move, yes—but, if you move the hands too *much,* it means nothing . . . You do *this,*" [Maria raised her hands] "but—by the time you *have* to do this, nobody believes you. It's like the story of the [boy who cried] wolf . . . Frankly, Mario, with a voice like yours I would use your hands *less* possible [*sic*]. It's very old *style* . . . It's like the cinema without words—the old-fashioned movies, you see them now?" She mimicked mime in silent films. " '*Oh,* Valentino—my *heart*'—you can't *do* that. It makes you laugh. It makes *me* laugh too—*everybody.* Today, I mean—we're dressing in *slacks* and everything is more *real* . . . Things are becoming more *real*—even if we see bad manners which I detest—*also.*"[127]

"It's not just a habit," Fusco explained. "I sang a lot in restaurant-type—"

"Well, *don't,*" she broke him off almost disparagingly. "You're *not* gonna sing in that anymore."

And Maria was trying her best to make sure of it. Though she and Fusco didn't become friends like her and Barrie Smith, he was likely the most gifted of her students based on voice alone. Already thirty-nine years old, Fusco had signed a contract with the New York City Center Opera. According to his résumé, he had been forced to cancel it as a result of financial struggles and family illness.[128]

With him Maria may have been most natural: a venerant colleague as opposed to a towering teacher. "I want more *passion,*" she instructed as he sang the "Bimba dagli occhi" *Madam Butterfly* duet with Zenaida Luz. "This whole duet should be more *passionate.* 'Cause you're Neapolitan and there's no *excuse.*"[129] So ebullient in enamorment and vocal splendor was Mario's "Recondita armonia" from *Tosca,* Maria lauded the tenor by laughing.

"Did you say you were not *well,* or you were tired? Don't you give me *that* again!"

"Well . . . I've worked hard—it's the curse of—"

"*Curse?!* This is no curse—*heaven!*"[130]

Playing favorites may have gone against the axiom of teaching but with Fusco pushing forty she was loath to let him go. Two weeks before the classes ended, Maria had Lorna Levant write Lawrence Kelly a letter: "Miss Callas has said you might be able to help Mario Fusco, a member of her classes at Juilliard, who hopes to receive the financial aid necessary to leave his job and study full time. I am therefore attaching his resume, with enclosures."[131]

Sadly Fusco lacked the impetus or luck to make a prominent career. He continued performing in "restaurant-type" venues for most of his life.[132]

Other students were not privy to that kind of feedback from Maria. Intending to study musical theatre, soprano Cynthia Clarey had wound up in the department by chance. "I just got thrown into it, but really had no interest in being in Juilliard's Opera Center," she later recalled.

When Maria learned that Clarey—who had offered a strong "Casta diva" during lessons—was undecided when it came to her vocation, she confronted her. "What do you want to be, a songster or an opera singer?!"—"A songster," Clarey clarified, walking offstage.[133] At Maria's bidding Wriston Locklair wrote a letter of dismissal.[134] Squeezing through the elevator doors weeks later, Clarey crossed paths with her former teacher. Maria couldn't help but quip to Peter Mennin, "Well, here's the young lady who thinks she has the world at her feet!"

Clarey bore no resentment. "She was very down to earth, very matter of fact about everything," she remembered. "She always looked beautiful. She wore glasses, the thick 'Coke bottle' lenses."[135]

That February Maria had her teeth capped partly on account of vocal reasons.[136] She would later recommend a London dentist to Montserrat Caballé, insisting that teeth played a great role in singing.[137]

Greek director Michael Cacoyannis—later known for his film *Zorba the Greek*—was staging the student production of *La bohème* with Thomas Schippers conducting. After the latter's eleventh-hour withdrawal, Maria heard young student James Conlon leading an orchestra during rehearsal and signaled to Mennin: "That's your man. Take him; he's going to have a great future."[138] While Georganne Mennin would insist her husband had selected Conlon, the soprano's input had most likely been a factor.[139] Barbara Hendricks called her "a kind of consultant to the production."[140]

With a double cast sharing the roles and two of Maria's students, Barbara Hendricks and Kyu-Do Park, performing the lead of Mimì,[141] on the opening night of 10 February Maria sat between Georganne and Peter. Soon she had to be inelegantly shuffled through the theatre; unbeknownst to her Jacqueline Onassis was attending. Precautions were immediately taken to prevent the two from crossing paths.[142]

Opening night received rave reviews. "Talented kids were on stage and a talented kid, the 21-year-old James Conlon, was in the pit. Everybody sang ardently and, with one exception, acted in a completely believable manner," Harold C. Schonberg wrote.[143] The following night the reception was no less elated. Director Cacoyannis came backstage together with Maria to give Barbara Hendricks hugs.[144]

Preparing her instrument for a potential performance, a terrified Maria tested out her voice a few days later at the Juilliard Theater with an audience of two. "I've just come back from the dentist, so I'm not in very good voice," she preemptively apologized to Cacoyannis. But following a brief recital neither he nor Peter Mennin had a great deal of encouragement to offer.[145]

*

As Maria busied her free hours by responding to the mounds of correspondence mailed to Juilliard from fans—including a writer's collection of "lyrical poetry created by me in the Communist jails from my native

Romania"—it brought her comfort to discover that her old friend Giuseppe Di Stefano was in town.[146] After attending one of her classes he sent her a bouquet of roses that read, *"Felicità, Pippo"*—"Congratulations from Pippo," his nickname.[147]

At the time Maria and Di Stefano had common ground: both were battling vocal struggles they had steadfastly resolved to overcome. Differences however greatly separated their predicaments. While Maria was exaggerating the void drama of her private life, Di Stefano's eighteen-year-old daughter Luisa had been diagnosed with Hodgkin's lymphoma. In large part he continued to perform to fund the costs of treatment and support his other children.

When Di Stefano caught Maria that February he noted a downtrodden woman.[148] A Tokyo impresario had offered him ten thousand dollars a concert if he could manage to convince her to join him on tour. He paid her a visit at the Plaza, where they discussed her voice endlessly. Di Stefano declared that he could rehabilitate it.

The following day they went to see Alberta Masiello and Maria attempted to sing. It was a bad day for her vocally; almost nothing came out. Witnessing Maria horribly upset, he stressed: "Come on, let's go out and take a walk in Central Park." She continued crying. Di Stefano urged her to study with him; Maria persistently told him that there was no use.[149] But he wouldn't take no for an answer. Maria began meeting with him frequently. The pair was spotted at the restaurant Quo Vadis;[150] Marko Lámpas would drive them around.[151]

At the same time a new recording of Maria's was released: arias she had denied permission to be published some eleven years before. It was called *Callas: By Request*. Upon receipt of a persuasive missive scribed by EMI's devoted Peter Andry, she had finally agreed to its exhibit.[152] A relic of a stronger voice, the album met with rapturous reviews.[153]

Pressured by the "media circus" provoked by the lessons, the teacher's motives seemed a little suspect to soprano Barbara Hendricks. "Even if the comments that Maria gave the students were sincere, Maria Callas always seemed to be performing, aware of being judged as a teacher . . ." Hendricks would write. "[But] little by little, this person that I had at first found arrogant began to touch me. Her vulnerability was palpable. She seemed not to trust the masquerade of sycophants surrounding her and constantly reminding her of how great she 'had been.'"

Though Hendricks was at first a little wary, in retrospect she conceded to having learnt about "the importance of breathing, of vocal support. She insisted a lot on that. And then, emotion . . . That said, I can't say that she taught me really a lot."[154] Nevertheless, the soprano's performance of "Io son l'umile ancella" from *Adriana Lecouvreur* left Maria bedazzled.[155]

Meanwhile Marko Lámpas was experiencing more problems with his wife. One morning when Maria rang and Sonia answered, the latter passed her husband the receiver: "Here, it's for you, another one of your whores calling." Outraged and fearful for her reputation, the soprano yelled: "I want you to leave that house at once! I heard what she said. Does she know who I am? How dare she speak about me like that! She's a terrible woman, and I'm extremely angry. I want you to call me at the hotel. Good-bye [sic]." She slammed the phone down.

Loath to get involved in Lámpas' affairs when he admitted he was getting a divorce, Maria told him in her typical maternal fashion: "It is your decision, Marko. If you have tried everything and still cannot have peace with each other, then I think it is better to separate. Now, about the trouble with your voice . . ." and she offered him the names of two successful New York doctors.

As Lámpas drove Maria back to her hotel after a dinner with Onassis one night she advised him, "Marko, you need to make a serious decision about your career, eh? You need to perform with small theatres to get the proper experience on stage. You don't have much time left. There aren't that many small opera companies here in America, so if you decide to come to Europe, I can help you start in some small theatres there."

Lámpas had a six-year-old son and insisted he couldn't leave home. "Remember what I told you once. You are a sentimental Greek, and you'll never put your career first. If you want to have a success in opera, your career must come first! You hear me? You must come first! You can stay with me in Paris until you get engaged in some opera company, and the Olympic flights to Paris always have some empty seats. I'll arrange for you to fly free. You have to think very seriously, eh, before you make a decision. I don't want you to come and be miserable thinking about your children."[156]

He may not have been as talented as Mario Fusco but the tenor had a luscious voice. Before the end of the classes Maria advised him to ask Costa Gratsos, her and Onassis' mutual friend, to get in touch with her if he needed help. "I spoke to him about you. He'll contact me in Paris or wherever I may be. Do not ask anyone else, especially Mr. Onassis. Only Gratsos, you understand?"

Though he decided against staying with Maria in Paris and attempting to launch a European career, Lámpas was "ripped apart" when he learned of her death.[157]

Overall her impact on the school was positive. As with her performances, detractors always loitered in the midst. "Some of the sopranos, because of their stupid envy, criticized and contradicted her during that time," Lámpas would write. "It was not until some years later when I stood on the stage performing that I began to comprehend the importance of Maria's advice and vast knowledge."[158] He recalled standing up in the Juilliard cafeteria and defending Maria before other students.[159]

The petty ones were few. And while she didn't change the lives or the techniques or the artistic attitudes of the majority, a great deal nurtured tender feelings for her. Soprano Anita Terzian wrote a Christmas card with the message, "I am so grateful for the chance of working with you. Words cannot express my joy . . . I have already learned so much from you."[160] Marilyn Horne would relate, "I know some of those students that were in those classes, and one of them said that she was very loving and very supportive."[161]

More teachers openly begrudged Maria than did students. She would remember the enquiry of one: "How do I *warm* up the theatre, literally—be the *fire* onstage? I mean . . . the stage itself is so *cold*."—"Lesson Number One," came Maria's response, "*you* are the fire."—"Oh, but that's too tiring," the unspecified colleague replied.[162]

With the exception of Peter Mennin's support, few Juilliard professionals embraced Maria's pedagogical period. "She was there to guide their [the students'] acting . . . some of the teachers were afraid that she would take their places," Georganne Mennin remembered.[163]

Soprano Jeanie Tourel was especially embittered. The teacher of Barbara Hendricks, she lambasted Hendricks upon hearing how her "Io son l'umile ancella" had been "tainted" by Callas, offering a lecture on the "dangers" of the latter's tuition.[164]

Tourel would casually observe to Leo Lerman, "Look, you know Maria's voice. You know she can't do it . . . We're not friends. She isn't a voice teacher."[165] Florence Page Kimball—Leontyne Price and later Cynthia Clarey's teacher—would tell the latter, "Maybe if [Callas] had sung more songs, she'd still be singing!"[166]

Only a drama teacher—actress Marian Seldes—heaped praise on Maria in the form of letter:

I am faced with trying to articulate a very personal and almost mystical impression because the force of an artist's personality is so difficult to describe and the way I have interpreted your teaching methods with singers and adapted it to the way I feel about teaching actors is so instinctive and basic to the way I feel about all theater work that it is difficult to separate what has inspired me in your classes with what I love about the theater in the first place.[167]

People stood around the block for tickets to the last class; some attendees even sat along the floor.[168] When Barrie Smith performed the final scene of *La forza del destino* with Mario Fusco and bass Willard White, Maria signaled for Barrie to release Leonora's fraught scream.

There was silence.

"Why didn't you do it?" Maria asked.

"Because you were nodding your head."

"I *am* in my head—*you* weren't!" the teacher exclaimed as the audience laughed.

"No—I said you were *nodding* your head! I thought we were going to go back and do it *again* . . ."[169]

Her final words were humble and respectful:

"I want you to *remember*—possibly, whatever I've said—I don't know whether I'll be here next year; we haven't figured it out—but I want you to *please* try and remember—please try and make it that all this effort is not *wasted*. That you should take whatever *little* I've given you and bring it into the other scores and *increase* it; in courage, in phrasing, in *diction*, in— *courage*, again, I say, because it's *not* an easy career, don't *ever* think that it's an easy career . . . So, for *thanks*, the only thing I want is that you all *sing* properly, that you *apply* whatever knowledge I've given you—*to* your scores; that's the only thing I *can* say . . . the time *being*. Each and every *one* of you. It doesn't stop *here*. It has to keep on going 'cause you're supposed to follow up what we *have* done. Whether I keep on singing or not doesn't make any difference—you are the younger generation and you must *apply* it. And it's the only thanks that I really *do* want. Keep on going—and the proper *way*. Not fireworks, not with an easy applause, but with the expression of the words; with the diction, feeling—whatever it is. This is what I want to say— I'm not good at words. So er—that's that."

A cocktail reception was held in her honor.[170] Wriston Locklair prepared a selection of tapes from the classes and sent them to her.[171] Maria alerted Irving Kolodin that she intended to return later that year, perhaps in the summer, to resume studying with Alberta Masiello.[172]

The experience left her sullen. "I found some good voices in New York, but I also found that one cannot teach personality," she later told Alan Sievewright.[173] To conductor Jeffrey Tate she readily admitted, "I'm not a teacher, I discovered that in New York. I can only tell people to imitate me, and that's not what teaching's about."[174]

So another new venture had folded. And Maria was restless again.

Juilliard soprano Pamela Hebert had once asked if it was wise to regulate expressions with the mirror as her aid. Maria countered: "*Inside* is your mirror. Never use a mirror—which is *frightening*. Dancers can use it—not singers. You have to make a *mental* memory."[175]

She had that self-awareness in abundance as an artist. Real life was another question.

20.

"Calculate in the dark"

"Opera is a dead corpse without singers." The overstatement came loose from Maria's lips in 1973. Of contemporary colleagues she remarked, "Some have brains and sensibilities, others just sing and act like fools. I've never frequented them. They have nothing to talk about but their beautiful homes and their jewels and their furs. Some of them have a way with the press and with management so they get reputations. They're good—anywhere but the stage. Who is great? Sutherland? A beautiful instrument. She said she followed my path. The trouble is she didn't. I used embellishments, those fireworks, for expression. She uses them for fireworks."[1]

Ironically Maria was bestowing copious attention on a firework-reliant singer. Returned to Paris shortly after Juilliard's unfavorable auspices in mid-March 1972, she soon conveyed herself to the house of Giuseppe and Maria Di Stefano in San Remo, Italy. With the renewal of her voice in mind, she spent Easter with the couple and their three teenage children: ailing Luisa, her sister Floria and their brother Giuseppe.[2]

Plagued with marital and money problems at the time, Di Stefano had never been an easy man. "When he flies into a temper just remember he is a Sicilian peasant—that explains all," Maria precised.[3] Too many times his unprofessional behavior had threatened to endanger her performances. This was the tenor who had slammed the door shut on her *Traviata* after witnessing their opening night's rapturous ovation;[4] the one whose ill-explained delay had summoned an eleventh-hour substitute to a live broadcast of Maria's "Golden Hour" concert.[5]

Di Stefano enjoyed a world ideal for him: every sign of disrespect, each slip up, every middle finger gesture of his went unnoticed. In a 2000 profile of him Jonathan Kandell wrote: "The tenor flaunted his affairs, ate heartily and seemed to relish an image of unpredictability." Rudolf Bing proclaimed that had it not been for his "lack of discipline" Di Stefano's career might have been equal to Caruso's. Where many singers would grow sentimental

442 The Callas Imprint: A Centennial Biography

for a role, Di Stefano described the plot of *La bohème* as a sad tale in which "she's a prostitute [Mimì is actually a seamstress], he's an intellectual, she falls ill, he doesn't even go looking for her in the hospital [Mimì dies in his arms]."

Proof of his memory's mishaps.[6]

Yet the tenor's indiscreet Lothario nature meant he was a magnet for the ladies. Plácido Domingo bemoaned that his eventual wife Marta "was not interested in me" in their conservatoire days because "there was a very famous singer who studied with us, Giuseppe Di Stefano, and all the girls were crazy about him."[7]

Together with Maria the Di Stefanos returned to their apartment in Milan where Giuseppe—known as "Pippo" to his friends—began rehearsing *Carmen* at La Scala. The production was being conducted by Maria's old collaborator and good friend Georges Prêtre. Festively received at *Carmen*'s dress rehearsal by her peers on April 13th, she was deluged in nostalgia.

As discussions about possible engagements persevered, the trio descended on Rome, where Di Stefano was singing *Pagliacci* at the Teatro dell'Opera. Staying at Residence Palace, now known as Duke Hotel,[8] Maria continued to consider propositions from Juilliard. Peter Mennin had suggested "two periods of approximately three or possibly four weeks each semester" of teaching. He urged Maria to mull over working at the school's American Opera Center as either "Artistic Consultant to the President" or "Guest Artist Consultant to the President," or any ad hoc title she would opt to choose.[9]

That was old hat. "I said 'no' to Juilliard because I was too busy and then I didn't feel like it," was the elementary explanation she wrote to Alberta Masiello.[10]

Meanwhile she fielded other offers. In Rome Maria met with Italian actor Raf Vallone; rumor had it he was hankering to make an opera-centric film with Callas as the leading lady.[11] She toyed with the idea—but not especially, as was her wont.

When she finally returned to Paris, the Théâtre Gabriel Château de Versailles was presenting a production of *La Cenerentola*. Among the invited were representatives from the Teatro Regio of Turin, an opera house that had burnt down in 1936 and was still undergoing restoration. Its superintendent Giuseppe Erba arrived at her apartment brandishing a box of chocolates and a challenging proposal. The theatre's administration was looking for artists to host its reopening in 1973. Having pondered over Leonard Bernstein and Dmitri Shostakovich, what they really sought was an opera *director*.

As usual the response was not immediate. Maria promised she would think about it.[12]

After spending most of uneventful June in Paris she retreated to San Remo early in July; accommodated by Giuseppe and his wife Maria in their spare apartment. For the purpose of retraining her voice she and Di Stefano listened to old records and practiced with an accompanist as pestiferous paparazzi encircled his home.[13]

To her friends in New York Maria apologized for not having surfaced. "I hoped to be back May but had to stay at home and tend to things that had developed while I was away and I was away too much this year," was her justification to Irving Kolodin.[14] To Alberta Masiello she scribed:

And then the Di Stefanos' daughter became ill, she is still and seriously with cancer of the glands [Hodgkin's lymphoma] and I had to stay with them to give both him and his wife a little support.

The girl has been operated on—had her spleen removed. The hope is that with some new medicine she could get better—But!

It's summer now and here in San Remo they have two apartments . . . I hope that we'll have some kind of holiday. But the weather is so cold. Every now and then you see the sun but often there's wind—it blusters!

I want to know your news? What are you doing—what programs do you have? I need to know in order to adjust my schedule.[15]

Here Maria was in a unique, peculiar situation: depending on a questionable tenor to revive her voice as he endured a fractured marriage and the trauma of a terminally ill young daughter. Did her selfishness provoke her to be blind to this? Most likely. But by letting her impose on his extremely troubled family, Di Stefano failed likewise to be prudent.

During this period Maria had a series of EKG tests conducted at the hospital where Luisa Di Stefano was receiving her treatment, the Istituto Nazionale per lo Studio e la Cura dei Tumori in Milan.[16] Cross-legged in the front row of an awe-struck, ailing audience, she watched Di Stefano perform a concert for the patients of the hospital on 24 July.[17] Later Maria wrote to Nadia Stancioff to inform her she would "probably be travelling thru Spain to visit George Moore & wife—then San Remo & Paris," and didn't neglect to "give [her] family my love" and express "deep sorrow for [her] father's illness."[18] Careful was she to continue honing her attentive character in a consistent craftsmanship of etiquette.

By early August she had verbally consented to direct the opera that would open the newly restored Teatro Regio in Turin, Verdi's *I vespri siciliani*.[19] Maria had performed it at La Scala back in January 1952. Escaping to the house of her old friend George Moore, Treasurer of the Metropolitan Opera, she, the Di Stefanos and Luisa stayed at his villa in Sotogrande. There Maria wasted time going around in a golf cart as Di Stefano batted the ball singing " 'O sole mio." They spent their evenings playing his recordings while he dubbed them jokingly into his brand of broken English.[20]

"Do you accept advice when it comes to singing?" a journalist had asked her two years previously. "That depends on who's giving it, evidently. Great conductors can give you indications about sparing yourself, about breathing, but not when it comes to technical problems, which you learn about at the conservatoire or onstage over many years."[21]

Following their Spanish sojourn[22] she was ready to accept advice from almost anyone. Di Stefano felt smug for being selected to restore her obviously defective instrument: "It was a debacle," he remembered. "She had to start everything from scratch. We began here, right in this room. Maria subjected herself to the training of a beginner ... We would record our rehearsals and then listen to them. Often I would give her tapes of our sessions so she could re-listen to them. She had lost her muscles. Muscles must be conserved in vocal exercise ... Maria was singing notes purely thanks to her enormous musical instinct. They were correct, perfect in pitch, their tone was right but they were hollow inside. So she would try to help herself by forcing them to make a sound that had no body since it wasn't founded on support. I taught her to breathe, I taught her how to work her diaphragm ... Witnessing the progress she was making week to week, sometimes even on a daily basis, gave her an extraordinary courage, even joy."[23]

The trouble was Di Stefano was not a voice instructor. Though he had studied with some singers he had never finished a whole vocal training course, let alone completed a degree.

He offered a colossal and imperforable instrument. And yet the artistry was monolithic: militant regardless of the role. If ever there was anyone who pandered to the old style and outmoded fads of opera—outstretched arms, long-held top notes and weighty proclamations—it was Giuseppe Di Stefano, who once shocked an accompanist with his "wayward and unmusical" singing.[24]

Emanating an intrepid, boastful boyishness, he couldn't help show off a medal Toscanini had once given him and brassily insist Maria owed him "everything": "She couldn't sing a note when we met again."[25]

The tenor's tutelage encompassed little. "Open your throat" was its principal axiom; in Italian, "Aperta, la gola". It was his conviction that Maria's problems had originated in the absence of this skill.[26]

In the grand scheme of vocalization "open your throat" is a basic requirement. Most singers do it without thinking and do not know it involves an increase of the pharyngeal space to amplify one's resonance. The notion that Maria had been closing off her instrument since the beginning of her training seemed facetious but the tenor was determined to prove otherwise. Different vocalists rely on different muscles quite unwittingly: some feel the resonance more in the "head" or "chest" voice; others less so. Some choose to vibrate all the time; others less frequently. Di Stefano was not sufficiently familiar with the facets of the vocal apparatus to identify Maria's ailment.

In her attempt to imitate him nonetheless, she sought to sing more homogeneously and loudly; surrendering the vocal molds that had composed her characters.[27] Yet on account of both her scarcely heeding muscles and artistic differences, pure mimicking remained impossible. "I'll never get there," she would cry out before bursting into tears.[28] One and a half years later she lamented, "I've tried now for two years to sing his way but I still can't find it."[29]

And it was not as though Di Stefano's own voice was in resplendent form. Tarnished by wear and tear and possibly irregular technique, the instrument was functioning more poorly than it had throughout his peak. It boasted the full-bodied sound Maria craved nevertheless.

With their continued efforts to renew her voice, rumors began to blare toward the end of August that Maria was "in love" with him.[30] Sadly the talk was not unfounded.

The soprano's attention once again stroked a less famous, less popular ego. "For a long time, we were the protagonists of romantic stories onstage all over the world, forming an envied, unique couple," Di Stefano would tell a Callas biographer. The narrative was not so rigidly linear. Franco Corelli had been Maria's choice tenor for a recording of opera duets; Di Stefano had slipped her mind when she had combed through possible Alfredos for the mused-upon La traviata. "That time, my relationship with my wife was merely formal," he avowed. "We stayed together simply because our family was going through a terrible drama."

Yet Maria Di Stefano—who filed for divorce after the death of Luisa[31]—would write a book about Maria called Nemica mia ("My enemy").

Despite the fragile nature of their ill-timed love affair Di Stefano rewrote the happenings in retrospect; pilfering a portion of Maria's legacy to lend his own fresh sparkle. "We were very much in love. We understood each other perfectly, which meant, at the same time, that we could be free. We were not only passionate, but there was something more: infinite tenderness, artistic complicity of the highest level, the desire to win again, mature love . . ."[32]

For her part, Luisa's sister Floria Di Stefano did not begrudge Maria openly. She acknowledged the romance as an unpleasant hindrance. "In our spare time we [Luisa and I] had to play cards with her so I would always find a way of getting out of it by meeting up with friends. One time she told me she respected me for my independence and recklessness." In a 2012 interview she was quick to emphasize that despite Maria and Di Stefano's affair, her stepmother Monika was responsible for her parents' eventual divorce.[33]

In this not so shining hour Maria finally agreed to the direction of I vespri siciliani on one condition: Di Stefano would join as Co-Director.[34] It was 8 September and they were alone at her Paris apartment. Four days later the press caught the scoop, publishing the telegram of confirmation in full.[35]

Pelted with the shots of speculative questions, immediately Maria was compelled to yield an explanation for this sudden change in her career.

The responses she unveiled were hardly eye-opening. Asked whether she had a "particular idea", she replied: "Well—a 'particular' idea, you know . . .

I think I'll do everything to make it as modern as *possible*. But naturally it's a little early to be thinking of our *idea*. Our first duty will be to put the singers at ease and foresee the million difficulties that don't always occur to us."[36] Painter and stage designer Aligi Sassù had been contacted to discuss visual elements.

"Did you ever quit studying music?" a paparazzo was desperate to know. "No, I always have a score under my arm. I never quit music."—"Does this mean you'll make no future ventures into cinema?"—"Not at all ... You know, I have a name I must deign to defend and the privilege of being able to choose. If the right kind of situation befalls me, a role of my standard, I will return to the cinema."[37]

Together with her underscored obliviousness to moral matters she was fast becoming readily defensive. Asked about her marriage to Meneghini, it was not enough to cite her privacy or spout a cursory remark. "You know that every marriage has to end ... I should never have got married in the first place," Maria professed. Questioned on her happiness, she went into unnecessary detail: "You can make yourself happy every day—just on account of a pretty flower you see, or a ray of sunshine. Through your own motives, in any case, and not waiting for others to impose it on you."[38]

After the initial choice of conductor, Francesco Molinari-Pradelli, committed to a Metropolitan Opera engagement, Teatro Regio's administration recruited Gianandrea Gavazzeni, Maria's beloved old colleague.

He dropped out unceremoniously days later. "It's a question of principle," the press release quoted him. Upon learning the identities of the production's two directors he had bolted. Grilled about the volte-face of events, Maria called Gavazzeni "a friend" and confessed she "could hardly believe it."[39] He would later explain that the hype around the Callas-Di Stefano pairing had caught him off guard. The maestro had no intention of joining the media circus.[40]

Striving to stave off Maria Di Stefano's growing suspicion and suppress her remorse, Maria invited the couple to stay at her apartment and took them to see her *Medea* film.[41] The wife subsequently left the singers to prepare for their upcoming Philips duet compilation; rumors of the secretive venture slipped out of their stronghold.

At the end of September Maria and Di Stefano came to Turin to meet with the theatre's technicians and Umberto Tirelli, a costume designer she knew from her days at La Scala.[42] After dining with the president of the Cassa di Risparmio bank division of Turin to negotiate funding, she visited the unopened theatre.

Canvassing the premises at night, she studied an elliptical, red auditorium that looked like bleeding gums. In lieu of tiers long rows of boxes with white borders were aligned along its scarlet entrails: teeth and braces. "Where do the acoustics sound?" her question echoed. Strolling backstage, Maria scrutinized the colors of the walls; shooing photographers arrived to capture nascent moments of her new experiment.[43]

From Turin she, Di Stefano and his wife journeyed to Munich for Oktoberfest.[44] The impromptu excursion was brief: at home Maria exchanged telephonic tirades with Gorlinsky on the subject of potential orchestras for their duet recording, considering the London Symphony before rejecting them.[45] She flirted with the notion of a concert with Di Stefano in Tokyo.[46] To keep preparations for the Philips compilation under wraps, the pair travelled to the French resort of Juan-les-Pins to practice singing in the company of Eugene Kohn, Maria's Juilliard accompanist.[47] Shortly thereafter they voyaged to New York for the photoshoot that would accompany the release of the record,[48] staying for the sake of their privacy at Leonidas Lantzounis' Upper East Side apartment.[49]

Panic instantly unsheathed its claws. On 25 October Gorlinsky alerted Philips' producer Erik Smith that Maria wanted the sessions postponed "until May". Now that the deadline loomed, she flung impediments at everyone in charge, alleging that Di Stefano had been accorded insufficient funds and suffered "shabby" treatment at their hands. Suddenly she wanted to record for EMI: a company with which she had suspended ties. Gorlinsky was flabbergasted. "You showed very great interest in Philips . . . very much liked Erik Smith, and now all these nice thoughts disappear in one second and suddenly they become inconsiderate and mean people, whereas E.M.I, whom you despised, are suddenly your favourites."[50]

Maria wasn't being irrational but consciously conniving. The idea of the Philips record daunted her. After spending more time with Di Stefano, his wife and Luisa as the guests of George Moore in Madrid,[51] she trained in November with French pianist Jean-Claude Ambrosini.[52]

By the 30th she and Di Stefano were finally in London—involuntarily stirring up gossip. "Maria and Di Stefano have been inseparable for several months," a Dutch gossip columnist wrote. Matters weren't helped by the tenor's confidences. With a dying daughter and a jealous wife discretion could have been expected of him. Instead he boasted of the nature of their closeness to a journalist: "Of course we are more than friends. You could say that our feelings include more romanticism than just two old acquaintances who work with each other . . . [but] it would be very wrong to talk about our personal relationship—for precisely because of what it is, personal—and I will wait for Miss Callas to say something."[53]

Obfuscated amid pillars of the hallowed St Giles Church was the renowned pair that November 30th. On the first day of recording the production crew was still oblivious to what they sought to sing. Stocked in the church was all manner of scores. Maria and Di Stefano elected to try the duet from L'elisir d'amore. Its intricacy meant it yielded less than positive results. Anxiously she asked Erik Smith to keep a close eye on the work of Harold Lawrence, Philips' sound engineer. The ambience grew volatile, imploding into raucous rows between the singers.[54]

Never released, the final document is a composed approach to the material compared to nerve-racked Normas of the 1960s. Maria fashions a voice feeble into Elisabeth de Valois' vulnerability in *Don Carlos'* "Io vengo a domandar," infuses innocence into "Ah, per sempre" from *La forza del destino* and elicits an exquisite Desdemona in "Già nella notte densa," the newlyweds' duet from *Otello*.

Deviating from Di Stefano's insistence on a bright and full voice, the soprano shrinks the timbre down enough for us to hear a wistful wife exulting in her husband's might. The work is fraught with breathing problems on her part and lacks the requisite support of her frayed stomach muscles likely worsened by the "hernia on [the] diaphragm" Maria had described.

Among her last interpretations, it is also one of the scant few to glisten with a bolt of character.

On 2 December the Philips production crew took Maria out to celebrate her fiftieth birthday.[55] That same day eighty-six-year-old George Callas died when complications from a middle ear infection triggered a severe attack of diabetes.[56]

The closeness of the pair had collapsed in recent years. After learning of his death on 4 December Maria developed a hoarseness and canceled her sessions that day.[57] Invited to the funeral by her sister, she feared seeing Evangelia, and leaned on the excuse of her recording.

At the same time she fretted the pernicious press would misconstrue her absence with the speculation that Maria's choice had been vindictive.[58] Sessions continued for two weeks but were suspended on 20 December before they could record *Aïda's* "Pur ti riveggo." Initially postponed until the start of February, they would finally resume in May.[59]

The last days of the year awoke a new accostment: pyrrhic pokes of speculation about who would be successor to the late Goeran Gentele, the Met's general manager.[60] George Moore proposed Maria's name to Schuyler Chapin, Vice President of Lincoln Center. After Moore exposed this proposition to Maria she agreed to dine with Chapin at the Plaza's Oak Room restaurant. Her godfather's apartment was her hideout once again.

Rising to meet her at 1 pm on 22 December, Chapin greeted a woman wearing "reddish-brown tweed" and a ring with a blinding bright ruby. "We must become such good friends," she insisted, sitting down beside him.

Prattling caught flame as Maria sermonized about contemporary opera houses and their managers—not letting Chapin get a word in edgeways. He invited her to attend the Met's production of *Otello* the forthcoming Saturday to "start with this opera as a base for her theories of reorganization."[61]

Maria spent that Christmas in the company of Maria Di Stefano's family in the Bronx.[62] On 29 December Schuyler Chapin and his guests sat waiting at *Otello*: a production featuring soprano Grace Bumbry, tenor James McCracken and baritone Sherrill Milnes. Arriving just before the second act, Maria bowed to onlookers and greeted Chapin and his entourage. In the course of its duration she bombarded him with penetrative stares. He "gathered we were sharing a conspiracy about how awful everything was up on the stage."

During the second interval he took Maria, Di Stefano and his wife back to his office and offered them a round of champagne. "Of course, you know the whole production is dreadful. No one on the stage sings or acts with any authority. The set is really awful and we're going to have to do something about all this," she griped. Before they could engage in a productive discourse the soprano snatched a quick glance at her watch. "My goodness, we must go!" exclaimed Maria. Excusing herself and her guests, she explained it was "Pippo's birthday, you know, and we must all be at his birthday dinner." (Di Stefano's birthday was 24 July).[63]

It was, on the other hand, Luisa Di Stefano's birthday the following day. The company celebrated by dining at New York's hot spot, Quo Vadis. Maria bought the girl a diamond-studded, little heart-shaped pendant.[64]

Scarcely had a few days passed when Chapin got a phone call. During their next meeting in his office he was ready to behave professionally, launching a discussion of "the fourteen unions, the over two million dollars in building maintenance costs, the board, the shops, the scheduling complications . . ." Cutting him short, Maria insisted on a tour of the building. "You know the dressing room, the stage, and the rehearsal halls," he guided her. "What you don't know are the shops and the sewing rooms and the administrative offices, the accountants, the artistic staff, both musical and administrative, the house directors, the chorus master, the chorus, the orchestra personnel manager, and the orchestra committee."

All this terrified Maria. As an artist she most likely felt this scope of information went beyond her "security clearance". "Not now, please," Maria stressed. "There will be time for all that later. We must talk about that dreadful *Otello*. We must not have things like that on our stage."[65] It wasn't long before she rose and took her fur coat with her, announcing she was leaving once again for Sotogrande, Spain to see George Moore. She would resume contact "in a few months when I return to New York. I'll let you know."[66]

That expectedly did not ensue. Chapin himself was assigned to the post five months later.[67]

Back in Paris in mid-January, Maria staved off rumors of a romance with Di Stefano[68] and vented to Leo Lerman in writing: "Mckraken? & Milnes & Zeffirelli's staging. Very bad—all around. The tenor should not sing & Milnes is swallowing his voice—what in heaven's name is wrong with them! My pupils sang better in comparison."[69] Writing to Lantzounis, she informed him she was "studying", still intending to finish the Philips record in February—and had placed a new antenna on the "little television" in his apartment.[70]

Maria also kept up correspondence with Bettina Brentano, the niece of France's Minister for Cultural Affairs Jacques Duhamel. Several years before she and the teenager had met. Her introduction to the prepubescent girl had been "Je suis chanteuse" ("I'm a singer"), met with the response, "You mean like Sylvie Vartan?" a popular French disco star.[71]

Fleetingly enthused by a new confidence that winter, Maria scribed to Leo Lerman:

> *In the meantime I'm singing duets records with Di Stefano—I must saying [sic] that working together made my comeback in records less difficult than if I were alone. We are finishing the record mid February—with Philips— then I have to finish some arias with Emi-Angel. Then—Japan—very good contract—end of May. I don't think I'll be doing Torino [Turin]. They have not respected one agreement and it's too late to prepare a good mis-en-scene [sic]. To work in Italy is nowadays very difficult. It's all politics.*
>
> *I'm struggling with my weight. Last year I was too thin. This year it is <u>hard</u> to diet—but I must lose 3 kilos. Why can't the doctors find a pill that does no harm but makes you consume <u>all</u> you eat-! We go to the moon but they can't cure a cold nor how to make our glands work properly-![72]*

With the prospect of becoming a director now behind her, Maria was immersed in singing once again. Nine days after she sent that letter Onassis' twenty-five-year-old son Alexander was killed in a plane crash. In San Remo at the time,[73] Maria's reaction was difficult to anticipate. Eventually she helped Onassis with this "final blow" as she would later term it, granting him "moral support, which I gave him in the best way I could."[74] At the time her urge to flee all kinds of pain delayed this offering. Just one week later she and the Di Stefanos were basking in the sun in Acapulco, where they visited old friends.[75]

Goaded by Giuseppe Erba and the Teatro Regio administration, by 1 February Maria had reversed her decision and re-signed the contract. Together with Di Stefano she had another meeting with designer Aligi Sassù and technical director Aulo Brasaola in Milan before flying to Mexico via New York.[76]

Sun-drenched and "extremely tanned,"[77] Maria sent postcards from Acapulco—among them one to Leo Lerman with the phrase "It's lovely here." Keeping company with Cousin Mary Annexy, she rolled a tennis ball along the beach to her small daughter Lydia.[78] Late one night some friends of the Di Stefanos awakened her with their rambunctious mariachi band, prompting the soprano to demand whoever "is playing the radio so high to turn down the volume."[79] Acquaintances of old revived her spirits by remembering her Mexican performances.[80]

After three weeks at the Hotel Condesa del Mar[81] Maria returned to her home with Di Stefano while his wife went to visit her New York-based relatives.[82] The trio then spent several days at the Di Stefanos' apartment in Milan, attending the premiere of Visconti's epic movie *Ludwig II* on 6 March.[83]

With the opening of *Vespri* and the new Teatro Regio now less than a month away, Maria threw herself into musical history; paying a visit to the Casa Ricordi—an archive of scores where she encountered her colleague

Luisa Mandelli and announced to Di Stefano: "Here are our glories!"— "Signora—you mean *your* glories!" Mandelli responded.[84]

Despite having just panned his *Otello*, despairingly Maria called her old friend Franco Zeffirelli to ask if she could come to Rome in mid-March and consult him on the costumes and the visuals.

At his home she dined with Anna Magnani—who was dying of terminal cancer—nearly genuflecting to the queen of the screen: "I watch all your films, I learn so much. Your Medea on stage was perfect. I've sung it many times, but you act it so much better than me," Maria avowed. Magnani was not that impressed.[85]

Seeking distraction from the mounting pressure of assembling a production with a stunted number of rehearsals due to technical impediments, Maria took Di Stefano and his disgruntled wife to tea at Princess Grace's palace.[86] She alternated between Paris, Milan and Turin to continue preparations and retrain her voice.[87]

When rehearsals finally commenced in late March they were inauspicious. Facing a cast and crew of some one hundred fifty with an eighty-six-year-old conductor in Vittorio Gui, she was overwhelmed and claustrophobic. The production's press agent Piero Robba would describe her as "very closed-off and taciturn both onstage and off. She was very kind and polite to me, but cold and reserved. She would only ask me information about certain people, shops and places in Turin, but rarely make comments and never about the work."[88]

Robba alluded to the operatic panorama as "a sea of people with various problems. Dancers, extras, artists, the chorus, technicians, teachers, set designers—all waited for her to cue them with a gesture, a decision, an idea, a solution that she was unable to give or even indirectly to hint at. Obviously in her naïve enthusiasm—and once again surrounded by a horde of inexperienced fans—she believed that being the creator of a production would be easier than it was . . . she found herself immersed in a complex, multifarious machine."

Rather than being guided by one rudder, the ensemble endured contradictory advice from several people: Di Stefano, Maria, assistant director Fabrizio Melano—an old friend of Maria's; Giuseppe Erba, Vittorio Gui and occasionally others. "There was no pulse, and therefore no direction," Robba recollected.[89]

Paparazzi craved to catch a glimpse of Callas the Director. Stationed in the theatre late one Thursday night, Hubert Saal observed Maria as she "stood suspended in midair, remote and impenetrable—as though a cloud had secluded her from the rest of the world. She came onto the stage of the brand-new Teatro Regio . . . she sat down, luminous in a magnificent black outfit reminiscent of Eugene O'Neill's play *Mourning Becomes Electra*. With her vast Aegean eyes she dazzled the singers and the mass of the company and Aligi Sassù's freshly painted designs, still dripping with color—and was silent.

"Only from time to time would she exchange a glance with Giuseppe Di Stefano. After a moment of suspense he would convey their message to the people ... But La Callas never said a word; she was mute: fixated in a melancholic mystery that no one could unseal. At eleven, at four, at eight in the evening Maria would come into the theatre repeating her ritual. The neo-director would stride in like a goddess and go and sit down ... Always in the same order, it was Di Stefano on one side, the Italian American [Fabrizio] Melano on the other. And she would observe attentively, providing only fleeting interventions or conveying her advice through a third party."[90]

The scant footage that remains of her direction shows Maria casually attired in a peach pink top and raven pants, raising her arms and smiling radiantly to signal to a singer to let loose. Elsewhere she rushes to soprano Raina Kabaivanska—the voice of leading lady Elena—to lift up her arm. When Kabaivanska fell ill during rehearsals Maria substituted for her and moved down the chorus singing "Il vostro fato è in vostro man," stunning the company with her power. "The next day everyone showed up with tape recorders,"[91] wrote Saal for *Newsweek*.

Fabrizio Melano remembered Maria as reliant on Di Stefano, girlish and devoutly in love. Clueless as to how to organize the opera, the disoriented soprano still came across as "a wonderful person".[92] Kabaivanska similarly spoke of Maria's enamorment with Di Stefano, whom she described as a director with "this luminous spontaneity; a sunny, Sicilian one."[93]

When lead tenor Gianni Raimondi was fearful of cracking a high note, Maria's imperiousness made itself known. "You have to be generous with singing. So you crack? What's a tenor who doesn't crack? If you don't risk, you don't win."[94] During disputes between her and Di Stefano she sought to have costumier Umberto Tirelli on *her* side. He had originally been called upon to sew the costumes sketched by stage designer Aligi Sassù. Tirelli found them to be "very colorful: not like the ones Callas had worn in her Visconti productions." Adhering to instructions, he had no choice but to realize them.[95]

Most of Maria's work centered on Kabaivanska, whom she was keen to befriend as a fellow soprano. Training her for the part of Elena, she tried to indoctrinate her with Di Stefano's dubious methods: opening the throat and singing "chiaro" ("brightly") as opposed to "scuro" ("darkly"). This came as a shock to Kabaivanska. "*You* sang *scuro* all your life, and now you revoke it all? Your entire career?" she demanded to know of Maria. "Yes, because I was wrong . . .[96] that's why I can no longer sing. Because I did it wrong all my life."[97] Maria proceeded to sing the entire opera to Kabaivanska, who called her "a natural explosion".[98]

Being taught was *one* craft but imparting art entirely another. Maria had remarked once, "It is panic, not knowing one thing before you go on stage. When I'm there I don't know what gestures to do, until they come pouring out. Each gesture goes with the word. I did not learn them anywhere. I am not a tragedienne like [Katina] Paxinou or Judith Anderson. I have to calculate in the dark and go by instinct."[99] Like a model well-tuned to the contours of her face, she had adapted all her features in the virtue of the operatic art; a practice she could execute with eyes closed.

Memorizing others' faces, limbs and costumes, finding art in other miens and movements would be the responsibility of a photographer; a panoramic scrutinizer. Maria had undoubtedly spent years exerting efforts in the interest of the opera world—but only through *herself.*

In one rehearsal octogenarian maestro Vittorio Gui was accused of conducting too slowly. Natalia Makarova—a supremely gifted ballerina— urged him as she danced: *"Maître—vite, vite, vite!"* ("Maestro, faster, faster, faster!"). At the session's culmination Gui collapsed and lost consciousness. He was hospitalized and young Fulvio Vernizzi was chosen to substitute him.

Costumier Tirelli's interference stretched into directing singers' movements: he chose specific poses to accentuate his garments. Meanwhile the lighting design was being crafted by a team of technicians who were professionals but "not the lighting designers that we have in today's productions," Piero Robba noted in 2007.

In the midst of the bustle Maria made herself less and less visible; tending to stand at the same spot onstage in rehearsals.[100] Stuck at Kabaivanska's side for the most part, she conversed additionally about music with Makarova, the prima ballerina. When the latter pointed out that dancers in the West were hard-pressed to use hands for their expression—showcasing a gesture from *Giselle* where the heroine "pats the hem of her gold-threaded dress"—Maria raised her hand and "instantly performed the very movement with such sovereign grace and simplicity that I was stunned. The turn of the head, the neck, the expression in her eyes—everything came of itself and was absolutely right," scribed Makarova.[101]

Thus Maria the director became more immersed in being guided than the opposite. "How did you distribute the division of labor?" one journalist asked shortly before opening night. "There was no division," she insisted. "We executed everything together, in perfect harmony ... We have the same artistic intuitions." Di Stefano followed suit with a similar, albeit much more elaborative message about his and Maria's "ideal" joint venture.[102]

"Have there been any problems so far?" asked Burt Quint of CBS News. "I hear something about a strike."—"Well, those are very little; in fact, we only had one in the *beginning,* and the chorus very *sweetly* said that they were *sorry* that we had to start this—no, there've been no problems." Maria smiled forcibly.

"I wonder, do you get as much pleasure out of *commanding*—as you did out of *directing* as you did out of *singing*?"—"Yes—there's one *sadistic* pleasure; I don't have to sing!" She laughed. Asked if she had deemed it a "challenge," Maria—who had always spoken of adoring "challenges"—responded almost bluntly, "Why should I see it as a 'challenge'? Must we always search for words like 'challenge' and this and that? It's just a continuation of something we've been doing."[103]

While chaos festered on the inside of the theatre, *outside* tickets were sold out and crowds of Callas fans frenetically assembled.[104] Maria embarked on the last day of rehearsals observing, "Even today everyone wants to rest." Nevertheless she remained "icily calm".

On the stage was a peculiar amalgam of contrasting tastes. Depicting thirteenth-century Sicily, the vista opened up "a still life, given over completely to the music and to the visual pleasure of weather-beaten, colorful, Mediterranean blue and gold sets and costumes brilliantly designed by the distinguished Italian painter, Aligi Sassù," in Saal's words.[105] These included sketches that suggested fuchsia pink tights, feathered hats and flagrant purple tunics—for the *men*.

"It wasn't an ugly production," Piero Robba countered. "The designs were too colorful . . . Aligi Sassù had justifiably specified that those were the colors of Sicily: sun, warmth, light and sea. Perhaps critics were expecting a Gothic ambience: Nordic, dark, cold. But that was not the atmosphere of *Vespri* . . . the costumes were very beautiful but Tirelli had exaggerated the poses of the singers and they didn't suit the direction; it was as though he wanted to present them this way, exhibition-style . . . the lighting wasn't full of errors, but technicians were using new, as yet untested equipment and they didn't have much direction."[106]

Mirroring the practice Visconti had once used for her 1955 La Scala *Sonnambula*, Maria had the house lights raised on one occasion—only for a critic to complain that simultaneously the stage had been "enshrouded in a useless darkness".[107]

Set during the Franco-Italian war, the opera illustrates the grievances of the Sicilian people in a melancholy fashion typical of Verdi—a composer whose entrancing melodies emblematize his feverish compatriots' oppression. Another tale of taboo love—this time between Sicilian duchess Elena and Arrigo, secret son of the French governor Montforte—the music features mirthful moments but remains for the large part lugubrious. Its productions tend to overflow with the obtrusive shades of black, scarlet and oak.

Italy's president Giovanni Leone was on hand together with the first lady at the premiere on 10 April 1973. "The feeling in Turin and in most of the Italian press was that the opening night's direction was unimaginative, the décor catastrophic," reported *The New York Times*. "Duilio Courir, critic for Milan's *Corriere della Sera*, described them as "an example of probably insuperable figurative banality."[108]

Other reviews were almost universally condemnatory. "The singing was less than great," Hubert Saal, a defender of the designs, wrote for *Newsweek*. "Best was baritone Licinio Montefusco, sharp and resonant as the French tyrant. Bass Bonaldo Giaiotti, as the Sicilian leader Procida, chopped and chopped but no chips flew. Kabaivanska blew her 'Bolero' at the end, and Gianni Raimondi, in the pivotal role of Arrigo, held back in the upper register as if afraid he might crack."[109] Taking issue with the "static direction,"[110] critiques cuttingly crafted their soundbites.

"Callas' work ... consisted of little more than adjusting the lighting (with some improvement between the general rehearsal and opening night) and the typically Callasian gestures of soprano Raina Kabaivanska. The chorus and the extras were reduced to static poses to the point of ridicule," remarked Alfredo Mandelli.[111]

Some articles and headlines offered hate. "No one could dare imagine that the staging bears the signature of Maria Callas," one read;[112] *"Non regge al 'Regio' la regia della Callas"*—"Callas' direction at the 'Royal' Theatre doesn't *rule*," another remarked.[113]

Then there came the personal attacks. As a social affair the event was conducive to further one's fifteen minutes of fame. Wally Toscanini couldn't wait to confide in the press, "It was a very painful evening for me. I felt great sadness in witnessing two artists, who were once great singers, create such an ugly production."[114] Antonio Ghiringhelli revealed how much the staging had left him displeased.[115]

Though the opening night audience reacted warmly to the spectacle— applauding, in the words of one reviewer, "at every act, at every scene, at every aria"[116]—the stinging rancor in the air was palpable. Electing not to attend the gala organized at the Hotel Principi di Piemonte,[117] Maria instead went to the restaurant at the Hotel Ducs d'Aoste with Raina Kabaivanska and her husband. In the elevator she bumped into Paolo Grassi, La Scala's then superintendent. He deliberately snubbed her. Maria started to cry.[118]

Such was the fallout that Maria and Di Stefano were forced to hold a roundtable press conference the following day at Palazzo Madama. Joining them were Aligi Sassù, conductor Fulvio Vernizzi and superintendent of the Teatro Regio Giuseppe Erba.

Admitting she had earlier requested a postponement of the opening night,[119] Maria was on the defensive. When it emerged that an inquisitive reporter hadn't seen *I vespri siciliani* she demanded that he leave.[120]

Journalist Renzo Allegri of *Gente*, one of Di Stefano's friends, was enlisted to publish her statement. "A little while ago Giuseppe Erba, the theatre's superintendent, telephoned me to let me know that tickets are still being requested from all of Europe: from France and from England, Germany and many Italian regions, especially Emilia-Romagna. They had to say 'no' to everyone because the performances are already sold out. I have the public on my side, and that's what counts. The critics often come with preconceived notions. The public, on the other hand, is simple; they love instinctively, they understand many things a critic disregards." Allegri asked whether she expected the overall panning of *Vespri*. "Yes, I expected it—Maestro Gianandrea Gavazzeni, after he pulled out of the production, decided to wage war against me. It is normal that the Italian critics should take his side, not mine."

It was a concept being promulgated by Di Stefano: "The company had been prepared and he liked the idea of Maria Callas. It was when Maria wanted to work with me that Gavazzeni pulled out, leaving us in grave circumstances."

She expelled a litany of arguments—insisting that a roundtable discourse be held on directorial criteria, reminding Allegri that "music is what counts in opera, scenic action takes second place . . . I studied Verdi's *Vespri* thoroughly. I contemplated it and sought to realize what Verdi would have wanted. This is a particular opera; it's neither a love story, nor a patriotic work. It's a work about paternal love [Governor Montforte's for his secret son, Arrigo]. It is a static work. There are scenes where two singers sing for ten, twenty minutes. Even if we wanted to, we couldn't have given this work one, single rhythm . . . Some opera productions insist too heavily on the purpose of making a spectacle. Opera is neither cinema, nor prose . . . After twenty-five years I don't think I'm completely ignorant in this field."

In her words she and Di Stefano were planning to pursue the new profession; already fielding offers from Monaco, England and Dallas. "If this *Vespri siciliani* had been mounted by other directors, and hadn't borne the names Maria Callas and Giuseppe Di Stefano, the reviews would have been very positive," Maria declared.[121]

In all likelihood she was both right and wrong. Given the non-controversial, banal nature of the spectacle, reviews of it would probably have been lukewarm if its directors had remained anonymous. Yet it was also undeniable that the incongruous production had met many mishaps. Maria's study of the score may have been thorough—but beholding painted walls, props, huddled chorus members and her colleagues likely left her frightened and befuddled. The role of architect was one beyond her cultural domain.

Walter Legge reached out amidst this hour of inexorable flagellation. "Thank you for your wishes and your letter," she wrote to him nine days after the opening. "And I am sorry to hear that you cannot find peace and quiet. I know, I imagine how you are bored with yourself, and I do agree that you should not have stopped working. But, as everything is destiny, you should not feel so restless, as you have done the most beautiful work during your lifetime. Also remember that the artistic level was much higher than now."[122]

Faced with the incisive question of her destiny by a reporter mid-rehearsal, Maria had dashed off the answer: "Oh, you mean in the future?" A nervous laugh followed. "Well, I don't *know* what I'd do in the *future*."—"No programs," Di Stefano clarified. "No programs," came Maria's echo.[123]

Like a foreign object threatens blood flow in the body, that unnatural stasis couldn't thrive in her internal habit.

21.

"The illusion of a better world"

In the whirlwind of absurdity that swarmed around events unfolding in the early 1970s—the erosion of the Soviet Union, Watergate, curled mustaches and feathered hairstyles—authoritarian figures lost their status. Independence and self-government were new ideals. An embracer of the principles before their time, in middle age Maria struggled to commit to them.

Returned to London with Di Stefano to finish their duets recording after *Vespri*'s flop, Maria was a spectator at a recital by the tenor on May 9th.[1] As she watched her partner tread the boards the visions of performing in her head began to swirl into a vortex.

Meanwhile they paired up for a scarcely publicized event: a masterclass seminar for the winners of Nagasaki's Madama Butterfly Competition that summer. Soprano Eugenia Moldoveanu and tenor Emil Gherman were selected as victors—with Maria lavishing on the former an honorary "Madama Butterfly kimono"[2] and on both singers trophies and prizes of one million yen.[3]

Tired of plastering her face with neon smiles, when it was time for her to give the masterclass to both the pair and the four runners-up at Osaka Festival Hall, she "mercilessly" cited the singers' mistakes according to local newspaper *The Asahi Shinbun*.[4]

With the tenor's wife on hand the trio travelled through both Tokyo and Hong Kong before advancing to the temples of Bangkok and then Tehran. Iran's last Shah, Mohammad Reza Pahlavi, had promised to receive Maria but was absent for the length of her short stay. Delegates led her and the Di Stefanos around bazaars and mosques;[5] the Minister for Culture introduced Maria to his singer-wife where they were staying at the Sheraton Hotel. A waft of opulence and luxury and infinite indulgence was aloft. Maria's mind was elsewhere—*sometimes*.

"The trip was beautiful but it's hard for me, having <u>her</u> always near us," Maria lamented in a letter to Bruna weeks later. "She [Maria Di Stefano] is so kind, but we're not used to always having people around."

Back home in Paris by mid-June she rested—solitary for a while. "At the moment I know that I just want to be alone and work. I can't see clearly vocally—that is to say, feel sure of myself," she wrote in the same missive. "I only hope that I'll manage to have the instrument back under control, by myself one of these days—otherwise I'll have to go back to him and I feel at ease here."[6]

The latter was inevitable. Intermittently Maria worked with Di Stefano on a gamut of scores[7] before paying a visit to her old friend conductor Vittorio Gui in the town of Fiesole. En route she took the wrapping off another present of distraction—stopping by the family abode of her butler Ferruccio Mezzadri in Villanova sull'Arda. Having visited the clan before in 1964, Maria dithered helplessly in the small town. As she walked into a bar to use the telephone, her entrance was accompanied by "oohs" and "aahs". Together with "Hey, that's the singer! That's Callas!", they earned her free coffee.[8]

During her visit to the maestro she endured another sudden drop in blood pressure; the first since a likely stress-induced episode on 5 April in Turin.[9]

Rumors circled in Milan—where once again Maria stopped to visit Biki. "It must have been you in that smart Mini Cooper who hooted and waved in Via Manzoni," Walter Legge wrote in mid-July. "Why didn't you stop? We should have loved to chat, even though it would have meant keeping Alain [Reynaud] waiting. You're a *monster*, but sacré. We are delighted that you are both getting down, or rather up, to singing again at long last."[10]

Little by little an anticipated concert tour began to be announced—with the first notice in the press appearing on 19 May.[11] On August 8th it was made known that Maria and Di Stefano's inaugural concert would take place at London's Royal Festival Hall on 22 September.[12] "We always work for a public," Maria had told a journalist in 1970. "We always need a mirror. We can't look at ourselves in a wall. We need a public to offer to them this force that we carry in the depths of our being."[13]

Understanding that her vocal vehicle was not prepared for liftoff, the soprano sabotaged the series early on. "I am not pleased with the amount you are giving me for the concerts," she wrote to Gorlinsky. "If years ago, with an orchestra, without the dollar not devaluated you gave me the same arrangement—why now when everything has gone up. I should still have not the same but less [by which she probably means "more"]—because of the various devaluation plus cost of life."[14]

Spending part of summer in San Remo in the company of the Di Stefanos, she was forced to pit her guilt against her nerves and vice versa. When Maria learnt the terminally ill Luisa was about to visit London, she requested that Gorlinsky transfer funds: "The exchange is bad now. So if you can advance her some money and when Pippo or I get our royalties on the concert in London you can take it off. 100 pounds £."[15] By this point her "qualms" about her concert salary had either fallen by the wayside or been overlooked.

While Maria submitted herself to a number of hospital tests and was "certified" as "not show[ing] any signs of a recurrence of a pathological nature,"[16] Luisa's health escalated. Such was her deterioration that en route to London from San Remo she was forced to make a stopover in Paris, staying with Maria till she once again felt fit to travel.[17]

Shortly after this horrific episode Maria and Di Stefano attempted to immerse themselves into full training for the tour. As well as Di Stefano's former accompanist Ivor Newton, young pianist Robert Sutherland was recruited to work with the pair. It was August. Heat could justify inertia. Terrified before each session like a child who hadn't practiced the piano, she depended on Di Stefano's insouciance to make excuses: "It's so hot in Paris we've decided to go for a holiday in San Remo," he alerted the accompanists. It was the conclusion of the first rehearsal. The vacation was beginning *now*.[18]

In early September Maria wrote to Leonidas Lantzounis. "I'm scared stiff—but I hope that I will be calm & well by my first one [concert] on the 22 of this month Sept because the expectation is great and of course I am not what I was at 35 years. Let's hope for the best."[19]

Among her reinforcements was a huge humidifier hauled to each hotel room to help soothe her chronic sinusitis."[20]

Procrastination battled with a selfless love of music. Every day Maria received Sutherland alone; Ivor Newton being too unwell to come to Paris and Di Stefano reluctant to attend. Espresso would be gulped; grind for the rumor mill exchanged. An operatic discourse would be offered from Maria—who would argue against changing a work's key to suit the singer: "That's cheating—I've got to be honest to the composer."

Listening to records of the past was once again her recourse. Sutherland was lured into these sessions after practice. "Don't you think I sang well that night?" the soprano would ask.[21] Reminders of the generous libations she had brought to great composers' altars helped defuse her horror.

Three weeks were left until the concert when Maria wrote to Leo Lerman.

I've been busy trying to collect my nerves—not to close my throat while singing and fighting the heat-!

It seems that when I'm supposed to work it's always hot—and I hate it—plus the tiredness heat causes me-!

Well my love, in twenty days—the day of truth *is to be seen-!*

Right now I'm not nervous—because it is such a great risk that I can't take it seriously. Probably that night I'll die of fear—but I know all I can do is study words. (My usual terror!)

This weekend I have to decide on the program—that is my own pieces & I find them all so trying. Probably it's fear in disguise—Well![22]

Di Stefano's "technique" was taking precedence. Some of the time. "Pippo is irritating me with his way of doing things," Maria wrote to Bruna, who was

taking care of her ill mother in Italy, on 4 September. "We had a little argument because he kept playing at the casino, and I told him clearly and
firmly that I don't like gambling and love suffers from it. He got angry with
me and we decided to remain friends, colleagues and that's it. He hasn't
telephoned in three days."[23]

The man's patience shrank to the size of a nub as the concert drew near.
Once again the problem was all owing to Maria—who was reticent to "keep
[her] throat open". With his cries of "Aperta, la gola, aperta, la gola," he
kindled their sessions with rage; turning their last chance for work into
spitfires' clashes.

Though she unleashed a diatribe Maria held back her explosion. They
headed to the Di Stefanos' Milan apartment on Via Omenoni where the tenor
escorted Maria and Sutherland into his studio. Pointing crudely at the latter,
he reviled: "He played a wrong note!"—"No, he didn't," Maria corrected. "It's
your piano, it's out of tune."[24]

After several days of this cacophony Maria's stress broke through her
psyche—exacerbating her glaucoma, tanking her blood pressure and
advancing her hiatal hernia pain.[25] Three days before the concert her
tension and health left her no choice but to forewarn Gorlinsky:

DEAR SANDER THE EXTREME PRESSURE OF THE PAST WEEKS
HAS AGGRAVATED MY GLAUCOMA AND I HAVE BEEN
ORDERED BY MY EYE SPECIALIST TO REST FOR AT LEAST SIX
WEEKS
    I AM MOST UNHAPPY TO DISAPOINT [sic] MY PUBLIC AT
THIS TIME HOWEVER MY DOCTOR ASSURES ME THAT I WILL
BE ABLE TO PERFORM BY THE END OF NOVEMBER—AS EVER,
MARI [sic][26]

He immediately telephoned the Royal Festival Hall.[27] Shortly thereafter the
press learnt the next concert in Amsterdam was also being rescheduled.[28] A
note from her physician was supplied as evidence: Dr. Enrico Bozzi observed
"acute laryngitis and influenza; she needs a period of rest and recuperation of
at least thirty days. After this interval she will be considered entirely cured."[29]

In Paris Maria and Di Stefano also coached from time to time with Janine
Reiss. "Everything was a worry for her but at the same time she was feeling a
kind of—an extraordinary source of rejuvenation . . ." Reiss remembered. "I
was very moved to see Maria in this marvelous state, one which usually foresees creation but, in this instance, led to something extremely painful. I'm
sure it was a shock for her."[30]

On 21 October the soprano and tenor arrived in Hamburg for their first
concert. Plaza Hotel had been reserved an extra three days in advance to
give Maria time to scrutinize the modern concert hall, Congress Centrum.[31]
Staying in the suite with her on-off maid and cook Elena Pozzan, she was
buoyed somewhat by the phone calls of Onassis: now a distant friend.[32]

Eschewing loyalty toward his colleagues, Di Stefano had failed to memorize the lyrics. Urgently he strived to have Gorlinsky send his favorite "souffleur" (prompter) from Milan. Upon discovering that he would have to cover all the man's expenses he abruptly changed his mind. It then fell on Robert Sutherland to mouth the lyrics as he turned the pages of the sheet music for Ivor Newton.³³

Congealed in fear at the rehearsal, the soprano practiced for a while and afterward went shopping.³⁴ The concert introduced an undiscovered Callas to the public: a soprano comprising a lissome legato and rein-tethered rhythms, slick speed and coils of coloratura. Yet her natural timbre was as slender as elastic: perforable bubble gum.

The effects of the hiatal hernia—likely in conjunction with her previous ones—had slaughtered her support system; her instrument was weightless. Confronting pieces she had never before sung in public or recorded—such as the duets "Una parola, o Adina" from Donizetti's light-hearted opera L'elisir d'amore and Gounod's "Il se fait tard . . . Laissez-moi contemplez ton visage" from his Faust, Maria's fragile instrument became her characters' naivety. Simultaneously it was grating.

Di Stefano appeared to muster all his strength into the purpose of outsinging her. His work across the concerts was coarse, feral, unrestrained: triple the dynamics of inebriated patrons' "Auld Lang Syne"s on New Year's Eve.

Though Maria suffered issues with her breathing in the Hamburg concert there was worse to come. Photographers were planted everywhere. Elizabeth Taylor stormed in twenty minutes late to the applause of ear-perked Germans.³⁵ A white orchid plant had been sent by the actress to Maria's hotel suite.³⁶

Few felt they had attended a true Callas concert. "Of Callas' once-fascinating voice, its once radiant glow, its volume, the expression that once dominated the musical world and held it in awe, only the trace of a hint is available," wrote Heinz Josef Herbort in Die Zeit. Yet he likewise wasn't loath to mention "her extraordinarily characteristic colors: she uses dark vocals in the areas between seduction and despair; occasionally in the vicinity of the vulgar depths of the timbre, with a slightly guttural quality in the voice. Tones colored in this way were nevertheless isolated phenomena; their impression and effect immediately forgotten when a couple of bars later unclean notes burst through the middle register: a dentist pulling on a nerve."³⁷

"This was the worst night of all," Maria commented. "I can go on from here and learn all over again. I thought at one time I would never beat my nerves. But I have. It took courage." A party was held at the Plaza Hotel where Maria stood up in her green chiffon gown, raising a glass to Di Stefano. "He has been at my side for two years, encouraging and helping me. Without him, tonight would not have been possible."³⁸

Regally received in Berlin some days thence, Maria was invited to inscribe the city's Golden Book.³⁹ Reviews regrettably appeared before her eyes: Maria had a positive reaction to a critic who alleged her voice "would become stronger with the run." She had instructed Elena and Ferruccio to cut out the caustic reactions and censor the ones they passed on to her.[40]

"I don't want to *read* them and *this* way disturb my peace of *mind* and my *nerves*," the soprano would insist to David Holmes weeks later. "So I feel that if I *don't* read criticisms, it's *better*. I know *exactly* what I do. Much before the *critics*. But, er—the *best* critic *is* the public. Now if the public was as happy as they *were*, then why should I *complain?*"[41] CBS's Mike Wallace went so far as to cite a quotation: "The world tour *might* turn out to be a *grandiose* finale. Or it could turn out to be an artistic *tragedy*." To this Maria responded, "So far it hasn't been a *tragedy*. And, I *belong* to the category— the difference between ancient Greeks and *me—is* that I don't *cry* on tragedies . . . if they *happen*. *If* they happen then I don't cry *on* the tragedies. I *cope* with them. So, er . . . Let's hope for the *best*."[42]

Charming her devoted fans was one of the tour's only balms. Following her Dusseldorf recital the soprano happened in the Hilton on a Scottish bagpipe player who had featured as a guardsman in her 1964 London *Tosca*. Subsequently she received him at dinner the following evening.[43]

Clad in a black velvet dress for her concert in Munich, Maria revisited her mime in a mirror; experimenting with her silk shawl. She clung to her custom of converting the accessory into a prop. In the words of Robert Sutherland, "As Queen Elizabeth in *Don Carlo* she wore it as a cloak of sovereign authority; as Santuzza, in the *Cavalleria* duet, it became a village girl's neck scarf; but for 'O mio babbino caro' she left it off altogether, her shoulders pulled in to give the appearance of a girl thirty-five years her junior."[44]

Her reception was so warm that by the next concert in Frankfurt her approach had shifted northward. "I'm quite happy, dear Leo," she wrote to Lantzounis. "People love me. Of course they know I am not as I was 15 years ago, but they are extremely happy so why should I complain . . . Well working does me good anyway."[45] The influx of delusion was fast-flowing.

It was in that very concert that Maria gave a poor performance: more notes slid off-pitch, Newton's accompaniment fell out of sync with the *Carmen* duet of "C'est toi, c'est moi"; *Gianni Schicchi*'s "O mio babbino caro" was recklessly rushed. Two days later nonetheless she was at peace. In a rehearsal prior to the Mannheim concert she took the score of *Cavalleria rusticana*, didn't comply with Di Stefano's suggestions and plucked memories of her teenage Athenian Santuzza from the back of her mind. Not having yet performed its aria "Voi lo sapete" as part of the concert tour, Maria asked Sutherland to lend her his score. Di Stefano grunted. "Yes, no sex for you tonight—you only take that score to bed." Maria shrugged this off with an expression that had failed to gauge the subtext.[46]

Decked in scarlet for the concert in Madrid on 20 November, Maria was "free of nervousness" before an audience that included her old acquaintance, Princess Sophie of Greece and Denmark.[47] Reviews commiserated rather than reviled. "Maria Callas sang with a voice of uneven color, yet of a unique seductive force; with an impressive technique and a personality that overrode everything . . . she created around herself a climate of sensational-ism . . . [but] the truth is that as the program evolved, many grew more and more disillusioned . . . While Maria Callas may not fail us when it comes to the clarity of her vocal line and her charisma, the condition of the voice did not reach the criteria necessary for the ears to feel aesthetic pleasure," wrote Antonio Fernández-Cid.[48]

A few days later Maria and Di Stefano welcomed Peter Andry of EMI to their Savoy Hotel, London suite. Scarcely self-aware, the pair was studying their repertoire (completely clothed) in bed. She was "relaxed and happy":[49] the Royal Festival Hall had seen sixty thousand applications for her upcom-ing two concerts.[50]

That 26 November she glided onstage in a gleaming, full-length ivory dress and a navy-blue cape made by Alain Reynaud.[51] Before a crowd of diehard fans including Elisabeth Schwarzkopf and Jessye Norman[52] Maria performed with a little more freedom than usual. There was more intensity throughout the *Don Carlos* duet; a wounded girl's tenderness percolated *Cavalleria*'s "Voi lo sapete" and infused it with lachrymose longing.

Caught on film are the soprano's restless changes in expression. As her Santuzza begs Di Stefano's Turiddu not to leave her in the fierce "Tu qui, Santuzza," she defers to her ex-lover; clasping his hand pleadingly in both of hers. The supplication borders on a threat: "No, no, Turiddu—rimani, rimani ancora" ("No, no, Turiddu; stay, please stay . . ."). Tenacious emotional blackmail. When Di Stefano's Turiddu finally unchains himself, she glowers with the seething scorn of shock. "Bada!" ("Beware!") she blasts Turiddu.

Vestiges of the original Bernstein *Medea* float ashore.

Taken hostage by the raptures of her London public, Maria faced them in embarrassment—a little gawky in her physical comportment: "I must say this evening holds a little more emotion . . . because when my public loves me *that* much, I have to give that much *more*—and there's no *end* to it . . ." She laughed. "So I'll try a little more and I'll . . . do the usual song: 'O mio babbino caro' for my *public* caro."

As she released that final note of "Papà, pietà . . . pietà" ("Papa, have pity, have pity"), her hands dropped from their pose unceremoniously. The trance of becoming her past secure self was exhausted.

Critics were not universally disdainful. "On her low notes in Ponchielli's 'Suicidio' and at the words 'fra le tenebre . . . dentro l'avel' we heard once more that majestic, cutting enunciation," Philip Hope-Wallace wrote for *The Guardian*.[53]

After being showered with bouquets and people's sweaty palms as she paraded through the audience, Maria met with supplementary praises at a dinner party in her honor. Luisa and her mother were both also present. Once again she toasted the self-pleased Di Stefano; employing the exact same words used in her Hamburg toast.[54]

Stelios Galatopoulos paid her a visit immediately afterward. She was melancholy. "Yes, it is wonderful that they love me so much in London, even though they love me a little bit more than they should. But they really love me for what I have been and not for what I am now."[55]

The soprano's transient illusions seemed to be confined to the elusive dwellings of her arias. She would enter and leave periods of disassociation: at times pretending not to care about her practice, at times believing a sublime performance was in store; at times resigned in her depression.

During this period she insisted to Robert Sutherland that she had always been interested in psychology. "They don't do enough for mental illness these days. All this stress on cancer, but they don't spend enough money for the mentally sick."[56] Obviously she wasn't speaking of herself; Maria wasn't suffering from something clinical. Yet she was not her most emotionally balanced self. Considering the route her life had taken that had been inevitable.

Brief respite would be rent asunder by Di Stefano. Racked by her muddy conscience, Maria spent the days between her London concerts Christmas shopping with Luisa and her lover's wife at Harrods, commenting aside to Sutherland, "She never leaves us alone."[57]

Hoary-haired, obese and having reached the age of fifty-two, Di Stefano still thought himself a ladies' man. He would pick up twenty-something women and invite them back to his hotel suite; never striving to conceal them from his spouse or mistress. So unabashed was his approach, their German tour manager's wife had discovered his amorous escapades.[58] Elena Pozzan often overheard Maria and Di Stefano's disputes about his other women.[59]

In public Maria presented herself as closed-off and withdrawn—stating for a Japanese interview, "I'm a bit *old-fashioned* and also I *hide* as I'm a shy person; I hide my *real* feelings."[60] Among her posse however she still toured with her one-woman show. There were sentiments she was reluctant to unveil; never elaborating too much on her voice's manifold impediments. Yet her blabbing circle—who relied on anecdotes about Onassis' phone calls for their relishment, together with the latest gossip on Di Stefano's affairs and their unending quarrels—scarcely knew that she *had* other problems.

It was still in her interest to present an unflappable image to those she knew little. Attending EMI's 75th anniversary concert on 29 November, Maria was seated next to future prime minister Edward Heath.[61] At a dinner afterward she spoke to Ger Oord, the director of EMI Netherlands, insisting that she had "become younger and especially happier".[62] "In a year's time I will be much better than now. You cannot deny that I am not what I once was. But on the other hand I have become a better musician. I am more driven by passion."[63]

Once an intolerable burden, Onassis knew how to support her with his telephonic words of reassurance. He would send Maria flowers before concerts[64] and she openly told Sutherland, "We're close friends . . . We have a basic understanding. He can talk to me about his business problems and he knows there's always his favourite champagne in my house."[65] On one occasion Onassis even spoke to Sutherland himself, enquiring whether Maria was happy; on another he conversed of the concerts with Mario de Maria, the United States tour manager. Wary of Di Stefano's infuriating antics, he advised his friend: "If he doesn't turn up to sing, just give me a call and I'll come over and appear with you. The audience will be just as pleased."[66]

Alexander's unforeseen death had ameliorated him in his ex-lover's eyes. "When his son died he lost the craving to conquer, which was his lifeblood," Maria would tell Galatopoulos. "Unfortunately we were not complementary, but we understood each other sufficiently to make our friendship eventually . . .[67] My affair with Onassis was a failure but my friendship with him was a success."[68]

"Happy Birthday" was sung at Maria's second concert the day she turned fifty-one. By the Paris concert on the 7th Sutherland had been recruited to accompany the singers full-time. Soon a rehearsal detonated into a terse altercation; stretching far into the concert as Di Stefano began to joust with the soprano during intermission. He was competing to observe who had the greater popularity. "The fairies are all there," Di Stefano attempted to joke, crudely referring to the gay opera-loving community. "They don't like me, but they just adore you."[69]

The ambience of rancor left a stain on their performance. Decades later it was still too sad to dwell upon for Janine Reiss.[70] Critics weren't entirely repulsed. "Always young, beautiful, fresh, smiling, she walks onstage in a swishing gown of raspberry veil and a studied assurance . . ." one scribed. "The great aria from Ponchielli's La Gioconda no longer has the dramatic poignancy it once offered. It was a lesson in the art of singing, a lesson in vocal technique rather than the visionary impression I used to behold . . . Only Santuzza, who sighs and who suffers, who simultaneously curses and begs her lover, crying on his shoulder—this is Callas Rediscovered: with that fleshy voice, that soulful cry; that fissured sonority we knew well in her golden age."[71]

Maria on the other hand was replenished. "Pippetto, I couldn't sleep tonight and so I mustered up the courage to listen to the concert on the 8th [7th]," she wrote him. "I was amazed. My voice, as you said, is making enormous progress. Just think, if I'd not had my dreadful stomach! My voice is so much more focused and firm! I'm on the right road at last, Jesus!!! I'm getting used to the good old sounds. I can't believe it. Thank God we have these tapes . . ."[72]

The armistice was brief. In her Amsterdam hotel room three days later Di Stefano again sought to bully Maria into vocal submission. "I can't sing like that at the concert," she insisted. "I haven't the nerve—and it rings so in my ears."[73] Clandestinely the paparazzi perched atop the roof of the hotel and dangled a marauding microphone to snatch a snippet of Maria's practice. Catching them red-handed, she absconded to the home of concert manager Charles Aerts, where she accompanied herself in tacit practice on his Kemble grand piano.[74]

"The almost proverbial Callas intensity has ceded to caution," was the Dutch verdict in a review by Charles Fabius.[75] A recording exposes a Maria who suffers from strenuous breathing and frightening stridency; flawfully fragile.

*

A polemic sparked anew at Christmas. At home Maria was hard-pressed again to fight Di Stefano's "technique",[76] denouncing his intention to drown out her voice. "My admirers don't like it—nor do I. He'd better do something about it for the USA or I'll just give up," she vented to Sutherland.[77]

Immersing herself in the ritual of listening to pirate recordings, she heard "O mio babbino caro" from a May 1963 concert. Melodramatically she commented to her accompanist: "It was about that time that my boyfriend started to influence me away from music and I gave it up. I was so tired of all the fuss and problems in opera houses, and intrigues between sopranos and tenors. But in the end I learned it wasn't worth giving up everything for him. He was only interested in his family. After all, music is the only thing I have in my life, and he took it away from me."[78]

Ironically in June of 1963 she had insisted to a journalist, "Today I'd like to be a woman like all the others. Have a house, children, a dog . . . I'd like to have a real life, a private life." After his rejoinder, "Would you give all of this up?" Maria had mysteriously stayed silent.[79]

It was a new narrative that had been gaining steam since 1970 when she had met with Giulietta Simionato after the Rome premiere of *Medea*: Onassis had compelled her to renounce her music; she had "begun dying" on account of him.[80] Evidently the real reasons for avoiding stage work had been polymorphous. There were sinus problems and her hernia and fraught relations with embittered general managers; there were drops in blood pressure and spiking stress that had bedeviled opening nights. The high E flat that she had cracked in her November 1959 *Lucia di Lammermoor* had sounded an alarm. Together with the fallout from her fractured bond with Meneghini, sour luck had made her take long stage-free intervals.

Those were complicated answers. This was easy scapegoating.

To Barbara Walters—the gossip-hungry journalist of CBS' *Today Show*—she offered an identical excuse in early 1974. Maria was told point-blank, "It's been said, 'Maria Callas gave up singing for Aristotle Onassis.'"

She concurred. "I *thought* that when I met a man I loved that I didn't *need* to sing. Because I think that a *woman*, necess—the most *important* thing in a woman is to have a man of her *own*, and to make *him* happy. Because I don't think that, er . . . *singing* is a woman's *job* . . . I *didn't* give up, I kept *on—singing*, but you see, in *our* kind of *work*, we have to keep *on* and *on*—you just cannot *sing* once or twice a year. Then you lose your muscles. Then you lose your—training; the habits, the reflexes. So—*naturally*, any man who is in *love* with you the way he *was*—I'm sure he *was*—did *not* want me to sing. But I had to sing, as I—as we *both*, or I would not make up my mind about *marriage*, 'cause I also had a husband, remember, who was making a lot of *trouble* . . ."[81]

And to Mike Wallace of *60 Minutes*, Maria likewise explained: "I sang less and less because evidently he did not like me to sing . . . If the person is in love he does not want to see you onstage. That is, er, comprehensible."[82]

Just two years earlier she had insisted to a Greek reporter, "Rumors spread that Callas lost her voice and stopped singing. To those I respond that I did not stop singing, that I work the old roles every day, that I take a lesson every day and that when I am ready I will return."[83]

Apparently her lack of children was no fault of hers. "I would like to have had children, but my husband . . . oh, there is no point in blaming anyone," she told a Miami reporter. "I would like to have had them and I did not."[84]

It was delicious bait for journalists: finally an exposé on Callas from the horse's mouth. And yet what kind of "tell-all" could it be if it emerged from someone so unstoppable she spilled her guts to almost anyone at four am? In the same Barbara Walters interview Maria was defensive and occasionally caustic, offering a string of soundbites such as: "I think love is so much better when you're *not* married . . . Why should I *marry*? Give me one good reason why I should marry. I'm well-*off*." Bitterly she stressed about her singing, "I'm *already* better than nine years ago, I'm sorry."[85]

Thus Maria's "confidences" largely sounded like they ran on auto-pilot—often skewing to her audience and the genre. A serious conversation—like her talks with Stelios Galatopoulos years later—would conclude Onassis hadn't had a bearing on her work life.[86] An emotional soliloquy distinctly reminiscent of bad theatre would allege he *had*—and thrive on fatuous exaggerations.

Perhaps at times Maria liked to think it true. Blaming someone else was preferable to thinking that her voice had disappeared without a concrete explanation, or attributing its defects to irreparably damaged stomach muscles. If she had *surrendered* singing she could be regarded as a sacrificial operatic heroine. If her voice had collapsed for no apparent reason she was no more than a has-been.

Finger-pointing was significantly simpler. Not only did the act relay the huge responsibility and vilify a man already scorned by many, it deflected focus from the soreful subject. Were there occasions when Maria told herself she had said "no" to an engagement at Onassis' behest? Probably. Inasmuch as an old friend invited to a Christmas party twenty miles away attributes her inevitable absence to a snowy forecast. Rewriting history can save a person.

"You can't believe half you read about me," Maria would insist in the same period's press conferences. "I stopped singing because I wasn't happy the way I was singing. I knew well it wasn't like it used to be."[87]

In other circumstances she was more explicit but stand-offish. "As a matter of fact I think that on the whole I have improved. I had acquired a sort of a . . . as they called it, a 'wobble' in the high notes, which is a *pulsation*. And I managed to *improve* that. Now, during the *concerts*, I will improve even *more* the whole status of the *voice* . . . there's nothing like the *stage* that can make you work *properly*. The *muscles*, properly. That's why I had to, er . . . go through certain—for instance, in a *year*'s time I'm sure that I will be much better than . . . what I actually am *now*. *Because* I have not worked certain muscles for eight long *years*," was her faulty explanation for her present vocal problems. "Every *evening* is an *improvement*," she insisted. "And only on *stage* can you improve certain *things*. *Unfortunately*."[88]

1974 began depressingly. In an act of charity Maria and Di Stefano performed at Milan's Istituto Nazionale per lo Studio alla Cura dei Tumori: the Institute for the Study and Cure of Tumors where Luisa was receiving her treatment.[89] It was a confidential concert of which nobody had been apprised. Fearing raucous riots, the soprano had elected to forsake the whole of Italy throughout her global concert tour. When she confronted—in her own words—"the children I know are among the public," she immediately swiped her spectacles to blind herself to the four hundred patients.[90] This didn't better her performance. Not managing to use enough support, she was profusely out of breath and frequently forgot her lyrics.[91]

The following day she and Di Stefano were already in Stuttgart. They publicly discussed the possibility of directing *Carmen* for the Dallas Opera, in the tenor's words: "because Maria is on the Board of Directors there and they've got enough money to have sufficient rehearsals." By the time of the concert on 23 January, the ailing Di Stefano was unable to sing.

Having made a pact that neither would perform if one fell ill, Di Stefano and Maria agreed to announce their cancellation onstage. As the pair stepped out, spectators still imagined they were going to sing. After discovering their last-minute dismissal, one man yelled: "Let Callas sing then."

Sutherland had brought the music. A conceding Maria began with "O mio babbino caro." Jealous of her rapturous reception, Di Stefano attempted to return onstage but was obstructed by the guards, who failed to recognize him. Maria announced her next aria, "Suicidio". In response an audience member booed and launched into a lengthy rant about the concert's cancellation though it was already underway. "I'm sorry," she replied. "But I can do nothing about it." The audience member stormed off. "Do you want me to sing?" A rowdy series of disputes among the public escalated; most were urging her to sing. The insurrection gnawed at the scant remnants of her confidence. Unsettled, she walked off the stage.

Back at her hotel she criticized an artist of unflagging energy. A television program reminded her of the support Marlon Brando had pledged to the Native Americans; ten months before he had enlisted an activist to decline the Academy Award for his role in *The Godfather* on his behalf. "He made a film about them," Maria observed. "If he objects so much to their treatment why doesn't he give them the money he made on the film?"[92]

*

In the weeks that led up to the daunting New York concert the soprano travelled with Di Stefano to Puerto Rico for a brief vacation and a visit to her cousin Mary Annexy.[93] It was cut short by unexpected rain[94] and the two singers soon came to Manhattan. Dressed in pond green satin and colossal bubble-gum sized beads, Maria fielded questions at the press conference.[95] "Why did she come back?" one press release wrote. "Because she felt like it is her simpler answer. Actually she's never really been away from music. She has continued studying—teaching." Asked if she would happily assist the Met, a taut Maria answered: "I have always helped the Met when I sang there."

One journalist enquired whether she desired to remarry. Accustomed to defaulting to the same excuse—that she was married still to Meneghini—Maria momentarily forgot her recently legitimized divorce. "But, I am already married." Reporters were befuddled. "To whom?" Hurriedly she eyed the room in search of the least likely man. "To Mr. Hurok!" Maria cast a look toward the impresario responsible for both this concert and her 1958–59 U.S. tours. The room burst out laughing.[96]

"You're making a *tour* but, that is not the compelling thing that it *was* and one wonders—what is at the *core* of your life? What is at the center of your life *today*, Madame Callas?" Mike Wallace ventured to interrogate her for the program *60 Minutes*.

Maria wouldn't give an inch. "The center of my life *is* to be *peaceful* with yourself, and erm . . . To be able to not be bored. Which is already a *lot*."[97]

The U.S. debut was not felicitous. At the Academy of Music in Philadelphia Maria squawked through many arias. She was perilously shaky; petrified. Unlike the European crowd of adulators, most Americans were focused on the more mass-market aspects of her life. When Di Stefano took a taxi to a local supermarket, the driver courteously asked him what his plans were in the States. "I'm singing here, with Maria Callas."—"Maria Callas?" verified the driver. "Ah, yes," he remembered. "The girlfriend of Onassis." Never one to shun insensitivity, Di Stefano vivaciously returned to their hotel to greet Maria: "Ciao, 'girlfriend of Onassis'!" She didn't find the joke amusing.[98]

Ahead of the Carnegie Hall endeavor the soprano's psyche teemed with such a speedy tension it spilled over. Following the last rehearsal, she was counting on a tranquil drive through Central Park—only to chance upon Maria Di Stefano at the stage door. At 2:00 am Maria's ritualistic phone calls started—to Robert Sutherland, then to Mario de Maria, the tour organizer. "Please, pray for me," she told the former.

A note pushed through the door instructed part-time maid-cook Consuelo not to rouse her. At around midday the maid entered the room and found Maria lying unconscious on the floor by her bed. Once more she had accidentally ingested an excess of sleeping pills, having already taken two before calling Sutherland and Mario de Maria the previous night. Dr. Louis Parrish was called. He ordered Di Stefano to walk with Maria, slap her to awaken her and make her drink coffee. When he arrived he gave the half-asleep Maria an emetic.[99]

Although lucidity returned to her with ease a while would pass before she could recover the capacity to sing. She supplicated Dr. Parrish to allow her to perform but he forbade it. While her cousin Helen Arfaras visited her in her hotel suite[100] the concert was cancelled. Parrish was appointed to field questions in the middle of Carnegie Hall's vast auditorium. He explained that "Miss Callas had an acute inflammation of the upper respiratory tract, bordering on influenza": the truth with the omission of its cause. "There is no way she could have sung tonight."[101]

On February 21st the pair performed their first Canadian concert in Toronto. Feeling ill again, Di Stefano gave way to just one solo; leaving Maria to taxingly fill out the rest of the concert.[102]

Washington's recital was a statelier affair. Regaled with red roses upon her arrival at National Airport, the soprano was collected in a limousine by impresario Patrick Hayes. As they drove through Pennsylvania Avenue she set her eyes upon the White House. "It will be there for a long time, for the world," she remarked in the car. "If not, we might as well all commit suicide."[103]

Accommodated at the Hay-Adams Hotel, Maria slipped into an elevator dressed in white mink, camouflaging against poodle Pixie. Close by a long-time fan was dithering: Ruth Bader Ginsburg, future United States Supreme Court justice. "I was in town to make an argument at the Court," the judge would later recall. "I mumbled something about how much joy she had given me through her recordings and then I felt as if I had been touched by magic—that there was no way that I was going to lose that argument—and as things turned out a couple of months later, the decision of the U.S. Supreme Court was unanimously in favor of my client."[104]

"I always sing beautifully in Washington," Maria had earlier observed.[105] This case was no different. Its recording proves that evening heralded the most successful concert up to then.

"She Came, She Sang, She Conquered," ran the headline by Paul Hume for his critique. "The flame of former years flared highest in the duet for Santuzza and Turiddu, beginning 'Tu qui, Santuzza.' Here all that the program intimated came out. There was phrasing to shame today's leading dramatic sopranos. All that made Callas uniquely great at her peak was glimpsed in the catch of a single breath, the change of inflection from jealous anger to helpless pleading."[106]

Meanwhile Di Stefano was once again unwell. The day of their Boston concert, 26 February 1974, he awoke barely able to speak.[107] For the first time since the tour's inception the soprano was compelled to sing a concert totally alone. And it wasn't even a case of Di Stefano playing the "divo". At the last minute Maria's pianist friend, Vasso Devetzi, was recruited to play works by Schumann, Chopin and Handel to alternate with the vocal performance.[108] At the Ritz-Carlton Hotel Maria learned she shared her suite with unexpected guests. As a precautionary measure she set mattresses against the walls to soundproof her surroundings.[109]

Her stylist Alexandre de Paris was asked what the color of Symphony Hall was. Learning it was gold-white and that Nana Mouskouri had worn pink for a concert, Maria selected a salmon dress.[110]

Terrified of solitary stage time, she took care of something that she *could* control: her knowledge of the lyrics. This she handled by requesting they be legible on notecards with large print the audience could unfortunately notice, "1½ inches high". During the concert nonetheless she barely looked at them. While the execution fell prey to explosions of crescendo, "Vissi d'arte" gained in confidence together with *Don Carlos*' "Tu che le vanità." "This was very important to me," Maria confessed at the end.[111]

Critics weren't enamored with the concert. " 'O mio babbino caro' was impossible," one Callas-devotee wrote. "The piece doesn't work as a cornet solo—but the girlish skip with which Callas rounded the bend of the piano, the pleading of the eyes, the testing of the mouth was irresistible."[112]

Maria on the other hand felt blissfully encouraged. "In America there was so much confusion," she wrote eleven months later to Alberta Masiello. "And I was not calm. So I gave the least of myself—Boston was the best."[113] To Chicagoan critic Claudia Cassidy she would insist, "I wish you had heard me in Boston. It was better."[114]

Embracing cohorts of her fans backstage, she beamed with smiles and offered autographs and greetings of "God bless you."[115]

Ever the male chauvinist, Di Stefano was uninspired by this newfound poise. Though he had come to Drake Hotel, Chicago for their next recital, the receptionist had erringly alerted him they lacked his reservation. Di Stefano had thus switched lodgings. When Maria came to see him at his new hotel he stubbornly refused to leave. It took hours for him to begrudgingly appear and finally agree to sing with her at Civic Opera House.[116]

Resentment reared its ugly head after Di Stefano elected to perform. Maria cautioned the Chicago public: "If I don't sing they say I am temperamental and am doing it on purpose. I am tired and Giuseppe has a cold."[117] As they launched into their second duet, *Don Carlos*' "Io vengo a domandar," Di Stefano cut short his singing, bitterly informing spectators: "I tried it for Maria."

Following an awkward pause she saved the moment. "No, not for me, let's say we are doing it for our Chicago public. We are among friends here and I'm sure they will understand. You go and rest and I will sing a song."[118]

Her partner took this as contemptuous derision. After disappearing offstage during Maria's "Voi lo sapete" Di Stefano re-emerged, suddenly well enough to perform. The crowd warmed to Maria; one even shouting "Thank you" after she announced "Vissi d'arte." "You are welcome, though I can't promise how I'm going to sing it," Maria answered unprofessionally.[119]

Governor of Illinois Dan Walker had invited her to dinner. Fatigue led her to veto the proposal but she took him and his wife to her hotel suite for champagne. Walker gallantly offered to carry Maria to dinner himself; she politely declined.[120]

With both bronchitis and a burst blood vessel in the trachea, Di Stefano was unfit to realize the following Carnegie Hall concert. James Conlon—who had conducted Juilliard's *La bohème* in February 1972—was contacted and summoned to New York. "There'd been a crisis that day: Di Stefano had for one reason or another decided that he didn't want to continue at all," Conlon recalled. "What they were proposing to me was, 'Could we make up a program with an orchestra, and we would alternate overtures, intermezzi, all sorts of things, to give her time in between her arias.' "[121]

On the day of their anticipated concert impresario Sol Hurok was frequenting his Manhattan bank when suddenly he had a heart attack, keeled over and died instantly.[122] Conlon was contacted anew: his services were not required as Di Stefano had now agreed to sing.[123]

That evening Maria addressed her public more intimately to explain Hurok's passing. "Please bear with us," she entreated them. "We bear with you," a spectator responded.[124]

Following a poor performance and possessive plaudits by the melomanes, Maria dived into a diatribe: complaining of the degradation of the Metropolitan, its administration, directors and composers—and insisting to her public that she would "be willing to sing opera once again in New York if new productions could be created."[125]

Greeting her admirers at the stage door, Maria threw them roses Hurok had dispatched to her that morning.[126] While critics were quick to disparage her, one admitted: "the art, even perceived through the wrong end of the telescope, remains extraordinary; and the skill of the presentation was spectacular."[127]

The following day she paid a visit to a throat specialist. He informed her that her pharynx and soft palate were inflamed and counseled her to talk less.[128]

Concert-centered quarrels vexed Di Stefano so much that he decamped to Elysée Hotel.[129] For the duration of an arduous invective he kept Sutherland hostage one night; whining of how Maria had assigned Consuelo the maid to instruct him not to have his wife around any longer,[130] of her pride, of her ego, of her control freak persona. "She thinks she's strong after Boston—she's nothing without me. WE HAVE AWAKENED A MONSTER . . . I AM A PRIMO DONNO! Meraviglioso! Machossissimo! Magnificent!"[131]

It was inevitable that Maria would perform alone at the next concert in Detroit. As young Grecian Tess Nepi made her up at the St. Regis Hotel, the soprano repined of having scalded her throat with hot coffee that morning. Excusing Di Stefano, she explained he would "be unable to go on because of a bad throat."

The evening unwound into torturous singing: strings of hollow notes and impromptu loud shrieks. Eager to report on this catastrophe, the local press remarked: "The kindest thing one heard at the Maria Callas concert Saturday in the Masonic Auditorium was: 'Isn't it sad!', or, with more intense feeling: 'It's so tragic!' "[132]

As their embroilment grew more feverish, Maria stumbled on Di Stefano one morning in a coffee shop where he sat lightly dressed in wintry weather. She sang alone in Dallas. With mismatched lyrics and flat notes, it was the worst of all her concerts.

Increasingly irritable, Di Stefano departed for Italy and returned to his wife, Luisa, Floria and little Giuseppe.[133] Six days later he was back in the States with Maria Di Stefano. Another swap of insults almost prompted a fourth solo concert by Maria till Di Stefano decided to show up. Before a Florida audience of thousands, he flippantly quipped, "I'm only on holiday here."[134] Mary Annexy was among them—dazzled by "magnificent Maria" as always.[135]

Insulted by the audience's ovation for his colleague, Di Stefano abandoned curtain calls to rush backstage and change into an orange t-shirt and "a pair of baggy pants". Catching him as he slipped out of the stage door with "a plastic water jug under his arm," the press captured his words: "I'm just a leeetle man so I'm getting out of here fast. Let her have the glory," he declared, barging past a path of photo-waving fans to reach his car.[136]

With the aggravation of his malady the duo's impasse became icier. Complaints about his wife threatening to divorce him fell on Maria's deaf ears. On the phone they shouted at each other.[137] Eventually the second Carnegie Hall concert—to be held on 2 April—was cancelled.[138]

By that date Maria and Di Stefano had reached a stalemate and advanced from New York to Ohio, where they ventured to Columbus to perform. WFCR's Mary Roscow was met with civility at the airport: "Do you see new and better prospects artistically for the Metropolitan now that Rudolf Bing is no longer in charge of that organization?" she wanted to know. "Now that's a question—you know the answer better than I do! You do the answering to that!" a jocose Maria insisted.[139]

The performance didn't bode well for the singers. Maria disliked Di Stefano's reliance on popular Italian songs: "He makes it difficult for me to get the audience back to my arias."[140] She hoped to cancel the impending concert in Long Island scheduled for 9 April but eventually changed her mind.[141]

Her former Juilliard student Barbara Hendricks had been gifted tickets for the evening by a date. Sat in the front row, she bowed her head each time she thought Maria might catch sight of her. "Her look expressed, simultaneously, how much she wanted but feared to emit the notes her vocal cords could no longer produce," Hendricks would later recall.[142] Maria was off-pitch and sang the wrong words in the "Habanera". To this Di Stefano responded with an even more animalistic attitude than usual in his rendering.

At Carnegie Hall six days later the public embraced her with unquench-able fire: "You are opera!" shouted one fan.[143] Encouraging roars became almost chaotic: impossible to quell or dispel. A spectator yelled "TOSCA!"; Maria responded with: "I'm going to try something else," announcing "Adieu, notre petite table" from Massenet's *Manon*.

Hearing her voice teeter off-pitch in a tape of it, one wonders if the paradox between her failing instrument and the voracious public's over-tures had kindled frazzlement.

Alarmed by nerves in Cincinnati three days later, Maria sang the wrong phrase in *Carmen*'s "Habanera" then repeated it; going so far as to stop her performance, apologize and start over. Her singing was scrambled and confused in the "C'est toi, c'est moi" duet: nothing could save the recital.

The next one was Seattle. In attendance was renowned ghost singer Marni Nixon—who had substituted and supplanted work for Audrey Hepburn in *My Fair Lady*, as well as for *West Side Story*'s Natalie Wood. In her words Maria "did it very effectively because of her emotional skills and imagination—that's where she was really effective."[144]

"I've had enough," was the following day's proclamation. Maria asked to be booked on the next plane to Paris.[145] Her exacerbating nerves and inner conflict had begun to push her to the precipice of self-destruction.

By holding up a mirror to her vocal atrophy the concert tour had lost its status as a work of art; now it was just an incidental hobby. Like her effort to act in *Medea*, her counsel to Juilliard students, her partial direction of *I vespri siciliani*, Maria was passing the time. Did she really feel this was a service to the music gods? Unlikely. Fans' cries were insufficient to restore an ego damaged almost totally beyond repair.

Sander Gorlinsky and Mario de Maria extracted Maria from real life. Performing in Portland, she and Di Stefano later moved on to Vancouver. Gorlinsky was proposing future concert dates: 31 August for the France Gourdon Festival, 5 September for Istanbul, 9 September for Tehran; Greece's Piraeus Municipal Theatre on September 13th and then Brussels.[146]

Maria wasn't in the mood.

In Vancouver a roiled Di Stefano repacked his suitcase, left his suite, caught a cab and asked the driver to escort him to a new hotel "near the water so that I can breathe." He neglected purposely to let Maria know that he was staying at the Sands.[147] The next day he insisted he was ill. A visiting physician found an empty pill bottle at his bedside, assuring Maria that her partner "was play-acting". Nonetheless it landed him in hospital, where doctors diagnosed him with a middle ear infection and advised him against singing.[148] Pianist Daniel Pollack was recruited in his stead.

When the time came, Di Stefano was loath to suffer inattention. Sneaking in backstage, he surfaced suddenly to grab Maria's arm and help-lessly insist: "We'll do *Carmen*."

It didn't bode well.[149]

Staying at the Bel Air Hotel in Los Angeles days later, Maria socialized with Walter Legge and Elisabeth Schwarzkopf. In Santa Barbara she met a legendary soprano and idol of hers, Lotte Lehmann, who resided nearby. The conversation must have raised her spirits; in the concert at Shrine Auditorium on 5 May Maria was securer. Though problems with her breath control persisted she performed *Werther*'s "Air des lettres" with a gentle diminuendo on the final, portentous warning of "Tu frémiras" ("You will tremble").

Saluting the soprano in the sparkling scarlet gown embroidered with green, gold and violet shapes, Governor of California Ronald Reagan later signaled to his guards and offered: "Let me give you my boys to see you home, Maria."[150]

On a trip to Las Vegas Di Stefano gambled away most of his fortune.[151] Maria moved on to San Francisco, where he arrived with a novel demand: he wanted her to write to his wife. "He's *pazzo!* [crazy!]" she insisted to Sutherland.[152] Once again her artistry unraveled at the concert; nerves chewed up her confidence and spit out collapsing notes.

Horrified before their final North American event in Montreal, Maria left a note for maid Elena one night at the Ritz-Carlton suite.[153] "Tell the doctor not to wake me so I can be in my best form—I must become a singer—I NO LONGER LOOK LIKE A DIVA, and must BECOME one."[154]

It was no use. Their concert in the city laid bare a Maria Callas almost serially off-pitch.

Two days later she returned to Paris. Local doctor Yves Hecht wrote a note to confirm that her "state of health contraindicates any kind of prolonged or distant travel for a period of two or three months."[155] The leftover concerts to Japan and Korea were provisionally cancelled.[156]

"I'm fine—recovering!" Maria wrote to Robert Sutherland a few days later. "My blood test proved better than ever. (Don't tell anyone!) So you see, work does one good, even with all the madness that went on—!"[157] Gorlinsky attempted to entice her to record songs and lieder by Handel and Grieg. Maria labeled the concept "a pop record" and expressed her contempt.[158]

As for engagements, she responded promptly to her manager on 23 May: "Let's resume—first—we will discuss about <u>any</u> artistical [*sic*] proposals after I am in good health due to the stress and fatigue after having to working [*sic*] under such conditions, as you also said that it was a miracle how I managed. So accept <u>no</u> engagements without my formal agreement. The only thing I would be willing to discuss would be <u>opera</u>—with the conditions you and I agreed upon—full control of designs, colleagues & mis en scène [*sic*]."[159]

Hearing that Di Stefano was planning to record duets with Montserrat Caballé, she was rankled. "I don't know if it's worth my while singing when Caballé is doing so well. She has such a beautiful voice," Maria told Sutherland during a practice at home. He responded by quoting a taxi driver: the soprano's voice was "Very nice, but nothing on Callas."

"Why didn't you tell me that earlier?"[160]

In a bid to patch up with Di Stefano Maria summoned him to spend the weekend with her in the company of Princess Grace in Monaco.[161] His wife was so irate she took the items left by the soprano at their San Remo apartment and arranged them all in plastic bags across the floor. Di Stefano proceeded to vacation with Maria in Monte Carlo.[162]

Future concerts remained undecided. Not only did Maria not know when and how she would perform in the planned Asian cities, she lamented to Gorlinsky her compulsory tuition at the hands of Robert Sutherland. These grievances elicited the answer, "I agree to your suggestion that you should be completely independent and have no obligation . . . If, and when you wish Robert to return to Paris, you make arrangements directly with him, and we will make the financial settlement on this basis, and charge it to you." Another vacation was planned. Maria promised she would come to a decision.[163]

A couple of weeks were spent with Di Stefano in Menton, France.[164] On 21 July Maria was watching Montserrat Caballé's *Norma* on television. It was a production designed by her old friend, music critic Jacques Bourgeois at the Orange Festival. Immediately she telephoned the man: "I'm not saying anything against Caballé, she sings very well. But she is no Norma!"—"Maria," responded Bourgeois, "You think that one shouldn't sing the roles you have sung but me—I happen to think one should at least try!"—"You do what you think." Maria slammed down the phone.[165]

Subsequently she sent Montserrat Caballé the earrings Visconti had given her on the occasion of her 1955 Scala *Norma*s.[166]

Early that September Di Stefano and Maria rehearsed at the Théâtre des Champs-Élysées for their tour's final leg: the Korean and Japanese concerts. Following an annexation of the theatre by reporters as they left, they severed that routine. Maria flipped-flopped between committing to the concerts and abandoning them; Di Stefano strived to persuade her to "make it up" with his wife.[167]

It was an absurd postmodern play.

Renzo Allegri—the *Gente* reporter who had chronicled her and Di Stefano's defense of the *Vespri* production—tried to convince her to sit down and tackle her memoirs for the Italian weekly. Maria kept the man on tenterhooks. "I'm not convinced . . . I trust you . . . But weekly magazines are full of headlines and subheadings, even captions under photographs. The journalist doesn't make them up—the editor does. I know because I've had many discussions of this kind with journalist friends from various theatre magazines . . . You would have to assure me that you would have full control over the headlines. But I know you can't do it. And then I'm fed up with reading the usual horrible and stupid things such as, 'Callas kisses Onassis,' 'Callas is running away with Onassis,' 'Callas is getting divorced for Onassis,' 'Callas has been dumped by Onassis.' It's torment." She promised to get back to him after her Asian concerts.[168]

With little left to do before embarking on the Oriental tour, Maria was invited to attend a Verdi-focused academic conference in Chicago. Musicologists took turns reading belabored dissertations; listening to an interpreter convey their colleagues' words in headphones.[169] The magnitude of the convention lent it the impression of a UN meeting. Her old friend Carol Fox, former director of the Civic Opera House, was also in tow.[170]

Asked about performances of Verdi, a journalist noted Maria's response: " 'There is too much intellectualism. It depresses genius,' said the genius, depressed."[171] She was referring to the practice of staging classical operas in modern or irrelevant settings: a phenomenon slowly usurping the opera world.

Defending opera's purpose, the soprano cited Serafin and underlined that some conductors "often know better than the composer."[172] Certain operas were too long and it was *their* role to determine cuts and modernize them. "I nearly died when I read how some scholars had found even *more* music for *Don Carlos*. The opera is far too long already," she expressed, unaware that several of the critics present were responsible for such a restoration.[173]

Dismay was the reaction of the musicologists—especially when the soprano asserted Germont's aria from *La traviata*—"Di Provenza al mar"— ought to be cut. Charles Osborne rose in order to redress her: "You seem to forget, Miss Callas, that the composer is not there to serve you or your high notes. You are there to serve the composer. You are an interpreter, not a creator. Singers like yourself will come and go, but the genius of Verdi will outlive us all."

Coldly Maria quipped, "If Verdi were alive today, he would agree with me."[174]

Mistaking her desire to make cuts for egomania, the scholars publicly reviled her comments. One alleged that "producers, singers and conductors" (including Maria) would "ignore the composer's intentions and continue to perpetuate bad traditions."[175] It seemed to have escaped them that the nineteenth century had heralded the trend of cuts—not Serafin or Callas.

Before commencing the last concerts Di Stefano and Maria ventured to Honolulu for another vacation. An unusual venue hosted their first Asian concert: the auditorium of Seoul's Ewha University for Women.[176] Following a wan performance the soprano took to spending time in the seclusion of her hotel suite. Sampling delicacies at the opening of its Italian eatery Caffe Centro, Di Stefano told *The Korean Herald*: "Whenever I come to Korea I enjoy the spicy flavour of Korean food. It is as good as Italian food. Maria Callas? Well, she prefers to stay in her room."[177]

Paraded round like an Olympic torch in later days, Maria was the subject of an unrelenting focus. At their interview in Tokyo on October 10th she kindled a rapport with her new public. "You're all so very *reserved* and all that and *yet* . . . so *passionate* and so *generous* in er . . . in *giving* yourself.

And *appreciating* so, I mean . . . What *more* can we *ask?* I wish I could speak the language and thank the *public* for this great *reception* . . . I've noticed the Japanese—they do *everything, like* the *others*—better than the others. So they've managed *this* with us *too.*"[178]

Excerpts from the first two Tokyo concerts in NHK Hall were compiled for one televised broadcast.[179] Performing the "Habanera," Maria relied as she had in the sixties on placing her hands on her hips. Once more she mixed up the words. Her confidence had grown nevertheless—and she was vitriolic tossing Don José the ring that he had given Carmen, almost growling "Tiens!" ("Here!").

"I'm here in Japan. I'm working and it's going wonderfully," Maria wrote to cousin Helen Arfaras. "A thousand times better than last season. I get better with each day."[180]

Soon after the first concert she complained of pain from her hiatal hernia.[181]

The Fukuoka concert on the 24th met with a fuller, rounder voice throughout the middle register. *Don Carlos'* "Tu che le vanità" became imbued with sentiments for the first time since 1959 to fashion what was likely her most liberal concert.

Sick prior to the recital at Osaka Festival Hall, Maria had to be examined anew by otolaryngologist Taiji Nishikawa, who observed that her throat had swelled up.[182] She was persuaded to sing on the condition that an announcement reflecting her illness be made. After performing *Manon Lescaut's* "Sola, perduta, abandonnata" with precarious frailty, she willed herself to do better—spontaneously announcing "Tu che le vanità." Taunted by her weak rendition of the ode, Maria smiled. Backstage she burst into tears.[183]

In the wings before the Hiroshima concert an unnerved Maria told Di Stefano she simply couldn't do it. "What do you mean, can't," he yelled. "You are Callas, I know you can do it, don't tell me you can't."

Her final performance took place on 11 November at the Hokkaido Kosei Nenkin Kaikan concert hall in Sapporo. There the Park Hotel's management had dismantled and reassembled the rooftop piano to have it conveyed to her suite.[184] Bolstered by a lucky outing in Hiroshima, she was goaded by Di Stefano to join both him and Sutherland for his impending series of Australian concerts. Uneager, she returned to Paris as Di Stefano and the accompanist went south.[185]

"It's an illusion of a better world," Maria had once said of opera.[186] Yet love of it was not enough for her or any artist. Defective instruments accord art a disservice detrimental: sacrilege.

Noble the endeavor *hadn't* been. Maria knew that. Throughout the year that knowledge had at times sat in the depths of her subconscious; at times leapt to the summit of her mind. Intermittent moments of mild mirth had posed as an illusion. That trance was stitched from gossamer: a flimsy web.

22.

"Carte blanche"

Acrid after-effects swelled like growing ink stains as Maria's concert tour unwound. "I finished the tour very well but arriving in Paris I collapsed—and I'm not joking," she wrote to Louis Parrish, the doctor who had treated her several times in the States. "They couldn't wake me up (and I had taken no pills). I'm off them as they are not on the market and coming back after such a long trip you certainly don't need pills to sleep."[1]

Maria was referring to just one of many struggles. The first was much severer pain from her hiatal hernia. "It had left me alone for years. Probably I'm working my diaphragm more & better and it starts kicking. I try to ignore [it]—but the pain is quite severe during the two weeks attack—and food then becomes a problem," she wrote to Leo Lerman,[2] elaborating in her note to Dr. Parrish two weeks later that because of it "my whole tour was a torment of weakness and great pain."[3] Shortly after her return to Paris she had also suffered from internal hemorrhaging likely owing to accompanying stomach ulcers.[4]

Then there was inner ear imbalance: "As a result of the cold, they say, I had my <u>labyrinth</u> [sic] disturbed. I couldn't stand straight, sit straight, I had lost most of my reflexes and couldn't see for nearly 12 hrs. I'm still terrified thinking about it. Now I'm fine—never been so well—because my doctor here called a neurologist. Thank heavens I regained all reflexes in 2 or 3 days so no hospitalizing was necessary . . ."[5]

By late November Di Stefano had finished his Australian tour and was back in Milan, where Maria would call him at night.[6] Talk began to bluster: a *Tosca* in Japan was once again in sight. John Coveney of Angel (a U.S. branch of EMI) wrote on 27 November to Tito Gobbi to enquire about his availability in "May or June next year . . . [they] want you to join them."[7] Robert Sutherland was contacted in order to prepare the pair again[8] and by 2 January 1975 they had drawn up a contract.[9]

Distracting herself during Christmas with a search for a house on the Côte d'Azur,[10] Maria spent New Year with Di Stefano and his family in Milan.[11]

"The world is going haywire," she scribed to Leo Lerman on 8 January.

What a pity, things were so nice in the fifties, remember? Music—people—theatre maybe. Now crisis all over!

I try to live in a world of my own. In my home if not travelling for pleasure or work—and am very peaceful for the time being . . .

I'll write soon and give you more details about my life. (Nothing sentimental, love—It's more peaceful this way!!!)[12]

As she wrote to Alberta Masiello, *Tosca* was a certainty for the time being but she had declined to sing at a memorial concert honoring the recently departed Richard Tucker. Rudolf Bing had invited her to take part in this "benefit for the Met. I would do it willingly for Tucker but why for the Met-!" was her semi-indignant response.[13]

Onassis paid Maria a visit. He was suffering from myasthenia gravis, an autoimmune disease that had left him debilitated.[14] In this state he couldn't do much to improve his friend's impoverished confidence. "I don't have the resistance anymore," Maria wrote to Dr. Parrish on 23 January. "Also I ask too much of my singing to be happy with even these good results. But right now—calm and lucid as I am—I think my decision will be to dub some of my best records and perform them for films so they will see Callas on stage (or nearly) and it will remain for posterity as all say I should leave documents of my acting ability. Maybe it might capture my stage appearance. This way, I keep busy—and the tension is reduced to the minimum."[15]

On 4 February influenza began to aggravate Onassis' condition, compelling American specialists to travel to Athens to treat him.[16] When this proved ineffective he was flown to Paris and hospitalized at the American Hospital in Neuilly.[17] The following day he underwent emergency gallbladder surgery.[18]

Contrasting sources both attest to and deny the story that Maria paid Onassis visits in the ward. While reports on his condition came to her via Vasso Devetzi, whose mother was simultaneously hospitalized,[19] as well as butler-chauffeur Ferruccio, who knew one of the doctors,[20] the latter insisted he never escorted her there.[21]

Contrarily Stelios Galatopoulos remembered Maria telling him about seeing Onassis "on his deathbed at the hospital" where "he was calm and I think at peace with himself." It was difficult for her to stop by at the public place unnoticed—especially with the rapacious press. Wherever it occurred, the last time that Maria saw Onassis was a warm exchange.[22]

At times Maria's mind was elsewhere on the spectrum of bad health. "Pippo's daughter is not doing very well as you expect," she wrote to her godfather on 24 February. "She's lost a lot of sight, has difficulty to breath [*sic*]—but she has a great will to live and she fights. I'm afraid it's a lost battle, don't you think? What a shame—such a young girl—intelligent, beautiful. Life is so strange at times."[23]

As another means of escapism Maria flew to Palm Beach, Florida on March 10th and rented a house at 12 Golf View Road.[24] Coming to visit from their home in Tarpon Springs,[25] Cousin Helen Arfaras and her daughter Mary Annexy found a woman who was so "down to earth" that she would "wear these unfeminine bedroom slippers and a robe. She would slouch. She was very low key."[26]

Circumstances didn't invite customary elegance. Eager to avoid contentious isolation and the confrontation of her thoughts, Maria goaded Nadia Stancioff to arrive with a proposal sent by telegram: "OFFER YOU ROOM, BOARD AND CHATS BY THE POOL."[27]

Five days after her arrival Onassis succumbed to pneumonia and died.[28] Four days later Luisa Di Stefano passed away aged twenty-one.[29]

Likely in response to the pleas of Di Stefano—who had several times tried to convince Maria to allay his wife's well-founded fears—she sent a wreath to Maria Di Stefano.[30] Six days after Luisa's death, she drafted an aspiring letter of condolences:

> I'm thinking of you so much these days.
>
> You must be going thru hell—especially now that you have to pack Luisa's things. It revives all back to you.
>
> But, on the other hand it is better this way. She really had no chance. I know it from my godfather [Lantzounis was a doctor]. He told me from the beginning that no cure would avoid the end. That is why I was nervous when you left her for a long trip. I was afraid something would happen while you were away and that would of [sic] been terrible. You would have that on your conscious [sic] all your life. I'm also glad Pippo was there.
>
> Now probably everything has come back to, nearly, normal. What are your plans—if any—when you find a little time I'd like some direct news from you.[31]

"I am a very simple woman, and I am a very moral woman," Maria had specified in a 1970 interview. "I do not mean that I claim to be a 'good' woman, as the word is, that is for others to judge; but I am a moral woman in that I see clearly what is right or wrong for me and I do not confuse them or evade them."[32]

That axiom had faltered.

Evidently the epistle didn't earn a favorable response. Fleeing the domestic torment, Di Stefano left his family three weeks after his daughter's death to join Maria in Palm Beach.[33] Feebly he chose to justify his rash departure with the explanation that he had to help her find a summer home.[34]

Meanwhile Maria scrutinized the "Spanish style" residence she was renting. "I always wanted a house in a place where it's always sunny, and in a civilized country . . ." she wrote to old friend Ben Meiselman. "Five minutes to the ocean on foot . . . a lot of magnificent mosaics, a beautiful swimming pool and plenty of gardenia bushes. My favorite flower as you know."[35] Surrounding neighbors were disturbed as the new resident performed her exercises to an unseen audience every morning.[36]

After signing a one-year rental lease on the house[37] Maria consulted with Mary Annexy's uncle and decided not to purchase the property.[38]

Back in Paris on around 15 April,[39] she accrued many condolences because of Onassis' death; even hearing "sorry for your loss" from a hair stylist, Jacques Clemente. Not one to share her grief, Clemente merely heard from her that she had "loved him for himself—not his fortune or his power. That was the most intimate dialogue we've ever had."[40]

With all this free time on her hands Maria welcomed guests to her Parisian home. One of these was Bettina Brentano, the teenager she had befriended. Now sixteen and still a superfan, Bettina watched Maria pick the phone up and respond to greetings of "Bonjour, Monsieur!" with, "This is no Monsieur; this is the voice of the morning!"

Maria offered the girl tea, berated her for nail-biting, bid her to sit up straight and found her garrulous soliloquies exasperating. The teenager blushed every time she heard Maria moan to Bruna, "Children are so tiring!" Somewhat misleadingly she promised her that if Bettina got admitted to "one of those British establishments such as Oxford," she would allow her to work as her secretary in between terms.[41]

That was contingent on there being a *Tosca*. On 14 May Maria wrote to Nadia Stancioff to tell her, "I'm fine—working very hard—I have Japan *Tosca* in November. God willing!"[42] She and Giuseppe Di Stefano were still an item—even though her feelings for him had been cooling off. That June she updated her godfather, "I'm still with Pippo . . . I cannot find anyone else better. Richer maybe, but poorer in feelings, and all that goes with the brain . . . I only wish we had fallen in love when he was famous—and had a fabulous voice—because he has many human qualities."[43]

Soon she returned to the ill-fated Teatro dell'Opera, where clandestine rehearsals for *Tosca* were due to begin. Counsel from her *Vespri* costumier, Umberto Tirelli, as well as the advice of Piero Tosi, *Medea*'s costume designer, and recommendations from opera director Alberto Fassini were sought.

Tirelli joined Maria in the Teatro dell'Opera's empty auditorium one afternoon. After singing the whole second act she turned to him with, "So, Umberto, what do you think?" Apparently he didn't have a very subtle poker face. Before he could say anything Maria spoke on his behalf. "No, it's useless. Don't say anything at all; I have already understood."

The conceit of the Rome *Tosca* was velociously abandoned. News of its cancellation only surfaced in the press months later—when the cause for it was said to be Maria's cerebral anemia.[44] Soon after she wrote to Tirelli to announce she would never again sing in opera   only in concerts. This time her theory on the reason for her vocal problems was another new discovery. "My true nature has resurfaced. I've become timid again. I no longer feel worthy of command-ing a stage for three or four acts. I no longer have the guts or the desire for it."[45]

It seemed as though *Maria*'s human qualities were slowly atrophying.

Taking their toll, her traumas had erected a colossal iron fortress in her soul; a depersonifying dogma. Sensibility had slowly turned into a deck of cards she couldn't gamble.

With her tunnel vision clinging to the prospect of potential future operas, she reserved few spaces in her conscience for all other matters. Etiquette was rarely lacking; altruism was another matter. That July she and Di Stefano went—despite his wife knowing—to vacation in Roquebrune-Cap-Martin, not far from Monaco.[46] Shortly afterward they began rehears-als at Di Stefano's Milan apartment with baritone Arturo Testa, who was singing the role of Sacristan. Maria complained that "she needed more time to prepare."[47] That led to the following announcement to her godfather:

"I have come to a big decision. I'm stopping singing. I'm fed up with the whole business! . . . After my last tour I came back so sick that I'm terrified now that the months are coming to that date. My nerves can't stand the strain anymore."[48] While Maria spent most of that summer in pain from an inflammation in her right elbow[49] she and Gorlinsky agreed she would take a year off and recommence concerts in 1976.[50]

Her thoughts scrambled hither-thither—resulting in confusion rather than congratulation when she heard her former lawyer Walter Cummings was engaged:

All that seems strange to me. Getting married and everything. I suppose that my past relationships exhausted me so much, getting married would be like a prison for me, and for me only! But I am passionate, romantic, sentimental, all the qualities you no longer find today.

I'd like to find someone who is well-off, who looks good, who has good manners . . . Very difficult to find, don't you think!

Don't tell your fiancée about all this nonsense I'm writing to you. I'm still so old-fashioned.[51]

To her godfather she admitted regarding Di Stefano:

I still care for him but of course not as I did—but how does one say it to him. After the death of his daughter he lives for this love of ours. I am hoping that destiny will take care of things so as the hurt and shock will not be hard on him. He is not the type to fall in love with another woman. I would hope for that but I doubt.

Maybe I might meet someone and that would be the ideal solution. This way I would not care whether he gets hurt or not (Terrible of me, isn't it?) . . .

You are right. I have had a long and fantastic career. I can never top that. My nervous system cannot take the wear and tear of a career anymore . . .[52]

Spending summer without work at home, she tried to tackle John Galsworthy's *The Forstye Saga*[53] and scribed to old friends such as Mexican critic Carlos Díaz Du-Pond to enquire about her past colleagues: "I would like to hear from you. I would like also to know how [Antonio] Caraza Campos is. There was really a great man of theatre. He knew talent, he risked, he payed [*sic*] and he had the best this time could have offered him. I wish there were more men like that now. If you see him remember me to him."[54]

With Di Stefano still planning to perform the *Tosca* in Japan Maria summoned Montserrat Caballé to replace her.[55] Having spent time coaching the soprano for *Norma* the previous year,[56] she provided her counsel in telephone calls; striving to foster a friendship.[57] "Real friends are very special," Caballé remembered her saying. "But you have to be careful because sometimes you have a friend and you think they are made of rock, then suddenly you realise they're only made of sand. It's a terrible thing to go through life thinking that you have a rock on your side when you haven't."[58]

Scheduled to perform with the Pasadena Symphony Orchestra at Ambassador College, Los Angeles on January 20, 1976, Maria cancelled her appearance in September. Predictably she was replaced by Renata Tebaldi and Franco Corelli.[59]

Observing events from the sidelines, she was not a recluse. Unlike *Sunset Boulevard*'s Norma Desmond—who notoriously produced a cult around herself—Maria took an avid interest in the opera world; subjecting it to scrutiny in her new role as spectator. "Paris is coming back to life after the summer and there are the usual galas dinners etc.," she wrote to her old friend Joan Crawford on 19 September.[60] In the company of mezzo-soprano Régine Crespin that evening she attended a Ravel concert conducted by Leonard Bernstein at the Théâtre des Champs-Élysées. When a musician blurted out the wrong note the soprano whispered to her colleague, "How can they play like this knowing I'm in the audience?"[61]

Canvassing the social scene, she went to a function at the Palais des Sports six days later[62] and the French film premiere of Michael Cacoyannis' *Attilas '74* on 4 November.[63] By this time Maria was professing openly the punctured nature of her kinship with Di Stefano. "He's just like the rest of them. I don't feel like talking about it, but it's over," she noted to Nadia Stancioff,[64] confiding that the attachment had "become an unhappy love affair" to her godfather.

Yet she had no idea how to conduct her new approach to training. "Maybe start practicing again and recording <u>on my own</u>. I might love singing again—but I have to sing alone and with orchestra. The offers are a lot—but I have to look into myself deeply and know what I want," she wrote to Lantzounis.

Indolence was loath to grant her a reward. After spending time recovering from an external swollen cyst,[65] on 22 November, Maria learned Pier

Paolo Pasolini had been brutally, mysteriously murdered. Startled by the inexplicable assassination of the fifty-three-year-old director, she "lost her sang-froid" according to Bettina Brentano, and started to vent irrationally about a fear of being "killed in her own home by a cleaner".[66]

Nothing could deter Maria nonetheless from her persistent efforts to appear composed and nonchalant. That December she discussed the possibility of acting in a film inspired by the life of Marcel Proust with Michael Cacoyannis,[67] later flying to Milan to attend the opening night of La Scala's 1975–76 season. Her colleague Teresa Berganza was singing the titular role of Rossini's La Cenerentola. Embracing her at the theatre's bar, Berganza excitedly notified her: "Maria, I have to tell you something: I think that I can sing Adalgisa now."—"Well, it's too late," she responded. "As I can no longer sing Norma." She asked Berganza to call her and pay her a visit in Paris.[68]

The soprano was not in hiding. During her sojourn in Milan Maria bumped into another colleague, Greek bass Costantino Ego, who had sung Il pirata with her. They chatted amiably on the street.[69]

Reticent to save his marriage, Di Stefano retreated to Miami to visit Maria again that January 1976. The hours spent together likely weren't felicitous; their fraught relationship was over and Maria didn't seek his company. While she remained in Palm Beach for three weeks[70] Di Stefano continued his vacation down in Puerto Rico.[71]

The Royal Opera's general administrator John Tooley had been attempting to persuade Maria to sing Santuzza in Cavalleria rusticana for years. Hoping at last to stage it with her, in early 1976 he sent accompanist Jeffrey Tate to rehearse with Maria both at home and at the Théâtre des Champs-Élysées. Her excuses and self-justifications were quickly forthcoming: at times she didn't feel well; at others Tate would be dismissed before the lesson. Though Tooley and Maria stayed in touch Santuzza would remain a role unsung in her adult career.[72]

Another plan shone into view: a Royal Opera House concert with orchestra. For this Maria called on Robert Sutherland for help.[73]

Working again toward the restoration of her voice, she studied pieces she had never sung before including Schumann's "Im wunderschönen Monat Mai" from his song cycle "Dichterliebe." The sound emerged both wan and flimsy; frequently off-pitch. "I plan and study our records of Lucia and Tosca and then try to get back to those vocal positions I used then," she informed Walter Legge when he asked what she did with her time.

It was a new kind of "starting from scratch": the pursuit of the earliest state of her instrument; the time she had sung, in her words, "like a wildcat."[74] "Did you know that . . . she wanted nothing more, and repeated it many times to my husband and me, than to find her Mexico-voice?" Legge's wife's Elisabeth Schwarzkopf would write to a friend decades later. "Both of us tried to convince her that in her later years she would be able to give a new dimension to many other operatic roles—for instance Salome or even Electra. But it was the Mexican Wonder-voice which she kept in her head and wanted restored."[75]

Among other ailments her skin was in awful condition again. Having tolerated acne her entire life, she didn't deem this a surprise. Dr. Mario Giacovazzo, the physician of statesman Aldo Moro—who in 1958 had bestowed on Maria the honorary title of "Commendatore"[76]—paid her a visit. According to his remembrances he diagnosed her with the autoimmune disorder dermatomyositis. The doctor subsequently prescribed her prednisone, an anti-inflammatory drug.

Upon observing that Maria had "a violet tinge on her neck" and "warts on her hands," he ascribed her chronic muscle weakness and her painful joints to this especial malady.

Giacovazzo likewise noted that her larynx had been touched by it—arguing that this accounted for her vocal degradation.

While it's highly likely that dermatomyositis contributed to the escalation of it from around 1970 onward, it is improbable that she had suffered the disease for well over ten years. Reviewing a group of seventy-five patients from 1969–1985, a 2006 medical paper attested the median life expectancy for someone receiving treatment was 12.3 years.[77] Maria's vocal problems had begun in 1954 and grown more manifest by 1957. Judging by her constant medical examinations from 1957 to 1975, she would have struggled to survive the illness without medication for a span of eighteen years. Thus the disease does not serve to explain entirely her instrument's decline.[78]

"Maria's voice would be different from one session to another," Janine Reiss observed of this period. "She searched for the reason for her irregularity *very* often—all the reasons that she offered made sense, and all of them were justifiable." But Reiss herself could never pinpoint just one cause.[79]

*

Late-night phone calls multiplied again. She would speak to Jacques Leiser—an old friend who worked at EMI—and ask him: "Pray for me that I'll awake tomorrow with my voice."[80] Tuition would comprise her conversations with soprano Caballé: "I learned more in those three hours than I had as a student," the singer remembered.[81] At times Maria's speech devolved into long-winded rants, complaints, and monologues. Robert Sutherland's suggestion that she give up her career and find romance was met with, "Where am I going to find such a man? They're all taken up and anyway, it would be difficult to be Mr. Callas."[82]

Impromptu forecasts on her part could turn out to be accurate. In a clairvoyant real life plot twist, Maria envisaged that Montserrat Caballé's upcoming appearance on the televised *Prestige de la musique* wasn't to be. "Believe me, the program will not take place," she assured Jacques Bourgeois. Suddenly a chorus strike occurred and the producer of the show was mystified by how she had "divined" the incident.[83]

In these months she was also in contact with Jackie Callas, not having spoken to her since the death of their father in December 1972. Still fielding Jackie's claims about her struggle to "subsist," Maria had supported her financially for many years.[84]

Later she would tell Galatopoulos how the frayed rapport pained her: "Why have my mother and sister never, never enquired whether I am well or not. Even strangers do! It hurts me very much. Do you know I cannot really get over this, even though, with time, I was able to forget terrible things said to me in moments of anger. I, too, have been harsh when pushed too far."[85]

And yet it seemed Maria's rancor had been spent. Despite feeling that her family exploited her, she sent them a check for two hundred dollars. Though she didn't maintain regular contact with Jackie, there were nights when she phoned to exchange thoughts on trivial topics: "Godfather says you have a nice place, a beautiful garden on the terrace. So tell me . . ." She would ask about the people they had known in wartime Athens; who was still among the living.[86]

By March 1976 Maria was determined to reenter the fray. Rumors announced that she would sit on the jury of a Dutch opera and operetta competition to be broadcast on the Netherlands' NCRV network, together with Walter Legge, Elisabeth Schwarzkopf and others.[87] A couple of weeks later, on 17 March 1976, Visconti died. Maria missed the funeral: attendance of services like these was not her forte. But she sent flowers and wrote Zeffirelli "anguished, confused messages".[88]

In the early days of April she was still rehearsing with accompanist Jeffrey Tate for either the series of concerts then planned or her unrealizable *Cavalleria*. The administrator of the theatre Charles Vannes had assured them total privacy.[89] As the pair worked on Beethoven's "Ah! perfido," on April 3rd a photographer surprised them by taking a shot of Maria: desolate and in tears from the practice. Published in the tabloid *Le Journal du Dimanche*, the image made its way across Italian weeklies.[90] Following the incident Maria never again used the theatre.[91]

A lawsuit was immediately underway: Gorlinsky wrote to Bernard Baudelot, a French lawyer, demanding that he "institute proceedings against Journal du Dimanche and the journalists concerned, and keep us informed."[92]

By 8 July Maria had won her case[93] and been rewarded three hundred thousand francs in damages; less than a thousand dollars at the time.[94]

Discussions with Gorlinsky swirled around the concept of a concert tour with orchestra "all over the world" that October.[95] Suddenly Maria was diagnosed with tracheitis; the same infection that had scrapped her concert in Ostende in 1960.[96]

That spring Maria gave an interview for the radio program *Quotidien Musique* ("Music Daily") hosted by Philippe Caloni for French classical music station, France Musique.[97] She expressed her shock over what she perceived to be the degradation of society and its loss of values: "I don't know if you say this in French but—'integrity', well, that no longer exists. The kind of mother who would sacrifice herself for her children and all that—today, that no longer exists. Having children means nothing at all today; nothing at all . . ."[98]

It was a theme that she had been expressing since the advent of the hippie: "I find society becoming too permissive," she had confided to Kenneth Harris in 1970. "Today young people too much criticize their parents. They do not realise that parents have something valuable, the young ones do not have a sense of values which may easily slip from their grasp and which it may be harder than they realise to recover."[99]

Now that people were dressing more casually and behaving more loosely, Maria was aghast at the stagnant aesthetics. "Why—my God—are we removing the most beautiful things from life? That beauty that remains, it has a tendency to vanish with all this revolution and with *too* much liberty—too much of *this*, too much of *that*—because today we have an excess of *everything*."

Without determination, hard work and self-discipline, people lacked grit and verve. Born into lighter times, the baby boomers were deprived of the ambition that had been germane to both Maria and her colleagues: "A sense of wanting to *better* yourself, to tell yourself: 'I am *nothing* today, but *tomorrow*—I will have something to say, and you will listen to me.' You see, in a poor neighborhood, you will have that. Because you will be stimulated."

Unlike her socialist colleague Pasolini, Maria was at loss to understand what she believed was a growing aversion to opulence. "We need luxury to feed workers," she explained. "Today—you say, 'Luxury must *go*.' But *why* must it go? It gives work to *thousands* of workers. Not just factory workers. But women's clothes, the shopgirls who work on them, the thousands of professions that offers . . . We are attacking something that allows a great deal of people to live. When I sang at La Scala, a gown, for instance—would involve the work of *millions* of people . . . The jewels, the outer garment, the undergarments, the buttons, the zipper—thousands of things that put people to work."

As for her future projects, Maria told Caloni she lacked "the excitement, the reason to catch fire and be able to give the *best* of myself. Me—I'm *certain*—I'm ready to give what I can to the young; I am *ready*. But people don't *want* that. My colleagues could profit from that—but no; they're too embarrassed to come to Callas and ask for advice. Because if others were to find out, someone might say—I don't know—'She went to see Callas—isn't she ashamed! What did she go and do *that* for?' " In response to this Caloni asked whether Maria felt she was "becoming useless". "Exactly," she responded. "I am completely useless. *Completely* useless, you see."

Yet she had ideas—ideas about directing a production of *Werther*, an opera she loved but had never performed except for the "Air des Lettres." She recognized why few would seek her counsel. "I'm part of an elite, shall we say, that's a pain in the neck for them. What they have is a machine that functions ... how should I put it? Too *well*. They give each other compliments, throw flowers at each other. Well—I don't throw flowers; I say things as they are. So I'm no longer part of that circle ... I tell the truth and that ... you know, it irritates a lot of people ... Rolf Liebermann [Artistic Director of the Opéra de Paris] has never even asked me anything."[100]

A recent discovery didn't allay the impression that most of her colleagues were negligent. Dallas music critic John Ardoin—a dear friend—had published a biography of her including his transcriptions of their private conversations without seeking her consent. The book also cited the opinions of Maria's former colleagues. Franco Zeffirelli claimed, "Maria is a stupid woman, so professional that if she cannot cope with all the notes written or expected, she will not do a piece. This is a crime. She could have done so many *Norma*s if she had cheated a bit, but she couldn't accept the principle."

Furthermore, Ardoin resolved to write another tome that featured all her Juilliard classes. Maria had denied the public access to recordings of them. Now she targeted Ardoin point-blank: "So I see that you exploited me beautifully," she scribed in response to his letter.[101]

As the critic inched toward his goal she wrote to Peter Mennin, who was still president of The Juilliard School, to demand that he tether Ardoin.[102] The author promised her a fixed percentage of the royalties. She declined, attempting to resolve the matter with Mennin's assistant, Wriston Locklair. Although his written notes showed disapproval of Ardoin, the cause was not considered worthy of a fight on Juilliard's part.[103]

And so Maria didn't beat around the bush. Confronting Ardoin, she penned a missive:

> I have not answered your letter because I thought that an intelligent man should have understood before doing what you did that I could have been unhappy about your book and the fact that you took my tapes without my permission.
>
> The least you could have done—to be correct—was to inform me of your intentions and ask me whether I could be in agreement with such an idea.
>
> Instead of that you continue hiding behind the so called royalties flag ...
>
> I <u>should say</u> you have been thoughtless thinking that accounting me for your royalties would make me think that you are an excellent friend.
>
> My feeling therefore is that John Ardoin has never understood and most probably will never understand Maria Callas.[104]

This same John Ardoin would base his whole career on posing as a "Callas expert": narrating and writing two documentaries and multiple books.

When Stelios Galatopoulos—a writer who'd obtained permission before scribing his biographies[105]—later reminded Maria that she had "learned to live with the lies and irresponsible accusations of publicity-seeking people, believing in the long run she would be vindicated," she replied wearisomely: "Yes, you are absolutely right. But it has been far too long a run."[106]

That summer Maria retreated to Ibiza for a short stay. Evelynne Archer, sister of Anastasia Gratsos—the wife of Maria and Onassis' mutual friend Costa—lived on the island. Surveying the boutiques, she spent time on the Roca Llisa beach and even on the golf course running out of boredom.[107]

Three weeks later she was on Mount Athos, a site of twenty Byzantine monasteries, trying to gain access to a male-only community of monks. Even female animals were not admitted.[108] Staying together with Vasso Devetzi at Eagles Palace Hotel in Ouranoupoli, Maria was visited by the Mayor of Thessaloniki.[109]

Paparazzi lay in wait and caught their prey. "They are beasts! All dressed, they are not interested, but in a bathing suit, ah, that's what they want—am I fat—am I thin—who is with me!" Maria complained in a letter to Nadia Stancioff on 23 August.[110] That said, she was allegedly happy to have come back "beautifully bronze" and "full of health"—as she notified Irving Kolodin—and was planning to visit New York.[111]

The gift of a pirate recording of her 1952 Turin concert from fan Oscar Coltellacci elated her. "You don't know how much pleasure I got from the discs that you sent me," she scribed. "God how I sang well! I got the record on the 15 August, my name day according to my religion (Greek Orthodox!) . . . I am happy with hearing Lakmé! The rest I'll listen to by the end of the week—I'll have plenty of time."[112]

Seeking to impart a sliver of her wisdom, that November Maria received Leonard Bernstein's new friend with the maestro in tow: Hungarian soprano Sylvia Sass. "What did you bring to sing with me?" she asked. "Some *Tosca* arias . . ."—"It's too easy." Instinctively Maria rummaged through the singer's scores and pulled out *Traviata*. Thus began another lecture: "I explained to her that that you must look to the dynamics," Maria recollected in a conversation with theatrical producer Alan Sievewright. "Why won't they, having gone through the entire role, go back, break it down phrase by phrase, bar by bar? You know I also would really like to get at the conductors; so often in Mozart you will find that the rhythms for the Queen of Night are not what they should be."[113]

Appointing Elvira de Hidalgo to accept an award on her behalf in Milan,[114] Maria kept in touch with many friends. "I thank you for remembering me as usual on my birthday," she wrote Leo Lerman that Christmas. "And I am happy to hear that they also remembered at the radio."[115]

Low blood pressure tormented her again in early 1977. "It makes me feel low and without desire for anything—but in a week I'll be back to normal,"[116] she alerted her godfather on February 21st. At around that time she also travelled to London to visit Galatopoulos "in excellent spirits" and "again interested in singing". He entertained Maria with a pirate recording of her 1957 Athenian concert. "Her joy was great," he would later remember, "and at certain passages in the 'Liebestod' she sang along with the recording."[117]

In their subsequent conversations at her Paris apartment she seemed more composed than the nocturnal Maria who battled her sleeplessness with perpetual phone calls. Repeating statements that had constituted her initial creed, she claimed: "I am never theatrical in life . . . Decorum has always been fundamental," though it had taken a backseat in recent years. Despite her frequent self-aggrandizement she still knew well, "The moment we get too big for our boots, we are really finished."[118]

When Galatopoulos attempted to open up her feelings regarding Onassis' death, Maria conceded, "Of course I miss him but I do try not to become a complete sentimental fool, you know!"[119] Less inclined to receive guests than previously, she nevertheless often dined with Prince Rainier and Princess Grace.[120]

Early in March Maria sat down with Italian journalist Dora Ossenska to record a documentary interview for a program entitled "La Scala e i suoi protagonisti" ("La Scala and Its Heroes"). Filmed at her apartment, the footage presented Maria reminiscing about her relationship with La Scala and referring to it as "such a happy marriage—an unforgettably happy marriage." She recalled coming home after every rehearsal. "There would begin the real creation; I would look back at what I had tried doing that day and think about what I would try the next, what was about to happen, how I should construct the character, how I should sing . . . Creation exactly."[121]

Zeffirelli wanted to persuade her to sing Monteverdi's *The Coronation of Poppaea*. "Poppaea doesn't have the biggest part." He offered her *The Merry Widow*. "Callas, in musical comedy? Me in an operetta?"[122]

Conversing with Galatopoulos that May, she was determined to drive home her strength: "living alone was not a great calamity."[123] A month before she had sought refuge in the snowy valleys of Swiss haven Crans-Montana; canvassing its corners with a group of friends.[124] While a lot of media focused on her "loneliness" in these years, solitude remained her choice. She was now fifty-three years old and not intent on scouting for another man. Both social and professional proposals were being flung at her incessantly. Living at times in isolation was no terminal disease. If Maria Callas had a plan, she tended at the very least to try to execute it. Socializing more did not occur to her.

As for her moods, they swung continuously. Maintaining her manners, she responded to an invitation from Stephen Bill, Executive Director for The Festival of Sydney, to decline his request for a vocal performance.[125] Finally that June Maria made a trip to New York—lunching at the Plaza with an old Scarpia to her Tosca, George London[126] and paying Montserrat Caballé a visit with familiar recommendations: "Pay attention to this passage; it's difficult. Pay attention to this phrase, because it goes like this . . . You *can* sing it; even I couldn't do any better."[127]

She attended a party hosted by co-founder of the New York City Ballet, Lincoln Kirstein. Present at the occasion, Lord Harewood found in her "a rather more subdued, and, curiously enough, more relaxed version of what I had known."[128]

So there was resignation. This was not the Callas who had told reporters that her voice was coming back; that she was singing "better" than nine years before. Acceptance nonetheless did not accompany the state of mind. To Andy Embiricos of the Embiricos clan she responded to a remark that she "wasn't herself" with "But the real me doesn't exist anymore."[129]

When that July Galatopoulos enquired if she might write her memoirs, Maria replied, "My memoirs are in the music I interpret—the only way I can write about my art or about myself—and my recordings, for what they are worth, have preserved my story. In any case, you have already written about me." After a contemplative pause she completed the answer. "Listen Stelios, don't you think I am too young to write my memoirs? I am not eighty yet, you know."[130]

Often her response to why she wasn't singing didn't center so much on her struggles as it did on opera's perilous condition. "Even when I was extremely busy, I would notice that the quality of the conductor . . . wasn't what it used to be," she had told Philippe Caloni in April 1976.[131] Variously she would uncover thoughts about the opera stagings she *did* see: among them a *Medea* televised from the Chorégies d'Orange Festival. Its performers had tossed the Golden Fleece carelessly onto the ground. "Why did the singers allow the director to do that kind of thing. I do not understand why so many singers do not stand up for what they know to be right."[132]

There was the second act of a *Faust* she had also beheld: set in a Manhattan ghetto, boasting linen dangling on the clotheslines. "It's a real *downfall*," Maria would say. "The *worst* that could exist . . ." Likewise she cited a *Don Giovanni* at the Paris Opéra set "instead of at a palace—I mean, I can see it was a sort of palace—but shall we say, it was more like a house where men worked on a scaffold . . . Let's forget about whether or not I'd be able to sing—say you gave me *carte blanche*. I'll respond very honestly: I couldn't do it. And it's not a question of the production. It's a question of *quality*. I don't have the conductor for a—a *Traviata*. Who could do it—[Carlo Maria] Giulini, yes. But he no longer conducts opera."[133]

Despite the use of these examples to deflect from her defective voice, many of Maria's peers were in agreement with her for a gamut of both similar and different reasons. In 1987 Georges Prêtre would lament, "Stars of today are intolerable, professionally speaking, with rare exceptions."[134]

Fifteen years later Joan Sutherland would admit having discussed the deterioration of training with sopranos Birgit Nilsson and Sena Jurinac. "Today the young singers do not develop a basic vocal technique," she professed. "They don't know how to breathe and support and project the sound. They breathe from here," Sutherland signaled to her chest, "and they don't support anything. They sing from here," she pointed at her throat, "but they don't project the sound into the cavities of the mouth and use the high palate. You see them holding on like this, down in their throat. It's so unrelaxed ... The old manuals were right. [Manuel] García, [Giovanni Battista] Lamperti, the others. People don't learn how to breathe, support and project ... I don't know where the teachers have gone."[135]

A 2013 conversation on the New York classical music station WQXR between Marilyn Horne and conductor James Levine centered on the "death of good singers" on both sides of the Atlantic. Both conceded "it would be impossible to stage a great, traditional opera with the right singers today."[136]

Thus even if Maria's harsh appraisal of the opera scene was prematurely scathing at a time when Karajan and Bernstein still conducted and sopranos Caballé and Sutherland held sway, it may have been prophetic.

The problem was she didn't plan to remedy it. Singing was her art; directing and teaching were not. Eventually that summer she alerted Galatopoulos she was preparing to record *Werther*. Alfredo Kraus—who had shared her stage in a 1958 Lisbon production of *La traviata*—would embody the titular role; Georges Prêtre had agreed to conduct. "I am still a little down because of my recent bout of influenza and can't take antibiotics but, God willing, I will be all right in the autumn," she confided to him. "You know how the dryness of the summer affects my voice."

To demonstrate what she believed was an improved condition of her voice Maria sang "Pleurez, pleurez mes yeux" from Massenet's *Le Cid* to her friend, followed by *La sonnambula*'s "Ah, non credea mirarti."[137] A private recording of her singing "Deh! Non m'abbandonar!" from Verdi's *La forza del destino* was made in this period.

That summer Teresa Berganza was singing *Carmen* in Edinburgh. Maria didn't neglect to send her a basket of flowers to wish her good luck.[138] Janine Reiss worked hard with her on *Werther*'s Charlotte: a character who, in the coach's words, "[Maria] believed was someone of duty and discipline who matched her personality."[139] Charlotte's unwavering fidelity toward her husband leads her to reject Werther, the man she is in love with; plunging him into a self-destructive spiral ending in his suicide.

Appearing in good spirits, Maria received Georges Prêtre and his wife for dinner.[140] She was spending time immersed in books about spirituality, such as a tome entitled *Spirits and Spiritual Words*.[141] It had evoked an interest in the character of Mary Magdalene. Maria kept wondering why an opera had never been written about her.[142] The apostle's sacrifice for Jesus was an act she found relatable: she drew a parallel between the woman's courage and her selflessness in music's inexhaustible domain.

"If we have managed to persuade and to *exhilarate* you, that means we have *earned* our reality,"[143] Maria had explained to Caloni the previous year.

Even if *carte blanche* had been an option she no longer had hers.

23.

"Beauty is truth."

Lamenting a lost summer early that September, Maria planned to spend a period vacationing once more at George Moore's house in Sotogrande, Spain that month.[1] On the 1st she wrote to her old friend, costumier Umberto Tirelli:

> I was sorry that I was not able to come to Capri. This year travelling seems like such an enormous thing to me (almost a crisis) that I deprived myself of a joyous, tranquil holiday on which you would have spoiled me (something I adore) . . .
> I am here in Paris amidst these beautiful scores of Rossini and Donizetti, working for my own sake, for no reason other than to seek the right proportions in each piece and, if the desire should come back to me, to put this work I'm doing on a record. I must find again my enthusiasm for singing. But for the moment it's exhausted, with the exception of the fun I have discovering how many splendid things there are in music and how much they ruin them—singing as they do today.
> And yet it's so easy, simple the way I look at music, why is it so impossible for them? . . .
> Today I need support even though my faith in my own musicality remains unshakeable.[2]

That summer she had telephoned Dorle Soria and mentioned "not feeling well".[3] Now she received Eliette von Karajan and regaled her with loops of her lacy remembrances.[4]

Another day that September 1977 she attended a breakfast at Princess Grace's Paris apartment. Franco Mannino—an old composer friend whom she had known since 1949—was present, together with young Princess Caroline. A monologue of jabbering about the past ensued. "She shared little anecdotes about certain colleagues of hers who had gone out of their way to take the first bows at the end of performances. She spoke of Herbert von Karajan, Giuseppe Di Stefano, Tito Gobbi, Mario Del Monaco—and a whole lot of pushing and shoving that had gone on to be first at the curtain call," Mannino wrote.[5]

For the 10 or 11 September Maria had scheduled a meeting with opera director and choreographer Maurice Béjart; tentative discussions regarding a film had begun.[6] Ringing her doorbell, Béjart was informed that Maria was ill and would rather receive him upon her recovery. Ferruccio proffered him the note that she had left:

> Next week I'll be able to see you both healthy and happy. For now I've been prescribed a week of total rest. Tell me if you can't make it. All my best, Maria

Having spoken on the phone, the pair rescheduled their appointment.[7] Training wasn't off her schedule, nonetheless. That 15 September she had her usual session with Janine Reiss, who was scheduled to fly to New York to work with Herbert von Karajan. She and Maria had been studying Werther's Charlotte; the concept of a record was still on the cards. "It's not very nice, you know, having a coach who travels all the time the way you do!" Maria jokingly rebuked her. "You're leaving me here alone! And then you know I want to record Charlotte and Georges Prêtre wants to do it with me." Reiss promised to return as soon as possible and the two women warmly parted.[8]

On the morning of Friday 16 September Bettina Brentano was in hospital about to have an appendectomy. Babbling with Maria on the phone, the girl had to suspend their conversation for her surgery and said that she would call her back that afternoon.[9]

Maria had a boiled egg, toast and coffee for her breakfast. For that day she had planned a visit to the hairdresser. Heading to the bathroom to get dressed, she felt a sudden headache overcome her and lay down in bed.[10] Of late she had been suffering from back pain on the left side that a doctor had allegedly attributed to flu and rheumatism. Bruna rushed to her and offered spoonfuls of her coffee while Ferruccio tried in vain to call a handful of Maria's doctors. Suffering a heart attack, she failed to respond to their efforts to keep her alert. At 1:30 pm Paris time Maria died from cardiac arrest. Arriving shortly before 2:15, the doctor was unable to revive her. At four the press announced her death.[11]

Reiss arrived at JFK airport the following day. A porter—in her words, a "big black man"—immediately offered to carry her luggage. They were heavy; packed with bulging scores. "Ma'am, do you work in fashion?" he enquired. "Not at all—I'm coming to New York to work at the Met."—"Did you know that a famous opera singer died yesterday?"—"No. Who's that?"— "Maria Callas." Reiss was silent. "That's impossible. I spoke to her a couple days ago."[12]

For her funeral attire Bruna dressed Maria in a "long gray silken dress".[13] Beholding her stretched out along her bed, Michel Glotz paid his respects. "She had become again the Traviata I had seen in 1955," he wrote. "A very long braid curving around her face, radiating with a poignant, yet a peaceful beauty."[14]

Maria was going to be cremated. No concrete evidence supported this decision; her casual friend Vasso Devetzi merely claimed this was her wish to sister Jackie. It was an odd happenstance. Asked about Devetzi some months earlier by Galatopoulos, Maria had "with a typical Greek wave of the hand, dismissed the idea of a friend."[15] Even if cremation *had* been her desire, it was doubtful she had shared it shortly before passing.[16] Through inexplicable and unknown means, Devetzi enlisted the help of a lawyer and record executive,[17] Jean Roire, to preclude the compulsory autopsy. Despite being evident, the cause of death was never stated by a coroner.[18]

The funeral took place on 20 September at the Cathédrale grecque Saint-Étienne de Paris, a Greek Orthodox church on rue Georges Bizet.[19] The following week Maria was cremated. Her urn of ashes was buried at the Père Lachaise Cemetery.[20] Less than two years later, on 3 June 1979, they were scattered across the Aegean Sea.[21]

The fate of Maria's estate devolved into macabre. Vasso Devetzi ingratiated herself with Jackie Callas, insisting that Maria hadn't signed a will.[22] Peter Andry of EMI—one of the few who saw Maria on her deathbed—would remember hearing at the time of how "Devetzi had instantly assumed control of the apartment, seized the keys, and removed practically all of Maria's private papers."[23]

Multiple bidders were found for the goods. Meneghini eagerly resurfaced after a brief silence in the press, claiming Maria had produced a will on 24 April 1954 leaving her fortune to him.[24] It was a single sentence on a tiny note that any modern court would easily have disregarded. Nonetheless it managed to be taken seriously.[25]

Devetzi convinced Jackie and Evangelia Callas that without the presence of a will they would automatically be entitled to Maria's estate. After a court decreed that all of it be halved between them and the designated Meneghini, she insisted that she "look after it all" on Evangelia and Jackie's behalf, later arranging for the boxes of Maria's possessions to be sent straight to her.

In 1979 Devetzi appeared in court with a typed letter conferring to her the title of Executor of Maria's estate. Clumsily pasted at the bottom was a photocopy of Maria's signature Devetzi had obtained from a completely unrelated letter from her.[26] The court approved the document's validity and granted her the title.

Jackie was stunned to see Devetzi and her lawyer, Jean Roire, bring "only seven parcels" from the estate to her and her mother. According to Jackie there were supposed to be another "ninety". Devetzi accused Meneghini of stealing them—simultaneously promising ninety-five parcels from the collection to the City of Paris to open a Maria Callas museum. While an exhibition would take place that year, a museum never opened.[27]

Items from Maria's estate that Devetzi had taken were eventually sold by her various descendants to private collectors and bidders at auctions.[28] Meneghini kept a large amount of letters she had sent to him and others through the period of their marriage, as well as half her fortune.[29]

Ironically in 1961 Maria had asked her secretary, Teresa d'Addato, to respond to a letter regarding her estate to the American Guild of Musical Artists: "Madame Callas has given your kind request her attention, but she does not wish for the moment to designate anybody as her beneficiary. I am therefore returning unfilled the card you sent her to be completed."[30] During these posthumous arrangements the letter remained undiscovered.

Papers and television programs were abundant in their tributes. Among them Vittorio Gui sent Maria a telegram: "An era ends with you, but your immortality begins. With love, Your Vittorio."[31]

That immortality has been of greater worth to most than any part or parcel of her bounteous estate. It is the lifeblood on which tabloids run over four decades after her untimely death, intrepid grind for rumor mills and crass intrusions on the study of her art; dust-costumed tomes in thrift stores.

In its natural form of pure and unadulterated gold, it is a band of irrepressible recordings that attest to art's superiority to perishable matter. All too often its consumers have to squint to seize a glimpse of it behind a guise of cheap vermeil; a sparkling margin visible through artifice. Or else they have to purchase it ensconced in a dull shade of copper alloy: diatribes attributing her magic to the bulging belly of the paparazzi beast; the claim that she was little more than operatic dynamite.

Sometimes Maria's words were elementary to the point that listeners believed she struggled to identify her source of power. "There are marvelous voices, and marvelous young girls full of respect for me . . ." she told a journalist in 1970. "But you know, you have to go *further* than that in opera. I tried to go *further*. They—they remain in normality, there is nothing original in their interpretation. It's not their fault: they understand me and respect me, but they can't go where I could go."[32]

In 1958 a scribe relayed a conversation with her. Callas had stressed that she no longer wanted to be deemed a "haughty freak;" she hoped one day the public would discover she was "here only to sing and perform art" because "time shows up the truth . . . time shows up everything."[33]

Love of singing was the only element that made her "bent," if one can even call it that. There was no unusual cruelty; no Marlon Brando-esque explosions or pretensions in the vein of the "divine one" of the nineteenth century, Sarah Bernhardt. Across the spectrum of great artists she remained delectable outside her art.

"I don't know its source, but it seems to keep me going on and on. There are certain things you can't explain even to yourself," was how Maria described her devotion.[34] "Miraculous things happen when one is onstage;

one is in a second state; hypersensitive."[35] The elixir that she drank when in the spell of her creations made the other forces in her life look stumped.

It was gravity in her eyes. Even when she wanted otherwise.

In the words of Swiss scribe Denis de Rougemont, "Love ceases to be a demon only when he ceases to be a god."[36] This love of her art controlled her—call it holy, call it poisonous. It steered her every action, stilled her other thirsts in life and sterilized her secondary wants.

Like many effervescent characters and artists, she was the victim of a zealous and insatiable passion. It was simply not the kind that fills the reams of nineteenth-century novels or the scripts of HBO shows. It was neither controversial, nor salacious, nor taboo. But you can't call it unoriginal.

"Callas stands as queen of the music mountain, having broken every rule and convention," Lawrence Kelly wrote in 1959.[37] We know that much. We know her fame was such that a sports writer cited a beloved tennis player's "Callas touch at Wimbledon;"[38] we know her records were the only operatic ones whose sales could rival those of Elvis Presley.[39]

Yet there's no magic potion to acquire it; no imbibable opiate to sniff even a hint. "It was, to use her own words, like trying to find the combination of a safe," wrote Stelios Galatopoulos. "More often than not she succeeded in opening the safe but without confiding in her audience the combination; nor did she remember it herself, for every time she had to find it anew."[40]

You cannot be inoculated with it. In spite of surgical advances human brains cannot be altered to possess it; neither can the rest of the anatomy. "There was one thing that could make her very sad," Janine Reiss would remember. "She had this feeling a little while before her death that the moment she would be gone, a certain way of working and conceiving an interpretation would vanish together with her."[41]

And it did.

It didn't help that Maria was not the most learned of artists—and incurred the dislike of a number of scholars and critics. She hadn't spent her hours analyzing Wieland Wagner's revolutionary stage direction or the creed of Stanislavsky. None of her attitude could be confined to a specific "method" ready for a pocket book of bullet-sized advice.

Observation was a great part of her work—not just of fellow singers but of pianists and violinists, cabaret dancers, actors and ballerinas. And yes—an artist has a temperament. Who doesn't have a temperament? *Boston Globe* theatre critic Cyrus Durgin scribed in Maria's defense: "In recent years there has been a certain amount of drivel about artists being like any other people. Well, in the basic physical aspects they are like other people, but that is where the comparison stops. Otherwise artists are not, they could not be, like other people. They are highly talented, sometimes to the point of genius. But they must involve themselves in art with a concentration amounting to fury ... Artists live at a higher emotional voltage than ordinary people. It is not only natural to them to do so, it is a necessity."[42]

A compulsion to decrypt and codify thrives in the age of the technocracy. Emotions can be read in neuroimaging; psychotropic drugs can alter inner states and labels can—apparently—account for *everything*. Scholarly research is inane unless it can extract a formula: a social or else scientific lesson; an algebraic calculation or a triple-barreled novel term. Writing in 1959, Maria mused, "In a strange way I really have nothing to do with my own career. Intentions gather up inside me no matter what I think. Decisions are borne in upon me. Whether I like it or not I am a fatalist."[43]

You do not work toward being a "Callas" any more than you might work toward being a "Plato" or a "Beethoven" or "Shakespeare". She engraved her name in time with such a sharp knife that millennia would have to pass before the climate weathered it.

Yet anyone can work toward creating ... *something*. In never being satisfied—in restless, endless study and immoveable resolve to fuel her self-improvement—Maria Callas proved that nothing is enough. The outgrowth of her glory did not breed a herd of mini-Callases—and yet it tipped the scales of operatic standards for a while. There was a period, now gone, when it was popular to stage bel canto operas; to perform them was a profitable thing for a soprano. Her legacy convinced critics acting was a *sine qua non*.

The propulsive work ethic insisted on everyone doing their best—no matter the subject at hand. "Nothing is a sacrifice for those who love their work," she said in 1969. "I think that in *all* professions—whatever it is— even the job of cleaning this table, there is someone who will do it *well*, and there is someone who will do it *badly*. You can't escape that; it's not a sacrifice, it is a *duty*."[44]

There was no subconscious ranking of professions. "Even the least utility man, even those who play the smallest parts and with whom I sang during my long career, have given me something and have in a certain way contributed to my artistic forming. In our work everybody, independently of the position they hold in the musical or artistic world, can teach you something which enriches your personality," she said in 1957.[45]

The lessons learnt? Being resigned is not in anybody's interests. As David Frost played "Casta diva" from her 1954 studio recording of *Norma*, Maria was asked, "Did you hear faults when you were listening?" She was coy; a little playful. "No."—"Good."—"But I *could've* made it better *always*— that's our *hope*; all our lives—I'll *die*, never having achieved the perfection I would have *wanted*."[46]

Give and take is not a part of it—because the goal is *always* out of reach. "If you love music truly you can only feel humble before its infinite potentialities and recognize one's own limitations in serving it—perhaps at the cost of never knowing any lasting, consistent happiness," averred the soprano.[47]

Great art is obscure; it is intangible. Many people in the arts and elsewhere were and are career-obsessed; they will continue to insist their motive is its lofty prize. But what is art? And who decides what fits and what does not? "It is hard when you see the standards of those who twist the truth and manipulate the facts and who spread propaganda for their selfish ends being imposed upon the multitude," Maria remarked in 1961. "[They] do not know enough to recognise the lies and deceits for what they are. It is hard when you see the people swallowing as artistic values and achievement what businessmen select for them to suit their pockets."[48]

The establishment—whoever they may be—will often mask ulterior motives with a sheath of demagoguery. A professional who wants to make an impact has the duty to sustain the faith in their creative mind: to not be swayed.

Art does not consist of laboring a point, exposing all the entrails of one's soul or chronically perseverating with an argument. There is a vast difference between self-expression and creative urges. One is a catharsis; therapeutic. Many emotional and most neurotic individuals enjoy the process: it can happen in a journalistic column, blog or diary. Depending on selective artful instincts talent can be sparked. Sometimes.

The other has the interests of an audience in mind: one present and one never-to-be-seen. In order to divine that audience's tastes the artist must conserve a mental registry of everything: their discipline and others'; what has come before and after—without grudge and without bias. Excising clichés and preserving good traditions and creating novel shapes of rhythms, metaphors, inflections of the voice or brushstrokes means incessant and instinctive study. This creates a gift of panoramic observation: universal intuition that can leave the artist either stumped or spoilt for choice.

"What is the feeling you get when you hear an ovation at the end of a performance?" David Frost asked. "I mean, is it a thrill like no other, or . . ."—"No," came Maria's blunt response. "Not really—you feel a satisfaction; sometimes you feel that er . . . you don't deserve it . . . it's *gratifying*." She sighed. "It's not all that important; it *is* of course, but . . . you know, your *work* is more important."—"What's the longest ovation you can remember?" Maria sighed again. "I can't remember."—"Really? All the number of curtain calls."—"Not really." There was a pause. "It isn't that important."

In real art there is no prize; no site at which to pitch a flag. Comprehending one's ideal is unattainable; the concept is enrobed in mystery. "Certain modernists are trying to send romanticism and idealism down the drain," Maria remarked in 1971. "I maintain there will always be romanticism and idealism. In these things we do not change. Even though man can now go to the moon, the body continues to maintain its temperature."[49]

In the 1970s the value of aesthetics was diminishing. "They want to remove *beauty*," Maria lamented. "If you remove beauty—from anything—even from a person; in every person, in every trinket, in every book—we must look for the beauty *within*. If we remove beauty, what's left? That makes animals better than *us*."[50]

The ideal is abstract; unseizable, unquantifiable and indescribable. It's a rogue of which no sketch artist could draw a corresponding face; computer scientists could not hack into it. An artist does not know the pinnacle of happiness upon reception of a Nobel Prize or Oscar. The wily zenith dangles within reach at a specific moment in the midst of writing or onstage; mid-symphony or mid-recording. Teasily the tinge of an ephemeral intoxication offers the relieving knowledge that their craft has poked the never-ending sky.

Real art follows rules—about technique, about tradition—but encompasses no finite, comprehensive list. Void of a didactic purpose, it is empty of ulterior motives. It does not skew toward a demographic; neither does it pander to a herd or kowtow to a trend. Its purity and authenticity are those of Mount Vesuvius or the Grand Canyon. The only difference is that it is human-made—not sculpted by Earth's forces.

Maria Callas worked toward this kind of beauty. As with other human beings, there were times when she fell short of its fulfillment. Her legacy cannot transfer her gifts to others. Its novelty nevertheless can engineer constituents of *other* novelty; its risks can drive interpreters to gamble in the lottery of art.

And while it is beyond the dreams of most to mirror them; while many would prefer to fixate on their private lives or other kinds of work, no one is void of a select patch in their life in need of betterment; an area they could ameliorate with greater open-mindedness. Knowing something of Maria Callas gives an impetus.

"Music must always be beautiful and beauty is truth," she once told a reporter.[51]

Myths will be propagated, circled and distributed; they'll rise and swell and reach a greater visibility like smoke rings from a feverish volcano. And like those smoke rings they will dissipate throughout the ether and their texture shall be made diaphanous until they vanish into history.

History is not The Callas Imprint.

Legend

Correspondence and Documents

Alberta Masiello Papers, JPB 03-13. Music Division, The New York Public Library for the Performing Arts [AMAS]

Alexis Minotis Papers, The Katina Paxinou and Alexis Minotis Archive | National Bank of Greece Cultural Foundation–Hellenic Literary and Historical Archive (MIET–ELIA) [AMP]

Alfred A. Knopf, Inc. Records (Manuscript Collection MS-00062). Harry Ransom Center, The University of Texas at Austin [AKP]

Archives of the Juilliard School, New York [JSA]

Archives of the Metropolitan Opera, New York [AMO]

Collection of Bruno Antoniolli, Desenzano del Garda, bequeathed to him from the Estate of Elvira de Hidalgo [CBA]

Collection of Private Collector Fabio Gervasoni, Lecco [CFG]

Collection of Fondazione Marzotto: The Estate of Collector Bruno Tosi of Venice [CFM]

Collection of Giovanni Mion, Grandson of Callas' Lawyer Augusto Caldi Scalcini [CGM]

Collection of Collector Nicos Haralabopoulos, Athens [CNH]

Dorle Soria Papers, JPB 13-16. Music Division, The New York Public Library for the Performing Arts [DSP]

Harold Rosenthal Papers, Music Collections, British Library, London [HRP]

Herbert Weinstock Collection, JPB 92-2. Music Division, The New York Public Library for the Performing Arts [HWP]

Irving Kolodin Papers, JPB 06-40. Music Division, The New York Public Library for the Performing Arts [IKP]

Leo Lerman Papers, Rare Book & Manuscript Library, Columbia University in the City of New York [LLP]

Luchino Visconti Papers, Fondazione Gramsci, Rome [LVP]

Pier Paolo Pasolini Collection, Archivio Contemporaneo A. Bonsanti, Archivio Gabinetto Vieusseux, Florence [PPP]

Robert Baxter Collection (featuring reproductions of correspondence between Callas and her godfather, Leonidas Lantzounis), Stanford University Archive of Recorded Sound [RBC]

Sander Gorlinsky Collection, Victoria & Albert Museum Performing Arts Archive, Blythe House, London [SGC]

Selected Interviews with Callas

The Norman Ross Show (Norman Ross), WGN Radio Chicago, 17 November 1957 [Ross: 1957]

Person on Person (Edward Murrow), CBS, 24 January 1958 [Murrow: 1958]

Hy Gardner Calling (Hy Gardner), NBC, 26 February 1958 [Gardner: 1958]

Music Through the Night (Harry Fleetwood), WRCA New York, 13 and 27 March 1958 [Fleetwood: 1958]

Small World (Edward Murrow), CBS, 4 and 11 January 1959 [Murrow: 1959]

"Why They Call me 'Tigress'—and why it's wrong," (John Cruesemann), *Daily Express*, 6 April 1959 [Cruesemann: 1959]

Trois jours avec Maria Callas (Micheline Banzet), ORTF Radio, 5 February 1965 [Banzet: 1965]

William Weaver, Interview with Callas aired during the Metropolitan Opera's radio broadcast of Verdi's *Ernani*, 10 April 1965 [Weaver: 1965]

Les grands interprètes (Bernard Gavoty), ORTF Television, 2 May 1965 [Gavoty: 1965]

"Opera News on the Air" (Edward Downes), 30 December 1967 and 13 January 1968, Independent Metropolitan Opera Radio Network [Downes: 1967]

Callas on Opera and *Callas on Norma*, (Lord George Harewood), BBC Television, recorded on 24 April 1968 and broadcast on 24–27 June 1968. Published on *The Callas Edition: Volume Six*, IMC Music Ltd., 1998 [Harewood: 1968]

Collector's Corner (John Ardoin), WFMT Dallas Radio, 13 September 1968 [Ardoin: 1968]

L'invité du dimanche (Pierre Desgraupes), ORTF-TV, 20 April 1969 [Desgraupes: 1969]

Sylvie de Nussac & Michele Cotta, "L'Express va plus loin avec Maria Callas," *L'Express*, 19 January 1970 [de Nussac & Cotta: 1970]

Kenneth Harris, "Callas," (Interview), *The Observer*, 8 and 15 February 1970 [Harris: 1970]

The David Frost Show (David Frost), CBS, 10 December 1970 [Frost: 1970]

Naomi Barry, "The Singer Is Nothing But the Servant of the Genius," *The International Herald Tribune*, 30 June 1971 [Barry: 1971]

John Gruen, "I am a very normal human being," *The New York Times*, 31 October 1971 [Gruen: 1971]

60 Minutes (Mike Wallace), CBS, 3 February 1974 [Wallace: 1974]

France Musique (Philippe Caloni), April 1976. Published in *Maria Callas La Légende*, EMI France 2000 [Caloni: 1976]

Notes

All sources in other languages have been translated by the author unless otherwise stated.

Prologue: "Break normality."

1 Eugenio Gara, *Maria Callas: Great Concert Artists*, trans. Barbara Wall (Geneva: René Kister, 1958), 27.

2 William Weaver, "Remembering Callas: Some Confessions of a Fan" in Tosi, *The Young Maria Callas* (Toronto: Guernica Editions, 2010), 61.

3 Yves Saint Laurent, "The End of a Dream," trans. in David Lowe, *Callas: As They Saw Her* (London: Robson Books Ltd, 1987), 126–29.

4 "Callasite" ("The Talk of the Town," *The New Yorker*, 15 March 1958); "Callasiano" ("I Trucchi del mestiere," *Classic Voice*, no. 102, November 2007); "callasien" ("Cinéma et opéra: Portrait de l'artiste en belle dame," *Commentaire*, 13 January 1981, no. 13).

5 Photo caption in *The Illustrated London News*, 3 February 1962; Greg MacGregor, "Callas Devotees Wait At The Met," *The New York Times*, 15 March 1965.

6 Giovanni Battista Meneghini, *Maria Callas, mia moglie* (Milan: Rusconi Libri, 1981), 203.

7 Diana Vreeland & Christopher Hemphill, *Allure* (San Francisco: Chronicle Books, 2010), 8.

8 Harewood: 1968

9 Lord Harewood (George Lascelles), *The Tongs and Bones: The Memoirs of Lord Harewood* (London: Weidenfeld & Nicholson, 1981), 228.

10 Claudia Cassidy, "Maria 'touched by God's finger,'" *Chicago Tribune*, 18 September 1977.

11 "From Our Special Correspondent: Mme. Callas on Opera," *The Times*, 22 June 1959.

12 Ira Siff, "The Associate," *Opera News*, 10 April 2001.

13 Downes: 1967

14 Callas, "I am not guilty of those Callas scandals," *Life*, 21 April 1959.

15 Jane Boutwell, "Processo alla Callas," *The New Yorker*, 25 April 1971.

16 Peter Conrad, "The beast within the beauty: Review of Julie Kavanagh's *Rudolf Nureyev: The Life*," *The Guardian*, 23 September 2007.

17 April FitzLyon, *Maria Malibran: Diva of the Romantic Age* (London: Souvenir Press, 1987), 169.

18 Elizabeth Silverthorne, *Sarah Bernhardt* (New York: Chelsea House Publications, 2004), 36.

19 Dalya Alberge, "Letters and secret files reveal the tormented files of Lina Prokofiev," *The Guardian*, 10 March 2013.

20 Frost: 1970

21 Matthew Gurewitsch, "Forget the Callas Legend," The Atlantic, 1 April 1999, https://www.theatlantic.com/magazine/archive/1999/04/forget-the-callas-legend/377551.

22 Harris: 1970

23 Elvira de Hidalgo to Callas, 15 November 1976 [CNH].

24 Dorle Soria, "Greek Sorceress," *Opera News*, November 1977.

25 Eileen Farrell & Brian Kellow, *Can't Help Singing: The Life of Eileen Farrell* (Boston: Northeastern University Press, 1999), 131.

26 George Jellinek, *Callas: Portrait of a Prima Donna* (New York: Dover Publications, New Edition, 1986), 309.

27 Stelios Galatopoulos, *Sacred Monster* (London: Fourth Estate, 1998), 294.

28 Callas to Irving Kolodin, 25 January 1959 [IKP].

29 Michel Glotz, *La note bleue* (Paris: Lattès, 2003), 194.

30 Fleetwood: 1958

31 Giovanna Lomazzi, "Volle Dimagrire Contro La Volontà di Meneghini," *La Settimana Incom Illustrata*, 23 February 1961.

32 Harewood, 235.

33 Downes: 1967

34 Desgraupes: 1969

35 Callas to Renzo Rossellini, 26 July 1961, in Christie's: Live Auctions 2357, Lot 6 (Rome: Christie's Auctions, 15 June 1999). Accessed at https://www.christies.com/en/lot/lot-1531266.

36 Banzet: 1965

37 Murrow: 1958

38 Frost: 1970

39 Murrow: 1959

40 Isabelle Ayre, *Entretiens avec Janine Reiss* (Lyon: Kirographaires Editions, 2013), 93.

41 Alexis Minotis to Nicola Rescigno, 2 September 1958 [AMP].

42 Caloni: 1976

43 Callas to Giovanni Battista Meneghini, 18 November 1948 in Renzo Allegri, *Maria Callas: Lettere d'amore* (Milan: Mondadori, 2008), 97.

44 Cruesemann: 1959

45 Soria, "Greek Sorceress."

46 "From Our Special Correspondent: Mme. Callas on Opera."

47 Callas, "The Lyric Tradition," master classes at The Juilliard School of Music (class of 15 November 1971). Accessed at https://www.youtube.com/playlist?list=PLYKjA1MofMMSQdjc3uHGGgVT24acipZnq.

48 Callas to Meneghini, 18 November 1948 in Allegri, *Maria Callas: Lettere d'amore*, 96.

49 Leo Lerman ed. Stephen Pascal, *The Grand Surprise: The Journals of Leo Lerman* (New York: Knopf, 2007), 175.

50 Isaiah Berlin, *Enlightening: LETTERS 1946–1960* (London: Chatto & Windus, 2009), 691.

51 Boutwell, "Processo alla Callas."

52 Banzet: 1965

53 Cruesemann: 1959

54 Callas to Leo Lerman, 15 December 1963 [LLP].

55 Lerman, 506.

56 April Fitzlyon, *The Price of Genius: The Life of Pauline Viardot* (London: John Calder, 1964), 349–50.

1. "Voluptuous intoxication"

1 de Nussac & Cotta: 1970

2 In December 1967 Maria asked her friend Fabrizio Melano to obtain her birth certificate from the New York Bureau of Vital Statistics. He subsequently sent her the original and kept two copies, one of which he gave to the author. (Author's interview with Fabrizio Melano, New York, 24 March 2013).

3 Robert Sutherland in Alan Lewens & Alastair Mitchell, *Maria Callas: Life and Art*, EMI Classics, 1987.

4 Jackie Callas, *Sisters* (London: St. Martin's, 1990), 31.

5 ibid. 40.

6 Nicholas Petsalis-Diomidis, *The Unknown Callas: The Greek Years* (Portland: Amadeus Press, 2003), 25.

7 Evangelia Callas & Lawrence Blochman, *My Daughter Maria Callas* (New York: Fleet Press, 1960), 11–12.

8 Photocopy of Callas' birth certificate.

9 Derek Prouse, "Maria Callas Speaks," *The Sunday Times*, 2 April 1961.

10 Questionnaire to Callas from her friend Herbert Weinstock for an upcoming feature for *Opera News*, February 1965 [HWP].

11 Sewell Chan, "Where Callas Was Born 85 Years Ago," *The New York Times*, 2 December 2008.

12 Maria Callas' memoirs for January 1957 editions of *Oggi* magazine trans. in David Lowe, *Callas: As They Saw Her*, 17.

13 Author's telephone interview with Mary Annexy, 14 September 2012.

14 Born Maria Arfaras, Annexy's great-great aunt is Frosso Lourou, Callas' maternal grandmother. Her mother Helen Kritikou (later Arfaras) was Evangelia's first cousin once removed.

15 Michael Scott, *Maria Meneghini Callas* (London: Simon & Schuster, 1992), 5. The address written on Callas' birth certificate is located in Queens, yet given the fact that Evangelia gave birth in a hospital on Fifth Avenue, it seems unlikely that a woman in labor would have travelled well over six and a half miles to find a hospital. The exact dates of their residence at the address in Queens remain unclear.

16 "Let's Get It Right: Work Incentive Posters of the 1920s." Exhibition at the National Museum of American History, 27 July 2018–24 March 2019.

17 Scott, 5.

18 Callas, *Oggi* memoirs in Lowe, 18. Callas notes the order of her given names as "Maria Anna Cecilia Sophia Kalogeropoulos."

19 Nadia Stancioff, *Maria Callas Remembered: An Intimate Portrait of the Private Callas* (Colorado: Da Capo Press, 2000), 48.

20 Evangelia Callas, 16.

21 Callas, *Oggi* memoirs in Lowe, 24. Callas notes that her age was six but, as other examples attest, she often confused numbers, ages and dates. Jackie Callas records her being eleven at the time (*Sisters*, 45) which would make the year 1929. But while Evangelia notes that the family was then "living on 192nd Street in Washington Heights" (*My Daughter Maria Callas*, 17) and Maria's hospitalization at Saint Elizabeth's Hospital on Fort Washington Avenue supports this idea, by June 1929 they had already relocated to Hell's Kitchen on 34th Street. Therefore the most likely outcome was that Maria had the accident in July 1928, aged four.

22 Scott, 7. The exact address was 569 West 192nd Street.

23 Callas, *Oggi* memoirs in Lowe, 24.

24 Jackie Callas, 46.

25 Gara, 10.

26 Author's telephone interview with Mary Annexy.

27 Evangelia Callas, 22. Stancioff (53) contrarily states that according to a school nurse's report from Maria's last school, S. 189, she began to wear glasses in the seventh grade (at around age twelve). However Jackie Callas in *Sisters* (45) also mentions the age was five, making this the likelier verdict.

28 John Fleming, "Nurturing a Legend," *The Floridian*, 6 August 2002.

29 Dacia Maraini, *E tu come eri: 26 interviste sull'infanzia* (Milan: Rizzoli, 1998), 306-7.

30 Scott, 5.

31 Jackie Callas, 49; Galatopoulos, 17. Galatopoulos also notes that Evangelia spent a month at the psychiatric institution of Bellevue Hospital on the Lower East Side in New York, but does not cite a source for this finding.

32 Jackie Callas, 49.

33 Ross: 1957

34 Derek Prouse, "Maria Callas Speaks," *The Sunday Times*, 19 March 1961.

35 Jackie Callas, 50.

36 Scott, 7.

37 Jackie Callas, 47.

38 Gara, 12.

39 Maraini, 306.

40 Jackie Callas, 44; Evangelia Callas, 18.

41 Jackie Callas, 44-45.

42 Leonetta Bentivoglia, "Le verità di Maria divina e infelice," *La Domenica di Repubblica*, 16 September 2007.

43 Downes: 1967

44 Gardner: 1958

45 Jellinek, 7.

46 Maraini, 306-7.

47 Callas, *Oggi* memoirs in Lowe, 17.

48 Jackie Callas, 33.

49 Evangelia Callas, 37.

50 Murrow: 1958

51 Marlyse Schaeffer, "Aujourd'hui, La Callas," *Elle* France, 28 April 1969.

52 Scott (7) lists the following schools that Maria attended: S. 228M, S. 9, S. 43, S. 192M, S. 189 and S. 164. He claims to have discovered these in a letter from Marvin Goodman, then Assistant Director of the Board of Education of the City of New York, to music critic Joel Honig dated 16 January 1979 (280).

53 Murrow: 1958.

54 Lomazzi, "Volle Dimagrire Contro La Volontà di Meneghini."

55 Cruesemann: 1959

56 Scott, 7.

57 Jellinek, 10.

58 Callas, *Oggi* memoirs in Lowe, 18.

59 Jellinek, 8.

60 Callas' radio greeting with Rudolf Bing and her colleagues to the Metropolitan Opera radio audience prior to her performance of *Lucia di Lammermoor*, 8 December 1956 (MYTO Records, *Maria Callas: Lucia di Lammermoor*, Milan: 2013).

61 Arianna Stassinopoulos, *Maria Callas: The Woman Behind the Legend* (New York: Simon & Schuster, 1981), 25.

62 Jackie Callas, 54–55.

63 Weaver: 1965

64 Ross: 1957

65 Irving A. Fein, *Jack Benny: An Intimate Biography* (New York: Pocket Books, 1977), 138–39.

66 Murrow: 1958

67 Callas, *Oggi* memoirs in Lowe, 18.

68 Frost: 1970

69 Callas, *Oggi* memoirs in Lowe, 17.

70 Prouse, "Maria Callas Speaks," 19 March 1961.

71 Jackie Callas, 56; Evangelia Callas, 23–24.

72 Murrow: 1958

73 Callas, "Corrections of *Time* magazine article," unpublished document, c. December 1956 [CFM].

74 Frost: 1970

75 Murrow: 1958

76 Jellinek, 2.

77 Gardner: 1958

78 Ross: 1957

79 Cruesemann: 1959

2. "A sort of a straitjacket"

1 Harewood: 1968

2 Scott, 9.

3 Evangelia Callas, 27.

4 Petsalis-Diomidis, 612 n. 1. "The precise date of their arrival in Patras, 6 March 1937, is
   first stated on Mary's application for registration as an American citizen in Athens, on 15
   March 1938. (Photocopied document kindly provided by Jackie Kalogeropoulou)."

5 Evangelia Callas, 36.

6 Caloni: 1976.

7 Petsalis-Diomidis, 85.

8 Stassinopoulos, 33.

9 Jackie Callas, 70.

10 Author's telephone interview with Ninon Dimitriadou-Kambouri, 17 September 2012.

11 Jackie Callas, 72.

12 Evangelia Callas, 36.

13 Prouse, "Maria Callas Speaks," 19 March 1961.

14 Petsalis-Diomidis, 90.

15 ibid. 93.

16 Callas, *Oggi* memoirs in Lowe, 18.

17 Petsalis-Diomidis, 89–90.

18 ibid. 95.

19 ibid. 98. Trivella was born on Lesbos in 1894.

20 Yorgos Vokos, "Maria Callas Arrived Day Before Yesterday, Full of Emotion But Saying
   Nothing," *Acropolis*, 30 July 1957.

21 ibid. 96 (from P. Krineos, "A Heavenly Voice, a Frosty Eye": interview given by Trivella
   to an unnamed Athens newspaper, c. 10 Mar. 1957—found as a clipping in Trivella's
   papers).

22 Evangelia Callas, 36.

23 Harewood: 1968

24 Eugenio Gara, *I grandi interpreti: Maria Callas* (Milan: Ricordi, 1957), 12.

25 Harewood: 1968

26 Vokos, "Maria Callas Arrived Day Before Yesterday, Full of Emotion But Saying Nothing."

27 Petsalis-Diomidis, 98.

28 Evangelia Callas, 37–38.

29 Prouse, "Maria Callas Speaks," 19 March 1961.

30 Fleetwood: 1958

31 Frost: 1970

32 Petsalis-Diomidis, 100.

33 Galatopoulos, 23.

34 Y. Leontaritis, "From the Old Phonograph to the Triumph at Carnegie Hall," *Acropolis*,
   2 October 1977.

35 Prouse, "Maria Callas Speaks," 19 March 1961.

36 Petsalis-Diomidis, 104–5.

37 Harewood: 1968

38 Galatopoulos, 27.

39 Petsalis-Diomidis, 103 (from Y. Karakandas' letter in *Ta Simerina*, 21 July 1977, and his
   letter in *Embros*, 18 November 1977).

40 Undated letter from Manolis Kalomiris to Callas (c. 1950) translated for the author by Fani Kanatzia. Some linguistic adjustments have been made for clarity's sake. Copies were provided to the author by the Maria Callas Alumni Association of the Music School of Kalamata.

41 Jackie Callas, 61–62.

42 ibid. 81.

43 Petsalis-Diomidis, 130 (he does not cite a source).

44 Jackie Callas, 78.

45 Petsalis-Diomidis, 110. c.f. 614 n. 8: "The new address, Harilaou Trikoupi 70, is stated on Mary's application for registration as an American citizen in Athens, 15 March 1938. (Photocopied document kindly provided by Jackie Kaloyeropoulou)."

46 Jackie Callas, 80.

47 Polyvios Marchand, *Maria Callas* (Athens: Gnose, 1983), 19.

48 Petsalis-Diomidis, 130.

49 ibid. 130 (Interview with Elli Nikolaidi, chorus mistress at the National Conservatory, and the Bulletin for the Academic Year 1937–38 from the Archives of the National Conservatory).

50 ibid. 129 (Interview with Zoe Vlachopoulou, a friend of Maria's at the National Conservatory).

51 Prouse, "Maria Callas Speaks," 19 March 1961.

52 Murrow: 1958

53 Petsalis-Diomidis, 132 (Interview with Christos Magliveras, brother of baritone Evangelos Magliveras; a program of the Independence Day celebrations from Evangelos Magliveras' papers).

54 Stancioff, 89.

55 Petsalis-Diomidis, 132 (from P. Krineos, "A Heavenly Voice, a Frosty Eye," interview given by Trivella to an Athenian newspaper, c. 10 Mar. 1957, in Trivella's papers).

56 ibid. 133.

57 Interview with Elvira de Hidalgo in *Oggi*, 1 October 1959, in Tosi, *The Young Maria Callas*, trans. William Weaver, 138–39.

58 Petsalis-Diomidis, 134–35.

59 Weaver, 140.

60 Petsalis-Diomidis, 138.

61 ibid. 130.

62 ibid. 142 (Interviews with Vyron Simiriotis who sang the role of Turiddu in *Cavalleria rusticana* and Afroditi Kopanou, a pupil at the National Conservatory).

63 ibid. 142 (from Y. Orfanos, "Maria Callas, Anatomy of a Genius," *Odos Panos*, no. 32. Sept–Oct 1987).

64 Galatopoulos, 28.

65 Harris: 1970

66 Prouse, "Maria Callas Speaks," 3 April 1961.

67 Callas, *Oggi* memoirs in Lowe, 19.

68 Petsalis-Diomidis, 142 (Interview with Vyron Simiriotis).

69 ibid. 146 (Interview with Penelope Adali).

70 ibid. 148–49.

71 ibid. 150.

72 ibid. 203–5.

73 ibid. 165–66.

74 ibid. 185.

75 Harris: 1970

76 Prouse, "Maria Callas Speaks," 3 April 1961.

77 Callas, *Oggi* memoirs in Lowe, 19.

78 Prouse, "Maria Callas Speaks," 3 April 1961.

79 Petsalis-Diomidis, 187.

80 ibid. 234 (Interview with Lola Ritsou).

81 ibid. 176.

82 ibid. 160 (c.f. Petsalis-Diomidis, 620 n. 9: "The biographical material on Elvira de Hidalgo comes partly from a statement she made to some of her pupils and partly from various written sources. The two best are both by Yorgos Leotsakos: *Greek Opera: 100 Years: 1888–1988*, 122–127; and 'Elvira de Hidalgo: Her Life and Work,' *Proini*, 31 Jan. 1980.").

83 de Hidalgo to Callas, 6 May 1966 [CNH].

84 Callas to de Hidalgo, 18 February 1965 [CBA].

85 Callas, *Oggi* memoirs in Lowe, 19–20.

86 Tosi, *The Young Maria Callas*, 140.

87 Callas, *Oggi* memoirs in Lowe, 20.

88 Callas, "Corrections of *Time* magazine article," [CFM].

89 Petsalis-Diomidis, 623 n. 20 (Interview with Arda Mandikian and a telephone conversation with Lakadzis' widow, 17 May 1996).

90 ibid. 179 (Interviews with Spyros Salingaros and Arda Mandikian).

91 Cruesemann: 1959

92 Harris: 1970

93 Renzo Allegri trans. Thierry Laget, *La véritable histoire de Maria Callas* (Paris: Éditions Belfont, 1992), 54.

94 Downes: 1967

95 Harewood: 1968

96 ibid. 174 (Interview with Andreas Paridis).

97 ibid. 258.

98 ibid. 202.

99 ibid. 183 (Interview with Zoe Vlachopoulou).

100 ibid. 256 (Interview with Katie Makriyanni).

101 ibid. 183–84 (Interview with Zoe Vlachopoulou).

102 ibid. 221–22 (Interview with Galatea Amaxopoulou).

103 ibid. 215 (Interview with Nikos Papachristos).

104 Scott, 15.

105 Callas, *Oggi* memoirs in Lowe, 20.

106 Evangelia Callas to Maria, 18 September 1949 in Petsalis-Diomidis, 240.

107 Tosi, *The Young Maria Callas*, 141.

108 Callas, *Oggi* memoirs in Lowe, 20.

109 Ross: 1957.

110 Callas, *Oggi* memoirs in Lowe, 20.

111 Petsalis-Diomidis, 265 (Interview with Yorgos Goudelis).

112 ibid. 265 (Interview with Marika Papadopoulou).

113 Callas, *Oggi* memoirs in Lowe, 21.

114 Ross: 1957

115 Allegri, *La véritable histoire de Maria Callas,* 56.

116 Petsalis-Diomidis, 245 (Interview with Giulietta Simionato).

117 ibid. 545. c.f. 654 n. 23: "As told to the author by John Ardoin at the First International Congress Dedicated to Maria Callas, Athens, Zappeion Megaron, 11–14 September 1997."

118 Callas, *Oggi* memoirs in Lowe, 21.

119 Petsalis-Diomidis, 236 (from examination records at the Athens Conservatory).

120 ibid 240–41.

121 ibid. 253.

122 ibid. 273 (Interview with Lela Skourdouli).

123 ibid. 281 (Interview with Giulietta Simionato).

124 ibid. 287–288 (Interview with Andonis Kalaidzakis and Haris Vassiliadou; *Ethnikos Kiryx,* 11 August 1960).

125 ibid. 293.

126 ibid. 293 (Interview with former chorus member Stefanos Chiotakis).

127 Galatopoulos, 36.

128 Petsalis-Diomidis, 300.

129 ibid. 297 (Interviews with Spyros Salingaros and Andonis Kalaidzakis).

130 ibid. 300 (from Sotos Vassiliadis, article in *Mousiki,* 22 September 1979).

3. "Strings of the heart and *mind*"

1 Jackie Callas, *Sisters,* 98.

2 Petsalis-Diomidis, 635 n. 2.

3 The Maria Callas International Club, Video Interview with Jackie Callas by Jeanne Handzic, 8 October 1991. Accessed at https://www.youtube.com/watch?v=vXyT2SauyfU.

4 Jackie Callas, 121.

5 Petsalis-Diomidis, 314 (Interview with Mitsa Kourahani).

6 ibid. 325 (Interview with Lela Skourdouli).

7 ibid. 325–26.

8 ibid. 327 (from D. Gouliamos, *Ta Nea tis Kyriakis,* 12 May 1985).

9 ibid. 330 (Interviews with Andreas Paridis and Zoe Vlachopoulou).

10 ibid. 329 (from Alexandra Lalaouni, *Vradyni,* 19 July 1943).

11 Friedrich W. Herzog, "Maria Kalojeropoulou als Tosca," *Deutsche Nachrichten in Griechenland,* 20 July 1943.

12 Friedrich W. Herzog, "Konzertabend im Kosta Moussouri," *Deutsche Nachrichten in Griechenland,* 23 July 1943.

13 Petsalis-Diomidis, 331 (from Alexandra Lalaouni, 24 July 1943).

14 Friedrich W. Herzog, "Callas Athene . . ." *Die Wildente,* no. 21, October 1959.

15 Petsalis-Diomidis, 306.

16 Callas, *Oggi* memoirs in Lowe, 23.

17 Petsalis-Diomidis, 309 (from Stamatis Tsoutis, "Maria Callas: The First Authentic Biography of the Greek Soprano," *Niki*, 20 July–30 August 1963 [part I], and 31 August–18 September 1963 [parts 2 and 15]).

18 ibid. 309 (from Tsoutis and an interview with Lalaki Kamara, friend and patient of Dr. Papatestas).

19 Galatopoulos, 45–46.

20 Petsalis-Diomidis, 341 (Interview with Stefanos Chiotakis).

21 ibid. 340 (Interview with Kostas Dounias).

22 ibid. 341 (from Archives of the Greek National Opera).

23 ibid. 342 (c.f. 638 n. 18: "Handwritten summaries of the statements made to the board by Lakis Vassilakis (22 October 1943), and Mary Kaloyeropoulou (23 October 1943) from the latter's personal dossier, which has disappeared from the G.N.O. archives. Photocopies of these statements were given to Polyvios Marchand in 1982 at the request of Elli Nikolaidi.").

24 ibid. 350 (Interview with Takis Sigaras).

25 ibid. 352–53.

26 ibid. 354–55.

27 ibid. 641 n. 5.

28 ibid. 349 (Interview with Zoe Vlachopoulou).

29 Evangelia Callas, 68.

30 Robert Sutherland, *Maria Callas: Diaries of A Friendship* (London: Constable & Co., 1999), 207.

31 Petsalis-Diomidis, 361 (Interview with Zoe Vlachopoulou).

32 ibid. 362 (from his conversation with Eleni Mangou).

33 Callas, *Oggi* memoirs in Lowe, 20.

34 Petsalis-Diomidis, 367–68 (Interview with Mitsa Kourahani).

35 ibid. 371 (from *To Radiophonon*, no. 46, 7–13 May 1944).

36 Downes: 1967

37 Petsalis-Diomidis, 174 (Interview with Zoe Vlachopoulou).

38 Downes: 1967

39 Petsalis-Diomidis, 370 (Interview with Zoe Vlachopoulou).

40 ibid. 640 n. 26 (Interview with Xenia Kouroussopoulou).

41 ibid. 376 (from Alexandra Lalaouni, *Vradyni*, 23 April 1944).

42 Galatopoulos, 41.

43 Petsalis-Diomidis, 360 (Interview with Elvira Mataranga).

44 ibid. 389.

45 ibid. 379.

46 ibid. 642 n. 11 (Interview with Galatea Amaxopoulou; Letters from Callas to Magliveras, 2 January 1946 and 12 January 1947).

47 ibid. 641 n. 7: "The first person to make such an allegation in print was Friedrich Herzog, the critic of the *Deutsche Nachrichten in Griechenland*, who was living in Athens in 1944 and had met Mary and most probably Vangelis too . . . This statement, however, appeared only in a rather obscure local magazine in Germany, in 1959 (*Die Wildente*)."

48 Petsalis-Diomidis, 385 (from a letter from Callas to Evangelos Magliveras written in Greek on notepaper headed "Hotel Times Square, Forty Third Street, West of B'way, New York City," 2 January 1946).

49 Galatopoulos, 47.

50 Petsalis-Diomidis, 312 (Interview with Marika Papadopoulou).

51 ibid. 339 (Interview with Nicholas Zachariou [Nicola Zaccaria]).

52 ibid. 340 (Interview with Stefanos Chiotakis).

53 Frost: 1970

54 " 'Man Hat Mich Seelisch Gelyncht': Ein *Spiegel* Gespräch mit der Sopranistin Maria Meneghini Callas," *Der Spiegel,* 22 January 1958.

55 Callas, *Oggi* memoirs in Lowe, 21–22.

56 Petsalis-Diomidis, 407 (from Archives of the Greek National Opera and his interview with Mireille Fléri).

57 ibid. 409–11 (Interview with Andonis Kalaidzakis; Archives of the Greek National Opera).

58 Tosi, *Giovane Callas* (Venice: Maria Callas Associazione Culturale, 1997), 179.

59 Werner Schroeter, "L'arrêt de cœur de la prima donna," *L'Avant-Scène,* no. 44, October 1982.

60 Callas, *Oggi* memoirs in Lowe, 22.

61 Petsalis-Diomidis, 437; 646 n. 15 (from Ray Morgan's memoir of the period "Athens: October-December '44," *The Athenian* December 1987 and from his interview with Morgan).

62 Petsalis-Diomidis, 439–40.

63 ibid. 353 (Interview with Sigaras).

64 ibid. 439–44 (Interview with Morgan).

65 ibid. 442–43.

66 Gardner: 1958

67 Callas, *Oggi* memoirs in Lowe, 24–25.

68 Petsalis-Diomidis, 442-3; 446 (Interview with Ray Morgan); John Crace, "How Maria Callas Fell In Love With Me," *Daily Mail,* 9 July 1998.

69 Callas, *Oggi* memoirs in Lowe, 25.

70 Evangelia Callas, 78.

71 Galatopoulos, 46.

72 Evangelia Callas, 81-2.

73 Petsalis-Diomidis, 477 (from Maria's private photograph album, then owned by Renzo Allegri).

74 Petsalis-Diomidis, 485 ("Application for registration, affidavit by native American to explain protracted foreign residence, Athens, American Consular Service, 28 March 1945, and other related documents. [Photocopies kindly provided by Jackie Kaloyeropoulou])."

75 ibid. 464.

76 Callas, *Oggi* memoirs in Lowe, 23.

77 Fleetwood: 1958

78 Petsalis-Diomidis, 485 (Interview with Maria Alkeou).

79 ibid. 466 (from articles in *Nea Alithia* and *Makedonia,* 26 April 1945).

80 ibid. 469–70 (Interview with pianist Tonis Yeoryiou).

81 ibid. 483.

82 Petsalis-Diomidis, 491 (from *Ta Nea,* 8 August 1945).

83 Claudia Cassidy, "Pride and Honesty: Shining Traits of Maria Callas," *Chicago Tribune,* 21 November 1954.

84 Fleetwood: 1958
85 Callas, "Corrections of *Time* magazine article," [CFM].
86 Tosi, *The Young Maria Callas*, 141.
87 Callas, *Oggi* memoirs in Lowe, 27.
88 New York, U.S., "Arriving Passenger and Crew Lists (including Castle Garden and Ellis Island), 1820–1957."
89 Callas, *Oggi* memoirs in Lowe, 23–24.

4. "Thick as molasses"

1 Banzet: 1965
2 Address shown on the audition card for "Callas, Mary (Maria)," [AMO].
3 Jellinek, 27–28.
4 Callas, "'I miei anni terribili in Grecia', *Oggi*, 10 January 1957," published in Tosi, *Giovane Callas*, 58–59.
5 Gara, 12.
6 Petsalis-Diomidis, 127.
7 Galatopoulos, 51.
8 Callas to Elvira de Hidalgo, 28 January 1946 in Volf, *Maria Callas: Lettres et Mémoires* (Paris: Albin Michel, 2019), "1946," Kobo.
9 Callas' January 1957 *Oggi* memoirs in Tosi, *Giovane Callas*, 60.
10 ibid. 58.
11 Prouse, "Maria Callas Speaks," 19 March 1961.
12 Callas to de Hidalgo, 28 January 1946 in Volf, "1946."
13 Galatopoulos, 50.
14 Petsalis-Diomidis, 641 n. 10: Callas to Evangelos Magliveras, 2 January 1946 from the author's collection.
15 ibid. 505.
16 Audition Card for "Callas, Mary (Maria)," [AMO].
17 Banzet: 1965.
18 Callas to Elvira de Hidalgo, 28 January 1946 in Tosi, *Giovane Callas*, 165.
19 Tosi, *Giovane Callas*, 59.
20 Cristina Gastel Chiarelli, *Maria Callas: Vita, immagini, parole, musica* (Venice: Marsilio, 1981), 24.
21 Robert Neville, "Voice of an Angel," *Life*, 31 October 1955.
22 Fleetwood: 1958
23 Prouse, "Maria Callas Speaks," 2 April 1961.
24 Petsalis-Diomidis, 523–25 (Interview with Dino Yannopoulos).
25 David Gelman, "The Maria Callas Story," *The New York Post*, 2 March 1958.
26 de Nussac & Cotta: 1970
27 Tosi, *Giovane Callas*, 59.
28 Jellinek, 30.
29 Callas to Walter Cummings, 27 December 1960 in Jean-Jacques Hanine-Roussel, *Maria Callas* (Paris: Éditions Carpentier, 2015), 452.

30 Stancioff, 71.

31 Ida Cook, *Safe Passage: The Remarkable True Story of Two Sisters Who Rescued Jews from the Nazis* (New York: Harlequin, 2008), 57.

32 As related by Ida and Louise Cook to Elayne Reynolds Duke. Author's e-mail correspondence with Reynolds Duke, 23 January 2013.

33 James A. Drake & Rosa Ponselle, *Rosa Ponselle: A Centenary Biography* (Portland: Amadeus Press, 2003), 315.

34 Gara, 10.

35 Downes: 1967

36 Callas to Evangelos Magliveras, 12 January 1947 in Petsalis-Diomidis, 387.

37 Jellinek, 30.

38 Fleetwood: 1958

39 Callas' *Oggi* memoirs in Tosi, *Giovane Callas*, 60.

40 Mary Jane Matz, "We Introduce Maria Meneghini Callas," *Opera News*, 3 December 1956.

41 Callas' *Oggi* memoirs in Tosi, *Giovane Callas*, 59–61.

42 de Nussac & Cotta: 1970

43 Matz, "We Introduce Maria Meneghini Callas."

44 Galatopoulos, 50.

45 Barry: 1971

46 Roberto Tumbarello, "La Mia Baby-Sitter si chiamava Maria Callas," *Oggi*, 4 August 1994.

47 Callas to Elvira de Hidalgo, 28 January 1946 in Volf, "1946."

48 Tumbarello, "La Mia Baby-Sitter Si Chiamava Maria Callas."

49 Matilde Amorosi, "Maria Callas Era La Mia Cameriera," *Gente*, 28 March 1994.

50 Hanine-Roussel, 503 (Interview with bass Georges Daum).

51 Callas to Giovanni Battista Meneghini, 2 May 1949 in Allegri, *Maria Callas: Lettere d'amore*, 116.

52 Callas, "My Defense," unpublished document, c. December 1956 [CFM].

53 Matilde Amorosi, "Maria Callas Era La Mia Cameriera."

54 Callas' *Oggi* memoirs in Tosi, *Giovane Callas*, 59.

55 Callas to Bagarozy, 2 September and 20 August 1947 in Allegri, *Maria Callas: Lettere d'amore*, 69–70.

56 Weaver: 1965

57 Frost: 1970

58 Author's telephone interview with Mary Annexy.

59 Gillian Widdicombe, "The Great Survivor," *The Observer*, 20 August 1978.

60 Harewood, 235.

61 Callas to Evangelos Magliveras, 12 January 1947 in Petsalis-Diomidis, 386.

62 Galatopoulos, 53.

63 "U.S. Opera Company to Open Three Week Season Here Jan. 27.," *The New York Times*, 11 January 1947.

64 Callas' *Oggi* memoirs in Tosi, *Giovane Callas*, 61.

65 Jellinek, 34.

66 Testimony of a singer with the Chicago Opera Company, Herbert Eyre Moulton in "Odyssey Of An Opera Freak or Waiting for Callas" published by his son Charles E.J. Moulton. Accessed at https://www.writerscafe.org/writing/CEJM/1351367.

67 Danny Newman, *Tales of a Theatrical Guru* (Boston: University of Illinois Press, 2006), 185.
68 Jellinek, 34.
69 Scott, 29 (Interview with Rossi-Lemeni).
70 Interview with Nicola Rossi-Lemeni, 2 May 1978 in *Hommages à Maria Callas* (Paris: EMI France, 1997).
71 Jellinek, 36.
72 Banzet: 1965
73 Tosi, *Giovane Callas*, 185.
74 Banzet: 1965
75 Tosi, *Giovane Callas*, 185.
76 Petsalis-Diomidis, 36 f.
77 Galatopoulos, 55.
78 Jellinek, 37.
79 Callas' statements in "My Defense," [CFM].
80 Callas to Eddie Bagarozy, 2 September 1947 in Allegri, *Maria Callas: Lettere d'amore*, 69–70.
81 Callas' statements in "My Defense," [CFM].
82 Stancioff, 76.
83 Callas' *Oggi* memoirs in Tosi, *Giovane Callas*, 61.
84 Galatopoulos, 56.

5. "Like going to church"

1 Callas' *Oggi* memoirs in Tosi, *Giovane Callas*, 61–2.
2 ibid. 117.
3 Allegri, *La véritable histoire de Maria Callas*, 111.
4 Allegri, *Lettere d'amore*, 164–165.
5 Allegri, *La véritable histoire de Maria Callas*, 130–31.
6 Meneghini, 16.
7 Callas, *Oggi* memoirs in Tosi, *Giovane Callas*, 62–65.
8 Meneghini, 19.
9 Allegri, *La véritable histoire de Maria Callas*, 99.
10 Meneghini, 19.
11 Gardner: 1958
12 Maraini, 308.
13 George London, "Prima Donnas I Have Sung Against," *High Fidelity*, March 1957.
14 Callas to Meneghini, 1 November 1948 in Allegri, *Lettere d'amore*, 78–79.
15 Frost: 1970
16 Gruen: 1971
17 Meneghini to Callas, 2 July 1948 in Allegri, *Lettere d'amore*, 59.
18 Meneghini, 22.
19 Allegri, *La véritable histoire de Maria Callas*, 104–5.
20 Meneghini to Callas, 6 July 1947 in Allegri, *Lettere d'amore*, 59.
21 ibid. Meneghini to Callas, 8 July 1947, 60.

22 ibid. Meneghini to Callas, 24 July 1947, 108–9.

23 Murrow: 1958

24 Callas, *Oggi* memoirs in Tosi, *Giovane Callas*, 91.

25 Pia Meneghini, "Sette anni con Maria" in Tosi, *Giovane Callas*, 109.

26 Hanine-Roussel, 94 (Interview with Liliana Meneghini, wife of youngest brother Nicola).

27 Tosi, *Giovane Callas*, 195.

28 Meneghini, 25.

29 Galatopoulos, 79.

30 ibid. 80

31 de Nussac & Cotta: 1970

32 Frost: 1970

33 Harold C. Schonberg, *The Virtuosi: Classical Music's Great Performers from Paganini to Pavarotti* (New York: Vintage, 1988), 433.

34 Derek Prouse, "Maria Callas Speaks," *The Sunday Times*, 26 March 1961.

35 Galatopoulos, 81.

36 Interview with Nicola Rossi-Lemeni (*Hommages à Maria Callas*), 2 May 1978.

37 Galatopoulos, 81.

38 Downes: 1967.

39 John Ardoin & Gerald Fitzgerald, *Callas: The Art and the Life* (New York: Holt, Rinehart and Winston, 1974), 30. Quoted with kind permission of Fitzgerald's nephew Mark Q. Williams.

40 Harewood: 1968

41 James A. Drake, "Robert Merrill, Luciano Pavarotti, Jan Peerce, Eleanor Steber, and Richard Tucker," *The Opera Quarterly*, v. 20, issue 4, 689–693.

42 Callas' *Oggi* memoirs in Tosi, *Giovane Callas*, 65.

43 Meneghini, 30.

44 Lord George Harewood & Harold Rosenthal, "Maria Callas," *Opera*, November 1952.

45 Lord George Harewood, "Callas Remembered: Tributes to Callas," *Opera*, November 1977.

46 Review by Renato Ravazzin from *Il Gazzettino* in Jürgen Kesting trans. John Hunt, *Maria Callas*, 1983 (Boston: Northeastern University Press, 1983), 101.

47 Downes: 1967

48 John Ardoin, *The Callas Legacy* (Baltimore: Encore Editions, 1984), 5.

49 Desgraupes: 1969

50 Fleetwood: 1958

51 Elisabeth Schwarzkopf & Walter Legge, *On and Off the Record: A Memoir of Walter Legge* (London: Faber & Faber), 198.

52 Michel Clerc, "La Callas: 'J'ai décidé d'être douce,'" *Paris Match*, 15 June 1963.

53 John Freeman, "Callas Sings Norma," *Opera News*, 16 March 1953.

54 Jacques Bourgeois, Interview with Maria Callas, 30 September 1968. Published on "L'Art de Maria Callas" (Paris: Pathé Marconi, 1968).

55 Harewood: 1968

56 John Ardoin, "Callas Today," *Musical America*, 1964. Accessed at https://www.musicalamerica.com/features/?fid=303&fyear=1964.

57 Rual Askew, *The Dallas Morning News*, "Maria Callas Is Opera," 1 November 1959.

58 Allegri, *La véritable histoire de Maria Callas*, 111.

59 Galatopoulos, 1.
60 Meneghini, 114–15.
61 Allegri, *La véritable histoire de Maria Callas*, 120.
62 Callas to Bagarozy, 20 August 1947 in Allegri, *Lettere d'amore*, 68–69.
63 Galatopoulos, 82.
64 Callas, *Oggi* memoirs in Tosi, *Giovane Callas*, 67.
65 Matz, "We Introduce Maria Meneghini Callas."
66 Callas to Meneghini, 22 September 1947 in Allegri, *Lettere d'amore*, 64–65.
67 Jacopo Pellegrini, "Quel canto vulnerabile," *Classic Voice*, n. 102, November 2007, 10.
68 Lerman, 173.
69 Callas, "Il mio dramma di artista e di donna," *Oggi*, 16 January 1958.
70 Joan Sutherland, *The Autobiography of Joan Sutherland: A Prima Donna's Progress* (Washington D.C.: Regnery Publishing, 1997), 92.
71 Lomazzi, "Volle Dimagrire Contro La Volontà di Meneghini."
72 Murrow: 1958
73 David Holmes, Interview with Callas for BBC Radio, 20 June 1958.
74 Galatopoulos, 82.
75 Scott, 58.
76 Salvato Cappelli, "La malincolia di Maria Callas," *Gazzetta Ticinese*, 14 August 1980.
77 Fleetwood: 1958
78 Downes: 1967
79 Meneghini to Callas, 28 October 1947, in Allegri, *La véritable histoire de Maria Callas*, 136.
80 Callas to Meneghini, 30 October 1947, in Allegri, *Lettere d'amore*, 77.
81 ibid. 79, Callas to Meneghini, 1 November 1947.
82 ibid. 84, Callas to Meneghini, 4 November 1947.
83 Galatopoulos, 97.
84 George Callas to Maria, 23 February 1957 trans. Fani Kanatzia (Maria Callas Alumni Association of the Music School of Kalamata Exhibition).
85 "Il Loro Natale," *Oggi*, 31 December 1953.
86 Meneghini, 63.
87 ibid. 123.
88 Paolo Corsi, "Callas e Tebaldi, 70 anni fa le divine rivali all'Arena di Verona," *Opera Arena*, 29 July 2017.
89 Giovanna Lomazzi, "La Tebaldi Rifiutò di Fare Pace Con La Grande Rivale," *La Settimana Incom Illustrata*, 26 February 1961.
90 Ardoin, "Callas Today."
91 John Deathridge, *Wagner: Beyond Good and Evil* (Berkeley: University of California Press, 2008), 117–18. Reproduced with kind permission from UC Press.
92 Scott, 38 (Interview with Fedora Barbieri).
93 Paul Hume, "This Is A Rich Prize," *The Washington Post*, 27 March 1955.
94 Review in *Il Gazzettino*, 30 December 1947 in Gastel Chiarelli, 197.
95 Ardoin: 1968
96 Galatopoulos, 446.
97 Harewood: 1968
98 Galatopoulos, 446.

99 Newman, 180.

100 Fleetwood: 1958

101 Ardoin & FItzgerald, 84 (Interview with Nicola Rossi-Lemeni).

102 Lerman, 174.

103 Martin Mayer, "La Scala's New Queen," *High Fidelity*, September 1954.

104 Pia Meneghini, "Sette anni con Maria," 127.

105 Callas to Meneghini, 12 June 1949 in Allegri, *Lettere d'amore*, 135.

106 Callas, "The Lyric Tradition," 28 February 1972.

107 Unsigned article, "The Reality of Maria," *Harper's Bazaar*, August 1971.

108 Robert Sutherland, 19.

109 Tosi, *Giovane Callas*, 129.

110 Gruen: 1971

111 Gelman, "The Maria Callas Story."

112 Hanine-Roussel, 64 (Interview with Giorgio Alzanese).

113 Newman, 181.

114 Stancioff, 33.

115 Hanine-Roussel, 135 (Interview with Callas' cook Elena Pozzan); Georges Prêtre, *La Symphonie d'une vie: Entretiens avec Isabelle Prêtre* (Paris: Écriture, 2013), 135.

116 NHK TV Japan, Interview with Callas and Giuseppe Di Stefano at Bunka Kaikan Hall, Tokyo, 27 October 1974.

117 Soria, "Greek Sorceress."

118 Lerman, 175.

119 Harewood, 226.

120 Pia Meneghini, "Sette anni con Maria," 123.

121 Weaver, "Remembering Callas: Some Confessions of a Fan," 63.

122 Callas to Elvira de Hidalgo, 30 September 1948 [CBA].

123 Galatopoulos, 85.

124 Franco Carlo Ricci, *Francesco Siciliani: Sessant'anni di vita musicale in Italia* (Rome: Edizioni Scientifiche Italiane, 2003).

125 Ardoin & Fitzgerald, 53.

126 Callas to Elvira de Hidalgo, 9 November 1948 in Aste Bolaffi, *Libri rari e autografi*: Catalogue for Bolaffi Auctions (Milan: 14 May 2014).

127 Callas to de Hidalgo, 9 November 1948 in Volf, "1948."

128 Callas to Meneghini, 11 and 15 November 1948 in Allegri, *Lettere d'amore*, 94–95.

129 Callas to Meneghini, 16 April 1948 in Allegri, *Lettere d'amore*, 91.

130 Tosi, *Giovane Callas*, 77.

131 Gorlinsky to Callas, 29 May 1958 [SGA].

132 Pia Meneghini, "Sette anni con Maria," 111.

133 Harewood: 1968

134 Callas to Meneghini, 18 November 1948 in Allegri, *Lettere d'amore*, 97.

135 Prouse, "Maria Callas Speaks," 26 March 1961.

136 Ardoin & Fitzgerald, 30.

137 Prouse, "Maria Callas Speaks," 2 April 1961.

138 Harewood: 1968.

139 Galatopoulos, 443.

140 Michel Glotz, Interview with Callas for *Le magazine lyrique*, Europe 1 French Radio, 25 May 1963.

141 Mirto Picchi, *Un trono vicino al sol* (Ravenna: Edizioni del Girasole, 1978), 53.

142 Galatopoulos, 86.

143 Gualtiero Frangieri, "Il più puro Bellini: Norma," *La Nazione*, 1 December 1948.

144 Cassidy, "Pride and Honesty Shining Traits of Maria Callas."

145 Tosi, *Giovane Callas*, 71.

146 Allegri, *Lettere d'amore*, 100.

147 ibid. 77, Callas to Meneghini, 30 October 1948 and 128, Callas to Meneghini, 27 May 1949.

148 ibid. 122, Callas to Meneghini, 19 May 1949.

149 Thomas Glasow, "Dining with Divas (And Other Personal Encounters with Operatic Greats)," *The Opera Quarterly*, v. 20, issue 4, 657–714.

150 Stancioff, 33.

151 Lomazzi, "Volle Dimagrire Contro La Volontà di Meneghini."

152 Pia Meneghini, "Sette anni con Maria," 123.

153 Giovanna Lomazzi, "Della Madre Preferisce Non Dir Niente: Tutta La Sua Tenerezza E' Per Il Padre," *La Settimana Incom Illustrata*, 5 March 1961.

154 John Amis, "Callas via Legge," *Gramophone*, 14 March 2012.

155 Callas' interview with Lynne Reid-Banks for ITN, 31 January 1957; Callas, "I am not guilty of those Callas scandals."

156 Franco Mannino, *Genii* (Milan: Bompiani, 1987), 87–89.

157 Mario Nordio's review in *Gazzettino-Sera*, 10 January 1949, in Hanine-Roussel, 90.

158 Callas, *Oggi* memoirs in Tosi, *Giovane Callas*, 73.

159 Harewood: 1968

160 Ardoin: 1968

161 Downes: 1967

162 The comments of Franco Zeffirelli (an audience member then) in Ardoin & Fitzgerald, 53.

163 A. Vardanega in *Gazzettino-Sera*, trans. Henry Wisneski in Lowe, 137.

164 Galatopoulos, 88.

165 Callas to Meneghini, 28 January 1949 in Allegri, *Lettere d'amore*, 105.

166 Boutwell, "Processo alla Callas."

167 Callas to Meneghini, 30 January 1949 in Allegri, *Lettere d'amore*, 106.

168 ibid. 79, Callas to Meneghini, 1 November 1947.

169 ibid. 153, Callas to Meneghini, 14 May 1950.

170 Callas, *Oggi* memoirs in Tosi, *Giovane Callas*, 73.

171 Callas to Meneghini, 11 November 1948, in Allegri, *Lettere d'amore*, 95.

172 Ardoin & Fitzgerald, 162 (from their interview with Luchino Visconti).

173 Desgraupes: 1969

174 Ardoin & Fitzgerald, 90.

175 Riccardo Arragno, Interview with Callas for *Sunday Night at The London Palladium*, ITV Television, 22 April 1966.

176 Desgraupes: 1969

177 Mannino, 98.

178 Callas to Henry Dardick, 8 April 1949 in Volf, "1947."

179 Jackie Callas, 144–45.

180 Callas, *Oggi* memoirs in Tosi, *Giovane Callas*, 73.

181 Pia Meneghini, "Sette anni con Maria," 116–17.

182 Allegri, *Lettere d'amore*, 108.

183 Maraini, 310.

184 Callas to Meneghini, 17 June 1949 in Allegri, *Lettere d'amore*, 136.

185 " 'What is said about me is false,' says Callas," *Eleftheria*, 11 August 1960.

186 Frost: 1970

187 Letters from Callas to Henry Dardick, 8, 15 and 22 April 1949 in Volf, "1949."

188 Allegri, *Lettere d'amore*, 165.

189 Callas, *Oggi* memoirs in Tosi, *Giovane Callas*, 65.

190 Allegri, *Lettere d'amore*, 108–9.

191 Callas to Elvira de Hidalgo, 16 April 1949 [CBA].

192 Callas, *Oggi* memoirs in Tosi, *Giovane Callas*, 75.

193 Callas to Meneghini, 10 and 13 May 1949 in Allegri, *Lettere d'amore*, 118.

194 Mary Jane Phillips-Matz, *Leonard Warren: American Baritone* (Portland: Amadeus Press, 2003), 189.

195 Callas to Meneghini, 14 May 1949 in Allegri, *Lettere d'amore*, 119.

196 ibid. 122, Callas to Meneghini, 19 May 1949.

197 Callas, *Oggi* memoirs in Tosi, *Giovane Callas*, 76.

198 Jellinek, 53–54.

199 Callas to Meneghini, 8 June 1949 in Allegri, *Lettere d'amore*, 133.

200 Callas to Meneghini, 23 May 1949 in Allegri, *Lettere d'amore*, 125.

201 ibid. Callas to Meneghini, 128, 26 May 1949.

202 ibid. Callas to Meneghini, 130, 30 May 1949.

203 ibid. Callas to Meneghini, 135, 17 June 1949.

204 J. d'Arbano's review in *Critica* magazine, 18 June 1949 in Hanine-Roussel, 102.

205 Callas to Meneghini, 24 June 1949 in Allegri, *Lettere d'amore*, 140.

206 ibid. Callas to Meneghini, 3 July 1949, 141.

207 Pia Meneghini, "Sette anni con Maria," 119.

6. "In a room with little light"

1 Allegri, *Lettere d'amore*, 150.

2 Stassinopoulos, 83.

3 Callas to Meneghini, 14 April 1948 in Allegri, *Lettere d'amore*, 90.

4 Meneghini, 109.

5 Anthony Tommasini, "Maria Callas: A Voice and a Legend That Still Fascinate," *The New York Times*, 15 September 1999.

6 Jean-Luc Hees, Interview with Janine Reiss, Radio Classique, 4 September 2007. Accessed at https://www.youtube.com/watch?v=fVqs2mDwppA.

7 Meneghini, 107.

8 Allegri, *Lettere d'amore*, 150.

9 Pia Meneghini, "Sette anni con Maria," 119.
10 Weaver, "Remembering Callas: Some Confessions of a Fan," 75.
11 Cruesemann: 1959
12 Renzo Allegri, "Edda Zoraide Casali: 'I Miei Anni Con La Callas,'" *Chi* magazine, 8 December 2010.
13 Ferruccio Mezzadri and Elena Pozzan's interviews in Hanine-Roussel, 415–17.
14 George Callas to Maria, 10 November 1949 in Petsalis-Diomidis, 530.
15 Evangelia Callas to Maria, 18 September 1949 in Petsalis-Diomidis, 535.
16 Callas to Elvira de Hidalgo, 2 October 1949 in Aste Bolaffi: *Libri rari e autografi*: Catalogue for Bolaffi Auctions (Milan: 14 May 2014).
17 Robert Sutherland, 33.
18 Caloni: 1976
19 Callas to Meneghini, 16 December 1949 in Allegri, *Lettere d'amore*, 145.
20 ibid. 145–46, Callas to Meneghini, 20 December 1949.
21 ibid. 161, Callas to Meneghini, 6 June 1950.
22 Weaver, "Remembering Callas: Some Confessions of a Fan," 60.
23 Callas to Meneghini, 21 December 1949 in Allegri, *Lettere d'amore*, 148.
24 Galatopoulos, 96.
25 Allegri, *La véritable histoire de Maria Callas*, 161.
26 Jellinek, 57–58.
27 Galatopoulos, 445.
28 ibid. 97.
29 Daniela Romanò Marchetti, *La Scala: Racconti dal palcoscenico* (Milan: Valentina Edizioni, 2000), 13.
30 Meneghini, 122.
31 ibid. 161.
32 Dolores Rivellino-Walsh, *The Malibu Cookbook: A Memoir by THE GODMOTHER OF MALIBU* (Bloomington: AuthorHouse, 2007), 47.
33 Cruesemann: 1959
34 Galatopoulos, 113.
35 Birgit Nilsson trans. Doris Jung Popper, *La Nilsson: My Life in Opera* (Boston: Northeastern University Press, 2015), 204.
36 Galatopoulos, 97.
37 Callas, *Oggi* memoirs in Tosi, *Giovane Callas*, 80–81.
38 Alfredo Signorini, "Ecco le lettere, i documenti e le foto che conservo della mia amica Callas," *Gente*, 2 November 1992.
39 Callas to Meneghini, 19 May 1950 in Allegri, *Lettere d'amore*, 154.
40 ibid. 152–53, Callas to Meneghini, 14 May 1950.
41 ibid. 154, Callas to Meneghini, 19 May 1950.
42 ibid. 158, Callas to Meneghini, 29 May 1950.
43 ibid. 159, Callas to Meneghini, 1 June 1950.
44 Callas, "Corrections of *Time* magazine article," [CFM].
45 Petsalis-Diomidis, 537 (Interview with Giulietta Simionato).
46 Stancioff, 91 93.
47 Callas, "Corrections of *Time* magazine article," [CFM].

48 Galatopoulos, 100.

49 Petsalis-Diomidis, 536–37 (Interview with Giulietta Simionato).

50 Scott, 58.

51 Mariano Paes, *Excelsior* (undated clipping trans. David Herren) in Lowe, 141.

52 Scott, 58.

53 Harewood: 1968

54 Galatopoulos, 98–99.

55 Boutwell, "Processo alla Callas."

56 Mariano Paes' review in *Excelsior* in Lowe, 142 [c.f. Hanine-Roussel, 121: "Mariano Paes was allegedly the pen name of Sara María Esponisa de Pani"].

57 Isabel Farfán, "Escenarios: Teatro: Aida," *El Informador*, 10 June 1950.

58 Callas, "The Lyric Tradition," 4 November 1971.

59 Schwarzkopf & Legge, 199.

60 Callas to Meneghini, 1 June 1950 in Allegri, *Lettere d'amore*, 159.

61 ibid. 160, Callas to Meneghini, 5 June 1950.

62 ibid. 162, Callas to Meneghini, 8 June 1950.

63 Allegri, *La véritable histoire de Maria Callas*, 162.

64 Maraini, 308.

65 Galatopoulos, 101.

66 Callas to Leonidas Lantzounis, 3 November 1950 [RBC].

67 Galatopoulos, 102.

68 Fabio Gervasoni, Interview with Beppe Menegatti, Maria Callas International Archive DVD Collection, Volume I.

69 Francesco Siciliani in Alain Ferrari, *Vissi d'arte*: Documentary on RTF France aired 27 September 1979.

70 Harvey Sachs, *Toscanini: Musician of Conscience* (New York: Liveright Editions, 2017), 811.

71 James A. Drake & Rosa Ponselle, *Rosa Ponselle: A Centenary Biography*, 156.

72 Ardoin & Fitzgerald, 89.

73 Prouse, "Maria Callas Speaks," 26 March 1961.

74 Callas to Meneghini, 10 March 1948 in Allegri, *Lettere d'amore*, 89.

75 Weaver, "Remembering Callas: Some Confessions of a Fan," 66.

76 Gianandrea Gavazzeni, *Il sipario rosso: Diario (1950-1976)* (Turin: Einaudi, 1992), 317–18.

77 Scott, 65 (Interview with Gian Carlo Menotti).

78 Gian Carlo Menotti in Tony Palmer, *Callas: A Documentary* (Canada: Isolde Films, 1978).

79 Jellinek, 65.

80 Downes: 1967.

81 Allegri, *Lettere d'amore*, 164–67.

82 ibid. 150.

83 Mayer, "La Scala's New Queen."

84 Callas to Elvira de Hidalgo, 11 October 1950 [CBA].

85 Callas to Leonidas Lantzounis, 3 November 1950 [RBC].

86 Galatopoulos, 452.

87 Evangelia Callas to Maria, 14 August 1951 in Petsalis-Diomidis, 539–41.

88 Callas to Leonidas Lantzounis, 3 November 1950 [RBC].

89 Undated letter from Meneghini to Evangelia in Petsalis-Diomidis, 540–41.

90 Evangelia Callas on *The Tonight Show Starring Johnny Carson*, 3 December 1963. Published on the Maria Callas International Archive DVD Collection, Volume IV.

91 George de Carvalho, "The Prima Donna," *Time*, 29 October 1956.

92 Wallace: 1974

93 Petsalis-Diomidis, 539: "Clearly the tone must have been very unpleasant, but Maria always denied—even in private conversation with John Ardoin—that she had used the words and phrases attributed to her."

94 Gruen: 1971

95 Jackie Callas, 156.

96 Callas to Elvira de Hidalgo, 11 October 1950 [CBA].

97 Stassinopoulos, 95.

98 Frost: 1970

99 Downes: 1967

100 Jellinek, 63–64.

101 Piero Tosi's interview with Jacopo Pellegrini in Luca Aversano & Jacopo Pellegrini, *Mille e una Callas* (Macerata: Quodlibet Editions, 2017), 376.

102 Wilfrid Van Wyck to David Webster in Montague Haltrecht, *The Quiet Showman* (London: Harper Collins, 1975), 178.

103 Callas, *Oggi* memoirs in Lowe, 83.

104 Jellinek, 67.

105 Galatopoulos, 105.

106 Alan Sievewright, "Callas Remembered: Conversation with Maria Callas, July 1977," *Opera*, November 1977.

107 Newell Jenkins, "Russian Artists Make Debut in Florence," *Musical America*, August 1951.

108 Callas, "The Lyric Tradition," 14 October 1971.

109 Callas, *Oggi* memoirs in Tosi, *Giovane Callas*, 85.

110 Jellinek, 70.

111 Callas, *Oggi* memoirs in Tosi, 85.

112 Galatopoulos, 107.

113 Callas, *Oggi* memoirs in Tosi, 85.

114 ibid. 87.

115 Scott, 80 (Interview with Carlo Maria Giulini).

116 Ardoin, *The Callas Legacy*, 38.

117 Hanine-Roussel, 158.

118 ibid. 159 (Undated review from *Jornal do Commercio*).

119 Callas, *Oggi* memoirs in Tosi, 85.

120 Galatopoulos, 117.

121 Allegri, *La véritable histoire de Maria Callas*, 176–77.

122 Jellinek, 59.

123 Dorle Soria to John Ardoin, 4 January 1973 [DSP].

124 Claude-Pascal Perna, Interview with Janine Reiss for The Maria Callas International Club, 15 November 2003. Accessed at https://www.yumpu.com/fr/document/view/17086723/interview-de-janine-reiss-claveciniste-pianiste-ars-bxl.

125 Ardoin & Fitzgerald, 60 (Interview with Antonino Votto).

126 Hanine-Roussel, 165 (Interviews with Antonio Tonini and Eliana de Sabata).

127 Downes: 1967

128 Dora Ossenska, Interview with Callas for *La Scala e i suoi protagonisti*: Documentary aired on RAI Television, 23 March 1975.

129 Ardoin & Fitzgerald, 74.

130 Foreword by Montserrat Caballé in David Bret, *The Tigress and the Lamb* (London: Robson Books Ltd, 1999), xii.

131 Yvette Romi, "Ce Que La Callas N'Avait Encore Jamais Raconté," *Elle* France, 9 February 1970.

132 Maraini, 312.

133 Callas, *Oggi* memoirs in Tosi, 89.

134 Franco Abbiati, "I Vespri siciliani diretti da De Sabata," *Corriere della Sera*, 8 December 1951.

135 Emilio Radius in *L'Europeo* in Hanine-Roussel, 165.

136 Schwarzkopf & Legge, 192.

137 ibid. 194–95.

138 Fleetwood: 1958

139 Undated letter from Luchino Visconti to Meneghini in Meneghini, 178.

140 Emilio Pozzi, Interview with Callas for RAI Television, 19 July 1966.

141 Allegri, *La véritable histoire de Maria Callas*, 200.

142 Toni Stöckli, "Les souvenirs d'un organisateur," *Construire*, 11 February 1959.

143 Fleetwood: 1958

144 Callas, *Oggi* memoirs in Tosi, 43.

145 Allegri, *Lettere d'amore*, 179.

146 Allegri, *La véritable histoire de Maria Callas*, 178.

147 Jellinek, 78.

148 Emilio Radius, "Norma d'oro," *L'Europeo*, 29 January 1952.

149 Mario Quaglia in *Corriere del Teatro* (trans. Henry Wisneski) in Lowe, 149.

150 Jellinek, 318.

151 Galatopoulos, 447.

152 Niarchos Thanasis, "Maria Callas—Christos Lambrakis: The Eternal Anniversary," *Ta Nea*, 12 September 2014.

153 Galatopoulos, 119.

154 Caloni: 1976

155 Boutwell, "Processo alla Callas."

156 Norman Lebrecht, *Covent Garden: The Untold Story* (Boston: Northeastern University Press, 2001), 155.

157 Callas, "I am not guilty of those Callas scandals."

158 Cruesemann: 1959

159 Frost: 1970

160 Prouse, "Maria Callas Speaks," 26 March 1961.

161 Caloni: 1976

162 Barry: 1971

163 "Nada para mim foi fácil": Unsigned interview with Callas reproduced likely from another publication in *Jornal do Brasil*, 2 February 1960.

164 Cook, 273.

165 "From Our Special Correspondent: Mme. Callas on Opera."

7. "Everything seems in a dense fog"

1 Hanine-Roussel, 178.
2 Callas' interview with Mexican Radio on 3 June 1952 during the intermission of *La traviata* at Palacio de Bellas Artes. Published on BJR Records, BJR130. Accessed at https://www.youtube.com/watch?v=7pso325PKMI&ab_channel=CallasFan.
3 Scott, 89.
4 Downes: 1967
5 Galatopoulos, 123.
6 Chris Pasles, "Italian Lyric Tenor Inspired Pavarotti," *The Los Angeles Times*, 4 March 2008.
7 Scott, 88 (Interview with Giuseppe Di Stefano).
8 Galatopoulos, 122.
9 Downes: 1967
10 "Unsung Heroes," Interview with Sir Edward Downes, BBC Radio 4, 25 April 2011.
11 Francis Rizzo, "The Callas Class," *Opera News*, 15 April 1972.
12 Teodoro Celli, "La sua voce commuove perché contiene un dramma," *Oggi*, 3 April 1958.
13 Cassidy, "Pride and Honesty Shining Traits of Maria Callas."
14 Paul Hume, "Unusual, Handsome Disk Filled With Easter Music," *The Washington Post*, 15 March 1953.
15 Paul A. Jackson, *Start-Up At the New Met: The Metropolitan Opera Broadcasts, 1966–1976* (Portland: Amadeus Press, 2006), 449.
16 Haltrecht, 180.
17 Callas, *Oggi* memoirs in Tosi, 89.
18 Scott, 101 (Interview with Sir John Pritchard).
19 Harris: 1970
20 Unsigned article, "Playwright States Key to Success," *Hartford Courant*, 15 December 1969.
21 Berlin, 339–340.
22 Weaver, "Remembering Callas: Some Confessions of a Fan," 64.
23 Matz, "We Introduce Maria Meneghini Callas."
24 Robert Jacobson, "Callas, The Tiger Tamed?," *After Dark*, October 1969.
25 Banzet: 1965
26 Murrow: 1959
27 Frost: 1970
28 Jacques Leiser, "Chapter 13: Maria Callas" in Leiser, *A Life Among Legends: An Impresario Looks Back* (Amazon Kindle Editions, 2013).
29 Ardoin & Fitzgerald, 56.
30 Galatopoulos, 227.
31 Ardoin: 1968
32 Teodoro Celli in *Corriere Lombardo* in Galatopoulos, 125.
33 Author's interview with Janine Reiss, Paris, 19 December 2011.
34 Harewood: 1968
35 Giacomo Gambetti, "Sono per una Medea non aggressiva," in Pier Paolo Pasolini, *Il Vangelo secondo Matteo, Edipe Re, Medea* (Milan: Garzanti Editions, 2006), 465.
36 Weaver: 1965

37 Harewood: 1968

38 Irene Bottero, *Maria Callas: Croce e delizia* (Mondovì: Nuova Editrice Italiana, 1997), 170 (Interview with Aldo Protti).

39 Tommasini, "Maria Callas: A Voice and a Legend That Still Fascinate."

40 Lomazzi, "Volle Dimagrire Contro La Volontà di Meneghini."

41 Matz, "We Introduce Maria Meneghini Callas."

42 Harris: 1970

43 Callas to Teresa d'Addato, 13 January 1967 in Volf, "1967."

44 Calmels Chambre Cohen, *Maria Callas: Souvenirs d'une légende: 2–3 décembre 2000* (Paris: Calmels Chambre Cohen), 230.

45 Downes: 1967

46 Signorini, "Ecco le lettere, i documenti e le foto che conservo della mia amica Callas."

47 Bentivoglia, "Le verità di Maria divina e infelice."

48 Lomazzi, "Volle Dimagrire Contro La Volontà di Meneghini."

49 Lomazzi in Vittoria Crespi Morbio, *Maria Callas: Gli anni alla Scala* (Turin: Umberto Allemandi, 2008), 130.

50 Cook, 275.

51 Bottero, 214 (Interview with Giovanna Lomazzi).

52 Crespi Morbio, 139.

53 Author's interview with Giovanna Lomazzi, Lecco, 13 July 2012.

54 Galatopoulos, 406.

55 Banzet: 1965

56 Callas to Irving Kolodin, 17 March 1971 [IKP].

57 Signorini, "Ecco le lettere, i documenti e le foto che conservo della mia amica Callas."

58 Nancy Berryman, "Tony can put the powerful in their place," *The Sydney Morning Herald*, 14 February 1982.

59 Pia Meneghini, "Sette anni con Maria," 115.

60 Stancioff, 119.

61 Ross: 1957

62 Gorlinsky to Callas, 17 June 1960 [SGA].

63 Stancioff, 133.

64 Unsigned article, "Onassis Escorts Maria Callas to Supper Party," *The Washington Post*, 30 January 1970.

65 Hanine-Roussel, 465–66 (Interview with Antonio Tonini).

66 "Contract Between The British Broadcasting Corporation and Maria Meneghini Callas Represented by Sander Gorlinsky to Callas Ltd.," 2 January 1953 [SGA].

67 Scott, 115–16.

68 Lerman, 137–38.

69 Unsigned article, "People Are Talking About in . . . ROME," *Vogue*, 15 March 1953.

70 Pia Meneghini, "Sette anni con Maria," 133.

71 Tito Gobbi, *My Life* (London: Macdonald & Jane's, 1979), 95.

72 Questionnaire to Callas from her friend Herbert Weinstock for an upcoming feature for *Opera News*, February 1965 [HWP].

73 Downes: 1967

74 Frost: 1970

75 Lomazzi, "Volle Dimagrire Contro La Volontà di Meneghini."
76 Allegri, "Edda Zoraide Casali: 'I Miei Anni Con La Callas.'"
77 Callas, "Corrections of *Time* magazine article," [CFM].
78 Jellinek, 108.
79 Lomazzi, "Volle Dimagrire Contro La Volontà di Meneghini."
80 "BBC Presenter Gains Weight After Swallowing Tapeworm," *The Herald*, 30 January 2014.
81 Cassidy, "Pride and Honesty Shining Traits of Maria Callas."
82 Eugenio Gara's review in *Candido* magazine, 8 March 1953 in Hanine-Roussel, 201.
83 Callas, "The Lyric Tradition," 14 October 1971.
84 Jellinek, 80.
85 Allegri, *Lettere d'amore*, 169–170.
86 *Desert Island Discs*. Guest John Copley, BBC Radio 4, 6 June 2010, https://www.bbc.co.uk/sounds/play/b00pj3yy.
87 Harewood: 1968
88 Fleetwood: 1958
89 Réal La Rochelle, *Callas: La diva et la vinyle* (Montréal: Triptyque, 2005), 241.
90 John Rosenfield, "Callas and Dallas," *Theatre Arts*, March 1959.
91 Prouse, "Maria Callas Speaks," 26 March 1961.
92 Sievewright, "Callas Remembered: Conversation with Maria Callas, July 1977."
93 Cook, 272.
94 Gavoty: 1965
95 Interview with Jacques Bourgeois (*Hommages à Maria Callas*), 4 April 1978.
96 Eric Blom, "'Norma' and Others," *The Observer*, 16 November 1952.
97 Callas, "I am not guilty of those Callas scandals."
98 Neville Cardus, "The divine Callas: Having made a comeback against all expectations in . . .," *The Guardian*, 1 December 1973.
99 Harewood: 1968
100 Ardoin & Fitzgerald, 12.
101 Harewood: 1968
102 Elio Trovato, *Rolando Panerai, simpatia e comunicativa* (Parma: Azzali, 2009), 112–13.
103 Ardoin: 1968
104 Downes: 1967
105 Sievewright, "Callas Remembered: Conversation with Maria Callas, July 1977."
106 Schwarzkopf & Legge, 199.
107 Andrew Porter in *Opera*, July 1953, quoted in Galatopoulos, 126.
108 Petronella Wyatt, "On meeting Callas," *The Spectator*, 22 November 2003.
109 Caloni: 1976
110 Harewood: 1968
111 Christopher Cook, "The Tosca Sessions," *Gramophone*, June 2007.
112 Pia Meneghini, "Sette anni con Maria," 129.
113 Galatopoulos, 129.
114 ibid, 130.
115 Callas, *Oggi* memoirs in Tosi, 91.

116 Leonard Bernstein to Callas, 15 November 1954 in Sotheby's, *Maria Callas and Her Pygmalion* (Milan: Sotheby's Auctions, 2007), Lot 3. Accessed at https://www.sothebys. com/en/auctions/ecatalogue/2007/maria-callas-and-her-pygmalion-her-life-with-giovanni-battista-meneghini-mi0287/lot.3.html.

117 Margarete Wallman, *Sous le ciel de l'opéra: Mémoires* (Paris: Félin, 2004), 139–40.

118 Teodoro Celli, " 'Grido in Tre Atti' La Medea di Cherubini," *Corriere Lombardo*, 8–9 May 1953.

119 Galatopoulos, 130.

120 Callas, *Oggi* memoirs in Tosi, 93.

121 Lomazzi, "La Tebaldi Rifiutò di Fare Pace Con La Grande Rivale."

122 Callas to Dorle Soria, 26 November 1957 [DSP].

123 " 'Man Hat Mich *Seelisch* Gelyncht': Ein *Spiegel* Gespräch mit der Sopranistin Maria Meneghini Callas."

124 Harris: 1970

125 Callas, *Oggi* memoirs in Tosi, 89.

126 Martina Marchiorello, "Biki: la sarta della Callas," *La Repubblica*, 15 September 2011.

127 Paolo Romani, "Callas," *Epoca*, 28 September 1977.

128 Hélène Blignaut, *La scala di vetro* (Milan: Rusconi, 1995) quoted in Cosimo Capanni, "Maria e Biki (prima parte)," GBOpera.it, 7 August 2009. Accessed at http://www. gbopera.it/2009/08/maria-e-biki-prima-parte.

129 Romi, "Ce Que La Callas N'Avait Encore Jamais Raconté."

130 Robert Sutherland, 53.

8. "Extreme poetry"

1 "From Our Special Correspondent: Mme. Callas on Opera."

2 Arlene Dahl, "Maria Callas Accents Her Magnificent Eyes," *Long Island Star Journal*, 21 January 1959.

3 Jellinek, 310.

4 "Callas Dazzles—Without Gems," *The Washington Post*, 30 January 1959.

5 Henry Canals, *Hommage Maria Callas*: 1987 Musée de Neuilly Exhibition Brochure for 16 September–19 October 1987 (Paris: Musée de Neuilly, 1987), 2.

6 ibid. 31, diagram 56.

7 ibid. 20, diagrams 32 and 53.

8 Romanò Marchetti, 15.

9 Canals, 2.

10 "I vestiti della Callas," *Grazia*, 1 June 1958.

11 Scott, 128 (Interviews with Biki and Alain Reynaud).

12 Sadie Whitelocks, "Time for new shoes Anna? Ms Wintour steps out in ill-fitting heels at Milan Fashion Week—but she's been wearing the same style since the NINETIES," *Daily Mail*, 23 September 2013, https://www.dailymail.co.uk/femail/article-2429905/Anna-Wintour-wears-ill-fitting-Manolo-Blahnik-strappy-sandals-Milan-Fashion-Week.html.

13 *Mad About Music*, Interview with Nicola Bulgari, WQXR Radio New York, 2 November 2008.

14 Benedetta Perilli, "Vestivamo alla Maria Callas: ovvero come la Divina divenne icona di stile," *La Repubblica*, 15 September 2018.

15 Leonard Lyons, "No Matter What the Cost Opera Star Gets Her Way," *The New York Times*, 7 May 1956.

16 Stancioff, 108.

17 Jacques Bourgeois, "Douce et timide, Callas a gagné le cœur de Paris," *Arts*, 24–30 December 1958.

18 Michael White, "Callas: A Life for Sale," *The Independent*, 25 November 2000.

19 Murrow: 1958

20 Anita Pensotti, "Maria Callas" in Tosi, *Giovane Callas*, 33.

21 Lebrecht, 156.

22 Lomazzi, "Della Madre Preferisce Non Dir Niente: Tutta La Sua Tenerezza E' Per Il Padre."

23 Soria, "Greek Sorceress."

24 Bettina Brentano, "Grandir avec Callas," *L'Avant-Scène*, no. 44, October 1982, 123.

25 Richard Osborne, *Herbert von Karajan: A Life in Music* (London: Chatto & Windus, 1998), 352.

26 Schwarzkopf & Legge, 196.

27 Lanfranco Rasponi, *The Last Prima Donnas* (New York: Limelight Editions, 1998), 579.

28 Osborne, 352.

29 Hanine-Roussel, 225 (Interview with Rolando Panerai).

30 Richard Osborne, *Conversations with Karajan* (Oxford: Oxford Paperbacks, 1991), 73–75.

31 Ardoin & Fitzgerald, 24.

32 Stassinopoulos, 124.

33 Harris: 1970

34 Cook, 274.

35 Prouse, "Maria Callas Speaks," 26 March 1961.

36 Jellinek, 106.

37 Harewood: 1968

38 Callas, "Il faut réformer l'opéra," *Arts* magazine, 18 December 1958.

39 Harewood: 1968

40 Wolf Mittler, Interview with Callas for Bayerischer Rundfunk TV, Munich, 21 May 1959, https://www.youtube.com/watch?v=-WSViOnFWes&pp=ygUYd29sZiBtaXR0bGVyIGNhbGxhcyAxOTU5.

41 Fleetwood: 1958

42 Boutwell, "Processo alla Callas."

43 Galatopoulos, 409.

44 Peter Andry, *Inside the recording studio: Working with Callas, Domingo, Rostropovich and the Classical Elite* (Lanham, MD: Scarecrow Press, 2008), 48.

45 Caloni: 1976

46 Harris: 1970

47 FitzLyon, *Maria Malibran: Diva of the Romantic Age*, 93.

48 Meneghini, 219–22.

49 Galatopoulos, 132.

50 Wallman, 140.

51 Weaver: 1965

52 Jellinek, 108.

53 Pensotti, "Maria Callas," 27.

54 Interview with Mike Buongiorno for *Viva Maria*, Radio 3 Italy, 16 September 1997.

55 Henry Luce, "Publisher's Letter," *Time*, 29 October 1956. Accessed at https://content.time.com/time/subscriber/article/0,33009,867161,00.html.

56 Fleetwood: 1958

57 Pablo Corbalán, *El Informador*, "La Estela de Maria Callas," 28 June 1959.

58 Jellinek, 108.

59 Mayer, "La Scala's New Queen."

60 David Gregson, "Remembering Maria," *San Diego Magazine*, October 1997.

61 Galatopoulos, 264.

62 Allegri, *La véritable histoire de Maria Callas*, 183.

63 Ossenska, Interview with Callas for *La Scala e i suoi protagonisti*.

64 Mayer, "La Scala's New Queen."

65 Schwarzkopf & Legge, 194.

66 Robert Naur, "I have been a little spoiled," *Politiken*, 8 June 1963.

67 Matz, "We Introduce Maria Meneghini Callas."

68 Pia Meneghini, "Sette anni con Maria," 111.

69 WGN Radio Chicago, Interview with Callas, 1 September 1957.

70 Giancarlo Fusco, *Il gusto di vivere* (Rome: Editori Laterza, 2014), 215.

71 Matz, "We Introduce Maria Meneghini Callas."

72 Lerman, 306.

73 Prouse, "Maria Callas Speaks," 26 March 1961.

74 Crespi Morbio, 129.

75 Undated letter from Meneghini to Luchino Visconti, c. summer 1954 [LVP].

76 Scott, 131 (from Lawrence Kelly's interview with John Ardoin, 29 January 1973).

77 Giovanna Lomazzi, "Perché Vogliono A Tutti Costi Che Io E Grace Siamo Nemiche," *La Settimana Incom Illustrata*, 26 March 1961.

78 Visconti to Meneghini, Undated letter of June 1954 in Allegri, *Lettere d'amore*, 177.

79 Meneghini to Visconti, 22 June 1954 [LVP].

80 Prouse, "Maria Callas Speaks," 2 April 1961.

81 Schwarzkopf & Legge, 200–1.

82 Galatopoulos, 137–38.

83 Scott, 139.

84 Jellinek, 115.

85 Interview with Nicola Rescigno in John Ardoin, *Maria Callas In Her Own Words*: Four-Part Documentary, KUSC Los Angeles Radio, 2, 9, 16 and 23 February 1998.

86 Bottero, 214 (Interview with Giulietta Simionato).

87 "Maria Meneghini Callas," *Vogue*, 1 November 1955.

88 Newman, 181.

89 Keith Kreitman, "A 'master' in her element," *San Mateo Daily Journal*, 29 October 2011.

90 Lerman, 174.

91 Cassidy, "Maria 'touched by God's finger.' "

92 Hanine-Roussel, 236.

93 Lerman, 174.

94 Cassidy, "Pride and Honesty Shining Traits of Maria Callas."

95 "Special To The New York Times: Contract Breach Is Laid to Singer: New York Lawyer Charges Maria Meneghini-Callas With Failure to Pay Fee," *The New York Times*, 5 November 1954.

96 Callas, "My Defense" [CFM].

97 "BREACH OF CONTRACT IS DENIED BY SOPRANO," *The New York Times*, 6 November 1954.

98 "ILLINOIS APPELATE RULING DECIDES MARIA CAN BE SUED IN ILLINOIS," *The Dallas Morning News*, 24 November 1955.

99 Cassidy, "Maria 'touched by God's finger.' "

100 John von Rhein, "Callas Sang Here: Remembering A Great Love Affair in Our Musical History," *Chicago Tribune*, 9 February 1997.

101 Undated letter from Callas to Luchino Visconti c. 1–8 August 1954 [LVP].

102 Ira Siff, "Bellini's Norma," *Opera News*, 3 June 2003.

103 Beppe Menegatti, "Una 'Vestale' con Maria Callas e Mago Visconti," *La Rivista Illustrata del Museo Teatrale alla Scala*, no. 23, October 1993.

104 Galatopoulos, 176.

105 U.R., "Corelli fa le bizze a Parigi vuole il nome come la Callas," *Il Gazzettino Venezia*, 4 June 1964.

106 Ardoin & Fitzgerald, 90.

107 Laurence Schifano, *Luchino Visconti: The Flames of Passion* (London: Harper Collins, 1990), 289.

108 Joseph Turquan, *The Love Affairs of Napoleon* (Charleston: Nabu Press, 2012), 314.

109 Menegatti, "Una 'Vestale' con Maria Callas e Mago Visconti."

110 Gastel Chiarelli, 60.

111 René de Cecatty, *Maria Callas* (Paris: Folio, 2009), 201.

112 Lomazzi, "Della Madre Preferisce Non Dir Niente: Tutta La Sua Tenerezza E' Per Il Padre."

113 Ann Draper, "Dinner with Callas and More, Too," *The Dallas Morning News*, 17 August 1960.

114 Matz, "We Introduce Maria Meneghini Callas."

115 Galatopoulos, 178

116 Nigel Simeone, *The Leonard Bernstein Letters* (New Haven: Yale University Press, 2013), 324.

117 Jellinek, 124.

118 Lomazzi, "La Tebaldi Rifiutò di Fare Pace Con La Grande Rivale."

119 Jellinek, 145.

120 Ross: 1957

121 Jellinek, 146.

122 Galatopoulos, 207.

123 de Carvalho, "The Prima Donna."

124 Callas, "Corrections of *Time* magazine article," [CFM].

125 Telegram from Tullio Serafin to Callas, 1 January 1957 [CFM].

126 Callas, "I am not guilty of those Callas scandals."

127 Rual Askew, "Firing Doesn't Worry Callas," *The Dallas Morning News*, 8 November 1958.

128 Banzet: 1965.

129 Gobbi, 94–95.

130 Harris: 1970.

131 Prouse, "Maria Callas Speaks," 2 April 1961.

132 Galatopoulos, 181.

133 Mario Fedrigo, "Gigliola Frazzoni: *La fanciulla del West*: Quinta Parte," GBOpera.it, 13 January 2013, https://www.gbopera.it/gb/gigliola-frazzonila-fanciulla-del-west-quintaparte.

134 Helen Smith, *There's a Place For Us: The Musical Theatre Works of Leonard Bernstein* (Farnham, UK: Ashgate, 2011), 124.

135 Carla Fracci, "1955, davanti a pochi amici 'West Side Story' prima della prima. Il dono di Bernstein," *Corriere della Sera*, 9 July 2000.

136 Vasso Papantiou, Interview with Piero Tosi in the catalogue for *In the Constellation of Maria Callas: The Origins of a Myth*, Exhibition for the Association for the Building of the Opera House & The Academy of Lyric Arts "Maria Callas," 28 April—20 May 2004, Athens.

137 John Gruen's Interview with Leonard Bernstein in *Opera News*, September 1972 in Monica Stirling, *A Screen of Time: A Study of Luchino Visconti* (London: Secker & Warburg, 1979), 105.

138 Harewood: 1968

139 Hanine-Roussel, 255 (Interview with Eugenia Ratti).

140 Desgraupes: 1969

141 Matz, "We Introduce Maria Meneghini Callas."

142 Fleetwood: 1958

143 Simeone, 326.

144 Galatopoulos, 181.

145 Ardoin & Fitzgerald, 104.

146 ibid. 107 (Interview with Piero Tosi).

147 Gavoty: 1965

148 Franco Zeffirelli, *Zeffirelli: An Autobiography* (London: Weidenfeld & Nicholson, 1986), 131–32.

149 Simeone, 326.

150 Ossenska, Interview with Callas for *La Scala e i suoi protagonisti*.

9. "Chantilly"

1 Mittler, Interview with Callas for Bayerischer Rundfunk TV, Munich, 21 May 1959.

2 Prouse, "Maria Callas Speaks," 2 April 1961.

3 "Tosca, the truth," *The Telegraph*, 29 January 2000.

4 Cruesemann: 1959

5 "From Our Special Correspondent: Mme. Callas on Opera."

6 Ulrich Müller, "Regietheater/Director's Theater," in Helen M. Greenwald, *The Oxford Handbook of Opera* (New York: Oxford University Press), 2014.

7 "From Our Special Correspondent: Mme. Callas on Opera."

8 Downes: 1967

9 Glotz, 201.

10 Harewood, "Callas Remembered: Tributes to Callas."

11 Emilio Radius, *L'Europeo*, January 1953 in Crespi Morbio, 17.

12 Galatopoulos, 185.

13 Author's e-mail correspondence with Cristina Gastel Chiarelli, 14 June 2014.

14 Callas to Visconti, 9 December 1955 [LVP].

15 Pellegrini, "Quel canto vulnerabile."

16 Weaver, "Remembering Callas: Some Confessions of a Fan," 75.

17 Luchino Visconti, "Per Maria" (rehearsal notes for *La traviata* at La Scala, May 1955). Lot 93 in Sotheby's, *Maria Callas and Her Pygmalion* Auction Catalogue, 12 December 2007. Accessed at https://www.sothebys.com/en/auctions/ecatalogue/2007/maria-callas-and-her-pygmalion-her-life-with-giovanni-battista-meneghini-mi0287/lot.93.html.

18 Desgraupes: 1969

19 Arragno, Interview with Callas for *Sunday Night at The London Palladium*.

20 Galatopoulos, 249–250.

21 Ardoin & Fitzgerald, 90.

22 Desgraupes: 1969

23 Ardoin & Fitzgerald, 90.

24 Scott, 84.

25 Galatopoulos, 247.

26 Visconti to Callas, 2 August 1955 in Meneghini, 195.

27 ibid. 189.

28 Meneghini, 177.

29 Richard Burton, Entry of 6 November 1968, *The Richard Burton Diaries* (New Haven: Yale University Press, 2013), 218.

30 Galatopoulos, 251.

31 Desgraupes: 1969

32 Frost: 1970

33 Harewood: 1968

34 Ardoin & Fitzgerald, 115.

35 Hanine-Roussel, 260 (Interview with Edda Zoraide Casali).

36 Ardoin & Fitzgerald, 119 (Interview with Carlo Maria Giulini).

37 Glotz, 180.

38 Downes: 1967

39 Harewood, 228.

40 Fabio Gervasoni, Interview with Beppe Menegatti, Maria Callas International Archive DVD Collection, Volume I.

41 Fusco, 210.

42 Jacques Bourgeois, "La traviata du siècle," *L'Avant-Scène Opéra*, April 1983.

43 Harewood: 1968

44 Gastel Chiarelli, 65.

45 ibid. 202.

46 Jellinek, 134.

47 Harewood, 227.

48 Prouse, "Maria Callas Speaks," 2 April 1961.

49 Scott, 160.

50 Werner Oehlmann in *Der Tagesspiegel*, 1 October 1955 in Hanine-Roussel, 270.

51 Scott, 160.

52 Downes: 1967

53 Dr. Alfred Tomatis to Kalle Brewster, 11 February 1994 in Alfred A. Tomatis, *The Ear and the Voice* (Lanham, MD: Scarecrow Press, 2005), 76.

54 Osborne, *Herbert von Karajan: A Life in Music*, 354–55.

55 Glotz, 204.

56 Undated letter from Callas to Walter Legge (c. April 1956) in Alan Sanders, *Walter Legge: Words and Music* (London: Duckworth, 1998), 232–33.

57 Jellinek, 151.

58 Harold C. Schonberg, "Music: Maria Callas Sings in Lucia," *The New York Times*, 13 June 1956.

59 Prouse, "Maria Callas Speaks," 2 April 1961.

60 "From Our Special Correspondent: Mme. Callas on Opera."

61 Harewood: 1968

62 Undated letter from Visconti to Meneghini in Meneghini, 194.

63 Galatopoulos, 425.

64 " 'Butterfly' Flees Process Servers," *The New York Times*, 19 November 1955; "ILLINOIS APPELATE RULING DECIDES MARIA CAN BE SUED IN ILLINOIS," *The Dallas Morning News*, 24 November 1955.

65 Lomazzi, "Della Madre Preferisce Non Dir Niente: Tutta La Sua Tenerezza E' Per Il Padre."

66 Newman, 179.

67 Ross: 1957

68 Rudolf Bing to Meneghini, 20 September 1955 [AMO].

69 Meneghini, 227–28.

70 Rudolf Bing, 5000 *Nights at the Opera: The Memoirs of Sir Rudolf Bing* (New York: Doubleday, 1972), 237.

71 Newman, 178.

72 Cassidy, "Maria 'touched by God's finger.' "

73 "Music: The Most Exciting," *Time*, 21 November 1955. Accessed at https://content.time.com/time/subscriber/article/0,33009,866641-1,00.html.

74 Rasponi, 583.

75 Pensotti, "Maria Callas," 33.

76 Stancioff, 125.

77 NHK TV Japan, Interview with Callas and Giuseppe Di Stefano at Bunka Kaikan Hall.

78 Lomazzi, "Della Madre Preferisce Non Dir Niente: Tutta La Sua Tenerezza E' Per Il Padre."

79 National Endowment for the Arts, Interview with Leontyne Price, 3 June 2010, https://www.arts.gov/stories/video/nea-opera-honors-interview-leontyne-price, 10:48–13:00.

80 Jellinek, 140.

81 Richard Dyer, "She was marvelous," *Boston Globe*, 25 September 1977.

82 Scott, 164.

83 Soria, "Greek Sorceress."

84 Callas, "My Defense" [CFM].

85 Soria, "Greek Sorceress."

86 Callas, *Oggi* memoirs in Lowe, 97.

87 Soria, "Greek Sorceress."

88 Callas, "My Defense" [CFM].

89 Galatopoulos, 144.

90 Callas, "I am not guilty of those Callas scandals."

91 Newman, 179–80.

92 Callas, "My Defense," [CFM].

93 Callas to Nelly Failoni, 18 September 1956, in Tosi, *Giovane Callas*, 158.

94 Jellinek, 143.

95 Meneghini, 216.

96 "Court Upholds Maria Callas' Decorum," *Buffalo Courier-Express*, 22 March 1957.

97 "Miss Callas' Suit Upheld," *The New York Times*, 11 August 1959.

98 Fleetwood: 1958

99 Galatopoulos, 273.

100 ibid. 196.

101 Georges Farret, *Luigi Alva, L'Almaviva de la Scala* (Gémenos: Éditions Autres Temps, 2010), 85.

102 Ardoin & Fitzgerald, 139.

103 Author's interview with Luigi Alva, Milan, 11 July 2012.

104 Galatopoulos, 197.

105 Lomazzi, "Della Madre Preferisce Non Dir Niente: Tutta La Sua Tenerezza E' Per Il Padre."

106 Nilsson, *My Life in Opera*, 197.

107 Undated letter from Callas to Walter Legge (c. April 1956) in Sanders, 232–33.

108 Lomazzi, "Della Madre Preferisce Non Dir Niente: Tutta La Sua Tenerezza E' Per Il Padre."

109 Desgraupes: 1969

110 Lomazzi, "Della Madre Preferisce Non Dir Niente: Tutta La Sua Tenerezza E' Per Il Padre."

111 "La Callas in 'Fedora' nonostante la febbre," *Corriere Milanese*, 24–25 May 1956.

112 Ardoin & Fitzgerald, 148–49 (from interviews with Tatiana Pavlova and Franco Corelli).

113 Lomazzi, "Della Madre Preferisce Non Dir Niente: Tutta La Sua Tenerezza E' Per Il Padre."

114 Pierre-Jean Rémy, *Callas: Une vie* (Paris: Albin Michel, 1997), eBook, Kindle location 3281. Accessed at https://www.amazon.co.uk/Callas-Une-vie-Litt-Generale-French-ebook/dp/B009XF6P8Y.

115 "I'm A Fatalist Says Prima Donna," *The Toronto Daily Star*, 21 October 1958.

116 Callas to Giulietta Simionato, 20 June 1966 in Hanine-Roussel, 523.

117 Romi, "Ce Que La Callas N'Avait Encore Jamais Raconté."

118 Ardoin & Fitzgerald, 44.

119 Stancioff, 172.

120 "Lucia oder die Orgie des Belcanto," *Kunst und Kultur*, 14 June 1956.

121 Sander Gorlinsky to Callas, 23 July 1956 [SGC].

122 Vittorio Ragona in Nicolò de Rienzo, *Nessun problema: I segreti dei portieri dei grandi alberghi* (ADD editore, 2012), eBook, Kindle location 655.

123 Aversano & Pellegrini, 382.

124 Stancioff, 121.

125 Roderick Gilchrist, "Lady Walton, mischievous, energetic and intensely feminine," *The Telegraph*, 6 April 2010.

126 " 'Met' To Present American Opera, Samuel Barber's 'Vanessa' Slated For Next Season," *The New York Times*, 6 November 1956.

127 Barbara B. Heyman, *Samuel Barber: The Composer and His Music* (New York: Oxford University Press, 1992), 384.

128 Murrow: 1958

129 Jellinek, 179.

130 Bruno Berenguer, *Denise Duval* (Lyon: Symétrie, 2003), 115.

131 de Nussac & Cotta: 1970

132 Sir Georg Solti, *Solti on Solti* (Chicago: Chicago Review Press, 1998), 148.

133 Author's interview with Giovanna Lomazzi.

134 Stassinopoulos, 156.

135 Letters from Gorlinsky to Meneghini, 9 and 11 August 1956 [SGC].

136 Jellinek, 154–55.

137 Mario Giuseppe Genesi, *Anna Moffo: una carriera italo-americana* (Piacenza: Orion Editions, 2002), 45.

138 Callas, "The Lyric Tradition," 18 October 1971.

139 Romi, "Ce Que La Callas N'Avait Encore Jamais Raconté."

140 Max de Schauensee, "Opera Taped Where It Grew," *High Fidelity*, December 1956.

141 Lomazzi, "Della Madre Preferisce Non Dir Niente: Tutta La Sua Tenerezza E' Per Il Padre."

142 Jellinek, 159.

143 Allegri, *Lettere d'amore*, 67.

144 "Sour Note For Her Agent," *Daily Defender*, 8 May 1956.

145 "CALLAS TO FACE 300,000 SUIT FROM BAGAROZY," *The New York Times*, 11 October 1956.

146 "From *Morning Democrat*'s Leased Wires: 'Declines Plea,' " *The Quad City Times* of Davenport, Iowa, 2 November 1957.

147 "Maria Callas Settles Suit," *The New York Times*, 18 November 1957.

148 Galatopoulos, 149.

149 Stassinopoulos, 160.

150 John Briggs, "Rehearsals Begin at Full Blast As 'Met' Tunes Up for Season," *The New York Times*, 16 October 1956.

151 Meneghini, 203.

152 Lerman, 214.

153 Soria, "Greek Sorceress."

154 Lerman, 214.

155 Callas, "Corrections of *Time* magazine article," [CFM].

156 George Callas to Maria and Meneghini, 7 October 1957 in Volf, "1957."

157 Lomazzi, "Della Madre Preferisce Non Dir Niente: Tutta La Sua Tenerezza E' Per Il Padre."

158 Gardner: 1958

159 Murrow: 1959

160 Lomazzi, "Volle Dimagrire Contro La Volontà di Meneghini."

161 "Scenes By Dramatic Diva," *Life*, 12 November 1956.

162 Martha Graham to Francis Robinson, 11 November 1956 in Lowe, 232 (Francis Robinson Collection of Theatre, Music, and Dance at Special Collections at the Vanderbilt University Library).

163 Roger Dettmer in *Chicago American*, 30 October 1956 in Lowe, 172.

164 Irving Kolodin, "Callas in NORMA: Report on the Met Opening," *Saturday Review*, 10 November 1956.

165 Jellinek, 161.

166 Lorenza Cerbini, "L'atelier Maragoni e il cuore di cristallo finito in fondo all'oceano," *Corriere della Sera*, 17 March 2018.

167 Lerman, 356.

168 Dorothy Kilgallen, "Long-Haired Darling Triumphs at Met," *The Washington Post and Times Herald*, 1 November 1956.

169 Lomazzi, "La Tebaldi Rifiutò di Fare Pace Con La Grande Rivale."

170 Noël Coward ed. Graham Payn & Sheridan Morley, Entry of 4 November 1956, *The Noël Coward Diaries* (Boston: Little Brown, 1982), 336.

171 Petsalis-Diomidis, 303 f. (Interview with Dino Yannopoulos).

172 London, "Prima Donnas I Have Sung Against."

173 Ronald Eyer in *Musical America*, December 1956 in Lowe, 175.

174 James A. Drake & Rosa Ponselle, *Ponselle: A Singer's Life* (New York: Doubleday, 1982), 200.

175 Harewood: 1968

176 Barbara Cook, liner notes for *Candide: Original Broadway Cast Recording* (New York: Sony BMG, 2003).

177 Caloni: 1976

178 Fleetwood: 1958

179 Ross: 1957

180 Murrow: 1959

181 Jellinek, 173–74.

182 Lomazzi, "La Tebaldi Rifiutò di Fare Pace Con La Grande Rivale."

183 Jellinek, 174.

184 "An Irishman's Diary: Catching Up With Callas," *The Irish Times*, 20 April 1960.

185 de Nussac & Cotta: 1970

186 Callas, "Italia domanda Il Loro Natale Più Bello," *Oggi*, 22 December 1957.

187 Murrow: 1958

188 Cruesemann: 1959

189 John Briggs, "Onstage, The Prima Donna," *The New York Times*, 11 November 1959.

190 Ross: 1957

191 Prouse, "Maria Callas Speaks," 2 April 1961.

192 "The Observer Profile: Prima Donna," *The Observer*, 15 June 1958.

193 Cruesemann: 1959

10. "A human note"

1 "An Operatic Volcano, Maria Meneghini Callas," *The New York Times*, 30 October 1956.

2 Lomazzi, "Volle Dimagrire Contro La Volontà di Meneghini."

3 Jellinek, 305.
4 Matz, "We Introduce Maria Meneghini Callas."
5 Boutwell, "Processo alla Callas."
6 Callas, "Il faut réformer l'opéra."
7 Callas to Meneghini, 8 June 1948 in Allegri, *Lettere d'amore*, 162.
8 Jellinek, 177–78.
9 Peter Heyworth, "Callas Recalls the Golden Age," *The Manchester Guardian*, 3 February 1957.
10 Callas to Eugenio Gara, 5 February 1957 in Tosi, *Casta diva: L'incomparabile Callas* (Rome: Gallia, 1993), 195–96.
11 Hanine-Roussel, 315 (Interview with Jacques Bourgeois).
12 Undated letter from Callas to Harold Rosenthal, c. March 1957 [HRP].
13 Jellinek, 247.
14 Matt Dobkin, "All Hail the Queen," metopera.org, https://www.metopera.org/userinformation/nightly-met-opera-streams/articles/all-hail-the-queen.
15 Lomazzi, "Volle Dimagrire Contro La Volontà di Meneghini."
16 Author's interview with Giovanna Lomazzi.
17 Banzet: 1965
18 Rasponi, 577.
19 Ardoin & Fitzgerald, 151–155.
20 Cook, 275–76.
21 Gavazzeni, 360.
22 Signorini, "Ecco le lettere, i documenti e le foto che conservo della mia amica Callas."
23 Galatopoulos, 398.
24 Gianandrea Gavazzeni in "Processo alla Callas," *Radiocorriere TV*, no. 48, 30 November 1969.
25 Jellinek, 183.
26 Callas to Oscar and Carla Coltellacci, 25 April 1957 in Minerva Auctions Catalogue (Rome: Minerva Auctions, 24 March 2011).
27 Jellinek, 184.
28 Harris: 1970.
29 Allegri, *La véritable histoire de Maria Callas*, 246.
30 Jellinek, 184.
31 Eliette von Karajan, *À ses côtés* (Paris: L'Archipel, 2008), 192.
32 Callas, "I am not guilty of those Callas scandals."
33 Allegri, *La véritable histoire de Maria Callas*, 171.
34 ibid. 182.
35 Galatopoulos, 246.
36 Sievewright, "Callas Remembered: Conversation with Maria Callas, July 1977."
37 Harewood: 1968
38 Stirling, 127.
39 Ardoin & Fitzgerald, 162.
40 Sievewright, "Callas Remembered: Conversation with Maria Callas, July 1977."
41 Ardoin & Fitzgerald, 162.
42 Galatopoulos, 246.
43 Ardoin, *The Callas Legacy*, 124.

44 Giovanna Lomazzi, "Svelati Dopo Tre Anni Tutti I Retroscena Del Clamoroso Scandalo All'Opera di Roma," *La Settimana Incom Illustrata*, 12 March 1961.

45 Reporter's interview with Callas at Düsseldorf Airport, 18 May 1963, Maria Callas International Archive DVD Collection, Volume VIII.

46 Emilio Pozzi, Interview with Callas for *Radio Suite*, RAI Television, 6 July 1957.

47 Lowe, 185.

48 Ardoin, *The Callas Legacy*, 128.

49 Fleetwood: 1958

50 Galatopoulos, 256.

51 Allegri, *La véritable histoire de Maria Callas*, 247.

52 Meneghini in Allegri, *Lettere d'amore*, 146.

53 Robert Sutherland, 240.

54 Galatopoulos, 405.

55 John A. Holmes, "Congenital Abnormalities of The Uterus and Pregnancy," *The British Medical Journal* Vol. 1, No. 4976 (May 19, 1956): 1144–47.

56 For more on the difficulties of surgical procedures used to correct uterine malformation in the 1950s, see:

- G.A.J. Dunselman, "Congenital Malformations of the Uterus. Results of the Strassmann Metroplastic Operation," N. V. Boekdrukkerij, Helmond, Holland (1959).
- S Genell & A. Sjovall, "The Strassmann operation, results obtained in 58 cases," *Acta Obstetricia et Gynecologica Scandinavica*, vol. 38 (1959): 477.
- Anusuya Dass, F.R.C.O.G. and R. Gulati, M.D., "Pregnancy After Strassman's Operation for the Uterus Bicornis," *Journal of Obstetrics and Gynaecology of India* (February 1971): 83–87.
- Edward E. Wallach, M.D., "The Uterine Factor in Infertility," *Fertility and Sterility*, Vol.23, No. 2 (February 1972).
- Lisa Jane Jacobsen & Alan DeCherney, "Results of Conventional and Hysteroscopic Surgery," *Human Reproduction*, vol. 12: (January 1997): 1376–81.

57 P.A. Zourlas, "Surgical treatment of malformations of the uterus," *Surgery, Gynecology and Obstetrics*, Vol. 141 (July 1975: 57–58). Accessed at https://pubmed.ncbi.nlm.nih.gov/1154214.

58 Meneghini, 8; Allegri, *Lettere d'amore*, 146; Galatopoulos, 405.

59 Jesus Sierra-Oliva, "Callas in Mexico; Part I: May–June 1950," *The Maria Callas International Magazine*, Issue 29, 28.

60 Callas, *Oggi* memoirs in Tosi, 67.

61 Frost: 1970

62 Pensotti, "Maria Callas," 33–34.

63 Callas, Untitled Defense of What Happened in Athens, 5 August 1957 in Allegri, *La véritable histoire de Maria Callas*, 251.

64 Lomazzi, "Svelati Dopo Tre Anni Tutti I Retroscena Del Clamoroso Scandalo All'Opera di Roma."

65 Callas, Untitled Defense of What Happened in Athens, 5 August 1957, 249–50.

66 Petsalis-Diomidis, 308.

67 Callas, Untitled Defense of What Happened in Athens, 5 August 1957, 251–52.

68 "Callas Afraid to Face the Athenian Public," *Ta Nea*, 2 August 1957.

69 "Maria Callas Cancels Concert at Last Minute," *The New York Times*, 2 August 1957.

70 Jellinek, 192.

71 Achilles Hamakis, Interview with Callas in Athens for *Through the Microphone*, Greek radio program on 4 August 1957, in *The Unknown Recordings, Vol. 2* trans. Christo Misirlóglou and Petros Heliotis (Buenos Aires: Divina Records, 2000).

72 Jellinek, 306–7.

73 Meneghini on behalf of Callas to an unnamed young fan, Lot 877, Gonnelli Auctions, 31 January 2017 (Florence: Gonnelli Casa d'Aste). Accessed at https://www.gonnelli.it/uk/auction-0022/callas-maria-lettera-manoscritta-firmata-maria.asp.

74 Callas to unnamed fans, 16 February 1958 [Copy from CFG].

75 Gorlinsky to John Coveney of EMI Records, 24 February 1965 [SGC].

76 Scott, 193.

77 Galatopoulos, 257.

78 Allegri, *La véritable histoire de Maria Callas*, 248.

79 United Press International, "Departs Without Leaving a Note," *The New York Daily News*, 18 September 1957.

80 Callas, "I am not guilty of those Callas scandals."

81 Lomazzi, "Svelati Dopo Tre Anni Tutti I Retroscena Del Clamoroso Scandalo All'Opera di Roma."

82 Gastel Chiarelli, 78.

83 Emilio Pozzi, Interview with Callas for "Schermi e ribalte," RAI Radio, 30 August 1957.

84 Jellinek, 194.

85 Pozzi, Interview with Callas for "Schermi e ribalte."

86 WGN Radio Philadelphia, Interview with Callas, 1 September 1957.

87 Callas, "I am not guilty of those Callas scandals."

88 Allegri, *La véritable histoire de Maria Callas*, 255.

89 Prouse, "Maria Callas Speaks," 2 April 1961.

90 Allegri, *La véritable histoire de Maria Callas*, 283–84.

91 Galatopoulos, 266.

92 Christopher Silvester, "Book Review: *Inventing Elsa Maxwell*," *Spears* magazine, 30 May 2013.

93 Galatopoulos, 406.

94 ibid. 263.

95 Callas, "I am not guilty of those Callas scandals."

96 Callas to Hedda Hopper in Hopper, *The whole truth and nothing but* (Pyramid Books: New York, 1963), 224.

97 Signorini, "Ecco le lettere, i documenti e le foto che conservo della mia amica Callas."

98 Lomazzi, "Svelati Dopo Tre Anni Tutti I Retroscena Del Clamoroso Scandalo All'Opera di Roma."

99 Meneghini, 258. Carlo Trabattoni featured in "Il symposium di psicologia clinica 1952 di Milan" from 11 April–30 December 1952.

100 Ross: 1957

101 Lomazzi, "Volle Dimagrire Contro La Volontà di Meneghini."

102 "Coast Opera Signs Mme. Callas," *The New York Times*, 4 January 1957.

103 Callas to Kurt Adler, 11 September 1957 [RBC].

104   Adler to Callas, 13 September 1957 [RBC].

105   Callas, "I am not guilty of those Callas scandals."

106   Lomazzi, "Svelati Dopo Tre Anni Tutti I Retroscena Del Clamoroso Scandalo All'Opera di Roma."

107   Galatopoulos, 263.

108   Earl Wilson's Syndicated U.S. Column, 18 October 1957.

109   "Coast Opera Acts Against Callas," *The New York Times*, 18 September 1957.

110   Bing, *5000 Nights at the Opera*, 240.

111   Jellinek, 327.

112   Callas to Oscar and Carla Coltellacci, 25 April 1957.

113   Callas to Charles Johnson, 30 September 1957. Accessed at http://www.mariacallasmuseum.org/documents/mc-doc-003.htm.

114   Hanine-Roussel, 416 (Interview with Ferruccio Mezzadri).

115   Jellinek, 200.

116   Callas to Walter Cummings, 13 October 1957 in Hanine-Roussel, 336–37.

117   Callas, "I am not guilty of those Callas scandals."

118   Lomazzi, "Svelati Dopo Tre Anni Tutti I Retroscena Del Clamoroso Scandalo All'Opera di Roma."

119   Allegri, *La véritable histoire de Maria Callas*, 261.

120   Galatopoulos, 264.

121   Associated Press, "Flu Downs Callas," *The Spokesman Review* of Spokane, Washington, 2 October 1957.

122   Callas to Walter Cummings, 1 November 1957 in Hanine-Roussel, 337.

123   Callas to the Administration of Teatro alla Scala, 6 November 1957 in Allegri, *La véritable histoire de Maria Callas*, 262–64.

124   "Conversation Piece," *Opera News*, 4 December 1982.

125   Callas to Leo Lerman, 26 November 1957 [LLP].

126   Jellinek, 203.

127   Callas, "Il mio dramma di artista e di donna," 16 January 1958.

128   " 'Man Hat Mich Seelisch Gelyncht': Ein *Spiegel* Gespräch mit der Sopranistin Maria Meneghini Callas."

129   Callas, "Il mio dramma di artista e di donna."

130   Gardner: 1958

131   Callas, "Il mio dramma di artista e di donna."

132   Lomazzi, "Svelati Dopo Tre Anni Tutti I Retroscena Del Clamoroso Scandalo All'Opera di Roma."

133   Franco Corelli in Tosi, *Casta diva: L'incomparabile Callas*, 237.

134   " 'Man Hat Mich Seelisch Gelyncht': Ein *Spiegel* Gespräch mit der Sopranistin Maria Meneghini Callas."

135   Bernard Gavoty, "Je chante, ne vous déplaise," *Le Figaro Littéraire*, 27 May 1965.

136   Callas, "Il mio dramma di artista e di donna."

137   Callas, "I am not guilty of those Callas scandals."

138   Meneghini's planned announcement is published in Tosi, *Casta diva: L'incomparabile Callas*, 222 23.

139 Lomazzi, "Svelati Dopo Tre Anni Tutti I Retroscena Del Clamoroso Scandalo All'Opera di Roma."

140 David Gelman, "The Maria Callas Story," *The New York Post*, 2 March 1958.

141 Lomazzi, "Svelati Dopo Tre Anni Tutti I Retroscena Del Clamoroso Scandalo All'Opera di Roma."

142 " 'Man Hat Mich Seelisch Gelyncht': Ein *Spiegel* Gespräch mit der Sopranistin Maria Meneghini Callas."

143 Callas, "Il mio dramma di artista e di donna."

144 Lomazzi, "Svelati Dopo Tre Anni Tutti I Retroscena Del Clamoroso Scandalo All'Opera di Roma."

145 Paul Hofmann, "Rome Crowds Denounce Callas; Physicians Say Her Voice Failed," *The New York Times*, 4 January 1958.

146 Eugene Levin, "Soprano Sets Rome Ablaze in Fury Over Virus-or-Virago Operatic Balk," *The Washington Post*, 4 January 1958.

147 Review in *Il Giorno* in Kesting, trans. John Hunt, 194.

148 "Fifers Crack Down, Fifes Crack Up In Draw Battle Over Opera Walkout," *The Washington Post*, 7 January 1958.

149 Hanine-Roussel, 387 n. 24.

150 Callas, "Il mio dramma di artista e di donna."

151 "Rome Bars Opera Star To Prevent New Riots," *The Washington Post*, 7 January 1958.

152 " 'Man Hat Mich Seelisch Gelyncht': Ein *Spiegel* Gespräch mit der Sopranistin Maria Meneghini Callas."

153 Murrow: 1958

154 Jellinek, 213.

155 UPI, "Callas Welcomed by Milan Fans," *The Times Record* of Troy, New York, 10 January 1958.

156 "Callas Wins Her Case," *The Guardian*, 2 February 1968.

157 Galatopoulos, 273.

158 Undated birthday note from Callas to Meneghini (c. 23 October 1958) in Allegri, *Lettere d'amore*, 170.

159 "La Callas, 'Ça valait la peine de faire deux scandales pour Paris,' " *France-Soir*, 17 January 1958.

160 William J. Conway, "Callas' Note Pianissimo?," *The Washington Post*, 21 January 1958.

161 "Diva Callas Loses Brooch," *The Washington Post*, 24 January 1958.

162 Jellinek, 218.

163 Giannis Tsarouchis, "A stone which the builders imposed as a sanction," quoted on the *tales from the other side of town* blog, https://grsamsa.blogspot.com/2009/10/blog-post_02.html.

164 Tony Villecco, "Helen Vanni, The Met's Invaluable Trouper," *Classical Singer*, 1 September 2014.

165 Gelman, "The Maria Callas Story."

166 Rivellino-Walsh, 40–46.

167 Allegri, *Lettere d'amore*, 88.

168 Leiser, "Chapter 13: Maria Callas."

169 Douglas Watt, "Musical Events," *The New Yorker*, 15 February 1958.

170 Irving Kolodin in *Saturday Review* in Lowe, 190.

171 Allegri, *La véritable histoire de Maria Callas*, 270–73.

172 Massimo Mauri, "Fra Callas e Scala è scoppiata la guerra," *Epoca*, 30 March 1958.

173 AP, "Maria Callas, La Scala Are Not in Harmony," *Wilkes-Barre Times Leader* of Wilkes-Barre, Pennsylvania, 11 April 1958.

174 Callas, "I am not guilty of those Callas scandals."

175 Harewood, 230.

176 Jellinek, 227.

177 "Milan Audience Hails Callas On Her Return," *The New York Times*, 10 April 1958.

178 Galatopoulos, 279.

179 UPI, "Callas' Voice Melts Milan All Over Again," *The New York Daily News*, 11 April 1958.

180 Harewood, 230.

181 Ardoin & Fitzgerald, 158.

182 Allegri, *La véritable histoire de Maria Callas*, 340–41.

183 Callas to Herbert Weinstock c. 1958 in Lot 337, Fine Books & Manuscripts, Bonhams Auctions Catalogue, 22 March 2005 (London: Bonhams Auctions, 2005). Accessed at https://www.bonhams.com/auctions/13096/lot/5453.

184 Jellinek, 230.

185 de Nussac & Cotta: 1970

186 Review in *Corriere d'Informazione* in Hanine-Roussel, 366.

187 Allegri, *La véritable histoire de Maria Callas*, 277.

188 AP, "Maria Callas Quitting La Scala over 'Disagreement' with Management," *The New York Times*, 25 May 1958.

189 Callas, "I am not guilty of those Callas scandals."

190 Galatopoulos, 280; Meneghini, 268; Author's interview with Giovanna Lomazzi.

191 Callas, "I am not guilty of those Callas scandals."

192 Galatopoulos, 281.

193 Cruesemann: 1959

194 Lomazzi, "Svelati Dopo Tre Anni Tutti I Retroscena Del Clamoroso Scandalo All'Opera di Roma."

195 Jellinek, 229.

196 Gelman, "The Maria Callas Story."

11. "Pure stage"

1 Jellinek, 190.

2 Ardoin, *The Callas Legacy*, 88–89.

3 Callas to Elvira de Hidalgo, 28 January 1946 in Volf, "1946."

4 Osborne, *Herbert von Karajan: A Life in Music*, 353.

5 Claudia Cassidy's review in the *Chicago Tribune* in Kesting trans. John Hunt, 183.

6 René Leibowitz, "Le secret de Maria Callas," *Les Temps Modernes*, no. 161, 1958–59.

7 Cassidy, "Pride and Honesty Shining Traits of Maria Callas."

8 Menegatti, "Una 'Vestale' con Maria Callas e Mago Visconti."

9   Glotz, Interview with Callas for "Le magazine lyrique."

10 Fleetwood: 1958

11 Harewood, 231.

12 Lomazzi, "Perché Vogliono A Tutti Costi Che Io E Grace Siamo Nemiche."

13 AP, "Prima Donna and Queen Are Wowed," *Spokane Chronicle* of Spokane, Washington, 11 June 1958.

14 Paul Popper's photograph of Callas attempting to curtsey before Queen Elizabeth II taken on 10 June 1959. Accessed on Getty Images at https://www.gettyimages.co.uk/detail/news-photo/opera-singer-maria-callas-curtseys-as-she-meets-queen-news-photo/603329263.

15 Geoffrey Bocca, "Invite Bud Flanagan," *The Australian Women's Weekly*, 13 June 1962.

16 Jellinek, 235.

17 Haltrecht, 231.

18 Author's e-mail correspondence with Robert Matthew-Walker, 6 November 2011.

19 Harold Rosenthal, *My Mad World of Opera: Autobiography of the Editor of "Opera" Magazine* (New York: Holmes & Meier Publications, 1983), 137.

20 Harewood: 1968

21 Rosenthal, 137–38.

22 Scott, 211 (Interview with Nicola Rescigno).

23 Callas, "I am not guilty of those Callas scandals."

24 Prouse, "Maria Callas Speaks," 2 April 1961.

25 Rosenthal, 138.

26 "From Our Special Correspondent: Mme. Callas on Opera."

27 Fleetwood: 1958

28 Lomazzi, "Volle Dimagrire Contro La Volontà di Meneghini."

29 Meneghini, 109.

30 Leonard Lyons, "Lyons Den," *Daily Defender*, 16 July 1958.

31 Zeffirelli, 141–42.

32 Callas to Leo Lerman, 18 July 1958 [LLP].

33 Callas to Walter and Therese "Teedy" Cummings, 16 July 1958 in Hanine-Roussel, 368.

34 Galatopoulos, 2.

35 Maria's note to Meneghini, 21 April 1956 in Allegri, *Lettere d'amore*, 173.

36 Ross: 1957

37 Frost: 1970

38 Lerman, 506.

39 Schwarzkopf & Legge, 197.

40 Prouse, "Maria Callas Speaks," 2 April 1961.

41 Robert Sutherland, 206.

42 Leo Lerman's journal entry of 7 February 1971 in Lerman, 330.

43 Pia Meneghini, "Sette anni con Maria," 127.

44 Tosi, *Casta diva: L'incomparabile Callas*, 43.

45 Virginia Kachan (International News Service), "Hubby Is Girl's Best Friend," *The Miami Herald*, 10 April 1957.

46 Michael Scott, "Callas: fact and fiction," *The Spectator*, 8 August 1998.

47 Elly Schotte's comments in Karl H. Zoggel, *Maria Callas in Nederland en Belgie* (Zutphen: Walburg Pers, 2007), 106.

48 Ardoin: 1968

49 BBC Radio, Interview with Callas, 23 September 1959. Most of the audio has been lost but some features in John Ardoin, *Maria Callas In Her Own Words*.

50 Ross: 1957

51 Cruesemann: 1959

52 Giovanna Lomazzi, "Dopo La Crociera Maria Disse Al Marito: 'Dimentichiamo Tutto E Torniamo Insieme,' " *La Settimana Incom Illustrata*, 19 March 1961.

53 Gorlinsky to Callas, 12 November 1958 [SGC].

54 Gorlinsky to Callas, 26 September 1958 [SGC].

55 Gorlinsky to Callas, 23 December 1958 [SGC].

56 Callas, "Il faut réformer l'opéra."

57 Luchino Visconti to Meneghini, 13 August 1956 in Meneghini, 194.

58 Harewood: 1968

59 Jellinek, 335.

60 ibid. 239.

61 Bing, *5000 Nights at the Opera*, 241.

62 Ardoin & Fitzgerald, 36.

63 Callas, "I am not guilty of those Callas scandals."

64 Maraini, 312.

65 Eileen Farrell & Brian Kellow, 180.

66 Callas, "Il faut réformer l'opéra."

67 Callas to Rudolf Bing, 23 October 1958 in Christie's: Lot 20, 30 November 2005 (London: Christie's Auctions), https://www.invaluable.com/auction-lot/callas-maria-1923-1977-three-typed-letters-signed-20-c-wgilddsgp5?objectID=1923101&algIndex=archive_prod&queryID=6600335c50effc6ba309af2df435b459.

68 Bing, *5000 Nights at the Opera*, 242.

69 Callas to Bing, 27 October 1958, Lot 19.

70 Jellinek, 243.

71 Askew, "Firing Doesn't Worry Callas."

72 "La Callas: 'Le directeur du Met est un corporel prussien,' " *Paris-Jour*, 13 November 1958.

73 Harewood: 1968

74 Zeffirelli, 143–44.

75 John Rosenfield, " 'La traviata by 'Flashback,' " *The Dallas Morning News*, 12 October 1958.

76 Maria Thermou, "Callas: Eight Years After Her Death, She Remains Alive and Unsurpassed," *Ta Nea*, 15 September 1985.

77 Harewood: 1968

78 Nicola Rescigno to Alexis Minotis, 2 September 1958 [AMP]. Printed here with kind permission from Rescigno's nephew Joseph Rescigno.

79 Haltrecht, 183.

80 Ronald L. Davis, *La Scala West: The Dallas Opera Under Kelly and Rescigno* (Dallas: Southern Methodist University Press, 2001), 33.

81 Jeannie Williams, *Jon Vickers: A Hero's Life* (Boston: Northeastern University Press, 2007), 89–90.

82 Teresa Berganza, "Para mí la Callas era solo María," *XL Semanal*, no. 1037, 9 September 2007.

83 Stassinopoulos, 191.

84 Harris: 1970

85 Bing, *5000 Nights at the Opera*, 244.

86 ibid. 242.

87 Bing to Callas, 29 October 1958 in Christie's: Lot 19.

88 Wolf Mittler, Interview with Callas for Bayerischer Rundfunk TV, Munich, 12 March 1962.

89 Callas to Bing, 2 November 1958 in Jackson, 168–69.

90 "La Callas: 'Le directeur du Met est un corporel prussien.' "

91 Lerman, 231.

92 Williams, 91.

93 Stassinopoulos, 192.

94 "La Callas: 'Le directeur du Met est un corporel prussien.' "

95 Askew, "Firing Doesn't Worry Callas."

96 Reproduction of the telegram in Peter G. Davis, "How Good is the Met?," *New York Magazine*, 17 October 1983.

97 Jellinek, 244.

98 W. Hartering, "Peter Diamand zegt Holland Festival vaarwel, 'Nog iets anders doen voordat ik te oud ben,'" *De Telegraaf*, 3 April 1965.

99 Roger Dettmer, "Callas Sings an Immortal Medea," *Chicago American*, 2 November 1958.

100 Press footage of Callas in her dressing room after *Medea* at the Dallas Civic Opera on 6 November 1958 in Palmer, *Callas: A Documentary*, 1978.

101 Davis, 36.

102 Lerman, 232.

103 "Mme Callas Replies, Eight Days Needed To 'Re-Train' Voice," *The Manchester Guardian*, 8 November 1958.

104 Askew, "Firing Doesn't Worry Callas."

105 "Hume Asserts Met Ought to Fire Bing," *The Washington Post*, 8 November 1958.

106 John Rosenfield, "Bing, Bang and Callas," *The Dallas Morning News*, 8 November 1958.

107 Callas, "I am not guilty of those Callas scandals."

108 Galatopoulos, 290.

109 Gorlinsky to Callas, 22 August 1958 [SGC].

110 Galatopoulos, 292.

111 Henry Mitchell, "La Callas Descends Upon Washington," *The Washington Post*, 25 February 1974.

112 Paul Hume, "Callas Gets Tumultuous Ovation Here," *The Washington Post*, 23 November 1958.

113 ibid.

114 Rivellino-Walsh, 47.

115 Jellinek, 288.

116 "La Callas a Milano dopo due mesi di assenza," *Gazzetta del Popolo*, 4 December 1958.

117 Claude Azoulay, "Paris attend Maria Callas," *Paris Match*, 20 December 1958.

118 *Le Figaro* article in Rémy, Kindle location 3255.

119 Callas' Press Conference at the Paris Ritz Hotel on 16 December 1958 on Divina Records, *The Unknown Recordings, Vol. 2.*

120 Canals, 3.

121 Gobbi, 97–98.

122 Nicola Rescigno to Alexis Minotis, 11 December 1958 [AMP].

123 Meneghini in Allegri, *Lettere d'amore*, 182.

124 "La Callas Canta en Paris a Beneficio de Las Obras Asistenciales de La Legion de Honor," *Blanco y Negro*, 27 December 1958.

125 "Ce soir-là, Paris a donné son cœur à Maria Callas," *Paris Match*, 27 December 1958.

126 Glotz, 212.

127 Antoine Blondin, "Un père Noël nommé Callas a fait rêver 30 millions d'européens," *Arts*, 24–30 December 1958.

128 Lomazzi, "Dopo La Crociera Maria Disse Al Marito: 'Dimentichiamo Tutto E Torniamo Insieme.'"

129 de Nussac & Cotta: 1970

130 Callas to Walter and Therese "Teedy" Cummings, 31 December 1958 in Hanine-Roussel, 386–87.

131 Harewood, 232

132 Callas to Irving Kolodin, 25 January 1959 [IKP].

133 Jellinek, 310.

134 Claudia Cassidy, "Splendor in the Night," *Opera News*, November 1977.

135 Callas to Renzo Rossellini, 26 July 1961 in Christie's: Lot 5.

136 Hanine-Roussel, 101.

137 Herbert Weinstock to Callas, 21 February 1965 [HWP].

138 Rosenthal, 118.

139 "London Letter: Dog reporting dog, Fleet Street, Thursday Night," *The Manchester Guardian*, 13 June 1958.

140 Callas, "I am not guilty of those Callas scandals."

141 Murrow: 1958

142 Ardoin & Fitzgerald, 22.

143 Jellinek, 258.

144 Glenway Scott, *A Heaven of Words: Last Journals, 1956–1984* (Madison: University of Wisconsin Press, 2013), 41.

145 Renzo Allegri, "Quel Che Resta di Maria," *Classic Voice*, n. 102, November 2007.

146 Noel Goodwin, "Today Among The People (And Problems) in the Music World I Predict," *Daily Express*, 31 October 1958.

147 Callas, "I am not guilty of those Callas scandals."

148 "La Callas en octobre à l'opéra," *Le Figaro*, 24 April 1959.

149 A.M. Julien, General Administrator of the Opéra de Paris, to Callas, 3 July 1959 [AMP].

150 UPI, "Miss Callas in Italy," *The Buffalo Courier-Express*, 2 February 1959.

151 Callas to Herbert Weinstock and Ben Meiselman, 13 February 1959 in Volf, "1959."

152 Beniamino Dal Fabbro's review in *Il Giorno*, 29 May 1955 in Gastel Chiarelli, 202.

153 Allegri, *La véritable histoire de Maria Callas*, 225–26.

154 AP, "Soprano Callas Loses Against Critic," *The Washington Post*, 6 February 1959.

155 Callas to Herbert Weinstock and Ben Meiselman, 13 February 1959 in Lot 337 of Bonhams Auctions Catalogue, 22 March 2005 (London: Bonhams Auctions). Accessed at http://www.bonhams.com/auctions/13082/lot/337.

156 Express Staff Reporter, "Maria the Tigress calls on friend in the rival role," *Daily Express*, 17 February 1959.

157 Schwarzkopf & Legge, 197.

158 WGN Radio Philadelphia, Interview with Callas, 1 September 1957.

159 "From Our Special Correspondent: Mme. Callas on Opera."

160 Weaver, "Remembering Callas: Some Confessions of a Fan," 76.

161 Hanine-Roussel, 395 (Interview with Ferruccio Tagliavini).

162 Gorlinsky to Meneghini, 20 April 1959 [SGC].

163 Callas to Walter Cummings, 9 April 1959 in Hanine-Roussel, 397.

164 Callas to Leo Lerman, 19 April 1959 [LLP].

165 Jellinek, 262.

166 Antonio Fernández-Cid, "Musica: Criticas breves e noticiario," *ABC*, 3 May 1959.

167 Nicole Hirsch, "Le vrai visage de la Callas," *Chaix Musica*, August 1961.

168 Lomazzi, "Dopo La Crociera Maria Disse Al Marito: 'Dimentichiamo Tutto E Torniamo Insieme.'"

169 "Callas Does It Again, German Concert Off," *The Washington Post*, 11 May 1959.

170 Gorlinsky to Callas, 12 May 1959 [SGC].

171 Lomazzi, "Dopo La Crociera Maria Disse Al Marito: 'Dimentichiamo Tutto E Torniamo Insieme.'"

172 "Callas flies in," *Daily Express*, 12 June 1959.

173 Lomazzi, "Dopo La Crociera Maria Disse Al Marito: 'Dimentichiamo Tutto E Torniamo Insieme.'"

174 Irving Kolodin, "Music To My Ears: Medea in Callas, Glyndebourne Strauss," *Saturday Review*, 7 November 1959.

175 William Hickey, "William Hickey at the Onassis Party," *Daily Express*, 18 June 1959.

176 Paul Tanfield, "Black Market Night at the Opera," *Daily Mail*, 18 June 1959.

177 Allegri, *Lettere d'amore*, 183–84.

178 Galatopoulos, 294.

179 ibid. 297.

180 Berlin, 691–693.

181 Fleetwood: 1958

182 Interview in Italian for an unknown Portuguese radio station featured on *La traviata*, Live Recording from 27 March 1958 (Milan: MYTO Records, 2013).

183 Hamakis, Interview with Callas for *Through the Microphone*.

184 WGN Radio Philadelphia, Interview with Callas, 1 September 1957.

185 Holmes, Interview with Callas for BBC Radio, 20 June 1958.

186 Banzet: 1965

187 de Nussac & Cotta: 1970

188 Weaver, "Remembering Callas: Some Confessions of a Fan," 71.

189 Vreeland & Hemphill, 8.

190 Stancioff, 124.

191 Davis, 29.

192 Carla Nani Mocenigo in Romanò Marchetti, 15.

193 AP release, "Callas in Amsterdam Spats Over Spotlights," 3 July 1959.

194 Unsigned article, "Maria Callas: De Ongelukkige," *Elsevier* No. 35, 29 August 1987.

195 Galatopoulos, 406; 424 n. 3.

196 Jean Benoit, "Bruxelles: La Callas Fleurit La Malibran," *Combat*, 10 March 1958.

12. "Being conscientious"

1 A.M. Julien to Callas, 3 July 1959 [AMP].

2 Rual Askew, "Plans Already Afoot For Dallas Opera '60," *The Dallas Morning News*, 4 July 1959.

3 Allegri, *Lettere d'amore*, 184.

4 Lomazzi, "Dopo La Crociera Maria Disse Al Marito: 'Dimentichiamo Tutto E Torniamo Insieme.' "

5 Galatopoulos, 406.

6 Lomazzi, "Dopo La Crociera Maria Disse Al Marito: 'Dimentichiamo Tutto E Torniamo Insieme.' "

7 AP, "Movies Bid For Callas," *Arizona Republic*, 15 August 1959.

8 Prouse, "Maria Callas Speaks," 2 April 1961.

9 Lomazzi, "Dopo La Crociera Maria Disse Al Marito: 'Dimentichiamo Tutto E Torniamo Insieme.' "

10 AP, "Callas to Join Winnie," *The Kingston Daily Freeman*, Kingston, NY, 21 July 1959.

11 Jellinek, 268.

12 Celia Sandys, *Chasing Churchill: The Travels of Winston Churchill* (New York: Basic Books, 2004), 8-9.

13 Callas to Bruna Lupoli, 27 July 1959 in Volf, "1959."

14 AP, "Callas-Churchill Chat," *The Washington Post*, 17 August 1959.

15 Mary Greene, "Around the world with Winston: Churchill's granddaughter reveals tales from the Onassis yacht to Lawrence of Arabia," *Daily Mail*, 6 September 2008.

16 Peter Evans, "First Film for Callas!," *Daily Express*, 5 August 1959.

17 Gambetti, "Sono per una Medea non aggressiva," 465.

18 Allegri, *Lettere d'amore*, 185.

19 Galatopoulos, 325.

20 Anthony Montague Browne, *LONG SUNSET: Memoirs of Winston Churchill's Last Private Secretary* (London: Cassell, 1995), 255.

21 Sanche de Gramont, "The Little Millionaire," *The Saturday Evening Post*, 8 September 1968.

22 Willi Frischauer, *Onassis* (London: The Bodley Head Ltd, First Edition, 1968), 19.

23 Anne Olsen, "The Old Man: Exclusive Interview with Sir Winston Churchill," *The Australian Women's Weekly*, 10 November 1965.

24 Galatopoulos, 424 n. 7.

25 Lomazzi, "Dopo La Crociera Maria Disse Al Marito: 'Dimentichiamo Tutto E Torniamo Insieme.' "

26 Nicholas Fraser, Philip Jacobson, Mark Ottoway & Lewis Chester, *Aristotle Onassis* (London: Weidenfeld & Nicholson, 1977), 16-22.

27 "Nostro servizio particolare: Onassis non è solo ricco ma è pieno di fascino," *La Stampa*, 25 February 1966.

28 Harris: 1970

29 "Nostro servizio particolare: Onassis non è solo ricco ma è pieno di fascino."

30 Fraser, Jacobson, Ottoway & Chester, 82–83.

31 Montague Browne, 253.

32 Galatopoulos, 406–7.

33 Fraser, Jacobson, Ottoway & Chester, 237.

34 Galatopoulos, 406.

35 Lomazzi, "Perché Vogliono A Tutti Costi Che Io E Grace Siamo Nemiche."

36 Galatopoulos, 407.

37 Glotz, 326–27.

38 Galatopoulos, 407–8.

39 Christian Cafarkis, *The Fabulous Onassis: His Life and Loves* (New York: William Morrow, 1972), 105.

40 Charles Vannes, "La Callas n'est pas celle que l'on pense," *Jours de France*, 15 April 1961.

41 Lomazzi, "Dopo La Crociera Maria Disse Al Marito: 'Dimentichiamo Tutto E Torniamo Insieme.' "

42 Galatopoulos, 409.

43 Gorlinsky to Callas, 14 August 1959 [SGC].

44 Cafarkis, 105; Lomazzi, "Dopo La Crociera Maria Disse Al Marito: 'Dimentichiamo Tutto E Torniamo Insieme.' "

45 Vannes, "La Callas n'est pas celle que l'on pense."

46 Galatopoulos, 408.

47 Lomazzi, "Dopo La Crociera Maria Disse Al Marito: 'Dimentichiamo Tutto E Torniamo Insieme.' "

48 Avv. Bienni to Avv. Augusto Caldi Scalcini, 25 August 1959 [CGM].

49 Romi, "Ce Que La Callas N'Avait Encore Jamais Raconté."

50 Robert Sutherland, 108.

51 Frost: 1970.

52 Callas to Walter Cummings, 28 August 1959 in Hanine-Roussel, 412.

53 Prouse, "Maria Callas Speaks," 26 March 1961.

54 Onassis to Spyros P. Skouras, 18 December 1956 (Spyros P. Skouras Papers. M0509. Dept. of Special Collections, Stanford University Libraries, Stanford, Calif.).

55 Fraser, Jacobson, Ottoway & Chester, 77–103.

56 ibid. 173–74.

57 Cable from Gorlinsky to Callas, 26 August 1959 [SGC].

58 Giorgio Pecorini, "L'amico della tigre," *L'Europeo*, 13 September 1959.

59 Ardoin & Fitzgerald, 144.

60 Galatopoulos, 409.

61 Pecorini,"L'amico della tigre."

62 Lomazzi, "Dopo La Crociera Maria Disse Al Marito: 'Dimentichiamo Tutto E Torniamo Insieme.' "

63 Ardoin, *The Callas Legacy*, 158.

64 Galatopoulos, 327–28.

65 ibid. 337 n. 2.

66 Express Staff Reporter, "Aristotle and I are Business Partners," *Daily Express*, 10 September 1959.

67 Franco Vegliani, "Il Caso Callas-Onassis," *Tempo* magazine, 20 September 1959.

68 Galatopoulos, 330.

69 Hirsch, "Le vrai visage de la Callas."

70 AP, "Callas, Onassis Sail to Greece," *The New York Times*, 12 September 1959.

71 "Miss Callas, Onassis Go To Cabaret," *The Times from San Mateo, California*, 17 September 1959.

72 Lawrence Kelly to Alexis Minotis, 15 September 1959 [AMP].

73 AP, "Onassis Plane Whisks Callas to Spain," *The Washington Post*, 18 September 1959; "BERUFLICHES: JENNY ROCCA-SERRA," *Der Spiegel*, 20 December 1961.

74 "Maria Callas defrauda al publico bilbaíno," *ABC Sevilla, Edición de Andalucía*, 18 September 1959.

75 "Las Venticuatro Horas en Bilbao de Maria Callas," *¡Hola!* magazine, 26 September 1959.

76 "Ha cantato per Meneghini," *Epoca*, 23 September 1959.

77 UPI, "Audience Gives Callas a Low Grade on Test," *St. Joseph's Gazette*, 18 September 1959.

78 "Maria Callas defrauda al publico bilbaíno."

79 "Nada para mim foi fácil": Unsigned interview with Callas.

80 UPI, "Callas Rejoins Yacht," *The Irish Times*, 19 September 1959.

81 A.C. Sedgwick, "Callas Receives A Greek Ovation," *The New York Times*, 26 August 1960.

82 Kostas Bastias, Interview with Callas for Greek National Radio, 10 August 1960, trans. in "Interviews with Maria Callas—Part XLIX: The Press Conference in Athens on 10 August 1960," *The Maria Callas International Club Magazine*, No. 70, November 2013.

83 Jellinek, 279.

84 Cable from Callas to Gorlinsky, 22 September 1959 [SGC].

85 "La Callas Arrives in a Temper," *Daily Express*, 23 September 1959.

86 Henry Fielding, "Triumph and tears for Callas," *Daily Herald*, 24 September 1959.

87 Martin Cooper, "The Dramatic Art of Maria Callas," *The Daily Telegraph*, 24 September 1959.

88 H.J., *Evening Standard*, "Lamb-like Maria Conquers," 24 September 1959.

89 "All Smiles for Callas," *Daily Record*, 24 September 1959.

90 Clive Barnes, "But this wasn't the tigress I remember," *Daily Express*, 24 September 1959.

91 Harold Rosenthal, "Maria Callas' First London Concert," *Financial Times*, 24 September 1959; William Hickey, "MACBETH ANNOUNCED FOR 1960," *Daily Express*, 29 September 1959.

92 "£250,000? Plenty of time, says Callas . . .," *The Evening News*, 24 September 1959.

93 AP, "Conductor For Callas Has Swollen Hands," *Freeport Journal Standard* of Freeport, Illinois, 1 October 1959.

94 Telegram from Callas to Gorlinsky, 27 September 1959 [SGC].

95 "Mme Callas—'A Touch of Fever,'" *The Guardian*, 30 September 1959; UPI, "Callas Collapses At Mate's Suit On 'Other Man,'" *The Philadelphia Inquirer*, 30 September 1959.

96 Rual Askew, "Callas Assures Dallas Impresario 'All's Well,'" *The Dallas Morning News*, 2 October 1959.

97 Joan Sutherland's interview with Helena Matheopoulos in "Callas Remembered," *Gramophone*, September 1987. Sutherland mistakenly refers to this incident occurring

during her "La Scala" *Don Giovanni*. Judging by the context, however, it seems likelier that she was confusing her eventual Scala debut in the role with the concert performances as Donna Anna she sang at the Royal Festival Hall on 18 and 20 October 1959.

98 "Maria Callas: je souhaite chanter en décembre à l'Opéra," *Le Figaro*, 20 October 1959.

99 "La Callas à Paris," *Le Figaro*, 19 October 1959.

100 "Callas At Court," *Daily Express*, 24 October 1959.

101 Jellinek, 282.

102 "Opera Star Sang Despite Bomb Scare," *The Age*, 30 October 1959.

103 Lomazzi, "Dopo La Crociera Maria Disse Al Marito: 'Dimentichiamo Tutto E Torniamo Insieme.'"

104 Brian Burnes, *Harry S. Truman: His Life and Times* (Kansas City: Kansas City Star Books, 2003), 15.

105 AP; Reuters, "Singer Departs Incognito," *The Canberra Times*, 31 October 1959.

106 "Callas Skips Out On Dallas Flight," *The Dallas Morning News*, 31 October 1959.

107 UPI, "Maria Callas May File for Divorce in U.S.," 6 November 1959.

108 Lomazzi, "Dopo La Crociera Maria Disse Al Marito: 'Dimentichiamo Tutto E Torniamo Insieme.'"

109 Jellinek, 284.

110 Galatopoulos, 197.

111 Davis, 41.

112 Zeffirelli, 150.

113 Bentivoglia, "Le verità di Maria divina e infelice."

114 Davis, 42–43.

115 George Saxe, "Callas Again Stirs Dallas," *Musical Courier*, December 1959.

116 Jellinek, 285.

117 Zeffirelli, 150–51.

118 Author's interview with Giovanna Lomazzi.

119 Jellinek, 286.

120 Prouse, "Maria Callas Speaks," 19 March 1961.

121 Notes in Christie's: Lot 16 (London: Christie's Auctions, 30 November 2005), https://www.invaluable.com/auction-lot/callas-maria-1923-1977-two-typed-letters-signed-m-16-c-qnll49hz0q?objectID=1923097&algIndex=archive_prod&queryID=6600335c50eff c6ba309af2df435b459.

122 Reuters; AP, "FEUD ENDED BY MARIA CALLAS: To Sing Again At Met?," *The Guardian*, 10 November 1959.

123 Interview with Bing in Alain Ferrari, "Vissi d'arte."

124 Rudolf Bing, *A Knight at the Opera* (New York: Putnam, 1981), 97–99.

125 Jellinek, 287.

126 Callas to Walter Cummings, 25 July 1963 in Hanine-Roussel, 470.

127 Lomazzi, "Dopo La Crociera Maria Disse Al Marito: 'Dimentichiamo Tutto E Torniamo Insieme.'"

128 Davis, 46.

129 John Rosenfield, "Callas States Ferocities of Hellenic Soul," *The Dallas Morning News*, 20 November 1959.

130 Jellinek, 288.

131 Callas to A.M. Julien, 10 February 1961 in Volf, "1961."

132 "Tina Onassis Files For Divorce," *Daily Express*, 26 November 1959; Galatopoulos, 334.

133 UPI, "Callas, Boiling Mad, Denies Pregnancy," *The Los Angeles Times*, 1 December 1959; "Callas Angered By Milan Rumor," *The Dallas Morning News*, 1 December 1959. The timing of the rumor is made all the more ironic (and comedic) by the theory published in Nicholas Gage's 2000 *Greek Fire, The Story of Maria Callas and Aristotle Onassis* (New York: Knopf)—completely groundless and thus unexplored in this biography—that alleges Callas secretly gave birth to Onassis' son three months later in March 1960.

134 Callas to Walter Cummings, 30 November 1959 in Hanine-Roussel, 428.

135 Gorlinsky to Callas, 2 December 1959 [SGC].

136 Paul Hume, "Maria Callas Sits For Two Portraits," *The Washington Post*, 11 December 1960.

137 Callas to Emily Coleman, 15 December 1959 in Sale 1985, Lot 214 in Swann Galleries Auctions (New York: Swann Galleries, 13 November 2003). Accessed at https://www.lotsearch.net/lot/on-her-divorce-callas-maria-autograph-letter-signed-maria-to-emily-42011631?searchID=5811243.

138 Address on Wikimapia, https://wikimapia.org/10819604/Via-Clavadatsch-12. Today it is known as "Onassis Villa".

139 William Hickey, "The so silent voice of Maria Callas," *Daily Express*, 30 December 1959.

140 Fraser, Jacobson, Ottoway & Chester, 315.

141 Author's interview with Taki Theodoracopulos, London, 2 July 2012.

142 Nikos Nikolizas, "George Zacharias: Everything I experienced on the *Christina*," *Espresso* magazine, 9 February 2019, https://www.espressonews.gr/celebrities/138011/giorgoszacharias-ola-osa-ezisa-sti-christina.

143 "The Cretan chef of Onassis George Pervolianos talks about his experience with the Greek Croesus," *Agonas Tis Kritis*, 20 August 2019, 20 August 2019, https://agonaskritis.gr/o-κρητικός-σεφ-του-ωνάση-γιώργος-περβο.

144 George S. Moore, *The Banker's Life* (New York: Norton, 1987), 285–86.

145 Author's trip on the *Christina* on 4 April 2012; Frischauer, 19.

146 Fraser, Jacobson, Ottoway & Chester, 160.

147 Janice Selinger, "Restauranteur finds smooth sailing," *The Central New Jersey Home News*, 13 June 1978.

148 Robert Champion, "Chapter 13." Handwritten account of Champion's time on the *Christina* published at http://www.willishenry.com/auctions/05/autograph%20session%20two%2005/chapter_13.htm.

149 Galatopoulos, 409.

150 Murray Schumach, "Onassis Noted as Gracious Host," *The New York Times*, 18 October 1968.

151 Elvira de Hidalgo to Callas, 19 January 1968 [CNH].

152 Helmut Berger, "Maria Callas nahm mit einem Bandwurm ab, Onassis spottete über seinen 'Kanarienvogel,' " in *Ich: Die Autobiographie*, 2013, Kindle.

153 Pedro González-Sosa, "Onassis y Maria Callas pasaron por Las Palmas a Bordo del 'Christina,' " *El Eco de Canarias*, 6 July 1967.

154 Frischauer, 245.

155 "Maria Callas avait regagné Milan," *Le Figaro*, 18 March 1961.

156 Fraser, Jacobson, Ottoway & Chester, 11.

157 Flora Lewis, "At his table at Maxim's, he reminisced," *The New York Times*, 16 March 1975.

158 Margot Fonteyn, *Autobiography* (New York: Random House, 1976), 193.

159 Mete Akyol, "Onassis è il mio più caro amico," *Gente*, 26 July 1969.

160 Galatopoulos, 412.

161 "Chez la Callas, la musique reste la vraie maîtresse de maison," *Illustré* Switzerland, 24 April 1974.

162 Galatopoulos, 410.

163 Lomazzi, "Perché Vogliono A Tutti Costi Che Io E Grace Siamo Nemiche."

164 William Hickey, "The Kiss revisited," *Daily Express*, 21 January 1960.

165 Galatopoulos, 2.

166 Alberto Ceretto, "La Callas dichiara: 'Quando riprenderò, riprenderò alla Scala,' " *Corriere d'informazione*, 22–23 March 1960.

167 Prouse, "Maria Callas Speaks," 19 March 1961.

168 UPI, "Callas kreeg gelijk—maar miste trein," *Friese Koerier*, 2 February 1960; AP, "Churchill in Riviera for Month's Holiday," 2 January 1960.

169 "La Callas Une Nouvelle Fois À l'Opéra, Mais En Spectatrice Pour Applaudir 'La Dame aux Camélias,' " *France-Soir*, 12 February 1960.

170 Marlyse Schaeffer, "Une femme vous parle," *France-Soir*, 12 February 1960.

171 "Maria Callas a Parigi," *Settimo Giorno*, 19 February 1960.

172 ANSA, "Maria Callas nao deixara de cantar," *Folha de São Paulo*, 19 February 1960.

173 "Nada para mim foi fácil": Unsigned interview with Callas.

174 Bing, *Knight at the Opera*, 100.

175 Cable from Gorlinsky to Callas, 22 February 1960 [SGC].

176 Lawrence Kelly to Alexis Minotis, 4 March 1960 [AMP].

177 Callas to Herbert Weinstock, 12 March 1960 [HWP].

178 Stassinopoulos, 223.

179 Callas to Peggy Glanville-Hicks in James Murdoch, *Peggy Glanville Hicks: A Transposed Life* (Hillsdale, NY: Pendragon Press, 2003), 164.

180 Callas' secretary Teresa d'Addato to Sander Gorlinsky, 11 April 1960 [SGC].

181 "Maria Callas to Sing in Athens," *De Telegraaf*, 21 May 1960.

182 Lomazzi, "Perché Vogliono A Tutti Costi Che Io E Grace Siamo Nemiche."

183 Callas to Walter Cummings, 25 May 1960 in Hanine-Roussel, 438.

184 Rual Askew, "1960 Operas Shape Up," *The Dallas Morning News*, 12 June 1960.

185 Photo caption of Maria and Issac Stern in *Het Vrije Volk*, 28 June 1960.

186 Chambre Cohen, 154.

187 John Ardoin, *The Furtwängler Record* (Portland: Amadeus Press, 1994), 12.

188 Downes: 1967

189 Sutherland, 103–4.

190 AP, "Maria Callas, Onassis In Naples," *The Los Angeles Times*, 8 July 1960.

191 "A Milano La Callas," *Il Giorno*, 11 July 1960.

192 Galatopoulos, 341.

193 Lomazzi, "Perché Vogliono A Tutti Costi Che Io E Grace Siamo Nemiche."

194 Callas to Leo Lerman, 31 July 1960 [LLP].

195 Callas to Walter Cummings, 29 July 1960 in Hanine-Roussel, 440.

196 Callas to Augusto Caldi Scalcini, 31 July 1960 [CGM].

197 Letter forged by Meneghini with the date "28 May 1959" in Allegri, *Lettere d'amore*, 171. c.f. David Webster to Alexis Minotis, 24 April 1959: "On the morning of June 10th, which is the first day that Callas will be with us . . ." [AMP] and the article "Callas flies in" (*Daily Express*, 12 June 1959).

198 Meneghini's "Diary" in Allegri, *Lettere d'amore*, 190–93. Photos of it feature on unpaginated pages between 124–25. They are also visible in Sotheby's, Lot 71: "Giovanni Battista Meneghini, Diario autografo contenente il racconto della separazione dalla moglie Maria Callas" in Sotheby's, *Maria Callas and Her Pygmalion*. Accessed at https://www.invaluable.com/auction-lot/giovanni-battista-meneghini-diario-autografo-cont-71-c-yst6ctb92a?objectID=10656519&algIndex=archive_prod&queryID=37a43db2798047a27b6ab78b58dd56de.

199 "Maria Callas Cannot Get Married Again," *Leeuwarder Courant*, 3 October 1960.

200 Galatopoulos, 341.

201 A.C. Sedgwick, "Callas Receives a Greek Ovation," *The New York Times*, 26 August 1960.

202 Picchi, 141.

203 Hanine-Roussel, 444 (Interview with Kiki Morfoniou).

204 Picchi, 142.

205 Lomazzi, "Perché Vogliono A Tutti Costi Che Io E Grace Siamo Nemiche."

206 Author's telephone interview with Ninon Dimitriadou-Kambouri.

207 Author's interview with Marilena Patronicolas, step-niece of Aristotle Onassis, Athens, 28 September 2012.

208 Lomazzi, "Perché Vogliono A Tutti Costi Che Io E Grace Siamo Nemiche."

209 Galatopoulos, 341.

210 Author's interview with Marilena Patronicolas.

211 Review by Pier Maria Paoletti in an unnamed Bolognese newspaper in Tosi, *Casta diva: L'incomparabile Callas*, 89.

212 Lomazzi, "Perché Vogliono A Tutti Costi Che Io E Grace Siamo Nemiche."

213 Galatopoulos, 3.

214 ibid. 342.

215 William Hickey, "Callas Sails For Naples," *Daily Express*, 30 August 1960.

216 Interview with Robert Gooch featured on *The Callas Effect: Deluxe Edition* (London: EMI Classics, 2011).

217 Frost: 1970.

218 Callas, "I am not guilty of those Callas scandals."

219 Prouse, "Maria Callas Speaks," 2 April 1961.

13. "Little checking machines"

1 Lomazzi, "Perché Vogliono A Tutti Costi Che Io E Grace Siamo Nemiche."

2 "Roman Society Believes Callas and Onassis Will be Married Soon," *De Telegraaf*, 15 September 1960.

3 Wendy Leigh, *True Grace: The Life and Times of An American Princess* (New York: St. Martin's, 2007), 178.

4 Frischauer, 21.

5 Callas to Bruna Lupoli, 27 July 1959 in Volf, "1959."

6 Lomazzi, "Perché Vogliono A Tutti Costi Che Io E Grace Siamo Nemiche."

7 Champion, "Chapter 13."

8 AP, "Rose Grower Dies," *The Daily Mail* of Hagerstown, Maryland, 14 February 1971

9 Callas to Ben Meiselman, 9 April 1975 in Volf, "1975."

10 "La Callas, 'Ça valait la peine de faire deux scandales pour Paris.' "

11 Lina Sotis, "Il mito della Callas rivive con la moda," *Corriere della Sera*, 26 February 1994.

12 La Rochelle, 232.

13 Gorlinsky to Roberto Arias, 14 July 1960 [SGC].

14 Stassinopoulos, 274.

15 La Rochelle, 225 (Interview with Michel Glotz).

16 Gorlinsky to Roberto Arias, 26 June 1960 [SGC].

17 Lomazzi, "Volle Dimagrire Contro La Volontà di Meneghini."

18 Lomazzi, "Perché Vogliono A Tutti Costi Che Io E Grace Siamo Nemiche."

19 Joan Sutherland, 92.

20 UPI, "Visconti Ceases Work in Italy In Protest Against Censors," *De Tijd De Maasbode*, 18 November 1960.

21 Stirling, 128–29.

22 Callas to Tullio Serafin, 26 November 1960 [CFM].

23 "La Callas Back At La Scala: Theatre Personnel Threaten A Strike," *Nieuwsblad van het Noorden*, 6 December 1960.

24 Peter Hoffer, "It Was Callas' Night At La Scala," *Music and Musicians*, January 1961.

25 Rizzo, "The Callas Class."

26 Callas to Walter and Therese "Teedy" Cummings, 27 December 1960 in Hanine-Roussel, 452–53.

27 Callas to Walter Cummings, 9 April 1961 in Hanine-Roussel, 453.

28 Callas to Walter Cummings, 12 June 1963 in Volf, "1963."

29 "Medaglia d'oro di ammiratori di Maria Callas," *Corriere d'informazione*, 5–6 December 1960.

30 Callas to La Scala's Subscribers, 4 December 1960 in Volf, "1960."

31 "La Callas Back At La Scala: Theatre Personnel Threaten A Strike."

32 Galatopoulos, 345.

33 Frischauer, 224–25.

34 ibid. 264.

35 Galatopoulos, 415.

36 Ronald Singleton, "This Will Be A Changed Callas Singing Tomorrow," *Daily Express*, 6 December 1960.

37 Marco Blasé, Interview with Callas for RAI Television, 7 December 1960.

38 Aldo Trippini of UPI, "Maria Callas Elated at Milan Reception," *The Record* of Hackensack, New Jersey, 3 December 1960.

39 Signorini, "Ecco le lettere, i documenti e le foto che conservo della mia amica Callas."

40 Callas to Tullio Serafin, 13 December 1960 in Volf, "1960."

41 Marialivia Seni's review in *L'Espresso*, 18 December 1960 in Crespi Morbio, 27.

42 ibid. Mario Morini's report in *La Settimana Radio TV*, 18–24 December 1960.

43 Cook, 276–77.

44 Jacques Bourgeois in Jacques Lorcey, *L'Art de Maria Callas* (Biarritz: Atlantica, 1999), 165.

45 Prouse, "Maria Callas Speaks," 2 April 1961.

46 Untitled article in *Le Figaro*, 23 December 1960.

47 UPI, "Maria Callas Denies She Will Quit Opera," *Chicago Tribune*, 24 December 1960.

48 "Maria Callas: 'It Was No Goodbye,' " *De Telegraaf*, 23 December 1960.

49 Callas to Walter Cummings, 27 December 1960 in Hanine-Roussel, 452.

50 Photo Caption in *Leeuwarder Courant*, 4 January 1961.

51 Prouse, "Maria Callas Speaks," 2 April 1961.

52 Author's interviews with Korinna Spanidou, 26 September 2012 and with Marilena Patronicolas, 28 September 2012.

53 Karajan, 193.

54 Osborne, *Herbert von Karajan: A Life in Music*, 355.

55 Stassinopoulos, 230.

56 Banzet: 1965

57 Hanine-Roussel, 284 (Interview with Elefteria Zaccaria, wife of Nicola).

58 Callas to Giovanna Lomazzi, 6 December 1963 in Volf, "1963."

59 Galatopoulos, 2.

60 Herbert Weinstock and Ben Meiselman to Callas, 3 March 1965 [HWP].

61 Author's conversation with Giovanni Mion, grandson of Augusto Caldi Scalcini, 16 August 2013; E-mail from Giovanni Mion, 4 August 2013.

62 Galatopoulos, 410; Author's interview with Cordelia van Zuylen, granddaughter of Maggie van Zuylen, Chantilly, 14 March 2014.

63 Gorlinsky to Callas, 11 May 1966 [SGC].

64 Hôtel Lancaster, 7 rue Berri, Paris is cited as Callas' temporary residence in Glotz, 190.

65 Canals, 2.

66 Schaeffer, "Aujourd'hui, La Callas."

67 Perna, "Interview with Janine Reiss."

68 Dominique Fournier, *La passion prédominante de Janine Reiss: La voix humaine* (Arles: Actes Sud Editions, 2013), 49–54.

69 Perna, "Interview with Janine Reiss."

70 Fournier, 54.

71 Ayre, 106.

72 Author's interview with Janine Reiss, 19 December 2011.

73 "Churchill to Cruise Caribbean," *The New York Times*, 10 March 1961.

74 "Maria Callas commence à la salle Wagram une série d'enregistrements de grands airs," *Le Figaro*, 25 March 1961.

75 Crespi Morbio, 5.

76 Hirsch, "Le vrai visage de la Callas."

77 William Hickey, "Getty Gives Guests a Hint of On Phone Costs," *Daily Express*, 27 March 1961.

78 AP, "The World In Brief," *Guam Daily News*, 3 April 1961.

79 Hirsch, "Le vrai visage de la Callas."

80 Stan Huygens, "La Callas mocht er niet in," *De Telegraaf*, 31 March 1961.

81 Hirsch, "Le vrai visage de la Callas."

82 Interview with Janine Reiss (*Hommages à Maria Callas*), 28 February 1978.

83 Callas, "The Lyric Tradition," 1 November 1971.

84 "Maria Callas is Monegasque," *Nieuwsblad van het Noorden*, 5 April 1961.

85 Prouse, "Maria Callas Speaks," 19 March 1961.

86 Gardner: 1958

87 Desgraupes: 1969

88 Emily Coleman, "What Makes a Prima Donna?," *Newsweek*, 13 February 1961, vol. 57, issue 7.

89 Prouse, "Maria Callas Speaks," 19 March 1961.

90 Gorlinsky to Callas, 20 October 1961 [SGC].

91 Glotz, 203.

92 La Rochelle, 226.

93 Callas to Walter Cummings, 26 March 1961 in Hanine-Roussel, 453.

94 Gorlinsky to Callas, 13 April 1961 [SGC].

95 "Onassis allowed free lakes," *De Telegraaf*, 15 May 1961.

96 Lerman, 240.

97 Interview with Robert Sutherland in *Maria Callas: Life and Art*.

98 Caloni: 1976

99 Angela Cuccio, "Callas on Callas," *Women's Wear Daily*, 23 November 1970.

100 Galatopoulos, 413.

101 Frost: 1970

102 Galatopoulos, 411.

103 Cafarkis, 117.

104 Helena Smith, "Callas takes centre stage again as exhibition recalls Onassis's life," *The Guardian*, 6 October 2006, https://www.theguardian.com/world/2006/oct/06/arts. artsnews.

105 Author's interview with Marilena Patronicolas.

106 Fraser, Jacobson, Ottoway & Chester, 232–33.

107 Prouse, "Maria Callas Speaks," 26 March 1961.

108 Naur, "I have been a little spoiled."

109 Callas to Pier Paolo Pasolini, 21 July 1971 [PPP].

110 Caloni: 1976

111 Claire Alby & Alfred Caron, *Passion Callas* (Paris: Mille et une nuits, 1997), 111.

112 Rual Askew, "Legend or Not, Callas Still DCO Prospect," *The Dallas Morning News*, 28 May 1961.

113 Hirsch, "Le vrai visage de la Callas."

114 Prouse, "Maria Callas Speaks," 2 April 1961.

115 Askew, "Legend or Not, Callas Still DCO Prospect."

116 Undated letter from Callas to Paul Hume, c. April 1961 in Volf, "1961."

117 Gorlinsky to Teresa d'Addato, 19 June 1961 [SGC].

118 Robert Sutherland, 52.

119 Edward Heath, *Music: A Joy for Life* (London: Sidgwick & Jackson, 1974), 64.

120 "Names in the News," *The Knickerbocker News*, 29 June 1961.

121 Hedda Hopper, "Hollywood," *The Hartford Courant*, 15 July 1961.

122 Leonard Lyons, "Lyons Den," *Chicago Daily Defender*, 23 August 1961.

123 Barbara Martyn, "Onassis the Great is a Genial Host," *The Australian Women's Weekly*, 29 March 1967.

124 Hirsch, "Le vrai visage de la Callas."

125 Murrow: 1958

126 Stancioff, 31–32.

127 AP, "Estranged Husband Files New Suit Against Callas," *The Hartford Courant*, 25 July 1961.

128 Callas to Renzo Rossellini, 26 July 1961, in Christie's: Lot 6. Accessed at https://www.christies.com/en/lot/lot-1531266.

129 Photo caption in *Freise Koerier*, 9 August 1961.

130 Interview with Jon Vickers in Ferrari, "Vissi d'arte."

131 "Cherubini's Medea at Epidaurus," *The Times*, 9 August 1961.

132 Callas to Herbert Weinstock, 17 August 1961 in Volf, "1961."

133 Galatopoulos, 452.

134 In her memoir (*Sisters*, 1990) Jackie Callas mistakenly reports the performances of *Norma* and *Medea* at Epidaurus took place in one summer. While the last time the sisters likely saw each other must have been after the latter, *Makedonia* alleged that Jackie and George were waiting for Maria's visit at a Rhodes hotel in late September 1960 ("Passengers on the *Christina* Onassis and Callas and other friends surround the Gulf of Euboea and the Karpathos," *Makedonia*, 25 September 1960).

135 Jackie Callas, 189–95.

136 Galatopoulos, 453–54.

137 Callas to Leonidas Lantzounis, 19 November 1964 [RBC].

138 Callas to Lantzounis, 9 January 1963 [RBC].

139 Gorlinsky to Callas, 21 September 1961 [SGC].

140 Dorothy Kilgallen, "Oscar Talk Stirring Filmland Already," Syndicated Column, 3 October 1961.

141 Letters from Gorlinsky to Callas, 17 and 20 October 1961 [SGC].

142 Callas to Alexis Minotis, 26 October 1961 [AMP].

143 Raymond Ericson, "Callas Revisited—Exquisite As Ever," *The New York Times*, 12 March 1972.

144 Hanine-Roussel, 465 (Interview with Antonio Tonini).

145 Gorlinsky to Callas, 22 November 1961 [SGC].

146 Gorlinsky to Callas, 29 November 1961 [SGC].

147 Peter Dragadze, "My lonely world, a woman looking for her voice," *Life*, 30 October 1964.

148 Ardoin & Fitzgerald, 185–86.

149 Stancioff, 155.

150 Callas to Emily Coleman, 15 December 1961 in Swann Galleries Auction Catalogue, Sale 1985, Lot 215 (New York: Swann's Galleries, 13 November 2003). Accessed at https://www.lotsearch.net/lot/callas-maria-typed-letter-signed-maria-to-emily-coleman-thanking-42011632?searchID=5811243.

151 "Maria Callas: flu after operation," *The Observer*, 17 December 1961.

152 Callas to Eugenio and Rosetta Gara, 19 December 1961 in Tosi, *Casta diva: L'incomparabile Callas*, 199.

153 Fabrizio Melano, "Solo un pianto: Crying for Callas," undated article given to the author by Melano on 24 March 2013. Quoted with permission.

154 Dragadze, "My lonely world, a woman looking for her voice."

155 Callas to David Bicknell, 21 July 1963 (EMI Music Archives, Hayes).

156 Author's interview with Sir John Tooley, Cambridge, 13 October 2012.

157 "Notable Absentee," *The Evening Times*, 3 March 1962.

158 Neville Cardus, "Last Night: Maria Callas at the Royal Festival Hall," *The Guardian*, 28 February 1962.

159 Peter Heyworth, "Callas in the Concert Hall," *The Observer*, 4 March 1962.

160 Callas to Gerardo De Marco, c. March 1962, in Aste Bolaffi, *Libri Rari e Autografi* (Turin: Aste Bolaffi Auctions, 11 December 2019), 16–17.

161 Glotz, 195.

162 "An Evening of Magic with Radiant Callas," *The Star*, 24 September 1959.

163 Ardoin, "Callas Today."

164 Glotz, 206.

165 Callas to Elvira de Hidalgo, 12 January 1963 in Volf, "1963."

166 Prouse, "Maria Callas Speaks," 2 April 1961.

167 "Weeping Callas," *Daily Express*, 23 March 1962.

168 Glotz, 192; UPI, *Folha de São Paulo*, "Maria Callas with Inflamed Sight," 23 March 1962.

169 Callas to David Bicknell, 21 July 1963.

170 Callas to Kiki Morfoniou, 15 April 1961 in Volf, "1961."

171 Gorlinsky to Frederick Schang, 1 May 1962 [SGC].

172 AP, "Singer's Mother Is Hospitalized," *The Washington Post*, 27 April 1962; UPI, "La mère de Maria Callas va mieux," *L'Impartial*, 28 April 1962.

173 Callas to Leonidas Lantzounis, 5 February 1963 in Volf, "1963."

174 UPI, "La mère de Maria Callas va mieux."

175 Callas to Lantzounis, 5 February 1963 [RBC].

176 Welfare Center Amsterdam to Callas, 12 December 1962; Callas to Lantzounis, 9 January 1963 [RBC].

177 Callas to Lantzounis, 21 September 1961 [RBC].

178 Galatopoulos, 452–53.

179 Stancioff, 52.

180 Callas to Lantzounis, 2 June 1963 [RBC].

181 Callas to Lantzounis, 22 July 1963 [RBC].

182 Callas to Edward Konrad, 8 May 1962 in Swann Galleries Auctions, Sale 2211, Lot 146 (New York: Swann Galleries, 22 April 2010). Accessed at https://catalogue.swanngalleries.com/Lots/auction-lot/CALLAS-MARIA-Autograph-Letter-Signed-Maria?saleno=2211&lotNo=146&refNo=630908.

183 UPI, "Callas Keeps Date In Court," *The Hartford Courant*, 15 May 1962.

184 "Callas May Lose Fortune," *Daily Express*, 19 June 1962.

185 UPI, "Newsmen Fined," *The Hartford Courant*, 18 December 1962.

186 Keith Badman, *The Final Years of Marilyn Monroe: The True Story* (London: Aurum Press, 2012), 146.

187 Merriman Smith, "JFK, Marilyn Monroe, Maria Callas Together," *The Press-Courier*, 23 May 1962.

188 "Text of President's Garden Address," *The New York Times*, 20 May 1962.

189 Callas to Emily Coleman, 23 May 1962 in Swann's Galleries, Sale 1985, Lot 215. Accessed at https://www.lotsearch.net/lot/callas-maria-autograph-letter-signed-to-emily-coleman-thanking-her-for-42011633?perPage=80&page=4&orderBy=lot-startPrice&order=ASC.

190 "Notes From Abroad," *High Fidelity*, October 1962.

191 UPI, " 'I am not 'crazy' about Onassis," *Nieuwsblad van het Noorden*, 28 May 1962.

192 Stan Huygens, "Stan Huygens' Journal: Maria Callas and Aristotle Onassis: 'We are just good friends,' " *De Telegraaf*, 13 June 1962.

193 Gerald Fitzgerald's review in *Opera News* in Lowe, 214.

194 Gastel Chiarelli, 102.

195 Galatopoulos, 349.

196 Prouse, "Maria Callas Speaks," 2 April 1961.

197 Callas to David Bicknell, 21 July 1963.

198 "La Callas Ha La Sinusite," *Oggi*, 12 July 1962.

199 "Pet for Callas," *Daily Express*, 26 May 1965.

200 Princess Grace of Monaco to Callas, 31 August 1962 [CNH].

201 "Soprano Maria Callas is again in Athens," *To Vima*, 23 July 1962.

202 "The Garden Signs Callas," *Daily Express*, 9 July 1962.

203 Haltrecht, 279.

204 Callas to Ben Meiselman, 26 November 1962 in Volf, "1962."

205 "Will Maria Callas Soon Be an Alto?," *Leeuwarder Courant*, 19 December 1962.

206 Naur, "I have been a little spoiled."

207 Gorlinsky to Frederick Schang, 23 July 1962 [SGC].

208 Galatopoulos, 443.

209 La Rochelle, 186.

210 Telegram from Callas to Gorlinsky, 2 November 1962 [SGC].

211 John Tooley, *In House: The Story of Covent Garden* (London: Faber & Faber, 1999), 103–4.

212 Callas to Gorlinsky, 12 November 1962 [SGC].

213 UPI, "Onassis, Maria Callas Visit Isle of Capri," *The Los Angeles Times*, 7 December 1962.

214 Dragadze, "My lonely world, a woman looking for her voice."

215 David Holmes, Interview with Callas for BBC Television, 23 November 1973.

216 Korinna Spanidou, *Onassis As I Knew Him* (Athens: Hestia, 1996), 145.

217 "Maria Callas has Operation," *Het Vrije Volk*, 23 January 1963.

218 "Roses Every Day for Maria Callas," *The Irish Times*, 24 January 1963.

219 "Maria Callas has left the hospital," *Leeuwarder Courant*, 24 January 1963.

220 Callas to Dorle Soria, 5 February 1963 [DSP].

221 Callas to Giacomo Lauri Volpi, 25 January 1963 in E. Castiglione, *Maria Callas: Lettere, scritti, interviste, pensieri* (Rome: Pantheon), 60–61.

222 Callas to Walter Cummings, 26 January 1963 in Hanine-Roussel, 464.

223 Hirsch, "Le vrai visage de la Callas."

224 Rivellino-Walsh, 54.

225 AP, "Callas Visits Capri With Yachting Party," *The Hartford Courant*, 18 April 1963; "Callas sails in," *Daily Express*, 18 April 1963.

226 Dorothy Kilgallen, "Garner's New Hit—An Old Song," *The Oneonta Star* of Oneonta, New York, 15 June 1963.

227 Alex Freeman, " 'Rifleman' Buys A Model Agency!," *The Hartford Courant*, 13 May 1963.

228 Interview with Michel Glotz in Gérard Caillat, *Maria Callas: Passion* (Paris: EMI Classics, 2005).

229 Schwarzkopf & Walter Legge, 196.

230 Werner Oehlmann's review in *Der Tagesspiegel* trans. Brittain Smith in Lowe, 215.

231 "Huit Représentations de 'La Norma' A L'Opéra," *Le Figaro*, 18 May 1963.

232 Stassinopoulos, 235.

233 Reporter's interview with Callas at Düsseldorf Airport, 16 May 1963, Maria Callas International Archive DVD Collection, Volume VIII.

234 Schwarzkopf & Legge, 163.

235 Newman, 180.

236 Callas to fan John Robinson, 2 June 1963 in Lot 344, International Autograph Auctions Europe (Marbella: International Autograph Auctions, 13 July 2013). Accessed at https://www.autographauctions.eu/130713-lot-344-CALLAS-MARIA-1923-1977-American-born-Greek-Soprano-A-L-S-Maria-one-page-8vo-Paris-2nd-June?auction_id=101&view=lot_detail.

237 Prêtre, 135.

238 Olivier Merlin, "Callas Perdue et Retrouvée," *Le Monde*, 7 June 1963.

239 Callas, "The Lyric Tradition," 1 November 1971.

240 Marcel Schneider, "Maria Callas, un monstre sacré qui échappe à la critique," *Combat*, 6 June 1963.

241 Jacques Bourgeois, "La Callas, inouïe," *Arts* magazine, no. 964, 2 June 1964.

14. "Like a signature"

1 Callas to Cummings, 17 June 1963 in Hanine-Roussel, 470.

2 Callas to Lantzounis, 22 July 1963 [RBC].

3 Gavoty: 1965.

4 Herb Caen, "Callas May Go To San Francisco," *The Los Angeles Times*, 7 June 1963.

5 Callas to Cummings, 12 June 1963 in Frank Hamilton: *Maria Callas: Performance Annals and Discography*, 2010. Accessed at https://www.yumpu.com/it/document/view/10107616/maria-callas-performance-annals-1934-1977-frankhamiltonorg. Likely from the collection of Walter B. Loeve.

6 William Hickey, "Maria Callas will sing Tosca at the Royal Opera House," *Daily Express*, 12 June 1963.

7 Haltrecht, 281.

8 Gorlinsky to Frederick Schang, 4 July 1963 [SGC].

9 Gorlinsky to John Tooley, 2 July 1963 [SGC].

10 Callas to Leonidas Lantzounis, 22 July 1963 [RBC].

11 Callas to First Lady Jacqueline Kennedy, 21 July 1963 [Files and Programs of White House Entertainment, White House Archives, John F. Kennedy Presidential Library & Museum].

12 Callas to Cummings, 12 June 1963 in Hanine-Roussel, 470.

13 Callas to David Bicknell, 21 July 1963.

14 Andry, 49–50.

15 Gorlinsky to Walter Legge, 22 November 1963 [SGC].

16 Edward Greenfield, "Suvi Raj Grubb," *The Guardian*, 27 January 2000.

17 Schwarzkopf & Legge, 202.

18 Callas to Leonidas Lantzounis, 22 July 1963 [RBC].

19 AP London Image of Callas at Rome's Fiumicino Airport, 7 August 1963.

20 Schumach, "Onassis Noted as Gracious Host."

21 Cafarkis, 112.

22 Undated note in Callas' handwriting written on the *Christina*'s letterheaded paper to Ferruccio Mezzadri in the 1960s [CNH].

23 "Sérénade à la Callas," *Le Figaro*, 30 May 1963.

24 Diana Dubois, *In Her Sister's Shadow: An Intimate Biography of Lee Radziwill* (Boston: Little, Brown, 1995), 144.

25 Gorlinsky to Frederick Schang, 22 August 1963 [SGC].

26 "Princess Radizwill was not dressed for a visit to a monastery," *Leeuwarder Courant*, 27 August 1963.

27 "Onassis Is in Love with Princess Radziwill," *Folha de São Paulo*, 29 August 1963.

28 Leo Lerman's journal entry of 29 November 1970 in Lerman, 313; Stancioff, 162.

29 Galatopoulos, 415–16.

30 Leo Lerman's journal entry from Nov 29, 1970 in Lerman, 313.

31 Galatopoulos, 415–16.

32 ibid. 410.

33 Taki Theodoracopulos, "Famous Even in Albania," *The Spectator*, 13 September 1986.

34 Galatopoulos, 410.

35 Letters from Schang to Gorlinsky, 7 October 1963 and from Gorlinsky to John Coveney of EMI, 18 September 1963 [SGC].

36 AP, "Jackie to Depart for Athens and Cruise on Plush Yacht," *The Washington Post*, 1 October 1963.

37 Stancioff, 162.

38 Aileen Mehle, "How Suzy Ruled Society Gossip for Five Decades, as Told by Aileen Mehle," *Vanity Fair*, 4 January 2017.

39 "The night Onassis made a promise," *The Sunday Times*, 18 September 1977.

40 Galatopoulos, 412.

41 UPI, "Ship Owner Pays Visit To Widow," *The Courier Gazette* (McKinney, Texas), 2 December 1963.

42 Lerman, 265.

43 Gorlinsky to Schang, 27 October 1963 [SGC].

44 Crespi Morbio, 9.

45 Hanine-Roussel, 465–56 (Interview with Antonio Tonini).

46 "La Callas a Milano," *Corriere della Sera*, 26 March 1964.

47 Suzy Knickerbocker, "Ex-Waitress and Donohue Get Divorce," *The Philadelphia Inquirer*, 4 March 1964.

48 Callas to Elvira de Hidalgo, 10 November 1963 in Volf, "1963."

49 Dorothy Kilgallen, "Onassis Sitting on Headline News," *The Washington Post*, 7 November 1963.

50 Callas to Augusto Caldi Scalcini, 1 May 1964 [CGM].

51 Gavoty: 1965

52 Callas to Giulietta Simionato, 4 November 1963 in Claude Dufresne, *La Callas* (Paris: Perrin, 1990), 247.

53 Gorlinsky to Schang, 22 November 1963 [SGC].

54 Gorlinsky to Nicola Rescigno, 25 November 1963 [SGC].

55 "Tosca with Callas in the summer at the Athens Festival," *Eleftheria*, 19 February 1964.

56 Prouse, "Maria Callas Speaks," 26 March 1961.

57 Gavoty: 1965

58 John C. Bastias, "Maria Callas' Greek Adventure," *The Maria Callas International Club Magazine*, November 2013, no. 70.

59 Callas to Lawrence Kelly, 4 November 1963 in Volf, "1963."

60 ibid. Callas to Giovanna Lomazzi, 6 December 1963.

61 Leiser, "Chapter 13: Maria Callas."

62 Callas to Leo Lerman, 15 December 1963 [LLP].

63 "Maria Callas, Rescigno Set Record Date," *The New York Times*, 22 December 1963.

64 Suzy Patterson, "Maria Callas Contradicts Her Publicity Image," *The Journal Herald* of Dayton, Ohio, 11 January 1964.

65 William Hickey, "Callas' secret ambition—to be a film actress," *Daily Express*, 4 January 1964.

66 John Ardagh, " 'The Bible,' According to Dino De Laurentis," *The Washington Post*, 4 October 1964; "From Our Special Correspondent: Callas in Film," *De Telegraaf*, 9 January 1964.

67 Fleetwood: 1958.

68 Julie Andrews, *Home: A Memoir of My Early Years* (New York: Hachette Books, 2003), 210.

69 Undated note from Laurence Olivier to Callas [CNH].

70 Desgraupes: 1969

71 Interview with Alan Sievewright featured in Steve Cole, *Maria Callas: Living and Dying For Art and Love* (London: BBC 1, 17 January 2004).

72 Anjelica Huston, "Look Homeward, Anjelica," *Vanity Fair*, 22 October 2013, http://www.vanityfair.com/hollywood/2013/11/anjelica-huston-father-memoir.

73 Gorlinsky to Walter Wanger, 27 April 1965 [SGC].

74 Weaver: 1965

75 de Nussac & Cotta: 1970

76 Banzet: 1965

77 Ivor Newton, *At the Piano: The world of an accompanist* (London: Hamish Hamilton, 1966), 196.

78 Glotz, 123.

79 Marie-Jo Alibert, "C'était une personne très mélancolique qui enviait ma vie," *Le Tarn Libre*, 11 August 2014, https://web.archive.org/web/20201129011411/http://www.letarnlibre.com/2014/08/11/1219-janine-reiss-maitre-chant-maria-callas-etait-personne-tres-melancolique-qui-enviait-vie.html.

80 Galatopoulos, 372.
81 Downes: 1967
82 Stassinopoulos, 257.
83 Weaver: 1965
84 Interview with Tito Gobbi (*Hommages à Maria Callas*), 2 May 1978.
85 Author's interview with Sir John Tooley.
86 Interview with John Copley featured on *The Callas Effect: Deluxe Edition* (London: EMI Classics, 2011).
87 Hanine-Roussel, 483 (Interview with Carlo Felice Cillario).
88 Zeffirelli, 188–89.
89 Downes: 1967
90 Gastel Chiarelli, 111.
91 Gobbi, 97.
92 Tooley, 103.
93 Weaver: 1965
94 Philip Hope-Wallace, "New 'Tosca' at Covent Garden," *The Guardian*, 22 January 1964.
95 Hanine-Roussel, 483.
96 Ardoin & Fitzgerald, 218.
97 Gobbi, 96–97.
98 Hanine-Roussel, 483 (Interview with Carlo Felice Cillario).
99 Weaver: 1965
100 ibid.
101 "Renato Cioni's last interview: Remembering Callas," *Gramilano*, 4 March 2014, https://www.gramilano.com/2014/03/renato-cionis-last-interview-remembering-callas.
102 Philip Hope-Wallace, "New 'Tosca' at Covent Garden," *The Guardian*, 22 January 1964.
103 David Cairns, "Callas Athene," *The Spectator*, 31 January 1964.
104 Gobbi, 100.
105 Callas to Eugenio Gara, 21 February 1964 in Tosi, *Casta diva: L'incomparabile Callas*, 201.
106 Callas to Harold Rosenthal, 20 March 1964 [HRP].
107 Stassinopoulos, 261.
108 Callas to Lantzounis, 29 April 1964 [RBC].
109 Callas to Lantzounis, 21 April 1964 [RBC].
110 Gardner: 1958
111 George Callas to Maria, 23 February 1957 trans. Fani Kanatzia (Maria Callas Alumni Association of the Music School of Kalamata Exhibition).
112 Callas to Lantzounis, 21 April 1964 [RBC].
113 Callas to Lantzounis, 29 April 1964 [RBC].
114 Callas to Lantzounis, 19 November 1964 [RBC].
115 "Mme Callas tells of an 'affectionate legpulling,'" *The Guardian*, 19 April 1967.
116 Frank Goldsworthy, "Callas By Callas," *Daily Express*, 20 April 1967.
117 Ardoin, *The Callas Legacy*, 188.
118 René Seghers, *Corelli: Prince of Tenors* (Portland: Amadeus Press, 2008), 305–6.
119 Despite Corelli's behavior at this recording session Callas still invited him to attend her Juilliard classes in February 1971.

120 "Maria Callas a Commencé Les Répétitions de 'La Norma,'" *Combat*, 1 May 1964.

121 Callas to Augusto Caldi Scalcini, 1 May 1964 [CGM].

122 Interview with Franco Zeffirelli in Alain Ferrari, "Vissi d'arte."

123 Georges Prêtre in Crespi Morbio, 8.

124 Harewood: 1968

125 Harold C. Schonberg, "Music: Maria Callas Sings Norma: Pro and Anti Factions in Dispute in Paris," *The New York Times*, 23 May 1963.

126 Georges Conchon, "Lettre d'amour à Maria Callas," *Arts*, no. 964, 2 June 1964.

127 ibid. Jacques Bourgeois, "La Callas, inouïe."

128 Andrew Porter's review in *Musical Times* in Ardoin & Fitzgerald, 38.

129 Sylvie de Nussac's report in *Paris-Presse*, 9 June 1964.

130 "Right in The Heart of Paris," *Time*, 26 June 1964.

131 John Ellison, "Midnight In Paris," *Daily Express*, 12 June 1964.

15. "Consciously watching"

1 Lerman, 585.

2 Paul Hume, "With 'Tosca,' Callas Reclaimed Throne at the Met: Callas Tosca Now on Record," *The Washington Post*, 4 April 1965.

3 Esther Gelatt, "The New Prima Donna At Work: An Interview with Maria Callas," *High Fidelity*, February 1965.

4 Crespi Morbio, 7.

5 Desgraupes: 1969

6 Fournier, 83–84.

7 Harewood: 1968

8 Robert Sutherland, 212.

9 Harewood: 1968

10 La Rochelle, 17.

11 Howard Klein, "Maria Callas' Imperious Carmen," *The New York Times*, 24 January 1965.

12 "Callas Is Hoping To Return To Met," *The New York Times*, 11 July 1964.

13 Moore, 263.

14 Unsigned article, "La Callas e Onassis sbarcati a Capri," *Corriere della Sera*, 24 August 1964.

15 "Maria Callas: Impromptu Recital in Lefkada," *To Vima*, 1 September 1964.

16 Gorlinsky to John Coveney, 1 September 1964 [SGC].

17 Rudolf Bing to Luchino Visconti, 20 October 1964 [LVP].

18 Bing to Visconti, 7 October 1964 [LVP].

19 Banzet: 1965

20 Frost: 1970

21 Gorlinsky to Maxwell Simon, 6 January 1965 [SGC].

22 Frost: 1970

23 Dragadze, "My lonely world, a woman looking for her voice."

24 Ayre, 99–100.

25 Mary Annexy to Callas, 23 January 1969 [CNH].

26 Author's telephone interview with Mary Annexy.

27 Author's interview with Taki Theodoracopoulos.

28 Author's interview with Marilena Patronicolas.

29 Author's e-mail correspondence with Cristina Gastel Chiarelli.

30 Banzet: 1965

31 Glotz, 190.

32 Hanine-Roussel, 241 (Interview with Nicola Rescigno).

33 Stancioff, 163.

34 Dorle Soria, "Maria Paris April Wed 29 69" [DSP]. Quoted with kind permission from her great-nephew, David Winner.

35 Galatopoulos, 412.

36 Stancioff, 156.

37 Tosi, *Casta diva: L'incomparabile Callas*, 43.

38 Galatopoulos, 410.

39 Glotz, 329–33.

40 Robert Sutherland, 14–15; Lorcey, 179.

41 Spanidou, 157–58.

42 Robert Sutherland, 183.

43 David Gregson, "Remembering Maria," *San Diego Magazine*, October 1997.

44 Galatopoulos, 411–12.

45 Stancioff, 149.

46 Prêtre, 133–34.

47 Robert Sutherland, 181.

48 ibid. 178

49 Glotz, 327.

50 La Rochelle, 234.

51 Christopher Andersen, *Jackie after Jack: Portrait of a Lady* (Boston: Little, Brown, 1999), 188–89.

52 Cafarkis, 117.

53 Galatopoulos, 411.

54 Gastel Chiarelli, 117.

55 Dragadze, "My lonely world, a woman looking for her voice."

56 Ardoin, "Callas Today."

57 Hanine-Roussel, 483 (Interview with Carlo Felice Cillario).

58 Undated letter from Elvira de Hidalgo to Callas, c. June 1965 [CNH].

59 La Rochelle, 24.

60 "Maria Callas Came to Athens Yesterday (strictly incognito) for a vacation," *Eleftheria*, 24 December 1965.

61 Callas to Elvira de Hidalgo, 18 February 1965 [CBA].

62 Jacques Lonchampt, " 'La Tosca' à l'opéra avec Maria Callas et Tito Gobbi," *Le Monde*, 24 February 1965.

63 Callas to Herbert Weinstock, 24 February 1965 [HWP].

64 Author's e-mail correspondence with Lore and Lynn Taussig, 5 September 2014.

65 "Callas Fans Get in Line At Met Week Too Soon," *The New York Times*, 8 March 1965.

66 "50 Shouting Youths Greet Maria Callas," *The New York Times*, 16 March 1965.

67 Weaver: 1965

68 Hume, "With 'Tosca,' Callas Reclaimed Throne at the Met: Callas Tosca Now on Record."

69 Weaver: 1965

70 Gorlinsky to Callas, 22 April 1965 [SGC].

71 Gorlinsky to Walter Wanger, 30 April 1965 [SGC].

72 Contract for "Tosca" Film, 2 April 1965 between Callas, Gorlinsky's Interart and Walter Wanger Pictures [SGC].

73 Undated letter from Gorlinsky to Callas, c. late July 1965 [SGC].

74 "La Callas Ieri Sera in TV," *Corriere della Sera*, 19 May 1965.

75 Marlyse Schaeffer, "La Callas à la TV," *Elle* France, 20 May 1965.

76 Downes: 1967

77 Prouse, "Maria Callas Speaks," 2 April 1961.

78 de Nussac & Cotta: 1970

79 Galatopoulos, 357–58.

80 Jean-Pierre Lenoir, "Callas Conquers Illness and Paris," *The New York Times*, 16 May 1965.

81 Zeffirelli, 193–94.

82 Kesting trans. John Hunt, 264.

83 Romi, "Ce Que La Callas N'Avait Encore Jamais Raconté."

84 Callas to Elvira de Hidalgo, 4 June 1965 in Castiglione, 62.

85 Galatopoulos, 358.

86 ibid. 353.

87 Hanine-Roussel, 490 (Interview with Claude Calès).

88 Galatopoulos, 294.

89 Shirley Verrett, *I Never Walked Alone: The Autobiography of An American Singer* (Hoboken, NJ: Wiley, 2003), 107.

90 "Pet for Callas," *Daily Express*, 26 May 1965.

91 Prêtre, 135.

92 Interview with Michel Glotz in Alain Ferrari, "Vissi d'arte."

93 Hanine-Roussel, 510 (Interview with Gianfranco Cecchele).

94 Interview with Glotz in Ferrari, "Vissi d'arte."

95 "I must sing!," *Newsweek*, 14 June 1965.

96 Galatopoulos, 359.

97 Gastel Chiarelli, 123.

98 Undated telegram from Callas to Georges Auric in Hanine-Roussel, 516.

99 Cafarkis, 116.

100 Callas to Elvira de Hidalgo, 4 June 1965 in Castiglione, 62

101 "People In The News," *The Hartford Courant*, 23 June 1965.

102 Gorlinsky to Callas, 8 July 1965 [SGC].

103 Haltrecht, 288.

104 "Maria Callas Sings for Queen; Breaks 3 Other Engagements," *The New York Times*, 6 July 1965.

105 Solti, 148.

106 Prêtre, 129.

107 Frank Giles, "The actress in Callas," *The Sunday Times*, 11 July 1965.

108 "Ovation for Maria Callas," *The Guardian*, 6 July 1965.

109 Richard Norton-Taylor, "The general, the diva and the soul star," *The Guardian*, 29 July 2000.

110 Naur, "I have been a little spoiled."

111 Harold Rosenthal's review in *Opera*, August 1965 in Galatopoulos, 351.

112 Prouse, "Maria Callas Speaks," 2 April 1961.

16. "Redimensioning"

1   Notice by the Daily Telegraph Theatre Correspondent, *Daily Telegraph*, 6 July 1965.

2   Gorlinsky to Callas, 8 July 1965 [SGC].

3   Callas to Cristina Gastel, 8 August 1965 in Gastel Chiarelli, 123–27.

4   "Callas Takes A Swim," *Daily Express*, 11 August 1965.

5   "Georges Prêtre exaspéré par les stars du chant," *France-Soir*, 14 September 1987.

6   Prêtre, 132.

7   Stancioff, 149.

8   Peter Halley, "Princess Marianne, 2001," *Index Magazine*, http://www.indexmagazine.com/interviews/princess_marianne.shtml.

9   Gavoty: 1965

10 Berger, "Maria Callas nahm mit einem Bandwurm ab, Onassis spottete über seinen 'Kanarienvogel.'"

11 Robert Sutherland, 15.

12 Halley, "Princess Marianne, 2001."

13 Meneghini, 204.

14 Teresa Berganza & Olivier Bellamy, *Un monde habité par le chant* (Paris: Buchet-Chastel, 2013), 95.

15 Fleetwood: 1958

16 Gorlinsky to Callas, 13 July 1965 [SGC].

17 George Armstrong, "Callas' Career in Films Begins," *The Guardian*, 14 August 1965.

18 Galatopoulos, 363.

19 Andry, 53.

20 Gorlinsky to Callas, 21 October 1965 [SGC].

21 Zeffirelli, 208.

22 Gorlinsky to Callas, 20 August 1965 [SGC].

23 Gorlinsky to Onassis, 5 July 1967 [SGC].

24 Cable from Onassis to Jack Warner, 22 September 1965 [SGC].

25 Gorlinsky to John Coveney, 3 December 1965 [SGC].

26 Gorlinsky to Callas, 26 January 1966 [SGC].

27 Spyros P. Skouras of 20th Century Fox to Onassis, 19 May 1966 (Spyros P. Skouras Papers. M0509).

28 Zeffirelli, 207–9.

29 Galatopoulos, 411.

30 ibid. 365.

31 La Rochelle, 223 (Interview with Michel Glotz).

32 Goldsworthy, "Callas By Callas."
33 Gorlinsky to Onassis, 5 July 1967 [SGC].
34 Callas to Leonard Bernstein, 16 August 1965 in Volf, "1965."
35 Stassinopoulos, 273.
36 "Callas-Onassis row described," *The Irish Times*, 25 April 1967.
37 Gorlinsky to Callas, 26 January 1966 [SGC].
38 William Hickey, "Goodness! As Maria Callas sees the airport scales," *Daily Express*, 11 September 1965.
39 "Happy Birthday Mystic Garbo," *The Washington Post*, 19 September 1965.
40 Desgraupes: 1969
41 Fleetwood: 1958
42 Frost: 1970
43 Gorlinsky to John Coveney, 29 October 1965 [SGC].
44 Gorlinsky to Callas, 29 December 1965 [SGC].
45 "Two tragedies behind the triumph of Margot Fonteyn and Rudolf Nureyev," *De Telegraaf*, 20 November 1965.
46 Downes: 1967
47 de Nussac & Cotta: 1970
48 Harewood: 1968
49 George Jellinek, Interview with Richard Tucker for *The Vocal Scene with George Jellinek*, WQXR Radio, 23 January 1975.
50 Gastel Chiarelli, 129–30.
51 La Rochelle, 234 (Interview with Michel Glotz).
52 Hanine-Roussel, 416 (Interview with Ferruccio Mezzadri).
53 Fan Jacqueline Pétiard's account in *The Maria Callas International Club Magazine*, no.7, 7 February 1993.
54 Callas to an unknown fan, 4 April 1966 in Volf, "1966."
55 Undated letter from Olive and May Haddock to Gorlinsky, c. October 1962 [SGC].
56 Weaver: 1965
57 Gorlinsky to Callas, 26 January 1966 [SGC].
58 "Onassis ama la Lollobrigida?," *La Stampa*, 10 March 1966.
59 "In Egitto la Lollo con Callas e Onassis," *La Gazzetta del Mezzogiorno*, 3 March 1966.
60 Rosemary Feitelberg, "Q&A with Gina Lollobrigida," *WWD*, 8 April 2013.
61 "La Callas a causa dell'ex marito rinuncia alla cittadinanza americana," *La Stampa*, 30 March 1966.
62 "Maria Callas Renounces U.S. Citizenship, Solves Problem of Marriage, She Asserts," *Chicago Tribune*, 7 April 1966.
63 Callas' comments to reporters on 18 March 1966 featured in Palmer, *Callas: A Documentary*.
64 Frost: 1970
65 Paul J. Ioannidis, *Destiny Prevails: My Life with Aristotle, Alexander, Christina Onassis and her daughter, Athina* (New York: Significance Press, 2015), Kindle location 1215.
66 Galatopoulos, 339.
67 Cafarkis, 114.
68 Author's interview with Korinna Spanidou.

69 Frost: 1970
70 Galatopoulos, 416.
71 ibid. 13.
72 Dragadze, "My lonely world, a woman looking for her voice."
73 Stassinopoulos, 277–78.

N.B. The earliest assertion of a pregnancy was made by Arianna Stassinopoulos, now known as media mogul Arianna Huffington. "One of the most exciting dreams had to do with Maria's abortion," she told a reporter after the U.S. publication of her biography, *Maria Callas: The Woman Behind The Legend* (New York: Simon & Schuster) in 1981. "I actually woke up from the dream and knew that Callas had had an abortion. I didn't say this for a long time, because I didn't want to detract from the book's credibility." (John Guinn, "She Peers Beyond the Callas Legend," *Detroit Free Press*, 15 March 1981).

Stassinopoulos' first source was Edith Gorlinsky, wife of Sander. The two had been discussing a trip of Maria's when Stassinopoulos had posed her the question, "Was this the time when she had the abortion?" Edith Gorlinsky had asked "how she knew," leading Stassinopoulos to say that as a journalist she refused to unveil "[her] sources" (Joseph McLellan, "Stalking the Stormy Diva," *The Washington Post*, 3 March 1981).

Unlike Sander, Edith knew Callas little. In January of 1966 she had accused her husband of paying too little attention to her, in part because of Callas. "Edith, for whom you have a great regard, has always told me that my No. 1 loyalty, sometimes even before loyalty to her, was for you, and this is the case and I am not ashamed to say so." (Gorlinsky to Callas, 26 January 1966: SGC).

The next source who supported Stassinopoulos' thesis, Maria's onetime assistant Nadia Stancioff, gave an account in her 1987 book about Callas. (Stancioff, 161). The biography, although reliable in parts, contained highly dramaticized incidents, as well as anecdotes related in a melodramatic style. These included a story about Maria allegedly fearing pregnancy at the age of forty-eight and inviting Stancioff to experience the doctor's visit with her at the Grand Hotel, Rome in fall 1972 (ibid. 217–218). The concierge of the hotel at the time, Pino Buso—who vividly recalled Maria's visits at that and other hotels—did not remember Callas having stayed there any time from 1971 thereafter. (Author's e-mail and text message correspondence with Pino Buso, 3–4 September 2015).

Given Callas' exhaustive schedule in that period, few days are unaccounted for. The story would also be advanced by Callas' sometime friend John Ardoin, a Dallas music critic with whom Callas severed contact when he wrote a book about her without asking her permission. He would sustain another myth about the singer, admitting later in life that he had "got a certain kick out of pulling the wool over the public's eyes" by fabricating tales. (Author's e-mail correspondence with Ardoin's final assistant Gregor Benko, 14 August 2014).

In an interview with the author on 11 July 2012, Callas' best friend Giovanna Lomazzi asserted she had "never" spoken of any alleged pregnancy, and that she did not know whether or not this ever happened to her friend. Years later, likely due to her advancing age, she embraced Nicholas Gage's tale of the "lost son" to whom Callas had "secretly given birth" in 1960 (Gage, *Greek Fire*, New York: Knopf, 2000). This and other thoughts Lomazzi chose to voice in later years attest to how the press had colored her impressions of her friend, since they are very much at odds with the substantially detailed, lengthy testimonials she wrote in *La Settimana Incom Illustrata* in 1961.

However, even in the present day she has told press multiple times that she did not hear anything of an alleged pregnancy from Callas personally (c.f. https://www.ilgiornale.it/news/spettacoli/fu-veramente-divina-poi-incontr-mostro-onassis-1440614.html, as well as https://www.gramilano.com/2017/09/maria-callas-as-told-by-her-little-sister-giovanna-lomazzi-interview).

Onassis' physician Nikolaos Christeas—Director of the First Surgical Clinic at Laiko Hospital, Athens from 1956–71—claimed at the age of ninety-five to Greek newspaper *Tachydromos*, in response to rumors, "It is not true. I would've been the first to know. Maria never got pregnant by Aristo. He and I were always together and he told me everything." (c.f. https://www.abc.es/estilo/gente/abci-confidencias-medico-onassis-200106240300-30620_noticia.html).

Ultimately, given Stassinopoulos' active imagination, Edith Gorlinsky's vested interest in stirring mistruths about Callas and Stancioff's publicity-seeking book, the accounts seem spurious. What the abovementioned allege is a very long and painful experience of deliberating whether or not to have a then illegal abortion. Being someone who had difficulty masking her emotions, Callas would have been unable to conceal her trauma. There is no gap in her social activity or any anomalous pattern of behavior in either 1966 or any other year during her relationship with Onassis that suggests such an episode happened.

74 Fleming, "Nurturing a Legend."
75 Desgraupes: 1969
76 Caloni: 1976
77 Callas to Elvira de Hidalgo, 22 April 1966 in Castiglione, 63.
78 Elvira de Hidalgo to Callas, 6 May 1966 [CNH].
79 Rasponi, 584.
80 Walter Winchell, "Mad About Town," *The Cincinnati Enquirer*, 21 April 1966.
81 Callas to Eugenio Gara, 22 April 1966 in Tosi, *Casta diva: L'incomparabile Callas*, 201–2.
82 Gorlinsky to Jacques Weulf, Secrétaire Général of *Le Figaro*, 6 May 1966 [SGC].
83 Gorlinsky to Françoise Bellaigue of Pathé Marconi, 10 May 1966 [SGC].
84 "La Callas contre Bibi, un crime de lèse-diva," *Marie-Claire*, 15 June 1966.
85 Photo Caption: "Maria Callas va in Svizzera," *La Stampa*, 17 May 1966; Callas' interview with Catherine Charbon on 16 May 1966 for RTS Television, accessed at: http://www.rts.ch/archives/tv/information/carrefour/3467161-maria-callas.html.
86 Waverley Root, "Parisian Critics Eviscerate Met," *The Washington Post*, 2 June 1966.
87 Glotz, 208.
88 Photograph of Callas with Juliette Gréco after the concert on 1 June 1966 by Jacques Haillot, Collection of Sygma Via Getty Images accessed at https://www.gettyimages.fr/detail/photo-d%27actualit%C3%A9/american-born-greek-soprano-maria-callas-with-french-photo-dactualit%C3%A9/788564243.
89 Harewood: 1968
90 Nana Mouskouri, *Memoirs* (London: Orion Publishing, 2007), 74–75.
91 Renaud Machart, "Classical Nana," *Le Monde*, 20 September 2013.
92 Bernard Gavoty to Gorlinsky, 14 June 1966 [SGC].
93 Gorlinsky to Callas, 1 April 1966 [SGC].
94 Gorlinsky to Schuyler Chapin, 21 June 1966 [SGC].
95 Emilio Pozzi, Interview with Callas for RAI Television, 19 July 1966.
96 Callas to Giulietta Simionato, 21 June 1966 in Hanine-Roussel, 523.
97 Photograph of Callas with Margot Fonteyn taken on 21 June 1966 by KEYSTONE Pictures, Collection of KEYSTONE Pictures USA. Accessed at https://www.alamy.com/opera-singer-maria-callas-with-ballerina-margot-fonteyn-image69423089.html.

98 Gorlinsky to Callas, 1 July 1966 [SGC].

99 Gorlinsky to Jacques Weulf, 8 July 1966 [SGC].

100 "The Beautiful People This Summer," *Vogue*, 15 September 1966, 78.

101 Author's e-mail correspondence with Cristina Gastel Chiarelli.

102 Author's interview with Korinna Spanidou.

103 Author's interview with Marilena Patronicolas.

104 Osborne, *Conversations with Karajan*, 75.

105 Interview with Herbert von Karajan (*Hommages à Maria Callas*), 2 November 1977.

106 Osborne, *Herbert von Karajan: A Life in Music*, 546.

107 AP, "Singer Shares Separation Onus," *The Washington Post*, 19 June 1966.

108 Callas to Augusto Caldi Scalcini, 22 August 1966 [CGM].

109 Callas to Matilde Stagnoli, 13 September 1966 [CFM].

110 Gorlinsky to a "Madame Boucheron" of Olympic Maritime S.A., 24 January 1967 [SGC].

111 Maureen Footer & Hamish Bowles, *Dior and His Decorators: Victor Grandpierre, Georges Geoffroy and the New Look* (New York: Vendome, 2018), 222.

112 Marlyse Schaeffer, "Aujourd'hui, La Callas," *Elle* France, 28 April 1969.

113 Footer & Bowles, 222.

114 Callas to Teresa d'Addato, 13 January 1967 in Volf, "1967."

115 Gorlinsky to Callas, 11 January 1967 [SGC].

116 Gorlinsky to Callas, 8 September 1966 [SGC].

117 Gorlinsky to Callas, 14 October and 11 November 1966 [SGC].

118 Callas to Augusto Caldi Scalcini, 1 November 1966 [CGM].

119 "Callas at Old Met Next Season In Civic Opera 'Medea' Possible," *The Dallas Morning News*, 18 November 1966.

120 "Maria Callas may appear at the Athens Festival in 1967," *Ta Nea*, 31 December 1966.

121 "Compiled From Wire Reports: People, Jet Set Lands at St. Moritz," *The Dallas Morning News*, 21 December 1966.

122 "Starry Soirée Salutes the Lido," *Life*, 6 January 1967.

123 Scott, 281 n. 24.

124 Callas to Olive Haddock (c. late 1966) in Tosi, *The Young Maria Callas*, 130.

125 This was *The Dallas Morning News'* John Ardoin, a sometime friend of Callas who supported the notion in his 1984 book *The Callas Legacy*. Ardoin eventually confessed to his assistant Gregor Benko—who had been appointed to organize his affairs during the last months of his life—that he had "at a certain point realized that it was not [Maria], but got a certain 'kick' out of pulling the wool over the public's eyes." (E-mail from Gregor Benko to the author, 15 August 2014).

126 Lawrence Kelly to Alexis Minotis, 12 January 1967 [AMP].

127 Alexis Minotis to Larry Kelly, 1 February 1967 [AMP].

128 Pablo Segura, "Onassis y Maria Callas llegaron en el 'Christina,'" *Diario de Las Palmas*, 10 February 1967.

129 Callas to Bruna Lupoli, 16 February 1967 in Volf, "1967."

130 "People, Vintage Cars, Chaplin Era," *The Dallas Morning News*, 17 March 1967.

131 Helen Miley, "Nassau Gives Yachtsmen A Gala Welcome," *The Miami Herald*, 19 March 1967.

132 Frischauer, 13.

133 Callas to Walter Cummings, 4 April 1967 in Volf, "1967."

134 Andry, 55–56.

135 Plácido Domingo, *My First Forty Years* (New York: Knopf, 1999), 79.

136 Andry, 55–56.

137 Alvin Shuster, "Miss Callas Wins Suit on Freighter," *The New York Times*, 1 November 1968.

138 Lloyd's Law Reports: Onassis and Calogeropulos v. Vergottis. Court of Appeal. 11, 12, 15, 16, 17, 18, 19, 22, 23 January 1968.

139 "Around The World: Maria Callas Is Now A Shipowner," *The Washington Post*, 29 April 1967.

140 Lloyd's Law Reports: Onassis and Calogeropulos v. Vergottis. Court of Appeal.

141 "Mme Callas tells of an 'affectionate legpulling.' "

142 Shuster, "Miss Callas Wins Suit on Freighter."

143 "Callas action is called a 'frame-up,' " *The Irish Times*, 27 April 1967.

144 Goldsworthy, "Callas By Callas."

145 Fraser, Jacobson, Ottoway & Chester, 222.

146 Frank Goldsworthy, "Callas and I," *Daily Express*, 18 April 1967.

147 Galatopoulos, 408.

148 Fraser, Jacobson, Ottoway & Chester, 223.

149 "Callas, not very lucky," *The Irish Times*, 20 April 1967.

150 "Mme. Callas Saved a Journalist," *The Guardian*, 20 April 1967.

151 "Callas at after-opera party," *Daily Express*, 20 April 1967.

152 Bottero, 219–20 (Interview with Carlo Maria Giulini).

153 "Callas action is called a 'frame-up.' "

154 Gwen Morgan, "Maria Callas Wins Suit to Control Ship," *Chicago Tribune*, 29 April 1967.

155 "New trial of action which gave ship shares to Mme. Callas," *The Guardian*, 24 January 1968; "Maria Callas can appeal to Lords," *The Guardian*, 5 March 1968; "Shipowner's cross-appeal withdrawn," *The Guardian*, 19 July 1968; Shuster, "Miss Callas Wins Suit on Freighter."

156 Photographs of Callas in Cannes in summer 1967 by Pictorial Press Ltd.; Alamy Stock Photos accessed at https://www.alamy.com/stock-photo/maria-callas-in-cannes-1967.html.

157 Gorlinsky to Callas, 27 July 1967 [SGC].

158 Berger, "Maria Callas nahm mit einem Bandwurm ab, Onassis spottete über seinen 'Kanarienvogel.' "

159 James Reginato, "The High Life," *W Magazine*, 1 April 2009, https://www.wmagazine.com/story/marina-cicogna.

160 Francesco Canino, "Florinda Bolkan a FQMagazine: 'Io donna libera che ama senza limiti. Una storia con Gianni Agnelli? Io sapevo tutto di lui, lui di me,' " FQMagazine, 15 December 2020, https://www.ilfattoquotidiano.it/2020/12/15/florinda-bolkan-a-fqmagazine-io-donnalibera-che-ama-senza-limiti-una-storia-con-gianni-agnelli-io-sapevo-tutto-di-lui-lui-dime/6037742.

161 Berger, "Maria Callas nahm mit einem Bandwurm ab, Onassis spottete über seinen 'Kanarienvogel.' "

162 Jacques Pessis, "Rowena Forrest: Des robes pour la Callas," *Le Figaro*, 9 February 2013.

163 Karl Aage Rasmussen, *Sviatoslav Richter: Pianist* (Boston: Northeastern University Press, 2010), 269.

164 Byron Janis, *Chopin and Beyond: My Extraordinary Life in Music and the Paranormal* (Hoboken, NJ: Wiley Books, 2010), 126.

165 Callas to Tullio Serafin c. August 1967 in Nicla Sguotti, *Tullio Serafin: Il custode del bel canto* (Padua: Armelin Musica, 2014), 259.

166 Hamilton, *Maria Callas: Performance Annals and Discography*. Callas worked with Richard Nunn in Paris from 13 August–9 September 1967. This information likely comes from Hamilton's contact with Nunn.

167 Sarah Bradford, *America's Queen: The Life of Jacqueline Kennedy Onassis* (New York: Viking, 2000), 439.

168 Callas to Giulietta Simionato, 5 September 1967 in Tosi, *Casta diva: L'incomparabile Callas*, 207.

169 John Pettitt, "Report of The M.C.I.C. 81st Birthday Dinner in London on 2 December 2004: Former répétiteur Richard Nunn talks about his work with Maria Callas in 1967 and 1968 for a recording of 'La traviata' with Luciano Pavarotti," *The Maria Callas International Magazine*, Issue 44.

170 Prouse, "Maria Callas Speaks," 26 March 1961.

171 "From our Utrecht Correspondent: Maria Callas in an Exclusive Interview at Haar Castle," *Nieuwsblad van het Noorden*, 13 September 1967.

172 Andry, 47.

173 ibid. 52.

174 Downes: 1967

175 Harris: 1970

176 Gobbi, 98.

177 Stancioff, 134.

178 Callas to Elvira de Hidalgo, 18 February 1965: "You will find a check enclosed." (Volf, "1965.")

179 Elvira de Hidalgo to Callas, 10 November 1967 (CNH).

180 Jack O'Brian, "DeSeversky Still Pioneering," *The Herald Statesman*, 17 November 1967.

181 Callas to Elvira de Hidalgo, 17 November 1967 in Castiglione, 64.

182 Janis, 126–27.

183 Galatopoulos, 410.

184 Callas to Meneghini, 20 June 1949 in Allegri, *Maria Callas: Lettere d'amore*, 138.

185 Leonard Lyons, "Lyons Den," *The Pittsburgh Press* from Pittsburgh, Pennsylvania, 14 May 1966.

186 Fraser, Ottoway, Jacobson & Chester, 206.

187 ibid. 207–8.

188 "The News of the Day," *The Los Angeles Times*, 7 March 1967.

189 de Gramont, "The Little Millionaire."

190 Soria, "Maria Paris Wed April 29 69" [DSP].

191 Lerman, diary entry of August 30, 1971, 353.

192 Valerio Cappelli, "Elsa Martinelli: I miei anni '60 senza tabù," *Corriere della Sera*, 1 August 1994.

193 Cafarkis, 112–14.

194 Berger, "Maria Callas nahm mit einem Bandwurm ab, Onassis spottete über seinen 'Kanarienvogel.'"

195 Soria, "Greek Sorceress."

196 Harold C. Schonberg, "Opera: Suliotis As Norma," *The New York Times*, 10 November 1967.

197 Callas to John Ardoin, 16 June 1968 in Volf, "1968."

198 Frost: 1970

199 Ardoin: 1968

200 Harewood: 1968

201 Andry, 55.

202 Leo Lerman's journal entry for 14 November 1967 in Lerman, 293.

203 Callas to Lerman, 1 May 1964 [LLP].

204 Virginie Merlin, "Dans l'intimité de la Callas": interview with Frédéric Simogli, *Paris Match*, September 1987.

205 Bing to Callas, 12 December 1967 in Bing, *A Knight at the Opera*, 102–3; Bing to Callas, 5 May 1969: ibid. 116.

206 Author's interview with Fabrizio Melano, New York, 24 March 2013. Melano obtained Callas' birth certificate from the New York Bureau of Vital Statistics on 16 December 1967 (the date stamped on it).

207 Cruesemann: 1959

208 Banzet: 1965

209 Callas, *Oggi* memoirs in Tosi, *Giovane Callas*, 101.

17. "The 'intangible' "

1 "Nada para mim foi fácil": Unsigned interview with Callas.

2 Callas to de Hidalgo, 20 January 1968 in Castiglione, 65.

3 Gorlinsky to Callas, 5 February 1968 [SGC].

4 Bing to Callas, 31 January 1968 in Bing, *A Knight at the Opera*, 104.

5 Birthday note from Callas to Meneghini in Allegri, *Lettere d'amore*, 170.

6 Callas, "A.S.O Birthday Present," 30 January 1968 in Sophia Handaka, *Aristotle Onassis: Beyond His Myth*: Exhibition Catalogue for the Benaki Museum (Athens: Benaki Museum, 2006), 77. ["Alexander S. Onassis' Foundation Collection."].

7 Handwritten notes by Gorlinsky dated 31 January 1968 [SGC].

8 Hugh Lee Lyon, *Leontyne Price: Highlights of a Prima Donna* (New York: Authors Choice Press), 90.

9 Bernard Holland, "Leontyne Price, Skipping Opera This Year, Makes Only New York Appearance," *The New York Times*, 20 March 1981.

10 Undated letter from Leontyne Price to Callas, c. late December 1968 [CNH].

11 Jan Maguire, "Callas, Serafin and the Art of Bel Canto," *Saturday Review*, 30 March 1968.

12 Gorlinsky to Callas, 1 March 1968 [SGC].

13 Menu of the Air France Boeing Jet Intercontinental to Las Palmas, 16 February 1968 [CNH].

14 Callas to Bruna Lupoli, 4 March 1968 in Volf, "1968."

15 "Aristote Onassis et Maria Callas Au Sans Souci," *Le Nouvelliste* of Haiti, 6 March 1968.

16 "Maria Callas a Haiti ricevuta da Duvalier," *Il Piccolo*, 10 March 1968.

17 "M. Onassis et Maria Callas nous parlent d'Haïti et de leur rencontre avec le Président Duvalier," *Le Nouvelliste* of Haiti, 7 March 1968.

18 Donald Spoto, *Jacqueline Kennedy Bouvier Onassis: A Life* (New York: St. Martin's Press, 2000), 259.
19 Aileen Mehle, "Suzy Says, A Gatherin' of Greeks," *The Hartford Courant*, 21 April 1968.
20 Frederick M. Winship, "Jacqueline Lived In Publicity Glare," *The Dallas Morning News*, 20 October 1968.
21 Gorlinsky to Peter Andry, 9 April 1968 [SGC].
22 John Culshaw, "Callas: A Personal Footnote," *High Fidelity*, November 1977.
23 Harewood, 234–35.
24 Merlin, "Dans l'intimité de la Callas."
25 Schaeffer, "Aujourd'hui, La Callas."
26 Merlin, "Dans l'intimité de la Callas."
27 Stancioff, 169–70.
28 Dufresne, 267
29 Desgraupes: 1969
30 Gorlinsky to Callas, 26 January 1971 [SGC].
31 Leo Lerman's journal entry of 12 December 1970 in Lerman, 315.
32 Bing, *A Knight at the Opera*, 107.
33 Andry, 56.
34 J. Randy Taraborrelli, *After Camelot: A Personal History of the Kennedy Family, 1968 to the Present* (New York: Grand Central Publishing, 2012), 11. Citing Robert F. Kennedy's campaign worker Joan Braden's personal oral history kept at the John F. Kennedy Presidential Library, Taraborrelli reports that Joan and Ethel Kennedy sought to discourage the engagement until after Bobby's projected victory.
35 "People, Princess Gives Birth to Son," *The Dallas Morning News*, 28 May 1968.
36 Bradford, 451.
37 Banzet: 1965
38 Harewood: 1968
39 ibid.
40 Andry, 56.
41 Bottero, 220 (Interview with Carlo Maria Giulini).
42 Gorlinsky to Callas, 30 May 1968 [SGC].
43 Earl Wilson, "Lady Bird's Aide To Write A Book," *The Philadelphia Daily News*, 1 June 1968.
44 Callas to Elvira de Hidalgo, 16 June 1968 in Castiglione, 68.
45 Winship, "Jacqueline Lived In Publicity Glare."
46 Bradford, 448.
47 Bing, *A Knight at the Opera*, 110.
48 Aileen Mehle, "Suzy Says, Bobo Summers in New York," *The Hartford Courant*, 15 July 1968.
49 Lawrence Kelly to Alexis Minotis, 3 July 1968 [AMP].
50 Maryn Schwartz, "Callas cut quite a swath in Dallas," *The Dallas Morning News*, 22 August 1989.
51 Gorlinsky to Callas, 25 July 1968 [SGC].
52 Press Wire Service, "Onassis, Jackie … Callas Quit, 3 Was a Crowd on Island," *Boston Globe*, 18 October 1968.

53 Leo Lerman's journal entry of 30 August 1971 in Lerman, 352–53.

54 Soria, "Maria Paris April Wed 29 69" [DSP].

55 Stassinopoulos, 288–89.

56 UPI, "Greeks Deny Kennedy To Visit Premier," *The Hartford Courant*, 10 August 1968.

57 Callas, Telegram to "THE CAST OF HAIR," 28 July 1968 [Copy from CFG].

58 Desgraupes: 1969

59 Harris: 1970

60 Ardoin & Fitzgerald, 3.

61 Stancioff, 132.

62 James Jorden, Interview with John Ardoin, 17 December 1999, https://parterre.com/ardoin_interview.htm.

63 Tom Donnelly, "The Rich Are You and Me," *The Washington Post*, 21 April 1973.

64 Judy Williamson, "The dream world of resorts," *The Los Angeles Times*, 25 December 1983.

65 Jerry Hulse, "The Lure Of Santa Fe: Blue Skies. Blue Corn. Art. Adobe. Few Can Resist the Charms of New Mexico's Enchanting City. And That's the Problem," *The Los Angeles Times*, 3 June 1990.

66 Stassinopoulos, 289.

67 Florabel Muir, "Hollywood," *The New York Daily News*, 16 August 1968.

68 Marilyn Beck, "That's Showbiz," *The Hartford Courant*, 8 September 1968.

69 Callas to Teresa d'Addato, 15 August 1968 in Volf, "1968."

70 Herb Caen of San Francisco, "Scoops du jour," *Honolulu Star Bulletin*, 25 August 1968.

71 Kurt & Ive Adler, *Kurt Adler and the San Francisco Opera: Oral History Transcripts: 1994, vol. 3* (Memphis: General Books, 2010), 133.

72 John Ardoin, "Maria Callas and DCO," *The Dallas Morning News*, 30 March 1969.

73 Gorlinsky to Callas, 4 September 1968 [SGC].

74 Callas to Bruna Lupoli, 17 August 1968 in Volf, "1968."

75 ibid. Note from Callas to Lawrence Kelly, 23 August 1968.

76 "Maria Callas Due in Dallas," *The Dallas Morning News*, 28 August 1968.

77 Stassinopoulos, 289.

78 Callas to Lawrence Kelly, 26 November 1962 in Volf, "1962."

79 ibid. Memo from John Coveney to Peter Andry, "Mexican Conversations with Maria Callas," 3 September 1968.

79 ibid. John Coveney to Lawrence Kelly, 23 August 1968.

80 Stassinopoulos, 290.

81 UPI, "Callas to Revive Career," *The Dallas Morning News*, 5 September 1968.

82 Nikos Nikolizas, "Jackie sent Alexander to his death," *Espresso* magazine, 23 May 2015, https://www.espressonews.gr/reportaz/49985/i-tzaki-estile-ston-thanato-ton-alexan/.

83 Stancioff, 166.

84 Schwartz, "Callas cut quite a swath in Dallas."

85 Cruesemann: 1959

86 Frost: 1970

87 de Nussac & Cotta: 1970

88 Romi, "Ce Que La Callas N'Avait Encore Jamais Raconté."

89 UPI, "Callas to Revive Career."

90 "WPR to Present Callas Interview," *The Dallas Morning News*, 19 September 1968.

91 "Luncheon to Honor Opera Star," *The Dallas Morning News*, 9 September 1968.

92 "Maria Callas to Perform," *The Dallas Morning News*, 13 September 1968.

93 Francis Robinson, Assistant Manager of the Metropolitan Opera, to his mother, 13 September 1968 in Lowe, 231.

94 Charlotte Curtis, "Glamour Brigade Troops to Opera Opening, Maria Callas Gets Salute of 'Bravas' From the Crowd," *The New York Times*, 17 September 1968.

95 Renzo & Roberto Allegri, *Callas by Callas: The Secret Writings of La Maria* (New York: Universe, 1998), 142.

96 Renata Tebaldi to Callas, 20 September 1968 [CNH].

97 Jacques Chancel, "Onassis . . . C'est Fini!," *Paris Jour*, 16 September 1968.

98 Gorlinsky to Callas, 16 September 1968 [SGC].

99 Bing, *A Knight at the Opera*, 112.

100 Callas to John Ardoin, 27 September 1968 [AKP].

101 Callas to Elvira de Hidalgo, 3 October 1968 [CBA].

102 Diary entry of Richard Burton on 6 October 1968 in Burton, 200.

103 John Ellison, "Callas, 'Just a friendship,' " *Daily Express*, 18 October 1968.

104 Photograph of Callas and Hélène Rochas at the premiere of *Phèdre* taken 14 October 1968. Getty image accessed at https://www.gettyimages.co.uk/detail/news-photo/first-of-the-film-phaedra-by-pierre-jourdan-at-the-paris-news-photo/160748832.

105 Merlin, "Dans l'intimité de la Callas."

106 Callas to Elvira de Hidalgo, 29 October 1968 [CBA].

107 Galatopoulos, 413.

108 Franco Paoli, "La Consola 'Ex' Si Consola," *Tempo* magazine, 15 February 1969.

109 Photograph of Callas at the Paris premiere of *A Flea In Her Ear* by Ron Galella, 18 October 1968. Getty Images Collection accessed at https://www.gettyimages.co.uk/detail/news-photo/actress-maria-callas-attends-the-premiere-of-flea-in-her-news-photo/139569743.

110 Roger Ebert, "The Beattys' Affair To Remember," 23 October 1994, https://www.rogerebert.com/interviews/the-beattys-affair-to-remember.

111 Gambetti, "Sono per una Medea non aggressiva," 466.

112 Ayre, 100.

113 Author's interview with Thérèse Darras, Paris, 2 December 2013.

114 Recorded tape of Callas' speech featured in John Ardoin, *Maria Callas In Her Own Words*.

115 Ardoin & Fitzgerald, 45.

116 "Maria Callas Refuses Comments to the Press," *De Tijd*, 22 October 1968.

117 Callas to Irving Kolodin, 24 October 1968 [IKP].

118 de Nussac & Cotta: 1970.

119 Ardoin, "Maria Callas and DCO."

120 Leo Lerman's journal entry of 6 January 1969 in Lerman, 296.

121 Luigi Chini, *Il destino mi ha fatto incontrare Maria Callas: Ferruccio Mezzadri racconta.* (Piacenza: Edizioni L.I.R., 2017), 93.

122 Galatopoulos, 414.

123 de Nussac & Cotta: 1970

124 Interview with Jacques Bourgeois in Tony Palmer, *Maria Callas: La Divina—A Portrait* (London: London Trust Productions, 1987).

125 Leo Lerman's journal entry of 6 January 1969 in Lerman, 295.

126 Callas to Max Lorenz, 14 November 1968 in Association pour la promotion des arts, *Maria Callas: Exposition, Paris, Hôtel de Ville de Paris, Salle Saint-Jean*, Catalogue for Exhibition held 27 March 1998–28 June 1998 (Paris: Association pour la promotion des arts).

127 Callas to Nino Costa, a collector of pirate recordings, 20 November 1968 in Volf, "1968."

128 de Nussac & Cotta: 1970

129 Guido Mazzon, "Le mie estati con Pasolini e la Callas," *La Provincia Pavese*, 6 June 2011, https://laprovinciapavese.gelocal.it/pavia/cronaca/2011/06/05/news/le-mie-estati-con-pasolini-e-la-callas-1.322954.

130 Jack Buckley, "An Ancient Woman," *Opera News*, 13 December 1969.

131 Harris: 1970

132 Gorlinsky to Franco Rossellini, 30 November 1968 [SGC].

133 Gina Guandalini, *Maria Callas: L'interprete, La storia* (Rome: Curcio Musica, 2007), 204.

134 Callas to Elvira de Hidalgo in Castiglione, 26 April 1969, 70.

135 Soria, "Greek Sorceress."

136 Gorlinsky to Callas, 9 December 1968 [SGC].

137 Gorlinsky to Callas, 9 October 1968 [SGC].

138 Leo Lerman's journal entry of 6 January 1969 in Lerman, 296.

139 Callas to Teresa d'Addato, 2 January 1969 in Volf, "1969."

140 Gorlinsky to Callas, 6 January 1969 [SGC].

141 1969 undated, handwritten notes by Gorlinsky to Callas [SGC].

142 Gorlinsky to Callas, 6 June 1969 [SGC].

143 André Chabaud, Administrator of the Opéra de Paris, to Luchino Visconti, 30 May 1969 [LVP].

144 Desgraupes: 1969

145 Schaeffer, "Aujourd'hui, La Callas."

146 Andry, 54.

147 Gavoty: 1965

148 Galatopoulos, 484.

149 Callas to Walter Legge, 18 March 1969 in Sanders, 234.

150 Callas to Nicolas Nabokov, 18 March 1969 [Nicolas Nabokov Papers, MS-02981. The Harry Ransom Center, University of Austin, Texas].

151 Callas to Giacomo Lauri Volpi, 24 March 1969 in Volf, "1969."

152 "Callas Will Sing in Dallas," *The Washington Post*, 26 March 1969.

153 Schaeffer, "Aujourd'hui, La Callas."

154 John Ardoin, "Maria Callas Not to Appear In Opera Here," *The Dallas Morning News*, 29 April 1969.

155 Callas to Elvira de Hidalgo, 26 March 1969 [CBA]; Tosi, *Giovane Callas*, 148.

156 Desgraupes: 1969

157 Callas to Elvira de Hidalgo, 26 April 1969 in Bolaffi Auctions, *Libri rari e autografi* (Milan: Bolaffi Auctions, 14 May 2014).

158 Hella Pick, "Something for everyone: even the Gaekwar," *The Guardian*, 2 May 1969.

159 Legge to Callas, 29 May 1969 in Sanders, 235.

160 Contract between Maria Callas, represented by Avv. Ercole Graziadei and Compagnia Finanziaria San Marco S.A: First version, 15 March 1969; Second version, 10 April 1969 [SGC].
161 Romi, "Ce Que La Callas N'Avait Encore Jamais Raconté."
162 Harris: 1970
163 Gambetti, "Sono per una Medea non aggressiva," 470.
164 Jacobson, "Callas, The Tiger Tamed?"
165 Nico Naldini, *Pasolini, una vita* (Verona: Tamellini, 2014), 409.
166 Callas' interview for *Monitor*, BBC Television, 28 May 1969.
167 Boutwell, "Processo alla Callas."
168 Gorlinsky to Callas, 16 May 1969 [SGC].
169 Sylvie de Nussac, "Médée se transforme . . . en agneau," *L'Express*, 28 July 1969.
170 Stancioff, 15–22.
171 Roland Lommé, Interview with Callas for *Première Magazine* on Belgium channel BRT, 22 February 1970.
172 de Nussac & Cotta: 1970
173 Callas' interview with Roland Lommé.
174 Jacobson, "Callas, The Tiger Tamed?"
175 Giuseppe Gentile, *La medaglia (con)divisa. Il triplo. Pasolini e Maria Callas* (Arezzo: fuori|onda, 2012), 106–8.
176 Michael Guillen, "Pasolini and Davoli: A Resonant Friendship," *Fandor*, 21 October 2013. Originally published at https://www.fandor.com/keyframe/pasolini-and-davoli-a-resonant-friendship; reprinted at https://theeveningclass.blogspot.com/2022/11/throwback-thursdaya-resonant-friendship.html.
177 Stancioff, 179.
178 Buckley, "An Ancient Woman."
179 Gorlinsky to Callas, 4 June 1969 [SGC].
180 Stancioff, 28.
181 ibid. 32
182 Sander Vanocur, NBC News interview with Callas and Pasolini for *First Tuesday* at Cinecittà Studios, Rome, NBC, 5 August 1969.
183 Stancioff, 33.
184 Ardoin & Fitzgerald, 258.
185 Gentile, 108–9.
186 AP, "Maria Callas' Introduction To Film-Making Not Ideal," *Press and Sun Bulletin*, Binghamton, 25 June 1969.
187 Buckley, "An Ancient Woman."
188 Andrea Razza & Gerardo Di Cola, Interview with Rita Savagnone on 14 January 2012 for www.enciclopediadeldoppiaggio.it. Accessed at: https://www.youtube.com/watch?v=n7PqCU_8Pew, 26.06-30.52.
189 "Quando la Callas non cantava," *Il Piccolo*, 5 June 2006.
190 de Nussac, "Médée se transforme . . . en agneau."
191 Ardoin & Fitzgerald, 258.
192 Stancioff, xiv.
193 Giorgio Alzanese in Tosi, *Giovane Callas*, 199.
194 "Mme Callas Tells of 'My Father,' " *The Times*, 20 April 1967.

195 Gentile, 109.

196 Guillen, "Pasolini and Davoli: A Resonant Friendship."

197 Interview with Giuseppe Zigaina in Renzo & Roberto Allegri, 150.

198 Paolo Mauri, "L'amore impossibile Callas-Pasolini," *La Repubblica*, 27 May 2012.

199 Callas to Pasolini, 5 September 1971 in Tosi, *Casta diva: L'incomparabile Callas*, 63–65.

200 Gruen: 1971

201 Callas to J. Warren Perry c. 1958, in J. Warren Perry, Correspondence and Autograph Collection, Mus. Arc. 3.3, University of New York at Buffalo Music Library.

202 Galatopoulos, 252.

203 Vanocur, NBC News interview with Callas and Pasolini for *First Tuesday*.

204 Roberto Calabretto, "Avanza un corteo, è la Callas!" in Roberto Calabretto, *Pasolini e la musica* (Pordenone: Cinemazero, 1999), 441.

205 Jacobson, "Callas, The Tiger Tamed?"

206 Lorcey, 639.

207 Vanocur, NBC News interview with Callas and Pasolini for *First Tuesday*.

208 John Ardoin, "Visit with Maria Callas," *The Dallas Morning News*, 19 July 1970.

209 de Nussac & Cotta: 1970

210 Vanocur, NBC News interview with Callas and Pasolini for *First Tuesday*.

211 Henri Chapier, "Maria Callas, De La Diva à la Déesse," *Combat*, 16 February 1970.

212 de Nussac & Cotta: 1970

213 Signorini, "Ecco le lettere, i documenti e le foto che conservo della mia amica Callas."

214 Author's interview with Thérèse Darras.

215 Luciana Jorio, "La Callas 'Medea' non più tigre," *Corriere della Sera*, 1–2 August 1969.

216 Renzo & Roberto Allegri, 151.

18. "Espèce de vapeur"

1 "Lui Parla d'Amor e Lei Tace," *Grazia*, 17 August 1969, 29.

2 Charlotte Curtis, "Décor For A Gala Rivals Guests' Diamonds," *The New York Times*, 11 August 1969.

3 William Hickey, "Callas Makes It Up with Monte Carlo," *Daily Express*, 5 September 1969.

4 "Grace ha inaugurato il festival di Mentone," *La Stampa*, 12 August 1969; Janis, 127.

5 "La Callas trema a Venezia," *La Stampa*, 3–4 September 1969.

6 "From Our Correspondent: Pasolini Reports: 'The World Is a Pigsty,'" *De Tijd*, 5 September 1969.

7 Barth David Schwartz, *Pasolini Requiem* (New York: Pantheon, 1992), 503.

8 Aileen Mehle, "Suzy Says Maria and Pier Are in Love," *The Hartford Courant*, 26 September 1969; "Pasolini refuse d'assister à la projection de son film à Venise," *Paris-Presse L'Intransigeant*, 30 August 1969.

9 Henk van der Meijden, "The Guests at Haarzuilens," *De Telegraaf*, 17 September 1969.

10 "Callas in a Jury," *De Tijd*, 16 September 1969.

11 Photograph of Callas attending the premiere of *The Battle of Britain* on 19 September 1969 by Jean-Claude Deutsch. Getty image accessed at https://www.gettyimages.co.uk/

detail/news-photo/first-of-the-film-the-battle-of-britain-by-guy-hamilton-news-photo/160704226.

12 Gorlinsky to Callas, 23 September 1969 [SGC].

13 "Birthday Party Goes Ancient," *Chicago Tribune*, 3 October 1969.

14 Gorlinsky to Callas, 22 October 1969 [SGC].

15 Stancioff, 193.

16 Enrico Giuffreddi, "Metti Quattro Sere a Cena Onassis e Maria Callas," *Oggi*, 7 January 1970.

17 Galatopoulos, 413–14.

18 Cuccio, "Callas on Callas."

19 Judy Klemesrud, "Maria Callas speaks her mind on fashions and friendship," *The New York Times*, 30 November 1970.

20 Giuffreddi, "Metti Quattro Sere a Cena Onassis e Maria Callas."

21 Stancioff, 198.

22 "La Callas: 'Ti perdono Aristotile,' " *La Stampa*, 29 October 1969.

23 Giuffreddi, "Metti Quattro Sere a Cena Onassis e Maria Callas."

24 Gorlinsky to Callas, 19 November 1969 [SGC].

25 Stancioff, 87.

26 Signorini, "Ecco le lettere, i documenti e le foto che conservo della mia amica Callas."

27 Gambetti, "Sono per una Medea non aggressiva," 465.

28 de Nussac & Cotta: 1970

29 Aileen Mehle, "Suzy Says 'Maria's Been Silenced,' " *The Hartford Courant*, 6 January 1970.

30 Frost: 1970

31 Dmitry Gordon, "It's all gone with the diamonds . . .," *Bulvar Gazeta*, 23 January 2015.

32 Edgar Schneider, "Pas de 'pop' à l'Opéra," *Paris-Presse L'Intransigeant*, 10 January 1970.

33 Candida Morvillo, "Pier Paolo Pasolini e Maria Callas, storia di un amore impossibile," *iodonna.it*, 29 October 2015, www.iodonna.it/personaggi/interviste-gallery/10/29/lamore-impossibile-fra-pasolini-e-la-callas.

34 AFP, "La Callas à Dakar," *Paris-Presse, L'Intransigeant*, 13 January 1970.

35 "Maria Callas in Mali," *Makedonia*, 20 January 1970.

36 "Maria Callas: En Afrique avec Pasolini," *Paris-Presse L'Intransigeant*, 20 January 1970.

37 Dacia Maraini, *La grande festa* (Milan: Rizzoli, 2011), 15–16.

38 Dacia Maraini, *Caro Pier Paolo* (Milan: Neri Pozza, 2022), 157.

39 Annalisa Serpilli, "Dacia Maraini: 'Maria Callas, una diva che rimasta bambina,' " *Il Sole 24 Ore*, 11 September 2007, https://www.ilsole24ore.com/art/SoleOnLine4/Tempo%20libero%20e%20Cultura/2007/09/callas-intervista-maraini.shtml?uuid=7f93da20-603b-11dc-8742-00000e251029&DocRulesView=Libero.

40 Interviews with Dacia Maraini and Alberto Moravia in Tosi, *Casta diva: L' Incomparabile Callas*, 41–43.

41 Callas to Pier Paolo Pasolini, 1 February 1971 [PPP].

42 Callas to Pasolini, 13 July 1971 [PPP].

43 Frost: 1970

44 Romi, "Ce Que La Callas N'Avait Encore Jamais Raconté."

45 Maraini, *E tu chi eri? 26 interviste sull'infanzia*, 310–11.

46 "Onassis Escorts Maria Callas To Supper Party."

47 Klemesrud, "Maria Callas speaks her mind on fashions and friendship."

48 Barbara Walters, Interview with Callas for *Today*, NBC, 15 April 1974.

49 Robert Sutherland, 207.

50 Leo Lerman's journal entry of 30 August 1971 in Lerman, 353

51 Soria, "Maria Paris April Wed 29 69" [DSP].

52 Gruen: 1971

53 Yorgos Pilchos, "A tree: my only companion," *Ta Nea*, 29 March 1969.

54 "Mme Pompidou et la Callas au gala de Médée," *Le Parisien Libéré*, 30 January 1970.

55 Ivy Fernandes, "Maria Callas no Rio," *Manchete*, Issue 937, 4 April 1970.

56 "Maria Callas and Onassis dine at the Baroness Van Zuylen's," *De Telegraaf*, 3 February 1970.

57 International Herald Tribune, "Onassis Escorts Maria Callas To Supper Party."

58 Gruen: 1971

59 Jean Gênet, "Paris," *The New Yorker*, 21 February 1970.

60 Kevin Kelly, "Maria Callas a hypnotic 'Medea,' " *Boston Globe*, 20 March 1972.

61 Richard Roud, "The Callas sound of silence," *The Guardian*, 28 January 1970.

62 Filippo Sacchi, "Solo Maria Callas poteva essere una furente Medea," *Epoca*, 1 February 1970.

63 Henri Chapier quoted in Luis Angel Torres, "Mar Del Plata Press Conference on *Medea*," *Obertura* magazine, April 1970.

64 Schwartz, 561.

65 Guy Flatley, "Yes, He Threw No Tantrum," *The New York Times*, 27 June 1971.

66 Edgar Schneider, "Quand Callas Médée apprivoise les étudiants," *Paris-Presse L'Intransigeant*, 1 February 1970.

67 Ardoin, "Visit with Maria Callas."

68 Stancioff, 11.

69 Aileen Mehle, "Suzy Says Who They Were and What They Wore," *The Hartford Courant*, 1 December 1970.

70 Aileen Mehle, "Suzy Says He'll Return To Shake Everybody Up," *The Hartford Courant*, 8 March 1971.

71 Robert Sutherland, 62.

72 Curtis, "Décor For A Gala Rivals Guests' Diamonds."

73 Callas to Bruna Lupoli, 5 September 1971 in Volf, "1971."

74 Mehle, "Suzy Says He'll Return To Shake Everybody Up."

75 Curtis, "Décor For A Gala Rivals Guests' Diamonds."

76 Barry: 1971

77 Schaeffer, "Aujourd'hui, La Callas."

78 Jean-Paul Farkas, Interview with Callas on *Le Journal Inattendu*, recorded 24 February and aired on RTL TV Belgium, 31 July 1970.

79 "Photo Today," *Limburgsch dagblad*, 17 March 1970.

80 "Callas in Brazil," *Folha de São Paulo*, 11 March 1970; "Callas and Pasolini Pass Through Rio," *Folha de São Paulo*, 14 March 1970.

81 AFP, "Callas denies marriage," *Folha de São Paulo*, 16 March 1970.

82 Torres, "Mar Del Plata Press Conference on *Medea*."

83 AP, "Maria Callas Ends Stay in Argentina," *The Niagara Falls Gazette*, 20 March 1970; Luis García, "Ele é tão lindo quanto a mãe . . . e agora o rei em Nova York," *Intervalo*, Issue No. 379, 1970.

84 "People In The News: CALLAS HEADS NORTH," *The Hartford Courant*, 21 March 1970.

85 "Pasolini na Bahia," *Folha de São Paulo*, 26 March 1970.

86 G. de H, Untitled review in *Le Journal de Genève*, 1 April 1970, 11.

87 Gorlinsky to Callas, 8 May 1970 [SGC].

88 Gorlinsky to Callas, 26 March 1970 [SGC]; Photograph of Callas for the Blackgama campaign by Richard Avedon. An advertisement with Callas in the Blackgama coat featured in the 25 October 1970 edition of *The New York Times*.

89 As referenced in *The Indianapolis Star*, 18 October 1979, 53.

90 Scott Cantrell, "Christian Steiner Returns to Piano from his Camera," *Albany Times Union*, 25 May 1986.

91 Stancioff, 235.

92 Harris: 1970.

93 de Nussac & Cotta: 1970

94 Harris: 1970

95 Callas to Walter Cummings, 21 September 1961 in Hanine-Roussel, 457.

96 "Gordon Mackie Dies," *Musical Times*, September 1970, v. 111, no. 1531, 927.

97 Andry, 57.

98 Galatopoulos, 401.

99 Bottero, 220 (Interview with Carlo Maria Giulini).

100 Klemesrud, "Maria Callas speaks her mind on fashions and friendship."

101 Stassinopoulos, 306.

102 UPI, "Callas wins case against magazine," *The Irish Times*, 10 June 1970.

103 Klemesrud, "Maria Callas speaks her mind on fashions and friendship."

104 UPI, "Callas wins case against magazine."

105 Albin Krebs, "Notes On People," *The New York Times*, 5 November 1971.

106 Harris: 1970

107 Frost: 1970

108 "Esclusivo: La Prima Uscita della Callas Dopo Il 'Suicidio,' " *Gente* magazine, 15 June 1970.

109 "People In the News," *The Hartford Courant*, 17 June 1970.

110 "Maria Callas Lived in a Dacha in Bakovka" in Felix Nikolaevich Medvedev, *Ekaterina Furtseva: The Main Woman of the USSR* (Moscow: Algorithm, 2016).

111 Visiting card from Soviet Union Culture Minister Ekaterina Furtseva [CNH].

112 1970 Tchaikovsky Competition Program [CNH].

113 Dmitry Gordon, Interview with Tamara Sinyavskaya, *gordon.com*, 25 October 2011. Accessed at http://web.archive.org/web/20130403115047/http://www.gordon.com.ua/tv/t-sinyavskaya.

114 Programme of *Raymonda* at the Bolshoi Theatre, 23 June 1970 signed by Maria [CFG].

115 "People In The News," *The Hartford Courant*, 17 June 1970.

116 Marina Aleksinskaya Besedovala, "I have always been Russian," *Zavtra*, No. 28, 14 June 2010.

117 Gordon, Interview with Tamara Sinyavskaya.

118 Ardoin, "Visit with Maria Callas."

119 Verrett, 150–52.

120 Tommasini, "Maria Callas: A Voice and a Legend That Still Fascinate."

121 Montserrat Caballé in "Callas Remembered," *Gramophone*, September 1987.

122 Callas, "The Lyric Tradition," 28 October 1971.

123 Petsalis-Diomidis, 405 (Interview with Giulietta Simionato).

124 Frost: 1970

125 Banzet: 1965

126 Frost: 1970

127 Harewood: 1968

128 Desgraupes: 1969

129 John Ardoin in Palmer, *Maria Callas: La Divina—A Portrait*.

130 Frost: 1970

131 Romi, "Ce Que La Callas N'Avait Encore Jamais Raconté."

132 Maraini, *E tu chi eri ? 26 interviste sull'infanzia*, 311.

133 Frost: 1970

134 Stassinopoulos, 307–8.

135 E-mail from Aristides Embiricos to the author, 11 June 2021.

136 Stancioff, 204.

137 Morvillo, "Pier Paolo Pasolini e Maria Callas, storia di un amore impossibile."

138 UPI, "Maria Callas and Onassis," *The Washington Post*, 26 August 1970.

139 "Personalia Overleden," *De Tijd*, 27 August 1970.

140 Photo Caption in *Leeuwarder Courant*, 28 August 1970.

141 "From Our Correspondent: Callas Treads the Boards?," *De Telegraaf*, 11 September 1970.

142 Associated Press photograph of Maria and Pier Paolo Pasolini in Capri, 27 September 1970.

143 "La Callas Indifférent," *De Telegraaf*, 30 October 1970.

144 Photograph of Callas with Pasolini on 14 October 1970 in Naples by Mario Tursi [CFG].

145 Marian Christy, "Polluted Air Chips Statues; Think What It Does to Skin," *Santa Maria Times* of Santa Maria, California, 9 November 1970.

146 "Trudeau-Streisand Tryst Suspected," *The Hartford Courant*, 27 November 1970.

147 N.B. A list of reserved seating for Callas' Juilliard classes, 3 February 1971 lists Teresa d'Addato as her secretary, though the latter lived by now in Milan. [JSA].

148 Callas to Matilde Stagnoli, 14 November 1970 [CFM].

149 "Verdi et Des Bonnes Œuvres Pour Le Retour de la Callas," *Le Figaro*, 25 November 1970.

150 Gorlinsky to Callas, 21 December 1970 [SGC].

151 "Verdi et Des Bonnes Œuvres Pour Le Retour de la Callas."

152 John Ardoin, "Callas Will Conduct Master Class Series," *The Dallas Morning News*, 1 December 1970.

153 Giuliano Ranieri, "Maria Callas è sempre la primadonna," *Epoca*, 20 December 1970.

154 "Renata Scotto on slapping a tenor, the divine Callas, and ... Bocelli," *Gramilano*, 22 November 2015 https://www.gramilano.com/2015/11/renata-scotto-slappingtenors-divine-callas-bocelli.

155 Barry: 1971

156 Handwritten note by Gorlinsky regarding Callas' planned dates for working with Richard Nunn in January 1971 [SGC].

157 Ayre, 109.

158 David Stickelberg, "Miss Callas Insists, 'I'm Dearly Loved,' " Undated newspaper clipping, c. February 1971 [JSA].

159 Undated notes by Gorlinsky c. February 1971 [SGC].

160 Georges Prêtre to Gorlinsky, 3 August 1971 [SGC].

161 Gorlinsky to Callas, 26 January 1971 [SGC].

162 Gorlinsky to Callas, 25 June 1971 [SGC].

163 Callas had previously turned down an invitation to lead masterclasses by Lady Domini Crosfield in a letter to the latter on 23 June 1961. (Chambre Cohen, 266).

164 Peter Mennin to Callas, 2 December 1970 [JSA].

165 Schwarzkopf & Legge, 202.

166 Irving Kolodin to Callas, 31 December 1970 [JSA].

167 Stickelberg, "Miss Callas Insists, 'I'm Dearly Loved.' "

168 Allen Hughes, "Callas Talks on Any Topic But When She'll Sing," *The New York Times*, 5 February 1971.

169 Leo Lerman's journal entry of 3 February 1971 in Lerman, 328.

170 Harris: 1970

171 Klemesrud, "Maria Callas speaks her mind on fashions and friendship."

172 Leo Lerman's journal entry of 29 November 1970 in Lerman, 313.

173 de Nussac & Cotta: 1970

174 Gruen: 1971

175 Barry: 1971

176 Stancioff, 131.

177 ibid. 207.

178 Leo Lerman's journal entry of 7 February 1971 in Lerman, 330.

179 Boutwell, "Processo alla Callas."

180 AP, "Maria Callas Spends Weekend in Vermont," *The Burlington Free Press*, 17 February 1971.

181 AP, "People In The News," *The Philadelphia Inquirer*, 13 February 1971.

182 "In the News: Philadelphia: Callas Cuts Short Her Opera Classes," *Opera* magazine, April 1971.

183 "Schedule for Special Auditions in the Juilliard Theater," 16 February 1971 [JSA].

184 Leo Lerman's journal entries for 18 and 19 February 1971 in Lerman, 331.

185 Harold C. Schonberg, "Opera Revival of 'Werther' At The Met," *The New York Times*, 21 September 1971.

186 Marko Lámpas, *My Life in America and What Maria Callas Taught Me* (Lulu.com, 2010), 185–86.

187 Performance Cast Listings for the Metropolitan Opera [AMO].

188 Lámpas, 189–90.

189 Callas to Pasolini, 21 July 1971 [PPP].

190 AP, "Callas' Divorce Suspended," *Folha de São Paulo*, 6 March 1971.

191 Callas to Alberta Masiello, 9 March 1971 [AMAS].

192 Callas to Leo Lerman, 9 March 1971 [LLP].

193 Callas to Irving Kolodin, 9 March 1971 [IKP].

194 Callas to Peter Mennin, 16 March 1971 [JSA].

195 Callas to Kolodin, 17 March 1971 [IKP].

196 Fournier, 55.

197 Callas to Roland Bourdin, Director of the Orchestre de Paris, 24 March 1971 [CNH].

198 Callas to Gorlinsky, 26 March 1971 [SGC].

199 Jean-Pierre Cassel, *À mes amours* (Paris: Stock, 2004), 137–38.

200 "Tavares de Miranda," *Folha de São Paulo*, 12 May 1971.

201 Cassel, 137–41.

202 Telegram from Callas to Marlon Brando, 26 March 1971 in Christie's: Lot 251 (New York: Christie's Auctions, 30 June 2005). Accessed at https://www.invaluable.com/auction-lot/telegrams-251-c-t0dei8oayr?objectID=1732991&algIndex=archive_prod&queryID=6600335c50effc6ba309af2df435b459.

203 "Impar-Tv: Sélection de samedi," *L'Impartial*, 11 December 1971, 23.

204 "Une corrida imprévue pour Maria Callas!," *Le Parisien Libéré*, 26 April 1971.

205 Callas to Peter Mennin, 17 April 1971 [JSA].

206 Mennin to Geraldine Shephard, 15 April 1971 [JSA].

207 Lámpas, 190–91.

208 Leo Lerman's journal entry of 7 May 1971 in Lerman, 340.

209 ibid. 343.

210 Luba Tcheresky to Callas, 24 May 1971 [JSA]. Excerpted here with kind permission from Tcheresky's daughter, Freya Pruitt.

211 Memorandum of the Juilliard School, 10 May 1971 [JSA].

212 Template letter from Callas to auditionees who were rejected, 28 May 1971 [JSA].

213 Lámpas, 192–97.

214 Barry: 1971

215 Barbara Hendricks, *Ma voie: Mémoires* (Paris: Éditions Les Arènes, 2010), 164–65.

216 "Personalities," *The Washington Post*, 17 June 1971.

217 Callas to Monika Wiards, 17 June 1971 [CFM].

218 Callas to Pier Paolo Pasolini, 13 July 1971 [PPP].

219 Callas to Antonio Caraza Campos, 7 August 1971 in Aaron Polo López, Karla Zárate, Martha Miranda & Aurelio de Los Reyes, *Maria Callas: Una Mujer, Una Voz, Un Mito* (Mexico: Instituto Nacional de Bellas Artes, 2000), 28 (originally from the Archivo Ingeniero Guillermo Corvera Caraza).

220 Telegram from Wriston Locklair, Assistant to Peter Mennin, to Callas, 20 August 1971 [JSA].

221 Luba Tcheresky to Callas, 22 August 1971 [JSA].

222 Walter Legge to Callas, 30 August 1971 [JSA].

223 Harris: 1970

19. "Inside is your mirror"

1 Schwarzkopf & Legge, 83.

2 Leo Lerman's journal entry of 30 August 1971 in Lerman, 352.

3 Irving Kolodin to Callas, 31 Dec 1970 [JSA].

4 Jackson, 449.

5 Callas to Teresa d'Addato, 5 September 1971 in Volf, "1971."

6 Robert Ross, "The Ross Report: On Being Thankful for Celebrated Friends and Allies," https://web.archive.org/web/20070214045442/http://www.mda.org;ross/index991220. html.

7 Patsy Swank, Interview with John Ardoin, *Swank in the Arts*, KERA TV Dallas, 11 November 1978.

8 Robert Sutherland, 6.

9 Author's interview with Georganne Mennin, New York, 25 March 2013.

10 "Met Opera Opens 87th Season," *The New York Times*, 21 September 1971.

11 Author's telephone interview with Joan Lasker Sobel, 7 September 2015.

12 Earl Wilson, "Welk, ABC Still 'Furry' Friendly," *The Hartford Courant*, 13 October 1971.

13 Author's telephone interview with Joan Lasker Sobel.

14 Gerald Walker, " 'You're Singing Too Much'—'The More I Sing, The Better I Sound,' " *The New York Times*, 27 February 1972.

15 Callas to Lawrence Kelly, 4 October 1971 [JSA].

16 Bona Alterocca, "Callas, primo incontro," *La Stampa*, 28 September 1972.

17 "Audition Schedule for October 6, 1971 in the Juilliard Theater," [JSA].

18 Luba Tcheresky to Lorna Levant, 23 February 1972.

19 Barry: 1971

20 Undated memorandum of the Juilliard School, October 1971 [JSA].

21 Memorandum of the Juilliard School, 19 January 1972 [JSA].

22 Lámpas, 201.

23 Callas, "The Lyric Tradition," 11 October 1971.

24 Rizzo, "The Callas Class."

25 Gruen: 1971

26 Photograph of Callas sitting with Eugene Kohn during a masterclass in 1972 by Beth Bergman featured on the back cover of John Ardoin, *Callas at Juilliard: The Master Classes* (Pompton Plains, N.J.: Amadeus Press, 2001).

27 Jack Hiemenz, "Classics With Callas," *The Washington Post*, 28 November 1971.

28 Richard Roud, "Features: Richard Roud Reports on Maria Callas' Master Classes," *The Guardian*, 8 April 1972.

29 Wriston Locklair to Barbara Hendricks et al., 11 June 1971 [JSA].

30 Callas, "The Lyric Tradition," 11 October 1971.

31 Author's telephone interview with Marko Lámpas, 6 January 2012.

32 Lámpas, 200–2.

33 Callas, "The Lyric Tradition," 18 October 1971.

34 Legge to Louis Fritze c.o. Dario Soria, 14 March 1957 [DSP].

35 Callas, "The Lyric Tradition," 18 October 1971.

36 ibid. 19 November 1971.

37 ibid. 4 November 1971.

38 Wriston Locklair to Callas, 6 December 1971 [JSA].

39 ibid. Lorna Levant to Kyu Do Park, Chung-Ha Park, Zenaida Luz, Pamela Hebert and Mayda Prado-Testa, 7 February 1972.

40 ibid. Memorandum by Wriston Locklair: "Reserved Seating for the Callas Classes," 3 February 1971.

41 Callas, "The Lyric Tradition," 25 October 1971.

42 Hubert Saal, "New House, New Callas," *Newsweek*, 23 April 1973.

43 Callas, "The Lyric Tradition," 10 February 1972.

44 ibid. 28 October 1971.

45 ibid. 14 February 1972.

46 ibid. 9 March 1972.

47 ibid. 8 November 1971.

48 ibid. 28 February 1972.

49 ibid. 28 October 1971.

50 ibid. 28 February 1972.

51 ibid. 13 Mar 1972.

52 Hiemenz, "Classics With Callas."

53 Callas, "The Lyric Tradition," 4 November 1971.

54 Leo Lerman's journal entry of 12 October 1971 in Lerman, 354.

55 Author's interview with Georganne Mennin.

56 Caloni: 1976

57 Tony Villecco, "Walking Out on La Divina," *Classical Singer*, April 2012.

58 Sheila Nadler in "Tyne Daly on the legend of Maria Callas," *The Times*, 6 February 2012.

59 Klemesrud, "Maria Callas speaks her mind on fashions and friendship."

60 Cuccio, "Callas on Callas."

61 Callas, "The Lyric Tradition," 11 November 1971.

62 ibid. 19 November 1971.

63 ibid. 14 February 1972.

64 Eugene Kohn to Wriston Locklair, 17 May 1971 [JSA]. Quoted with kind permission from Kohn.

65 Kathryn Shattuck, "A Profile—Eugene Kohn, Maestro in Residence," *The Palisades Newsletter*, March 2012, issue 216.

66 Author's interview with Eugene Kohn, New York, 24 March 2013.

67 Undated letter from Eugene Kohn to Callas (c. April 1972) [JSA].

68 Memorandum from Eugene Kohn to all of Callas' students, 1 December 1971 [JSA].

69 Prouse, "Maria Callas Speaks," 19 March 1961.

70 Callas, "The Lyric Tradition," 9 March 1972.

71 ibid. 28 February 1972.

72 ibid. 13 March 1972.

73 ibid. 28 October 1971.

74 ibid. 14 October 1971.

75 Memorandum from The American Opera Center to Peter Mennin: "Length of membership information," 25 April 1971 [JSA].

76 Lynn B. Villela, "S.F. Opera: The Place to Watch for Barrie opening night," *Albuquerque Tribune*, July 1971 [Precise date obscured in clipping at JSA].

77 "Clifford Smith Obituary," *The Greenville* News, 8 June 2014, https://www.legacy.com/us/obituaries/greenvilleonline/name/clifford-smith-obituary?id=19367573.

78 Callas, "The Lyric Tradition," 8 November 1971.

79 ibid. 15 November 1971.

80 Christmas Card from Barrie Smith to Callas, 1971 [JSA].

81 Author's e-mail correspondence with Barrie Smith, 18 March 2012.

82 James A. Drake & Rosa Ponselle, *Ponselle: A Singer's Life*, 207.

83 Sheila Nadler's career is described at https://operawire.com/obituary-mezzo-sopranosheila-nadler-dies-at-82.

84 Sheila Nadler in "Tyne Daly on the legend of Maria Callas."

85 Sheila Nadler to Callas, 10 January 1972 [JSA].

86 Author's interview with Marko Lámpas.

87 Jorden, Interview with John Ardoin.

88 Leo Lerman's journal entry of 5 February 1972 in Lerman, 361.

89 Callas to Lawrence Kelly, 4 October 1971 [JSA].

90 Gobbi, 98.

91 Author's interview with Eugene Kohn.

92 Author's interview with Georganne Mennin.

93 Unsigned article, "The Reality of Maria."

94 Author's interview with Eugene Kohn.

95 John Gruen, *Callas Kissed Me . . . Lenny Too!: A Memoir* (Brooklyn, NY: powerHouse, 2008), 291.

96 Photograph of Callas kissing Pasolini during the shooting of *Medea* accessed at https://www.cittapasolini.com/post/pier-paolo-pasolini-e-maria-callas-lettere.

97 Lámpas, 207.

98 Unsigned interview, "Chez la Callas, la musique reste la vraie maîtresse de maison."

99 Author's interview with Georganne Mennin.

100 Ardoin, *The Callas Legacy*, 200.

101 Irving Kolodin, "What Makes Maria Sing?," *Saturday Review*, 9 February 1974.

102 Author's interview with Georganne Mennin.

103 Author's e-mail correspondence with Elayne Reynolds Duke.

104 Audrey Inman to Callas, 6 October 1971 [JSA].

105 Gorlinsky to Callas, 6 September 1971 [SGC].

106 Sievewright, "Callas Remembered: Conversation with Maria Callas, July 1977."

107 Joseph Wishy to Gorlinsky, 9 March 1972 [SGC].

108 F.L. Ammannati to Callas, 6 Dec 1971 and Callas' response, 7 January 1972 [JSA].

109 Hiemenz, "Classics With Callas."

110 Callas to Tim Lewis of *New York Magazine*, 26 November 1971 [JSA].

111 Leo Lerman's journal entry of 28 December 1971 in Lerman, 358.

112 Galatopoulos, 417.

113 Aileen Mehle, "Suzy Says, Dinner for a Diva," *The Dallas Morning News*, 5 February 1972.

114 Callas, "The Lyric Tradition," 14 October 1971.

115 Wriston Locklair to Lynne Silverman, 3 February 1972 [JSA].

116 Wriston Locklair to Luba Tcheresky, 8 May 1972 [JSA].

117 Lorna Levant to Maria Cessena-Yagzogiou, 5 January 1972 [JSA].

118 Downes: 1967

119 Callas, "The Lyric Tradition," 24 February 1972.

120 "Schedule for Miss Callas, Friday, January 21, in the Juilliard Theater" [JSA].

121 Joseph McLellan, "Offstage with the Opera Star," *The Washington Post*, 30 January 1992.

122 *Desert Island Discs.* Guest Willard White, BBC Radio 4, 12 November 1999, https://www.bbc.co.uk/programmes/p00941vr.

123 Callas, "The Lyric Tradition," 14 October 1971.

124 ibid. 17 February 1972.

125 ibid. 21 February 1972.

126 Jack Hiemenz, "Callas Banks Her Fires Coaching Young Singers," *The Washington Post*, 12 December 1971.

127 Callas, "The Lyric Tradition," 11 November 1971.

128 Mario Fusco, 1971 Handwritten Personal Résumé [JSA].

129 Callas, "The Lyric Tradition," 9 March 1972.

130 ibid. 28 October 1971.

131 Lorna Levant to Lawrence Kelly, 29 February 1972 [JSA].

132 Comments by YouTube user @TheMako990 Mako, nephew of Mario Fusco, on: "Mario Fusco, Core 'ngrato.'" Accessed at: https://www.youtube.com/wath?v=PA3k5iYb0PM&ab_channel=SuperFirewire1.

133 Villecco, "Walking Out on La Divina."

134 Wriston Locklair to Cynthia Clarey, 3 February 1972 [JSA].

135 Villecco, "Walking Out on La Divina."

136 Leo Lerman's journal entry of 5 February 1972 in Lerman, 361; Robert Sutherland, 103.

137 Marta Robles, "Montserrat Caballé, 'Por fortuna he cantado cuando no iban a la ópera a verte la figura,'" Marta Robles' Blog, 10 June 2012. Accessed at https://martaroblesdotorg.wordpress.com/2012/06/10/montserrat-caballe.

138 John von Rhein, "Conlon to handle Ravinia with Care," *Chicago Tribune*, 22 June 2005.

139 Author's interview with Georganne Mennin.

140 Barbara Hendricks, *Lifting My Voice: A Memoir* (Chicago: Chicago Review Press, 2014), 134.

141 Harold C. Schonberg, "Music, Young 'Bohème,'" *The New York Times*, 12 February 1972.

142 Author's interview with Georganne Mennin.

143 Schonberg, "Music, Young 'Bohème.'"

144 Hendricks, *Lifting My Voice*, 136.

145 Stassinopoulos, 316.

146 Scott, 245 (Interview with Giuseppe Di Stefano).

147 Robert Sutherland, 45.

148 Scott, 245 (Interview with Di Stefano).

149 Giuseppe Di Stefano in Allegri, *Lettere d'amore*, 23.

150 Earl Wilson, "It Happened Last Night," *The Dallas Morning News*, 7 March 1972.

151 Author's telephone interview with Marko Lámpas.

152 Peter Andry to Callas, 3 November 1971 [JSA].

153 Raymond Ericson, "Callas Revisited—Exquisite As Ever," *The New York Times*, 12 March 1972.

154 Barbara Hendricks, "Un art intransmissable," *L'Avant-Scène Opéra*, October 1982. Quoted with kind permission from Hendricks.

155 Callas, "The Lyric Tradition," 19 November 1971.

156 Lámpas, 203–7.

157 Author's telephone interview with Marko Lámpas.

158 Lámpas, 200.
159 Author's telephone interview with Marko Lámpas.
160 Christmas Card from Anita Terzian to Callas, 1971 [JSA].
161 James Jorden's interview with Marilyn Horne and James Levine on *Operavore*, WQXR Radio New York, 26 January 2013.
162 Caloni: 1976
163 Author's interview with Georganne Mennin.
164 Hendricks, *Ma voie*, 170–71.
165 Lerman, 361–2.
166 Villecco, "Walking Out on La Divina."
167 Marian Seldes to Callas, 20 November 1971 [JSA]. Quoted with kind permission from her daughter Katharine Andres.
168 Leo Lerman's journal entry of 17 March 1972 in Lerman, 363.
169 Callas, "The Lyric Tradition," 16 March 1972.
170 "Maria Callas Cocktail Reception," 3 March 1972 [JSA].
171 Wriston Locklair to Callas, 29 March 1972 [JSA].
172 Kolodin, "What Makes Maria Sing?"
173 Sievewright, "Callas Remembered: Conversation with Maria Callas, July 1977."
174 Michael Anthony, "A Chat with Jeffrey Tate," *The American Record Guide*, Nov–Dec 1997, 14.
175 Callas, "The Lyric Tradition," 18 October 1971.

20. "Calculate in the dark"

1 Saal, "New House, New Callas."
2 Maria Di Stefano & Francamaria Trapani, *Callas: Nemica mia* (Milan: Sonzogno Editore, 1992), 114.
3 Robert Sutherland, 4.
4 Galatopoulos, 186–87.
5 Tooley, 103.
6 Jonathan Kandell, "Stages of Di Stefano," *Opera News*, 1 January 2000.
7 Jenny Johnston, "Unlikely fan: Why opera's biggest star Plácido Domingo is crazy for Lady Gaga," *Daily Mail*, 3 May 2012.
8 Di Stefano & Trapani, 114.
9 Peter Mennin to Callas, 26 April 1972 [JSA].
10 Callas to Alberta Masiello, 9 July 1972 [AMAS].
11 Henryk Jablonski, "BERUFLICHES," *Der Spiegel*, 3 April 1972; Jack O'Brian, "Voice of Broadway," *The Leader Herald*, Johnstown, NY, 25 May 1972; Di Stefano & Trapani, 117.
12 Coverage of Théâtre Gabriel Château de Versailles' June 6 production of *La Cenerentola* is featured in *Opera*, Autumn 1972 Festival Issue.
13 Di Stefano & Trapani, 118.
14 Callas to Kolodin, 21 July 1972 [IKP].
15 Callas to Masiello, 9 July 1972 [AMAS].

16 "Callas' last blood tests, taken exactly four months before her death, as well as the EKGs she had done at the Istituto Nazionale per lo Studio e la Cura dei Tumori in Milan in the summer of 1972." [CNH].

17 "La Callas non ha cantato," *Corriere della Sera*, 25 July 1973.

18 Callas to Nadia Stancioff, 21 July 1972 in the cover of Stancioff, *Maria: Callas Remembered* (New York: Dutton, 1987, 1st ed.).

19 Guido Gerosa, "La regina omerica di Torino," *Epoca*, 8 April 1973.

20 Moore, 286.

21 de Nussac & Cotta: 1970

22 Gorlinsky's handwritten notes on Callas' itinerary written on 24 August 1972 [SGC].

23 Carlamaria Casanova, "Povera Callas, l'amico Di Stefano ci rivela i suoi ultimi penosi segreti," *Gente*, 22 April 1978.

24 Robert Sutherland, 20.

25 ibid. 199.

26 ibid. 22.

27 Stancioff, 225.

28 Allegri, *La véritable histoire de Maria Callas*, 364.

29 Robert Sutherland, 110.

30 "Opera star falls for Di Stefano," *The Dallas Morning News*, 27 August 1972.

31 Giuseppe Di Stefano, "Glielo dissi cantando 'Maria, ti amo,' " *La Domenica del Corriere*, 26 February 1987.

32 Interview with Giuseppe Di Stefano in Renzo & Roberto Allegri, 156.

33 Rainero Schembri, "Giuseppe Di Stefano Nei Ricordi della Figlia Floria," *Euronews*, 27 July 2012. Accessed at: https://www.facebook.com/397388985852/posts/giuseppe-di-stefano-nei-ricordi-della-figlia-floriaposted-by-rainero-schembri-on/10154053477890853.

34 Piero Robba, "Maria Callas a Torino e al Regio: Una voce dal futuro," in "Maria Callas a trent'anni dalla scomparsa (1977–2007), Convegno di studi a cura di Elio Battaglia," *MiTo-Settembre Musica*, 2007.

35 Bona Alterocca, "La Callas Regista Al Regio," *La Stampa*, 12 September 1972.

36 Bona Alterocca, "Callas, primo incontro," *La Stampa*, 28 September 1972.

37 Stefano Reggiani, "Parla la Soprano da Parigi, Un mito caparbio ritorna alla lirica," *La Stampa*, 12 September 1972.

38 Alterocca, "Callas, primo incontro."

39 Bona Alterocca, "Gavazzeni Rinuncia Ai Vespri," *La Stampa*, 13 September 1972.

40 Allegri, *Lettere d'amore*, 24–25.

41 Di Stefano & Trapani, 127–28.

42 Bona Alterocca, "La Callas già al lavoro (entro il mese a Torino), A Parigi la cantante prepara un disco," *La Stampa*, 14 September 1972.

43 Sandro Casazza, "La Callas scopre il Regio," *La Stampa*, 29 September 1972.

44 Alterocca, "Callas, primo incontro."

45 Gorlinsky to Callas, 21 September 1972 [SGC].

46 Gorlinsky to Callas, 11 October 1972 [SGC].

47 Author's interview with Eugene Kohn.

48 Di Stefano & Trapani, 128.

49 Handwritten note by Gorlinsky of Callas' address: "55 East End Avenue near 82nd Street, C/O Lantzounis . . . till 25 Oct." [SGC].

50 Gorlinsky to Callas, 25 October 1972 [SGC].

51 Di Stefano & Trapani, 128; Handwritten notes by Gorlinsky concerning Callas' requirements: "pianist for 8th-25th November; second half of November–Madrid." [SGC].

52 Hamilton, *Maria Callas: Performance Annals and Discography*.

53 Henk van der Meijden, "Privé," *De Telegraaf*, 30 November 1972.

54 Stancioff, 219.

55 Roland Mancini in *Opéra International*, numéro spécial 1977, 666.

56 Jackie Callas, 215.

57 Galatopoulos, 373.

58 Jackie Callas, 216

59 Callas to Leonidas Lantzounis, 13 January 1973 in Sale 2155, Lot 188 at Swann Galleries Auctions (New York: Swann Galleries Auctions, Catalogue of 25 September 2008).

60 Donal Henahan, "Chapin Due for Top Met Post Today," *The New York Times*, 8 May 1973.

61 Schuyler Chapin, *Musical Chairs* (iUniverse Edition, 2000), 319.

62 Di Stefano & Trapani, 131.

63 Chapin, 319-20.

64 Di Stefano & Trapani, 131.

65 Chapin, 320-21.

66 Moore, 286.

67 Henahan, "Chapin Due for Top Met Post Today."

68 "I do not need a man," *To Vima*, 13 January 1973.

69 Callas to Leo Lerman, 14 January 1973 [LLP].

70 Callas to Leonidas Lantzounis, 13 January 1973 [RBC].

71 Author's interview with Bettina Brentano, Paris, 28 March 2013; Brentano, "Grandir avec Callas."

72 Callas to Leo Lerman, 14 January 1973 [LLP].

73 Di Stefano & Trapani, 131.

74 Galatopoulos, 417.

75 Di Stefano & Trapani, 132.

76 Robba, "Maria Callas a Torino e al Regio: Una voce dal futuro,"; Aileen Mehle, "Suzy Says, Lady Lindsay goes to London,"; *The Dallas Morning News*, 19 February 1973; Bona Alterocca, "La Callas ha iniziato il lavoro di regia," *La Stampa*, 17 March 1973.

77 Postcard sent from Callas to Vasso Devetzi from Acapulco stamped February 1973 (the precise date is unclear) [CNH].

78 Author's interview with Mary Annexy.

79 Di Stefano & Trapani, 132.

80 María Eugenia Sevilla, "Maria Callas y el frío recibimiento que México le dio," *El Financiero*, 15 September 2017, https://www.elfinanciero.com.mx/after-office/mariacallas.

81 Postcard from Callas to Elena Pozzan stamped February 1973 (the precise date is unclear) [CFG]; Postcard from Callas to Leo Lerman [LLP].

82 López, Zárate, Miranda & de Los Reyes, 79; Di Stefano & Trapani, 133.

83 Vittorio Notarnicola, "Tutto Milano per Luchino," *Corriere della Sera*, 7 March 1973.

84 Hanine-Roussel, 262 (Interview with Luisa Mandelli).

85 Zeffirelli, 269.

86 Di Stefano & Trapani, 133.

87 Gerosa, "La regina omerica di Torino."

88 The remembrances of Piero Robba e-mailed to the author by his colleague Francesca Sgroi on 11 December 2012; "Callas, una storia torinese," *La Repubblica*, 15 September 2007.

89 Robba, "Maria Callas a Torino e al Regio: Una voce dal futuro."

90 Gerosa, "La regina omerica di Torino."

91 Saal, "New House, New Callas."

92 Author's interview with Fabrizio Melano.

93 Brunella Torresin Modena, "Quella voce faceva innamorare la Kabaiwanska e gli anni col maestro," *La Repubblica*, 4 March 2008.

94 Saal, "New House, New Callas."

95 Guido Vergani & Umberto Tirelli, "Questa è la vera Callas," *La Repubblica*, 23 April 1992.

96 Stancioff, 225.

97 Borja Mariño, "No sé si he cantado bien o mal pero lo he hecho siempre con alegría," codalrio.com, 1 January 2017, https://www.codalario.com/raina-kabaivanska/entrevistas/raina-kabaivanska--soprano-no-se-si-he-cantado-bien-o-mal-pero-lo-he-hecho-siempre-con-alegria_4913_4_14475_0_33_in.html.

98 Interviews with Kabaivanska quoted from unnamed Bulgarian newspapers at a fan site. Accessed at http://rainafan.314c.com/en/interview.html.

99 "From Our Special Correspondent: Mme. Callas on Opera."

100 Robba, "Maria Callas a Torino e al Regio: Una voce dal futuro."

101 Natalia Makarova, *A Dance Autobiography* (New York: Knopf, 1979), 120–21.

102 Renzo Allegri, "E stata una congiura," *Gente*, no. 17, 1973.

103 Burt Quint, Interview with Callas, CBS News, 31 March 1973.

104 Allegri, *Lettere d'amore*, 25.

105 Saal, "New House, New Callas."

106 The remembrances of Piero Robba e-mailed to the author by his colleague Francesca Sgroi.

107 Mario Rinaldi, "Il 'Viola' Porta Sfortuna," *La Fiera Letteraria*, 22 April 1973.

108 Brendan Fitzgerald, "An Opera in Turin Staged By Callas," *The New York Times*, 13 April 1973.

109 Saal, "New House, New Callas."

110 Fitzgerald, "An Opera in Turin Staged By Callas."

111 Alfredo Mandelli's review in *Oggi*, 26 April 1973, quoted in Roussel, 561.

112 Allegri, *Lettere d'amore*, 32.

113 Gian Galeazzo Severi's review in *Il Dramma*, March–April 1973 quoted in Roussel, 561.

114 Allegri, *Lettere d'amore*, 33.

115 Allegri, "E stata una congiura."

116 Laura Padellaro, "Luci, coloro e una grande musica," *Radiocorriere TV*, no. 17, 28 April 1973.

117 Robba, "Maria Callas a Torino e al Regio: Una voce dal futuro."

118 Hanine-Roussel, 558 (Interview with Raina Kabaivanska).

119 ibid. 562 (from clippings from French press).

120 "Riapre il Regio con la Callas," *La Repubblica*, 13 April 1973.

121 Allegri, "E stata una congiura."

122 Callas to Walter Legge, 19 April 1973 in Sanders, 236.

123 Quint, Interview with Callas for CBS News.

21. "The illusion of a better world"

1 Frank Hamilton, *Giuseppe Di Stefano: Performance Annals and Discography*, 2010, https://www.yumpu.com/it/document/view/12115806/giuseppe-di-stefanodiscography-of-concert-and-frank-hamilton.

2 "Eugenia Moldoveanu, soprana care a primit chimonoullui Cio-Cio-San din mâinile Mariei Callas," *Financiarul.ro*, 19 March 2014, https://financiarul.ro/ultimele-stiri/eugenia-moldoveanu-soprana-care-a-primit-chimonoul-lui-cio-cio-san-din-mainilemariei-callas.

3 "International News," *Billboard* magazine, 9 June 1973.

4 Toshisato Chikazawa, "Maria Callas in the Far East—Part I," *The Maria Callas International Magazine*, Issue 2, 14.

5 Di Stefano & Trapani, 135–36.

6 Callas to Bruna Lupoli, 3 June 1974 in Volf, "1974."

7 Di Stefano & Trapani, 137.

8 Renato Passerini, "Callas, la 'diva' in una inedita dimensione umana raccontata da Mezzadri e Chini," *Il Piacenza*, 31 October 2017, https://fiorenzuola.ilpiacenza.it/callas-la-diva-in-una-inedita-dimensione-umana-raccontata-da-mezzadri-e-chini.html.

9 Undated note from Callas to Ferruccio Mezzadri (c. June 1973) [CNH].

10 Sanders, 237.

11 UPI, "Maria Callas Sings Again," 25 May 1973.

12 UPI, "Temperamental Maria Callas, Opera Soprano, Returns to Stage After 8-Year Layoff," *Watertown Daily News*, 8 August 1973.

13 Romi, "Ce Que La Callas N'Avait Encore Jamais Raconté."

14 Callas to Gorlinsky, 25 July 1973 [SGC].

15 Callas to Gorlinsky, 1 August 1973 [SGC].

16 Doctor's note by Dr. Luciano Martini, Milan, 1 August 1973 [SGC].

17 Di Stefano & Trapani, 137.

18 Robert Sutherland, 5–6.

19 Callas to Leonidas Lantzounis, 1 September 1973 [RBC].

20 Johanna Steinmetz, "Callas' comeback tour raises speculation," *The Telegraph-Herald*, 15 March 1974; Mitchell, "La Callas Descends Upon Washington."

21 Robert Sutherland, 12–15.

22 Callas to Leo Lerman, 1 September 1973 [LLP].

23 Callas to Bruna Lupoli, 4 September 1973 in Volf, "1973."

24 Robert Sutherland, 21–25.

25 ibid. 31–32.

26 Callas to Gorlinsky, 19 September 1973 [SGC].

27 "Callas' Comeback Delayed by Glaucoma," *De Telegraaf*, 20 September 1973.

28 "La Callas Not Coming to the Netherlands," *Het Vrije Volk*, 20 September 1973.

29 Doctor's note by Dr. Enrico Bozzi, Milan, 20 September 1973 [SGC].

30 Interview with Janine Reiss (*Hommages à Maria Callas*), 28 February 1978.

31 Sydney Edwards, "Callas' Night, But Taylor Steals It," *The New York Times*, 11 November 1973.

32 Undated note from Callas to Ferruccio Mezzadri written at the Hamburg Plaza Hotel [CNH].

33 Robert Sutherland, 39.

34 ibid. 41.

35 Edwards, "Callas' Night, But Taylor Steals It."

36 Robert Sutherland, 41.

37 Heinz Josef Herbort, "Maria Callas versucht ihr Comeback," *Die Zeit*, 2 November 1973.

38 Edwards, "Callas' Night, But Taylor Steals It."

39 Robert Sutherland, 45.

40 ibid. 50.

41 Holmes, Interview with Callas for BBC Television, 23 November 1973.

42 Wallace: 1974

43 Robert Sutherland, 57–59.

44 ibid. 63.

45 Callas to Leonidas Lantzounis, 9 November 1973 [RBC].

46 Robert Sutherland, 67.

47 ibid. 78.

48 Antonio Fernández-Cid, "Maria Callas y Di Stefano Actuaron en Madrid," *Blanco y Negro*, 1 December 1973.

49 Andry, 58.

50 Charles Fabius, "Di Stefano In Great Shape; Maria Callas Legend Is Not True," *De Tijd*, 12 December 1973.

51 Canals, 2.

52 Robert Sutherland, 86–88.

53 Philip Hope-Wallace, "Maria Callas at the Festival Hall," *The Guardian*, 27 November 1973.

54 Sydney Edwards, "The courage of Callas," *Evening Standard*, 27 November 1973.

55 Galatopoulos, 375.

56 Robert Sutherland, 225.

57 ibid. 91.

58 ibid. 52.

59 Author's interview with Gianni Tanzi, Verona, 25 August 2012.

60 NHK TV Japan, Interview with Callas and Giuseppe Di Stefano at Bunka Kaikan Hall.

61 Andry, 127.

62 Henk van der Meijden, "Ger Oord's Party at London Festival Hall," *De Telegraaf*, 1 December 1973.

63 "Callas Weak and Loud," *Het Vrije Volk*, 1 December 1973.

64 Galatopoulos, 414.

65 Robert Sutherland, 263.

66 ibid. 145–46.

67 Galatopoulos, 412.

68 ibid. 417.

69 Robert Sutherland, 94–95.

70 Author's interview with Janine Reiss.

71 Henry-Louis de la Grange, "La Callas Huit ans après," *Le Nouvel Observateur*, 17 December 1973.

72 Callas to Di Stefano, 8 December 1973 in Renzo & Roberto Allegri, 157.

73 Robert Sutherland, 97.

74 Zoggel, 181.

75 Fabius, "Di Stefano In Great Shape; Maria Callas Legend Is Not True."

76 Robert Sutherland, 110.

77 ibid. 112.

78 ibid. 117.

79 Clerc, "La Callas: 'J'ai décidé d'être douce.' "

80 "Fu Onassis La Rovina Di Callas," *La Repubblica*, 16 September 1997.

81 Walters, Interview with Callas for *Today*.

82 Wallace: 1974

83 George Koumantou, "Maria Callas: My Life Is Music," *To Vima*, 5 November 1971.

84 Bill Hutchinson, Knight Newspapers Writer, "Even If She Is Maria Callas, She's Only Human," *The Cincinnati Enquirer*, 31 March 1974.

85 Walters, Interview with Callas for *Today*.

86 Galatopoulos, 411.

87 UPI, "Maria Callas Renounces Her Brooklyn Birth," *Tanawanda News*, 8 February 1974.

88 Holmes, Interview with Callas for BBC Television, 23 November 1973.

89 Robert Sutherland, 122–23.

90 "Callas-Di Stefano: concerto segreto," *La Domenica del Corriere*, 3 February 1974.

91 Martin Walker, "Open File," *The Guardian*, 24 January 1974.

92 Robert Sutherland, 125–28.

93 Di Stefano & Trapani, 149; Christina K. Cosdon, "Fine Arts Events: They Had A Ball," *The Tampa Bay Times*, 10 February 1974.

94 Robert Sutherland, 130.

95 Richard Dyer, "Maria Callas vocalizes for press," *Boston Globe*, 8 February 1974.

96 "Notes on The Maria Callas Press Conference," [scribbled in the margin: "Probably by Richard Altman"], 7 February 1974 [LLP].

97 Wallace: 1974

98 Interview with Giuseppe Di Stefano for "Callas day" on RAI Television, 16 September 1997.

99 Robert Sutherland, 137–38.

100 Author's telephone interview with Mary Annexy.

101 Steven R. Weisman, "Callas Abruptly Cancels Recital Here," *The New York Times*, 18 February 1974.

102 Robert Sutherland, 143.

103 Mitchell, "La Callas Descends Upon Washington."

104 Interview with Ruth Bader Ginsburg, WQXR Radio New York, 4 July 2004.

105 Mitchell, "La Callas Descends Upon Washington."

106 Paul Hume, "She Came, She Sang, She Conquered," *The Washington Post*, 25 February 1974.

107 Robert Sutherland, 146.

108 Stassinopoulos, 329–30.

109 Robert Sutherland, "Callas: Diary of a world tour—2," *The Sunday Telegraph*, 7 September 1980.

110 Marian Christy, "The voice next door," *Boston Globe*, 4 March 1974.

111 Michael Steinberg, "Callas struggles in Hub, but adds to operatic legend," *Boston Globe*, 28 February 1974.

112 Richard Dyer's review in *The Nation* in Lowe, 226.

113 Callas to Alberta Masiello, 15 January 1975 [AMAS].

114 Cassidy, "Splendor in the Night."

115 Christopher C. Purdy, "I heard Maria Callas in Boston, February 27, 1974," blog entry, 12 April 2012, http://christophercpurdy.blogspot.com/2012/04/i-heard-maria-callas-in-bostonfebruary.html.

116 Robert Sutherland, 151–52.

117 Thomas Willis' review for the *Chicago Tribune* in Lowe, 227.

118 Robert Sutherland, 153–54.

119 Willis' review for the *Chicago Tribune* in Lowe, 227.

120 Robert Sutherland, 153.

121 Interview with James Conlon in Caillat, *Maria Callas: Passion*.

122 Harlow Robinson, *The Last Impresario: The Life, Times and Legacy of Sol Hurok* (New York: Viking, 1994), 456–57.

123 Interview with James Conlon in Caillat, *Passion*.

124 Harold C. Schonberg, "Callas Returns to Fans' Adulation," *The New York Times*, 6 March 1974.

125 Steven R. Weisman, "Carnegie Hall Is Swept By Emotional Torrent," *The New York Times*, 6 March 1974.

126 Robinson, 457.

127 Desmond Shawe-Taylor, "Musical Events," *The New Yorker*, 18 March 1974.

128 Robert Sutherland, 159.

129 ibid. 155.

130 ibid. 138.

131 ibid. 161.

132 "Date with Diva Proves Delight," *The Detroit Free Press*, 12 March 1974.

133 Robert Sutherland, 163–64.

134 ibid. 175–77.

135 Author's telephone interview with Mary Annexy.

136 "Night Belonged to Callas," *The News-Press* from Fort Myers, Florida, 25 March 1974.

137 Robert Sutherland, 182.

138 "Callas Recital Canceled," *The New York Times*, 1 April 1974.

139 Mary Roscow, Interview with Callas and Di Stefano, WFCR Radio Columbus, 2 April 1974.

140 Robert Sutherland, 186.

141 ibid. 188.

142 Hendricks, *Ma voie*, 170–71.

143 Harold C. Schonberg, "Soprano Led Bel Canto Revival," *The New York Times*, 17 September 1977.

144 Marni Nixon, "Marni Nixon on Maria Callas," *Variety*, 8 February 2007.

145 Robert Sutherland, 198–99.

146 Gorlinsky to Callas, 25 April 1974 [SGC].

147 Jack Wasserman, "Peeper's Papers," *The Vancouver Sun*, 2 May 1974.

148 Robert Sutherland, 208.

149 Wasserman, "Peeper's Papers."

150 Robert Sutherland, 211–13.

151 Hanine-Roussel, 416 (Interview with Elena Pozzan).

152 Robert Sutherland, 214.

153 La Rochelle, 272 (citing "Colloque International Sur La Piraterie Des [sic] Callas," Radio-Canada, 4 February 1985).

154 Undated note from Callas to Elena Pozzan written in Montreal [CNH].

155 Medical certificate by Yves Hecht, Paris, 16 May 1974 [SGC].

156 Telegram from Gorlinsky to Callas, 14 June 1974 [SGC].

157 Callas to Robert Sutherland, 21 May 1974 in Robert Sutherland, 219.

158 Gorlinsky to Callas, 4 July 1974 [SGC].

159 Callas to Gorlinsky, 23 May 1974 [SGC].

160 Robert Sutherland, 223.

161 Di Stefano & Trapani, 164

162 ibid. 165

163 Gorlinsky to Callas, 4 July 1974 [SGC].

164 Di Stefano & Trapani, 166.

165 Jacques Bourgeois, "Diva Maria," *Télérama*, 16 September 1987.

166 Ira Siff, "Bellini Norma," *Opera News*, 3 June 2003.

167 Robert Sutherland, 244–46.

168 Allegri, *Lettere d'amore*, 40–41.

169 Charles Osborne, "Well above herself," *The Spectator*, 18–25 December 1999.

170 Newman, 179–80.

171 Marilynn Preston, "Maria Callas, the pussycat and the tiger," *Chicago Tribune*, 6 October 1974.

172 Rosenthal, 187.

173 Weaver, "Remembering Callas: Some Confessions of a Fan," 81.

174 Osborne, "Well above herself."

175 Rosenthal, 188.

176 Robert Sutherland, 249.

177 Toshisato Chikazawa, "Maria Callas in the Far East—Part II," *The Maria Callas International Magazine*, Issue No. 24, 10.

178 NHK TV Japan, Interview with Callas and Giuseppe Di Stefano at Bunka Kaikan Hall.

179 Robert Sutherland, 253.

180 Callas to Helen Arfaras, 28 October 1974 in Volf, "1974."

181 Robert Sutherland, 255.

182 Toshisato Chikazawa, "Maria Callas in the Far East—Part III," *The Maria Callas International Magazine*, Issue 25, 6.

183 Robert Sutherland, 259–61.

184 Chikazawa, "Maria Callas in the Far East—Part III."
185 Robert Sutherland, 263–66.
185 Holmes, Interview with Callas, BBC Radio, 20 June 1958.

22. "Carte blanche"

1 Callas to Louis Parrish, 23 January 1975 in Robert Sutherland, 266–67.
2 Callas to Leo Lerman, 8 January 1975 [LLP].
3 Robert Sutherland, 266–67.
4 Callas to Leonidas Lantzounis, 8 February 1975 in Volf, "1975."
5 Callas to Parrish, 23 January 1975.
6 Di Stefano & Trapani, 169.
7 John Coveney to Tito Gobbi, 27 November 1974 [Tito Gobbi Collection, Boston University Libraries, Howard Gotlieb Archival Research Center].
8 Robert Sutherland, 268.
9 Gorlinsky to Callas, 2 January 1975 [SGC].
10 Callas to Helen Arfaras, 8 January 1975 in Volf, "1975."
11 Di Stefano & Trapani, 170.
12 Callas to Leo Lerman, 8 January 1975 [LLP].
13 Callas to Alberta Masiello, 15 January 1975 [AMAS].
14 Galatopoulos, 402.
15 Callas to Louis Parrish, 23 January 1975.
16 AP, "Onassis Is Ailing With Two Diseases; Specialist on Way," *The New York Times*, 5 February 1975.
17 UPI, "Onassis 'a Bit Better,' Paris Hospital Reports," *The New York Times*, 9 February 1975.
18 Reuters, "Onassis Is Improving," *The New York Times*, 27 February 1975.
19 Stassinopoulos, 335.
20 Chini, 121.
21 Author's e-mail correspondence with Fabio Gervasoni, 9 May 2012. Gervasoni knew Ferruccio Mezzadri, who claimed never to have driven Callas to the American Hospital at Neuilly to visit Onassis.
22 Galatopoulos, 418.
23 Callas to Leonidas Lantzounis, 24 February 1975 [RBC].
24 Callas to Lantzounis, 1 March 1975, Volf, "1975."
25 Mary Annexy to Callas, 16 December 1976 [CNH].
26 Fleming, "Nurturing a Legend."
27 Stancioff, 232.
28 "Aristotle Onassis Is Dead Of Pneumonia in France," *The New York Times*, 16 March 1975.
29 William Hickey, "Giuseppe deserts Callas to comfort his wife," *Daily Express*, 14 April 1975; Di Stefano & Trapani, 171.
30 Di Stefano & Trapani, 172.
31 ibid. unpaginated sheets between 94–95.
32 Harris: 1970

33 Di Stefano & Trapani, 173.

34 Robert Sutherland, 269.

35 Callas to Ben Meiselman, 9 April 1975 in Volf, "1975."

36 Carleton Varney, "Palm Beach decorating: Dr. John will be remembered dearly," *Palm Beach Daily News*, 1 November 2019, https://web.archive.org/web/20191105131756/ https://www.palmbeachdailynews.com/lifestyle/20191101/palm-beach-decorating-dr-john-will-be-remembered-dearly.

37 Callas to Leonidas Lantzounis, 26 June 1975 [RBC].

38 Author's telephone interview with Mary Annexy.

39 Di Stefano & Trapani, 173.

40 Christy, "The voice next door."

41 Brentano, "Grandir avec Callas."

42 Stancioff, 233.

43 Callas to Leonidas Lantzounis, 26 June 1975 [RBC].

44 AFP, "La Callas à nouveau malade," *Le soleil*, 2 October 1975.

45 Vergani & Tirelli, "Questa è la vera Callas."

46 Di Stefano & Trapani, 175.

47 Hanine-Roussel, 579 (Interview with Arturo Testa).

48 Callas to Leonidas Lantzounis, 18 July 1975 [RBC].

49 Robert Sutherland, 269.

50 Gorlinsky to Bernard Baudelot, 10 May 1976 [SGC].

51 Callas to Walter Cummings, 9 August 1975 in Hanine-Roussel, 580–581.

52 Undated letter from Callas to Leonidas Lantzounis (c. August 1975) [RBC].

53 Callas to Sutherland, 27 August 1975 in Robert Sutherland, 270.

54 Callas to Carlos Díaz Du-Pond, 27 August 1975 in López, Zárate, Miranda & de los Reyes, 28 (originally published in *El Redondel* on 25 September 1977).

55 Robert Sutherland, 271.

56 Stassinopoulos, 346.

57 Interview with Montserrat Caballé (*Hommages à Maria Callas*), 10 December 1977.

58 Caballé in Bret, xii.

59 Joseph H. Firman, "Spectrum," *Progress Bulletin*, Pomona, California, 14 September 1975.

60 Callas to Joan Crawford, 19 September 1975 in Sale 1057, Lot 103 at Heritage Auctions, 27 November 2002, https://entertainment.ha.com/itm/autographs/maria-callas-rare-handwritten-letter-signed/a/1057-103.s?src=pr.

61 Régine Crespin, *À la scène, à la ville* (Arles: Actes Sud, 1999), 211.

62 Photograph of Callas with Count Manolino Borromeo, 25 September 1975 (credits missing). [CFG].

63 Photograph of Callas at the premiere of *Attila '74: The Rape of Cyprus* by Pool Lochon/ Maous, 4 November 1975. Gamma-Rapho via Getty Images, https://www.gettyimages.co.uk/detail/news-photo/maria-callas-american-born-greek-soprano-newsphoto/952412864.

64 Stancioff, 232.

65 Callas to Leonidas Lantzounis, 29 October 1975 [RBC].

66 Brentano, "Grandir avec Callas."

67 "Maria Callas' Film Plans," *De Telegraaf*, 4 December 1975.

68 Berganza, "Para mí la Callas era solo Maria."

69 Hanine-Roussel, 393–94 (from his Interview with Lina Ego Lazzarini, wife of Costantino Ego).

70 Callas to Helen Arfaras, 3 May 1976 in Volf, "1976."

71 Di Stefano & Trapani, 183–84.

72 Tooley, 104.

73 Robert Sutherland, 269.

74 Schwarzkopf & Legge, 199.

75 Schwarzkopf to Cristina Muñoz, 15 November 1999 in López, Zárate, Miranda & Reyes, 28.

76 Jellinek, 187.

77 A. Airio, H. Kautiainen and M. Hakala, "Prognosis and mortality of polymyositis and dermatomyositis patients," Clinical Rheumatology 25, March 2006, 234–39.

78 Interview with Mario Giacovazzo in Associated Press, "Why Callas lost that voice," The Sydney Morning Herald, 15 October 2002.

79 Interview with Janine Reiss in Hommages à Maria Callas.

80 Leiser, "Chapter 13: Maria Callas."

81 Interview with Montserrat Caballé in Hommages à Maria Callas.

82 Robert Sutherland, 272–73.

83 Dufresne, 280.

84 Callas to Leonidas Lantzounis, 21 February 1977 in Volf, "1977."

85 Galatopoulos, 451.

86 Jackie Callas, 218–19.

87 "Maria Callas will probably be in a jury, Channel Seven To Broadcast the NCRV Opera and Operetta Competition Live," Nieuwsblad van het Noorden, 1 March 1976.

88 Zeffirelli, 288.

89 Interview with Charles Vannes (Hommages à Maria Callas), 13 February 1978.

90 "Maria Callas in Lacrime per una Stecca," Oggi, 3 March 1976.

91 Interview with Charles Vannes in Hommages à Maria Callas.

92 Muriel Alpin, secretary of Sander Gorlinsky to Bernard Baudelot, 23 April 1976 [SGC].

93 "Maria Callas Wins Case Against French Magazine," Leeuwarder Courant, 8 July 1976.

94 Julia Ammerman Yebra, "The Voice of the Opera Singer and Its Protection: Another Look at the Maria Callas Case" in Filippo Annunziata & Giorgio Fabio Colombo, Law and Opera (New York: Springer International Publishing, 2018), 255.

95 Gorlinsky to Bernard Baudelot, 10 May 1976 [SGC].

96 Callas to Helen Arfaras, 3 May 1976 in Volf, "1976."

97 "Maria Callas sur France Musique," L'Humanité, 16 September 1992.

98 Caloni: 1976

99 Harris: 1970

100 Caloni: 1976

101 Callas to John Ardoin, 18 February 1976 [AKP].

102 Callas to Peter Mennin, 16 June 1976 [JSA].

103 Wriston Locklair, "Notes on Maria Callas—Wriston Locklair Conversation: July 1976," [JSA].

104 ibid. Callas to John Ardoin, 16 June 1976.

105 Undated letter from Callas to Stelios Galatopoulos (c. May 1975) in Galatopoulos, 5.

106 Galatopoulos, 5.

107 "Gente: María Callas," *El País*, 27 July 1976.

108 William Hickey ed. Alison Miller, "A bass refusal?," *Daily Express*, 11 August 1976.

109 Kostis Zafirakis, "Luxury Hideaways in Halkidiki," 10 December 2015, http://www. greece-is.com/luxury-hideaways-halkidiki; Teresa Machan, "Eagles Palace Hotel Review," *The Telegraph*, undated review, http://www.telegraph.co.uk/travel/destinations/europe/ greece/halkidiki/hotels/eagles-palace-hotel.

110 Callas to Nadia Stancioff, 23 August 1975 in Stancioff, 237.

111 Callas to Irving Kolodin, 19 August 1976 [IKP].

112 Callas to Oscar Coltellacci, 31 August 1976 in "Maria Callas. The Exhibition" at Arena Museo Opera, Verona, 11 March—18 September 2016.

113 Sievewright, "Callas Remembered: Conversation with Maria Callas, July 1977."

114 Elvira de Hidalgo to Callas, 15 November 1976 [CNH].

115 Callas to Leo Lerman, 24 December 1976 [LLP].

116 Stassinopoulos, 347.

117 Galatopoulos, 3–4.

118 ibid. 251.

119 ibid. 415.

120 Hanine-Roussel, 416 (Interview with Ferruccio Mezzadri).

121 Ossenska, Interview with Callas for *La Scala e i suoi protagonisti*.

122 Zeffirelli, 296.

123 Galatopoulos, 450.

124 "En Valais le retour de l'hiver a fait la joie des skieurs," *La Liberté*, 12 April 1977.

125 Callas to Stephen Bill, Executive Director, The Festival of Sydney, 17 May 1977. Featured on the blog of collector David Crothers at https://callasautographs.com/#jp-carousel-264.

126 Nora London, *George London: Of Gods and Demons* (Fort Worth: Baskerville Publishers, 2005), 96.

127 Interview with Montserrat Caballé in *Hommages à Maria Callas*.

128 Harewood, 236.

129 Petsalis-Diomidis, 656 n. 16 ("Statement by Andy Embirikos to Tassos Kriekoukis, then secretary of the Greek embassy in Paris; author's conversation with Tassos Kriekoukis, 6 June 1997.").

130 Galatopoulos, 6.

131 Caloni: 1976

132 Sievewright, "Callas Remembered: Conversation with Maria Callas, July 1977."

133 Caloni: 1976

134 "Georges Prêtre exaspéré par les stars du chant."

135 Martin Kettle, "I didn't want to be a diva," Interview with Joan Sutherland, *The Guardian*, 8 May 2002.

136 Jorden, Interview with Marilyn Horne and James Levine.

137 Galatopoulos, 6–7.

138 Berganza, "Para mí la Callas era solo Maria."

139 Interview with Michel Glotz (*Hommages à Maria Callas*), 16 March 1978.

140 Prêtre, 136.
141 Callas' copy of *Spirits and Spiritual Words* features in the Collection of Nicos Haralabopoulos.
142 Galatopoulos, 461.
143 Caloni: 1976

23. "Beauty is truth."

1   Moore, 287.
2   Callas to Umberto Tirelli, 1 September 1977 (incorrectly transcribed as 1 September 1975) in Tosi, *Casta diva: L'incomparabile Callas*, 273–4 and in Vergani & Tirelli, "Questa è la vera Callas."
3   Soria, "Greek Sorceress."
4   Karajan, 193.
5   Mannino, 115.
6   " 'Casta diva' de Béjart," *La Liberté*, 16 July 1980.
7   Undated note from Callas to Maurice Béjart (c. 10 or 11 September 1977) in Tosi, *Casta diva: L'incomparabile Callas*, 275.
8   Fournier, 59.
9   Brentano, "Grandir avec Callas."
10 Chini, 125.
11 Paolo Romani, "Sognava ancora il palcoscenico," *Epoca*, 28 September 1977.
12 Fournier, 59–60; Author's interview with Janine Reiss.
13 Andry, 59.
14 Glotz, 209.
15 Galatopoulos, 456.
16 Jackie Callas, 16.
17 "Jean Roire, 'Le Chant du Monde,' est éteint," *La Croix*, 3 May 2007.
18 Galatopoulos, 458.
19 Associated Press Archive, "FUNERAL OF SINGER MARIA CALLAS, IN PARIS," 20 September 1977. Published online on 24 July 2015 at https://www.youtube.com/watch?v=7FtVom97ZV4.
20 UPI, "Maria Callas to be Cremated In Paris in a Closed Ceremony," *The New York Times*, 18 September 1977.
21 AP Release, 4 June 1979.
22 Jackie Callas, 222.
23 Andry, 59.
24 The piece of paper is dated 24 April 1954 and entitled "Will". It reads: "I leave all my estate to my husband, Battista Meneghini." It features in Lot 90 in Sotheby's, *Maria Callas and Her Pygmalion*. Accessed at https://www.sothebys.com/en/auctions/ecatalogue/2007/maria-callas-and-her-pygmalion-her-life-with-giovanni-battista-meneghini-mi0287/lot.90.html.
25 Reuters, "Claim on Callas millions," 28 October 1977.
26 Jackie Callas, 278.

27 Hervé Guibert, "L'opéra secret de Maria Callas," *Le Monde*, 11 April 1979.

28 James Sherwood, "Mystery of the Callas millions resurfaces as jewels are put up for auction," *The Independent*, 26 October 2004; Will Bennett, "Object of the week," *The Telegraph*, 15 November 2004.

29 "Legal copy of the agreement between the Kalogeropoulos family and Giovanni Battista Meneghini on the succession of Maria Callas, signed by Vasso Devetzi," Lot 90, Sotheby's, *Maria Callas and Her Pygmalion*, https://www.sothebys.com/en/auctions/ecatalogue/2007/maria-callas-and-her-pygmalion-her-life-with-giovanni-battista-meneghini-mi0287/lot.90.html.

30 Teresa d'Addato to Mr. DeLloyd Tibbs, Assistant Exec. Secretary of the American Guild of Musical Artists, 11 April 1961 [SGC].

31 Posthumous telegram from Vittorio Gui to Callas [CNH].

32 de Nussac & Cotta: 1970

33 Richard Gehman, "Callas: Opera's Fiery Diva," *Coronet* magazine, September 1958.

34 Matz, "We introduce Maria Meneghini Callas."

35 Banzet: 1965.

36 C.S. Lewis' quotation of Denis de Rougemont in Will Vaus, *Mere Theology: A Guide to the Thought of C.S. Lewis* (Downers Grove: InterVarsity Press, 2004), 157.

37 Lawrence Kelly, "Queen of Musical Mountain Rips Convention for Purpose," *The Dallas Morning News*, 9 August 1959.

38 Alison Adburgham, "Storms in the tea cups of Wimbledon," *The Manchester Guardian*, 1 July 1959.

39 Leibowitz, "Le secret de Maria Callas."

40 Galatopoulos, 447.

41 Interview with Janine Reiss on *Hommages à Maria Callas*.

42 Cyrus Durgin, "Temperament, Or Is It Temper?," *Boston Globe*, 15 January 1958.

43 Cruesemann: 1959

44 Desgraupes: 1969

45 Jellinek, 318.

46 Frost: 1970

47 Prouse, "Maria Callas Speaks," 19 March 1961.

48 Banzet: 1965

49 Barry: 1971

50 Caloni: 1976

51 "I'm Fatalist Says Prima Donna," *The Toronto Daily Star*, 21 October 1958.

Selected Bibliography

Allegri, Renzo & Roberto. *Callas by Callas: The Secret Writings of La Maria.* New York: Universe, 1998.

Allegri, Renzo trans. Thierry Laget. *La véritable histoire de Maria Callas.* Paris: Éditions Belfont, 1992.

Allegri, Renzo. *Maria Callas: Lettere d'amore.* Milan: Mondadori, 2008.

Andry, Peter. *Inside the recording studio: Working with Callas, Domingo, Rostropovich and the Classical Elite.* Lanham, MD: Scarecrow Press, 2008.

Ardoin, John & Fitzgerald, Gerald. *Callas: The Art and the Life.* New York: Holt, Rinehart and Winston, 1974.

Ardoin, John. *The Callas Legacy.* Baltimore: Encore Editions, 1984.

Aversano, Luca & Pellegrini, Jacopo. *Mille e una Callas.* Macerata: Quodlibet Editions, 2017.

Ayre, Isabelle. *Entretiens avec Janine Reiss.* Lyon: Kirographaires Editions, 2013.

Berlin, Isaiah. *Enlightening: Letters: 1946–1960.* London: Chatto & Windus, 2009.

Bing, Rudolf. *5000 Nights at the Opera: The Memoirs of Sir Rudolf Bing.* New York: Doubleday, 1972.

Bing, Rudolf. *A Knight at the Opera.* New York: Putnam, 1981.

Bottero, Irene. *Maria Callas: Croce e delicia.* Mondovì: Nuova Editrice Italiana, 1997.

Bradford, Sarah. *America's Queen: The Life of Jacqueline Kennedy Onassis.* New York: Viking, 2000.

Burton, Richard. *The Richard Burton Diaries.* New Haven: Yale University Press, 2013.

Cafarkis, Christian. *The Fabulous Onassis: His Life and Loves.* New York: Morrow, 1972.

Callas, Evangelia. *My Daughter Maria Callas.* New York: Fleet Press, 1960.

Callas, Jackie. *Sisters.* London: St. Martin's, 1990.

Castiglione, E. *Maria Callas: Lettere, scritti, interviste, pensieri.* Rome: Pantheon, 2008.

Chambre Cohen, Calmels. *Maria Callas: Souvenirs d'une légende.* Paris: Chambre Cohen, 2000.

Chapin, Schuyler. *Musical Chairs.* Bloomington, IN: iUniverse Edition, 2000.

Chini, Luigi. *Il destino mi ha fatto incontrare Maria Callas: Ferruccio Mezzadri racconta.* Piacenza: Edizioni L.I.R., 2017.

Coward, Noël ed. Graham Payn & Sheridan Morley. *The Noël Coward Diaries.* Boston: Little Brown, 1982.

Cook, Ida. *Safe Passage: The Remarkable True Story of Two Sisters Who Rescued Jews from the Nazis.* New York: Harlequin, 2008.

Crespi Morbio, Vittoria. *Maria Callas: Gli anni alla Scala*. Turin: Umberto Allemandi, 2008.

Crespin, Régine. *À la scène, à la ville*. Arles: Actes Sud, 1999.

Davis, Ronald L. *La Scala West: The Dallas Opera Under Kelly and Rescigno*. Dallas: Southern Methodist University Press, 2001.

de Cecatty, René. *Maria Callas*. Paris: Folio, 2009.

de Rienzo, Nicolò. *Nessun problema: I segreti dei portieri dei grandi alberghi*. add editore, 2011.

Di Stefano, Maria & Trapani, Francamaria. *Callas: Nemica mia*. Milan: Sonzogno Editore, 1992.

Drake, James A. & Ponselle, Rosa. *Ponselle: A Singer's Life*. New York: Doubleday, 1982.

Drake, James A. *Rosa Ponselle: A Centenary Biography*. Portland: Amadeus Press, 1997.

Dufresne, Claude. *La Callas*. Paris: Perrin, 1990.

Farrell, Eileen & Kellow, Brian. *Can't Help Singing: The Life of Eileen Farrell*. Boston: Northeastern University Press, 1999.

Fournier, Dominique. *La passion prédominante de Janine Reiss: La voix humaine*. Arles: Actes Sud Editions, 2013.

Fraser, Nicholas; Jacobson, Philip; Ottoway, Mark & Chester, Lewis. *Aristotle Onassis*. London: Weidenfeld & Nicholson, 1st ed., 1977.

Frischauer, Willi. *Onassis*. London: The Bodley Head Ltd, 1st ed., 1968.

Galatopoulos, Stelios. *Sacred Monster*. London: Fourth Estate, 1998.

Gara, Eugenio. *I grandi interpreti: Maria Callas*. Milan: Ricordi, 1957.

Gara, Eugenio trans. Barbara Wall. *Maria Callas: Great Concert Artists*. Geneva: René Kister, 1958.

Gastel Chiarelli, Cristina. *Maria Callas*. Venice: Marsilio, 1995.

Gavazzeni, Gianandrea. *Il sipario rosso: Diario (1950–1976)*. Turin: Einaudi, 1992.

Gentile, Giuseppe. *La medaglia (con)divisa. Il triplo. Pasolini e Maria Callas*. Arezzo: fuori|onda, 2012.

Glotz, Michel. *La note bleue: Une vie pour la musique*. Paris: Lattès, 2010.

Gobbi, Tito. *My Life*. London: Macdonald & Jane's, 1979.

Guandalini, Gina. *Maria Callas: L'interprete, La storia*. Rome: Curcio Musica, 2007.

Haltrecht, Montague. *The Quiet Showman*. London: Harper Collins, 1975.

Hanine-Roussel, Jean-Jacques. *Maria Callas*. Paris: Éditions Carpentier, 2015.

Lord Harewood (George Lascelles), *The Tongs and Bones: The Memoirs of Lord Harewood*. London: Weidenfeld & Nicholson, 1981.

Heath, Edward. *Music: A Joy for Life*. London: Sidgwick & Jackson, 1976.

Hendricks, Barbara. *Ma voie: Mémoires*. Paris: Éditions Les Arènes, 2010.

_____ *Lifting My Voice: A Memoir*. Chicago: Chicago Review Press, 2014.

Heyman, Barbara B. *Samuel Barber, The Composer and His Music*. New York: Oxford University Press, 1992.

Ioannidis, Paul J. *Destiny Prevails: My Life with Aristotle, Alexander, Christina Onassis and her daughter, Athina*. Significance Press, 2015.

Jackson, Paul. *Sign-Off for the Old Met: The Metropolitan Opera Broadcasts, 1950–1966*. Portland: Amadeus Press, 1997.

Janis, Byron. *Chopin and Beyond: My Extraordinary Life in Music and the Paranormal.* Hoboken, NJ: Wiley Books, 2010.

Jellinek, George. *Callas: Portrait of a Prima Donna.* New York: Dover Publications, New Edition, 1986.

von Karajan, Eliette. *À ses côtés.* Paris: L'Archipel, 2008.

Kesting, Jürgen trans. John Hunt. *Maria Callas.* Boston: Northeastern University Press, 1993.

La Rochelle, Réal. *Callas: La diva et la vinyle.* Montréal: Triptyque, 2005.

Lámpas, Marko. *My Life in America and What Maria Callas Taught Me.* Lulu.com, 2010.

Lebrecht, Norman. *Covent Garden: The Untold Story.* Boston: Northeastern University Press, 2001.

Lerman, Leo ed. Stephen Pascal. *The Grand Surprise: The Journals of Leo Lerman.* New York: Knopf, 2007.

London, Nora. *George London: Of Gods and Demons.* Fort Worth: Baskerville Publishers, 2005.

López, Aaron Polo; Zárate, Karla; Miranda, Martha & de Los Reyes, Aurelio. *Maria Callas: Una Mujer, Una Voz, Un Mito.* Mexico: Instituto Nacional de Bellas Artes, 1997.

Lorcey, Jacques. *L'Art de Maria Callas.* Biarritz: Atlantica, 1999.

Lowe, David. *Callas: As They Saw Her.* London: Robson Books Ltd, 1987.

Mannino, Franco. *Genii.* Milan: Bompiani, 1987.

Maraini, Dacia. *E tu chi eri? 26 interviste sull'infanzia.* Milan: Rizzoli, 1998.

Meneghini, Giovanni Battista. *Maria Callas, mia moglie.* Milan: Rusconi, 1981.

Montague Browne, Anthony. *LONG SUNSET: Memoirs of Winston Churchill's Last Private Secretary.* London: Cassell, 1995.

Moore, George S. *The Banker's Life.* New York: Norton, 1987.

Mouskouri, Nana. *Memoirs.* London: Orion Publishing, 2007.

Murdoch, James. *Peggy Glanville Hicks: A Transposed Life.* Hillsdale, NY: Pendragon Press, 2003.

Naldini, Nico. *Pasolini, una vita.* Verona: Tamellini, 2014.

Newman, Danny. *Tales of a Theatrical Guru.* Urbana: University of Illinois Press, 2006.

Newton, Ivor. *At the Piano: The world of an accompanist.* London: Hamish Hamilton, 1966.

Nilsson, Birgit. *La Nilsson: My Life in Opera.* Boston: Northeastern University Press, 2015.

Osborne, Richard E. *Conversations with Karajan.* Oxford: Oxford Paperbacks, 1991.

_____ *Herbert von Karajan: A Life in Music.* London: Chatto & Windus, 1998.

Pasolini, Pier Paolo. *Il Vangelo secondo Matteo, Edipe Re, Medea.* Milan: Garzanti Editions, 2006.

Petsalis-Diomidis, Nicholas. *Callas: The Unknown Callas: The Greek Years.* Portland: Amadeus Press, 2003.

Picchi, Mirto. *Un trono vicino al sol.* Ravenna: Edizioni del Girasole, 1978.

Prêtre, Georges. *La Symphonie d'une vie: Entretiens avec Isabelle Prêtre.* Paris: Écriture, 2013.

Rasponi, Lanfranco. *The Last Prima Donnas.* New York: Limelight Editions, 1998.

Rémy, Pierre-Jean. *Callas: Une vie.* Paris: Albin Michel, 1997, Kindle.

Rivellino-Walsh, Dolores. *The Malibu Cookbook: A Memoir by THE GODMOTHER OF MALIBU.* Bloomington, IN: AuthorHouse, 2007.

Romanò Marchetti, Daniela. *La Scala: Racconti dal palcoscenico.* Milan: Valentina Edizioni, 2000.

Rosenthal, Harold. *My Mad World of Opera: Autobiography of the Editor of "Opera" Magazine.* New York: Holmes & Meier Publications, 1983.

Sanders, Alan. *Walter Legge: Words and Music.* London: Duckworth, 1998.

Schifano, Laurence. *Luchino Visconti: The Flames of Passion.* London: Harper Collins, 1990.

Schonberg, Harold C. *The Virtuosi: Classical Music's Great Performers from Paganini to Pavarotti.* New York: Vintage, 1988.

Schwartz, Barth David. *Pasolini Requiem.* New York: Pantheon, 1992.

Schwarzkopf, Elisabeth & Legge, Walter. *On and Off the Record: A Memoir of Walter Legge.* London: Faber & Faber, 1982.

Sachs, Harvey. *Toscanini: Musician of Conscience.* New York: Liveright, 2017.

Scott, Glenway. *A Heaven of Words: Last Journals, 1956–1984.* Madison: University of Wisconsin Press, 2013.

Scott, Michael. *Maria Meneghini Callas.* London: Simon & Schuster, 1992.

Seghers, René. *Corelli: Prince of Tenors.* Portland: Amadeus Press, 2008.

Servadio, Gaia. *Luchino Visconti: A Biography.* New York: Franklin Watts, 1983.

Sguotti, Nicla. *Tullio Serafin: Il custode del bel canto.* Padua: Armelin Musica, 2014.

Simeone, Nigel. *The Leonard Bernstein Letters.* New Haven: Yale University Press, 2013.

Solti, Sir Georg. *Solti on Solti.* Chicago: Chicago Review Press, 1998.

Spanidou, Korinna. *Onassis As I Knew Him.* Athens: Hestia, 1996.

Stancioff, Nadia. *Maria Callas Remembered: An Intimate Portrait of the Private Callas.* Colorado: Da Capo Press, 1st Da Capo Press ed., 2000.

Stassinopoulos, Arianna. *Maria Callas: The Woman Behind the Legend.* New York: Simon & Schuster, 1981.

Stirling, Monica. *A Screen of Time: A Study of Luchino Visconti.* London: Secker & Warburg, 1979.

Sutherland, Joan. *The Autobiography of Joan Sutherland: A Prima Donna's Progress.* Washington D.C.: Regnery Publishing, 1997.

Sutherland, Robert. *Maria Callas: Diaries of A Friendship.* London: Constable & Co., 1999.

Tomatis, Alfred A. *The Ear and the Voice.* Lanham, MD: Scarecrow Press, 2005.

Tooley, John. *In House: The Story of Covent Garden.* London: Faber & Faber, 1999.

Tosi, Bruno. *Casta diva: L'incomparabile Callas.* Rome: Gallia, 1993.

Tosi, Bruno. *Giovane Callas.* Venice: Associazione Maria Callas, 1997.

Tosi, Bruno trans. William Weaver. *The Young Maria Callas.* Toronto: Guernica Editions, 2010.

Volf, Tom. *Maria Callas: Lettres et Mémoires.* Paris: Albin Michel, 2019. Kobo.

Wallman, Margarete. *Sous le ciel de l'opéra: Mémoires.* Paris: Félin, 2004.

Williams, Jeannie. *Jon Vickers: A Hero's Life.* Boston: Northeastern University Press, 2007.

Zeffirelli, Franco. *Zeffirelli: An Autobiography.* London: Weidenfeld & Nicholson, 1986.

Index

Notes: Page numbers followed by "f" indicate footnotes; those by "n" are endnotes. Photographs are in two sections after pages 185 and 370; these are indicated by "*after*" and the page number in *italic*. The initials "M.C." refer to Maria Callas throughout.

Printed in Great Britain
by Amazon

33111483R00382